FICTION

Reading > Reacting > Writing

FICTION

Reading > Reacting > Writing

Laurie G. Kirszner
Philadelphia College of Pharmacy and Science

Stephen G. Mandell
Drexel University

HARCOURT BRACE COLLEGE PUBLISHERS
Fort Worth Philadelphia San Diego New York Orlando Austin San Antonio
Toronto Montreal London Sydney Tokyo

Editor-in-Chief: **Ted Buchholz**
Acquisitions Editor: **Michael Rosenberg**
Development Editor: **Camille Adkins**
Project Editor: **Barbara Moreland**
Production Manager: **Cynthia Young**
Book Designer: **Garry Harman**

Cover Artwork by: **Greta Vaught**

ISBN 0-15-501014-X
Library of Congress Card Number 93-79506

Address editorial correspondence to:
301 Commerce St., Suite 3700
Fort Worth, TX 76102

Address orders to:
6277 Sea Harbor Dr.
Orlando, FL 32887
1-800-782-4479 (outside Florida)
1-800-433-0001 (inside Florida)

Acknowledgments begin on page 634.

Printed in the United States of America

4567890123 090 987654321

Preface

The first edition of *Literature: Reading, Reacting, Writing* broke new ground and, perhaps as a result, received praise from both students and instructors. When we began work on the first edition, our goal was to move away from the predictability and familiarity that characterize traditional literature anthologies. In the process we wanted to demonstrate that a literature anthology could reflect the exciting changes taking place in literary studies. We also wanted to combine the study of literature with writing instruction based on the latest research from the field of composition. The success of the first edition demonstrates that the direction we chose was the right one.

In response to many requests from instructors, we have made the fiction and poetry sections of the second edition of *Literature: Reading, Reacting, Writing* available as separate volumes. These books make it possible for instructors who do not need or want a full sized literature anthology to have all the innovative features of *Literature: Reading, Reacting, Writing* in a format suited to their specific needs.

Fiction: Reading, Reacting, Writing begins with a chapter called "Understanding Literature," which helps students gain an appreciation of the complex issues surrounding the expansion of the literary canon. After surveying conventional literary themes, this chapter summarizes the reasons why many students of literature believe that the traditional canon needs to be revised. It then discusses the processes of interpreting and evaluating literature, placing special emphasis on how the personal responses of readers affect meaning. Finally, it examines the role of literary criticism and considers how it offers students perspectives that can help them expand their literary horizons.

Chapter 2, "Reading and Writing about Literature," offers a detailed discussion of writing about literature. As experienced writing teachers, and as coauthors of seven other writing texts, we know that writing about literature presents special problems for students. For this reason, we discuss the processes of reading and writing in the context of literature before we specifically discuss reading and writing about fiction. We demonstrate how students discover ideas about literature through a complex process of reading, rereading, questioning, and discussing as well as writing and rewriting. To help students see writing about literature as a process of exploring and testing ideas, of growing into a point of view or a critical stance, and of participating in an ongoing critical debate, we include writing instruction not as an afterthought, tucked away in an appendix, but in a full chapter that examines the writing process as it applies to all literature.

In Chapter 3, "Reading and Writing about Fiction," we narrow our focus to follow the progress of a student as he moves through the process of writing about Alberto Alvaro Rios's story, "The Secret Lion" (p. 37). We discuss concepts familiar to composition teachers and students of writing—gathering and arranging ideas, drafting and so on—and explain and illustrate how to apply these concepts to writing about fiction. In each of three drafts of the student essay, we show how revision and editing help strengthen an essay, making it clearer, more precise, and more compelling.

Of course, the heart of *Fiction: Reading, Reacting, Writing* is its reading selections. Throughout the book (in separate chapters focusing on plot; character; setting; point of view; style, tone, and language; symbol and allegory; and themes, as well as in the Stories for Further Reading section) we include a significant number of established favorites—those readings recognized by many instructors as excellent. Students and teachers like and expect to see these works, and their familiarity makes them good starting points for introducing students to fiction. We wanted, however, to include more than the "approved" readings—and, in fact, to do more than supplement the approved list with a few token selections representing contemporary voices.

We recognize that the literary canon has expanded to include an exciting diversity of contexts, cultures, and viewpoints, and we welcome this trend as long overdue. Accordingly, we have included high-quality representatives of these diverse voices. As a result of our efforts, this anthology includes short stories by noted writers from many regions and ethnic backgrounds in the United States, Canada, and the British Isles, as well as selections by writers from various countries in Asia, Africa, Latin America, and the Caribbean. In addition, we have sought younger writers whose reputations are still developing, and a significant number of stories by women, minorities, and non-Western writers.

Many anthologies, eager to include such works because of their obvious merit and appeal, are nevertheless reluctant to look too different; therefore, they may include "new" works that are new only to their text, not to the canon, choosing "safe" minority or foreign writers whose works, already given the stamp of approval by the critical hierarchy, have been anthologized frequently. Alternately, editors may limit the number of new works to a sprinkling, or even relegate "nontraditional" or "contemporary" works to separate sections of the text. Our practice has been to place such works where they belong, along side the "classics": to integrate new with old, familiar with unfamiliar, inviting students simultaneously to discover new works and to see familiar works in new contexts. Our goal in this anthology is not just to expand the literary canon, but also to expand the personal canons of both students and instructors.

Following the readings is a Casebook that is unique to this book. Although the student essay-in-progress in Chapter 3 does not make use of source-based research, we recognize that many literary essays do, including those assigned in introductory literature courses. At the same time, we know that instructors may be reluctant to assign such essays because of the limitations of library facilities or because they are not certain that students will be able to evaluate or even locate useful sources on their own. Still, we realize that learning to make use of critical, historical, and bibliographic sources can help students develop critical thinking skills, learn to make judgments about the validity and relevance of various ideas, and formulate critical positions of their own. For this reason, we have assembled a Casebook designed to supplement students' reading of Joyce Carol Oates's story "Where Are You Going, Where Have You Been?" In this Casebook we include song lyrics, a newspaper article by the author, articles by literary critics, and a complete student research paper based on this source material. Following the Casebook is a detailed appendix on MLA documentation format. The result is a self-contained resource that will enable students to write thoughtful critical essays on Oates's short story—and, eventually, on other stories as well.

Each of the features described above is designed to serve the text's dual goals: to encourage students to appreciate stories representing diverse literary subjects, styles, and perspectives, and to recognize their own role in bringing these diverse works into an expanded literary canon by reading, reacting to, and writing about them. We anticipate that students' responses will take a variety of forms: class discussion, collaborative activities, journals, informal essays, source-based literary criticism, and possibly even original fiction. Nevertheless, our goal in this text is not to turn students into literary critics or writers of fiction. If this anthology can encourage students to respond spontaneously and enthusiastically to what they read and to see their responses as involving them in an ongoing and stimulating (if sometimes unpredictable) dialogue—with peers, with critics, with instructors, with themselves, and with the work itself—then we will have accomplished our purpose.

From start to finish, this text has been a true collaboration for us, not only with each other, but also with our students and colleagues. We have worked hard on the book, and many people at Harcourt Brace have worked along with us. Camille Adkins, Shana Lum, and Michael Rosenberg gave us their time, support, and encouragement. Others at Harcourt Brace who were important to the book are Barbara Moreland, Margaret Allyson, Shelia Shutter, Garry Harmon, and Cindy Young. In addition, we would like to thank Carol Lea Clark, University of Texas at El Paso; Todd Stebbins, University of South Carolina; Gloria Underwood, Savannah College of Art and Design; Wayne Cox, Anderson College; Miriam Moore, University of South Carolina; Shelia Tombe, University of South Carolina; and Rudy Eastman, Jubilee Theatre, Fort Worth, Texas. We also appreciate the work of Anne Lesser, Carla Hahn-Clardy, and Publications Development Company.

We would like to thank all the reviewers who made valuable contributions through several drafts of the text. Reviewers of the second edition were Deborah Barberbousse, Horry-Georgetown Technical College; Bob Mayberry, University of Nevada Las Vegas; Shireen Carroll, University of Miami; Stephen Wright, Seminole Community College; Robert Dees, Orange Coast College; Larry Gray, Southeastern Louisiana University; Nancy Rayl, Cypress College; James Clemmer, Austin Peay State University; Roberta Kramer, Nassau Community College.

We would also like to thank our families—Mark, Adam, and Rebecca Kirszner and Demi, David, and Sarah Mandell—for being there when we needed them. And finally, we each thank the person on the other side of the ampersand for making our collaboration work one more time.

Detailed Contents

Chapter 1

Chapter 2

CHAPTER 5

CHAPTER 6

CHAPTER 7

CHAPTER 10

STORIES FOR FURTHER READING

APPENDICES

CHAPTER 1

UNDERSTANDING LITERATURE

WHAT IS LITERATURE?

IMAGINATIVE LITERATURE

Imaginative literature begins with a writer's need to convey his or her personal vision to readers. Even when writers use factual material—historical documents, newspaper stories, personal experience—their primary purpose is to give a unique view of experience, one that has significance beyond the moment. As the poet Ezra Pound said, "Literature is the news that *stays* news." To convey their views of experience, writers of imaginative literature frequently manipulate facts—change dates, invent characters, and create dialogue. For example, when the nineteenth-century American author Herman Melville wrote his novella *Benito Cereno,* he drew many of his facts from an eighteenth-century journal that gave an account of an actual slave revolt. In his story he reproduces court records and plot details from this primary source, but he leaves out many incidents that the original dwells on at length, and he adds material of his own. The result is an original work of literature with an emphasis that serves the author's purpose. Wanting to do more than tell the original story, Melville used the factual material as "a skeleton of actual reality" upon which to build a story that examines the nature of the truth.

Imaginative literature is more likely than other types of writing to include words chosen not only because they communicate the writer's ideas in a clear and straightforward manner, but also because they are memorable. Using vivid imagery and evocative comparisons, writers of imaginative literature strive to stretch language to its limits. By relying on the multiple connotations of words and images, a work of imaginative literature can evoke many possible meanings and interpretations. Thus imaginative literature encourages readers to see the possibilities of language and to move beyond the factual account of an event. Consider, for example, how William Wordsworth uses language in the following lines from his poem "Composed upon Westminster Bridge":

This City now doth, like a garment, wear
The beauty of the morning; silent, bare,
Ships, towers, domes, theaters, and temples lie
Open unto the fields, and to the sky;
All bright and glittering in the smokeless air.

Notice that Wordsworth does not present a picture of London that is scientifically or sociologically accurate. By comparing the city at dawn to a person wearing a beautiful garment, Wordsworth creates a striking picture that has its own kind of truth, one that enables readers to participate in the speaker's imaginative experience. The city, traditionally the antithesis of nature, is "open unto the fields, and to the sky" and is therefore a part of nature. By using a strikingly original comparison, the poet is able to convey the unity of the city, nature, and himself—an idea that is not easily communicated.

Even though imaginative literature can be divided into types—fiction, poetry, and drama—called **genres,** the nature of these literary forms varies from culture to culture. In fact, some literary forms that readers in the West take very much for granted are quite alien to those familiar with other literary traditions. For example, the poetic forms of non-Western literature are quite different from those of Western Europe and North America. The sonnet, although quite common in the West, is not a conventional literary form in Chinese or Arabic poetry. Similarly, the most popular theatrical entertainment in Japan since the mid-seventeenth century, the kabuki play, does not follow many of the dramatic conventions Western audiences have come to expect and has no exact counterpart in the West. In a kabuki play, which includes stories, scenes, dances, music, acrobatics, and elaborate costumes and stage settings, all of the actors are men, some of whom play the parts of females. Many of the kabuki plays have little plot and seem to be primarily concerned with spectacle. One feature of this form of drama is a walkway that extends from the stage through the audience to the back of the theater.

Finally, conventions of narrative organization and character development can vary considerably, especially in literature descended from an oral tradition. For example, narrative organization in some Native American stories (and, even more commonly, in some African stories) can be very different from what modern readers are accustomed to. Events may be arranged spatially instead of chronologically: First a story presents all the events that happened in one place, then it presents everything that happened in another location, and so on. Character development is also much less important in some traditional African and Native American stories than in modern short fiction. In fact, a character's name, description, and personality can change dramatically (and without warning) in the course of a story.

Despite such differences, the imaginative literature of all cultures has similar effects on readers. A short story, a play, or a poem can arrest readers' attention and cause them to marvel. Lifelike characters, vivid descriptions, imaginative use of language, and intricately developed plots can fascinate and delight readers. Finally, literature can take readers where they have never been before and, in so doing, can create a sense of wonder and adventure.

At another level, however, readers find more than just pleasure or escape in literature. Beyond transporting readers out of their lives and times, literature can enable readers to see their lives and times more clearly. Whether a work of imaginative literature depicts a young girl as she experiences the disillusionment of adulthood for the first time, as in David Michael Kaplan's "Doe Season" (p. 298), or examines the effect of a brutal war on young men's lives, as in Tim O'Brien's "The Things They Carried" (p. 243), it can enlighten readers and help them to understand their own experiences and the experiences of others. In this sense, literature offers readers increased insight and awareness. As the Chilean poet Pablo Neruda says, works of imaginative literature fulfill "the most ancient rites of our conscience in the awareness of being human and of believing in a common destiny."

CONVENTIONAL THEMES

The **theme** of a work of literature is its central or dominant idea. This idea is seldom stated explicitly; rather, it is conveyed through the selection and arrangement of details, through the emphasis of certain events or images, and through the actions and reactions of the characters.

Although one central theme may seem to dominate a literary work, most works explore a number of different themes or ideas. For example, the central theme of Mark Twain's *The Adventures of Huckleberry Finn* might be the idea that an individual's innate sense of right and wrong is superior to society's artificial and sometimes unnatural values. The main character, Huck, gains a growing awareness of this idea by witnessing feuds, duels, and all manner of human folly. As a result he makes a decision to help his friend Jim escape from slavery despite the fact that society, as well as his own conscience, condemns this action. However, *The Adventures of Huckleberry Finn* also examines other themes. Throughout his novel Twain criticizes many of the ideas that prevailed in the pre–Civil War South, such as the evils of slavery and the hypocrisy of the traditional religious values that dominated the towns along the Mississippi.

A literary work can explore any theme, but certain ideas occur so frequently that they have become conventions. These themes express ideas that have meaning to many individuals regardless of the time or place in which they live. One theme frequently explored in literature, a character's loss of innocence, appears in the biblical story of Adam and Eve and later finds its way into works such as Nathaniel Hawthorne's 1835 short story "Young Goodman Brown" (p. 264) and James Joyce's 1914 short story "Araby" (p. 219). Another conventional theme—the conflict between an individual's values and the values of society—is examined in the ancient Greek play *Antigone,* by Sophocles. Almost two thousand years later Norwegian playwright Henrik Ibsen deals with the same theme in *A Doll House.*

Other themes frequently examined in literary works include the individual's quest for spiritual enlightenment, the *carpe diem* ("seize the day") theme, the making of the artist, the nostalgia for a vanished past, the disillusionment of adulthood, the beauty of love, the subjugation of women, the conflict between parents and children, the clash between civilization and the wilderness, the evils of unchecked ambition, the inevitability of fate, the impact of the past on the present, the conflict between human beings and machines, and the tension between the ideal and the actual realms of experience. Modern works of literature sometimes treat such traditional themes in new ways. For example, in *1984* George Orwell explores the negative consequences of unchecked power by creating a nightmare world in which technology is used to control and dehumanize a population. Even though Orwell's novel is set in an imaginary future (it was written in 1948), its theme echoes ideas frequently examined in the plays of both Sophocles and Shakespeare.

Nearly every culture explores themes similar to those just mentioned, but writers from different cultures may develop these themes differently. A culture's history, a particular region's geography, or a country's social structure can suggest a unique way of developing a conventional theme. The assumptions, concerns, values, ideals, and beliefs of a particular country or society—or of a particular group within that society—can have an impact on the themes writers choose to explore and on the manner in which they do so.

Themes occurring repeatedly in North American literature include the loss of innocence, rites of passage, childhood epiphanies, coming to self-awareness, and the ability (or inability) to form relationships. American writers of color, in addition to exploring these themes, also develop themes that reflect their unique perspectives. African-American and Latino writers, for example, may express their frustration with the racism of the dominant society or celebrate their cultural identities. Even when they explore conventional themes, writers of color in North America may choose to do so in the context of their own experience. For example, the theme of loss of innocence may be presented as a first encounter with racial prejudice; a conflict between the individual and society may be presented as a conflict between a minority view and the values of the dominant group; and the theme of failure or aborted relationships may revolve around language difficulties or cultural misunderstandings.

THE LITERARY CANON

Originally the term *canon* referred to the authoritative or accepted list of books that made up the Christian Bible. The term was extended to include the **literary canon,** a group of works generally agreed upon by critics to be masterpieces. As standards change, the definition of what is "good" literature changes, and the canon is modified accordingly. For example, at different times Shakespeare's plays were thought by critics to be either mundane, immoral, commonplace, or brilliant. The eighteenth-century critic Samuel Johnson says of Shakespeare that "in his comick scenes he is seldom very successful" and in tragedy "his performance seems constantly to be worse, as his labor is more." Many people find it difficult to believe that a writer whose name today is synonymous with great literature could ever have been judged so harshly. But like all aesthetic works, the plays of Shakespeare affect individuals in different periods of history or in different societies in various ways.

In recent years, educators and literary scholars have charged that the traditional literary canon, like a restricted club, admits some authors and closes out all others. This fact is borne out, they say, by an examination of the literature curriculum that until recently was found at many North American colleges and universities. This curriculum typically began with Homer, Plato, Dante, and Chaucer, progressed to Shakespeare, Milton, the eighteenth-century novel, the Romantics, and the Victorians, and ended with some of the classics of modern British and American literature. Most of the writers of these works are white and male, and their writing reflects only their Western values. In educational institutions in other countries, the situation has been much the same: Students have typically studied works that reflect and reinforce their society's or their country's values.

In the United States during the past decade, critics of the traditional canon have sought to revise it to include more works by women, people of color, and writers from a variety of cultures. These additions are meant to open up the curriculum and redefine the standards by which literature is judged. For many years, literature courses in North American universities have overlooked South American, African, and Asian writers. Students of literature were not encouraged to consider the perspectives of women or of Latinos, Native Americans, or other ethnic or racial groups (let alone the perspectives of gay writers or those with disabilities). Now this situation is beginning to change. By revising and updating the list of works to be studied, critics of the traditional canon believe that we not only convey the diversity of both American and world cultures, but also expand the definition of great literature.

Consider the following brief story, "All About Suicide" by Luisa Valenzuela, an Argentinean writer. Not only is it experimental, moving freely in time, bending the facts, and speaking directly to readers, but it also focuses on the political realities of contemporary Argentina. Although such a story probably would not be included in a traditional syllabus at many North American universities, it does have literary value.

Luisa Valenzuela
(1938–   )

ALL ABOUT SUICIDE

(1967)

Translated by Helen Lane

Ismael grabbed the gun and slowly rubbed it across his face. Then he pulled the trigger and there was a shot. Bang. One more person dead in the city. It's getting to be a vice. First he grabbed the revolver that was in a desk drawer, rubbed it gently across his face, put it to his temple, and pulled the trigger. Without saying a word. Bang. Dead.

Let's recapitulate: the office is grand, fit for a minister. The desk is ministerial too, and covered with a glass that must have reflected the scene, the shock. Ismael knew where the gun was, he'd hidden it there himself. So he didn't lose any time, all he had to do was open the right-hand drawer and stick his hand in. Then he got a good hold on it and rubbed it over his face with a certain pleasure before putting it to his temple and pulling the trigger. It was something almost sensual and quite unexpected. He hadn't even had time to think about it. A trivial gesture, and the gun had fired.

There's something missing: Ismael in the bar with a glass in his hand thinking over his future act and its possible consequences.

We must go back farther if we want to get at the truth: Ismael in the cradle crying because his diapers are dirty and nobody is changing him.

5 Not that far.

Ismael in the first grade fighting with a classmate who'll one day become a minister, his friend, a traitor.

No, Ismael in the ministry without being able to tell what he knew, forced to be silent. Ismael in the bar with the glass (his third) in his hand, and the irrevocable decision: better death.

Ismael pushing the revolving door at the entrance to the building, pushing the swinging door leading to the office section, saying good morning to the guard, opening the door of his office. Once in his office, seven steps to his desk. Terror, the act of opening the drawer, taking out the revolver, and rubbing it across his face, almost a single gesture and very quick. The act of putting it to his temple and pulling the trigger—another act, immediately following the previous one. Bang. Dead. And Ismael coming out of his office (the other man's office, the minister's) almost relieved, even though he can predict what awaits him.

Certainly canon revision is not without its problems. Some critics point out that inherent in canon revision is the danger of including a work more for political reasons than for literary merit. Nevertheless, if the debate about the literary canon has accomplished anything, it has revealed that the canon is not fixed and that many works formerly excluded from the canon—African-American slave narratives and eighteenth-century women's diaries, for example—deserve to be included.

This is an exciting time in literary studies, and as the debate about the canon continues, new questions and new answers will continue to emerge. Some of the works included in this anthology are considered part of the traditional canon, and others reflect the diversity of the expanding literary canon.

THINKING CRITICALLY

INTERPRETING LITERATURE

When you *interpret* a literary work, you attempt to understand its various meanings. One commonly held idea about reading a literary work is that its meaning lies buried somewhere within it, waiting to be unearthed. This reasoning suggests that a clever reader has only to discover the author's intent to find out what a story or poem means. The one actual meaning of a work is, therefore, hidden between the lines, unaffected by a reader's experiences or interpretations. More recently, however, a different model of the reading process—one that takes into consideration the reader as well as the work he or she is interpreting—has emerged.

Many contemporary critics recognize that the reading process is *interactive:* Meaning comes about through the interaction between a reader and a text. The meaning of a particular work comes alive in the imagination of an individual reader, and no reader can determine a work's meaning without considering his or her reaction to the text. Meaning, therefore, is created partly by what is supplied by a work and partly by what is supplied by the reader.

The most obvious kind of meaning a work supplies is factual, the information that enables a reader to follow the plot of a story, the action of a play, or the development of a poem. For instance, the work itself will provide some factual details about the setting; the characters' names, ages, and appearances; the sequence of events; and the emotions and attitudes of a poem's speaker, a story's narrator, or the characters in a play or story. This factual information cannot be ignored: If a play's stage directions identify its setting as nineteenth-century Norway or the forest of Arden, that is where it is set.

In addition to facts, a work also conveys the social, political, class, and gender attitudes of the writer. Thus a work may have an overtly feminist or class bias or a subtle political agenda; it may confirm or challenge contemporary attitudes; it may communicate a writer's nostalgia for a vanished past or his or her outrage at a corrupt present; it may take an elitist, distant view of characters and events or present a sympathetic, involved perspective. A reader's understanding of these attitudes will contribute to his or her interpretation of the work.

Finally, a work also contains assumptions about literary conventions. A poet, for example, may have definite ideas about whether a poem should be rhymed or unrhymed or about whether a particular subject is appropriate for poetic treatment. A knowledge of the literary conventions of a particular period or the preferences of a particular writer may provide a starting point for your interpretation of literature.

As a reader you also bring to a work your own personal perspectives. Your experiences, your ideas about the issues discussed in the work, and your assumptions about literature color your interpretations; so do your religious, social, and cultural beliefs. In fact, virtually every literary work means different things to different people, depending on their age, gender, nationality, political and religious beliefs, ethnic background, social and economic class, education, knowledge, and experiences. Depending on your religious beliefs, for instance, you can react to a passage from the Old Testament as literal truth, symbolic truth, or fiction. Depending on your race, where you live, your biases, and the nature of your experience, a story about racial discrimination can strike you as accurate and realistic, exaggerated for dramatic effect, or understated and restrained.

In a real sense, then, the process of determining meaning is like a conversation, one in which both you and the text have a voice. Sometimes, by clearly dictating the terms of the discussion, the text determines the direction of the conversation; at other times, by using your knowledge and experience to interpret the text, you dominate. Because every reading of a literary work is actually an interpretation, it is a mistake to look for a single "correct" reading of a text.

The 1923 poem "Stopping by Woods on a Snowy Evening" by the American poet Robert Frost illustrates the flexibility of the process of interpretation. Readers may interpret the poem as being about the inevitability of death; as suggesting that the poet is tired or world weary; or as making a comment about duty and the need to persevere, or about the conflicting pulls of life and art. Beyond these possibilities, readers' own associations of snow with quiet and sadness could lead them to define the mood of the poem as sorrowful or melancholy. Information about Robert Frost's life or his ideas about poetry could add to readers' appreciation of the poem, and they might even develop ideas about the poem that are quite different from the poet's. In fact, on several occasions when he spoke about "Stopping by Woods on a Snowy Evening," Frost himself gave strikingly different, even contradictory, interpretations of the poem, sometimes insisting the poem had no hidden meaning and at other times saying that it required a good deal of explication. Literary critics also disagree about its meaning. When reading a work of literature, then, keep in mind that the meaning of the text is not fixed. Your best strategy is to open yourself up to the text's many possibilities and to explore the full range of your responses.

Although no single reading of a literary work is "correct," some readings are more plausible than others. Like a scientific theory, a literary interpretation must have a basis in fact, and the text supplies the facts against which your interpretations should be judged. For example, after you read Shirley Jackson's "The Lottery" (p. 276), a 1948 short story in which a randomly chosen victim is stoned to death by her neighbors, it would be reasonable for you to conclude that the ceremonial aspects of the lottery suggest a contemporary pagan ritual. Your understanding of what a pagan ritual is, combined with your observation that a number of specific details in the text suggest ancient fertility ceremonies, might lead you to this conclusion. Another possibility is that "The Lottery" provides a commentary on mob psychology. The way characters reinforce one another's violent tendencies lends support to this interpretation. However, the interpretation that the ritual of the lottery is a comment on the death penalty would be difficult to support. Certainly a character in the story is killed, but she is not accused of a crime, nor is she tried or convicted. The killing is random and seemingly without motivation. Still, although seeing the "The Lottery" as an endorsement of the death penalty may be far-fetched, this interpretation is a good beginning. A second, closer reading of the story will most likely lead you in different directions, allowing you to explore other, more plausible, interpretations.

As you read, do not be afraid to take chances and present unusual or creative interpretations of a work. "Safe" readings of a work often result in dull papers that simply state the obvious. An aggressive or "strong" reading of a work, however, can raise issues that lead to interesting and intellectually challenging conclusions. Even if your reading differs from established interpretations of a work, you should not assume it has no merit. Your special knowledge of the material discussed in the text—a regional practice, an ethnic custom, an attitude toward gender—may give you a unique perspective from which to view the work. Whatever interpretation you make, be sure that you justify it by supporting your assertions with specific references to the text. If your interpretation is based on your own experiences, explain those experiences and relate them clearly to the work you are discussing. As long as you can make a reasonable case, you have the right (and perhaps the obligation) to present your ideas. By doing so you may provide your fellow students and your instructor with a reading that gives them new insight into the work.

It is important to keep in mind, however, that some interpretations are *not* reasonable. Readers may contribute ideas based on their own perspectives, but they cannot ignore or contradict evidence in the text to suit their own biases. As you read and reread a text, continue to question and reexamine your judgments. The conversation between reader and text should be a dialogue, not a monologue or a shouting match.

EVALUATING LITERATURE

When you *evaluate* a work of literature, you do more than interpret it; you make a judgment about it. You reach conclusions concerning the work—not simply that the work is good or bad, but also how effectively the work presents itself to you, the reader. To evaluate a work, you *analyze* it, breaking it apart and considering its individual elements. As you evaluate a work of literature, remember that different works are designed to fulfill different needs—for entertainment, education, enlightenment, and so on. When you begin to evaluate a work, make certain that you determine its purpose and apply reasonable standards. Consider the following guidelines:

Begin your evaluation by considering how various elements function individually within a work. For instance, fiction may use dialogue and symbols. Plays are divided into scenes and acts and employ dialogue and special staging techniques. Poems may be arranged in regularly ordered groups of lines and use poetic devices such as rhyme and meter. Understanding the choices writers make can lead you to new insights and can help you make judgments about the work. For example, why does Alberto Alvaro Rios use a first-person narrator (*I* and *we*) in his story "The Secret Lion" (p. 38)? Would the story have been different had it been told in the third person (*they*) by a narrator who is not a participant in the action? How does unusual staging affect an audience's response to a play? What does an unusual stanzaic form contribute to a poem? Naturally, you cannot and should not focus on every aspect of a particular story, poem, or play. But you can and should focus on those that play a major role in determining your responses to a work.

As you read, ask yourself some questions. Do the characters in a short story seem real, or do they seem like cardboard cutouts? Are the stage directions of a play clear or ambiguous? Are the images in a poem original and thought-provoking, or are they clichéd?

As you continue your evaluation, decide whether or not the literary elements of a work interact to achieve a common goal. Well-crafted literary works are aesthetically pleasing, fitting together in a way that conceals the craft of the writer. Good writers are like master cabinetmakers; their skill makes it possible for them to disguise the actual work that goes into the process of creation. Consider the following stanza from the 1862 poem "Echo" by Christina Rosetti:

> Come to me in the silence of the night;
>   Come to me in the speaking silence of a dream;
> Come with soft round cheeks and eyes as bright
>   As sunlight on a stream;
>   Come back in tears,
> O memory, hope, love of finished years.

Throughout this stanza Rossetti repeats words (<u>Come</u> to me. . . . /<u>Come</u> with soft. . . . /<u>Come</u> back. . . .) and initial consonants (<u>s</u>peaking silence/sunlight on a stream) to create an almost hypnotic mood. The rhyme scheme is so subtle that it is hardly noticeable. Even so, the rhymes (*night/bright, dream/stream,* and *tears/years*) reinforce the mood by creating a musical undercurrent that extends throughout the poem. This stanza is effective because its sounds and rhyme scheme work together to create a single lyrical effect.

The chorus in *Antigone* by Sophocles also illustrates how the elements of a well-crafted work of literature function together. In ancient Greece plays were performed by masked male actors who played various roles—both male and female. A chorus of fifteen men would remain in a central circle called the *orchestra* and comment on and react to the action taking place around them. Along with the dialogue, characterization, and staging, the chorus contributes to the total effect of *Antigone.* It not only expresses the moral judgment of the community, but it also acts as a guide for the audience. Once modern audiences become accustomed to the presence of the chorus, it becomes an integral part of the play. It neither distracts the audience nor intrudes upon the action. In fact, eliminating the chorus would diminish the impact of the play.

Next, consider whether a work reinforces or calls into question your ideas about the world. The 1985 short story "Gryphon" by Charles Baxter (p. 123) is one that may lead readers to question their assumptions. It presents a boy in a rural town whose sick teacher is replaced by an eccentric substitute. In her idiosyncratic, even exotic, way, the substitute introduces the boy to a whole new range of intellectual possibilities. Because we, like the children in the story, have learned to expect substitute teachers to be dull and conventional, the story challenges our basic assumptions about substitute teachers and, by extension, about education itself.

Works of popular fiction—those aimed at a mass audience—usually do little more than reassure readers that what they believe is correct. Catering to people's prejudices, or to their desires (for wealth or success, for example), or to their fears, these works serve as escapes from life. Serious fiction, however, goes against the grain, challenging cherished beliefs and leading readers to reexamine long-held assumptions. In the 1977 short story "A Loaf of Bread" (p. 324) James Alan McPherson's protagonist, a white grocer, struggles with the conflict between his desire to fight the black customers who are protesting his high prices and his wife's view that he should settle the conflict by giving all his merchandise to his customers. His reluctance to follow his wife's advice underscores his conflict with the values of those who live in the neighborhood near his store. Serious literature provokes readers to confront and question their values and beliefs, just as the grocer does.

Then, consider whether or not a work is intellectually challenging. The extended comparison between a compass and two people in love in "A Valediction: Forbidding Mourning" by the seventeenth-century English poet John Donne illustrates how an intellectually challenging image can communicate ideas to a reader. Compressed into the comparison are ideas about the perfection of love, the pain of enforced separation, and the difference between sexual and spiritual love. As complex as the extended comparison is, it is nonetheless accessible to the careful reader. After all, many people have used a compass to draw a circle and, therefore, are able to understand the relationship between the two points of the compass and the two lovers.

A fine line exists, however, between works that are intellectually challenging and those that are intellectually obscure. An *intellectually challenging work* makes readers think; it requires some effort on the readers' part to unlock ideas that enrich and expand their understanding of themselves and the world. Although it is complex, the work gives readers a sense that they have gained something by putting forth the effort to read and interpret it. An *intellectually obscure work,* however, seems to exist solely to display a writer's erudition or intellectual idiosyncrasies. In such works allusions to other works and events are so numerous and arcane that the work seems more like a private code than an effort to communicate with or enlighten readers. Consider the following excerpt from "Canto LXXVI" by the twentieth-century American poet Ezra Pound:

Le Paradis n'est pas artificiel
        States of mind are inexplicable to us.
        δακρυων δακρυων δακρυων
L.   P.   gli onesti
                J'ai eu pitié des autres
probablement pas assez, and at moments that suited my own
        convenience
                Le paradis n'est pas artificiel,
                        l'enfer non plus.
Came Eurus as comforter
and at sunset la pastorella dei suini
        driving the pigs home, benecomata dea
                under the two-winged cloud
                as of less and more than a day

This segment contains lines in French, Greek, and Italian; a reference to Eurus, the ancient Greek personification of the east wind; and the initials L.P. (Loomis Pound?). Admittedly this passage demands a lot from readers; the question is whether the reward is worth the effort. No hard and fast rule exists for determining whether a work is intellectually challenging or simply obscure. Just as a poem has no fixed meaning, it also has no fixed value. Some readers would say that the passage is good, even great, poetry. Others might argue that these lines do not yield enough pleasure and insight to justify the work needed to analyze them. As a careful reader, you must draw your own conclusions and justify them in a clear and reasonable way. Do not assume that just because a work is difficult, it is obscure. (Nor should you assume that all difficult works are great literature or that all accessible literature is trivial.) Some of the most beautiful and inspiring literary works demand a great deal of effort from readers. Most readers would agree, however, that the time spent exploring such works yields tremendous rewards.

Finally, and perhaps most importantly, consider whether a work gives you pleasure. One of the primary reasons that literature endures is that it gives readers enjoyment. As subjective as this assessment is, it is a starting point for critical judgment. When readers ask themselves what they liked about a work, why they liked it, or what they learned, they begin the process of evaluation. Although this process is largely uncritical, it can lead to an involvement with the work and to a critical response. When you encounter great literature, with all its complexities, you may lose sight of the idea of literature as a source of pleasure. But literature should touch you on a deep emotional or intellectual level, and if it does not—despite its technical perfection—it has failed to achieve one of its primary aims.

THE FUNCTION OF LITERARY CRITICISM

Sometimes your personal reactions and knowledge cannot give you enough insight into a literary work. For example, archaic language, obscure references, historical allusions, and textual inconsistencies can make reading a work particularly difficult. Similarly, an intellectual or philosophical movement such as Darwinism, Marxism, naturalism, structuralism, or feminism may influence a work, and if this is the case, you will need some knowledge of the movement before you can interpret the work. In addition, you may not have the background to appreciate the technical or historical dimension of a work. To widen the context of your reading, you may choose to read **literary criticism**—books and journal articles written by experts who describe, analyze, interpret, or evaluate a work of literature. Reading literary criticism not only enables you to expand your knowledge of a particular work, but also allows you to participate in the public dialogue about literature. In a sense you become part of a community of scholars who share their ideas and who are connected to one another through their writing.

Just because literary criticism is written by experts, do not assume you must accept it automatically. You have to evaluate literary criticism just as you do any new opinion that you encounter. Not all criticism is valid, timely, or responsible, and not all literary criticism is pertinent to your assignment or useful for your purposes. Some critical comments will strike you as plausible, but others will seem unfounded or biased. Quite often two critics will reach strikingly different conclusions about the skill or importance of the same work or writer, or interpret a character, a symbol, or even the entire work quite differently. The Fiction Casebook that closes this section of the text contains articles in which critics disagree in just this fashion. In "In Fairyland, without a Map: Connie's Exploration Inward in Joyce Carol Oates' 'Where Are You Going, Where Have You Been?'" Gretchen Schulz and R. J. R. Rockwood examine the parallels between a character, Arnold

Friend, and a real-life psychopathic killer. They see Arnold in mythological terms and conclude that he is the "exact transpositional counterpart of the real-life Pied Piper of Tucson." In Mike Tierce and John Michael Crafton's "Connie's Tambourine Man: A New Reading of Arnold Friend," however, the authors explicitly reject this suggestion as well as other critical interpretations, concluding instead that "The key question . . . is who is this musical messiah, and the key to the answer is the dedication 'For Bob Dylan.'"

As you can see, critics may disagree, but even conflicting ideas can help you to reach your own conclusions about a work. It is up to you to sort out the various opinions and decide which have merit and which do not. The following questions can help you to evaluate literary criticism:

- What is the main point of the critical article you are reading?
- Does the critic supply enough examples to support his or her conclusions?
- Does the critic acknowledge and refute the most obvious arguments against his or her position?
- Does the critic ignore any information in the text that might call his or her conclusions into question?
- Does the critic present historical information? Biographical information? Literary information? How does this information shed light on significant aspects of the work or works being discussed?
- Does the critic exhibit any prejudices or beliefs that might interfere with his or her critical judgment?
- Does the critic slant the facts, or does he or she offer a fair and objective reading of the text?
- Does the critical book or article support its assertions with documentation? Does it contain a list of works cited? Are these works current? Are explanatory notes included where necessary?
- Do other critical works mention the book or article you are reading? What do they say about its conclusions?

With your instructor's help, you might also try to answer these questions:

- Does the critic identify with a particular critical school of thought—deconstruction, Marxism, or feminism, for example? What unique perspective does this school of thought provide?
- Is the critic well known and respected or unknown?
- Does the critic take into consideration the most important critical books and articles on his or her subject? Are there works that should have been mentioned that were not? Do these gaps cast doubts on the critic's conclusions?
- Is the critical work's publication date of any significance?

CHAPTER 2

READING AND WRITING ABOUT LITERATURE

READING LITERATURE

The process of writing about literature actually starts the moment you begin to read. At that point you begin interacting with a work and start to discover ideas about the text. As soon as you decide to write about a work, you should start recording your reactions to it. These reactions will not only help you to interpret the material, but they will also enable you to organize your ideas into a clear and logical paper.

Three strategies in particular will help you to become a more effective reader: *previewing, highlighting,* and *annotating.* As you engage in these activities, remember that the process of reading and responding to what you read is not an orderly or a sequential one. You will most likely find yourself simultaneously engaging in more than one of the strategies described here—annotating at the same time you highlight, for example. For the sake of clarity, however, we discuss each strategy separately in the pages that follow.

PREVIEWING

The first time you encounter a text you should **preview** it to get a general sense of what to look for later, when you read it more carefully. At this stage you simply want to glance through the work, looking for physical characteristics that can help you to identify some of its most noteworthy features.

These physical characteristics, which can call attention to a stylistic, structural, or even thematic feature of a work, are often fairly easy to identify. For example, a glance is enough to identify a play's cast of characters or to show a short story's brevity. Literary texts also exhibit a wide variety of experiments with form. For example, a contemporary short story may be presented entirely in a question and answer format, it may be organized as diary entries, as Lorrie Moore's "How to Talk to Your Mother (Notes)" (p. 78) is, or it may be divided into sections by headings. Previewing may identify poems that seem to lack formal structure, those written in traditional forms (such as sonnets), and those written in experimental forms—for example, those whose shape on the page reflects their subject.

Other physical characteristics—such as the breaks between sections of stories, stanzas of poems, chapters of books, and acts and scenes of plays—are also easy to identify. Perhaps the most physically distinctive element of a text is its title. Not only can the title give you an idea what a work is about, but it can also introduce a word or phrase that is central to the work, or it can be a symbol or an allusion to another work. Other, more subtle, physical elements—such as paragraphing, capitalization, italics, and punctuation—can also provide clues about how to read a work.

Previewing is a useful strategy because it suggests questions to ask later as you read more closely—for instance, *why* does William Faulkner use italics in "Barn Burning" (p. 187)? Remember, however, that although physical elements such as those described above may be noticeable even as you preview, they are likely to be more obvious as you read more carefully and review your notes.

HIGHLIGHTING

When you go on to read a work closely, you notice stylistic features, thematic patterns, and other elements that you may want to examine further. At this point, you should begin **highlighting**—physically marking the text to identify key points and to note relationships among ideas.

What should you highlight? As you read, ask yourself whether repeated words or phrases form a pattern, as they do in Ernest Hemingway's short story "A Clean, Well-Lighted Place" (p. 225), in which the Spanish word *nada* ("nothing") appears again and again. Because this unusual word appears so frequently, and because it appears at key points in the story, it helps to reinforce the story's theme—that all human experience amounts to *nada,* or nothingness. As you read, then, you should highlight your text to identify such repeated words and phrases.

You should also pay particular attention at this stage to images that occur repeatedly in a work; such repeated images may form patterns that can help you to interpret the work, and for this reason they should be highlighted. During the previewing stage, you may have been able only to identify repeated images. When you reread the work, however, you can begin to determine the pattern the images form and perhaps try to decide how this pattern enhances the work's ideas. When previewing Robert Frost's "Stopping By Woods on a Snowy Evening" for instance, you might simply have made a mental note of the poem's related images of silence, cold, and darkness. Now you can highlight those images so that later you can consider their significance.

When you highlight, you emphasize portions of the text with a system of symbols. As you become experienced with the techniques of active reading, you will develop the system of shorthand that works best for you. For the time being, however, you can experiment with the symbols listed here:

- Underline important ideas that you should read again.
- Box or circle repeated words, phrases, or images.
- Question (?) confusing segments, unfamiliar references, or words that need to be defined.
- Draw lines or arrows to connect related ideas or images.
- Number incidents that occur in sequence.
- Set off a long portion of the text with a vertical line in the margin.
- Star (*) a particularly important idea.

The following poem by Maya Angelou has been highlighted by a student preparing to write about it. Notice how the student uses symbols to help him identify stylistic features, key points, and patterns of repetition that he may want to examine later.

Maya Angelou
(1928–)

MY ARKANSAS
(1978)

There is a deep brooding
in Arkansas.
? Old crimes like moss pend ?
from poplar trees.
The sullen earth
is much too
red for comfort.

Sunrise seems to hesitate
and in that second
lose its
incandescent aim, and
dusk no more shadows
than the noon.
* The past is brighter yet.

Old hates and
ante-bellum lace are rent ?
but not discarded.
* Today is yet to come
in Arkansas.
It writhes. It writhes in awful
waves of brooding.

This student identifies repeated words and phases ("brooding"; "it writhes") and places question marks beside the two words ("pend" and "rent") whose meanings he plans to look up in a dictionary. He also questions the possible meanings of "old crimes" and "ante-bellum lace," two references he needs to think more about. Finally, he stars what he tentatively identifies as the poem's key ideas. When he rereads the poem, his highlighting will make it easier for him to react to and interpret the writer's ideas.

ANNOTATING

At the same time you highlight a text, you also **annotate**, making marginal notes on the page. By engaging in this activity, you record your reactions and perhaps begin to map out a preliminary plan for your paper. Your notes may define new words, identify allusions, identify patterns of language or imagery, summarize complex plot relationships, list a work's possible themes, suggest the motivations of certain characters, or examine the possible significance of particular images or symbols. You may also use annotations to record questions that occur to you as you read. Many works contain unresolved issues that you must try to explain. For example, what motivates Sammy to quit his job at the end of John Updike's 1961 short story "A&P" (p. 93)? The following paragraph from "A&P" was highlighted and annotated by a student in an introduction to literature course who was writing an essay in response to this question:

> Lengel sighs and begins to look very patient and old and gray. He's been a friend of my parents for years. "Sammy, you don't want to do this to your Mom and Dad," he tells me. It's true, I don't. But it seems to me that once you begin a gesture it's fatal not to go through with it. I fold the apron, "Sammy" stitched in red on the pocket, and put it on the counter, and drop the bow tie on top of it. The bow tie is theirs, if you've ever wondered. "You'll feel this for the rest of your life," Lengel says, and I know that's true, too, but remembering how he made the pretty girl blush makes me so scrunchy inside I punch the No Sale tab and the machine whirs "pee-pul" and the drawer splats out. One advantage to this scene taking place in summer, I can follow this up with a clean exit, there's no fumbling around getting your coat and galoshes, I just saunter into the electric eye in my white shirt that my mother ironed the night before, and the door heaves itself open, and outside the sunshine is skating around on the asphalt.

Action does not seem to be the result of thought. Sammy reacts to the girls' embarrassment

cowboy – John Wayne

* need for a clean exit – reinforce immature romantic ideas

Romantic cowboy, but his mother irons his shirt. Irony.

Because the student's instructor had discussed the story in class and because the student had a specific assignment—to explain Sammy's actions at the end of the story—her annotations are quite focused. In addition to highlighting important information in this paragraph, she notes her reactions to the story and tries to interpret Sammy's actions. Sometimes, however, you may annotate before you have decided on a topic—in fact, the process of reading and responding to your text can help you to focus on a topic. In the absence of a topic, your annotations are likely to be less focused, and you will need to highlight and annotate again when your paper's direction is more firmly fixed in your mind.

WRITING ABOUT LITERATURE

Writing about literature—or about anything else, for that matter—is an idiosyncratic process during which many activities occur at once: As you write, you think of ideas; as you think of ideas, you clarify the focus of your essay; and as you clarify your focus, you reshape your paragraphs and sentences and refine your word choice. Even though this process sounds chaotic, it may be described as having three stages: *planning, drafting,* and *revising and editing*. Remember, however, that although for the sake of clarity we discuss these stages separately, they actually overlap.

PLANNING AN ESSAY

Considering Your Audience

Sometimes—for example, in a journal entry—you write primarily for yourself. At other times, however, you write for an **audience**. As you write an essay, you should consider the special requirements of that audience. Is your audience your classmates or your instructor? Can you assume your readers are familiar with your paper's topic and with any technical terms you will use, or will they need brief plot summaries or definitions of key terms? If your audience is your instructor, remember that he or she is a representative of a larger academic audience and therefore expects accurate information; standard English; correct grammar, mechanics, and spelling; logical arguments; and a certain degree of stylistic fluency. In addition, your instructor expects you to support your assertions with specific information, to express yourself clearly and explicitly, and to document your sources. In short, your instructor wants to see how well you think and whether you are able to arrange your ideas into a well-organized, coherent essay.

In addition to being a member of a general academic audience, your instructor is also a member of a particular community of scholars—in this case, those who study literature. By writing about literature, you engage in a dialogue with this community. For this reason, you should adhere to the specific *conventions*—procedures that by habitual use have become accepted practice—its members follow. Many of the conventions that apply specifically to writing about literature—matters of style, format, and the like—will be discussed in this book.

Understanding Your Purpose

In addition to considering your audience, you need to consider your **purpose** (or purposes) for writing. Sometimes you write with a single purpose in mind; at other times a single assignment or writing task may suggest more than one purpose. In general terms, you may write for any of the following reasons:

Writing to Respond When you write to *respond,* your goal is to discover and express your reactions to a work. To record your responses you engage in relatively informal, personal activities, such as brainstorming, listing, and journal writing (see p. 22–24). As you write you explore your own ideas, forming and reforming your impressions of the work.

Writing to Interpret When you write to *interpret,* you explain a work's possible meanings. To do so, you may summarize, identify examples, or compare and contrast the work to other works or to your own experiences. Then, you may go on to analyze the work, studying each of its elements in turn, putting complex statements in your own words, defining difficult concepts, or placing ideas in context.

Writing to Evaluate When you write to *evaluate,* your purpose is to assess a work's literary merits. You may consider not only its aesthetic appeal, but also its ability to retain that appeal over time and across national or cultural boundaries. As you write, you use your own critical sense and the opinions of experts in the field to help you make judgments about the work.

Choosing a Topic

When you write an essay about literature, you develop an idea about a literary work or works—an analysis of the point of view of a story, a discussion of the theme of a poem, an examination of a character in a play, or a comparison between two works, for example. Before you begin your writing, you should make certain that you understand your assignment. Do you know how much time you have to complete your essay? Are you expected to rely on your own ideas, or are you able to consult journal articles in the library? Is your essay to focus on a specific work or on a particular element of literature? Do you have to write on an assigned topic, or are you free to choose a topic? About how long should your essay be? Do you understand exactly what the assignment is asking you to do?

Sometimes your assignment limits your options by telling you what you are to discuss:

- Write an essay in which you analyze Robert Frost's use of the color white in his poem "Design."
- Discuss Hawthorne's use of allegory in his short story "Young Goodman Brown."
- Write a short essay in which you explain Nora's actions at the end of Ibsen's *A Doll House.*

Sometimes, however, your instructor will give you no specific guidelines other than a paper's length and format. In such situations, where you must choose a topic on your own, you can find a topic by brainstorming or by writing journal entries. As you engage in these activities, however, keep in mind that you have many options for writing papers about literature. Some of these options are listed here.

- Compare two works of literature.
- Compare two characters or some attribute of those characters.
- Trace a common theme—jealousy, revenge, repression, coming of age—in several works.
- Consider how a common subject—war, love, nature—is treated in several works.
- Examine a single element in one or more works—for instance, plot, point of view, or figurative language.
- Focus on a single aspect of that element, such as the role of flashbacks, the effect of a shifting narrative perspective, or the use of metaphors.
- Apply a critical theory to a work of literature—for instance, apply a feminist perspective to Tillie Olsen's "I Stand Here Ironing."
- Examine connections between an issue treated in a work of literature—for instance, child abuse in James Joyce's "Counterparts"—and that same issue as it is treated in sociological or psychological journals or in the popular press.
- Examine some aspect of history or biography and consider its impact on a literary work—for instance, the influence of his World War I experiences on Ernest Hemingway's fiction.
- Explore a problem within a work and propose a possible solution—for example, what is the narrator's true reason for killing the old man in Edgar Allan Poe's "The Tell-Tale Heart"?

Any of the options above may lead you to an interesting topic. Remember, however, that you will still have to narrow the scope of your topic so that it fits within the limits of your assignment.

Finding Something to Say

Once you have a topic, you have to find something to say about it. The information that you collected when you highlighted and annotated will help you to formulate the statement that will be the central idea of your essay and lead you to ideas that can support that statement.

A number of strategies can help you to find supporting material:

- You can discuss ideas with others—friends, classmates, instructors, or parents, for example.
- You can ask questions.

- You can do research.
- You can **freewrite**—that is, keep writing on your topic for a given period of time without pausing to consider style, structure, or content.

Three other strategies—*brainstorming, keeping a journal,* and *listing*—are especially helpful.

Brainstorming When you **brainstorm**, you jot down ideas—single words, phrases, or sentences; statements or questions; quotations, paraphrases, summaries, or your own ideas—as they occur to you, moving as quickly as possible. Your starting point may be a general assignment, a particular work (or works) of literature, a specific topic, or even a thesis statement; in fact, you can brainstorm at any stage of the writing process, and you can repeat this activity as often as you like.

The brainstorming notes that follow were made by a student preparing to write a paper on the relationships between children and parents in four poems. She began by brainstorming about each poem in turn and went on to consider thematic relationships among the poems. These notes represent her preliminary reactions to one of the four poems she planned to study, Adrienne Rich's 1984 poem "A Woman Mourned by Daughters."

Brainstorming Notes

Memory: then and now
    Then: leaf, straw, dead insect (= light); ignored
    Now: swollen, puffed up, weight (= heavy); focus of attention.
        controls their movements.
*Kitchen = a "universe"
    Teaspoons, goblets, etc. = concrete representations of mother;
        also = obligations, responsibilities (like plants and father)
    → (weigh on them, keep them under her spell)

Milestones of past: weddings, being fed as children
"You breathe upon us now"
    PARADOX? (Dead, she breathes, has weight, fills house and sky. Alive, she was a dead insect, no one paid attention to her.)

Keeping a Journal You can use a journal to find ideas—and, later, to help you to find a topic or a thesis. In a **journal** you expand your marginal annotations and go on to record your responses to works you have read, note questions, explore emerging ideas, experiment with possible paper topics, try to paraphrase or summarize difficult concepts, or speculate about a work's ambiguities. A journal is the place to take chances, to try out ideas that may seem frivolous or irrelevant; here you can think on paper until connections become clear or ideas crystallize. You can also use your journal as a convenient place to collect your brainstorming notes and, later, your lists of related ideas.

As he prepared to write a paper analyzing the role of Jim, the "gentleman caller" in Tennessee Williams's play *The Glass Menagerie* a student explored ideas in the following journal entry:

> When he tells Laura that being disappointed is not the same as being discouraged, and that he's disappointed but not discouraged, Jim reveals his role as a symbol of the power of newness and change—a "bulldozer" that will clear out whatever is in its path, even delicate people like Laura. But the fact that he is disappointed shows Jim's human side. He has run into problems since high school, and these problems have blocked his progress toward a successful future. Working at the warehouse, Jim needs Tom's friendship to remind him of what he used to be (and what he still can be?), and this shows his insecurity. He isn't as sure of himself as he seems to be.

This journal entry reflects the student's initial response to a character; it is personal and subjective. Even so, these preliminary explorations can eventually help him to decide on a specific direction for his essay.

Listing After you have actively read a work, you should have a good many underlinings and marginal notes. Some of this material will relate to your topic, and some will be irrelevant. **Listing** is the process of examining the notes you collected through brainstorming, keeping a journal, and annotating your text; deciding what material is pertinent; and arranging that material into categories so that you can determine a direction for your essay. As you prepare to list, review your information and consider the categories your notes suggest. Then, after writing down these categories, list specific information under each heading. As you list information, you will discover new ideas and new connections among ideas. Listing enables you to discover patterns: to see repeated images, similar characters, recurring words and phrases, and interrelated themes or ideas. Identifying these patterns helps you to decide which points to make in your paper and what information you will use to support these points. Remember that the lists you make do not yet reflect the order or emphasis of the ideas you will develop in your paper. As your ideas become more focused, you will add, delete, and rearrange material.

After reading Lorrie Moore's "How to Talk to Your Mother (Notes)," a student arranged material from her annotations, brainstorming notes, and journal entries into the following lists of related details. Her topic was the relationship between the details of the narrator's personal life and the events of the larger world. This topic suggested categories under which she could arrange her material.

PERSONAL/COMMONPLACE
- Details of day-to-day life
  - Laundromat
  - Apple crisp
  - Dishwasher
  - Meals
  - Party
  - Funeral
- Babies
  - Abortions
  - Kids on public transportation
  - Stretch marks
  - Doll ("the Sue")
  - Brother's children

WORLD
- Songs
  - "You'll Never Walk Alone"
  - "Oklahoma!"
  - "Three Little Fishies"
  - "Shoofly Pie"
- Historical Events
  - Dead Sea Scrolls discovered
  - Elections
  - Germany invades Poland
  - Bicentennial
  - Grandma Moses dies
  - Kennedy is shot
- Scientific/Medical Events
  - Polyurethane heart
  - Temporary artificial heart
  - Moon landing

Deciding on a Thesis

After completing your listing, you should try to express the direction of your thinking in a tentative **thesis**—a statement, often expressed in a single sentence, that the rest of your essay supports. This idea, which you will develop as you write, should emerge out of your highlighting, annotations, brainstorming notes, journal entries, and lists of related points. (In many cases, in fact, you will decide on a tentative thesis at an earlier stage of the writing process.)

An effective thesis tells readers what your essay will discuss and how you will approach your material. Consequently, it should be precisely worded, making its point clear to your readers. It should contain no vague words or inexact diction that will make it difficult for readers to follow your discussion. Although the statement "The use of sound in Tennyson's poem 'The Eagle' is interesting" is accurate, it does not convey any clear idea to your readers because the words *sound* and *interesting* are not specific enough. An effective thesis might be "Unity in 'The Eagle' is achieved by Tennyson's use of alliteration, assonance, and rhyme throughout the poem." In addition to being specific, your thesis should give your readers an accurate sense of the scope and direction of your essay. It should not make promises that you do not intend to fulfill or contain extraneous details that might confuse your readers. If, for example, you are going to write a paper about the dominant image in a poem, your thesis should not imply that you will focus on setting or tone.

Remember that as you organize your ideas and as you write, you will probably modify and sharpen your tentative thesis. Sometimes you will even begin your essay with one idea about a work and end it with an entirely different idea. If this happens, be sure to revise your support paragraphs so that they are consistent with your changes and so that the points you include support your new thesis. If you find that your thoughts about your topic are changing, remember that this is how the writing process works. As you write you will discover new ideas, and your essay will be stronger as a result.

Preparing an Outline

Once you have decided on a tentative thesis and have some idea of how you will support it, you can begin to plan your essay's structure. Quite often, an outline can help you to shape your essay. Not all writers outline, but many do at some point in the writing process because it helps them to clarify their ideas and the relationship of these ideas to one another. Realizing, however, that they will discover many new ideas as they write, even these writers seldom use a detailed formal outline, preferring a scratch outline that lists just the major points they plan to make.

A **scratch outline**, perhaps the most useful kind of outline for a short paper, is an informal list of the main points you will discuss in your essay in the order in which they will be introduced. As its name implies, a scratch outline is rough, lacking the detail and the degree of organization of a more formal outline. The main purpose of a scratch outline is to give a sense of the shape and order of your paper and thus enable you to begin writing. A student writing a short essay on American poet Edwin Arlington Robinson's use of irony in his 1910 poem "Miniver Cheevy" used the following scratch outline as a guide:

SPEAKER'S ATTITUDE
- Ironic
- Cynical
- Critical

USE OF DICTION
- Formal
- Detached

USE OF ALLUSIONS
- Thebes
- Camelot
- Priam
- Medici

USE OF REPETITION
- "Miniver"
- "thought"
- repetitious rhyme

Once this outline was complete, the student was ready to write a first draft.

DRAFTING

Your first draft is not a finished product but a preliminary version of your paper, something to react to and revise. Still, before you begin to write, you should be familiar with one of the most common ways of arranging information: thesis and support. In a **thesis and support** paper you present your thesis in your introduction, support your thesis in the body paragraphs of your essay, and restate your thesis or summarize your points in your conclusion. Knowing this basic method of organizing information will not only help you to write your first draft, but also help you with the revision that you do later.

Before you draft your paper, you should review the material you have collected to support your thesis.

First, make sure that you have collected enough information to support your thesis. The judgments you make are only as convincing as the evidence you present to support them. As you read and took notes, you collected examples from the work or works about which you are writing—summaries, paraphrases, or quoted lines of narrative, verse, or dialogue—to back up your assertions. Just how many of these examples you need to use in your draft depends on the nature of your thesis and how skeptical you believe your audience to be. In general, the more inclusive your thesis, the more material you need to support it. For example, if you were supporting the rather narrow thesis that the dialogue of a certain character in the second scene of a play was wooden or awkward, only a few examples would be enough. However, if you wanted to support the inclusive thesis that Nora and Torvald Helmer in Henrik Ibsen's 1879 play *A Doll House* are trapped in their roles, you would need to present quite a number of examples.

Second, see if the work includes any examples that contradict your thesis. Before you can establish your thesis with a high degree of certainty, you should look for examples that contradict it. For example, if you plan to support the thesis that in *A Doll House* Ibsen makes a strong case for the rights of women, you should look for counterexamples. Can you find subtle hints in the play that suggest women should remain locked in their traditional roles and continue to defer to their fathers and husbands?

Finally, consider whether you need to use literary criticism to help you support your thesis. You could strengthen the thesis that *A Doll House* challenged contemporary attitudes about marriage by including the fact that when the play first opened, Ibsen was convinced by an apprehensive theater manager to write another ending. In the new ending, Ibsen had Nora decide, after she stopped briefly to look in at her sleeping children, that she could not leave her family. In some cases, information from another source can lead you to change your thesis. For example, after reading *A Doll House,* you could decide that Ibsen's purpose was to make a strong case for the rights of women. In class, however, you might learn that Ibsen repeatedly said that his play was about the rights of all human beings, not just women. This information could lead you to a thesis that suggests Torvald is just as trapped in his role as Nora is in hers. Naturally, Ibsen's interpretation of his work does not invalidate your first judgment, but it does suggest another conclusion that is worth investigating.

After you have carefully evaluated your supporting material, you can begin drafting your essay, using your scratch outline as your guide. Your goal is to get your ideas down on paper, so you should write quickly. Once you have a draft, you will be able to examine the connections among ideas and to evaluate preliminary versions of your paragraphs and sentences. Do not worry about constructing the "perfect" introduction and conclusion. Many writers, knowing that their ideas will change as they write, postpone writing these paragraphs until a later draft, preferring instead to begin with just their tentative thesis. Your first draft is naturally going to be rough and will probably not achieve the clarity of thought that you want; still, it enables you to see the ideas that you have outlined begin to take shape.

REVISING AND EDITING

As soon as you begin to draft your essay, you begin the process of revision. Before you are satisfied with your essay, you will probably write several drafts, each more closely focused and more coherent than the previous one.

Strategies for Revision

Two strategies can help you to revise your drafts: *peer review* and a *dialogue with your instructor.*

Peer review is a process in which students assess each other's work. This activity may be carried out in informal sessions, during which one student comments on another's draft, or it may be a formal process in which a student responds to specific questions on a form supplied by the instructor. In either case, one student's reaction can help another student develop a draft. Peer review can be carried out on any draft, and questions can focus on style, essay structure, or any other issue.

A **dialogue with your instructor**—in conference or in writing—can give you a sense of how to proceed with your revision. Establishing such an oral or written dialogue can help you learn how to respond critically to your own writing, and your reactions to your instructor's comments on any draft can help you to clarify your essay's goals. (If your instructor is not available, you may be able to schedule a conference at a writing center, if your college has such a facility.) Using your own responses as well as those of your classmates and your instructor, you can write drafts that are increasingly more consistent with these goals.

The Revision Process

As you move through successive drafts, the task of revising your essay about literature will be easier if you follow a systematic process. As you read and react to your essay, assess the effectiveness of the larger elements—thesis and support, for instance—and proceed to examine increasingly smaller details.

Thesis First, reconsider your thesis. Is it carefully and precisely worded? Does it provide a realistic idea of what your essay will cover? Does it make a point that is worth supporting? It is not enough, for instance, to base an essay about literature on a vague thesis like one of the following:

Vague: Many important reasons exist to explain why Margot Macomber's shooting of her husband was probably intentional.

Vague: Dickens's characters are a lot like those of Addison and Steele.

To give focus and direction to your essay a thesis statement must be more pointed and more specific, as the following revisions are:

Revised: Although Hemingway's text states that Margot Macomber "shot at the buffalo," a careful analysis of her relationship with her husband suggests that in fact she intended to kill him.

Revised: With their extremely familiar, almost caricature-like physical and moral traits, many of Charles Dickens's minor characters reveal a debt to the "characters" created by the seventeenth-century essayists Joseph Addison and Richard Steele for the newspaper The Spectator.

Supporting Ideas Next, assess the appropriateness of your **supporting ideas** and consider whether you present enough support for your thesis. Make sure that you have supported all points with specific, concrete examples from the work or works you are discussing, briefly summarizing key events, quoting dialogue or description, describing characters or settings, or paraphrasing key ideas. Make certain, however, that your own ideas control the essay and that you have not substituted plot summary for analysis and interpretation. Your goal is to draw a conclusion about one or more works and to support that conclusion with pertinent details. If a plot detail supports a point you wish to make, include a *brief* summary of the event or series of events, showing its relevance by explicitly connecting the summary to the point you are making. For example:

> At the end of "Counterparts," when Farrington returns home after a day of frustration and abuse at work, his reaction is to strike out at his son Tom. This act shows that while he and his son are similarly victimized, Farrington is also the counterpart of his tyrannical boss.

Introduction The **introduction** of an essay about literature should specifically identify the works to be discussed and indicate the emphasis of the paper to follow. Depending on your paper's topic, you may want to provide some historical background or biographical information or to discuss the work in relation to other, similar works. Like all introductions, the one you write for an essay about literature should create interest in your topic and include a clear statement of the essay's thesis. The following introduction, while more than adequate for a first draft, is in need of revision:

> Revenge, which is defined as "the chance to retaliate, get satisfaction, take vengeance, or inflict damage or injury in return for an injury, insult, etc.," is a major component in many of the stories we have read. The storiesthat will be discussed here deal with a variety of ways to seek revenge. In my essay, I will show some of these differences.

Although the student clearly identifies her paper's topic, she does not specify the works she will discuss or indicate the particular point she will make about revenge. Her tired opening strategy, a dictionary definition, is not likely to arouse interest in her topic, and her announcement of her intention in the last sentence is intrusive and unnecessary. The following revision is much more effective:

> In Edgar Allan Poe's "The Cask of Amontillado" Montresor vows revenge on Fortunato for an unspecified

"insult"; in Ring Lardner's "Haircut" Paul, a young retarded man, gets even with a cruel practical joker who has taunted him for years. Both of these stories present characters who seek revenge, and both stories end in murder. However, the murderers' motivations are presented very differently. In "Haircut" the unreliable narrator is unaware of the significance of many events, and his ignorance helps to create sympathy for the murderer. In "The Cask of Amontillado," where the untrustworthy narrator is the murderer himself, Montresor's inability to offer a convincing motive turns the reader against him.

Conclusion In your conclusion you restate your thesis or sum up your essay's main points and also make a graceful exit. The concluding paragraph below represents an acceptable effort for a first draft, but it communicates little:

> Although the characters of Montresor and Paul were created by different authors at different times, they do have similar motives and goals. However, they are portrayed very differently.

One possible revision echoes the introductory paragraph on page 000, incorporating a brief quotation from one of the stories.

> In fact, then, what is significant is not whether or not each murderer's acts are justified, but rather how each murderer, and each victim, is portrayed by the narrator. Montresor—driven by a thirst to avenge "a thousand injuries" as well as a final insult—is shown to be sadistic and unrepentent; in "Haircut" it is Jim, the victim, whose sadism and lack of remorse are revealed to the reader.

Topic Sentences When you have revised your introduction and conclusion, you should begin to focus on your body paragraphs. In particular, be sure you have communicated the direction of your ideas, and the precise relationships of ideas to one another, with clearly worded **topic sentences,** statements that present the main ideas of your paragraphs.

Be especially careful to avoid abstractions and vague generalities in topic sentences.

Vague: One similarity revolves around the dominance of the men by women. (*What exactly is the similarity?*)

Revised: In both stories, a man is dominated by a woman.

Vague: There is one reason for the fact that Jay Gatsby remains a mystery. (*What is the reason?*)

Revised: Because The Great Gatsby is narrated by the outsider Nick Carraway, Jay Gatsby himself remains a mystery.

When revising the key topic sentences that are intended to move readers from one point (or section of your paper) to another, be sure that the relationship between the ideas they link is clear.

Relationship between ideas unclear: Now the poem's imagery will be discussed.

Revised: Another reason for the poem's effectiveness is its unusual imagery.

Relationship between ideas unclear: The sheriff's wife is another interesting character.

Revised: Like her friend Mrs. Hale, the sheriff's wife also has mixed feelings about what Mrs. Wright has done.

Sentences and Words After reviewing your paper's topic sentences, turn your attention to **transitions,** particularly the words and phrases that link sentences. Be sure that every needed transitional element has been supplied, and that each word or phrase you have selected conveys an accurate relationship (sequence, contradiction, and so on) between ideas. When you are satisfied with the clarity and appropriateness of your paper's transitions, move on to stylistic considerations such as diction and sentence variety.

Next, focus on the special stylistic conventions that govern essays about works of literature. For instance, use present tense verbs when discussing literary works (Jake Barnes *is* a major character in Ernest Hemingway's novel *The Sun Also Rises*). Use past tense verbs only when discussing historical events (Stephen Crane's *The Red Badge of Courage* deals with a battle that *took* place during the American Civil War), presenting biographical data (Samuel Taylor Coleridge *was* a close friend of William Wordsworth's), or referring to events that took place before the time of the work's main action (Hamlet's father *was* murdered by Claudius, his mother's new husband). In addition, eliminate subjective expressions, such as *I think, in my opinion, I believe, it seems to me,* and *I feel.* These phrases weaken your argument by suggesting that its ideas are "only" opinions and have no objective validity.

Source Material and Documentation Make certain that all references to sources are integrated smoothly and documented appropriately (see Appendix A, Documenting Sources).

- Acknowledge all sources, including the work or works under discussion, using the documentation style of the Modern Language Association (MLA).

- Combine paraphrases, summaries, and quotations with your own interpretations, weaving quotations smoothly into your paper. Introduce the words or ideas of others with a phrase that identifies their source, and end with appropriate parenthetical documentation.
- Use quotations *only* when something vital would be lost if you did not reproduce the author's exact words.
- Integrate quotations shorter than four lines smoothly into your paper. Make sure that you set off quotations with quotation marks.
- Set off quotations of more than four lines by indenting ten spaces from the margin. Double space, and do not use quotation marks. If you are quoting a single paragraph, do not indent the first line.
- Use the correct reference formats for fiction, poetry, and drama. When citing a part of a short story or novel, supply the page number (143); for a poem, give the line numbers (3–5); for a play, include the act, scene, and line numbers (II.ii.17–22).

Editing

Once you have finished revising, edit your paper to make certain that grammar, punctuation, spelling, and mechanics are correct. As you edit, pay particular attention to the mechanical conventions of literary essays. For instance, titles of short works and titles of parts of long works—short stories, short poems, and magazine or journal articles—should be in quotation marks ("A Rose for Emily"); titles of long works—books, long poems, plays, and newspapers and journals, for example—should be underlined or set in italics (*Invisible Man;* the *Washington Post*).

In addition, refer to authors of literary works by their full names in your first reference to them and by their last names in subsequent references. Never refer to them by their first names, and never use titles that indicate marital status (*Willa Cather* or *Cather,* never Willa or Miss Cather). Also, make sure you have used literary terms accurately. For example, be careful to avoid confusing **narrator** or **speaker** with author; feelings or opinions expressed by a narrator or character do not necessarily represent those of the author. Do not say, "In the poem 'Patterns' Amy Lowell expresses her anger" when you mean that the **persona**—the speaker in the poem, who may or may not be the poet—expresses anger.

When your editing is complete, give your essay a descriptive title; before you retype or reprint it, make sure that its format conforms to your instructor's requirements.

CHAPTER 3

READING AND WRITING ABOUT FICTION

UNDERSTANDING FICTION

A **narrative** is a recounting of a story through the presentation of events in some logical or orderly way. Works of narrative fiction originate in the imagination of the author, not in history or fact. Certainly some fiction—historical or autobiographical, for example—focuses on real people and actual events, but the interaction of the characters and the unfolding of the plot are the author's invention.

Even before they know how to read, most people have learned how narratives are structured. Once a child can tell a story, he or she also knows how to exaggerate, how to add or delete details, how to rearrange events, and how to bend facts—in other words, how to fictionalize a narrative to achieve a desired effect. This kind of informal, personal narrative is in many ways quite similar to the more structured literary narratives included in this anthology.

Our earliest examples of narrative fiction are stories and songs that were part of a prehistoric oral tradition. These stories, embellished with each telling, were often quite long, embodying the history, the central myths, and the religious beliefs of the cultures in which they developed. Eventually transcribed, these extended narratives became epics—Homer's *The Iliad* and *The Odyssey,* the ancient Babylonian *Epic of Gilgamesh,* the Hindu *Bhagavad-Gita,* and the Anglo-Saxon *Beowulf,* for example. Many of the tales of the Old Testament also came out of this tradition. An **epic** is a long narrative poem about a heroic figure upon whose actions depend the fate of a nation or an entire race. The setting of an epic is vast—sometimes worldwide or cosmic, including heaven and hell—and the action commonly involves a battle or a perilous journey. Quite often the gods participate in the action and influence the outcome of events, as they do in the Trojan War in *The Iliad* and in the founding of Rome in Virgil's *The Aeneid.*

Folktales and **fairy tales** also come out of the oral tradition. These tales, which developed concurrently with other narrative forms, have influenced works as diverse as Chaucer's *The Canterbury Tales* and D. H. Lawrence's "The Rocking-Horse Winner" (p. 438). The folktales and fairy tales that survive (such as "Cinderella" and Aesop's *Fables*) are contemporary versions of old, even ancient, tales that can be traced back centuries through many different cultures. Despite their variety these narrative forms have several elements in common. First, they have straightforward characterizations, often contrasting distinctly different personality types. Much of the appeal of "Cinderella," for example, depends on the contrast between the selfish, sadistic stepsisters and poor, gentle, victimized Cinderella. In addition, the folktale or fairy tale has an obvious theme or moral—good triumphing over evil, for instance. The stories move directly to their conclusions, never interrupted by ingenious or unexpected twists of plot. Love is temporarily thwarted, but the prince eventually finds Cinderella and marries her. Finally, these tales are anchored not in specific times or places but in "Once upon a time" settings, green worlds of prehistory replete with royalty, talking animals, and magic.

During the Middle Ages, the **romance** supplanted the epic. Written initially in verse but later in prose, the romance replaced the epic's gods and heroes with knights, kings, and damsels in distress. Events were controlled by enchantments rather than by the will of the gods. *Sir Gawain and the Green Knight* and other tales of King Arthur and the Knights of the Round Table are examples of the romance form. Eventually the romance gave way to other types of narratives. The **novella,** a short prose tale such as the ones collected in Giovanni Boccaccio's *The Decameron,* originated in fourteenth-century Italy, and the **picaresque,** an episodic, often satirical work about a rogue or rascal, such as Miguel de Cervantes's *Don Quixote,* emerged in seventeenth-century Spain. The **pastoral romance,** a prose tale set in an idealized rural world, and the **character,** a brief satirical sketch illustrating a type of personality, both became popular in Renaissance England.

From these diverse sources emerged the **novel.** Daniel Defoe is commonly given credit for writing the first novel. His *Robinson Crusoe* (1719) is an episodic narrative similar to the picaresque but unified not only by a central character but also by a single setting. By the nineteenth century the novel reached a high point in its development, supplanting other kinds of extended narratives. Because of its ability to present a wide range of characters in realistic settings and to develop them in depth, the novel appealed to the rising middle class who seemingly had an insatiable desire to see itself portrayed. Writers such as George Eliot, Charles Dickens, William Thackeray, and Charlotte and Emily Brontë appealed to this desire by creating large fictional worlds populated by many different characters who reflected the complexity—and at times the melodrama—of Victorian society. The novel as a literary form has continued to develop in the twentieth century.

THE SHORT STORY

The short story, like the novel, evolved from the various forms of narrative discussed above. Because the short story comes from so many different sources from all over the world, it is difficult to determine where it originated. We can say with certainty, however, that in the United States during the nineteenth century a group of writers—most pointedly Nathaniel Hawthorne and Edgar Allan Poe—took it seriously and exploited its fictional possibilities. Because the short story was embraced so readily and developed so quickly in the United States, it is commonly, although not quite accurately, thought of as an American art form.

Whereas the novel is an extended piece of narrative fiction, the **short story** is limited in length and scope. These limitations account for the characteristics that distinguish the short story from longer prose forms. Unlike the novelist, the short story writer usually cannot devote a great deal of space to developing a complex plot or a large number of characters. As a result, the short story commonly begins close to or at the height of action and develops one character in depth. In most cases concentrating on a single incident, the writer develops a character by showing his or her responses to events. (This attention to character development, as well as its detailed description of setting, is what distinguishes the short story from earlier short narrative forms, such as folktales and fairy tales.) Often a character will experience an **epiphany,** a moment of illumination in which something hidden or not understood becomes immediately clear. Examples of epiphany are found in this anthology in James Joyce's "Araby," John Updike's "A&P," and David Michael Kaplan's "Doe Season."

Today the term *short story* is applied to a wide variety of prose narratives: short stories such as Chinua Achebe's "Vengeful Creditor" (p. 99), which runs about twelve pages; **short short stories,** such as Luisa Valenzuela's "All About Suicide" (p. 6), which are under five pages in length; and long stories, such as Franz Kafka's "The Metamorphosis" (p. 393), which may more accurately be called short novels or **novellas.**

The possibilities of the short story are infinite. A short story may be comic or tragic; its subject may be growing up, marriage, crime and punishment, war, sexual awakening, death, or any number of other human concerns. The setting can be an imaginary world, the old West, rural America, the jungles of Uruguay, nineteenth-century Russia, precommunist China, or modern Egypt. The story's form may be conventional, with a definite beginning, middle, and end, or it may be structured as a letter, a diary entry, or even random notes. The narrator of a story may be trustworthy or unreliable, involved in the action or a disinterested observer, sympathetic or deserving of scorn, extremely ignorant or highly insightful, limited in vision or able to see inside the minds of all the characters. And, as the stories in this anthology show, the conventions of short fiction are constantly changing.

READING FICTION

As you read more and more works of short fiction, you will eventually get into the habit of paying careful attention to elements such as plot; character; setting; point of view; style, tone, and language; symbol and allegory; and theme. The following guidelines, designed to guide your exploration of works of fiction, focus on issues that will be examined in depth in chapters to come.

- Look at the **plot** of the story (see Chapter 4). How do the events in the story relate to one another, and how do they relate to the story as a whole? What conflicts occur in the story, and how are these conflicts developed or resolved? Does the story include any noteworthy plot devices, such as flashbacks or foreshadowing?
- Analyze the **characters** of a story (see Chapter 5). What are the traits of the characters of a short story? How do these individuals interact with one another? Are the characters fully fleshed out, or are they stereotypes whose sole purpose is to express a single trait (good, evil, generosity) or to move the plot along?
- Identify the **setting** of the story (see Chapter 6). At what time period and in what geographic location does the action of the story occur? How does the setting affect the characters of the story? How does it determine the relationships among the characters? How does the setting affect the plot? Does the setting create a mood for the story? In what way does the setting reinforce the central ideas that the story examines?
- Examine the narrative **point of view** of the story (see Chapter 7). What person or persons are telling the story? Is the story told in the first person (*I* or *we*) or in the third person (*he, she,* or *they*)? Is the narrator all-knowing, or is the story restricted to the perspective of one person—a major character, a minor character, or just an observer? How much does the narrator know about the events in the story? Does the narrator present an accurate or inaccurate picture of events? Does the narrator understand the full significance of the story he or she is telling?
- Analyze the **style, tone,** and **language** of the story (see Chapter 8). Does the writer make any unusual use of diction or syntax? Does the writer use figures of speech? Patterns of imagery? What styles or levels of speech are associated with particular characters? What words or phrases are repeated throughout the work? Does the narrative style of the story seem plain or elaborate? Does the narrator's tone reveal his or her attitude toward characters or events? Are there any discrepancies between the narrator's attitude and the attitude of the author? Is the tone of the story playful, humorous, ironic, satirical, serious, somber, solemn, bitter, condescending, formal, informal—or does the tone suggest some other attitude?
- Focus on **symbolism** and **allegory** (see Chapter 9). Does the author use any objects or ideas symbolically? What characters or objects in the story are part of an **allegorical framework?** How does an object establish its symbolic or allegorical significance in the story? Does the same object have different meanings at different places in the story? Are the symbols or

allegorical figures conventional or unusual? At what points in the story do symbols or allegorical figures appear?

- Identify the **themes** of the story (see Chapter 10). What is the central theme? How is this idea or concept made concrete in the work? What elements of the story develop the central theme? How do character, plot, setting, point of view, and symbols reinforce the central theme? How does the title of the story contribute to readers' understanding of the central theme? What other themes are explored?

ACTIVE READING

John Frei, a student in an introduction to literature course, was assigned to write a two- to three-page essay on a topic of his choice, focusing on any short story in this literature anthology. After considering a number of possible choices, John selected Alberto Alvaro Rios's "The Secret Lion," which appears on the pages that follow.

Alberto Alvaro Rios (1952–) was born and raised in the border town of Nogales, Arizona, the son of a Mexican father and an English mother. He has published many poems and short stories, including the poetry collection *Whispering to Fool the Wind* (1982), which won the American Academy of Poets Walt Whitman Award, and *The Iguana Killer: Twelve Stories of the Heart* (1984), from which "The Secret Lion" is drawn. Rios lives in Chandler, Arizona, and teaches at Arizona State University in Tempe.

Reviewer Mary Logue, writing in the October 1982 *Village Voice Literary Supplement,* says that Rios's writings "carry the feel of another world. . . . Rios's tongue is both foreign and familiar," reflecting an upbringing "where one is neither in this country nor the other." In many of his stories, Rios expresses the seeming "other-ness" of Anglo culture as seen through the eyes of Chicano children: a little boy frightened by the sight of his first snowfall, or (as in "The Secret Lion") boys amazed by the other-worldly sight of "heaven." Through Rios's children, we see our own world with new eyes.

Alberto Alvaro Rios

THE SECRET LION

(1984)

I was twelve and in junior high school and something happened that we didn't have a name for, but it was there nonetheless like a lion, and roaring, roaring that way the biggest things do. Everything changed. Just that. Like the rug, the one that gets pulled—or better, like the tablecloth those magicians pull where the stuff on the table stays the same but the gasp! from the audience makes the staying-the-same part not matter. Like that.

What happened was there were teachers now, not just one teacher, teach-erz, and we felt personally abandoned somehow. When a person had all these teachers now, he didn't get taken care of the same way, even though six was more than one. Arithmetic went out the door when we walked in. And we saw girls now, but they weren't the same girls we used to know because we couldn't talk to them anymore, not the same way we used to, certainly not to Sandy, even though she was my neighbor, too. Not even to her. She just played the piano all the time. And there were words, oh there were words in junior high school, and we wanted to know what they were, and how a person did them—that's what school was supposed to be for. Only, in junior high school, school wasn't school, everything was backward-like. If you went up to a teacher and said the word to try and find out what it meant you got in trouble for saying it. So we didn't. And we figured it must have been that way about other stuff, too, so we never said anything about anything—we weren't stupid.

But my friend Sergio and I, we solved junior high school. We would come home from school on the bus, put our books away, change shoes, and go across the highway to the arroyo. It was the one place we were not supposed to go. So we did. This was, after all, what junior high had at least shown us. It was our river, though, our personal Mississippi, our friend from long back, and it was full of stories and all the branch forts we had built in it when we were still the Vikings of America, with our own symbol, which we had carved everywhere, even in the sand, which let the water take it. That was good, we had decided; whoever was at the end of this river would know about us.

At the very very top of our growing lungs, what we would do down there was shout every dirty word we could think of, in every combination we could come up with, and we would yell about girls, and all the things we wanted to do with them, as loud as we could—we didn't know what we wanted to do with them, just things—and we would yell about teachers, and how we loved some of them, like Miss Crevelone, and how we wanted to dissect some of them, making signs of the cross, like priests, and we would yell this stuff over and over because it felt good, we couldn't explain why, it just felt good and for the first time in our lives there was nobody to tell us we couldn't. So we did.

5 One Thursday we were walking along shouting this way, and the railroad, the Southern Pacific, which ran above and along the far side of the arroyo, had dropped a grinding ball down there, which was, we found out later, a cannonball thing used in mining. A bunch of them were put in a big vat which turned around and crushed the ore. One had been dropped, or thrown—what do caboose men do when they get bored—but it got down there regardless and as we were walking along yelling about one girl or another, a particular Claudia, we found it, one of these things, looked at

it, picked it up, and got very very excited, and held it and passed it back and forth, and we were saying "Guythisis, this is, geeGuythis . . .": we had this perception about nature then, that nature is imperfect and that round things are perfect: we said "GuyGodthis is perfect, thisisthis is perfect, it's round, round and heavy, it'sit's the best thing we'veeverseen. Whatisit?" We didn't know. We just knew it was great. We just, whatever, we played with it, held it some more.

And then we had to decide what to do with it. We knew, because of a lot of things, that if we were going to take this and show it to anybody, this discovery, this best thing, was going to be taken away from us. That's the way it works with little kids, like all the polished quartz, the tons of it we had collected piece by piece over the years. Junior high kids too. If we took it home, my mother, we knew, was going to look at it and say "throw that dirty thing in the, get rid of it." Simple like, like that. "But ma it's the best thing I" "Getridofit." Simple.

So we didn't. Take it home. Instead, we came up with the answer. We dug a hole and buried it. And we marked it secretly. Lots of secret signs. And came back the next week to dig it up and, we didn't know, pass it around some more or something, but we didn't find it. We dug up that whole bank, and we never found it again. We tried.

Sergio and I talked about that ball or whatever it was when we couldn't find it. All we used were small words, neat, good. Kid words. What we were really saying, but didn't know the words, was how much that ball was like that place, that whole arroyo: couldn't tell anybody about it, didn't understand what it was, didn't have a name for it. It just felt good. It was just perfect in the way it was that place, that whole going to that place, that whole junior high school lion. It was just iron-heavy, it had no name, it felt good or not, we couldn't take it home to show our mothers, and once we buried it, it was gone forever.

The ball was gone, like the first reasons we had come to that arroyo years earlier, like the first time we had seen the arroyo, it was gone like everything else that had been taken away. This was not our first lesson. We stopped going to the arroyo after not finding the thing, the same way we had stopped going there years earlier and headed for the mountains. Nature seemed to keep pushing us around one way or another, teaching us the same thing every place we ended up. Nature's gang was tough that way, teaching us stuff.

10 When we were young we moved away from town, me and my family. Sergio's was already out there. Out in the wilds. Or at least the new place seemed like the wilds since everything looks bigger the smaller a man is. I was five, I guess, and we had moved three miles north of Nogales where we had lived, three miles north of the Mexican border. We looked across the highway in one direction and there was the arroyo; hills stood up in the other direction. Mountains, for a small man.

When the first summer came the very first place we went to was of course the one place we weren't supposed to go, the arroyo. We went down in there and found water running, summer rain water mostly, and we went swimming. But every third or fourth or fifth day, the sewage treatment plant that was, we found out, upstream, would release whatever it was that it released, and we would never know exactly what day that was, and a person really couldn't tell right off by looking at the water, not every time, not so a person could get out in time. So, we went swimming that summer and some days we had a lot of fun. Some days we didn't. We found a thousand ways to explain what happened on those other days, constructing elaborate stories about the neighborhood dogs, and hadn't she, my mother, miscalculated her step before, too? But she knew something was up because we'd come running into the house those days, wanting to take a shower, even—if this can be imagined—in the middle of the day.

That was the first time we stopped going to the arroyo. It taught us to look the other way. We decided, as the second side of summer came, we wanted to go into the mountains. They were still mountains then. We went running in one summer Thursday morning, my friend Sergio and I, into my mother's kitchen, and said, well, what'zin, what'zin those hills over there—we used her word so she'd understand us—and she said nothingdon'tworryaboutit. So we went out, and we weren't dumb, we thought with our eyes to each other, ohhoshe'stryingtokeepsomethingfromus. We knew adults.

We had read the books, after all; we knew about bridges and castles and wildtreacherousraging alligatormouth rivers. We wanted them. So we were going to go out and get them. We went back that morning into that kitchen and we said, "We're going out there, we're going into the hills, we're going away for three days, don't worry." She said, "All right."

"You know," I said to Sergio, "if we're going to go away for three days, well, we ought to at least pack a lunch."

15 But we were two young boys with no patience for what we thought at the time was mom-stuff: making sa-and-wiches. My mother didn't offer. So we got out little kid knapsacks that my mother had sewn for us, and into them we put the jar of mustard. A loaf of bread. Knivesforksplates, bottles of Coke, a can opener. This was lunch for the two of us. And we were weighed down, humped over to be strong enough to carry this stuff. But we started walking anyway, into the hills. We were going to eat berries and stuff otherwise. "Goodbye." My mom said that.

After the first hill we were dead. But we walked. My mother could still see us. And we kept walking. We walked until we got to where the sun is straight overhead, noon. That place. Where that is doesn't matter; it's time to eat. The truth is we weren't anywhere close to that place. We just agreed that the sun was overhead and that it was time to eat, and by tilting our heads a little we could make that the truth.

"We really ought to start looking for a place to eat."

"Yeah. Let's look for a good place to eat." We went back and forth saying that for fifteen minutes, making it lunchtime because that's what we always said back and forth before lunchtimes at home. "Yeah,

I'm hungry all right." I nodded my head. "Yeah, I'm hungry all right too. I'm hungry." He nodded his head. I nodded my head back. After a good deal more nodding, we were ready, just as we came over a little hill. We hadn't found the mountains yet. This was a little hill.

And on the other side of this hill we found heaven.

It was just what we thought it would be.

Perfect. Heaven was green, like nothing else in Arizona. And it wasn't a cemetery or like that because we had seen cemeteries and they had gravestones and stuff and this didn't. This was perfect, had trees, lots of trees, had birds, like we had never seen before. It was like "The Wizard of Oz," like when they got to Oz and everything was so green, so emerald, they had to wear those glasses, and we ran just like them, laughing, laughing that way we did that moment, and we went running down to this clearing in it all, hitting each other that good way we did.

We got down there, we kept laughing, we kept hitting each other, we unpacked our stuff, and we started acting "rich." We knew all about how to do that, like blowing on our nails, then rubbing them on our chests for the shine. We made our sandwiches, opened our Cokes, got out the rest of the stuff, the salt and pepper shakers. I found this particular hole and I put my Coke right into it, a perfect fit, and I called it my Coke-holder. I got down next to it on my back, because everyone knows that rich people eat lying down, and I got my sandwich in one hand and put my other arm around the Coke in its holder. When I wanted a drink, I lifted my neck a little, put out my lips, and tipped my Coke a little with the crook of my elbow. Ah.

We were there, lying down, eating our sandwiches, laughing, throwing bread at each other and out for the birds. This was heaven. We were laughing and we couldn't believe it. My mother was keeping something from us, ah ha, but we had found her out. We even found water over at the side of the clearing to wash our plates with—we had brought plates. Sergio started washing his plates when he was done, and I was being rich with my Coke, and this day in summer was right.

When suddenly these two men came, from around a corner of trees and the tallest grass we had ever seen. They had bags on their backs, leather bags, bags and sticks.

We didn't know what clubs were, but I learned later, like I learned about the grinding balls. The two men yelled at us. Most specifically, one wanted me to take my Coke out of my Coke-holder so he could sink his golf ball into it.

Something got taken away from us that moment. Heaven. We grew up a little bit, and couldn't go backward. We learned. No one had ever told us about golf. They had told us about heaven. And it went away. We got golf in exchange.

We went back to the arroyo for the rest of that summer, and tried to have fun the best we could. We learned to be ready for finding the grinding ball. We loved it, and when we buried it we knew what would happen. The truth is, we didn't look so hard for it. We were two boys and twelve summers then, and not stupid. Things get taken away.

We buried it because it was perfect. We didn't tell my mother, but together it was all we talked about, till we forgot. It was the lion.

Previewing

John Frei began the reading process by previewing his text. A quick glance at the story showed John that it was quite short (under five pages), that it was written in the first person ("I was twelve"), that it included dialogue as well as narrative, and that it had a provocative title.

Previewing "The Secret Lion" prepared John to read it more closely and, eventually, to write about it. In preparation for writing, he read and reread the story, highlighting and annotating it as he went along.

Highlighting and Annotating

As he reread the story, John highlighted words and ideas that he thought might be useful to him, indicated possible connections among ideas, and noted questions and comments as they occurred to him. During this process, he paid close attention to the meaning of the term *secret lion* and to the narrator's voice. The highlighted and annotated passage below illustrates his responses to the last five paragraphs of the story.

> When suddenly these two men came, from around a corner of trees and the tallest grass we had ever seen. They had bags on their backs, leather bags, bags and sticks.
>
> We didn't know what clubs were, but I learned later, like I learned about the grinding balls. The two men yelled at us. Most specifically, one wanted me to take my Coke out of my Coke-holder so he could sink his golf ball into it. *[pt of view]*
>
> Something got taken away from us that moment. Heaven. We grew up a little bit, and couldn't go backward. We learned. No one had ever told us about golf. They had told us about heaven. And it went away. We got golf in exchange. *[Heaven = innocence] [Golf = adulthood]*
>
> We went back to the arroyo for the rest of that summer, and tried to have fun the best we could. We learned to be ready for finding the grinding ball. We loved it, and when we buried it we knew what would happen. The truth is, we didn't look so hard for it. We were two boys and twelve summers then, and not stupid. Things get taken away. *[Lose their magic & specialness. Also—loss of innocence, trust, belief in things being perfect.]*
>
> We buried it because it was perfect. We didn't tell my mother, but together it was all we talked about, till we forgot. It was the lion. *[ball?] [Lion = knowledge that growing up = loss? or is lion growing up itself?]*

John's highlighting and annotations suggested a number of interesting possibilities for his paper. First, John noticed that the story reveals both the narrator's childhood innocence and his adult knowledge. John's highlighting also identified some unusual stylistic features, such as words run together ("Getridofit") and repetition of words like *neat* and *perfect*. Finally, John noticed that four items—the arroyo, the grinding ball, the golf course, and the lion—were mentioned again and again. This emphasis led him to suspect that one or more of these items—particularly the secret lion, prominently mentioned in the story's title—might have some special, even symbolic, significance.

WRITING ABOUT FICTION

Planning an Essay

At this stage, John had not yet thought of a topic; he knew only that he would be writing a paper on "The Secret Lion." However, his previewing, highlighting, and annotations had helped him to move toward a topic, revealing some interesting ideas about style and point of view—and, possibly, about symbolism. Now, because his paper was to be at most three pages long, he decided to select one element on which to concentrate.

Choosing a Topic To help him settle on a direction for his paper, John decided to explore possible topics in his journal. When he examined the story's style and point of view, John found little he was interested in pursuing further. His journal entry on these two elements of literature appears below.

Journal Entry

Style—Style is informal, with lots of contractions and slang terms like "neat." Words are run together. Most of the time, the boys combine words to indicate something unimportant to them. When they're packing the lunch, they include "knivesforksplates." They're not interested in packing the lunch--they just want to get to the "mountains." Packing lunches is very important to the mother, so she does the opposite of combining words: She breaks them down ("sa-and-wiches"). Also, the words running together can be compared to the days of a child, especially in the summer, when days just blend together. This style gets pretty annoying after a while, though—it's too cute.

Point of view—We see the story through the eyes of the narrator, who is a participant in the story. Sergio is developed along with the narrator as part of a "we." It's unusual that the characters are not really individuals—they function as "we" for most of the story, and nothing is done to give them separate voices. We don't see into the minds of the boys to any extent greater than what the narrator tells us, but the narrator has a double perspective: He takes the reader back to childhood, and this helps us understand the boys' excitement and disappointment, but he also shows us how much more he knows now, so we know that too.

John had no trouble writing paragraphs on style and point of view in his journal, but he ran out of ideas quickly; he knew that he did not have enough material to write a paper about either of these two topics. When he started to write a journal entry about the possible symbolic significance of certain items, however, he immediately found himself becoming involved. As a result, he chose "Symbols in 'The Secret Lion'" as his paper's topic. His journal entry on symbolism appears below.

Symbolism—The arroyo, the grinding ball, the golf course, and of course the secret lion all seem to mean something beyond their literal meanings as objects and places. (Maybe the "mountains" do too.) For one thing, they're all repeated over and over again. Also, they all seem to be related somehow to magic and perfection and surprise and expectation and idealism (and, later, to disillusionment and disappointment). If this is a story about growing up, these things could be related somehow to that theme.

Finding Something to Say

Brainstorming Once he had decided to write about symbolism, John moved on to brainstorm about his topic, focusing on what he considered the story's most important—and most obvious—symbol: the secret lion itself.

Brainstorming Notes: Symbols in "The Secret Lion"

Lion = "roaring, roaring that way the biggest things do"

EVERYTHING CHANGED (=secret because it's something they have to find out on their own, not from adults?)

Tablecloth- - rug (=magic). "Staying-the-same part" is most important - - why?

Arroyo: not supposed to go (=rebellion) - - Mississippi, "friend from long back"; freedom. Place that doesn't change.

Grinding ball- - Perfection in imperfect world, innocence in adult world. "Nature is imperfect," but "round things are perfect" - - "the best thing." ("That ball was like that place, that whole arroyo")

Buried and "gone forever" - - "taken away" (like arroyo)

Mountains: "everything looks bigger the smaller a man is"; hills = "Mountains for a small man." (Mother calls them hills)

Arroyo = polluted with sewage (never know when it's coming) - - went to mts.

On other side of hills = golf course (=heaven) - - perfect "perfect" x3

*Like Oz - - green, emerald

*Place to act "rich"

*Men with clubs = reality, future - -they go back to arroyo (=end of innocence)

"Things get taken away" (heaven, ball - - something buried and lost - - arroyo)

"We buried it because it was perfect. . . . It was the lion." Lion = secret place inside us that still craves childhood (as adults, we learn we have to keep it buried, like ball).

How can a roaring lion be secret?

Listing When he looked over his brainstorming notes in search of an organizing scheme for his paper, John saw that most of his information was about four items: the secret lion, the arroyo, the grinding ball, and the golf course. Clearly, his most obvious option was to discuss one item at a time. But he knew that he needed to find a common denominator among the four separate things, a thematic connection that would relate them to one another. When he noticed that each seemed to have different meanings at different periods of the boys' lives, he realized that his essay could trace the changes in meaning of the four items as the boys move from childhood to adolescence to adulthood. He experimented with this possibility in the following lists.

Listing: Symbols in "The Secret Lion"

The secret lion
Beginning: "raging beast" inside of them (6th grade class) = frustration, puberty
Beginning: "roaring, roaring that way the biggest things do"
Middle: "that whole junior high school lion"
End: Lion = greatness, something important
(also = puberty?)
Also = great discoveries they expect to make in their lives.
End: "It was the lion."

Arroyo
Place that doesn't change (= childhood); constant in changing lives. (But it changes too)
Mississippi—horizons
Freedom of childhood
Waste dump

Grinding ball
Perfection (in imperfect world)
Childhood innocence (in adult world)
Undiscovered knowledge?
Secrets of childhood (buried)
Something lost: "Things get taken away"

Golf course
Heaven—knowledge that there is no heaven, that it's a fraud, like the Wizard of Oz.
Adulthood—men with clubs
Scene of remembered humiliation
End of innocence (realization that it's just a golf course)

John's lists confirmed what he had suspected—the meanings of the four items did seem to change as the boys grew up. To the boys, the arroyo, the grinding ball, and the golf course are all magical and special, but when they grow up, all three turn out to be disappointingly ordinary. The secret lion, however, seemed more complex than the other three, and John knew that he would have to develop his ideas further before he could show how the lion's meaning changes and how these changes affect the story as a whole.

Deciding on a Thesis

With his key ideas organized into lists that clarified some possible relationships among them, John began to see a tentative thesis emerging. Although he still was not sure he would limit his essay to the four items on his lists, he now felt certain that these items functioned in the story as symbols: Prominently and repeatedly mentioned, they helped to convey the story's theme. As a result, he was able to decide on the main idea he wanted his essay to communicate, and he used this idea as his tentative thesis, the keystone of his essay's first draft:

> The meanings of the story's key symbols change as the boys move from childhood to adolescence to adulthood; these changes reveal corresponding changes in the boys' view of the world from idealism to frustration to resignation.

Preparing an Outline

Even though his essay was to be short, John felt a need to prepare an outline that would map out a simple arrangement for his ideas. He decided that discussing the four key symbols one by one and drawing conclusions about their common purpose in his essay's opening and closing paragraphs would be the most effective strategy. This arrangement would allow him to group his information into the four by-now-familiar categories. He also decided to discuss the lion last because he saw it as the story's pivotal symbol, the one he believed to be the most important.

Looking back over all his notes, and paying close attention to his thesis, John constructed the following scratch outline.

Scratch Outline: Symbols in "The Secret Lion"

<u>Arroyo</u>
  Mississippi
  Rebellion
  Waste dump
<u>Grinding ball</u>
  [Not yet discovered]
  Lost perfection
  "Things get taken away."
<u>Golf course</u>
  Heaven
  Humiliation
  Golf course
<u>Lion</u>
  [Not yet discovered]
  "roaring"; "raging beast"
  Just the lion

Drafting

Guided by his scratch outline, his thesis, and his notes, John Frei wrote the following first draft. Because his notes included many ideas not included on his scratch outline, and because he discovered new ideas and connections among ideas as he wrote, the draft does not follow the scratch outline exactly.

Symbols in "The Secret Lion": First Draft

"The Secret Lion" is a story that is rich in symbols. It is also a story about change. The meanings of the story's key symbols change as the boys move from childhood to adolescence to adulthood; these changes reveal corresponding changes in the boys' view of the world from idealism to frustration to resignation.

The arroyo, or river, is special to the narrator and his friend Sergio when they are boys. Literally, it is a place to play. Symbolically, it is a place to rebel (they're not supposed to be there; they yell forbidden words). It could also symbolize the continuum of discoveries they will make before they are completely grown up. To the young boys, the arroyo symbolizes a retreat from the disappointment of the golf course; it is their second choice. Later, it represented adventure, the uncertainty and unpredictability of adolescence, as illustrated by the fact that they could not tell just by looking at it from the riverside whether the river was going to be tainted with sewage. When they are children, it is their Mississippi. When they are adolescents, it is a place to hang out and a symbol of adolescent rebellion; as an adult, the narrator looks back at it for what it was: an ordinary river polluted by sewage. The arroyo doesn't change, but the boys' view of it changes as they change.

At first, when they find the grinding ball, it stands for everything that is perfect and fascinating (and therefore forbidden and unattainable) in life. Like a child's life, it is perfect. They knew they couldn't keep it forever, just as they couldn't be children forever, so they buried it. When they tried to look for it again, they couldn't find it. They admit later that they don't look very hard. (People always wish they can find youth again, but they can't.) The ball represents perfection in an imperfect world, childhood innocence in an adult world. They hide it from their mother because they know she won't see it as perfect; she'll make them "getridofit" (39). They hide it because they want to retain the excitement of the undiscovered, but once they've used it and seen it and buried it, it's not new anymore. Even if they'd been able to find it, it would still be lost. To the adult narrator, it's just an ordinary object used in mining.

The golf course, which they wander into at age five, is, for a short period of time, "heaven" (41). It is lush and green and carefully cared for, and it is the opposite of the polluted arroyo. It is also another world, as mysterious as the Land of Oz. With the realization that it is not heaven to the golfers, the boys see what outsiders they really are. They may start "acting 'rich'" (41), but it will be just an act. There are no Coke-holders, no Oz, no heaven. The adolescents see the golf course as a scene of defeat and embarrassment, the setting for the confrontation that sent them back to the arroyo. To the adult, the golf course is just a golf course.

The secret lion is the most complex symbol in the

story. In a sense it stands for the innocence of childhood, something we lose when we learn more. The lion symbolizes a great "roaring" disturbance (37). It is a change that unsettles everything for a brief time and then passes, leaving everything changed in irrevocable, indescribable ways. It symbolizes the boys' growing up: they are changed, but still the same people. The "secret lion" is that thing that changes little boys into men. It is secret because no one notices it happening; before it is noticed, the change has occurred, and the little boy is gone forever. It is a lion because it "roars" through the boy like a storm, and makes all of the growing up changes which can be "the biggest things" (37). In a more specific sense, the lion stands for puberty, reflected in their rage and frustration when they shout profanity. In the beginning of the story, the lion is rage (puberty, adolescence); in the middle, it suggests greatness (passing through adolescence into manhood); at the end it's just the lion ("It was the lion" [42]), without any symbolic significance.

By the time they bury the ball, they have already learned one lesson, and the force of adulthood is pushing childhood aside. The golf course changes from heaven to shame to golf course; the ball changes from a special, perfect thing to something ordinary; the arroyo changes from grand river to polluted stream. Maybe it is the knowledge that life is not perfect, the knowledge that comes with growing up, that is the secret lion.

First Draft: Commentary

As John reviewed his first draft, he made a number of changes in content, style, and organization. He decided to delete wordiness and repetition; add more specific references, including quotations, from the story; sharpen transitions and add clearer topic sentences; and reorganize paragraphs to make logical and causal connections more obvious. He also planned to revise his introduction and conclusion.

Discussions with students and with his instructor gave him some additional insights. The students' major criticism of his essay was that his thesis seemed to make a claim he could not support: that the development of all four symbols follows the three stages that parallel the boys' development. One student pointed out that two of the four symbols (the grinding ball and the secret lion) do not even enter the boys' lives until adolescence, and John's treatment of the story's most prominent symbol—the lion—does not convincingly show it to change in any significant way. The group decided that his thesis should be modified to focus on the way the four symbols all reflect the story's theme about the inevitability of change.

John's instructor agreed with the students' suggestions and supported John's own assessment of his essay's strengths and weaknesses. In addition, he helped John with the arrangement of his essay, suggesting that he discuss the golf course first because it is the setting for the event that occurred first in time, and because the disillusionment associated with it influences the subsequent events.

John also discussed ideas for his introduction and conclusion with his instructor, deciding to use these paragraphs to stress the common theme that all four symbols convey instead of focusing on the different ways in which each of the four separate symbols changes.

Finally, John's instructor was concerned with John's tendency in this draft to engage in "symbol hunting." Rather than focusing on finding equivalents for each of the four items ("the ball represents perfection," "the lion stands for puberty," and so on), he suggested John consider how the use of these symbols opens up the story, how they work together to communicate the story's theme. His instructor pointed out that in looking for neat equivalent values for each symbol, John was oversimplifying very complex, suggestive symbols. And, as John's own draft indicates, the symbols seem to suggest different things at different stages in the boys' lives.

Revising and Editing

The revisions John decided on are reflected in his second draft.

Symbols in "The Secret Lion": Second Draft

"The Secret Lion" is a story about change. The first paragraph of the story gives a twelve-year-old's view of growing up: Everything changes. When the child watches the magician, he is amazed at the "staying-the-same part" (38); adults focus on the tablecloth. As adults, we lose the ability to see the world through innocent eyes. We have the benefit of experience, confident the trick will work as long as the magician pulls the tablecloth in the proper way. The "staying-the-same part" is less important than the technique. In a story full of prominent symbols, the magician's trick does not seem very important, but all the key symbols, like the sleight of hand, are about change. In fact, each of the story's key symbols highlights the theme of the inevitability of change that permeates the lives of the narrator and his friend Sergio.

The golf course is one such symbol. When the boys first see it, it is "heaven" (41). Lush and green and carefully cared for, it is completely different from the dry brown Arizona countryside and the polluted arroyo. In fact, to the boys it is another world, as mysterious as Oz - - and just as unreal. Almost at once, the Emerald City becomes black and white again, the "Coke-holders" disappear, and the boys stop "acting 'rich'" (41). Heaven becomes a golf course, and the boys are changed forever.

The arroyo, or river, is another symbol that reinforces the theme of the inevitability of change.

It is a special place for the boys - - a place to rebel, to shout forbidden words, to swim in waters polluted by a sewage treatment plant. Although it represents a retreat from the disillusionment of the golf course, clearly second choice, it is the boys' "personal Mississippi" (38), full of possibilities. Eventually, though, the arroyo too disappoints the boys, and they stop going there. "Nature seemed to keep pushing us around one way or another, teaching us the same thing every place we ended up" (39). The lesson they keep learning is that nothing is permanent.

The grinding ball, round and perfect, seems to suggest permanence and stability. But when the boys find it, they realize at once that they cannot keep it forever, just as they cannot remain children forever. Like a child's life, it is perfect - - but temporary. Burying it is their futile attempt to make time stand still, to preserve perfection in an imperfect world, innocence in an adult world, and they have already learned Nature's lesson well enough to know that this is not possible. They do not look very hard for the ball, but even if they'd been able to find it, the perfection and the innocence it represents would still be unattainable.

The secret lion, the most complex symbol, suggests the most profound kind of change: moving from innocence to experience, from childhood to adulthood. When the narrator is twelve, he says, "something happened that we didn't have a name for, but it was there nonetheless like a lion, and roaring, roaring that way the biggest things do. Everything changed" (37). School is different, girls are different, language is different. Innocence was lost. The lion is associated with a great "roaring" disturbance, a change that unsettles everything for a brief time and then passes, leaving everything changed in irrevocable, indescribable ways. The secret lion is the thing that changes little boys into men. It is a lion because it "roars" through the boy like a storm; everything changes.

In an attempt to make things stay the same, to make time stand still, the boys bury the grinding ball "because it was perfect. . . . It was the lion" (39). The grinding ball is "like that place, that whole arroyo" (39): secret and perfect. In other words, the ball and the arroyo and the lion are all tightly connected. By the time the boys bury the ball, they have already learned one sad lesson and are already on their way to adulthood. Heaven is just a golf course; the round, perfect object is only "a cannonball thing used in mining" (38); the arroyo is no Mississippi but a polluted stream; and childhood does not last forever. "Things get taken away" (42), and this knowledge that things do not last is the secret lion.

Second Draft: Commentary

John felt fairly satisfied with his second draft. His revised thesis seemed more reasonable, and it seemed to be convincingly supported, with topic sentences that introduced support paragraphs and connected them to the thesis. The second draft was also a good deal less wordy and more focused than the first, notably in the paragraphs about the arroyo and the grinding ball, and the introduction and conclusion were more fully developed. Moreover, he had given up his search for the one true "meaning" of each symbol, focusing instead on the many possibilities of each.

Now that John felt comfortable with the larger concerns of his essay, he was ready to turn his attention to smaller items such as style, grammar, mechanics, punctuation, and format. For instance, he planned to eliminate contractions, to check all verb tenses carefully, to review documentation and work quotations into his text more smoothly, to make his thesis more precise and his title more interesting, and to revise the language of his introduction and conclusion further. In addition, he planned to scrutinize this draft carefully, aiming to make his final paper more concise.

Frei 1

John Frei

Professor Nyysola

English 102

15 April 1993

Opening paragraph identifies work and author

Parenthetical documentation identifies source of quotation

Thesis statement

Topic sentence identifies one key symbol

"The Secret Lion": Everything Changes

The first paragraph of Alberto Alvaro Rios's "The Secret Lion" presents a twelve-year-old's view of growing up: Everything changes. When the magician pulls a tablecloth out from under a pile of dishes, the child is amazed at the "staying-the-same part" (38); adults focus on the tablecloth. As adults, we have the benefit of experience; we know the trick will work as long as the technique is correct. We gain confidence, but we lose our innocence, and we lose our sense of wonder. The price we pay for knowledge is a permanent sense of loss, and this tradeoff is central to "The Secret Lion," a story whose key symbols reinforce its central theme: that change is inevitable, and that change is always accompanied by loss.

The golf course is one symbol that helps to convey this theme. When the boys first see the golf course, it is "heaven" (41). Lush and green and carefully tended, it is the antithesis of the dry, brown Arizona landscape and the polluted arroyo. In fact, to the boys it is another world, as exotic as Oz and ultimately as unreal. Before long the Emerald City becomes black and white again. They learn that there is no such thing as a "Coke-holder," that their "acting 'rich'" is just an act, and that their heaven is only a golf course (41). As the narrator acknowledges,

Frei 2

"Sometimes got taken away from us that moment. Heaven" (41).

Topic sentence identifies another key symbol

The arroyo, or river, is another symbol that reflects the idea of the inevitability of change, and of the loss that accompanies change. It is a special, Eden-like place for the boys - - a place where they can rebel by shouting forbidden words and by swimming in forbidden waters. Although it is a retreat from the disillusionment of the golf course, it is still their "personal Mississippi" (38), full of possibilities. Eventually, though, the arroyo too disappoints the boys, and they stop going there. As the narrator says, "Nature seemed to keep pushing us around one way or another, teaching us the same thing every place we ended up" (39). The lesson they keep learning is that nothing is permanent.

Topic sentence identifies another key symbol

The grinding ball, round and perfect, suggests permanence and stability. But when the boys find it, they realize at once that they cannot keep it forever, just as they cannot remain balanced forever between childhood and adulthood. Like a child's life, the ball is perfect - - but temporary. Burying it is their desperate attempt to stop time, to preserve perfection in an imperfect world, innocence in an adult world. But the boys are already twelve years old, and they have learned nature's lesson well enough to know that this action will not work. Even if they had been able to find the ball, the perfection and the innocence it suggests to them would still be unattainable. Perhaps that is why they do not try very hard to find it.

Frei 3

Topic sentence identifies final (and most important) symbol to be discussed

Like the story's other symbols, the secret lion itself suggests the most profound kind of change: the movement from innocence to experience, from childhood to adulthood, from expectation to disappointment to resignation. The narrator explains that when he was twelve, "something happened that we didn't have a name for, but it was there nonetheless like a lion, and roaring, roaring that way the biggest things do. Everything changed" (37). School was different, girls were different, language was different. Despite its loud roar, the lion remained paradoxically "secret," unnoticed until it passed. Like adolescence, the secret lion is a roaring disturbance that unsettles everything for a brief time and then passes, leaving everything changed.

Conclusion

In an attempt to make things stay the same, to make time stand still, the boys bury the grinding ball "because it was perfect. . . . It was the lion" (41). The grinding ball is "like that place, that whole arroyo" (39): secret and perfect. The ball and the arroyo and the lion are all perfect, but all, ironically, are ephemeral. The first paragraph of "The Secret Lion" tells us "Everything changed" (37); by the last paragraph we learn what this change means: "Things get taken away" (42). In other words, change implies loss. Heaven turns out to be just a golf course; the round, perfect object only "a cannonball thing used in mining" (38); the arroyo just a polluted stream; and childhood just a phase. "Things get taken away," and this knowledge that things do not last is the lion, secret yet roaring.

Final Draft: Commentary

As he revised and edited his second draft, John made many changes in word choice and sentence structure. He also changed his title, edited to eliminate errors in mechanics and punctuation, and ran a spell check on his computer. In this final draft he made his thesis even more precise, to communicate the idea of the relationship between change and loss that is central to the essay. In addition, he worked all quoted material smoothly into his essay, making sure he used quotations only when the author's words added something vital to the paper. Finally, John checked all his references to page numbers in the story, so readers would be able to return to his source if necessary to check the accuracy and appropriateness of his quotations.

CHAPTER 4

PLOT

Alfred Hitchcock's 1951 film *Strangers on a Train,* based on a suspense novel by Patricia Highsmith, offers an intriguing premise: Two men, strangers, can both murder someone the other wishes dead; because they have no apparent connection to their victims, both can escape suspicion. Many people would describe this ingenious scheme as the film's "plot," but in fact it is simply the gimmick around which the complex plot revolves. Certainly a clever twist can be an important ingredient of a story's plot, but plot is more than "what happens"; it is how what happens is presented. **Plot** is the way in which a story's events are arranged, and it is shaped by causal connections—historical, social, and personal—by the interaction between characters, and by the juxtaposition of events.

The way in which a writer presents incidents influences the way in which readers respond to them. For example, the reintroduction of a particular event, or the presence of a series of related incidents, can suggest a pattern, adding emphasis or revealing a new or unexpected meaning. More specifically, a writer may choose to present a sequence of events with distinct clarity or with some degree of ambiguity; in chronological order or in a confusing or even obscure sequence; from a single perspective or from several different viewpoints—in each case with a different effect. In *Strangers on a Train,* as in many well-developed works of fiction, the plot that unfolds is complex, with one character directing the events and determining their order while the other is drawn into the action against his will. The same elements that enrich the plot of the film—unexpected events, conflict, suspense, flashbacks, foreshadowing—can also enrich the plot of a work of short fiction.

CONFLICT

Readers' interest and involvement in a story are heightened by its **conflict,** the struggle between opposing forces that emerges as the story's action develops. This conflict is a clash between the **protagonist,** a story's principal character, and an **antagonist,** someone or something presented in opposition to the protagonist. Sometimes the antagonist is easily identified as a villain; more often, he or she simply represents a conflicting point of view or advocates a course of action different from the one the protagonist chooses to follow. Sometimes the antagonist is not a character at all but a situation (war, poverty) or an event (a natural disaster, such as a flood or a storm) that challenges the protagonist. In other stories, the protagonist may struggle against a supernatural force, or the conflict may be internal, occurring within a character's mind. It may, for example, be a struggle between two moral choices, such as whether to stay at home and care for an aging parent or leave to make a new life. In such a case, the parent is not the antagonist; rather, the conflict occurs within the protagonist's mind.

STAGES OF PLOT

A work's plot explores one or more conflicts, moving from exposition through a series of complications to a climax, and, finally, to a resolution.

In a story's **exposition** the writer presents the basic information readers need to understand the events that follow. Typically, the exposition sets the story's scene, introduces the major characters, and perhaps suggests the major events or conflicts that will follow. In a very brief story, a single sentence like "Knowing that Mrs. Mallard was afflicted with a heart trouble, great care was taken to break to her as gently as possible the news of her husband's death" can present exposition clearly and economically. This sentence, which opens Kate Chopin's classic "The Story of an Hour," provides readers with two pieces of information vital to their understanding of the plot that will unfold: Mrs. Mallard is physically delicate, and she is about to hear news of her husband's death. In a longer story, John Updike's "A&P" (p. 93), a more fully developed exposition section establishes the story's setting, introduces the main characters, and suggests possible conflicts. In more experimental stories a distinct exposition component may be absent, as it is in Lorrie Moore's "How to Talk to Your Mother (Notes)" (p. 78).

As the plot progresses, the story's conflict unfolds through a series of complications that will eventually lead readers to the story's climax. The action may include several crises. A **crisis** is a peak in the story's action, a moment of considerable tension or importance; the **climax** is the point of greatest tension or importance, the scene which presents a story's decisive action.

The final stage of plot, the **resolution**, or **denouement** (French for "untying of the knot"), draws the action to a close and ties up all remaining loose ends. Here the outcome of the story's events is presented. Sometimes this resolution is achieved by virtue of a **deus ex machina** (Latin for "a god from a machine"), an intervention of some force or agent previously extraneous to the story—the appearance of a long-lost relative or a fortuitous inheritance, the discovery of a character's true identity, a last-minute rescue by a character not previously introduced. Usually, however, the resolution is more plausible: All the events lead logically and convincingly (although not necessarily predictably) to the resolution. Sometimes the ending of a story is indefinite—that is, readers are not quite sure what the protagonist will do, or what will happen next. This kind of resolution, although it may leave some readers feeling cheated, has its advantages: It mirrors the complexity of life, where closure rarely occurs, and it can draw readers into the action as they try to understand the significance of the story's ending or to decide how conflicts should have been resolved.

ORDER AND SEQUENCE

A writer may present a story's events in strict chronological order, with the event that actually occurred first presented first and each subsequent event presented in the sequence in which it took place. More often, however, especially in relatively modern fiction, writers do not present events chronologically. Instead, they present incidents out of expected order, or in no apparent order. For example, a writer may choose to begin **in medias res** (Latin for "in the midst of things"), starting with a key event and later going back in time to explain events that preceded it, as Tillie Olsen does in "I Stand Here Ironing" (p. 148). Or, a writer can decide to begin a work of fiction at the end and then move back to reconstruct events that led up to the final outcome, as William Faulkner does in "A Rose for Emily" (p. 70). Many sequences are possible as the writer manipulates events to create interest, suspense, confusion, wonder, or other effects.

Writers commonly use established techniques such as flashbacks and foreshadowing to vary chronological order. A **flashback** moves out of sequence to examine an event or situation that occurred before the time in which the story's action takes place. A character can remember an earlier event, or a story's narrator can recreate an earlier situation. For example, in Alberto Alvaro Rios's "The Secret Lion" (p. 37) the adult narrator looks back at events that occurred when he was twelve years old—and then moves back further in time to consider related events that occurred when he was five. In Edgar Allan Poe's "The Cask of Amontillado" (p. 180) the entire story is recounted in the form of a flashback. Flashbacks are valuable because they can substitute for or supplement formal exposition by presenting background vital to the readers' understanding of a story's events. One disadvantage is that flashbacks, because they interrupt the natural flow of events, may be intrusive or distracting. Such distractions, however, can be an advantage if the writer wishes to reveal events gradually and subtly or to obscure causal links.

Foreshadowing is the introduction early in a story of situations, events, characters, or objects that seem to have no special importance but are later revealed to have great significance. For example, a casual mention of a character's unusually accurate memory for faces may become significant only when his or her fate turns out to hinge on recognizing a person from the distant past. Using foreshadowing allows a writer to hint provocatively at what is to come, so that readers only gradually become aware of a particular detail's role in a story. Thus foreshadowing helps to create suspense as readers begin to sense what will occur and grow increasingly involved as they see the likelihood (or even the inevitability) of a particular outcome.

In addition to employing conventional techniques like flashbacks and foreshadowing, writers may experiment with sequence by substantially tampering with—or even dispensing with—chronological order. One experimental option for presenting a story's events is using an unconventional sequence, such as the scrambled chronology of "A Rose for Emily" or the reverse chronology of "How to Talk to Your Mother (Notes)." In such instances the experimental form enhances interest and encourages readers to become involved with the story as they work to untangle or reorder the events and determine their logical and causal connections.

A FINAL NOTE

In examining a story's plot, remember that plot is only one element in a work of fiction. In some popular forms of fiction, plot is likely to be the dominant element. For example, in mystery or adventure stories, which may lack fully developed characters, complex themes, and elaborately described settings, the plot line will be clear and easy to follow. In richer, more complicated works of fiction, however, plot, like other elements, may be more complex and less obvious.

Checklist for Writing about Plot

- What happens in the story?
- Where does the story's formal exposition section end? What do readers learn about characters in this section? What do readers learn about setting? What possible conflicts are suggested here?
- What is the story's central conflict? What other conflicts are presented? Who is the protagonist? Who (or what) serves as the antagonist?
- Identify the story's crisis or crises.
- Identify the story's climax.
- How is the story's central conflict resolved? Is this resolution plausible? Satisfying? Logical?
- Which portion of the story constitutes the resolution? Do any problems remain unresolved? Does any uncertainty remain? If so, does this uncertainty strengthen or weaken the story? Would another ending be more effective?
- How are the story's events arranged? Are they presented in chronological order? What events are presented out of logical sequence? Does the story use foreshadowing? Flashbacks? Are the causal connections between events clear? Logical? If not, can you explain why?
- How does the story's plot depart from convention?

Nadine Gordimer (1923–), winner of the 1991 Nobel Prize in literature, has been publishing short stories, essays, and novels about South Africa, her native country, since she was fifteen. Gordimer once explained that after growing up as a middle-class child of Jewish immigrants, becoming a politically aware writer in South Africa was like "peeling an onion. You're sloughing off all the conditioning that you've had since you were a child." The prevailing attitude of her extensive work has evolved from cautious optimism to pessimism in accord with the changing nature of Africa in her lifetime. Michiko Kakutani of the *New York Times* suggests that in the attempt to illustrate that apartheid debases the lives of both blacks and whites, "she has mapped out the social, political and emotional geography of that troubled land with extraordinary passion and precision."

Gordimer's novels include *The Lying Days* (1953), *Occasion for Loving* (1963), *A Guest of Honor* (1970), *Burger's Daughter* (1979), *July's People* (1981), and *A Sport of Nature* (1987). Her short stories have been collected in *Face to Face* (1949), *The Soft Voice of the Serpent, and Other Stories* (1952), *Friday's Footprint, and Other Stories* (1960), *Livingston's Companions* (1971), *Something Out There* (1984), and *Jump and Other Stories* (1991).

Though her work has often been banned in her own country because of its condemnation of apartheid, Gordimer continues to live in Johannesburg.

Nadine Gordimer

ONCE UPON A TIME

(1991)

Someone has written to ask me to contribute to an anthology of stories for children. I reply that I don't write children's stories; and he writes back that at a recent congress/book fair/seminar a certain novelist said every writer ought to write at least one story for children. I think of sending a postcard saying I don't accept that I 'ought' to write anything.

And then last night I woke up—or rather was wakened without knowing what had roused me.

A voice in the echo-chamber of the subconscious?

A sound.

5 A creaking of the kind made by the weight carried by one foot after another along a wooden floor. I listened. I felt the apertures of my ears distend with concentration. Again: the creaking. I was waiting for it; waiting to hear if it indicated that feet were moving from room to room, coming up the passage—to my door. I have no burglar bars, no gun under the pillow, but I have the same fears as people who do take these precautions, and my windowpanes are thin as rime, could shatter like a wineglass. A woman was murdered (how do they put it) in broad daylight in a house two blocks away, last year, and the fierce dogs who guarded an old

widower and his collection of antique clocks were strangled before he was knifed by a casual labourer he had dismissed without pay.

I was staring at the door, making it out in my mind rather than seeing it, in the dark. I lay quite still—a victim already—but the arrhythmia of my heart was fleeing, knocking this way and that against its body-cage. How finely tuned the senses are, just out of rest, sleep! I could never listen intently as that in the distractions of the day; I was reading every faintest sound, identifying and classifying its possible threat.

But I learned that I was to be neither threatened nor spared. There was no human weight pressing on the boards, the creaking was a buckling, an epicentre of stress. I was in it. The house that surrounds me while I sleep is built on undermined ground; far beneath my bed, the floor, the house's foundations, the stopes and passages of gold mines have hollowed the rock, and when some face trembles, detaches and falls, three thousand feet below, the whole house shifts slightly, bringing uneasy strain to the balance and counterbalance of brick, cement, wood and glass that hold it as a structure around me. The misbeats of my heart tailed off like the last muffled flourishes on one of the wooden xylophones made by the Chopi and Tsonga migrant miners who might have been down there, under me in the earth at that moment. The stope where the fall was could have been disused, dripping water from its ruptured veins; or men might now be interred there in the most profound of tombs.

I couldn't find a position in which my mind would let go of my body—release me to sleep again. So I began to tell myself a story; a bedtime story.

In a house, in a suburb, in a city, there were a man and his wife who loved each other very much and were living happily ever after. They had a little boy, and they loved him very much. They had a cat and a dog that the little boy loved very much. They had a car and a caravan trailer for holidays, and a swimming-pool which was fenced so that the little boy and his playmates would not fall in and drown. They had a housemaid who was absolutely trustworthy and an itinerant gardener who was highly recommended by the neighbours. For when they began to live happily ever after they were warned, by that wise old witch, the husband's mother, not to take on anyone off the street. They were inscribed in a medical benefit society, their pet dog was licensed, they were insured against fire, flood damage and theft, and subscribed to the local Neighbourhood Watch, which supplied them with a plaque for their gates lettered YOU HAVE BEEN WARNED over the silhouette of a would-be intruder. He was masked; it could not be said if he was black or white, and therefore proved the property owner was no racist.

It was not possible to insure the house, the swimming pool or the car against riot damage. There were riots, but these were outside the city, where people of another colour were quartered. These people were not allowed into the suburb except as reliable housemaids and gardeners, so there was nothing to fear, the husband told the wife. Yet she was afraid that some day such people might come up the street and tear off the plaque YOU HAVE BEEN WARNED and open the gates and stream in . . . Nonsense, my dear, said the husband, there are police and soldiers and tear-gas and guns to keep them away. But to please her—for he loved her very much and buses were being burned, cars stoned, and schoolchildren shot by the police in those quarters out of sight and hearing of the suburb—he had electronically-controlled gates fitted. Anyone who pulled off the sign YOU HAVE BEEN WARNED and tried to open the gates would have to announce his intentions by pressing a button and speaking into a receiver relayed to the house. The little boy was fascinated by the device and used it as a walkie-talkie in cops and robbers play with his small friends.

10 The riots were suppressed, but there were many burglaries in the suburb and somebody's trusted housemaid was tied up and shut in a cupboard by thieves while she was in charge of her employers' house. The trusted housemaid of the man and wife and little boy was so upset by this misfortune befalling a friend left, as she herself often was, with responsibility for the possessions of the man and his wife and the little boy that she implored her employers to have burglar bars attached to the doors and windows of the house, and an alarm system installed. The wife said, She is right, let us take heed to her advice. So from every window and door in the house where they were living happily ever after they now saw the trees and sky through bars, and when the little boy's pet cat tried to climb in by the fanlight to keep him company in his little bed at night, as it customarily had done, it set off the alarm keening through the house.

The alarm was often answered—it seemed—by other burglar alarms, in other houses, that had been triggered by pet cats or nibbling mice. The alarms called to one another across the gardens in shrills and bleats and wails that everyone soon became accustomed to, so that the din roused the inhabitants of the suburb no more than the croak of frogs and musical grating of cicadas' legs. Under cover of the electronic harpies' discourse intruders sawed the iron bars and broke into homes, taking away hi-fi equipment, television sets, cassette players, cameras and radios, jewellery and clothing, and sometimes were hungry enough to devour everything in the refrigerator or paused audaciously to drink the whisky in the cabinets or patio bars. Insurance companies paid no compensation for single malt, a loss made keener by the property owner's knowledge that the thieves wouldn't even have been able to appreciate what it was they were drinking.

Then the time came when many of the people who were not trusted housemaids and gardeners hung about the suburb because they were unemployed. Some importuned for a job: weeding or painting a roof; anything, *baas,* madam. But the man and his wife remembered the warning about taking on anyone off the street. Some drank liquor and fouled the street with discarded bottles. Some begged, waiting for the man or his wife to drive the car out of the electronically-operated gates. They sat about with their feet in the gutters, under the jacaranda trees that made a green tunnel of the street—for it was a beautiful suburb, spoilt only by their presence—and sometimes they fell asleep lying right before the gates in the midday sun. The wife could never see anyone go hungry. She sent the trusted housemaid out with bread and tea, but the trusted housemaid said these were loafers and *tsotsis,* who would come and tie her up and shut her in a cupboard. The husband said, She's right. Take heed of her advice. You only encourage them with your bread and tea. They are looking for their chance . . . And he brought the little boy's tricycle from the garden into the house every night, because if the house was surely secure, once locked and with the alarm set, someone might still be able to climb over the wall or the electronically-closed gates into the garden.

You are right, said the wife, then the wall should be higher. And the wise old witch, the husband's mother, paid for the extra bricks as her Christmas present to her son and his wife—the little boy got a Space Man outfit and a book of fairy tales.

But every week there were more reports of intrusion: in broad daylight and the dead of night, in the early hours of the morning, and even in the lovely summer twilight—a certain family was at dinner while the bedrooms were being ransacked upstairs. The man and his wife, talking of the latest armed robbery in the suburb, were distracted by the sight of the little boy's pet cat effortlessly arriving over the seven-foot wall, descending first with a rapid bracing of extended forepaws down on the sheer vertical surface, and then a graceful launch, landing with swishing tail within the property. The whitewashed wall was marked with the cat's comings and goings; and on the street side of the wall there were larger red-earth smudges that could have been made by the kind of broken running shoes, seen on the feet of unemployed loiterers, that had no innocent destination.

When the man and wife and little boy took the pet dog for its walk round the neighbourhood streets they no longer paused to admire this show of roses or that perfect lawn; these were hidden behind an array of different varieties of security fences, walls and devices. The man, wife, little boy and dog passed a remarkable choice: there was the low-cost option of pieces of broken glass embedded in cement along the top of walls, there were iron grilles ending in lance-points, there were attempts at reconciling the aesthetics of prison architecture with the Spanish Villa style (spikes painted pink) and with the plaster urns of neoclassical façades (twelve-inch pikes finned like zigzags of lightning and painted pure white). Some walls had a small board affixed, giving the name and telephone number of the firm responsible for the installation of the devices. While the little boy and the pet dog raced ahead, the husband and wife found themselves comparing the possible effectiveness of each style against its appearance; and after several weeks when they paused before this barricade or that without needing to speak, both came out with the conclusion that only one was worth considering. It was the ugliest but the most honest in its suggestion of the pure concentration-camp style, no frills, all evident efficacy. Placed the length of walls, it consisted of a continuous coil of stiff and shining metal serrated into jagged blades, so that there would be no way of climbing over it and no way through its tunnel without getting entangled in its fangs. There would be no way out, only a struggle getting bloodier and bloodier, a deeper and sharper hooking and tearing of flesh. The wife shuddered to look at it. You're right, said the husband, anyone would think twice . . . And they took heed of the advice on a small board fixed to the wall: Consult DRAGON'S TEETH The People for Total Security.

Next day a gang of workmen came and stretched the razor-bladed coils all round the walls of the house where the husband and wife and little boy and pet dog and cat were living happily ever after. The sunlight flashed and slashed, off the serrations, the cornice of razor thorns encircled the home, shining. The husband said, Never mind. It will weather. The wife said, You're wrong. They guarantee it's rust-proof. And she waited until the little boy had run off to play before she said, I hope the cat will take heed . . . The husband said, Don't worry, my dear, cats always look before they leap. And it was true that from that day on the cat slept in the little boy's bed and kept to the garden, never risking a try at breaching security.

One evening, the mother read the little boy to sleep with a fairy story from the book the wise old witch had given him at Christmas. Next day he pretended to be the Prince who braves the terrible thicket of thorns to enter the palace and kiss the Sleeping Beauty back to life: he dragged a ladder to the wall, the shining coiled tunnel was just wide enough for his little body to creep in, and with the first fixing of its razor-teeth in his knees and hands and head he screamed and struggled deeper into its tangle. The trusted housemaid and the itinerant gardener, whose 'day' it was, came running, the first to see and to scream with him, and the itinerant gardener tore his hands trying to get at the little boy. Then the man and his wife burst wildly into the garden and for some reason (the cat, probably) the alarm set up wailing against the screams while the bleeding mass of the little boy was hacked out of the security coil with saws, wire-cutters, choppers, and they carried it—the man, the wife, the hysterical trusted housemaid and the weeping gardener—into the house.

READING AND REACTING

1. This story's events are presented in strict chronological order. Give some examples of phrases that move readers from one time period to another.
2. Imagine Gordimer's story dramatized, perhaps as a television documentary. Where would you interrupt the story to provide commercial breaks or station identification? Explain your decisions.

3. Throughout the story, various objects and events (and even specific warnings) foreshadow the grim ending. Give several examples of such hints, and explain how each anticipates the ending.
4. The story's title suggests a fairy tale. In what respects is the *plot* of "Once Upon a Time" like that of a fairy tale? In what respects is it different?
5. Like many fairy tales, "Once Upon a Time" has a flat, emotionless tone. How does this detached tone affect your reaction to the story?
6. What portion of the story constitutes the basic exposition? What vital information about characters and setting is *not* presented in this section? Why do you think such information is not provided?
7. What characters are set in opposition in this story? Does the story have a hero? A villain? What larger forces are in conflict? Are the conflicts between these forces resolved at the end? Explain.
8. What tendencies in her society do you think the author of "Once Upon a Time" means to criticize? Do you agree that these tendencies are dangerous?
9. **JOURNAL ENTRY:** "Once Upon a Time" is set in South Africa. Could it have been set in the United States?

William Faulkner (1897–1962), winner of the 1949 Nobel Prize for literature and the 1955 and 1963 Pulitzer prizes for fiction, was an unabashedly "Southern" writer whose work continues to transcend the regional label. His nineteen novels, notably *The Sound and the Fury* (1929), *As I Lay Dying* (1930), *Light in August* (1932), *Absalom, Absalom!* (1936), and *The Reivers* (1962), explore a wide range of human experience—from high comedy to tragedy—as seen in the life of one community, Faulkner's fictional "Yoknapatawpha County" (modeled on the area around Faulkner's own hometown of Oxford, Mississippi). Faulkner's Yoknapatawpha stories—a fascinating blend of complex Latinate prose and primitive Southern dialect—paint an extraordinary portrait of a community bound together by ties of blood, by a shared belief in moral "verities," and by an old grief (the Civil War). Faulkner's grandfather raised "Billy" on Civil War tales and local legends, including many about the "Old Colonel," the writer's great-grandfather, who was a colorful Confederate officer. But Faulkner was no Margaret Mitchell. Like Mitchell's *Gone With the Wind,* his stories elegize the agrarian virtues of the Old South, but his look unflinchingly at that world's tragic flaw: the "peculiar institution" of slavery.

Local legends and gossip frequently served as the spark for Faulkner's stories. As John B. Cullen, writing in *Old Times in Faulkner Country,* notes, "A Rose for Emily," Faulkner's first nationally published short story, was based on the tale of Oxford's aristocratic "Miss Mary" Neilson, who married Captain Jack Hume, the charming Yankee foreman of a street-paving crew, over her family's shocked protests. But Hume didn't meet the fate of "Miss Emily's" lover. He lived on to a ripe old age and lovingly cared for his wife during her final illness. According to Cullen, one of Faulkner's neighbors said he created his story "out of fears and rumors"—the dire predictions of what *might* happen if Mary Neilson married her Yankee.

William Faulkner

A ROSE FOR EMILY

(1930)

I

When Miss Emily Grierson died, our whole town went to her funeral: the men through a sort of respectful affection for a fallen monument, the women mostly out of curiosity to see the inside of her house, which no one save an old manservant—a combined gardener and cook—had seen in at least ten years.

It was a big, squarish frame house that had once been white, decorated with cupolas and spires and scrolled balconies in the heavily lightsome style of the seventies, set on what had once been our most select street. But garages and cotton gins had encroached and obliterated even the august names of that neighborhood; only Miss Emily's house was left, lifting its stubborn and coquettish decay above the cotton wagons and the gasoline pumps—an eyesore among eyesores. And now Miss Emily had gone to join the representatives of those august names where they lay in the cedar-bemused cemetery among the ranked and anonymous graves of Union and Confederate soldiers who fell at the battle of Jefferson.

Alive, Miss Emily had been a tradition, a duty, and a care; a sort of hereditary obligation upon the town, dating from that day in 1894 when Colonel Sartoris, the mayor—he who fathered the edict that no Negro woman should appear on the streets without an apron—remitted her taxes, the dispensation dating from the death of her father on into perpetuity. Not that Miss Emily would have accepted charity. Colonel Sartoris invented an involved tale to the effect that Miss Emily's father had loaned money to the town, which the town, as a matter of business, preferred this way of repaying. Only a man of Colonel Sartoris' generation and thought could have invented it, and only a woman could have believed it.

When the next generation, with its more modern ideas, became mayors and aldermen, this arrangement created some little dissatisfaction. On the first of the year they mailed her a tax notice. February came, and there was no reply. They wrote her a formal letter, asking her to call at the sheriff's office at her convenience. A week later the mayor wrote her himself, offering to call or to send his car for her, and received in reply a note on paper of an archaic shape, in a thin, flowing calligraphy in faded ink, to the effect that she no longer went out at all. The tax notice was also enclosed, without comment.

5 They called a special meeting of the Board of Aldermen. A deputation waited upon her, knocked at the door through which no visitor had passed since she ceased giving china-painting lessons eight or ten years earlier. They were admitted by the old Negro into a dim hall from which a stairway mounted into still more shadow. It smelled of dust and disuse—a close, dank smell. The Negro led them into the parlor. It was furnished in heavy, leather-covered furniture. When the Negro opened the blinds of one window, they could see that the leather was cracked; and when they sat down, a faint dust rose sluggishly about their thighs, spinning with slow motes in the single sun-ray. On a tarnished gilt easel before the fireplace stood a crayon portrait of Miss Emily's father.

They rose when she entered—a small, fat woman in black, with a thin gold chain descending to her waist and vanishing into her belt, leaning on an ebony cane with a tarnished gold head. Her skeleton was small and spare; perhaps that was why what would have been merely plumpness in another was obesity in her. She looked bloated, like a body long submerged in motionless water, and of that pallid hue. Her eyes, lost in the fatty ridges of her face, looked like two small pieces of coal pressed into a lump of dough as they moved from one face to another while the visitors stated their errand.

She did not ask them to sit. She just stood in the door and listened quietly until the spokesman came to a stumbling halt. Then they could hear the invisible watch ticking at the end of the gold chain.

Her voice was dry and cold. "I have no taxes in Jefferson. Colonel Sartoris explained it to me. Perhaps one of you can gain access to the city records and satisfy yourselves."

"But we have. We are the city authorities, Miss Emily. Didn't you get a notice from the sheriff, signed by him?"

10 "I received a paper, yes," Miss Emily said. "Perhaps he considers himself the sheriff . . . I have no taxes in Jefferson."

"But there is nothing on the books to show that, you see. We must go by the—"

"See Colonel Sartoris. I have no taxes in Jefferson."

"But, Miss Emily—"

"See Colonel Sartoris." (Colonel Sartoris had been dead almost ten years.) "I have no taxes in Jefferson. Tobe!" The Negro appeared. "Show these gentlemen out."

II

15 So she vanquished them, horse and foot, just as she had vanquished their fathers thirty years before about the smell. That was two years after her father's death and a short time after her sweetheart—the one we believed would marry her—had deserted her. After her father's death she went out very little; after her sweetheart went away, people hardly saw her at all. A few of the ladies had the temerity to call, but were not received, and the only sign of life about the place was the Negro man—a young man then—going in and out with a market basket.

"Just as if a man—any man—could keep a kitchen properly," the ladies said; so they were not surprised when the smell developed. It was another link between the gross, teeming world and the high and mighty Griersons.

A neighbor, a woman, complained to the mayor, Judge Stevens, eighty years old.

"But what will you have me do about it, madam?" he said.

"Why, send her word to stop it," the woman said. "Isn't there a law?"

20 "I'm sure that won't be necessary," Judge Stevens said. "It's probably just a snake or a rat that nigger of hers killed in the yard. I'll speak to him about it."

The next day he received two more complaints, one from a man who came in diffident deprecation. "We really must do something about it, Judge. I'd be the last one in the world to bother Miss Emily, but we've got to do something." That night the Board of Aldermen met—three graybeards and one younger man, a member of the rising generation.

"It's simple enough," he said. "Send her word to have her place cleaned up. Give her a certain time to do it in, and if she don't . . ."

"Dammit, sir," Judge Stevens said, "will you accuse a lady to her face of smelling bad?"

So the next night, after midnight, four men crossed Miss Emily's lawn and slunk about the house like burglars, sniffing along the base of the brickwork and at the cellar openings while one of them performed a regular sowing motion with his hand out of a sack slung from his shoulder. They broke open the cellar door and sprinkled lime there, and in all the outbuildings. As they recrossed the lawn, a window that had been dark was lighted and Miss Emily sat in it, the light behind her, and her upright torso motionless as that of an idol. They crept quietly across the lawn and into the shadow of the locusts that lined the street. After a week or two the smell went away.

25 That was when people had begun to feel really sorry for her. People in our town, remembering how old lady Wyatt, her great-aunt, had gone completely crazy at last, believed that the Griersons held themselves a little too high for what they really were. None of the young men were quite good enough for Miss Emily and such. We had long thought of them as a tableau, Miss Emily a slender figure in white in the background, her father a spraddled silhouette in the foreground, his back to her and clutching a horsewhip, the two of them framed by the back-flung front door. So

when she got to be thirty and was still single, we were not pleased exactly, but vindicated; even with insanity in the family she wouldn't have turned down all of her chances if they had really materialized.

When her father died, it got about that the house was all that was left to her; and in a way, people were glad. At last they could pity Miss Emily. Being left alone, and a pauper, she had become humanized. Now she too would know the old thrill and the old despair of a penny more or less.

The day after his death all the ladies prepared to call at the house and offer condolence and aid, as is our custom. Miss Emily met them at the door, dressed as usual and with no trace of grief on her face. She told them that her father was not dead. She did that for three days, with the ministers calling on her, and the doctors, trying to persuade her to let them dispose of the body. Just as they were about to resort to law and force, she broke down, and they buried her father quickly.

We did not say she was crazy then. We believed she had to do that. We remembered all the young men her father had driven away, and we knew that with nothing left, she would have to cling to that which had robbed her, as people will.

III

She was sick for a long time. When we saw her again, her hair was cut short, making her look like a girl, with a vague resemblance to those angels in colored church windows—sort of tragic and serene.

The town had just let the contracts for paving the sidewalks, and in the summer after her father's death they began the work. The construction company came with niggers and mules and machinery, and a foreman named Homer Barron, a Yankee—a big, dark, ready man, with a big voice and eyes lighter than his face. The little boys would follow in groups to hear him cuss the niggers, and the niggers singing in time to the rise and fall of picks. Pretty soon he knew everybody in town. Whenever you heard a lot of laughing anywhere about the square, Homer Barron would be in the center of the group. Presently we began to see him and Miss Emily on Sunday afternoons driving in the yellow-wheeled buggy and the matched team of bays from the livery stable.

At first we were glad that Miss Emily would have an interest, because the ladies all said, "Of course a Grierson would not think seriously of a Northerner, a day laborer." But there were still others, older people, who said that even grief could not cause a real lady to forget *noblesse oblige*[1]—without calling it *noblesse oblige*. They just said, "Poor Emily. Her kinsfolk should come to her." She had some kin in Alabama; but years ago her father had fallen out with them over the estate of old lady Wyatt, the crazy woman, and there was no communication between the two families. They had not even been represented at the funeral.

---

[1] The obligation of those of high birth or rank to behave in an honorable fashion.

And as soon as the old people said, "Poor Emily," the whispering began. "Do you suppose it's really so?" they said to one another. "Of course it is. What else could . . ." This behind their hands; rustling of craned silk and satin behind jalousies closed upon the sun of Sunday afternoon as the thin, swift clop-clop-clop of the matched team passed: "Poor Emily."

She carried her head high enough—even when we believed that she was fallen. It was as if she demanded more than ever the recognition of her dignity as the last Grierson; as if it had wanted that touch of earthiness to reaffirm her imperviousness. Like when she bought the rat poison, the arsenic. That was over a year after they had begun to say "Poor Emily," and while the two female cousins were visiting her.

"I want some poison," she said to the druggist. She was over thirty then, still a slight woman, though thinner than usual, with cold, haughty black eyes in a face the flesh of which was strained across the temples and about the eye-sockets as you imagine a lighthouse-keeper's face ought to look. "I want some poison," she said.

"Yes, Miss Emily. What kind? For rats and such? I'd recom—"

"I want the best you have. I don't care what kind."

The druggist named several. "They'll kill anything up to an elephant. But what you want is—"

"Arsenic," Miss Emily said. "Is that a good one?"

"Is . . . arsenic? Yes, ma'am. But what you want—"

"I want arsenic."

The druggist looked down at her. She looked back at him, erect, her face like a strained flag. "Why, of course," the druggist said. "If that's what you want. But the law requires you to tell what you are going to use it for."

Miss Emily just stared at him, her head tilted back in order to look him eye for eye, until he looked away and went and got the arsenic and wrapped it up. The Negro delivery boy brought her the package; the druggist didn't come back. When she opened the package at home there was written on the box, under the skull and bones: "For rats."

IV

So the next day we all said, "She will kill herself"; and we said it would be the best thing. When she had first begun to be seen with Homer Barron, we had said, "She will marry him." Then we said, "She will persuade him yet," because Homer himself had remarked—he liked men, and it was known that he drank with the younger men in the Elks' Club—that he was not a marrying man. Later we said, "Poor Emily" behind the jalousies as they passed on Sunday afternoon in the glittering buggy, Miss Emily with her head high and Homer Barron with his hat cocked and a cigar in his teeth, reins and whip in a yellow glove.

Then some of the ladies began to say that it was a disgrace to the town and a bad example to the young people. The men did not want to interfere, but at last the ladies forced the Baptist minister—Miss Emily's people were Episcopal—to call upon her. He would never divulge what happened during that interview, but he refused to go back again. The next Sunday they again drove about the streets, and the following day the minister's wife wrote to Miss Emily's relations in Alabama.

45 So she had blood-kin under her roof again and we sat back to watch developments. At first nothing happened. Then we were sure that they were to be married. We learned that Miss Emily had been to the jeweler's and ordered a man's toilet set in silver, with the letters H. B. on each piece. Two days later we learned that she had bought a complete outfit of men's clothing, including a nightshirt, and we said, "They are married." We were really glad. We were glad because the two female cousins were even more Grierson than Miss Emily had ever been.

So we were not surprised when Homer Barron—the streets had been finished some time since—was gone. We were a little disappointed that there was not a public blowing-off, but we believed that he had gone on to prepare for Miss Emily's coming, or to give her a chance to get rid of the cousins. (By that time it was a cabal, and we were all Miss Emily's allies to help circumvent the cousins.) Sure enough, after another week they departed. And, as we had expected all along, within three days Homer Barron was back in town. A neighbor saw the Negro man admit him at the kitchen door at dusk one evening.

And that was the last we saw of Homer Barron. And of Miss Emily for some time. The Negro man went in and out with the market basket, but the front door remained closed. Now and then we would see her at a window for a moment, as the men did that night when they sprinkled the lime, but for almost six months she did not appear on the streets. Then we knew that this was to be expected too; as if that quality of her father which had thwarted her woman's life so many times had been too virulent and too furious to die.

When we next saw Miss Emily, she had grown fat and her hair was turning gray. During the next few years it grew grayer and grayer until it attained an even pepper-and-salt iron-gray, when it ceased turning. Up to the day of her death at seventy-four it was still that vigorous iron-gray, like the hair of an active man.

From that time on her front door remained closed, save for a period of six or seven years, when she was about forty, during which she gave lessons in china-painting. She fitted up a studio in one of the downstairs rooms, where the daughters and granddaughters of Colonel Sartoris' contemporaries were sent to her with the same regularity and in the same spirit that they were sent to church on Sundays with a twenty-five-cent piece for the collection plate. Meanwhile her taxes had been remitted.

50 Then the newer generation became the backbone and the spirit of the town, and the painting pupils grew up and fell away and did not send their children to her with boxes of color and tedious brushes and pictures cut from the ladies' magazines. The front door closed upon the last one and remained closed for good. When the town got free

postal delivery, Miss Emily alone refused to let them fasten the metal numbers above her door and attach a mailbox to it. She would not listen to them.

Daily, monthly, yearly we watched the Negro grow grayer and more stooped, going in and out with the market basket. Each December we sent her a tax notice, which would be returned by the post office a week later, unclaimed. Now and then we would see her in one of the downstairs windows—she had evidently shut up the top floor of the house—like the carven torso of an idol in a niche, looking or not looking at us, we could never tell which. Thus she passed from generation to generation—dear, inescapable, impervious, tranquil, and perverse.

And so she died. Fell ill in the house filled with dust and shadows, with only a doddering Negro man to wait on her. We did not even know she was sick; we had long since given up trying to get any information from the Negro. He talked to no one, probably not even to her, for his voice had grown harsh and rusty, as if from disuse.

She died in one of the downstairs rooms, in a heavy walnut bed with a curtain, her gray head propped on a pillow yellow and moldy with age and lack of sunlight.

V

The Negro met the first of the ladies at the front door and let them in, with their hushed, sibilant voices and their quick, curious glances, and then he disappeared. He walked right through the house and out the back and was not seen again.

The two female cousins came at once. They held the funeral on the second day, with the town coming to look at Miss Emily beneath a mass of bought flowers, with the crayon face of her father musing profoundly above the bier and the ladies sibilant and macabre; and the very old men—some in their brushed Confederate uniforms—on the porch and the lawn, talking of Miss Emily as if she had been a contemporary of theirs, believing that they had danced with her and courted her perhaps, confusing time with its mathematical progression, as the old do, to whom all the past is not a diminishing road but, instead, a huge meadow which no winter ever quite touches, divided from them now by the narrow bottle-neck of the most recent decade of years.

Already we knew that there was one room in that region above stairs which no one had seen in forty years, and which would have to be forced. They waited until Miss Emily was decently in the ground before they opened it.

The violence of breaking down the door seemed to fill this room with pervading dust. A thin, acrid pall as of the tomb seemed to lie everywhere upon this room decked and furnished as for a bridal: upon the valance curtains of faded rose color, upon the rose-shaded lights, upon the dressing table, upon the delicate array of crystal and the man's toilet things backed with tarnished silver, silver so tarnished that the monogram was obscured. Among them lay collar and tie, as if they had just been removed, which, lifted, left upon the surface a pale crescent in the dust. Upon a chair hung the suit, carefully folded; beneath it the two mute shoes and the discarded socks.

The man himself lay in the bed.

For a long while we just stood there, looking down at the profound and fleshless grin. The body had apparently once lain in the attitude of an embrace, but now the long sleep that outlasts love, that conquers even the grimace of love, had cuckolded him. What was left of him, rotted beneath what was left of the nightshirt, had become inextricable from the bed in which he lay; and upon him and upon the pillow beside him lay that even coating of the patient and biding dust.

60 Then we noticed that in the second pillow was the indentation of a head. One of us lifted something from it, and leaning forward, that faint and invisible dust dry and acrid in the nostrils, we saw a long strand of iron-gray hair.

READING AND REACTING

1. Arrange these events in the sequence in which they actually occur: Homer's arrival in town, the aldermen's visit, Emily's purchase of poison, Colonel Sartoris's decision to remit Emily's taxes, the development of the odor around Emily's house, Emily's father's death, the arrival of Emily's relatives, Homer's disappearance. Then, list the events in the sequence in which they are presented in the story. Why do you suppose Faulkner presents events out of their actual chronological order?
2. Despite the story's confusing sequence, many events are foreshadowed. Give some examples of this technique. How does the foreshadowing enrich the story?
3. Where does the exposition end and the movement toward the story's climax begin? Where does the resolution stage begin?
4. Emily is clearly the story's protagonist. In the sense that he opposes her wishes, Homer is the antagonist. What other characters—or what larger forces—are set in opposition to Emily?
5. Explain how each of these phrases moves the story's plot along: "So she vanquished them, horse and foot . . ." (15); "After a week or two the smell went away" (24); "And that was the last we saw of Homer Barron" (47); "And so she died" (52); "The man himself lay in the bed" (58).
6. The narrator of the story is an observer, not a participant. Who might this narrator be? How do you suppose the narrator might know so much about Emily? Why do you think the narrator uses *we* instead of *I*?
7. It has been suggested that Miss Emily Grierson is a kind of symbol of the Old South, the last defender of its outdated ideas of chivalry, formal manners, and tradition. Do you think this interpretation is justified? Explain.

8. Do you think the story might be a comment on the status of women in the Old South? Would you characterize Miss Emily as a victim of the values her town tries to preserve?
9. **JOURNAL ENTRY:** When asked at a seminar at the University of Virginia about the meaning of the title "A Rose for Emily," Faulkner replied, "Oh, it's simply the poor woman had no life at all. Her father had kept her more or less locked up and then she had a lover who was about to quit her, she had to murder him. It was just 'A Rose for Emily'—that's all." How do you interpret Faulkner's response? Can you offer other possible interpretations of the title's significance?

Lorrie Moore (1957–) gives this advice in her story "How to Become a Writer": "First, try to become something, anything, else. A movie star/astronaut. A movie star/missionary. A movie star/kindergarten teacher. President of the World. Fail miserably." Born in Glens Falls, New York, Moore was educated at St. Lawrence University and at Cornell University. Her first book was *Self-Help* (1985), a collection of short stories—including "How to Talk to Your Mother (Notes)," which rated an enthusiastic front-page review in the *New York Times Book Review.* More recent works include *Anagrams* (1986), *The Forgotten Helper* (1987), and *Like Life* (1990). Moore divides her time between New York City and her teaching job at the University of Wisconsin, Madison.

Of the origins of her writing career, Moore is typically humorous. In a 1985 interview printed in the magazine *Vanity Fair* she explains, "I signed up for a course called 'The Romance and Reality of Words' in high school and got put in the creative writing class by mistake." Her voice is what *New York Times* reviewer Michiko Kakutani describes as the "wry, crackly" and vulnerable voice of the women in her stories: women who fend off anxiety with irreverent, self-bolstering humor. The stories of *Self-Help* are, according to Moore's comments in *Contemporary Authors,* "second person, mock-imperative narratives . . . what happens when one appropriates the 'how-to' form for a fiction, for an irony, for a 'how-not-to.'"

Lorrie Moore

HOW TO TALK TO YOUR MOTHER (NOTES)

(1985)

1982. Without her, for years now, murmur at the defrosting refrigerator, "What?" "Huh?" "Shush now," as it creaks, aches, groans, until the final ice block drops from the ceiling of the freezer like something vanquished.

Dream, and in your dreams babies with the personalities of dachshunds, fat as Macy balloons, float by the treetops.

The first permanent polyurethane heart is surgically implanted.[1]

Someone upstairs is playing "You'll Never Walk Alone" on the recorder. Now it's "Oklahoma!" They must have a Rodgers and Hammerstein book.[2]

1981. On public transportation, mothers with soft, soapy, corduroyed seraphs glance at you, their faces dominoes of compassion. Their seraphs are small and quiet or else restlessly counting bus-seat colors: "Blue-blue-blue, red-red-red, lullow-lullow-lullow." The mothers see you eyeing their children. They smile sympathetically. They believe you envy them. They believe you are childless. They believe they know why. Look quickly away, out the smudge of the window.

1980. The hum, rush, clack of things in the kitchen. These are some of the sounds that organize your life. The clink of the silverware inside the drawer, piled like bones in a mass grave. Your similes grow grim, grow tired.

Reagan is elected President, though you distributed donuts and brochures for Carter.

Date an Italian. He rubs your stomach and says, "These are marks of stretch, no? Marks of stretch?" and in your dizzy mind you think: Marks of Harpo, Ideas of Marx, Ides of March, Beware.[3] He plants kisses on the sloping ramp of your neck, and you fall asleep against him, your underpants peeled and rolled around one thigh like a bride's garter.

1979. Once in a while take evening trips past the old unsold house you grew up in, that haunted rural crossroads two hours from where you now live. It is like Halloween: the raked, moonlit lawn, the mammoth, tumid trees, arms and fingers raised into the starless wipe of sky like burns, cracks, map rivers. Their black shadows rock against the side of the east porch. There are dream shadows, other lives here. Turn the corner slowly but continue to stare from the car window. This house is embedded in you deep, something still here you know, you think you know, a voice at the top of those stairs, perhaps, a figure on the porch, an odd apron caught high in the twigs, in the too-warm-for-a-fall-night breeze, something not

---

[1] The Jarvik-7, created by Robert K. Jarvik, was implanted in Barney Clark by Dr. William C. DeVries on December 2, 1982.

[2] The American songwriting team of composer Richard Rodgers (1902–1979) and lyricist Oscar Hammerstein II (1895–1960) created many modern classics, including "You'll Never Walk Alone" (from *Carousel*) and "Oklahoma!" (from the musical of the same name).

[3] The narrator's "free association," prompted by "marks of stretch" (stretch marks) alludes to comedian Arthur 'Harpo' Marx (1893–1964), philosopher Karl Marx (1818–1883), and the warning the soothsayer issues ("Beware the Ides of March") in Shakespeare's *Julius Caesar.*

right, that turret window you can still see from here, from outside, but which can't be reached from within. (The ghostly brag of your childhood: "We have a mystery room. The window shows from the front, but you can't go in, there's no door. A doctor lived there years ago and gave secret operations, and now it's blocked off.") The window sits like a dead eye in the turret.

You see a ghost, something like a spinning statue by a shrub.

1978. Bury her in the cold south sideyard of that Halloweenish house. Your brother and his kids are there. Hug. The minister in a tweed sportscoat, the neighborless fields, the crossroads, are all like some stark Kansas. There is praying, then someone shoveling. People walk toward the cars and hug again. Get inside your car with your niece. Wait. Look up through the windshield. In the November sky a wedge of wrens moves south, the lines of their formation, the very sides and vertices mysteriously choreographed, shifting, flowing, crossing like a skater's legs. "They'll descend instinctively upon a tree somewhere," you say, "but not for miles yet." You marvel, watch, until, amoeba-slow, they are dark, faraway stitches in the horizon. You do not start the car. The quiet niece next to you finally speaks: "Aunt Ginnie, are we going to the restaurant with the others?" Look at her. Recognize her: nine in a pile parka. Smile and start the car.

1977. She ages, rocks in your rocker, noiseless as wind. The front strands of her white hair dangle yellow at her eyes from too many cigarettes. She smokes even now, her voice husky with phlegm. Sometimes at dinner in your tiny kitchen she will simply stare, rheumy-eyed, at you, then burst into a fit of coughing that racks her small old man's body like a storm.

Stop eating your baked potato. Ask if she is all right.

She will croak: "Do you remember, Ginnie, your father used to say that one day, with these cigarettes, I was going to have to 'face the mucus'?" At this she chuckles, chokes, gasps again.

Make her stand up.

Lean her against you.

Slap her lightly on the curved mound of her back.

Ask her for chrissakes to stop smoking.

She will smile and say: "For chrissakes? Is that any way to talk to your mother?"

At night go in and check on her. She lies there awake, her lips apart, open and drying. Bring her some juice. She murmurs, "Thank you, honey." Her mouth smells, swells like a grave.

1976. The Bicentennial. In the laundromat, you wait for the time on your coins to run out. Through the porthole of the dryer, you watch your bedeviled towels and sheets leap and fall. The radio station piped in from the ceiling plays slow, sad Motown; it encircles you with the desperate hopefulness of a boy at a dance, and it makes you cry. When you get back to your apartment, dump everything on your bed. Your mother is knitting crookedly: red, white, and blue. Kiss her hello. Say: "Sure was warm in that place." She will seem not to hear you.

1975. Attend poetry readings alone at the local library. Find you don't really listen well. Stare at your crossed thighs. Think about your mother. Sometimes you confuse her with the first man you ever loved, who ever loved you, who buried his head in the pills of your sweater and said magnificent things like "Oh god, oh god," who loved you unconditionally, terrifically, like a mother.

The poet loses his nerve for a second, a red flush through his neck and ears, but he regains his composure. When he is finished, people clap. There is wine and cheese.

Leave alone, walk home alone. The downtown streets are corridors of light holding you, holding you, past the church, past the community center. March, like Stella Dallas,[4] spine straight, through the melodrama of street lamps, phone posts, toward the green house past Borealis Avenue, toward the rear apartment with the tilt and the squash on the stove.

Your horoscope says: Be kind, be brief.

You are pregnant again. Decide what you must do.

1974. She will have bouts with a mad sort of senility. She calls you at work. "There's no food here! Help me! I'm starving!" although you just bought forty dollars' worth of groceries yesterday. "Mom, there is too food there!"

When you get home the refrigerator is mostly empty. "Mom, where did you put all the milk and cheese and stuff?" Your mother stares at you from where she is sitting in front of the TV set. She has tears leaking out of her eyes. "There's no food here, Ginnie."

There is a rustling, scratching noise in the dishwasher. You open it up, and the eyes of a small rodent glint back at you. It scrambles out, off to the baseboards behind the refrigerator. Your mother, apparently, has put all the groceries inside the dishwasher. The milk is spilled, a white pool against blue, and things like cheese and bologna and apples have been nibbled at.

1973. At a party when a woman tells you where she bought some wonderful pair of shoes, say that you believe shopping for clothes is like masturbation—everyone does it, but it isn't very interesting and therefore

---

[4] Originally introduced in Olive Higgins Prouty's novel *Stella Dallas;* also the main character in the radio show of the same name, which the announcer introduced as a "world famous drama of mother love and sacrifice." *Stella Dallas* was filmed three times, in 1926 (with Belle Bennett), 1937 (with Barbara Stanwyck), and 1990 (with Bette Midler).

should be done alone, in an embarrassed fashion, and never be the topic of party conversation. The woman will tighten her lips and eyebrows and say, "Oh, I suppose you have something more fascinating to talk about." Grow clumsy and uneasy. Say, "No," and head for the ginger ale. Tell the person next to you that your insides feel sort of sinking and vinyl like a Claes Oldenburg toilet.[5] They will say, "Oh?" and point out that the print on your dress is one of paisleys impregnating paisleys. Pour yourself more ginger ale.

1972. Nixon wins by a landslide.

Sometimes your mother calls you by her sister's name. Say, "No, Mom, it's me. Virginia." Learn to repeat things. Learn that you have a way of knowing each other which somehow slips out and beyond the ways you have of not knowing each other at all.

Make apple crisp for the first time.

1971. Go for long walks to get away from her. Walk through wooded areas; there is a life there you have forgotten. The smells and sounds seem sudden, unchanged, exact, the papery crunch of the leaves, the mouldering sachet of the mud. The trees are crooked as backs, the fence posts splintered, trusting and precarious in their solid grasp of arms, the asters spindly, dry, white, havishammed (Havishammed!)[6] by frost. Find a beautiful reddish stone and bring it home for your mother. Kiss her. Say: "This is for you." She grasps it and smiles. "You were always such a sensitive child," she says.

Say: "Yeah, I know."

1970. You are pregnant again. Try to decide what you should do.

Get your hair chopped, short as a boy's.

1969. Mankind leaps upon the moon.

Disposable diapers are first sold in supermarkets.

Have occasional affairs with absurd, silly men who tell you to grow your hair to your waist and who, when you are sad, tickle your ribs to cheer you up. Moonlight through the blinds stripes you like zebras. You laugh. You never marry.

1968. Do not resent her. Think about the situation, for instance, when you take the last trash bag from its box: you must throw out the box by putting it in that very trash bag. What was once contained, now must contain. The container, then, becomes the contained, the enveloped, the held. Find more and more that you like to muse over things like this.

---

[5] Claes Oldenburg (1929–   )—American artist noted for his oversized soft sculptures of everyday objects, made from such materials as canvas and vinyl.

[6] Miss Havisham, in Charles Dickens's *Great Expectations,* is an elderly recluse who lives surrounded by the decaying remnants of her aborted wedding, called off years earlier by her fiancé.

1967. Your mother is sick and comes to live with you. There is no place else for her to go. You feel many different emptinesses.

The first successful heart transplant is performed in South Africa.[7]

1966. You confuse lovers, mix up who had what scar, what car, what mother.

1965. Smoke marijuana. Try to figure out what has made your life go wrong. It is like trying to figure out what is stinking up the refrigerator. It could be anything. The lid off the mayonnaise, Uncle Ron's honey wine four years in the left corner. Broccoli yellowing, flowering fast. They are all metaphors. They are all problems. Your horoscope says: Speak gently to a loved one.

1964. Your mother calls long distance and asks whether you are coming home for Thanksgiving, your brother and the baby will be there. Make excuses.

"As a mother gets older," your mother says, "these sorts of holidays become increasingly important."

Say: "I'm sorry, Mom."

1963. Wake up one morning with a man you had thought you'd spend your life with, and realize, a rock in your gut, that you don't even like him. Spend a weepy afternoon in his bathroom, not coming out when he knocks. You can no longer trust your affections. People and places you think you love may be people and places you hate.

Kennedy is shot.

Someone invents a temporary artificial heart, for use during operations.

1962. Eat Chinese food for the first time, with a lawyer from California. He will show you how to hold the chopsticks. He will pat your leg. Attack his profession. Ask him whether he feels the law makes large spokes out of the short stakes of men.

1961. Grandma Moses dies.[8]

You are a zoo of insecurities. You take to putting brandy in your morning coffee and to falling in love too easily. You have an abortion.

1960. There is money from your father's will and his life insurance. You buy a car and a green velvet dress you don't need. You drive two hours to meet your mother for lunch on Saturdays. She suggests things for you to write about, things she's heard on the radio: a woman with telepathic twins, a woman with no feet.

---

[7] By Dr. Christiaan Barnard (1923–).

[8] Grandma Moses (Anna Mary Robertson Moses, 1860–1961)—American artist, famous for her "primitive" paintings depicting rural life. Completely self-taught, she did not begin painting seriously until the age of 67.

1959. At the funeral she says: "He had his problems, but he was a generous man," though you know he was tight as a scout knot, couldn't listen to anyone, the only time you remember loving him being that once when he got the punchline of one of your jokes before your mom did and looked up from his science journal and guffawed loud as a giant, the two of you, for one split moment, communing like angels in the middle of that room, in that warm, shared light of mind.

Say: "He was okay."

"You shouldn't be bitter," your mother snaps. "He financed you and your brother's college educations." She buttons her coat. "He was also the first man to isolate a particular isotope of helium, I forget the name, but he should have won the Nobel Prize." She dabs at her nose.

Say: "Yeah, Mom."

1958. At your brother's wedding, your father is taken away in an ambulance. A tiny cousin whispers loudly to her mother, "Did Uncle Will have a hard attack?" For seven straight days say things to your mother like: "I'm sure it'll be okay," and "I'll stay here, why don't you go home and get some sleep."

1957. Dance the calypso with boys from a different college. Get looped on New York State burgundy, lose your virginity, and buy one of the first portable electric typewriters.

1956. Tell your mother about all the books you are reading at college. This will please her.

1955. Do a paint-by-numbers of Elvis Presley. Tell your mother you are in love with him. She will shake her head.

1954. Shoplift a cashmere sweater.

1953. Smoke a cigarette with Hillary Swedelson. Tell each other your crushes. Become blood sisters.

1952. When your mother asks you if there are any nice boys in junior high, ask her how on earth would you ever know, having to come in at nine! every night. Her eyebrows will lift like theater curtains. "You poor, abused thing," she will say.

Say, "Don't I know it," and slam the door.

1951. Your mother tells you about menstruation. The following day you promptly menstruate, your body only waiting for permission, for a signal. You wake up in the morning and feel embarrassed.

1949. You learn how to blow gum bubbles and to add negative numbers.

70 *1947.* The Dead Sea Scrolls are discovered.[9]

You have seen too many Hollywood musicals. You have seen too many people singing in public places and you assume you can do it, too. Practice. Your teacher asks you a question. You warble back: "The answer to number two is twelve." Most of the class laughs at you, though some stare, eyes jewel-still, fascinated. At home your mother asks you to dust your dresser. Work up a vibrato you could drive a truck through. Sing: "Why do I have to do it now?" and tap your way through the dining room. Your mother requests that you calm down and go take a nap. Shout: "You don't care about me! You don't care about me at all!"

1946. Your brother plays "Shoofly Pie" all day long on the Victrola.

Ask your mother if you can go to Ellen's for supper. She will say, "Go ask your father," and you, pulling at your fingers, walk out to the living room and whimper by his chair. He is reading. Tap his arm. "Dad? Daddy? Dad?" He continues reading his science journal. Pull harder on your fingers and run back to the kitchen to tell your mother, who storms into the living room, saying, "Why don't you ever listen to your children when they try to talk to you?" You hear them arguing. Press your face into a kitchen towel, ashamed, the hum of the refrigerator motor, the drip in the sink scaring you.

1945. Your father comes home from his war work. He gives you a piggyback ride around the broad yellow thatch of your yard, the dead window in the turret, dark as a wound, watching you. He gives you wordless pushes on the swing.

75 Your brother has new friends, acts older and distant, even while you wait for the school bus together.

You spend too much time alone. You tell your mother that when you grow up you will bring your babies to Australia to see the kangaroos.

Forty thousand people are killed in Nagasaki.

1944. Dress and cuddle a tiny babydoll you have named "the Sue." Bring her everywhere. Get lost in the Wilson Creek fruit market, and call softly, "Mom, where are you?" Watch other children picking grapes, but never dare yourself. Your eyes are small, dark throats, your hand clutches the Sue.

1943. Ask your mother about babies. Have her read to you only the stories about babies. Ask her if she is going to have a baby. Ask her about the baby that died. Cry into her arm.

80 *1940.* Clutch her hair in your fist. Rub it against your cheek.

1939. As through a helix, as through an ear, it is here you are nearer the dream flashes, the other lives.

---

[9] Parchment scrolls containing Hebrew and Aramaic scriptural texts, as well as communal writings. Generally dated from 100 B.C. to A.D. 100, they were discovered in a cave near the Dead Sea, between Israel and Jordan.

There is a tent of legs, a sundering of selves, as you both gasp blindly for breath. Across the bright and cold, she knows it when you try to talk to her, though this is something you never really manage to understand.

Germany invades Poland.

The year's big song is "Three Little Fishies" and someone, somewhere, is playing it.

READING AND REACTING

1. What do you think the word *notes* in the story's title means?
2. Who is the story's protagonist? With whom (or what) is the protagonist in conflict? Explain the nature of this conflict.
3. What does the writer gain by arranging the story's events in reverse chronological order? What, if anything, does she lose?
4. What do the dates and the references to historical events contribute to the story?
5. Despite its unconventional sequence of events, does the story contain any foreshadowing? Explain.
6. Does this story include any of the conventional stages of plot (exposition, resolution, and so on)? If so, where?
7. Identify several crises (peaks of tension). Does the story have a climax? Explain.
8. What is the effect of the narrator's use of the second person, as in the title and in phrases like "The mothers see you eyeing their children"? Explain the impact of the imperative mood, as in "Date an Italian."
9. A student, encountering this story for the first time, commented, "It's hard to follow because it has no plot." Do you agree with this student's assessment? Why or why not?
10. **JOURNAL ENTRY:** Although the story's title is "How to Talk to Your Mother (Notes)," the narrator actually does *not* talk to her mother. What do you think she wants to tell her mother? What stops her?

WRITING SUGGESTIONS: PLOT

1. Write your own life story, imitating the style and structure of "How to Talk to Your Mother (Notes)." That is, use reverse chronology, use *you* instead of *I,* and divide your story into sections according to year. Be sure to include mentions of world events, song titles, and the like, as well as recurring themes in your life, to provide continuity and unify your "notes" into a story.
2. Find a newspaper story that disturbs you. Then, write a "once upon a time" story like Gordimer's in which you retell the story's events in a detached tone without adding analysis or commentary.

3. Consider the possible effect on the plot of one of this chapter's stories of the appearance of a *deus ex machina* (p. 61), an outside force or agent that suddenly appears to change the course of events. What might this outside force be in each story? How might it change the story's action? How plausible would such a dramatic turn of events be in each story?

4. Both "A Rose for Emily" and "How to Talk to Your Mother (Notes)" are formally divided into sections. Write a paper in which you discuss what these visual divisions contribute to each story.

5. Read the following article from the January 30, 1987, *Philadelphia Inquirer.* After listing some similarities and differences between the events in the article's story and those in "A Rose for Emily," write an essay in which you discuss how the presentation of events differs. Can you draw any conclusions about journalistic and fictional treatments of similar incidents?

A Woman's Wintry Death Leads to a Long-Dead Friend

by Dick Pothier and Thomas J. Gibbons Jr.

For more than two years, Frances Dawson Hamilton lived with the body of her long-time companion, draping his skeletonized remains with palm fronds and rosary beads.

Yesterday, the 70-year-old woman was found frozen to death in the home in the 4500 block of Higbee Street where she had lived all her life—the last year without heat or hot water. Her body was found by police accompanying a city social worker who came bearing an order to have her taken to a hospital.

Police investigators said the body of Bernard J. Kelly, 84, was found in an upstairs bedroom of the two-story brick home in the Wissinoming section, on the twin bed where he apparently died at least two years ago.

Two beds had been pushed together, and Hamilton apparently had been sleeping beside Kelly's remains since he died of unknown causes, police said.

Kelly's remains were clothed in long johns and socks, investigators said. The body was draped with rosary beads and palm fronds, and on the bed near his body were two boxes of Valentine's Day candy.

"It was basically a funeral—we've seen it before in such cases," said one investigator who was at the scene but declined to be identified.

Neighbors and investigators said Hamilton and Kelly had lived together in the house for at least 15 years. Several neighbors said Hamilton came from an affluent family, was educated in Europe, and lived on a trust fund until a year or so ago.

Last winter, said John Wasniewski, Hamilton's next-door neighbor, the basement of the home was flooded and the heater destroyed. "There was no heat in that house last winter or this winter," he said.

An autopsy will be performed on Hamilton today, but she apparently froze to death sometime since Monday, when a friend spoke to her on the telephone, investigators said.

Over the last two years, neighbors said, Hamilton had become increasingly reclusive and irrational. Just last week, a city social worker summoned by a friend arranged for a Philadelphia Gas Works team to visit the home and try to repair the furnace—but she refused to let them in.

The friend was James Phillips, 44, of Horsham, a salesman for Apex Electric in Souderton.

In October 1985, he said, Hamilton visited the Frankford Avenue electrical shop where he was then working, told him that she had an electrical problem in her house and had no lights, and asked whether he could help.

Phillips said he visited the house, fixed the problem and gave her some light bulbs.

"She was really paranoid," Phillips said. "She believed that all her problems were from people doing things to her. For some reason or other, she took to me."

Phillips said that he began visiting her, taking her shopping and doing some shopping for her. But, he said, he never saw the body on the second floor.

Hamilton told him there was a man up there. "I thought it was a story she was telling to protect herself," Phillips said.

He provided her with electric heaters and also contacted a caseworker with the city's Department of Human Services whom Phillips identified as Albert Zbik.

Between the two of them, he said, "we got her through last winter." Phillips said Zbik helped her obtain food stamps and Social Security assistance.

When the snowstorm hit last week, Phillips became concerned because he knew Hamilton would have trouble getting food. On Saturday, he took her a plate of hot food and bought more food from a local store.

On Monday, she telephoned him. "I didn't like the way she sounded," he said. He called Zbik and told him he felt it was time that they forced her to go to a hospital.

Phillips said Zbik went to her home yesterday, carrying a form authorizing an involuntary admission to a hospital for observation or required medical treatment.

Phillips told police that he was never allowed above the first floor and was often told by Hamilton that "Bernie is not feeling well today."

Neighbors and police investigators said Kelly was last seen alive about two years ago, and appeared to be quite ill at the time.

"As recently as last month, I asked Frances how Bernard was and whether she should get a doctor, and she said it wasn't necessary. She said 'He's sick, but I'm taking care of him—I'm feeding him with an eye-dropper,'" Wasniewski said.

"I told her in December that if he was that sick, she should call a doctor, but she'd say she was taking care of him very well." Wasniewski said.

CHAPTER 5

CHARACTER

Interaction between characters creates the conflict that drives a story's plot. A **character** is a fictional representation of a person—usually (but not necessarily) a psychologically realistic depiction.

Characterization is the way writers develop characters and reveal those characters' traits to readers. Writers may portray characters through their actions, through their reactions to situations or to other characters, through their physical appearance, through their speech and gestures and expressions, and even through their names.

Generally speaking, characters are developed in two ways. First, readers can be *told* about characters. Third-person narrators can give us information about what characters are doing and thinking, what experiences they have had, what they look like, how they are dressed, and so on. They can even provide analysis of and judgments about a character's behavior. For instance, the narrator of Chinua Achebe's "Vengeful Creditor" (p. 99) tells us, "Vero was a good girl and very sharp. . . . She had the sense of a girl twice her age and was amazingly quick to learn." Similarly, first-person narrators can tell us about themselves or about other characters. Thus Sammy in John Updike's "A&P" (p. 93) tells us that he lives with his parents and that he disapproves of the supermarket's customers. He also tells us what various characters are wearing and describes their actions, attitudes, and gestures.

Alternatively, characters may be developed more subtly, with key personality traits and explanations of motivation not summarized or described but rather *revealed* through actions, dialogue, or thoughts. For instance, Sammy's vivid fantasies and his rejection of his customers' lives suggest to readers that he is not suited for conventional supermarket society, that he is something of a nonconformist; however, Sammy himself does not actually tell us this information.

ROUND AND FLAT CHARACTERS

In his influential 1927 work *Aspects of the Novel,* English novelist E. M. Forster classifies characters as **round** (well developed, closely involved in and responsive to the action) or **flat** (barely developed or stereotypical). In an effective story the major characters will usually be complex and fully developed; if they are not, readers will not care what happens to them. In much modern fiction, readers are encouraged to become involved with the characters, even to identify with them. This empathy is possible only when we know something about the characters—their strengths and weaknesses, for example, or their likes and dislikes. We must know at least enough to understand why characters act the way they do. In some cases, of course, a story can be effective even when its central characters are not well developed. Sometimes, in fact, a story's effectiveness is enhanced by an *absence* of character development, as in Shirley Jackson's "The Lottery" (p. 276).

Readers often expect characters to behave as "real people" in their situation might behave. Real people are not perfect, and realistic characters cannot be perfect either. The flaws that are revealed as round characters are developed—greed, gullibility, naïveté, shyness, a quick temper or a lack of insight or judgment or tolerance or even intelligence—make them believable. In modern fiction, the protagonist is seldom if ever the noble "hero"; more often, he or she is at least partly a victim, someone to whom some unpleasant things happen, and someone who is sometimes ill-equipped to cope with events.

Unlike a story's major characters, its minor characters are frequently not well developed. Often they are flat, perhaps acting as foils for the protagonist. (A **foil** is a supporting character whose role in the story is to highlight a major character by presenting a contrast with him or her. For instance, in "A&P," Stokesie, another young checkout clerk, is a foil for Sammy. Because he is a little older than Sammy and shows none of Sammy's imagination, restlessness, or nonconformity, Stokesie suggests what Sammy might become if he were to continue to work at the A&P.) Some flat characters are **stock characters,** easily identifiable types who behave so consistently that readers can readily recognize them. The kindly old priest, the young bully, the ruthless business executive, and the reckless adventurer are all stock characters. Some flat characters can even be **caricatures,** characterized by a single dominant trait, such as miserliness, or even by one physical trait, such as nearsightedness.

DYNAMIC AND STATIC CHARACTERS

Characters may also be classified as either dynamic or static. **Dynamic** characters grow and change in the course of a story, developing as they react to events and to other characters. In "A&P," for instance, Sammy's decision to speak out in defense of the girls—and the events that lead him to do so—changes him. His view of the world is different at the end of the story, and as a result his position in that world will be different too. A **static** character may face the same challenges a dynamic character might encounter but will remain essentially unchanged: A static character who was selfish and arrogant will still be selfish and arrogant, regardless of the nature of the story's conflict. In the fairy tale "Cinderella," for example, the title character is as sweet and good-natured at the end of the story—despite her mistreatment by her family—as she is at the beginning. Her situation may have changed, but her character has not.

Whereas round characters tend to be dynamic, flat characters tend to be static. But even a very complex, well-developed major character may be static; sometimes, in fact, the point of a story may hinge on a character's inability to change. A familiar example is the title character in William Faulkner's "A Rose for Emily" (p. 70), who lives a wasted, empty life, at least in part because she is unwilling or unable to accept that the world around her and the people in it have changed. Similarly, Mrs. Emenike's view of the world is not changed by the events of "Vengeful Creditor." At the story's end she still believes the social order must be maintained as it is, and she remains as unconcerned and unenlightened about the lives of people such as Vero as she is when the story begins. Her blindness and inflexibility help to create the story's tension.

A story's minor characters are often static; their growth is not usually relevant to the story's development. Moreover, we usually do not learn enough about a minor character's traits, thoughts, actions, or motivation to determine whether or not the character changes significantly.

MOTIVATION

Because round characters are complex, they are not always easy to understand. They may act differently in similar situations, just as real people do. They wrestle with decisions, resist or succumb to temptation, make mistakes, ask questions, search for answers, hope and dream, rejoice and despair. What is important is not whether we approve of a character's actions but whether those actions are *plausible*—whether the actions make sense in light of what we know about the character. We need to see a character's **motivation**—the reasons behind that character's behavior—or we will not believe or accept that behavior. For instance, given Sammy's dissatisfaction with his job and his desire to impress the young woman he calls Queenie, his sudden resignation is perfectly plausible. Without having established his motivation, Updike could not have expected readers to accept Sammy's actions.

Even when readers get to know a character, they still are not able to predict how a complex, round character will behave in a given situation; only a flat character is predictable. The tension that develops as readers wait to see how a character will act or react, and thus how a story's conflict will be resolved, is what holds readers' interest and keeps them involved as a story's action unfolds.

Checklist for Writing about Character

- Who is the story's protagonist? Who is the antagonist? Who are the other major characters?
- Who are the minor characters? What role does each play in the story?

- What do the major characters look like? Is their physical appearance important?
- What are the major characters' most noticeable traits?
- What are the major characters' likes and dislikes? Their strengths and weaknesses?
- What are we told about the major characters' backgrounds and prior experiences? What can we infer?
- Are characters developed for the most part directly (through the narrator's comments and descriptions) or indirectly (through the characters' actions and dialogue)?
- Are the characters round or flat?
- Are the characters dynamic or static?
- Does the story include any stock characters? Any caricatures? Does any character serve as a foil?
- Do the characters act in a way that is consistent with how readers expect them to act?
- With which characters are readers likely to be most (and least) sympathetic?

John Updike (1932–) is a prolific writer of novels, short stories, essays, poems, plays, and children's tales. Updike's earliest ambition was to be a cartoonist for *The New Yorker.* He attended Harvard hoping to draw cartoons for *The Lampoon,* studied drawing and fine art at Oxford, and in 1955 went to work for *The New Yorker*—not as a cartoonist, but as a "Talk of the Town" reporter. Updike left *The New Yorker* after three years to write full time, but (over thirty years later) is still contributing stories, reviews, and essays to the magazine. Among his best-known novels are *Rabbit, Run* (1960), *The Centaur* (1963), *Rabbit Redux* (1971), *Rabbit Is Rich* (1981), *The Witches of Eastwick* (1985), *Rabbit at Rest* (1990), and *Memories of the Ford Administration* (1992).

In early stories such as "A&P" (1961), Updike draws on memories of his childhood and teenage years for the sort of "small" scenes and stories for which he quickly became famous. "There is a great deal to be said about almost anything," Updike comments in an interview in *Contemporary Authors.* "All people can be equally interesting. . . . Now either nobody is a hero or everybody is. I vote for everybody. My subject is the American Protestant small-town middle class. I like middles. It is in middles that extremes clash. . . ."

"What John Updike does for a living," writes John Romano in the *New York Times Book Review,* "is remind us of the human costliness of an everyday situation." In "A&P" there is cost, and a small triumph—and a young man's growing awareness of the "hard" world ahead.

John Updike

A&P
(1961)

In walks these three girls in nothing but bathing suits. I'm in the third check-out slot, with my back to the door, so I don't see them until they're over by the bread. The one that caught my eye first was the one in the plaid green two-piece. She was a chunky kid, with a good tan and a sweet broad soft-looking can with those two crescents of white just under it, where the sun never seems to hit, at the top of the backs of her legs. I stood there with my hand on a box of HiHo crackers trying to remember if I rang it up or not. I ring it up again and the customer starts giving me hell. She's one of these cash-register-watchers, a witch about fifty with rouge on her cheekbones and no eyebrows, and I know it made her day to trip me up. She'd been watching cash registers for fifty years and probably never seen a mistake before.

By the time I got her feathers smoothed and her goodies into a bag—she gives me a little snort in passing, if she'd been born at the right time they would have burned her over in Salem—by the time I get her on her way the girls had circled around the bread and were coming back, without a push-cart, back my way along the counters, in the aisle between the check-outs and the Special bins. They didn't even have shoes on. There was this chunky one, with the two-piece—it was bright green and the seams on the bra were still sharp and her belly was still pretty pale so I guessed she just got it (the suit)—there was this one, with one of those chubby berry-faces, the lips all bunched together under her nose, this one, and a tall one, with black hair that hadn't quite frizzed right, and one of these sunburns right across under the eyes, and a chin that was too long—you know, the kind of girl other girls think is very "striking" and "attractive" but never quite makes it, as they very well know, which is why they like her so much—and then the third one, that wasn't quite so tall. She was the queen. She kind of led them, the other two peeking around and making their shoulders round. She didn't look around, not this queen, she just walked straight on slowly, on these long white prima-donna legs. She came down a little hard on her heels, as if she didn't walk in her bare feet that much, putting down her heels and then letting the weight move along to her toes as if she was testing the floor with every step, putting a little deliberate extra action into it. You never know for sure how girls' minds work (do you really think it's a mind in there or just a little buzz like a bee in a glass jar?) but you got the idea she had talked the other two into coming in here with her, and now she was showing them how to do it, walk slow and hold yourself straight.

She had on a kind of dirty-pink—beige maybe, I don't know—bathing suit with a little nubble all over it and, what got me, the straps were down. They were off her shoulders looped loose around the cool tops of her arms, and I guess as a result the suit had slipped a little on her, so all around the top of the cloth there was this shining rim. If it hadn't been there you wouldn't have known there could have been anything whiter than those shoulders. With the straps pushed off, there was nothing between the top of the suit and the top of her head except just *her,* this clean bare plane of the top of her chest down from the shoulder bones like a dented sheet of metal tilted in the light. I mean, it was more than pretty.

She had sort of oaky hair that the sun and salt had bleached, done up in a bun that was unravelling, and a kind of prim face. Walking into the A&P with your straps down, I suppose it's the only kind of face you *can* have. She held her head so high her neck, coming up out of those white shoulders, looked kind of stretched, but I didn't mind. The longer her neck was, the more of her there was.

5 She must have felt in the corner of her eye me and over my shoulder Stokesie in the second slot watching, but she didn't tip. Not this queen. She kept her eyes moving across the racks, and stopped, and turned so slow it made my stomach rub the inside of my apron, and buzzed to the other two, who kind of huddled against her for relief, and they all three of them went up the cat-and-dog-food-breakfast-cereal-macaroni-rice-raisins-seasonings-spreads-spaghetti-soft-drinks-crackers-and-cookies aisle. From the third slot I look straight up this aisle to the meat counter, and I watched them all the way. The fat one with the tan sort of fumbled with the cookies, but on second thought she put the packages back. The sheep pushing their carts down the aisle—the girls were walking against the usual traffic (not that we have one-way signs or anything)—were pretty hilarious. You could see them, when Queenie's white shoulders dawned on them, kind of jerk, or hop, or hiccup, but their eyes snapped back to their own baskets and on they pushed. I bet you could set off dynamite in an A&P and the people would by and large keep reaching and checking oatmeal off their lists and muttering "Let me see, there was a third thing, began with A, asparagus, no, ah, yes, applesauce!" or whatever it is they do mutter. But there was no doubt, this jiggled them. A few houseslaves in pin curlers even looked around after pushing their carts past to make sure what they had seen was correct.

You know, it's one thing to have a girl in a bathing suit down on the beach, where what with the glare nobody can look at each other much anyway, and another thing in the cool of the A&P, under the fluorescent lights, against all those stacked packages, with her feet paddling along naked over our checkerboard green-and-cream rubber-tile floor.

"Oh Daddy," Stokesie said beside me. "I feel so faint."

"Darling," I said. "Hold me tight." Stokesie's married, with two babies chalked up on his fuselage already, but as far as I can tell that's the only difference. He's twenty-two, and I was nineteen this April.

"Is it done?" he asks, the responsible married man finding his voice. I forgot to say he thinks he's going to be manager some sunny day, maybe in 1990 when it's called the Great Alexandrov and Petrooshki Tea Company or something.

10 What he meant was, our town is five miles from a beach, with a big summer colony out on the Point, but we're right in the middle of town, and the women generally put on a shirt or shorts or something before they get out of the car into the street. And anyway these are usually women with six children and varicose veins mapping their legs and nobody, including them, could care less. As I say, we're right in the middle of town, and if you stand at our front doors you can see two banks and the Congregational church and the newspaper store and three real-estate offices and about twenty-seven old freeloaders tearing up Central Street because the sewer broke again. It's not as if we're on the Cape; we're north of Boston and there's people in this town haven't seen the ocean for twenty years.

The girls had reached the meat counter and were asking McMahon something. He pointed, they pointed, and they shuffled out of sight behind a pyramid of Diet Delight peaches. All that was left for us to see was old McMahon patting his mouth and looking after them sizing up their joints. Poor kids, I began to feel sorry for them, they couldn't help it.

Now here comes the sad part of the story, at least my family says it's sad but I don't think it's sad myself. The store's pretty empty, it being Thursday afternoon, so there was nothing much to do except lean on the register and wait for the girls to show up again. The whole store was like a pinball machine and I didn't know which tunnel they'd come out of. After a while they come around out of the far aisle, around the light bulbs, records at discount of the Caribbean Six or Tony Martin Sings or some such gunk you wonder they waste the wax on, sixpacks of candy bars, and plastic toys done up in cellophane that fall apart when a kid looks at them anyway. Around they come, Queenie still leading the way, and holding a little gray jar in her hand. Slots Three through Seven are unmanned and I could see her wondering between Stokes and me, but Stokesie with his usual luck draws an old party in baggy gray pants who stumbles up with four giant cans of pineapple juice (what do these bums *do* with all that pineapple juice? I've often asked myself) so the girls come to me. Queenie puts down the jar and I take it into my fingers icy cold. Kingfish Fancy Herring Snacks in Pure Sour Cream: 49¢. Now her hands are empty, not a ring or a bracelet, bare as God made them, and I wonder where the money's coming from. Still with that prim look she lifts a folded dollar bill out of the hollow at the center of her nubbled pink top. The jar went heavy in my hand. Really, I thought that was so cute.

Then everybody's luck begins to run out. Lengel comes in from haggling with a truck full of cabbages on the lot and is about to scuttle into that door marked MANAGER behind which he hides all day when the girls touch his eye. Lengel's pretty dreary, teaches Sunday school and the rest, but he doesn't miss that much. He comes over and says, "Girls, this isn't the beach."

Queenie blushes, though maybe it's just a brush of sunburn I was noticing for the first time, now that she was so close. "My mother asked me to pick up a jar of herring snacks." Her voice kind of startled me, the way voices do when you see the people first, coming out so flat and dumb yet kind of tony, too, the way it ticked over "pick up" and "snacks." All of a sudden I slid right down her voice into her living room. Her father and the other men were standing around in ice-cream coats and bow ties and the women were in sandals picking up herring snacks on toothpicks off a big plate and they were all holding drinks the color of water with olives and sprigs of mint in them. When my parents have somebody over they get lemonade and if it's a real racy affair Schlitz in tall glasses with "They'll Do It Every Time" cartoons stencilled on.

"That's all right," Lengel said. "But this isn't the beach." His repeating this struck me as funny, as if it had just occurred to him, and he had been thinking all these years the A&P was a great big dune and he was the head lifeguard. He didn't like my smiling—as I say he doesn't miss much—but he concentrates on giving the girls that sad Sunday-school-superintendent stare.

Queenie's blush is no sunburn now, and the plump one in plaid, that I liked better from the back—a really sweet can—pipes up, "We weren't doing any shopping. We just came in for the one thing."

"That makes no difference," Lengel tells her, and I could see from the way his eyes went that he hadn't noticed she was wearing a two-piece before. "We want you decently dressed when you come in here."

"We *are* decent," Queenie says suddenly, her lower lip pushing, getting sore now that she remembers her place, a place from which the crowd that runs the A&P must look pretty crummy. Fancy Herring Snacks flashed in her very blue eyes.

"Girls, I don't want to argue with you. After this come in here with your shoulders covered. It's our policy." He turns his back. That's policy for you. Policy is what the kingpins want. What the others want is juvenile delinquency.

All this while, the customers had been showing up with their carts but, you know, sheep, seeing a scene, they had all bunched up on Stokesie, who shook open a paper bag as gently as peeling a peach, not wanting to miss a word. I could feel in the silence everybody getting nervous, most of all Lengel, who asks me, "Sammy, have you rung up this purchase?"

I thought and said "No" but it wasn't about that I was thinking. I go through the punches, 4, 9, GROC, TOT—it's more complicated than you think, and after you do it often enough, it begins to make a little song, that you hear words to, in my case "Hello (*bing*) there, you (*gung*) hap-py *pee*-pul (*splat*)!"—the *splat* being the drawer flying out. I uncrease the bill, tenderly as you may imagine, it just having come from between the two smoothest scoops of vanilla I had ever known were there, and pass a half and a penny into her narrow pink palm, and nestle the herrings in a bag and twist its neck and hand it over, all the time thinking.

The girls, and who'd blame them, are in a hurry to get out, so I say "I quit" to Lengel quick enough for them to hear, hoping they'll stop and watch me, their unsuspected hero. They keep right on going, into the electric eye; the door flies open and they flicker across the lot to their car, Queenie and Plaid and Big Tall Goony-Goony (not that as raw material she was so bad), leaving me with Lengel and a kink in his eyebrow.

"Did you say something, Sammy?"

"I said I quit."

"I thought you did."

"You didn't have to embarrass them."

"It was they who were embarrassing us."

I started to say something that came out "Fiddle-de-doo." It's a saying of my grandmother's, and I know she would have been pleased.

"I don't think you know what you're saying," Lengel said.

"I know you don't," I said. "But I do." I pull the bow at the back of my apron and start shrugging it off my shoulders. A couple customers that had been heading for my slot begin to knock against each other, like scared pigs in a chute.

Lengel sighs and begins to look very patient and old and gray. He's been a friend of my parents for years. "Sammy, you don't want to do this to your Mom and Dad," he tells me. It's true, I don't. But it seems to me that once you begin a gesture it's fatal not to go through with it. I fold the apron, "Sammy" stitched in red on the pocket, and put it on the counter, and drop the bow tie on top of it. The bow tie is theirs, if you've ever wondered. "You'll feel this for the rest of your life," Lengel says, and I know that's true, too, but remembering how he made that pretty girl blush makes me so scrunchy inside I punch the No Sale tab and the machine whirs "pee-pul" and the drawer splats out. One advantage to this scene taking place in summer, I can follow this up with a clean exit, there's no fumbling around getting your coat and galoshes, I just saunter into the electric eye in my white shirt that my mother ironed the night before, and the door heaves itself open, and outside the sunshine is skating around the asphalt.

I look around for my girls, but they're gone, of course. There wasn't anybody but some young married screaming with her children about some candy they didn't get by the door of a powder-blue Falcon station wagon. Looking back in the big windows, over the bags of peat moss and aluminum lawn furniture stacked on the pavement, I could see Lengel in my place in the slot, checking the sheep through. His face was dark gray and his back stiff, as if he'd just had an injection of iron, and my stomach kind of fell as I felt how hard the world was going to be to me hereafter.

READING AND REACTING

1. Summarize the information Sammy gives readers about his tastes and background. Why is this exposition vital to the story's development?

2. List some of the most obvious physical characteristics of the A&P's customers. How do these characteristics make them foils for Queenie and her friends?
3. What is it about Queenie and her friends that appeals to Sammy?
4. Is Queenie a stock character? Explain.
5. What rules and conventions are customers expected to follow in a supermarket? How does the behavior of Queenie and her friends violate these conventions?
6. What indications are there that Sammy believes Queenie and her friends come from a higher socioeconomic level than he does? Do you think this perception is accurate? Does it affect Sammy's actions? Explain.
7. How accurate are Sammy's judgments about the other characters? How might the characters be portrayed if the story were told by Lengel?
8. In what sense, if any, does the supermarket itself achieve the status of a character in the story? Would the story have the same impact if it were set in a car wash? In a fast-food restaurant?
9. Given what you learn about Sammy during the course of the story, what do you see as his *primary* motivation for quitting his job? What other factors motivate him?
10. **JOURNAL ENTRY:** Where do you think Sammy will find himself in ten years? Why?

Chinua Achebe (1930–) was born in eastern Nigeria, the son of a mission school teacher. He received his degree from University College, Ibadan, in 1953 and soon after joined the Nigerian Broadcasting Service, first as a producer of radio "talks" and later as the director in charge of all Voice of Nigeria broadcasts. Achebe won critical acclaim for his first novel, *Things Fall Apart* (1958), a story of the effect of white civilization on African tribal unity. More novels followed—*No Longer at Ease* (1962), *Arrow of God* (1964), *A Man of the People* (1966), and *Anthills of the Savannah* (1987)—as did a collection of short stories, *Girls at War* (1972), from which "Vengeful Creditor" is drawn. Today, Achebe divides his time between Nigeria and the United States, where he teaches at several universities, including Stanford and the University of Massachusetts, Amherst.

Beyond his reputation as a writer, Achebe has deeply influenced both the direction and the development of African literature. He was for many years the editor of the notable African Writers Series, and, as such, encouraged the careers of many other Nigerian writers—most of whom worked all day in offices and wrote fiction at night. Achebe's stories, though restrained, are full of humor, understated irony, and telling insight into the realities of contemporary African life. As in "Vengeful Creditor," his fiction puts a human face on abstract social issues, forcing the reader to confront not just "ideas," but also their effect on the "real" people of his stories.

Chinua Achebe

VENGEFUL CREDITOR

(1972)

"Madame, this way," sang the alert, high-wigged salesgirl minding one of a row of cash machines in the supermarket. Mrs. Emenike veered her fullstacked trolley ever so lightly to the girl.

"Madame, you were coming to me," complained the cheated girl at the next machine.

"Ah, sorry my dear. Next time."

"Good afternoon, Madame," sang the sweet-voiced girl already unloading Madame's purchases on to her counter.

5 "Cash or account, Madame?"

"Cash."

She punched the prices as fast as lightning and announced the verdict. Nine pounds fifteen and six. Mrs. Emenike opened her handbag, brought out from it a wallet, unzipped it and held out two clean and crisp five-pound notes. The girl punched again and the machine released a tray of cash. She put Madame's money away and gave her her change and a foot-long receipt. Mrs. Emenike glanced at the bottom of the long strip of paper where the polite machine had registered her total spending with the words THANK YOU COME AGAIN, and nodded.

It was at this point that the first hitch occurred. There seemed to be nobody around to load Madame's purchases into a carton and take them to her car outside.

"Where are these boys?" said the girl almost in distress. "Sorry, Madame. Many of our carriers have gone away because of this free primary . . . John!" she called out, as she caught sight of one of the remaining few, "Come and pack Madame's things!"

10 John was a limping forty-year-old boy sweating profusely even in the air-conditioned comfort of the supermarket. As he put the things into an empty carton he grumbled aloud.

"I don talk say make una tell Manager make e go fin' more people for dis monkey work."

"You never hear say everybody don go to free primary?" asked the wigged girl, jovially.

"All right-o. But I no go kill myself for sake of free primary."

Out in the car-park he stowed the carton away in the boot of Mrs. Emenike's grey Mercedes and then straightened up to wait while she opened her handbag and then her wallet and stirred a lot of coins there with one finger until she found a threepenny piece, pulled it out between two fingers and dropped it into the carrier's palm. He hesitated for a while and then limped away without saying a word.

Mrs. Emenike never cared for these old men running little boys' errands. No matter what you gave them they never seemed satisfied. Look at this grumbling cripple. How much did he expect to be given for carrying a tiny carton a few yards? That was what free primary education had brought. It had brought even worse to the homes. Mrs. Emenike had lost three servants including her baby-nurse since the beginning of the school year. The baby-nurse problem was of course the worst. What was a working woman with a seven-month-old baby supposed to do?

However the problem did not last. After only a term of free education the government withdrew the scheme for fear of going bankrupt. It would seem that on the advice of its experts the Education Ministry had planned initially for eight hundred thousand children. In the event one million and a half turned up on the first day of school. Where did all the rest come from? Had the experts misled the government? The chief statistician, interviewed on the radio, said it was nonsense to talk about a miscalculation. The trouble was simply that children from neighbouring states had been brought in in thousands and registered dishonestly by unscrupulous people, a clear case of sabotage.

Whatever the reason the government cancelled the scheme. The *New Age* wrote an editorial praising the Prime Minister for his statesmanship and courage but pointing out that the whole dismal affair could have been avoided if the government had listened in the first place to the warning of many knowledgeable and responsible citizens. Which was true enough, for these citizens had written on the pages of the *New Age* to express their doubt and reservation about free education. The newspaper, on throwing open its pages to a thorough airing of views on the matter, had pointed out that it did so in the national cause and, mounting an old hobby-horse, challenged those of its critics who could see no merit whatever in a newspaper owned by foreign capital to come forward and demonstrate an equal or a higher order of national commitment and patriotism, a challenge that none of those critics took up. The offer of space by the *New Age* was taken up eagerly and in the course of ten days at the rate of two or even three articles a day a large number of responsible citizens—lawyers, doctors, merchants, engineers, salesmen, insurance brokers, university lecturers, etc.—had written in criticism of the scheme. No one was against education for the kids, they said, but free education was premature. Someone said that not even the United States of America in all its wealth and power had introduced it yet, how much less . . .

Mr. Emenike read the various contributions with boyish excitement. "I wish civil servants were free to write to the papers," he told his wife at least on three occasions during those ten days.

"This is not bad, but he should have mentioned that this country has made tremendous strides in education since independence because parents know the value of education and will make any sacrifice to find school fees for their children. We are not a nation of Oliver Twists."

His wife was not really interested in all the argument at that stage, because somehow it all seemed to hang in the air. She had some vague, personal doubts about free education, that was all.

"Have you looked at the paper? Mike has written on this thing," said her husband on another occasion.

"Who is Mike?"

"Mike Ogudu."

"Oh, what does he say?"

"I haven't read it yet . . . Oh yes, you can trust Mike to call a spade a spade. See how he begins: 'Free primary education is tantamount to naked Communism'? That's not quite true but that's Mike all over. He thinks someone might come up to nationalize his shipping line. He is so scared of Communism."

"But who wants Communism here?"

"Nobody. That's what I told him the other evening at the Club. But he is so scared. You know one thing? Too much money is bad-o."

The discussion in the Emenike family remained at this intellectual level until one day their "Small Boy," a very bright lad of twelve helping out the cook and understudying the steward, announced he must go home to see his sick father.

"How did you know your Father was sick?" asked Madame.

"My brodder come tell me."

"When did your brother come?"

"Yesterday for evening-time."

"Why didn't you bring him to see me?"

"I no no say Madame go wan see am."

"Why you no talk since yesterday?" asked Mr. Emenike looking up from his newspaper.

"At first I tink say I no go go home. But today one mind tell me say make you go see-am-o; perhaps e de sick too much. So derefore . . ."

"All right. You can go but make sure you are back by tomorrow afternoon otherwise . . ."

"I must return back by morning-time sef."

He didn't come back. Mrs. Emenike was particularly angry because of the lies. She didn't like being outwitted by servants. Look at that little rat imagining himself clever. She should have suspected something from the way he had been carrying on of late. Now he had gone with a full month's pay which he should lose in lieu of notice. It went to show that kindness to these people did not pay in the least.

A week later the gardener gave notice. He didn't try to hide anything. His elder brother had sent him a message to return to their village and register for free education. Mr. Emenike tried to laugh him out of this ridiculous piece of village ignorance.

"Free primary education is for children. Nobody is going to admit an old man like you. How old are you?"

"I am fifteen years of old, sir."

"You are three," sneered Mrs. Emenike. "Come and suck breast."

"You are not fifteen," said Mr. Emenike. "You are at least twenty and no headmaster will admit you into a primary school. If you want to go and try, by all means do. But don't come back here when you've gone and failed."

"I no go fail, oga," said the gardener. "One man for our village wey old pass my fader sef done register everyting finish. He just go for Magistrate Court and pay dem five shilling and dey swear-am for Court juju wey no de kill porson; e no fit kill rat sef."

"Well it's entirely up to you. Your work here has been good but . . ."

"Mark, what is all that long talk for? He wants to go, let him go."

"Madame, no be say I wan go like dat. But my senior brodder . . ."

"We have heard. You can go now."

"But I no de go today. I wan give one week notice. And I fit find anoder gardener for Madame."

"Don't worry about notice or gardener. Just go away."

"I fit get my pay now or I go come back for afternoontime?"

"What pay?"

"Madame, for dis ten days I don work for dis mont."

"Don't annoy me any further. Just go away."

But real annoyance was yet to come for Mrs. Emenike. Abigail, the baby-nurse, came up to her two mornings later as she was getting ready for work and dumped the baby in her lap and took off. Abigail of all people! After all she had done for her. Abigail who came to her full of craw-craw,[1] who used rags for sanitary towels, who was so ignorant she gave the baby a full bowl of water to stop it crying and dropped some through its nose. Now Abigail was a lady; she could sew and bake, wear a bra and clean pants, put on powder and perfumes and stretch her hair; and she was ready to go.

From that day Mrs. Emenike hated the words "free primary" which had suddenly become part of every-day language, especially in the villages where they called it "free primadu." She was particularly angry when people made jokes about it and had a strong urge to hit them on the head for a lack of feeling and good taste. And she hated the Americans and the embassies (but particularly the Americans) who threw their money around and enticed the few remaining servants away from Africans. This began when she learnt later that her gardener had not gone to school at all but to a Ford Foundation man who had offered him seven pounds, and bought him a bicycle and a Singer sewing-machine for his wife.

"Why do they do it?" she asked. She didn't really want or need an answer but her husband gave one all the same.

---

[1] Itching skin disease.

"Because," said he, "back home in America they couldn't possibly afford a servant. So when they come out here and find them so cheap they go crazy. That's why."

Three months later free primary ended and school fees were brought back. The government was persuaded by then that its "piece of hare-brained socialism" as the *New Age* called it was unworkable in African conditions. This was a jibe at the Minister of Education who was notorious for his leftist sympathies and was perpetually at war with the formidable Minister of Finance.

"We cannot go through with this scheme unless we are prepared to impose new taxes," said the Finance Minister at a Cabinet meeting.

"Well then, let's impose the taxes," said the Minister of Education, which provoked derisive laughter from all his colleagues and even from Permanent Secretaries like Mr. Emenike who were in attendance and who in strict protocol should not participate in debate or laughter.

"We can't," said the Finance Minister indulgently with laughter still in his mouth. "I know my right honourable friend here doesn't worry whether or not this government lasts its full term, but some of us others do. At least I want to be here long enough to retire my election debts . . ."

This was greeted with hilarious laughter and cries of "Hear! Hear!" In debating skill Education was no match for Finance. In fact Finance had no equal in the entire Cabinet, the Prime Minister included.

"Let us make no mistake about it," he continued with a face and tone now serious, "if anyone is so foolish as to impose new taxes now on our long-suffering masses . . ."

"I thought we didn't have masses in Africa," interrupted the Minister of Education starting a meagre laughter that was taken up in good sport by one or two others.

* * *

"I am sorry to trespass in my right honourable friend's territory; communist slogans are so infectious. But as I was saying we should not talk lightly about new taxes unless we are prepared to bring the Army out to quell tax riots. One simple fact of life which we have come to learn rather painfully and reluctantly—and I'm not so sure even now that we have all learnt it—is that people do riot against taxes but not against school fees. The reason is simple. Everybody, even a motor-park tout, knows what school fees are for. He can see his child going to school in the morning and coming back in the afternoon. But you go and tell him about general taxation and he immediately thinks that government is stealing his money from him. One other point, if a man doesn't want to pay school fees he doesn't have to, after all this is a democratic society. The worst that can happen is that his child stays at home which he probably doesn't mind at all. But taxes are different; everybody must pay whether they want to or not. The difference is pretty sharp. That's why mobs riot." A few people said "Hear! Hear!" Others just let out exhalations of relief or agreement. Mr. Emenike who had an unrestrainable admiration for the Finance Minister and had been nodding like a lizard through his speech shouted his "Hear! Hear!" too loud and got a scorching look from the Prime Minister.

A few desultory speeches followed and the government took its decision not to abolish free primary education but to suspend it until all the relevant factors had been thoroughly examined.

One little girl of ten, named Veronica, was broken-hearted. She had come to love school as an escape from the drabness and arduous demands of home. Her mother, a near-destitute widow who spent all hours of the day in the farm and, on market days, in the market left Vero to carry the burden of caring for the younger children. Actually only the youngest, aged one, needed much looking after. The other two, aged seven and four, being old enough to fend for themselves, picking palm-kernels and catching grasshoppers to eat, were no problem at all to Vero. But Mary was different. She cried a lot even after she had been fed her midmorning foo-foo[2] and soup saved for her (with a little addition of water to the soup) from breakfast which was itself a diluted left-over from last night's supper. Mary could not manage palm-kernels on her own account yet so Vero half-chewed them first before passing them on to her. But even after the food and the kernels and grasshoppers and the bowls of water Mary was rarely satisfied, even though her belly would be big and tight like a drum and shine like a mirror.

Their widowed mother, Martha, was a hard-luck woman. She had had an auspicious beginning long, long ago as a pioneer pupil at St. Monica's, then newly founded by white women-missionaries to train the future wives of native evangelists. Most of her schoolmates of those days had married young teachers and were now wives of pastors and one or two even of bishops. But Martha, encouraged by her teacher, Miss Robinson, had married a young carpenter trained by white artisan-missionaries at the Onitsha Industrial Mission, a trade school founded in the fervent belief that if the black man was to be redeemed he needed to learn the Bible alongside manual skills. (Miss Robinson was very keen on the Industrial Mission whose Principal she herself later married.) But in spite of the bright hopes of those early evangelical days carpentry never developed very much in the way teaching and clerical jobs were to develop. So when Martha's husband died (or as those missionary artisans who taught him long ago might have put it—when he was called to higher service in the heavenly mansions by Him who was Himself once a Carpenter on earth) he left her in complete ruins. It had been a bad-luck marriage from the start. To begin with she had had to wait twenty whole years after their marriage for her first child to be born, so that now she was virtually an old woman with little children to care for and

---

[2] Food made from mashed yams, casaba, and coco.

little strength left for her task. Not that she was bitter about that. She was simply too overjoyed that God in His mercy had lifted her curse of barrenness to feel a need to grumble. What she nearly did grumble about was the disease that struck her husband and paralysed his right arm for five years before his death. It was a trial too heavy and unfair.

Soon after Vero withdrew from school Mr. Mark Emenike, the big government man of the village who lived in the capital, called on Martha. His Mercedes 220S pulled up on the side of the main road and he walked the 500 yards or so of a narrow unmotorable path to the widow's hut. Martha was perplexed at the visit of such a great man and as she bustled about for colanut she kept wondering. Soon the great man himself in the hurried style of modern people cleared up the mystery.

"We have been looking for a girl to take care of our new baby and today someone told me to inquire about your girl . . ."

At first Martha was reluctant, but when the great man offered her £5 for the girl's services in the first year—plus feeding and clothing and other things—she began to soften.

"Of course it is not money I am concerned about," she said, "but whether my daughter will be well cared for."

"You don't have to worry about that, Ma. She will be treated just like one of our own children. My wife is a Social Welfare Officer and she knows what it means to care for children. Your daughter will be happy in our home, I can tell you that. All she will be required to do is carry the little baby and give it its milk while my wife is away at the office and the older children at school."

"Vero and her sister Joy were also at school last term," said Martha without knowing why she said it.

"Yes, I know. That thing the government did is bad, very bad. But my belief is that a child who will be somebody will be somebody whether he goes to school or not. It is all written here, in the palm of the hand."

Martha gazed steadily at the floor and then spoke without raising her eyes. "When I married I said to myself: My daughters will do better than I did. I read Standard Three in those days and I said they will all go to College. Now they will not have even the little I had thirty years ago. When I think of it my heart wants to burst."

"Ma, don't let it trouble you too much. As I said before, what any one of us is going to be is all written here, no matter what the difficulties."

"Yes. I pray God that what is written for these children will be better than what He wrote for me and my husband."

"Amen! . . . And as for this girl if she is obedient and good in my house what stops my wife and me sending her to school when the baby is big enough to go about on his own? Nothing. And she is still a small girl. How old is she?"

"She is ten."

"You see? She is only a baby. There is plenty of time for her to go to school."

He knew that the part about sending her to school was only a manner of speaking. And Martha knew too. But Vero who had been listening to everything from a dark corner of the adjoining room did not. She actually worked out in her mind the time it would take the baby to go about on his own and it came out quite short. So she went happily to live in the capital in a great man's family and looked after a baby who would soon be big enough to go about on his own and then she would have a chance to go to school.

Vero was a good girl and very sharp. Mr. Emenike and his wife were very pleased with her. She had the sense of a girl twice her age and was amazingly quick to learn.

Mrs. Emenike, who had almost turned sour over her recent difficulty in getting good servants, was now her old self again. She could now laugh about the fiasco of free primadu. She told her friends that now she could go anywhere and stay as long as she liked without worrying about her little man. She was so happy with Vero's work and manners that she affectionately nicknamed her "Little Madame." The nightmare of the months following Abigail's departure was mercifully at an end. She had sought high and low then for another baby-nurse and just couldn't find one. One rather over-ripe young lady had presented herself and asked for seven pounds a month. But it wasn't just the money. It was her general air—a kind of labour-exchange attitude which knew all the rights in the labour code, including presumably the right to have abortions in your servants' quarters and even have a go at your husband. Not that Mark was that way but the girl just wasn't right. After her no other person had turned up until now.

Every morning as the older Emenike children—three girls and a boy—were leaving for school in their father's Mercedes or their mother's little noisy Fiat, Vero would bring the baby out to the steps to say bye-bye. She liked their fine dresses and shoes—she'd never worn any shoes in her life—but what she envied them most was simply the going away every morning, going away from home, from familiar things and tasks. In the first months this envy was very, very mild. It lay beneath the joy of the big going away from the village, from her mother's drab hut, from eating palm-kernels that twisted the intestines at midday, from bitter-leaf soup without fish. That going away was something enormous. But as the months passed the hunger grew for these other little daily departures in fine dresses and shoes and sandwiches and biscuits wrapped in beautiful paper-napkins in dainty little school bags. One morning, as the Fiat took the children away and little Goddy began to cry on Vero's back, a song sprang into her mind to quieten him:

Little noisy motor-car
If you're going to the school
Please carry me
Pee—pee—pee!—poh—poh—poh!

All morning she sang her little song and was pleased with it. When Mr. Emenike dropped the other children home at one o'clock and took off again Vero taught them her new song. They all liked it and for days it supplanted "Baa Baa Black Sheep" and "Simple Simon" and the other songs they brought home from school.

"The girl is a genius," said Mr. Emenike when the new song finally got to him. His wife who heard it first had nearly died from laughter. She had called Vero and said to her, "So you make fun of my car, naughty girl." Vero was happy because she saw not anger but laughter in the woman's eyes.

"She is a genius," said her husband. "And she hasn't been to school."

"And besides she knows you ought to buy me a new car."

"Never mind, dear. Another year and you can have that sports car."

"Na so."

"So you don't believe me? Just you wait and see."

More weeks and months passed by and little Goddy was beginning to say a few words but still no one spoke about Vero's going to school. She decided it was Goddy's fault, that he wasn't growing fast enough. And he was becoming rather too fond of riding on her back even though he could walk perfectly well. In fact his favourite words were "Cayi me." Vero made a song about that too and it showed her mounting impatience:

Carry you! Carry you!
Every time I carry you!
If you no wan grow again
I must leave you and go school
Because Vero e don tire!
Tire, tire e don tire!

She sang it all morning until the other children returned from school and then she stopped. She only sang this one when she was alone with Goddy.

* * *

One afternoon Mrs. Emenike returned from work and noticed a redness on Vero's lips.

"Come here," she said, thinking of her expensive lipstick. "What is that?"

It turned out, however, not to be lipstick at all, only her husband's red ink. She couldn't help a smile then.

"And look at her finger-nails! And toes too! So, Little Madame, that's what you do when we go out and leave you at home to mind the baby? You dump him somewhere and begin to paint yourself. Don't ever let me catch you with that kind of nonsense again; do you hear?" It occurred to her to strengthen her warning somehow if only to neutralize the smile she had smiled at the beginning.

"Do you know that red ink is poisonous? You want to kill yourself? Well, little lady you have to wait till you leave my house and return to your mother."

That did it, she thought in glowing self-satisfaction. She could see that Vero was suitably frightened. Throughout the rest of that afternoon she walked about like a shadow.

When Mr. Emenike came home she told him the story as he ate a late lunch. And she called Vero for him to see.

"Show him your finger-nails," she said. "And your toes, Little Madame!"

"I see," he said waving Vero away. "She is learning fast. Do you know the proverb which says that when mother cow chews giant grass her little calves watch her mouth?"

"Who is a cow? You rhinoceros!"

"It is only a proverb, my dear."

A week or so later Mrs. Emenike just home from work noticed that the dress she had put on the baby in the morning had been changed into something much too warm.

"What happened to the dress I put on him?"

"He fell down and soiled it. So I changed him," said Vero. But there was something very strange in her manner. Mrs. Emenike's first thought was that the child must have had a bad fall.

"Where did he fall?" she asked in alarm. "Where did he hit on the ground? Bring him to me! What is all this? Blood? No? What is it? My God has killed me! Go and bring me the dress. At once!"

"I washed it," said Vero beginning to cry, a thing she had never done before. Mrs. Emenike rushed out to the line and brought down the blue dress and the white vest both heavily stained red!

She seized Vero and beat her in a mad frenzy with both hands. Then she got a whip and broke it all on her until her face and arms ran with blood. Only then did Vero admit making the child drink a bottle of red ink. Mrs. Emenike collapsed into a chair and began to cry.

Mr. Emenike did not wait to have lunch. They bundled Vero into the Mercedes and drove her the forty miles to her mother in the village. He had wanted to go alone but his wife insisted on coming, and taking the baby too. He stopped on the main road as usual. But he didn't go in with the girl. He just opened the door of the car, pulled her out and his wife threw her little bundle of clothes after her. And they drove away again.

Martha returned from the farm tired and grimy. Her children rushed out to meet her and to tell her that Vero was back and was crying in their bedroom. She practically dropped her basket and went to see; but she couldn't make any sense of her story.

"You gave the baby red ink? Why? So that you can go to school? How? Come on. Let's go to their place. Perhaps they will stay in the village overnight. Or else they will have told somebody there what happened. I don't understand your story. Perhaps you stole something. Not so?"

"Please Mama don't take me back there. They will kill me."

"Come on, since you won't tell me what you did."

She seized her wrist and dragged her outside. Then in the open she saw all the congealed blood on whipmarks all over her head, face, neck and arms. She swallowed hard.

"Who did this?"

"My Madame."

"And what did you say you did? You must tell me."

"I gave the baby red ink."

"All right, then let's go."

Vero began to wail louder. Martha seized her by the wrist again and they set off. She neither changed her work clothes nor even washed her face and hands. Every woman—and sometimes the men too—they passed on the way screamed on seeing Vero's whip-marks and wanted to know who did it. Martha's reply to all was "I don't know yet. I am going to find out."

She was lucky. Mr. Emenike's big car was there, so they had not returned to the capital. She knocked at their front door and walked in. Mrs. Emenike was sitting there in the parlour giving bottled food to the baby but she ignored the visitors completely neither saying a word to them nor even looking in their direction. It was her husband who descended the stairs a little later who told the story. As soon as the meaning dawned on Martha—that the red ink was given to the baby *to drink* and that the motive was to encompass its death—she screamed, with two fingers plugging her ears, that she wanted to hear no more. At the same time she rushed outside, tore a twig off a flowering shrub and by clamping her thumb and forefinger at one end and running them firmly along its full length stripped it of its leaves in one quick movement. Armed with the whip she rushed back to the house crying "I have heard an abomination!" Vero was now screaming and running around the room.

"Don't touch her here in my house," said Mrs. Emenike, cold and stern as an oracle, noticing her visitors for the first time. "Take her away from here at once. You want to show me your shock. Well I don't want to see. Go and show your anger in your own house. Your daughter did not learn murder here in my house."

This stung Martha deep in her spirit and froze her in mid-stride. She stood rooted to the spot, her whiphand lifeless by her side. "My Daughter," she said finally addressing the younger woman, "as you see me here I am poor and wretched but I am not a murderer. If my daughter Vero is to become a murderer God knows she cannot say she learnt from me."

"Perhaps it's from me she learnt," said Mrs. Emenike showing her faultless teeth in a terrible false smile, "or maybe she snatched it from the air. That's right, she snatched it from the air. Look, woman, take your daughter and leave my house."

"Vero, let's go; come, let's go!"

"Yes, please go!"

Mr. Emenike who had been trying vainly to find an opening for the clearly needed male intervention now spoke.

"It is the work of the devil," he said. "I have always known that the craze for education in this country will one day ruin all of us. Now even children will commit murder in order to go to school."

This clumsy effort to mollify all sides at once stung Martha even more. As she jerked Vero homewards by the hand she clutched her unused whip in her other hand. At first she rained abuses on the girl, calling her an evil child that entered her mother's womb by the back of the house.

"Oh God, what have I done?" Her tears began to flow now. "If I had had a child with other women of my age, that girl that calls me murderer might have been no older than my daughter. And now she spits in my face. That's what you brought me to," she said to the crown of Vero's head, and jerked her along more violently.

"I will kill you today. Let's get home first."

Then a strange revolt, vague, undirected began to well up at first slowly inside her. "And that thing that calls himself a man talks to me about the craze for education. All his children go to school, even the one that is only two years; but that is no craze. Rich people have no craze. It is only when the children of poor widows like me want to go with the rest that it becomes a craze. What is this life? To God, what is it? And now my child thinks she must kill the baby she is hired to tend before she can get a chance. Who put such an abomination into her belly? God, you know I did not."

She threw away the whip and with her freed hand wiped her tears.

READING AND REACTING

1. Vero is one of the story's major characters, yet she is not introduced until almost halfway through the story. What does Achebe gain by establishing Mrs. Emenike's character first? What, if anything, does he lose by keeping Vero offstage for so long?
2. What is the function of the story's opening scene in the supermarket? How does it help to introduce conflicts important to the story?
3. In paragraph 20 we learn that Mrs. Emenike has "some vague, personal doubts about free education." How does her position change during the course of the story? Why?
4. What do the following statements reveal about Mrs. Emenike's character: "Mrs. Emenike never cared for these old men running little boys' errands" (15); "She didn't like being outwitted by servants" (39); "Abigail of all people! After all she had done for her" (56)?
5. What role does Vero's mother, Martha, play in the story? Why are we told so much about her background and so little about anyone else's?

6. What role does Mr. Emenike play in the story? Could the story have communicated its ideas just as effectively without this character? Explain.
7. Is it important for readers to know that Mrs. Emenike is a Social Welfare Officer or that Mr. Emenike is a "big government man"? Why or why not?
8. **JOURNAL ENTRY:** Explain Mr. Emenike's final statement ("I have always known that the craze for education in this country will one day ruin all of us"). Explain Martha's response ("All his children go to school . . . but that is no craze"). What do these contrasting statements reveal about the two characters? What do you think they reveal about the society in which they live?

Louise Erdrich (1954–) was born in Little Falls, Minnesota, and grew up in North Dakota. Erdrich, of German-American and Chippewa descent, is a member of the Turtle Mountain Band of Chippewa. Her father, a teacher with the Bureau of Indian Affairs, "used to give me a nickel for every story I wrote," she recalls in an interview in *Contemporary Authors,* "and my mother wove strips of construction paper together and stapled them into book covers. So at an early age I felt myself to be a published author earning substantial royalties." In 1972, she graduated with the first group of women admitted to Dartmouth College, and she went on to receive a master's degree in creative writing from Johns Hopkins University.

Though her first major published work was a volume of poetry (*Jacklight,* 1984), she has won widespread acclaim for her novels *Love Medicine* (1984), *The Beet Queen* (1986), and *Tracks* (1988) (which relates more of the story of Fleur Pillager). In 1991 she and her husband, Michael Dorris, coauthored a novel, *The Crown of Columbus.* Her short stories have won two national magazine awards and are found in *The Pushcart Prize VIII* and in the *O. Henry Prize Story Collection* of 1985 and 1987.

Erdrich's stories combine stark realism with legend and folktelling, magic, and, says fellow writer Peter Mathiessen, "the funkiness, humor, and great unspoken sadness of the Indian reservations. . . ." A reviewer in the *New York Times Book Review* observes, "Ms. Erdrich's novels . . . are 'about' the experience of Native Americans the way Toni Morrison's are about black people. . . . The specificity implies nothing provincial or small."

Louise Erdrich

FLEUR

(1986)

The first time she drowned in the cold and glassy waters of Lake Turcot, Fleur Pillager was only a girl. Two men saw the boat tip, saw her struggle in the waves. They rowed over to the place she went down, and jumped in. When they dragged her over the gunwales, she was cold to the touch and stiff, so they slapped her face, shook her by the heels, worked her arms back and forth, and pounded her back until she coughed up lake water. She shivered all over like a dog, then took a breath. But it wasn't long afterward that those two men disappeared. The first wandered off, and the other, Jean Hat, got himself run over by a cart.

It went to show, my grandma said. It figured to her, all right. By saving Fleur Pillager, those two men had lost themselves.

The next time she fell in the lake, Fleur Pillager was twenty years old and no one touched her. She washed onshore, her skin a dull dead gray, but when George Many Women bent to look closer, he saw her chest move. Then her eyes spun open, sharp black riprock, and she looked at him. "You'll take my place," she hissed. Everybody scattered and left her there, so no one knows how she dragged herself home. Soon after that we noticed Many Women changed, grew afraid, wouldn't leave his house, and would not be forced to go near water. For his caution, he lived until the day that his sons brought him a new tin bathtub. Then the first time he used the tub he slipped, got knocked out, and breathed water while his wife stood in the other room frying breakfast.

Men stayed clear of Fleur Pillager after the second drowning. Even though she was good-looking, nobody dared to court her because it was clear that Misshepeshu, the waterman, the monster, wanted her for himself. He's a devil, that one, love-hungry with desire and maddened for the touch of young girls, the strong and daring especially, the ones like Fleur.

5 Our mothers warn us that we'll think he's handsome, for he appears with green eyes, copper skin, a mouth tender as a child's. But if you fall into his arms, he sprouts horns, fangs, claws, fins. His feet are joined as one and his skin, brass scales, rings to the touch. You're fascinated, cannot move. He casts a shell necklace at your feet, weeps gleaming chips that harden into mica on your breasts. He holds you under. Then he takes the body of a lion or a fat brown worm. He's made of gold. He's made of beach moss. He's a thing of dry foam, a thing of death by drowning, the death a Chippewa cannot survive.

Unless you are Fleur Pillager. We all knew she couldn't swim. After the first time, we thought she'd never go back to Lake Turcot. We thought she'd keep to herself, live quiet, stop killing men off by drowning in the lake. After the first time, we thought she'd keep the good ways. But then, after the second drowning, we knew that we were dealing with something much more serious. She was haywire, out of control. She messed with evil, laughed at the old women's advice, and dressed like a man. She got herself into some half-forgotten medicine, studied ways we shouldn't talk about. Some say she kept the finger of a child in her pocket and a powder of unborn rabbits in a leather thong around her neck. She laid the heart of an owl on her tongue so she could see at night, and went out, hunting, not even in her own body. We know for sure because the next morning, in the snow or dust, we followed the tracks of her bare feet and saw where they changed, where the claws sprang out, the pad broadened and pressed into the dirt. By night we heard her chuffing cough, the bear cough. By day her silence and the wide grin she threw to bring down our guard made us frightened. Some thought that Fleur Pillager should be driven off the reservation, but not a single person who spoke like this had the nerve. And finally, when people were just about to get together and throw her out, she left on her own and didn't come back all summer. That's what this story is about.

During that summer, when she lived a few miles south in Argus, things happened. She almost destroyed that town.

When she got down to Argus in the year of 1920, it was just a small grid of six streets on either side of the railroad depot. There were two elevators, one central, the other a few miles west. Two stores competed for the trade of the three hundred citizens, and three churches quarreled with one another for their souls. There was a frame building for Lutherans, a heavy brick one for Episcopalians, and a long narrow shingled Catholic church. This last had a tall slender steeple, twice as high as any building or tree.

No doubt, across the low, flat wheat, watching from the road as she came near Argus on foot, Fleur saw that steeple rise, a shadow thin as a needle. Maybe in that raw space it drew her the way a lone tree draws lightning. Maybe, in the end, the Catholics are to blame. For if she hadn't seen that sign of pride, that slim prayer, that marker, maybe she would have kept walking.

10 But Fleur Pillager turned, and the first place she went once she came into town was to the back door of the priest's residence attached to the landmark church. She didn't go there for a handout, although she got that, but to ask for work. She got that too, or the town got her. It's hard to tell which came out worse, her or the men or the town, although the upshot of it all was that Fleur lived.

The four men who worked at the butcher's had carved up about a thousand carcasses between them, maybe half of that steers and the other half pigs, sheep, and game animals like deer, elk, and bear. That's not even mentioning the chickens, which were beyond counting. Pete Kozka owned the place, and employed Lily Veddar, Tor Grunewald, and my stepfather, Dutch James, who had brought my mother down from the reservation the year before she disappointed him by dying. Dutch took me out of school to take her place. I kept house half the time and worked the other in the butcher shop, sweeping floors, putting sawdust down, running a hambone across the street to a customer's bean pot or a package of sausage to the corner. I was a good one to have around because until they needed me, I was invisible. I blended into the stained brown walls, a skinny, big-nosed girl with staring eyes. Because I could fade into a corner or squeeze beneath a shelf, I knew everything, what the men said when no one was around, and what they did to Fleur.

Kozka's Meats served farmers for a fifty-mile area, both to slaughter, for it had a stock pen and chute, and to cure the meat by smoking it or spicing it in sausage. The storage locker was a marvel, made of many thicknesses of brick, earth insulation, and Minnesota timber, lined inside with sawdust and vast blocks of ice cut from Lake Turcot, hauled down from home each winter by horse and sledge.

A ramshackle board building, part slaughterhouse, part store, was fixed to the low, thick square of the lockers. That's where Fleur worked. Kozka hired her for her strength. She could lift a haunch or carry a pole of sausages without stumbling, and she soon learned cutting from Pete's wife, a string-thin blonde who chain-smoked and handled the razor-sharp knives with nerveless precision, slicing close to her stained fingers. Fleur and Fritzie Kozka worked afternoons, wrapping their cuts in paper, and Fleur hauled the packages to the lockers. The meat was left outside the heavy oak doors that were only opened at 5:00 each afternoon, before the men ate supper.

Sometimes Dutch, Tor, and Lily ate at the lockers, and when they did I stayed too, cleaned floors, restoked the fires in the front smokehouses, while the men sat around the squat cast-iron stove spearing slats of herring onto hardtack bread. They played long games of poker or cribbage on a board made from the planed end of a salt crate. They talked and I listened, although there wasn't much to hear since almost nothing ever happened in Argus. Tor was married, Dutch had lost my mother, and Lily read circulars. They mainly discussed about the auctions to come, equipment, or women.

15 Every so often, Pete Kozka came out front to make a whist, leaving Fritzie to smoke cigarettes and fry raised doughnuts in the back room. He sat and played a few rounds but kept his thoughts to himself. Fritzie did not tolerate him talking behind her back, and the one book he read was the New Testament. If he said something, it concerned weather or a surplus of sheep stomachs, a ham that smoked green or the markets for corn and wheat. He had a good-luck talisman, the opal-white lens of a cow's eye. Playing cards, he rubbed it between his fingers. That soft sound and the slap of cards was about the only conversation.

Fleur finally gave them a subject.

Her cheeks were wide and flat, her hands large, chapped, muscular. Fleur's shoulders were broad as beams, her hips fishlike, slippery, narrow. An old green dress clung to her waist, worn thin where she sat. Her braids were thick like the tails of animals, and swung against her when she moved, deliberately, slowly in her work, held in and half-tamed, but only half. I could tell, but the others never saw. They never looked into her sly brown eyes or noticed her teeth, strong and curved and very white. Her legs were bare, and since she padded around in beadwork moccasins they never saw that her fifth toes were missing. They never knew she'd drowned. They were blinded, they were stupid, they only saw her in the flesh.

And yet it wasn't just that she was a Chippewa, or even that she was a woman, it wasn't that she was good-looking or even that she was alone that made their brains hum. It was how she played cards.

Women didn't usually play with men, so the evening that Fleur drew a chair up to the men's table without being so much as asked, there was a shock of surprise.

20 "What's this," said Lily. He was fat, with a snake's cold pale eyes and precious skin, smooth and lily-white, which is how he got his name. Lily had a dog, a stumpy mean little bull of a thing with a belly drum-tight from eating pork rinds. The dog liked to play cards just like Lily, and straddled his barrel thighs through games of stud, rum poker, vingt-un.[1] The dog snapped at Fleur's arm that first night, but cringed back, its snarl frozen, when she took her place.

"I thought," she said, her voice soft and stroking, "you might deal me in."

There was a space between the heavy bin of spiced flour and the wall where I just fit. I hunkered down there, kept my eyes open, saw her black hair swing over the chair, her feet solid on the wood floor. I couldn't see up on the table where the cards slapped down, so after they were deep in their game I raised myself up in the shadows, and crouched on a sill of wood.

I watched Fleur's hands stack and ruffle, divide the cards, spill them to each player in a blur, rake them up and shuffle again. Tor, short and scrappy, shut one eye and squinted the other at Fleur. Dutch screwed his lips around a wet cigar.

"Gotta see a man," he mumbled, getting up to go out back to the privy. The others broke, put their cards down, and Fleur sat alone in the lamplight that glowed in a sheen across the push of her breasts. I watched her closely, then she paid me a beam of notice for the first time. She turned, looked straight at me, and grinned the white wolf grin a Pillager turns on its victims, except that she wasn't after me.

25 "Pauline there," she said, "how much money you got?"

We'd all been paid for the week that day. Eight cents was in my pocket.

"Stake me," she said, holding out her long fingers. I put the coins in her palm and then I melted back to nothing, part of the walls and tables. It was a long time before I understood that the men would not have

---

[1] Vingt-un—twenty-one, a card game.

seen me no matter what I did, how I moved. I wasn't anything like Fleur. My dress hung loose and my back was already curved, an old woman's. Work had roughened me, reading made my eyes sore, caring for my mother before she died had hardened my face. I was not much to look at, so they never saw me.

When the men came back and sat around the table, they had drawn together. They shot each other small glances, stuck their tongues in their cheeks, burst out laughing at odd moments, to rattle Fleur. But she never minded. They played their vingt-un, staying even as Fleur slowly gained. Those pennies I had given her drew nickels and attracted dimes until there was a small pile in front of her.

Then she hooked them with five-card draw, nothing wild. She dealt, discarded, drew, and then she sighed and her cards gave a little shiver. Tor's eye gleamed, and Dutch straightened in his seat.

"I'll pay to see that hand," said Lily Veddar.

Fleur showed, and she had nothing there, nothing at all.

Tor's thin smile cracked open, and he threw his hand in too.

"Well, we know one thing," he said, leaning back in his chair, "the squaw can't bluff."

With that I lowered myself into a mound of swept sawdust and slept. I woke up during the night, but none of them had moved yet, so I couldn't either. Still later, the men must have gone out again, or Fritzie come out to break the game, because I was lifted, soothed, cradled in a woman's arms and rocked so quiet that I kept my eyes shut while Fleur rolled me into a closet of grimy ledgers, oiled paper, balls of string, and thick files that fit beneath me like a mattress.

The game went on after work the next evening. I got my eight cents back five times over, and Fleur kept the rest of the dollar she'd won for a stake. This time they didn't play so late, but they played regular, and then kept going at it night after night. They played poker now, or variations, for one week straight, and each time Fleur won exactly one dollar, no more and no less, too consistent for luck.

By this time, Lily and the other men were so lit with suspense that they got Pete to join the game with them. They concentrated, the fat dog sitting tense in Lily Veddar's lap, Tor suspicious, Dutch stroking his huge square brow, Pete steady. It wasn't that Fleur won that hooked them in so, because she lost hands too. It was rather that she never had a freak hand or even anything above a straight. She only took on her low cards, which didn't sit right. By chance, Fleur should have gotten a full or flush by now. The irritating thing was she beat with pairs and never bluffed, because she couldn't, and still she ended up each night with exactly one dollar. Lily couldn't believe, first of all, that a woman could be smart enough to play cards, but even if she was, that she would then be stupid enough to cheat for a dollar a night. By day I watched him turn the problem over, his hard white face dull, small fingers probing at his knuckles, until he finally thought he had Fleur figured out as a bit-time player, caution her game. Raising the stakes would throw her.

More than anything now, he wanted Fleur to come away with something but a dollar. Two bits less or ten more, the sum didn't matter, just so he broke her streak.

Night after night she played, won her dollar, and left to stay in a place that just Fritzie and I knew about. Fleur bathed in the slaughtering tub, then slept in the unused brick smokehouse behind the lockers, a windowless place tarred on the inside with scorched fats. When I brushed against her skin I noticed that she smelled of the walls, rich and woody, slightly burnt. Since that night she put me in the closet I was no longer afraid of her, but followed her close, stayed with her, became her moving shadow that the men never noticed, the shadow that could have saved her.

August, the month that bears fruit, closed around the shop, and Pete and Fritzie left for Minnesota to escape the heat. Night by night, running, Fleur had won thirty dollars, and only Pete's presence had kept Lily at bay. But Pete was gone now, and one payday, with the heat so bad no one could move but Fleur, the men sat and played and waited while she finished work. The cards sweat, limp in their fingers, the table was slick with grease, and even the walls were warm to the touch. The air was motionless. Fleur was in the next room boiling heads.

Her green dress, drenched, wrapped her like a transparent sheet. A skin of lakeweed. Black snarls of veining clung to her arms. Her braids were loose, half-unraveled, tied behind her neck in a thick loop. She stood in steam, turning skulls through a vat with a wooden paddle. When scraps boiled to the surface, she bent with a round tin sieve and scooped them out. She'd filled two dishpans.

"Ain't that enough now?" called Lily. "We're waiting." The stump of a dog trembled in his lap, alive with rage. It never smelled me or noticed me above Fleur's smoky skin. The air was heavy in my corner, and pressed me down. Fleur sat with them.

"Now what do you say?" Lily asked the dog. It barked. That was the signal for the real game to start.

"Let's up the ante," said Lily, who had been stalking this night all month. He had a roll of money in his pocket. Fleur had five bills in her dress. The men had each saved their full pay.

"Ante a dollar then," said Fleur, and pitched hers in. She lost, but they let her scrape along, cent by cent. And then she won some. She played unevenly, as if chance was all she had. She reeled them in. The game went on. The dog was stiff now, poised on Lily's knees, a ball of vicious muscle with its yellow eyes slit in concentration. It gave advice, seemed to sniff the lay of Fleur's cards, twitched and nudged. Fleur was up, then down, saved by a scratch. Tor dealt seven cards, three down. The pot grew, round by round, until it held all the money. Nobody folded. Then it all rode on one last card and they went silent. Fleur picked hers up and blew a long breath. The heat lowered like a bell. Her card shook, but she stayed in.

Lily smiled and took the dog's head tenderly between his palms.

"Say, Fatso," he said, crooning the words, "you reckon that girl's bluffing?"

The dog whined and Lily laughed. "Me too," he said, "let's show." He swept his bills and coins into the pot and then they turned their cards over.

Lily looked once, looked again, then he squeezed the dog up like a fist of dough and slammed it on the table.

Fleur threw her arms out and drew the money over, grinning that same wolf grin that she'd used on me, the grin that had them. She jammed the bills in her dress, scooped the coins up in waxed white paper that she tied with string.

"Let's go another round," said Lily, his voice choked with burrs. But Fleur opened her mouth and yawned, then walked out back to gather slops for the one big hog that was waiting in the stock pen to be killed.

The men sat still as rocks, their hands spread on the oiled wood table. Dutch had chewed his cigar to damp shreds, Tor's eye was dull. Lily's gaze was the only one to follow Fleur. I didn't move. I felt them gathering, saw my stepfather's veins, the ones in his forehead that stood out in anger. The dog had rolled off the table and curled in a knot below the counter, where none of the men could touch it.

Lily rose and stepped out back to the closet of ledgers where Pete kept his private stock. He brought back a bottle, uncorked and tipped it between his fingers. The lump in his throat moved, then he passed it on. They drank, quickly felt the whiskey's fire, and planned with their eyes things they couldn't say out loud.

When they left, I followed. I hid out back in the clutter of broken boards and chicken crates beside the stock pen, where they waited. Fleur could not be seen at first, and then the moon broke and showed her, slipping cautiously along the rough board chute with a bucket in her hand. Her hair fell, wild and coarse, to her waist, and her dress was a floating patch in the dark. She made a pig-calling sound, rang the tin pail lightly against the wood, froze suspiciously. But too late. In the sound of the ring Lily moved, fat and nimble, stepped right behind Fleur and put out his creamy hands. At his first touch, she whirled and doused him with the bucket of sour slops. He pushed her against the big fence and the package of coins split, went clinking and jumping, winked against the wood. Fleur rolled over once and vanished in the yard.

The moon fell behind a curtain of ragged clouds, and Lily followed into the dark muck. But he tripped, pitched over the huge flank of the pig, who lay mired to the snout, heavily snoring. I sprang out of the weeds and climbed the side of the pen, stuck like glue. I saw the sow rise to her neat, knobby knees, gain her balance, and sway, curious, as Lily stumbled forward. Fleur had backed into the angle of rough wood just beyond, and when Lily tried to jostle past, the sow tipped up on her hind legs and struck, quick and hard as a snake. She plunged her head into Lily's thick side and snatched a mouthful of his shirt. She lunged again, caught him lower, so that he grunted in pained surprise. He seemed to ponder, breathing deep. Then he launched his huge body in a swimmer's dive.

55 The sow screamed as his body smacked over hers. She rolled, striking out with her knife-sharp hooves, and Lily gathered himself upon her, took her foot-long face by the ears and scraped her snout and cheeks against the trestles of the pen. He hurled the sow's tight skull against an iron post, but instead of knocking her dead, he merely woke her from her dream.

She reared, shrieked, drew him with her so that they posed standing upright. They bowed jerkily to each other, as if to begin. Then his arms swung and flailed. She sank her black fangs into his shoulder, clasping him, dancing him forward and backward through the pen. Their steps picked up pace, went wild. The two dipped as one, box-stepped, tripped each other. She ran her split foot through his hair. He grabbed her kinked tail. They went down and came up, the same shape and then the same color, until the men couldn't tell one from the other in that light and Fleur was able to launch herself over the gates, swing down, hit gravel.

The men saw, yelled, and chased her at a dead run to the smokehouse. And Lily too, once the sow gave up in disgust and freed him. That is where I should have gone to Fleur, saved her, thrown myself on Dutch. But I went stiff with fear and couldn't unlatch myself from the trestles or move at all. I closed my eyes and put my head in my arms, tried to hide, so there is nothing to describe but what I couldn't block out, Fleur's hoarse breath, so loud it filled me, her cry in the old language, and my name repeated over and over among the words.

The heat was still dense the next morning when I came back to work. Fleur was gone but the men were there, slack-faced, hung over. Lily was paler and softer than ever, as if his flesh had steamed on his bones. They smoked, took pulls off a bottle. It wasn't noon yet. I worked awhile, waiting shop and sharpening steel. But I was sick, I was smothered, I was sweating so hard that my hands slipped on the knives, and I wiped my fingers clean of the greasy touch of the customers' coins. Lily opened his mouth and roared once, not in anger. There was no meaning to the sound. His boxer dog, sprawled limp beside his foot, never lifted its head. Nor did the other men.

They didn't notice when I stepped outside, hoping for a clear breath. And then I forgot them because I knew that we were all balanced, ready to tip, to fly, to be crushed as soon as the weather broke. The sky was so low that I felt the weight of it like a yoke. Clouds hung down, witch teats, a tornado's green-brown cones, and as I watched one flicked out and became a delicate probing thumb. Even as I picked up my heels and ran back inside, the wind blew suddenly, cold, and then came rain.

60 Inside, the men had disappeared already and the whole place was trembling as if a huge hand was pinched at the rafters, shaking it. I ran straight through, screaming for Dutch or for any of them, and then I

stopped at the heavy doors of the lockers, where they had surely taken shelter. I stood there a moment. Everything went still. Then I heard a cry building in the wind, faint at first, a whistle and then a shrill scream that tore through the walls and gathered around me, spoke plain so I understood that I should move, put my arms out, and slam down the great iron bar that fit across the hasp and lock.

Outside, the wind was stronger, like a hand held against me. I struggled forward. The bushes tossed, the awnings flapped off storefronts, the rails of porches rattled. The odd cloud became a fat snout that nosed along the earth and sniffled, jabbed, picked at things, sucked them up, blew them apart, rooted around as if it was following a certain scent, then stopped behind me at the butcher shop and bored down like a drill.

I went flying, landed somewhere in a ball. When I opened my eyes and looked, stranger things were happening.

A herd of cattle flew through the air like giant birds, dropping dung, their mouths opened in stunned bellows. A candle, still lighted, blew past, and tables, napkins, garden tools, a whole school of drifting eyeglasses, jackets on hangers, hams, a checkerboard, a lampshade, and at last the sow from behind the lockers, on the run, her hooves a blur, set free, swooping, diving, screaming as everything in Argus fell apart and got turned upside down, smashed, and thoroughly wrecked.

Days passed before the town went looking for the men. They were bachelors, after all, except for Tor, whose wife had suffered a blow to the head that made her forgetful. Everyone was occupied with digging out, in high relief because even though the Catholic steeple had been torn off like a peaked cap and sent across five fields, those huddled in the cellar were unhurt. Walls had fallen, windows were demolished, but the stores were intact and so were the bankers and shop owners who had taken refuge in their safes or beneath their cash registers. It was a fair-minded disaster, no one could be said to have suffered much more than the next, at least not until Fritzie and Pete came home.

Of all the businesses in Argus, Kozka's Meats had suffered worst. The boards of the front building had been split to kindling, piled in a huge pyramid, and the shop equipment was blasted far and wide. Pete paced off the distance the iron bathtub had been flung—a hundred feet. The glass candy case went fifty, and landed without so much as a cracked pane. There were other surprises as well, for the back rooms where Fritzie and Pete lived were undisturbed. Fritzie said the dust still coated her china figures, and upon her kitchen table, in the ashtray, perched the last cigarette she'd put out in haste. She lit it up and finished it, looking through the window. From there, she could see that the old smokehouse Fleur had slept in was crushed to a reddish sand and the stockpens were completely torn apart, the rails stacked helter-skelter. Fritzie asked for Fleur. People shrugged. Then she asked about the others and, suddenly, the town understood that three men were missing.

There was a rally of help, a gathering of shovels and volunteers. We passed boards from hand to hand, stacked them, uncovered what lay beneath the pile of jagged splinters. The lockers, full of the meat that was Pete and Fritzie's investment, slowly came into sight, still intact. When enough room was made for a man to stand on the roof, there were calls, a general urge to hack through and see what lay below. But Fritzie shouted that she wouldn't allow it because the meat would spoil. And so the work continued, board by board, until at last the heavy oak doors of the freezer were revealed and people pressed to the entry. Everyone wanted to be the first, but since it was my stepfather lost, I was let go in when Pete and Fritzie wedged through into the sudden icy air.

Pete scraped a match on his boot, lit the lamp Fritzie held, and then the three of us stood still in its circle. Light glared off the skinned and hanging carcasses, the crates of wrapped sausages, the bright and cloudy blocks of lake ice, pure as winter. The cold bit into us, pleasant at first, then numbing. We must have stood there a couple of minutes before we saw the men, or more rightly, the humps of fur, the iced and shaggy hides they wore, the bearskins they had taken down and wrapped around themselves. We stepped closer and tilted the lantern beneath the flaps of fur into their faces. The dog was there, perched among them, heavy as a doorstop. The three had hunched around a barrel where the game was still laid out, and a dead lantern and an empty bottle, too. But they had thrown down their last hands and hunkered tight, clutching one another, knuckles raw from beating at the door they had also attacked with hooks. Frost stars gleamed off their eyelashes and the stubble of their beards. Their faces were set in concentration, mouths open as if to speak some careful thought, some agreement they'd come to in each other's arms.

* * *

Power travels in the bloodlines, handed out before birth. It comes down through the hands, which in the Pillagers were strong and knotted, big, spidery, and rough, with sensitive fingertips good at dealing cards. It comes through the eyes, too, belligerent, darkest brown, the eyes of those in the bear clan, impolite as they gaze directly at a person.

In my dreams, I look straight back at Fleur, at the men. I am no longer the watcher on the dark sill, the skinny girl.

The blood draws us back, as if it runs through a vein of earth. I've come home and, except for talking to my cousins, live a quiet life. Fleur lives quiet too, down on Lake Turcot with her boat. Some say she's married to the waterman, Misshepeshu, or that she's living in shame with white men or windigos, or that she's killed them all. I'm about the only one here who ever goes to visit her. Last winter, I went to help out in her cabin when she bore the child, whose green eyes and skin the color of an old penny made more talk, as no one could decide if the child was mixed blood or what, fathered in a smokehouse, or by a man with brass scales, or by the lake. The girl is bold, smiling in her sleep, as if she knows what people wonder, as if she hears the old men talk, turning the story over. It comes up different every time and has no ending, no beginning. They get the middle wrong too. They only know that they don't know anything. ✪

READING AND REACTING

1. Describe Fleur Pillager. What does she look like? Why is her physical appearance important to the story? Why are people afraid of her?
2. What are Fleur's most striking character traits? Through what different methods does Erdrich characterize her?
3. In paragraph 2 the narrator says, "By saving Fleur Pillager, those two men had lost themselves"; in paragraph 7 the narrator says, "She almost destroyed that town." How do these statements prepare readers for the story's events?
4. Describe the story's narrator. Is she in any sense a foil for Fleur? Explain.
5. Does the narrator's use of qualifiers in passages like "*Some say* she kept the finger of a child in her pocket . . ." (6); "*No doubt* . . . Fleur saw that steeple rise . . ." (9); and "*Some say* she's married to the waterman . . ." (70) weaken her credibility, or does it reveal her to be a careful storyteller? Explain.
6. Are the four men who work at the butcher's—Pete, Lily, Tor, and Dutch—round or flat characters? Explain.
7. How does the fact that Fleur is a woman help to create the story's conflict? What is the significance of the fact that she is a Chippewa Indian?
8. At the end of the story the narrator says, "In my dreams, I look straight back at Fleur, at the men. I am no longer the watcher on the dark sill, the skinny girl." Explain this statement.
9. The story is called "Fleur." Who is the protagonist—Fleur or the narrator? Explain.
10. **JOURNAL ENTRY:** Do you think the narrator's drastic action at the end of the story is justified? Why or why not?

Charles Baxter (1947–   ) was born in Minneapolis and educated at Macalester College and at the State University of New York, Buffalo. He is currently a professor of English at the University of Michigan. Baxter is the author of three much-praised collections of short stories, *Harmony of the World* (1984), *Through the Safety Net* (1985), and *A Relative Stranger:*

Stories (1990); two novels, *First Light* (1987) and *Shadow Play* (1993); and one book of poetry, *Imaginary Paintings and Other Poems* (1989).

Baxter's critics often mention the compassion he shows in writing about his fictional characters: a couple who lose their child, a hospital worker who wants to be famous, a tired businessman who really wants to paint. In many of the short stories of *Through the Safety Net* (from which "Gryphon" is taken), unexpected events jar Baxter's characters out of their routines—forcing them to consider different choices, to call on inner strengths, or to swim against the tide of "middle America's" conventions.

Charles Baxter

GRYPHON

(1985)

On Wednesday afternoon, between the geography lesson on ancient Egypt's hand-operated irrigation system and an art project that involved drawing a model city next to a mountain, our fourth-grade teacher, Mr. Hibler, developed a cough. This cough began with a series of muffled throat clearings and progressed to propulsive noises contained within Mr. Hibler's closed mouth. "Listen to him," Carol Peterson whispered to me. "He's gonna blow up." Mr. Hibler's laughter—dazed and infrequent—sounded a bit like his cough, but as we worked on our model cities we would look up, thinking he was enjoying a joke, and see Mr. Hibler's face turning red, his cheeks puffed out. This was not laughter. Twice he bent over, and his loose tie, like a plumb line, hung down straight from his neck as he exploded himself into a Kleenex. He would excuse himself, then go on coughing. "I'll bet you a dime," Carol Peterson whispered, "we get a substitute tomorrow."

Carol sat at the desk in front of mine and was a bad person—when she thought no one was looking she would blow her nose on notebook paper, then crumble it up and throw it into the wastebasket—but at times of crisis she spoke the truth. I knew I'd lose the dime.

"No deal," I said.

When Mr. Hibler stood us up in formation at the door just prior to the final bell, he was almost incapable of speech. "I'm sorry, boys and girls," he said. "I seem to be coming down with something."

5 "I hope you feel better tomorrow, Mr. Hibler," Bobby Kryzanowicz, the faultless brown-noser said, and I heard Carol Peterson's evil giggle. Then Mr. Hibler opened the door and we walked out to the buses, a clique of us starting noisily to hawk and cough as soon as we thought we were a few feet beyond Mr. Hibler's earshot.

Five Oaks being a rural community, and in Michigan, the supply of substitute teachers was limited to the town's unemployed community college graduates, a pool of about four mothers. These ladies fluttered, provided easeful class days, and nervously covered material we had mastered weeks earlier. Therefore it was a surprise when a woman we had never seen came into the class the next day, carrying a purple purse, a checkerboard lunchbox, and a few books. She put the books on one side of Mr. Hibler's desk and the lunchbox on the other, next to the Voice of Music phonograph. Three of us in the back of the room were playing with Heever, the chameleon that lived in the terrarium and on one of the plastic drapes, when she walked in.

She clapped her hands at us. "Little boys," she said, "why are you bent over together like that?" She didn't wait for us to answer. "Are you tormenting an animal? Put it back. Please sit down at your desks. I want no cabals this time of the day." We just stared at her. "Boys," she repeated, "I asked you to sit down."

I put the chameleon in his terrarium and felt my way to my desk, never taking my eyes off the woman. With white and green chalk, she had started to draw a tree on the left side of the blackboard. She didn't look usual. Furthermore, her tree was outsized, disproportionate, for some reason.

"This room needs a tree," she said, with one line drawing the suggestion of a leaf. "A large, leafy, shady, deciduous . . . oak."

10 Her fine, light hair had been done up in what I would learn years later was called a chignon, and she wore gold-rimmed glasses whose lenses seemed to have the faintest blue tint. Harold Knardahl, who sat across from me, whispered "Mars," and I nodded slowly, savoring the imminent weirdness of the day. The substitute drew another branch with an extravagant arm gesture, then turned around and said, "Good morning. I don't believe I said good morning to all you yet."

Facing us, she was no special age—an adult is an adult—but her face had two prominent lines, descending vertically from the sides of her mouth to her chin. I knew where I had seen those lines before: *Pinocchio.* They were marionette lines. "You may stare at me," she said to us, as a few more kids from the last bus came into the room, their eyes fixed on her, "for a few more seconds, until the bell rings. Then I will permit no more staring. Looking I will permit. Staring, no. It is impolite to stare, and a sign of bad breeding. You cannot make a social effort while staring."

Harold Knardahl did not glance at me, or nudge, but I heard him whisper "Mars" again, trying to get more mileage out of his single joke with the kids who had just come in.

When everyone was seated, the substitute teacher finished her tree, put down her chalk fastidiously on the phonograph, brushed her hands, and faced us. "Good morning," she said. "I am Miss Ferenczi, your teacher for the day. I am fairly new to your community, and I don't believe any of you know me. I will therefore start by telling you a story about myself."

While we settled back, she launched into her tale. She said her grandfather had been a Hungarian prince; her mother had been born in some place called Flanders, had been a pianist, and had played concerts for people Miss Ferenczi referred to as "crowned heads." She gave us a knowing look. "Grieg," she said, "the Norwegian master, wrote a concerto for piano that was," she paused, "my mother's triumph at her debut concert in London." Her eyes searched the ceiling. Our eyes followed. Nothing up there but ceiling tile. "For reasons that I shall not go into, my family's fortunes took us to Detroit, then north to dreadful Saginaw, and now here I am in Five Oaks, as your substitute teacher, for today, Thursday, October the eleventh. I believe it will be a good day: All the forecasts coincide. We shall start with your reading lesson. Take out your reading book. I believe it is called *Broad Horizons,* or something along those lines."

Jeannie Vermeesch raised her hand. Miss Ferenczi nodded at her. "Mr. Hibler always starts the day with the Pledge of Allegiance," Jeannie whined.

"Oh, does he? In that case," Miss Ferenczi said, "you must know it *very* well by now, and we certainly need not spend our time on it. No, no allegiance pledging on the premises today, by my reckoning. Not with so much sunlight coming into the room. A pledge does not suit my mood." She glanced at her watch. "Time *is* flying. Take out *Broad Horizons.*"

She disappointed us by giving us an ordinary lesson, complete with vocabulary word drills, comprehension questions, and recitation. She didn't seem to care for the material, however. She sighed every few minutes and rubbed her glasses with a frilly perfumed handkerchief that she withdrew, magician style, from her left sleeve.

After reading we moved on to arithmetic. It was my favorite time of the morning, when the lazy autumn sunlight dazzled its way through ribbons of clouds past the windows on the east side of the classroom, and crept across the linoleum floor. On the playground the first group of children, the kindergartners, were running on the quack grass just beyond the monkey bars. We were doing multiplication tables. Miss Ferenczi had made John Wazny stand up at his desk in the front row. He was supposed to go through the tables of six. From where I was sitting, I could smell the Vitalis soaked into John's plastered hair. He was doing fine until he came to six times eleven and six times twelve. "Six times eleven," he said, "is sixty-eight. Six times twelve is . . ." He put his fingers to his head, quickly and secretly sniffed his fingertips, and said, "seventy-two." Then he sat down.

"Fine," Miss Ferenczi said. "Well now. That was very good."

"Miss Ferenczi!" One of the Eddy twins was waving her hand desperately in the air. "Miss Ferenczi! Miss Ferenczi!"

"Yes?"

"John said that six times eleven is sixty-eight and you said he was right!"

"*Did* I?" She gazed at the class with a jolly look breaking across her marionette's face. "Did I say that? Well, what *is* six times eleven?"

"It's sixty-six!"

25 She nodded. "Yes. So it is. But, and I know some people will not entirely agree with me, at some times it is sixty-eight."

"When? When is it sixty-eight?"

We were all waiting.

"In higher mathematics, which you children do not yet understand, six times eleven can be considered to be sixty-eight." She laughed through her nose. "In higher mathematics numbers are . . . more fluid. The only thing a number does is contain a certain amount of something. Think of water. A cup is not the only way to measure a certain amount of water, is it?" We were staring, shaking our heads. "You could use saucepans or thimbles. In either case, the water *would be the same*. Perhaps," she started again, "it would be better for you to think that six times eleven is sixty-eight only when I am in the room."

"Why is it sixty-eight," Mark Poole asked, "when you're in the room?"

30 "Because it's more interesting that way," she said, smiling very rapidly behind her blue-tinted glasses. "Besides, I'm your substitute teacher, am I not?" We all nodded. "Well, then, think of six times eleven equals sixty-eight as a substitute fact."

"A substitute fact?"

"Yes." Then she looked at us carefully. "Do you think," she asked, "that anyone is going to be hurt by a substitute fact?"

We looked back at her.

"Will the plants on the windowsill be hurt?" We glanced at them. There were sensitive plants thriving in a green plastic tray, and several wilted ferns in small clay pots. "Your dogs and cats, or your moms and dads?" She waited. "So," she concluded, "what's the problem?"

35 "But it's wrong," Janice Weber said, "isn't it?"

"What's your name, young lady?"

"Janice Weber."

"And you think it's wrong, Janice?"

"I was just asking."

40 "Well, all right. You were just asking. I think we've spent enough time on this matter by now, don't you, class? You are free to think what you like. When your teacher, Mr. Hibler, returns, six times eleven will be sixty-six again, you can rest assured. And it will be that for the rest of your lives in Five Oaks. Too bad, eh?" She raised her eyebrows and glinted herself at us. "But for now, it wasn't. So much for that. Let us go to your assigned problems for today, as painstakingly outlined, I see, in Mr. Hibler's lesson plan. Take out a sheet of paper and write your names in the upper left-hand corner."

For the next half hour we did the rest of our arithmetic problems. We handed them in and went on to spelling, my worst subject. Spelling always came before lunch. We were taking spelling dictation and looking at the clock. "Thorough," Miss Ferenczi said. "Boundary." She walked in the aisles between the desks, holding the spelling book open and looking down at our papers. "Balcony." I clutched my pencil. Somehow, the way she said those words, they seemed foreign, Hungarian, mis-voweled and mis-consonanted. I stared down at what I had spelled. *Balconie.* I turned my pencil upside down and erased my mistake. *Balconey.* That looked better, but still incorrect. I cursed the world of spelling and tried erasing it again and saw the paper beginning to wear away. *Balkony.* Suddenly I felt a hand on my shoulder.

"I don't like that word either," Miss Ferenczi whispered, bent over, her mouth near my ear. "It's ugly. My feeling is, if you don't like a word, you don't have to use it." She straightened up, leaving behind a slight odor of Clorets.

At lunchtime we went out to get our trays of sloppy joes, peaches in heavy syrup, coconut cookies, and milk, and brought them back to the classroom, where Miss Ferenczi was sitting at the desk, eating a brown sticky thing she had unwrapped from tightly rubber-banded wax paper. "Miss Ferenczi," I said, raising my hand. "You don't have to eat with us. You can eat with the other teachers. There's a teachers' lounge," I ended up, "next to the principal's office."

"No, thank you," she said. "I prefer it here."

"We've got a room monitor," I said. "Mrs. Eddy." I pointed to where Mrs. Eddy, Joyce and Judy's mother, sat silently at the back of the room, doing her knitting.

"That's fine," Miss Ferenczi said. "But I shall continue to eat here, with you children. I prefer it," she repeated.

"How come?" Wayne Razmer asked without raising his hand.

"I talked with the other teachers before class this morning," Miss Ferenczi said, biting into her brown food. "There was a great rattling of the words for the fewness of ideas. I didn't care for their brand of hilarity. I don't like ditto machine jokes."

"Oh," Wayne said.

"What's that you're eating?" Maxine Sylvester asked, twitching her nose. "Is it food?"

"It most certainly *is* food. It's a stuffed fig. I had to drive almost down to Detroit to get it. I also bought some smoked sturgeon. And this," she said, lifting some green leaves out of her lunchbox, "is raw spinach, cleaned this morning before I came out here to the Garfield-Murry school."

"Why're you eating raw spinach?" Maxine asked.

"It's good for you," Miss Ferenczi said. "More stimulating than soda pop or smelling salts." I bit into my sloppy joe and stared blankly out the window. An almost invisible moon was faintly silvered in the daytime autumn sky. "As far as food is concerned," Miss Ferenczi was saying, "you have to shuffle the pack. Mix it up. Too many people eat . . . well, never mind."

"Miss Ferenczi," Carol Peterson said, "what are we going to do this afternoon?"

"Well," she said, looking down at Mr. Hibler's lesson plan, "I see that your teacher, Mr. Hibler, has you scheduled for a unit on the Egyptians."

Carol groaned. "Yessss," Miss Ferenczi continued, "that is what we will do: the Egyptians. A remarkable people. Almost as remarkable as the Americans. But not quite." She lowered her head, did her quick smile, and went back to eating her spinach.

After noon recess we came back into the classroom and saw that Miss Ferenczi had drawn a pyramid on the blackboard, close to her oak tree. Some of us who had been playing baseball were messing around in the back of the room, dropping the bats and the gloves into the playground box, and I think that Ray Schontzeler had just slugged me when I heard Miss Ferenczi's high-pitched voice quavering with emotion. "Boys," she said, "come to order right this minute and take your seats. I do not wish to waste a minute of class time. Take out your geography books." We trudged to our desks and, still sweating, pulled out *Distant Lands and Their People.* "Turn to page forty-two." She waited for thirty seconds, then looked over at Kelly Munger. "Young man," she said, "why are you still fossicking in your desk?"

Kelly looked as if his foot had been stepped on. "Why am I what?"

"Why are you . . . burrowing in your desk like that?"

"I'm lookin' for the book, Miss Ferenczi."

Bobby Kryzanowicz, the faultless brown-noser who sat in the first row by choice, softly said, "His name is Kelly Munger. He can't ever find his stuff. He always does that."

"I don't care what his name is, especially after lunch," Miss Ferenczi said. *"Where is your book?"*

"I just found it." Kelly was peering into his desk and with both hands pulled at the book, shoveling along in front of it several pencils and crayons, which fell into his lap and then to the floor.

"I hate a mess," Miss Ferenczi said. "I hate a mess in a desk or a mind. It's . . . unsanitary. You wouldn't want your house at home to look like your desk at school, now, would you?" She didn't wait for an answer. "I should think not. A house at home should be as neat as human hands can make it. What were we talking about? Egypt. Page forty-two. I note from Mr. Hibler's lesson plan that you have been discussing the modes of Egyptian irrigation. Interesting, in my view, but not so interesting as what we are about to cover. The pyramids and Egyptian slave labor. A plus on one side, a minus on the other." We had our books open to page forty-two, where there was a picture of a pyramid, but Miss Ferenczi wasn't looking at the book. Instead, she was staring at some object just outside the window.

"Pyramids," Miss Ferenczi said, still looking past the window. "I want you to think about the pyramids. And what was inside. The bodies of the pharaohs, of course, and their attendant treasures. Scrolls. Perhaps," Miss Ferenczi said, with something gleeful but unsmiling in her face, "these scrolls were novels for the pharaohs, helping them to pass the time in their long voyage through the centuries. But then, I am joking." I was looking at the lines on Miss Ferenczi's face. "Pyramids,"

Miss Ferenczi went on, "were the repositories of special cosmic powers. The nature of a pyramid is to guide cosmic energy forces into a concentrated point. The Egyptians knew that; we have generally forgotten it. Did you know," she asked, walking to the side of the room so that she was standing by the coat closet, "that George Washington had Egyptian blood, from his grandmother? Certain features of the Constitution of the United States are notable for their Egyptian ideas."

Without glancing down at the book, she began to talk about the movement of souls in Egyptian religion. She said that when people die, their souls return to Earth in the form of carpenter ants or walnut trees, depending on how they behaved—"well or ill"—in life. She said that the Egyptians believed that people act the way they do because of magnetism produced by tidal forces in the solar system, forces produced by the sun and by its "planetary ally," Jupiter. Jupiter, she said, was a planet, as we had been told, but had "certain properties of stars." She was speaking very fast. She said that the Egyptians were great explorers and conquerors. She said that the greatest of all the conquerors, Genghis Khan, had had forty horses and forty young women killed on the site of his grave. We listened. No one tried to stop her. "I myself have been in Egypt," she said, "and have witnessed much dust and many brutalities." She said that an old man in Egypt who worked for a circus had personally shown her an animal in a cage, a monster, half bird and half lion. She said that this monster was called a gryphon and that she had heard about them but never seen them until she traveled to the outskirts of Cairo. She said that Egyptian astronomers had discovered the planet Saturn, but had not seen its rings. She said that the Egyptians were the first to discover that dogs, when they are ill, will not drink from rivers, but wait for rain, and hold their jaws open to catch it.

"She lies."

We were on the school bus home. I was sitting next to Carl Whiteside, who had bad breath and a huge collection of marbles. We were arguing. Carl thought she was lying. I said she wasn't, probably.

"I didn't believe that stuff about the bird," Carl said, "and what she told us about the pyramids? I didn't believe that either. She didn't know what she was talking about."

"Oh yeah?" I had liked her. She was strange. I thought I could nail him. "If she was lying," I said, "what'd she say that was a lie?"

"Six times eleven isn't sixty-eight. It isn't ever. It's sixty-six, I know for a fact."

"She said so. She admitted it. What else did she lie about?"

"I don't know," he said. "Stuff."

"What stuff?"

"Well." He swung his legs back and forth. "You ever see an animal that was half lion and half bird?" He crossed his arms. "It sounded real fakey to me."

"It could happen," I said. I had to improvise, to outrage him. "I read in this newspaper my mom bought in the IGA about this scientist, this mad scientist in the Swiss Alps, and he's been putting genes and chromosomes and stuff together in test tubes, and he combined a human being and a hamster." I waited, for effect. "It's called a humster."

"You never." Carl was staring at me, his mouth open, his terrible bad breath making its way toward me. "What newspaper was it?"

"The *National Enquirer,*" I said, "that they sell next to the cash registers." When I saw his look of recognition, I knew I had bested him. "And this mad scientist," I said, "his name was, um, Dr. Frankenbush." I realized belatedly that this name was a mistake and waited for Carl to notice its resemblance to the name of the other famous mad master of permutations, but he only sat there.

"A man and a hamster?" He was staring at me, squinting, his mouth opening in distaste. "Jeez. What'd it look like?"

When the bus reached my stop, I took off down our dirt road and ran up through the back yard, kicking the tire swing for good luck. I dropped my books on the back steps so I could hug and kiss our dog, Mr. Selby. Then I hurried inside. I could smell Brussels sprouts cooking, my unfavorite vegetable. My mother was washing other vegetables in the kitchen sink, and my baby brother was hollering in his yellow playpen on the kitchen floor.

"Hi, Mom," I said, hopping around the playpen to kiss her, "Guess what?"

"I have no idea."

"We had this substitute today, Miss Ferenczi, and I'd never seen her before, and she had all these stories and ideas and stuff."

"Well. That's good." My mother looked out the window behind the sink, her eyes on the pine woods west of our house. Her face and hairstyle always reminded other people of Betty Crocker, whose picture was framed inside a gigantic spoon on the side of the Bisquick box; to me, though, my mother's face just looked white. "Listen, Tommy," she said, "go upstairs and pick your clothes off the bathroom floor, then go outside to the shed and put the shovel and ax away that your father left outside this morning."

"She said that six times eleven was sometimes sixty-eight!" I said. "And she said she once saw a monster that was half lion and half bird." I waited. "In Egypt, she said."

"Did you hear me?" my mother asked, raising her arm to wipe her forehead with the back of her hand. "You have chores to do."

"I know," I said. "I was just telling you about the substitute."

"It's very interesting," my mother said, quickly glancing down at me, "and we can talk about it later when your father gets home. But right now you have some work to do."

"Okay, Mom." I took a cookie out of the jar on the counter and was about to go outside when I had a thought. I ran into the living room, pulled out a dictionary next to the TV stand, and opened it to the G's. *Gryphon:* "variant of griffin." *Griffin:* "a fabulous beast with the head and wings of an eagle and the body of a lion." Fabulous was right. I shouted with triumph and ran outside to put my father's tools back in their place.

Miss Ferenczi was back the next day, slightly altered. She had pulled her hair down and twisted it into pigtails, with red rubber bands holding them tight one inch from the ends. She was wearing a green blouse and pink scarf, making her difficult to look at for a full class day. This time there was no pretense of doing a reading lesson or moving on to arithmetic. As soon as the bell rang, she simply began to talk.

She talked for forty minutes straight. There seemed to be less connection between her ideas, but the ideas themselves were, as the dictionary would say, fabulous. She said she had heard of a huge jewel, in what she called the Antipodes, that was so brilliant that when the light shone into it at a certain angle it would blind whoever was looking at its center. She said that the biggest diamond in the world was cursed and had killed everyone who owned it, and that by a trick of fate it was called the Hope diamond. Diamonds are magic, she said, and this is why women wear them on their fingers, as a sign of the magic of womanhood. Men have strength, Miss Ferenczi said, but no true magic. That is why men fall in love with women but women do not fall in love with men; they just love being loved. George Washington had died because of a mistake he made about a diamond. Washington was not the first *true* President, but she did not say who was. In some places in the world, she said, men and women still live in the trees and eat monkeys for breakfast. Their doctors are magicians. At the bottom of the sea are creatures thin as pancakes which have never been studied by scientists because when you take them up to the air, the fish explode.

There was not a sound in the classroom, except for Miss Ferenczi's voice, and Donna DeShano's coughing. No one even went to the bathroom.

Beethoven, she said, had not been deaf; it was a trick to make himself famous, and it worked. As she talked, Miss Ferenczi's pigtails swung back and forth. There are trees in the world, she said, that eat meat: their leaves are sticky and close up on bugs like hands. She lifted her hands and brought them together, palm to palm. Venus, which most people think is the next closest planet to the sun, is not always closer, and, besides, it is the planet of greatest mystery because of its thick cloud cover. "I know what lies underneath those clouds," Miss Ferenczi said, and waited. After the silence, she said, "Angels. Angels live under those clouds." She said that angels were not invisible to everyone and were in fact smarter than most people. They did not dress in robes as was often claimed but instead wore formal evening clothes, as if they were about to attend a concert. Often angels *do* attend concerts and sit in the aisles where, she said, most people pay no attention to them. She said the most terrible angel had the shape of the Sphinx. "There is no running away from that one," she said. She said that unquenchable fires burn just under the surface of the earth in Ohio, and that the baby Mozart fainted dead away in his cradle when he first heard the sound of a trumpet. She said that someone named Narzim al Harrardim was the greatest writer who ever lived. She said that planets control behavior, and anyone conceived during a solar eclipse would be born with webbed feet.

"I know you children like to hear these things," she said, "these secrets, and that is why I am telling you all this." We nodded. It was better than doing comprehension questions for the readings in *Broad Horizons*.

"I will tell you one more story," she said, "and then we will have to do arithmetic." She leaned over, and her voice grew soft. "There is no death," she said. "You must never be afraid. Never. That which is, cannot die. It will change into different earthly and unearthly elements, but I know this as sure as I stand here in front of you, and I swear it: you must not be afraid. I have seen this truth with these eyes. I know it because in a dream God kissed me. Here." And she pointed with her right index finger to the side of her head, below the mouth, where the vertical lines were carved into her skin.

Absent-mindedly we all did our arithmetic problems. At recess the class was out on the playground, but no one was playing. We were all standing in small groups, talking about Miss Ferenczi. We didn't know if she was crazy, or what. I looked out beyond the playground, at the rusted cars piled in a small heap behind a clump of sumac, and I wanted to see shapes there, approaching me.

On the way home, Carl sat next to me again. He didn't say much, and I didn't either. At last he turned to me. "You know what she said about the leaves that close up on bugs?"

"Huh?"

"The leaves," Carl insisted. "The meat-eating plants. I know it's true. I saw it on television. The leaves have this icky glue that the plants have got smeared all over them and the insects can't get off 'cause they're stuck. I saw it." He seemed demoralized. "She's tellin' the truth."

"Yeah."

"You think she's seen all those angels?"

I shrugged.

"I don't think she has," Carl informed me. "I think she made that part up."

"There's a tree," I suddenly said. I was looking out the window at the farms along County Road H. I knew every barn, every broken windmill, every fence, every anhydrous ammonia tank, by heart. "There's a tree that's . . . that I've seen . . ."

"Don't you try to do it," Carl said. "You'll just sound like a jerk."

I kissed my mother. She was standing in front of the stove. "How was your day?" she asked.

"Fine."

"Did you have Miss Ferenczi again?"

"Yeah."

"Well?"

"She was fine. Mom," I asked, "can I go to my room?"

"No," she said, "not until you've gone out to the vegetable garden and picked me a few tomatoes." She glanced at the sky. "I think it's going to rain. Skedaddle and do it now. Then you come back inside and watch your brother for a few minutes while I go upstairs. I need to clean up before dinner." She looked down at me. "You're looking a little pale, Tommy." She touched the back of her hand to my forehead and I felt her diamond ring against my skin. "Do you feel all right?"

"I'm fine," I said, and went out to pick the tomatoes.

Coughing mutedly, Mr. Hibler was back the next day, slipping lozenges into his mouth when his back was turned at forty-five minute intervals and asking us how much of the prepared lesson plan Miss Ferenczi had followed. Edith Atwater took the responsibility for the class of explaining to Mr. Hibler that the substitute hadn't always done exactly what he would have done, but we had worked hard even though she talked a lot. About what? he asked. All kinds of things, Edith said. I sort of forgot. To our relief, Mr. Hibler seemed not at all interested in what Miss Ferenczi had said to fill the day. He probably thought it was woman's talk; unserious and not suited for school. It was enough that he had a pile of arithmetic problems from us to correct.

For the next month, the sumac turned a distracting red in the field, and the sun traveled toward the southern sky, so that its rays reached Mr. Hibler's Halloween display on the bulletin board in the back of the room, fading the scarecrow with a pumpkin head from orange to tan. Every three days I measured how much farther the sun had moved toward the southern horizon by making small marks with my black Crayola on the north wall, ant-sized marks only I knew were there, inching west.

And then in early December, four days after the first permanent snowfall, she appeared again in our classroom. The minute she came in the door, I felt my heart begin to pound. Once again, she was different: this time, her hair hung straight down and seemed hardly to have been combed. She hadn't brought her lunchbox with her, but she was carrying what seemed to be a small box. She greeted all of us and talked about the weather. Donna DeShano had to remind her to take her overcoat off.

When the bell to start the day finally rang, Miss Ferenczi looked out at all of us and said, "Children, I have enjoyed your company in the past, and today I am going to reward you." She held up the small box. "Do you know what this is?" She waited. "Of course you don't. It is a tarot pack."

Edith Atwater raised her hand. "What's a tarot pack, Miss Ferenczi?"

"It is used to tell fortunes," she said. "And that is what I shall do this morning. I shall tell your fortunes, as I have been taught to do."

"What's fortune?" Bobby Kryzanowicz asked.

120 "The future, young man. I shall tell you what your future will be. I can't do your whole future, of course. I shall have to limit myself to the five-card system, the wands, cups, swords, pentacles, and the higher arcanes. Now who wants to be first?"

There was a long silence. Then Carol Peterson raised her hand.

"All right," Miss Ferenczi said. She divided the pack into five smaller packs and walked back to Carol's desk, in front of mine. "Pick one card from each of these packs," she said. I saw that Carol had a four of cups, a six of swords, but I couldn't see the other cards. Miss Ferenczi studied the cards on Carol's desk for a minute. "Not bad," she said. "I do not see much higher education. Probably an early marriage. Many children. There's something bleak and dreary here, but I can't tell what. Perhaps just the tasks of a housewife life. I think you'll do very well, for the most part." She smiled at Carol, a smile with a certain lack of interest. "Who wants to be next?"

Carl Whiteside raised his hand slowly.

"Yes," Miss Ferenczi said, "let's do a boy." She walked over to where Carl sat. After he picked his five cards, she gazed at them for a long time. "Travel," she said. "Much distant travel. You might go into the Army. Not too much romantic interest here. A late marriage, if at all. Squabbles. But the Sun is in your major arcana, here, yes, that's a very good card." She giggled. "Maybe a good life."

125 Next I raised my hand, and she told me my future. She did the same with Bobby Kryzanowicz. Kelly Munger, Edith Atwater, and Kim Foor. Then she came to Wayne Razmer. He picked his five cards, and I could see that the Death card was one of them.

"What's your name?" Miss Ferenczi asked.

"Wayne."

"Well, Wayne," she said, you will undergo a *great* metamorphosis, the greatest, before you become an adult. Your earthly element will leap away, into thin air, you sweet boy. This card, this nine of swords here, tells of suffering and desolation. And this ten of wands, well, that's certainly a heavy load."

"What about this one?" Wayne pointed to the Death card.

130 "That one? That one means you will die soon, my dear." She gathered up the cards. We were all looking at Wayne. "But do not fear," she said. "It's not really death, so much as change." She put the cards on Mr. Hibler's desk. "And now, let's do some arithmetic."

At lunchtime Wayne went to Mr. Faegre, the principal, and told him what Miss Ferenczi had done. During the noon recess, we saw Miss Ferenczi drive out of the parking lot in her green Rambler. I stood under the slide, listening to the other kids coasting down and landing in the little depressive bowl at the bottom. I was kicking stones and tugging at my hair right up to the moment when I saw Wayne come out to the playground. He smiled, the dead fool, and with the fingers of his right hand he was showing everyone how he had told on Miss Ferenczi.

I made my way toward Wayne, pushing myself past two girls from another class. He was watching me with his little pinhead eyes.

"You told," I shouted at him. "She was just kidding."

"She shouldn't have," he shouted back. "We were supposed to be doing arithmetic."

"She just scared you," I said. "You're a chicken. You're a chicken, Wayne. You are. Scared of a little card," I singsonged.

Wayne fell at me, his two fists hammering down on my nose. I gave him a good one in the stomach and then I tried for his head. Aiming my fist, I saw that he was crying. I slugged him.

"She was right," I yelled. "She was always right! She told the truth!" Other kids were whooping. "You were just scared, that's all!"

And then large hands pulled at us, and it was my turn to speak to Mr. Faegre.

In the afternoon Miss Ferenczi was gone, and my nose was stuffed with cotton clotted with blood, and my lip had swelled, and our class had been combined with Mrs. Mantei's sixth-grade class for a crowded afternoon science unit on insect life in ditches and swamps. I knew where Mrs. Mantei lived: she had a new house trailer just down the road from us, at the Clearwater Park. She was no mystery. Somehow she and Mr. Bodine, the other fourth-grade teacher, had managed to fit forty-five desks into the room. Kelly Munger asked if Miss Ferenczi had been arrested, and Mrs. Mantei said no, of course not. All that afternoon, until the buses came to pick us up, we learned about field crickets and two-striped grasshoppers, water bugs, cicadas, mosquitoes, flies, and moths. We learned about insects' hard outer shell, the exoskeleton, and the usual parts of the mouth, including the labrum, mandible, maxilla, and glossa. We learned about compound eyes and the four-stage metamorphosis from egg to larva to pupa to adult. We learned something, but not much, about mating. Mrs. Mantei drew, very skillfully, the internal anatomy of the grasshopper on the blackboard. We learned about the dance of the honeybee, directing other bees in the hive to pollen. We found out about which insects were pests to man, and which were not. On lined white pieces of paper we made lists of insects we might actually see, then a list of insects too small to be clearly visible, such as fleas; Mrs. Mantei said that our assignment would be to memorize these lists for the next day, when Mr. Hibler would certainly return and test us on our knowledge.

READING AND REACTING

1. In classical mythology a gryphon (also spelled *griffin*) is a monster that has the head and wings of an eagle and the body of a lion. Why is this story called "Gryphon"?
2. The story's narrator indicates that he is an adult looking back at incidents from his childhood. (In paragraph 10, for instance, he says that Miss Ferenczi's hair was arranged in "what I would learn years later was called a chignon.") How do you think this adult view colors his story? How might a child's view be different?
3. Describe Miss Ferenczi's physical appearance, including her personal belongings. Why is her appearance important to the story? How does it change as the story progresses?
4. How is Miss Ferenczi different from other teachers? From other substitute teachers? From other people in general? How is her differentness communicated to her pupils? To the story's readers?
5. What is the significance of the narrator's comment, in paragraph 11, that the lines on Miss Ferenczi's face remind him of Pinocchio?
6. What is Miss Ferenczi's attitude toward Mr. Hibler and his methods? Toward the other teachers? What do these attitudes reveal about her character?
7. Is Miss Ferenczi a round or a flat character? Explain.
8. In what sense is the narrator's mother a foil for Miss Ferenczi?
9. Why does the narrator defend Miss Ferenczi, first in his argument with Carl Whiteside and later on the playground? What does his attitude toward Miss Ferenczi reveal about his character?
10. Are all of Miss Ferenczi's "substitute facts" lies, or is there some truth in what she says? Is she correct when she says that substitute facts cannot hurt anyone?
11. Could it be argued that much of what is taught in schools today could be viewed as "substitute facts"? Explain.
12. **JOURNAL ENTRY:** Is Miss Ferenczi a good teacher? Why or why not?

WRITING SUGGESTIONS: CHARACTER

1. Both "Gryphon" and "Vengeful Creditor" examine the issue of education. Taking into account your own experiences with education as well as those of the characters in the two stories, write an essay in which you discuss what you believe the purpose of education should (and should not) be.

2. In "Fleur" and "Vengeful Creditor" major characters (the narrator and Vero, respectively) are led by circumstances to take drastic actions. Write a paper in which you outline each character's motivation, consider possible alternative courses of action, and explain why the course of action taken by each was (or was not) the only available option.
3. In each of the four stories in this chapter, a child or adolescent struggles against adult rules and authority and inflexible social systems. Choose two stories, and compare and contrast the nature of the struggle.
4. In both "Fleur" and "Gryphon" a young narrator watches as another character (one with whom the narrator sides emotionally) faces disapproval from the rest of society, yet only one narrator acts decisively. Write an essay in which you discuss alternate actions that could have been taken by either child, or by any of the story's other characters.
5. Both Sammy in "A&P" and Miss Ferenczi in "Gryphon" are nonconformists. Write an essay in which you compare and contrast these two characters with their peers in order to illustrate the nature, extent, and impact of their antisocial attitudes and actions.

CHAPTER 6

SETTING

The **setting** of a work of fiction establishes its historical, geographical, and physical location. *Where* a work is set—on a tropical island; in a dungeon; at a crowded party; in a tent in the woods—influences our interpretation of the story's events and characters. *When* a work takes place—during the French Revolution, today, in the future, or at an unspecified time—is equally important. Setting, however, means more than just the approximate time and place in which the work is set; setting also encompasses a wide variety of physical and cultural features.

Clearly, setting is more important in some works than in others. In some stories—such as Nadine Gordimer's "Once Upon a Time" (p. 64)—no particular time or place is specified, or even suggested, perhaps because the writer does not consider a specific setting to be important or because the writer wishes the story's events to seem timeless and universal. In other stories a writer may provide only minimal information about setting, telling readers little more than where and when the action takes place. In still other instances setting may be of obvious importance, helping to define the action as well as to explain characters' behavior, as it does in Charlotte Perkins Gilman's "The Yellow Wall-Paper" (p. 155). In such cases setting is clearly identified and fully described. In fact, setting may be so important that it is the key factor influencing the characters or the plot development.

One function of setting is its ability to highlight some aspect of a character's behavior or some feature of plot development. This emphasis is frequently achieved when a character is set in opposition to the setting. Alice in Wonderland; a northerner in the South; a naive, unsophisticated American tourist in an old European city; a sane person in a mental hospital; a moral person in a corrupt environment; an immigrant in a new world; a city person in the country—all these characters are set in opposition to the setting in which they find themselves, and this opposition helps to define the characters and creates a conflict central to the story.

In much the same way, a contrast between situation and setting can create interest—for example, the intrusion of nuclear war into a typical suburban neighborhood, the intrusion of modern social ideas into an old-fashioned world, or the intrusion of a brutal, senseless murder into a peaceful English village. In each of these cases, the setting enhances the plot.

HISTORICAL CONTEXT

A particular historical period, and the events associated with it, can be important in a story; therefore, some familiarity with a period can be useful (or even essential) to readers who wish to understand a story fully. Historical context establishes a social, cultural, economic, and political environment. Knowing, for instance, that "The Yellow Wall-Paper," written in 1892, is set in a period in which doctors treated women as delicate and dependent helps to explain the narrator's emotional state. Likewise, it may be important to know that a story is set during a particularly volatile (or static) political era, during a time of permissive (or repressive) attitudes toward sex, during a war, or during a period of economic prosperity or recession. Any one of these factors may determine—or help to explain—characters' actions: Historical events or cultural norms may, for instance, limit or multiply a character's options, and our knowledge of history may reveal to us a character's incompatibility with his or her milieu. In F. Scott Fitzgerald's "Bernice Bobs Her Hair," set in the 1920s in a midwestern town, a young girl is goaded into cutting her long hair. To understand the significance of Bernice's act—and to understand the reactions of others to that act—readers must know that during that era only racy "society vampires," not nice girls from good families, bobbed their hair.

Knowing the approximate year or historical period during which a story takes place can explain forces that act on characters, help to account for their behavior, clarify circumstances that influence the story's action, and help to justify a writer's use of plot devices that might otherwise seem improbable. For instance, stories set before the development of modern transportation and communication systems may hinge on plot devices readers would not accept in a modern story. In "Paul's Case," a 1904 story by Willa Cather, a young man who steals a large sum of money in Pittsburgh is able to spend many days enjoying it before the news of the theft reaches New York, where he has fled. In other stories we see such outdated plot devices as characters threatened by diseases that have now been eradicated (and subjected to outdated medical or psychiatric treatment). In addition, characters may be constrained by social conventions different from those that operate in our own society.

GEOGRAPHICAL CONTEXT

In addition to knowing when a work takes place, readers need to know *where* it takes place. A story's geographical context can also help readers to understand characters' behavior. For instance, knowing whether a story is set in the United States, in Europe, or in a developing nation can help to explain anything from why language and customs are unfamiliar to us to why characters act in ways we find improbable. Even if a story is set in our own country, regional differences may account for differences in plot development and characters' motivation. For example, knowing that William Faulkner's "A Rose for Emily" (p. 70) is set in the post–Civil War American South helps to explain why the townspeople are so chivalrously protective of Miss Emily. Similarly, the fact that Bret Harte's "The Outcasts of Poker Flat" is set in the American West accounts for its unusual cast of characters—including a gambler, a prostitute, and a traveling salesman.

The size of the town or city in which a story takes place may also be important. In a small town, for example, a character's problems are more likely to be subject to intense scrutiny by other characters, as they are in stories of small-town life such as those in Sherwood Anderson's *Winesburg, Ohio.* In a large city, characters may be more likely to be isolated and anonymous, like Mrs. Miller in Truman Capote's "Miriam," who is so lonely that she creates an imaginary companion. Characters are also more likely to be alienated by their big-city surroundings, as Gregor Samsa is in Franz Kafka's "The Metamorphosis" (p. 393).

Of course, a story may lack any recognizable historical context, or it may be set in a fantasy world with no particular geographical location. Such settings may free writers from the constraints placed on them by familiar environments, allowing them to experiment with situations and characters, unaffected by readers' expectations or associations with familiar settings.

PHYSICAL CONTEXT

A work's physical context includes such factors as the time of day, whether a story unfolds primarily inside or out-of-doors, what the weather is like, and the story's general atmosphere.

The *time of day* can clearly influence a story's mood as well as its development. The gruesome murder described in Edgar Allan Poe's "The Cask of Amontillado" (p. 180) takes place in an appropriate setting: at night, underground. Conversely, the horrifying events of Shirley Jackson's "The Lottery" (p. 276) take place in broad daylight, contrasting dramatically with the darkness of the society that permits—and even participates in—such events. Many stories, of course, move through several time periods as the action unfolds, and changes in time may also be important. For instance, the approach of evening, or of dawn, can signal the end of a crisis in the plot.

Whether a story is set primarily *inside* or *out-of-doors* may also be significant. The characters may be physically constrained by a closed-in setting or liberated by an expansive landscape. Some interior settings may be psychologically limiting. For instance, the narrator in "The Yellow Wall-Paper" feels suffocated by her room, whose ugly wallpaper comes to haunt her. In many of Poe's stories the central character is trapped, physically or psychologically, in a confined, suffocating space. In other stories an interior setting may serve a symbolic function. For instance, in "A Rose for Emily" the house is for Miss Emily a symbol of the South's past glory as well as a refuge, a fortress, and a hiding place. Similarly, a building or house may represent society, with its rules and norms and limitations. In John Updike's "A&P" (p. 93), for instance, the supermarket establishes social as well as physical limits. This is also the case in Katherine Mansfield's "Her First Ball," where a ballroom serves as the setting for a young girl's initiation into the rules and realities of adult society.

Conversely, an outdoor setting can free a character from social norms of behavior, as it does for Ernest Hemingway's Nick Adams, a war veteran who, in "Big Two-Hearted River," finds order, comfort, and peace only when he is away from civilization. Of course, an outdoor setting can also expose characters to physical dangers, such as untamed wilderness, uncharted seas, and frighteningly empty open spaces, as in Stephen Crane's classic story "The Open Boat."

Weather can be another important aspect of setting. A storm can threaten a character's life or just make the character—and readers—*think* danger is present, distracting us from other, more subtle threats. Extreme weather conditions can make characters act irrationally or uncharacteristically, as in Doris Lessing's "A Woman on a Roof" (p. 450), where the intense heat encourages desperate flirtation, or in Kate Chopin's "The Storm" (p. 143), where a storm provides the complication and determines the characters' actions. In numerous stories set in hostile landscapes, where extremes of heat and cold influence the action, weather may pose a test for characters, as in Jack London's "To Build a Fire," in which the main character struggles unsuccessfully against a brutally cold, hostile environment.

The various physical attributes of setting combine to create an **atmosphere,** or **mood,** that may be critical to a story. This atmosphere may emphasize a story's theme, helping to explain a character's reactions or state of mind, advancing or impeding the action. Characters may react one way in a crowded, busy, hectic atmosphere but behave very differently in a peaceful rural context. Darkness and isolation can cause (or reflect) behavior disturbances, while an idyllic, peaceful setting can change or reinforce a character's positive mood—or serve an ironic purpose, as it does in a story of horror such as "The Lottery." In "The Cask of Amontillado" several factors work together to create the eerie, intense atmosphere appropriate to the story's events: It is nighttime; it is the hectic carnival season; and the catacombs are dark, damp, and filled with the bones of the narrator's ancestors.

Checklist for Writing about Setting

- Is the setting specified or unidentified? Is it fully described or just sketched in?
- Is the setting important only as background, or is it a key force in the story?
- How does the setting influence the characters? Does it affect (or reflect) their emotional state? Does it help to explain their motivation?

- Are any characters set in opposition to their environment?
- Are any situations set in sharp contrast to the setting?
- How does the setting influence the story's plot? Does it cause characters to act?
- Does the setting add irony to the story?
- In what time period does the story take place? How can you tell? What social, political, or economic characteristics of the historical period might influence the story?
- In what geographical location is the story set? Is this location important to the story?
- At what time of day is the story set? Is time important to the development of the story?
- Is the story set primarily indoors or out-of-doors? What role does this aspect of the setting play in the story?
- What role do weather conditions play in the story?
- Is the story's general atmosphere dark or bright? Clear or murky? Tumultuous or calm? Gloomy or cheerful?
- Does the atmosphere change as the story progresses? Is this change significant?

Kate Chopin (1851–1904) must, in a sense, be considered a contemporary writer. Her honest, sexually frank stories (many of them out of print for more than half a century) were rediscovered in the 1960s and 1970s, influencing a new young generation of writers. Though she was a popular contributor of stories and sketches to the magazines of the day, Chopin scandalized many critics with her outspoken novel *The Awakening* (1899), in which a woman seeks sexual and emotional fulfillment.

Chopin was born Katherine O'Flaherty in St. Louis, the daughter of a wealthy Irish-born merchant and his aristocratic Creole wife. Educated at convent schools, she was married at nineteen to Oscar Chopin, a Louisiana cotton broker who took his young bride to live first in New Orleans, and later on a plantation in the Cajun country of southern Louisiana—a region she was to chronicle in her books *Bayou Folk* (1894) and *A Night in Arcadie* (1897). A busy wife and mother, Chopin seems to have begun writing only after she returned to St. Louis following her young husband's sudden death in 1883.

Chopin's style is realistic yet infused with a dense, sensual texture—perhaps, in part, Chopin's artistic response to her memories of the exotic Louisiana bayou country. Like her contemporary Gustave Flaubert (*The Awakening* has often been called a "Creole *Bovary*"), Chopin used the physical world—as in the charged atmosphere of "The Storm"—to symbolize the inner truths of her characters' minds and hearts. Unlike Flaubert, however, she depicts sex not as a frantic and destructive force, but as a joyous, elemental part of life. Apparently Kate Chopin knew how daring "The Storm" was: She never submitted it for publication.

Kate Chopin

THE STORM

(c. 1899)

I

The leaves were so still that even Bibi thought it was going to rain. Bobinôt, who was accustomed to converse on terms of perfect equality with his little son, called the child's attention to certain sombre clouds that were rolling with sinister intention from the west, accompanied by a sullen, threatening roar. They were at Friedheimer's store and decided to remain there till the storm had passed. They sat within the door on two empty kegs. Bibi was four years old and looked very wise.

"Mama'll be 'fraid, yes," he suggested with blinking eyes.

"She'll shut the house. Maybe she got Sylvie helpin' her this evenin'," Bobinôt responded reassuringly.

"No; she ent got Sylvie. Sylvie was helpin' her yistiday," piped Bibi.

5 Bobinôt arose and going across to the counter purchased a can of shrimps, of which Calixta was very fond. Then he returned to his perch on the keg and sat stolidly holding the can of shrimps while the storm burst. It shook the wooden store and seemed to be ripping great furrows in the distant field. Bibi laid his little hand on his father's knee and was not afraid.

II

Calixta, at home, felt no uneasiness for their safety. She sat at a side window sewing furiously on a sewing machine. She was greatly occupied and did not notice the approaching storm. But she felt very warm and often stopped to mop her face on which the perspiration gathered in beads. She unfastened her white sacque at the throat. It began to grow dark, and suddenly realizing the situation she got up hurriedly and went about closing windows and doors.

Out on the small front gallery she had hung Bobinôt's Sunday clothes to air and she hastened out to gather them before the rain fell. As she stepped outside, Alcée Laballière rode in at the gate. She had not seen him very often since her marriage, and never alone. She stood there with Bobinôt's coat in her hands, and the big rain drops began to fall. Alcée rode his horse under the shelter of a side projection where the chickens had huddled and there were plows and a harrow piled up in the corner.

"May I come and wait on your gallery till the storm is over, Calixta?" he asked.

"Come 'long in, M'sieur Alcée."

10 His voice and her own startled her as if from a trance, and she seized Bobinôt's vest. Alcée, mounting to the porch, grabbed the trousers and snatched Bibi's braided jacket that was about to be carried away by a sudden gust of wind. He expressed an intention to remain outside, but it

was soon apparent that he might as well have been out in the open: the water beat in upon the boards in driving sheets, and he went inside, closing the door after him. It was even necessary to put something beneath the door to keep the water out.

"My! what a rain! It's good two years sence it rain' like that," exclaimed Calixta as she rolled up a piece of bagging and Alcée helped her to thrust it beneath the crack.

She was a little fuller of figure than five years before when she married; but she had lost nothing of her vivacity. Her blue eyes still retained their melting quality; and her yellow hair, dishevelled by the wind and rain, kinked more stubbornly than ever about her ears and temples.

The rain beat upon the low, shingled roof with a force and clatter that threatened to break an entrance and deluge them there. They were in the dining room—the sitting room—the general utility room. Adjoining was her bed room, with Bibi's couch along side her own. The door stood open, and the room with its white, monumental bed, its closed shutters, looked dim and mysterious.

Alcée flung himself into a rocker and Calixta nervously began to gather up from the floor the lengths of a cotton sheet which she had been sewing.

"If this keeps up, *Dieu sait*[1] if the levees goin' to stan' it!" she exclaimed.

"What have you got to do with the levees?"

"I got enough to do! An' there's Bobinôt with Bibi out in that storm—if he only didn't left Friedheimer's!"

"Let us hope, Calixta, that Bobinôt's got sense enough to come in out of a cyclone."

She went and stood at the window with a greatly disturbed look on her face. She wiped the frame that was clouded with moisture. It was stiflingly hot. Alcée got up and joined her at the window, looking over her shoulder. The rain was coming down in sheets obscuring the view of far-off cabins and enveloping the distant wood in a gray mist. The playing of the lightning was incessant. A bolt struck a tall chinaberry tree at the edge of the field. It filled all visible space with a blinding glare and the crash seemed to invade the very boards they stood upon.

Calixta put her hands to her eyes, and with a cry, staggered backward. Alcée's arm encircled her, and for an instant he drew her close and spasmodically to him.

"*Bonté!*"[2] she cried, releasing herself from his encircling arm and retreating from the window, "the house'll go next! If I only knew w'ere Bibi was!" She would not compose herself; she would not be seated. Alcée

---

[1] God knows.

[2] "Goodness!"

clasped her shoulders and looked into her face. The contact of her warm, palpitating body when he had unthinkingly drawn her into his arms, had aroused all the old-time infatuation and desire for her flesh.

"Calixta," he said, "don't be frightened. Nothing can happen. The house is too low to be struck, with so many tall trees standing about. There! aren't you going to be quiet? say, aren't you?" He pushed her hair back from her face that was warm and steaming. Her lips were as red and moist as pomegranate seed. Her white neck and a glimpse of her full, firm bosom disturbed him powerfully. As she glanced up at him the fear in her liquid blue eyes had given place to a drowsy gleam that unconsciously betrayed a sensuous desire. He looked down into her eyes and there was nothing for him to do but to gather her lips in a kiss. It reminded him of Assumption.

"Do you remember—in Assumption, Calixta?" he asked in a low voice broken by passion. Oh! she remembered; for in Assumption he had kissed her and kissed and kissed her; until his senses would well nigh fail, and to save her he would resort to a desperate flight. If she was not an immaculate dove in those days, she was still inviolate; a passionate creature whose very defenselessness had made her defense, against which his honor forbade him to prevail. Now—well, now—her lips seemed in a manner free to be tasted, as well as her round, white throat and her whiter breasts.

They did not heed the crashing torrents, and the roar of the elements made her laugh as she lay in his arms. She was a revelation in that dim, mysterious chamber; as white as the couch she lay upon. Her firm, elastic flesh that was knowing for the first time its birthright, was like a creamy lily that the sun invites to contribute its breath and perfume to the undying life of the world.

The generous abundance of her passion, without guile or trickery, was like a white flame which penetrated and found response in depths of his own sensuous nature that had never yet been reached.

When he touched her breasts they gave themselves up in quivering ecstasy, inviting his lips. Her mouth was a fountain of delight. And when he possessed her, they seemed to swoon together at the very borderland of life's mystery.

He stayed cushioned upon her, breathless, dazed, enervated, with his heart beating like a hammer upon her. With one hand she clasped his head, her lips lightly touching his forehead. The other hand stroked with a soothing rhythm his muscular shoulders.

The growl of the thunder was distant and passing away. The rain beat softly upon the shingles, inviting them to drowsiness and sleep. But they dared not yield.

The rain was over; and the sun was turning the glistening green world into a palace of gems. Calixta, on the gallery, watched Alcée ride away. He turned and smiled at her with a beaming face; and she lifted her pretty chin in the air and laughed aloud.

III

30 Bobinôt and Bibi, trudging home, stopped without at the cistern to make themselves presentable.

"My! Bibi, w'at will yo' mama say! You ought to be ashame'. You oughtn' put on those good pants. Look at 'em! An' that mud on yo' collar! How you got that mud on yo' collar, Bibi? I never saw such a boy!" Bibi was the picture of pathetic resignation. Bobinôt was the embodiment of serious solicitude as he strove to remove from his own person and his son's the signs of their tramp over heavy roads and through wet fields. He scraped the mud off Bibi's bare legs and feet with a stick and carefully removed all traces from his heavy brogans. Then, prepared for the worst—the meeting with an over-scrupulous housewife, they entered cautiously at the back door.

Calixta was preparing supper. She had set the table and was dripping coffee at the hearth. She sprang up as they came in.

"Oh, Bobinôt! You back! My! but I was uneasy. W'ere you been during the rain? An' Bibi? he ain't wet? he ain't hurt?" She had clasped Bibi and was kissing him effusively. Bobinôt's explanations and apologies which he had been composing all along the way, died on his lips as Calixta felt him to see if he were dry, and seemed to express nothing but satisfaction at their safe return.

"I brought you some shrimps, Calixta," offered Bobinôt, hauling the can from his ample side pocket and laying it on the table.

35 "Shrimps! Oh, Bobinôt! you too good fo' anything!" and she gave him a smacking kiss on the cheek that resounded. *"J'vous réponds,*[3] we'll have a feas' tonight! umph-umph!"

Bobinôt and Bibi began to relax and enjoy themselves, and when the three seated themselves at table they laughed much and so loud that anyone might have heard them as far away as Laballière's.

IV

Alcée Laballière wrote to his wife, Clarisse, that night. It was a loving letter, full of tender solicitude. He told her not to hurry back, but if she and the babies liked it at Biloxi, to stay a month longer. He was getting on nicely; and though he missed them, he was willing to bear the separation a while longer—realizing that their health and pleasure were the first things to be considered.

V

As for Clarisse, she was charmed upon receiving her husband's letter. She and the babies were doing well. The society was agreeable; many of her old friends and acquaintances were at the bay. And the first free breath since her marriage seemed to restore the pleasant liberty of her maiden

---

[3] "I tell you."

days. Devoted as she was to her husband, their intimate conjugal life was something which she was more than willing to forego for a while.

So the storm passed and everyone was happy. ◌

READING AND REACTING

1. Trace the progress of the weather through the five parts of the story. Then, trace the stages of the story's plot. How does the progress of the storm parallel the developing plot?
2. How does the storm help to create the story's atmosphere? How would you characterize this atmosphere?
3. In Part I the "sombre clouds . . . rolling with sinister intention" introduce the storm. In what sense does this description introduce the story's action as well?
4. In what ways does the storm force the action of the story? List specific events that occur because of the storm. Is the presence of the storm essential to the story? Explain.
5. The weather is the most obvious element of the story's setting. What other aspects of setting are important to the story?
6. After Part II the storm is not mentioned again until the last line of the story. What signs of the storm remain in Parts III, IV, and V?
7. Besides denoting the weather, what else might the title suggest?
8. **JOURNAL ENTRY:** The storm sets in motion the chain of events that leads to the characters' adultery. Do you think the storm excuses them in any way from responsibility for their actions?

Tillie Olsen (1912 or 1913–) is known for her works of fiction about working-class Americans. Her short stories and one novel are inhabited by those she called the "despised people"—coal miners, farm laborers, packinghouse butchers, and housewives. Olsen was born in Nebraska into a working-class family. Though she has been described as a Depression-era dropout, Olsen has observed that she educated herself, with libraries as her college. According to an account in her nonfiction work *Silences* (1978), Olsen was at age fifteen inspired to write about working class people when she read Rebecca Harding Davis's *Life in the Iron Mills,* a tale of the effects of industrialization upon workers, in an 1861 issue of *Atlantic Monthly* bought for ten cents in a junk shop.

Shortly after she left high school, she was jailed for helping to organize packinghouse workers. Motivated by her experiences, she began to write a novel, *Yonnondio.* Under her maiden name, Tillie Lerner, she published two poems, a short story, and part of her novel in the 1930s. After her marriage she did not publish again for twenty-two years, spending her time raising four children and working at a variety of jobs. The book of short stories *Tell Me a Riddle* (1961), which includes "I Stand Here Ironing" (originally titled "Help Her to Believe"), was published when she was fifty. Her only other work of fiction is *Yonnondio* (1974), which she pieced together from drafts she wrote in the 1930s and edited for publication in 1974.

Saying that her own career was "ruined" by the passage of time when she could not write because of other responsibilities, she focuses on encouraging young writers by lecturing or reading her own works to writers' groups and holding writer-in-residency or visiting professorships at several major universities. She is also known for her efforts to rediscover long-forgotten works by other working-class women. In 1984, she edited *Mother to Daughter, Daughter to Mother: Mothers on Mothering,* a collection of poems, letters, short fiction, and diary excerpts written by famous and not-so-famous women. Olsen lives in San Francisco.

Tillie Olsen

I STAND HERE IRONING

(1961)

I stand here ironing, and what you asked me moves tormented back and forth with the iron.

"I wish you would manage the time to come and talk with me about your daughter. I'm sure you can help me understand her. She's a youngster who needs help and whom I'm deeply interested in helping."

"Who needs help." . . . Even if I came, what good would it do? You think because I am her mother I have a key, or that in some way you could use me as a key? She has lived for nineteen years. There is all that life that has happened outside of me, beyond me.

And when is there time to remember, to sift, to weigh, to estimate, to total? I will start and there will be an interruption and I will have to gather it all together again. Or I will become engulfed with all I did or did not do, with what should have been and what cannot be helped.

5 She was a beautiful baby. The first and only one of our five that was beautiful at birth. You do not guess how new and uneasy her tenancy in her now-loveliness. You did not know her all those years she was thought homely, or see her poring over her baby pictures, making me tell her over and over how beautiful she had been—and would be, I would tell her—and was now, to the seeing eye. But the seeing eyes were few or nonexistent. Including mine.

I nursed her. They feel that's important nowadays. I nursed all the children, but with her, with all the fierce rigidity of first motherhood, I did like the books then said. Though her cries battered me to trembling and my breasts ached with swollenness, I waited till the clock decreed.

Why do I put that first? I do not even know if it matters, or if it explains anything.

She was a beautiful baby. She blew shining bubbles of sound. She loved motion, loved light, loved color and music and textures. She would lie on the floor in her blue overalls patting the surface so hard in ecstasy her hands and feet would blur. She was a miracle to me, but when she was eight months old I had to leave her daytimes with the woman downstairs to whom she was no miracle at all, for I worked or looked for work and for Emily's father, who "could no longer endure" (he wrote in his good-bye note) "sharing want with us."

I was nineteen. It was the pre-relief, pre-WPA[1] world of the depression. I would start running as soon as I got off the streetcar, running up the stairs, the place smelling sour, and awake or asleep to startle awake, when she saw me she would break into a clogged weeping that could not be comforted, a weeping I can hear yet.

After a while I found a job hashing at night so I could be with her days, and it was better. But it came to where I had to bring her to his family and leave her.

It took a long time to raise the money for her fare back. Then she got chicken pox and I had to wait longer. When she finally came, I hardly knew her, walking quick and nervous like her father, looking like her father, thin, and dressed in a shoddy red that yellowed her skin and glared at the pockmarks. All the baby loveliness gone.

She was two. Old enough for nursery school they said, and I did not know then what I know now—the fatigue of the long day, and the lacerations of group life in the kinds of nurseries that are only parking places for children.

Except that it would have made no difference if I had known. It was the only place there was. It was the only way we could be together, the only way I could hold a job.

And even without knowing, I knew. I knew the teacher that was evil because all these years it has curdled into my memory, the little boy hunched in the corner, her rasp, "why aren't you outside, because Alvin hits you? that's no reason, go out, scaredy." I knew Emily hated it even if she did not clutch and implore "don't go Mommy" like the other children, mornings.

She always had a reason why we should stay home. Momma, you look sick. Momma, I feel sick. Momma, the teachers aren't there today, they're sick. Momma, we can't go, there was a fire there last night. Momma, it's a holiday today, no school, they told me.

But never a direct protest, never rebellion. I think of our others in their three-, four-year-oldness—the explosions, the tempers, the denunciations,

---

[1] Works Progress Administration, created in 1935 as part of President Franklin D. Roosevelt's New Deal program. The purpose of the WPA (renamed the Works Projects Administration in 1939) was to provide jobs for the unemployed during the Great Depression.

the demands—and I feel suddenly ill. I put the iron down. What in me demanded that goodness in her? And what was the cost, the cost to her of such goodness?

The old man living in the back once said in his gentle way: "You should smile at Emily more when you look at her." What *was* in my face when I looked at her? I loved her. There were all the acts of love.

It was only with the others I remembered what he said, and it was the face of joy, and not of care or tightness or worry I turned to them—too late for Emily. She does not smile easily, let alone almost always as her brothers and sisters do. Her face is closed and sombre, but when she wants, how fluid. You must have seen it in her pantomimes, you spoke of her rare gift for comedy on the stage that rouses laughter out of the audience so dear they applaud and applaud and do not want to let her go.

Where does it come from, that comedy? There was none of it in her when she came back to me that second time, after I had had to send her away again. She had a new daddy now to learn to love, and I think perhaps it was a better time.

Except when we left her alone nights, telling ourselves she was old enough.

"Can't you go some other time, Mommy, like tomorrow?" she would ask. "Will it be just a little while you'll be gone? Do you promise?"

The time we came back, the front door open, the clock on the floor in the hall. She rigid awake. "It wasn't just a little while. I didn't cry. Three times I called you, just three times, and then I ran downstairs to open the door so you could come faster. The clock talked loud. I threw it away, it scared me what it talked."

She said the clock talked loud again that night I went to the hospital to have Susan. She was delirious with the fever that comes before red measles, but she was fully conscious all the week I was gone and the week after we were home when she could not come near the new baby or me.

She did not get well. She stayed skeleton thin, not wanting to eat, and night after night she had nightmares. She would call for me, and I would rouse from exhaustion to sleepily call back: "You're all right, darling, go to sleep, it's just a dream," and if she still called, in a sterner voice, "now go to sleep, Emily, there's nothing to hurt you." Twice, only twice, when I had to get up for Susan anyhow, I went in to sit with her.

Now when it is too late (as if she would let me hold and comfort her like I do the others) I get up and go to her at once at her moan or restless stirring. "Are you awake, Emily? Can I get you something?" And the answer is always the same: "No, I'm all right, go back to sleep, Mother."

They persuaded me at the clinic to send her away to a convalescent home in the country where "she can have the kind of food and care you can't manage for her, and you'll be free to concentrate on the new baby." They still send children to that place. I see pictures on the society page of sleek young women planning affairs to raise money for it, or dancing at the affairs, or decorating Easter eggs or filling Christmas stockings for the children.

They never have a picture of the children so I do not know if the girls still wear those gigantic red bows and the ravaged looks on the every other Sunday when parents can come to visit "unless otherwise notified"—as we were notified the first six weeks.

Oh it is a handsome place, green lawns and tall trees and fluted flower beds. High up on the balconies of each cottage the children stand, the girls in their red bows and white dresses, the boys in white suits and giant red ties. The parents stand below shrieking up to be heard and the children shriek down to be heard, and between them the invisible wall: "Not to Be Contaminated by Parental Germs or Physical Affection."

There was a tiny girl who always stood hand in hand with Emily. Her parents never came. One visit she was gone. "They moved her to Rose Cottage," Emily shouted in explanation. "They don't like you to love anybody here."

She wrote once a week, the labored writing of a seven-year-old. "I am fine. How is the baby. If I write my leter nicly I will have a star. Love." There never was a star. We wrote every other day, letters she could never hold or keep but only hear read—once. "We simply do not have room for children to keep any personal possessions," they patiently explained when we pieced one Sunday's shrieking together to plead how much it would mean to Emily, who loved so to keep things, to be allowed to keep her letters and cards.

Each visit she looked frailer. "She isn't eating," they told us.

(They had runny eggs for breakfast or mush with lumps, Emily said later, I'd hold it in my mouth and not swallow. Nothing ever tasted good, just when they had chicken.)

It took us eight months to get her released home, and only the fact that she gained back so little of her seven lost pounds convinced the social worker.

I used to try to hold and love her after she came back, but her body would stay stiff, and after a while she'd push away. She ate little. Food sickened her, and I think much of life too. Oh she had physical lightness and brightness, twinkling by on skates, bouncing like a ball up and down up and down over the jump rope, skimming over the hill; but these were momentary.

She fretted about her appearance, thin and dark and foreign-looking at a time when every little girl was supposed to look or thought she should look a chubby blonde replica of Shirley Temple. The doorbell sometimes rang for her, but no one seemed to come and play in the house or be a best friend. Maybe because we moved so much.

There was a boy she loved painfully through two school semesters. Months later she told me how she had taken pennies from my purse to buy him candy. "Licorice was his favorite and I brought him some every day, but he still liked Jennifer better'n me. Why, Mommy?" The kind of question for which there is no answer.

School was a worry to her. She was not glib or quick in a world where glibness and quickness were easily confused with ability to learn. To her overworked and exasperated teachers she was an overconscientious "slow learner" who kept trying to catch up and was absent entirely too often.

I let her be absent, though sometimes the illness was imaginary. How different from my now-strictness about attendance with the others. I wasn't working. We had a new baby, I was home anyhow. Sometimes, after Susan grew old enough, I would keep her home from school, too, to have them all together.

Mostly Emily had asthma, and her breathing, harsh and labored, would fill the house with a curiously tranquil sound. I would bring the two old dresser mirrors and her boxes of collections to her bed. She would select beads and single earrings, bottle tops and shells, dried flowers and pebbles, old postcards and scraps, all sorts of oddments; then she and Susan would play Kingdom, setting up landscapes and furniture, peopling them with action.

Those were the only times of peaceful companionship between her and Susan. I have edged away from it, that poisonous feeling between them, that terrible balancing of hurts and needs I had to do between the two, and did so badly, those earlier years.

Oh there are conflicts between the others too, each one human, needing, demanding, hurting, taking—but only between Emily and Susan, no, Emily toward Susan that corroding resentment. It seems so obvious on the surface, yet it is not obvious. Susan, the second child, Susan, golden- and curly-haired and chubby, quick and articulate and assured, everything in appearance and manner Emily was not; Susan, not able to resist Emily's precious things, losing or sometimes clumsily breaking them; Susan telling jokes and riddles to company for applause while Emily sat silent (to say to me later: that was *my* riddle, Mother, I told it to Susan); Susan, who for all the five years' difference in age was just a year behind Emily in developing physically.

I am glad for that slow physical development that widened the difference between her and her contemporaries, though she suffered over it. She was too vulnerable for that terrible world of youthful competition, of preening and parading, of constant measuring of yourself against every other, of envy, "If I had that copper hair," "If I had that skin. . . ." She tormented herself enough about not looking like the others, there was enough of the unsureness, the having to be conscious of words before you speak, the constant caring—what are they thinking of me? without having it all magnified by the merciless physical drives.

Ronnie is calling. He is wet and I change him. It is rare there is such a cry now. That time of motherhood is almost behind me when the ear is not one's own but must always be racked and listening for the child cry, the child call. We sit for a while and I hold him, looking out over the city spread in charcoal with its soft aisles of light. "*Shoogily,*" he breathes and curls closer. I carry him back to bed, asleep. *Shoogily.* A funny word, a family word, inherited from Emily, invented by her to say: *comfort.*

In this and other ways she leaves her seal, I say aloud. And startle at my saying it. What do I mean? What did I start to gather together, to try and make coherent? I was at the terrible, growing years. War years. I do not remember them well. I was working, there were four smaller ones now, there was not time for her. She had to help be a mother, and housekeeper, and shopper. She had to set her seal. Mornings of crisis and near hysteria trying to get lunches packed, hair combed, coats and shoes found, everyone to school or Child Care on time, the baby ready for transportation. And always the paper scribbled on by a smaller one, the book looked at by Susan then mislaid, the homework not done. Running out to that huge school where she was one, she was lost, she was a drop; suffering over the unpreparedness, stammering and unsure in her classes.

45 There was so little time left at night after the kids were bedded down. She would struggle over books, always eating (it was in those years she developed her enormous appetite that is legendary in our family) and I would be ironing, or preparing food for the next day, or writing V-mail to Bill, or tending the baby. Sometimes, to make me laugh, or out of her despair, she would imitate happenings or types at school.

I think I said once: "Why don't you do something like this in the school amateur show?" One morning she phoned me at work, hardly understandable through the weeping: "Mother, I did it. I won, I won; they gave me first prize; they clapped and clapped and wouldn't let me go."

Now suddenly she was Somebody, and as imprisoned in her difference as she had been in anonymity.

She began to be asked to perform at other high schools, even in colleges, then at city and statewide affairs. The first one we went to, I only recognized her that first moment when thin, shy, she almost drowned herself into the curtains. Then: Was this Emily? The control, the command, the convulsing and deadly clowning, the spell, then the roaring, stamping audience, unwilling to let this rare and precious laughter out of their lives.

Afterwards: You ought to do something about her with a gift like that—but without money or knowing how, what does one do? We have left it all to her, and the gift has as often eddied inside, clogged and clotted, as been used and growing.

50 She is coming. She runs up the stairs two at a time with her light graceful step, and I know she is happy tonight. Whatever it was that occasioned your call did not happen today.

"Aren't you ever going to finish the ironing, Mother? Whistler painted his mother in a rocker. I'd have to paint mine standing over an ironing board." This is one of her communicative nights and she tells me everything and nothing as she fixes herself a plate of food out of the icebox.

She is so lovely. Why did you want me to come in at all? Why were you concerned? She will find her way.

She starts up the stairs to bed. "Don't get me up with the rest in the morning." "But I thought you were having midterms." "Oh, those," she comes back in, kisses me, and says quite lightly, "in a couple of years when we'll all be atom-dead they won't matter a bit."

She has said it before. She *believes* it. But because I have been dredging the past, and all that compounds a human being is so heavy and meaningful in me, I cannot endure it tonight.

I will never total it all. I will never come in to say: She was a child seldom smiled at. Her father left me before she was a year old. I had to work her first six years when there was work, or I sent her home and to his relatives. There were years she had care she hated. She was dark and thin and foreign-looking in a world where the prestige went to blondeness and curly hair and dimples, she was slow where glibness was prized. She was a child of anxious, not proud, love. We were poor and could not afford for her the soil of easy growth. I was a young mother, I was a distracted mother. There were other children pushing up, demanding. Her younger sister seemed all that she was not. There were years she did not want me to touch her. She kept too much in herself, her life was such she had to keep too much in herself. My wisdom came too late. She has much to her and probably little will come of it. She is a child of her age, of depression, of war, of fear.

Let her be. So all that is in her will not bloom—but in how many does it? There is still enough left to live by. Only help her to know—help make it so there is cause for her to know—that she is more than this dress on the ironing board, helpless before the iron. ✪

READING AND REACTING

1. "I Stand Here Ironing" focuses on incidents that took place in the "pre-relief, pre-WPA world of the depression." In light of social, political, and economic changes that have occurred since the 1930s, do you think the events the story presents could occur today? Explain.
2. In what sense is the image of a mother at an ironing board appropriate for this story?
3. The narrator is overwhelmed by guilt. What does she believe she has done wrong? What, if anything, do *you* think she has done wrong? Do you think she has been a good mother? Why or why not?
4. Who, or what, do you blame for the narrator's problems? For example, do you blame Emily's father? The Depression? The social institutions to which the narrator turns?
5. Do you see the narrator as a victim limited by the times in which she lives? Do you agree with the narrator that Emily is "a child of her age, of depression, of war, of fear"? Or do you believe both women have some control over their own destinies, regardless of the story's historical setting?
6. What do you think the narrator wants for her daughter? Do you think her goals for Emily are realistic ones?

7. **JOURNAL ENTRY:** Put yourself in Emily's position. What do you think she would like to tell her mother?

Charlotte Perkins Gilman (1860–1935) was a prominent feminist and social thinker at the turn of the century. Her essays, lectures, and nonfiction works—such as *Women and Economics* (1898), *Concerning Children* (1900), and *The Man-Made World* (1911)—are forceful statements of Gilman's opinions on women's need for economic independence and social equality. In the main, Gilman's fiction is a didactic expression of her social views. She is probably best known for three utopian feminist novels: *Moving the Mountain* (1911), *Herland* (1915; unpublished until 1978), and *With Her in Ourland* (1916). Gilman's fictional works are full of humor and satire: In *Herland,* for instance, a male sociologist (wandering in by accident from the outside world) is chagrined to find that the women of "Herland" want him for a friend, not a lover.

Although "The Yellow Wall-Paper" (1899) is not typical of Gilman's other fiction, it is considered her artistic masterpiece. The terse, clinical precision of the writing, conveying the tightly wound and distraught mental state of the narrator, is particularly chilling when it is read with a knowledge of Gilman's personal history. In the 1880s, she met and married a young artist, Charles Walter Stetson. Following the birth of their daughter, she grew increasingly depressed and turned to a noted Philadelphia neurologist for help. Following the traditions of the time, he prescribed complete bed rest and mental inactivity—a treatment that, Gilman said later, drove her "so near the borderline of utter mental ruin that I could see over." "The Yellow Wall-Paper" is not simply a psychological study. Like most of Gilman's work, it makes a point—this time about the dangers of women's utter dependence on a male interpretation of their needs.

Charlotte Perkins Gilman

THE YELLOW WALL-PAPER

(1899)

It is very seldom that mere ordinary people like John and myself secure ancestral halls for the summer.

A colonial mansion, a hereditary estate, I would say a haunted house, and reach the height of romantic felicity—but that would be asking too much of fate!

Still I will proudly declare that there is something queer about it.

Else, why should it be let so cheaply? And why have stood so long untenanted?

5 John laughs at me, of course, but one expects that in marriage.

John is practical in the extreme. He has no patience with faith, an intense horror of superstition, and he scoffs openly at any talk of things not to be felt and seen and put down in figures.

John is a physician, and *perhaps*—(I would not say it to a living soul, of course, but this is dead paper and a great relief to my mind—) *perhaps* that is one reason I do not get well faster.

You see he does not believe I am sick!

And what can one do?

10 If a physician of high standing, and one's own husband, assures friends and relatives that there is really nothing the matter with one but temporary nervous depression—a slight hysterical tendency—what is one to do?

My brother is also a physician, and also of high standing, and he says the same thing.

So I take phosphates or phosphites[1]—whichever it is, and tonics, and journeys, and air, and exercise, and am absolutely forbidden to "work" until I am well again.

Personally, I disagree with their ideas.

Personally, I believe that congenial work, with excitement and change, would do me good.

15 But what is one to do?

I did write for a while in spite of them; but it *does* exhaust me a good deal—having to be so sly about it, or else meet with heavy opposition.

I sometimes fancy that in my condition if I had less opposition and more society and stimulus—but John says the very worst thing I can do is to think about my condition, and I confess it always makes me feel bad.

So I will let it alone and talk about the house.

The most beautiful place! It is quite alone, standing well back from the road, quite three miles from the village. It makes me think of English places that you read about, for there are hedges and walls and gates that lock, and lots of separate little houses for the gardeners and people.

20 There is a *delicious* garden! I never saw such a garden—large and shady, full of box-bordered paths, and lined with long grape-covered arbors with seats under them.

There were greenhouses, too, but they are all broken now.

There was some legal trouble, I believe, something about the heirs and co-heirs; anyhow, the place has been empty for years.

---

[1] Both terms refer to salts of phosphorous acid. The narrator, however, means "phosphate," a carbonated beverage of water, flavoring, and a small amount of phosphoric acid.

That spoils my ghostliness, I am afraid, but I don't care—there is something strange about the house—I can feel it.

I even said so to John one moonlight evening, but he said what I felt was a *draught,* and shut the window.

I get unreasonably angry with John sometimes. I'm sure I never used to be so sensitive. I think it is due to this nervous condition.

But John says if I feel so, I shall neglect proper self-control; so I take pains to control myself—before him, at least, and that makes me very tired.

I don't like our room a bit. I wanted one downstairs that opened on the piazza and had roses all over the window, and such pretty old-fashioned chintz hangings! But John would not hear of it.

He said there was only one window and not room for two beds, and no near room for him if he took another.

He is very careful and loving, and hardly lets me stir without special direction.

I have a schedule prescription for each hour in the day; he takes all care from me, and so I feel basely ungrateful not to value it more.

He said we came here solely on my account, that I was to have perfect rest and all the air I could get. "Your exercise depends on your strength, my dear," said he, "and your food somewhat on your appetite; but air you can absorb all the time." So we took the nursery at the top of the house.

It is a big, airy room, the whole floor nearly, with windows that look all ways, and air and sunshine galore. It was nursery first and then playroom and gymnasium, I should judge; for the windows are barred for little children, and there are rings and things in the walls.

The paint and paper look as if a boys' school had used it. It is stripped off—the paper—in great patches all around the head of my bed, about as far as I can reach, and in a great place on the other side of the room low down. I never saw a worse paper in my life.

One of those sprawling flamboyant patterns committing every artistic sin.

It is dull enough to confuse the eye in following, pronounced enough to constantly irritate and provoke study, and when you follow the lame uncertain curves for a little distance they suddenly commit suicide—plunge off at outrageous angles, destroy themselves in unheard of contradictions.

The color is repellent, almost revolting; a smouldering unclean yellow, strangely faded by the slow-turning sunlight.

It is a dull yet lurid orange in some places, a sickly sulphur tint in others.

No wonder the children hated it! I should hate it myself if I had to live in this room long.

There comes John, and I must put this away,—he hates to have me write a word.

We have been here two weeks, and I haven't felt like writing before, since that first day.

I am sitting by the window now, up in this atrocious nursery, and there is nothing to hinder my writing as much as I please, save lack of strength.

John is away all day, and even some nights when his cases are serious.

I am glad my case is not serious!

But these nervous troubles are dreadfully depressing.

John does not know how much I really suffer. He knows there is no *reason* to suffer, and that satisfies him.

Of course it is only nervousness. It does weigh on me so not to do my duty in any way!

I meant to be such a help to John, such a real rest and comfort, and here I am a comparative burden already!

Nobody would believe what an effort it is to do what little I am able,—to dress and entertain, and order things.

It is fortunate Mary is so good with the baby. Such a dear baby!

And yet I *cannot* be with him, it makes me so nervous.

I suppose John never was nervous in his life. He laughs at me so about this wall-paper!

At first he meant to repaper the room, but afterwards he said that I was letting it get the better of me, and that nothing was worse for a nervous patient than to give way to such fancies.

He said that after the wall-paper was changed it would be the heavy bedstead, and then the barred windows, and then that gate at the head of the stairs, and so on.

"You know the place is doing you good," he said, "and really, dear, I don't care to renovate the house just for a three months' rental."

"Then do let us go downstairs," I said, "there are such pretty rooms there."

Then he took me in his arms and called me a blessed little goose, and said he would go down cellar, if I wished, and have it whitewashed into the bargain.

But he is right enough about the beds and windows and things.

It is an airy and comfortable room as any one need wish, and, of course, I would not be so silly as to make him uncomfortable just for a whim.

I'm really getting quite fond of the big room, all but that horrid paper.

Out of one window I can see the garden, those mysterious deep-shaded arbors, the riotous old-fashioned flowers, and bushes and gnarly trees.

Out of another I get a lovely view of the bay and a little private wharf belonging to the estate. There is a beautiful shaded lane that runs down there from the house. I always fancy I see people walking in these numerous paths and arbors, but John has cautioned me not to give way to fancy in the least. He says that with my imaginative power and habit of story-making, a nervous weakness like mine is sure to lead to all manner of excited fancies, and that I ought to use my will and good sense to check the tendency. So I try.

I think sometimes that if I were only well enough to write a little it would relieve the press of ideas and rest me.

But I find I get pretty tired when I try.

It is so discouraging not to have any advice and companionship about my work. When I get really well, John says we will ask Cousin Henry and Julia down for a long visit; but he says he would as soon put fireworks in my pillow-case as to let me have those stimulating people about now.

I wish I could get well faster.

But I must not think about that. This paper looks to me as if it *knew* what a vicious influence it had!

There is a recurrent spot where the pattern lolls like a broken neck and two bulbous eyes stare at you upside down.

I get positively angry with the impertinence of it and the everlastingness. Up and down and sideways they crawl, and those absurd, unblinking eyes are everywhere. There is one place where two breadths didn't match, and the eyes go all up and down the line, one a little higher than the other.

I never saw so much expression in an inanimate thing before, and we all know how much expression they have! I used to lie awake as a child and get more entertainment and terror out of blank walls and plain furniture than most children could find in a toy-store.

I remember what a kindly wink the knobs of our big, old bureau used to have, and there was one chair that always seemed like a strong friend.

I used to feel that if any of the other things looked too fierce I could always hop into that chair and be safe.

The furniture in this room is no worse than inharmonious, however, for we had to bring it all from downstairs. I suppose when this was used as a playroom they had to take the nursery things out, and no wonder! I never saw such ravages as the children have made here.

The wall-paper, as I said before, is torn off in spots, and it sticketh closer than a brother—they must have had perseverance as well as hatred.

Then the floor is scratched and gouged and splintered, the plaster itself is dug out here and there, and this great heavy bed which is all we found in the room, looks as if it had been through the wars.

But I don't mind it a bit—only the paper.

There comes John's sister. Such a dear girl as she is, and so careful of me! I must not let her find me writing.

She is a perfect and enthusiastic housekeeper, and hopes for no better profession. I verily believe she thinks it is the writing which made me sick!

But I can write when she is out, and see her a long way off from these windows.

There is one that commands the road, a lovely shaded winding road, and one that just looks off over the country. A lovely country, too, full of great elms and velvet meadows.

This wall-paper has a kind of sub-pattern in a different shade, a particularly irritating one, for you can only see it in certain lights, and not clearly then.

But in the places where it isn't faded and where the sun is just so—I can see a strange, provoking, formless sort of figure, that seems to skulk about behind that silly and conspicuous front design.

There's sister on the stairs!

Well, the Fourth of July is over! The people are all gone and I am tired out. John thought it might do me good to see a little company, so we just had mother and Nellie and the children down for a week.

Of course I didn't do a thing. Jennie sees to everything now.

But it tired me all the same.

John says if I don't pick up faster he shall send me to Weir Mitchell[2] in the fall.

But I don't want to go there at all. I had a friend who was in his hands once, and she says he is just like John and my brother, only more so!

Besides, it is such an undertaking to go so far.

I don't feel as if it was worth while to turn my hand over for anything, and I'm getting dreadfully fretful and querulous.

I cry at nothing, and cry most of the time.

Of course I don't when John is here, or anybody else, but when I am alone.

And I am alone a good deal just now. John is kept in town very often by serious cases, and Jennie is good and lets me alone when I want her to.

So I walk a little in the garden or down that lovely lane, sit on the porch under the roses, and lie down up here a good deal.

I'm getting really fond of the room in spite of the wall-paper. Perhaps *because* of the wall-paper.

It dwells in my mind so!

I lie here on this great immovable bed—it is nailed down, I believe—and follow that pattern about by the hour. It is as good as gymnastics, I assure you. I start, we'll say, at the bottom, down in the corner over there where it has not been touched, and I determine for the thousandth time that I *will* follow that pointless pattern to some sort of a conclusion.

I know a little of the principle of design, and I know this thing was not arranged on any laws of radiation, or alternation, or repetition, or symmetry, or anything else that I ever heard of.

It is repeated, of course, by the breadths, but not otherwise.

Looked at in one way each breadth stands alone, the bloated curves and flourishes—a kind of "debased Romanesque" with *delirium tremens*[3] go waddling up and down in isolated columns of fatuity.

But, on the other hand, they connect diagonally, and the sprawling outlines run off in great slanting waves of optic horror, like a lot of wallowing seaweeds in full chase.

---

[2] Silas Weir Mitchell (1829–1914)—a Philadelphia neurologist-psychologist who introduced the "rest cure" for nervous diseases.

[3] Mental confusion caused by alcohol poisoning and characterized by physical tremors and hallucinations.

The whole thing goes horizontally, too, at least it seems so, and I exhaust myself in trying to distinguish the order of its going in that direction.

They have used a horizontal breadth for a frieze, and that adds wonderfully to the confusion.

There is one end of the room where it is almost intact, and there, when the crosslights fade and the low sun shines directly upon it, I can almost fancy radiation after all,—the interminable grotesques seems to form around a common center and rush off in headlong plunges of equal distraction.

It makes me tired to follow it. I will take a nap I guess.

I don't know why I should write this.

I don't want to.

I don't feel able.

And I know John would think it absurd. But I *must* say what I feel and think in some way—it is such a relief!

But the effort is getting to be greater than the relief.

Half the time now I am awfully lazy, and lie down ever so much.

John says I mustn't lose my strength, and has me take cod liver oil and lots of tonics and things, to say nothing of ale and wine and rare meat.

Dear John! He loves me very dearly, and hates to have me sick. I tried to have a real earnest reasonable talk with him the other day, and tell him how I wish he would let me go and make a visit to Cousin Henry and Julia.

But he said I wasn't able to go, nor able to stand it after I got there; and I did not make out a very good case for myself, for I was crying before I had finished.

It is getting to be a great effort for me to think straight. Just this nervous weakness I suppose.

And dear John gathered me up in his arms, and just carried me upstairs and laid me on the bed, and sat by me and read to me till it tired my head.

He said I was his darling and his comfort and all he had, and that I must take care of myself for his sake, and keep well.

He says no one but myself can help me out of it, that I must use my will and self-control and not let any silly fancies run away with me.

There's one comfort, the baby is well and happy, and does not have to occupy this nursery with the horrid wall-paper.

If we had not used it, that blessed child would have! What a fortunate escape! Why, I wouldn't have a child of mine, an impressionable little thing, live in such a room for worlds.

I never thought of it before, but it is lucky that John kept me here after all, I can stand it so much easier than a baby, you see.

Of course I never mention it to them any more—I am too wise,—but I keep watch of it all the same.

There are things in that paper that nobody knows but me, or ever will.

Behind that outside pattern the dim shapes get clearer every day.

It is always the same shape, only very numerous.

And it is like a woman stooping down and creeping about behind that pattern. I don't like it a bit. I wonder—I begin to think—I wish John would take me away from here!

It is so hard to talk with John about my case, because he is so wise, and because he loves me so.

But I tried it last night.

It was moonlight. The moon shines in all around just as the sun does.

I hate to see it sometimes, it creeps so slowly, and always comes in by one window or another.

John was asleep and I hated to waken him, so I kept still and watched the moonlight on that undulating wall-paper till I felt creepy.

The faint figure behind seemed to shake the pattern, just as if she wanted to get out.

I got up softly and went to feel and see if the paper *did* move, and when I came back John was awake.

"What is it, little girl?" he said. "Don't go walking about like that—you'll get cold."

I thought it was a good time to talk, so I told him that I really was not gaining here, and that I wished he would take me away.

"Why, darling!" said he, "our lease will be up in three weeks, and I can't see how to leave before.

"The repairs are not done at home, and I cannot possibly leave town just now. Of course if you were in any danger, I could and would, but you really are better, dear, whether you can see it or not. I am a doctor, dear, and I know. You are gaining flesh and color, your appetite is better, I feel really much easier about you."

"I don't weigh a bit more," said I, "nor as much; and my appetite may be better in the evening when you are here, but it is worse in the morning when you are away!"

"Bless her little heart!" said he with a big hug, "she shall be as sick as she pleases! But now let's improve the shining hours by going to sleep, and talk about it in the morning!"

"And you won't go away?" I asked gloomily.

"Why, how can I, dear? It is only three weeks more and then we will take a nice little trip of a few days while Jennie is getting the house ready. Really dear you are better!"

"Better in body perhaps—" I began, and stopped short, for he sat up straight and looked at me with such a stern, reproachful look that I could not say another word.

"My darling," said he, "I beg of you, for my sake and for our child's sake, as well as for your own, that you will never for one instant let that idea enter your mind! There is nothing so dangerous, so fascinating, to a temperament like yours. It is a false and foolish fancy. Can you not trust me as a physician when I tell you so?"

So of course I said no more on that score, and we went to sleep before long. He thought I was asleep first, but I wasn't, and lay there for hours trying to decide whether that front pattern and the back pattern really did move together or separately.

On a pattern like this, by daylight, there is a lack of sequence, a defiance of law, that is a constant irritant to a normal mind.

The color is hideous enough, and unreliable enough, and infuriating enough, but the pattern is torturing.

You think you have mastered it, but just as you get well underway in following, it turns back-somersault and there you are. It slaps you in the face, knocks you down, and tramples upon you. It is like a bad dream.

The outside pattern is a florid arabesque, reminding one of a fungus. If you can imagine a toadstool in joints, an interminable string of toadstools, budding and sprouting in endless convolutions—why, that is something like it.

That is, sometimes!

There is one marked peculiarity about this paper, a thing nobody seems to notice but myself, and that is that it changes as the light changes.

When the sun shoots in through the east window—I always watch for that first long, straight ray—it changes so quickly that I never can quite believe it.

That is why I watch it always.

By moonlight—the moon shines in all night when there is a moon—I wouldn't know it was the same paper.

At night in any kind of light, in twilight, candlelight, lamplight, and worst of all by moonlight, it becomes bars! The outside pattern I mean, and the woman behind it is as plain as can be.

I didn't realize for a long time what the thing was that showed behind, that dim sub-pattern, but now I am quite sure it is a woman.

By daylight she is subdued, quiet. I fancy it is the pattern that keeps her so still. It is so puzzling. It keeps me quiet by the hour.

I lie down ever so much now. John says it is good for me, and to sleep all I can.

Indeed he started the habit by making me lie down for an hour after each meal.

It is a very bad habit I am convinced, for you see I don't sleep.

And that cultivates deceit, for I don't tell them I'm awake—O no!

The fact is I am getting a little afraid of John.

He seems very queer sometimes, and even Jennie has an inexplicable look.

It strikes me occasionally, just as a scientific hypothesis,—that perhaps it is the paper!

I have watched John when he did not know I was looking, and come into the room suddenly on the most innocent excuses, and I've caught him several times *looking at the paper!* And Jennie too. I caught Jennie with her hand on it once.

She didn't know I was in the room, and when I asked her in a quiet, a very quiet voice, with the most restrained manner possible, what she was doing with the paper—she turned around as if she had been caught stealing, and looked quite angry—asked me why I should frighten her so!

Then she said that the paper stained everything it touched, that she had found yellow smooches on all my clothes and John's, and she wished we would be more careful!

Did not that sound innocent? But I know she was studying that pattern, and I am determined that nobody shall find it out but myself!

Life is very much more exciting now than it used to be. You see I have something more to expect, to look forward to, to watch. I really do eat better, and am more quiet than I was.

John is so pleased to see me improve! He laughed a little the other day, and said I seemed to be flourishing in spite of my wall-paper.

I turned it off with a laugh. I had no intention of telling him it was *because* of the wall-paper—he would make fun of me. He might even want to take me away.

I don't want to leave now until I have found it out. There is a week more, and I think that will be enough.

I'm feeling ever so much better! I don't sleep much at night, for it is so interesting to watch developments; but I sleep a good deal in the daytime.

In the daytime it is tiresome and perplexing.

There are always new shoots on the fungus, and new shades of yellow all over it. I cannot keep count of them, though I have tried conscientiously.

It is the strangest yellow, that wall-paper! It makes me think of all the yellow things I ever saw—not beautiful ones like buttercups, but old foul, bad yellow things.

But there is something else about that paper—the smell! I noticed it the moment we came into the room, but with so much air and sun it was not bad. Now we have had a week of fog and rain, and whether the windows are open or not, the smell is here.

It creeps all over the house.

I find it hovering in the dining-room, skulking in the parlor, hiding in the hall, lying in wait for me on the stairs.

It gets into my hair.

Even when I go to ride, if I turn my head suddenly and surprise it—there is that smell!

Such a peculiar odor, too! I have spent hours in trying to analyze it, to find what it smelled like.

It is not bad—at first, and very gentle, but quite the subtlest, most enduring odor I ever met.

In this damp weather it is awful, I wake up in the night and find it hanging over me.

It used to disturb me at first. I thought seriously of burning the house—to reach the smell.

But now I am used to it. The only thing I can think of that it is like is the *color* of the paper! A yellow smell.

There is a very funny mark on this wall, low down, near the mop-board. A streak that runs round the room. It goes behind every piece of furniture, except the bed, a long, straight, even *smooch,* as if it had been rubbed over and over.

I wonder how it was done and who did it, and what they did it for. Round and round and round—round and round and round!—it makes me dizzy!

I really have discovered something at last.

Through watching so much at night, when it changes so, I have finally found out.

The front pattern *does* move—and no wonder! The woman behind shakes it!

Sometimes I think there are a great many women behind, and sometimes only one, and she crawls around fast, and her crawling shakes it all over.

Then in the very bright spots she keeps still, and in the very shady spots she just takes hold of the bars and shakes them hard.

And she is all the time trying to climb through. But nobody could climb through that pattern—it strangles so; I think that is why it has so many heads.

They get through, and then the pattern strangles them off and turns them upside down, and makes their eyes white!

If those heads were covered or taken off it would not be half so bad.

I think that woman gets out in the daytime!

And I'll tell you why—privately—I've seen her!

I can see her out of every one of my windows!

It is the same woman, I know, for she is always creeping, and most women do not creep by daylight.

I see her in that long shaded lane, creeping up and down. I see her in those dark grape arbors, creeping all around the garden.

I see her on that long road under the trees, creeping along, and when a carriage comes she hides under the blackberry vines.

I don't blame her a bit. It must be very humiliating to be caught creeping by daylight!

I always lock the door when I creep by daylight. I can't do it at night, for I know John would suspect something at once.

And John is so queer now, that I don't want to irritate him. I wish he would take another room! Besides, I don't want anybody to get that woman out at night but myself.

I often wonder if I could see her out of all the windows at once.

But, turn as fast as I can, I can only see out of one at one time.

And though I always see her, she *may* be able to creep faster than I can turn!

I have watched her sometimes away off in the open country, creeping as fast as a cloud shadow in a high wind.

If only that top pattern could be gotten off from the under one! I mean to try it, little by little.

I have found out another funny thing, but I shan't tell it this time! It does not do to trust people too much.

There are only two more days to get this paper off, and I believe John is beginning to notice. I don't like the look in his eyes.

And I heard him ask Jennie a lot of professional questions about me. She had a very good report to give.

She said I slept a good deal in the daytime.

John knows I don't sleep very well at night, for all I'm so quiet!

He asked me all sorts of questions, too, and pretended to be very loving and kind.

As if I couldn't see through him!

Still, I don't wonder he acts so, sleeping under this paper for three months.

It only interests me, but I feel sure John and Jennie are secretly affected by it.

Hurrah! This is the last day, but it is enough. John to stay in town over night, and won't be out until this evening.

Jennie wanted to sleep with me—the sly thing! But I told her I should undoubtedly rest better for a night all alone.

That was clever, for really I wasn't alone a bit! As soon as it was moonlight and that poor thing began to crawl and shake the pattern, I got up and ran to help her.

I pulled and she shook, I shook and she pulled, and before morning we had peeled off yards of that paper.

A strip about as high as my head and half around the room.

And then when the sun came and that awful pattern began to laugh at me, I declared I would finish it to-day!

We go away to-morrow, and they are moving all my furniture down again to leave things as they were before.

Jennie looked at the wall in amazement, but I told her merrily that I did it out of pure spite at the vicious thing.

She laughed and said she wouldn't mind doing it herself, but I must not get tired.

How she betrayed herself that time!

But I am here, and no person touches this paper but me,—not *alive!*

She tried to get me out of the room—it was too patent! But I said it was so quiet and empty and clean now that I believed I would lie down again and sleep all I could; and not to wake me even for dinner—I would call when I woke.

So now she is gone, and the servants are gone, and the things are gone, and there is nothing left but that great bedstead nailed down, with the canvas mattress we found on it.

We shall sleep downstairs to-night, and take the boat home tomorrow.

I quite enjoy the room, now it is bare again.

How those children did tear about here!

This bedstead is fairly gnawed!

But I must get to work.

I have locked the door and thrown the key down into the front path.

I don't want to go out, and I don't want to have anybody come in, till John comes.

I want to astonish him.

I've got a rope up here that even Jennie did not find. If that woman does get out, and tries to get away, I can tie her!

But I forgot I could not reach far without anything to stand on!

This bed will *not* move!

I tried to lift and push it until I was lame, and then I got so angry I bit off a little piece at one corner—but it hurt my teeth.

Then I peeled off all the paper I could reach standing on the floor. It sticks horribly and the pattern just enjoys it! All those strangled heads and bulbous eyes and waddling fungus growths just shriek with derision!

I am getting angry enough to do something desperate. To jump out of the window would be admirable exercise, but the bars are too strong even to try.

Besides I wouldn't do it. Of course not. I know well enough that a step like that is improper and might be misconstrued.

I don't like to *look* out of the windows even—there are so many of those creeping women, and they creep so fast.

I wonder if they all come out of that wall-paper as I did?

But I am securely fastened now by my well-hidden rope—you don't get *me* out in the road there!

I suppose I shall have to get back behind the pattern when it comes night, and that is hard!

It is so pleasant to be out in this great room and creep around as I please!

I don't want to go outside. I won't, even if Jennie asks me to.

For outside you have to creep on the ground, and everything is green instead of yellow.

But here I can creep smoothly on the floor, and my shoulder just fits in that long smooch around the wall, so I cannot lose my way.

Why there's John at the door!

It is no use, young man, you can't open it!

How he does call and pound!

Now he's crying for an axe.

It would be a shame to break down that beautiful door!

"John dear!" said I in the gentlest voice, "the key is down by the front steps, under a plaintain leaf!"

That silenced him for a few moments.

Then he said—very quietly indeed. "Open the door, my darling!"

"I can't," said I. "The key is down by the front door under a plaintain leaf!"

And then I said it again, several times, very gently and slowly, and said it so often that he had to go and see, and he got it of course, and came in. He stopped short by the door.

"What is the matter?" he cried. "For God's sake, what are you doing!"

I kept on creeping just the same, but I looked at him over my shoulder.

"I've got out at last," said I, "in spite of you and Jane. And I've pulled off most of the paper, so you can't put me back!"

Now why should that man have fainted? But he did, and right across my path by the wall, so that I had to creep over him every time!

READING AND REACTING

1. The story's narrator, who has recently given birth, is suffering from what doctors call "temporary nervous depression—a slight hysterical tendency." What is the relationship between this depression and the story's setting?
2. Describe the house and grounds. How do they affect the narrator's mood?
3. What aspects of the room in which the narrator lives upset her? Why?
4. Describe the wallpaper. What does the narrator actually see in it, and what does she imagine? How can you tell the difference?
5. What do the following comments reveal about the narrator's situation: "John laughs at me, of course, but one expects that in marriage" (5); "I must put this away,—he hates to have me write a word" (39); "He laughs at me so about this wall-paper" (51); "Then he took me in his arms and called me a blessed little goose" (56)?
6. What has probably caused the narrator's depression? What factors aggravate it? How much insight does the narrator seem to have into her situation?
7. How does the narrator's mood change as the story progresses? How do her descriptions of her setting change?
8. Aside from the physical setting—the room, the house, and the garden—what other aspects of the story's setting play an important role?
9. **JOURNAL ENTRY:** Do you think a present-day physician or psychiatrist would give the narrator different advice? Would a

present-day woman respond differently to advice from her husband or her doctor? Explain.

WRITING SUGGESTIONS: SETTING

1. Write an essay in which you consider the impact of changing the setting of each of this chapter's three stories to the present. What would change in each?
2. In all three of the stories in this chapter, social constraints determined by the story's historical context limit a woman's options. Explore the options each woman might reasonably exercise in order to break free of the limits that social institutions impose on her.
3. In stories in which setting is a strong presence, the danger always exists that the writer will neglect character development in favor of atmosphere. Does this problem occur in any of the stories in this chapter? Explain your answer.
4. Write an essay in which you consider how any one of the three stories in this chapter would be different if a major aspect of its physical or geographical setting were changed to a setting or settings of your choice. In your essay, examine the changes (in plot development as well as in the characters' conflicts, reactions, and motivation) that might be caused by the change in setting.
5. Select a story from another chapter, and write an essay in which you consider how setting affects plot—for example, how it creates conflict or crisis, how it forces characters to act, or how it determines how the plot is resolved.

CHAPTER 7

POINT OF VIEW

All works of fiction are told, or narrated, by someone, and one of the first choices writers make is who tells the story. This choice determines the story's **point of view**—the angle or vantage point from which events are presented. The implications of this choice are far reaching. Consider for a moment the following scenario. Five people witness a crime and are questioned by law enforcement officials. Their stories agree on certain points: A crime was committed, a body was found, and the crime occurred at noon. But in other ways their stories are very different. The man who fled the scene was either tall or of average height; his hair was either dark or light; he was either carrying an object or was empty handed. The events that led up to the crime and even the description of the crime itself are markedly different depending on who tells the story. Thus the perspective from which a story is told determines the details that are included in the story and the way they are arranged—in short, the plot. In addition, the perspective of the narrator affects the style, the language, and the themes of the story.

The narrator's voice in a work of fiction is not the same as the author's voice. Even when an author uses the first-person "I" to narrate a story, you should not assume that the narrator is speaking for the author. Authors create characters, sometimes with mannerisms and ideas far different from theirs, to tell their stories. Critics use the technical term **persona**—which literally means "mask"—to describe the self created by authors to tell a story. By assuming this mask, authors enhance the creative possibilities of their writing.

When deciding on a point of view for fiction, writers can choose to tell the story in the first person or in the third person.

FIRST-PERSON NARRATOR

In this situation the narrator is a character who uses the **first person** *I* (or sometimes *we*) to tell the story. This narrator may be a major character telling his or her own story or a minor character who plays only a small part (or no part at all) in the story's events. Both Sammy in John Updike's "A&P" (p. 93) and the boy in James Joyce's "Araby" (p. 219) are major characters who tell their own stories and are the focus of those stories. Sometimes, however, a first-person narrator may tell a story that is primarily about someone else. Such a narrator may be a minor character who plays a relatively small part in the story or simply an observer who reports events experienced or related by others. The narrator of William Faulkner's "A Rose for Emily" (p. 70), for example, is an unidentified witness to the story's events. By using *we* instead of *I,* this narrator seems to be speaking on behalf of all the residents of the town. (The focus of the story, however, is on neither the narrator nor the townspeople but on Miss Emily Grierson.)

> We did not say she was crazy then. We believed she had to do that. We remembered all the young men her father had driven away, and we knew that with nothing left, she would have to cling to that which had robbed her, as people will.

Writers gain a number of advantages with a first-person narrator. First, they are able to present incidents in a very convincing fashion. Readers are more willing to suspend disbelief and accept a statement such as "My sister changed a lot after that day" when it is presented as a personal account than when it is the impersonal observation of a third-person narrator. The first-person narrator also simplifies a writer's task of selecting details. Only the events and details that the narrator could have seen or experienced can logically be introduced into the story.

Another major advantage of first-person narrators is that their restricted view, as well as their own distinct perspectives, can create **irony**—a discrepancy between what a narrator says and what readers perceive to be true. Irony may be *dramatic, situational,* or *verbal.* **Dramatic irony** occurs when the narrator perceives less about the events he or she describes than the audience does. Dramatic irony occurs in the story "Greasy Lake" by T. Coraghessan Boyle (p. 341), when the narrator and his friends are involved in an attempted rape. Although readers are shocked by the events, the narrator never acknowledges the significance of his actions or understands the tragic consequences that might have resulted. **Situational irony** occurs when what happens is at odds with what the story leads readers to expect will happen; **verbal irony** occurs when the narrator says one thing but actually means another. "Gryphon" by Charles Baxter (p. 123) illustrates both situational and verbal irony. The setting of the story—a rural school—creates irony because it contrasts sharply with the unexpected events that unfold there. In addition, many of the narrator's comments have more meaning than they may seem to have. At the end of the story, for example, after the substitute, Miss Ferenczi, has been dismissed, the narrator relates another teacher's comment that life will now return to "normal" and their regular teacher will soon return to test them on their "knowledge." These comments are extremely ironic in light of all Miss Ferenczi has done to redefine the narrator's ideas about "normal" education.

Unreliable Narrators Sometimes first-person narrators may be self-serving, mistaken, confused, unstable, or even mad. These *unreliable narrators,* whether intentionally or unintentionally, misrepresent events and misdirect readers. In Edgar Allan Poe's "The Cask of Amontillado" (p. 180), for example, the narrator, Montresor, tells his story to justify a crime he committed fifty years before. Montresor's version of what happened and why is not accurate, and perceptive readers know it: His obvious self-deception, his sadistic manipulation of Fortunato, his detached description of the cold-blooded murder, and his lack of remorse lead readers to question his sanity (and, therefore, to distrust his version of events). This distrust creates an ironic distance between readers and narrator.

The narrator of Charlotte Perkins Gilman's "The Yellow Wall-Paper" (p. 155) is also an unreliable narrator. Suffering from "nervous depression," she unintentionally distorts the facts when she says that the shapes in the wallpaper of her bedroom are changing and moving. Moreover, she does not realize what is wrong with her or why, or how her husband's "good intentions" are hurting her. Readers, however, see the disparity between the narrator's interpretation of events and their own, and thus they realize the irony.

Some narrators are unreliable simply because they are naive. Because they are immature, sheltered, or innocent of evil, these narrators may not be aware of the full significance of the events they are relating. Readers, having the benefit of experience, interpret events differently from the way these narrators do. This ironic effect would be impossible if the stories were not presented in the first person. When we read a passage by a child narrator—such as the following from J. D. Salinger's novel *The Catcher in the Rye*—we are aware of the narrator's innocence, and we know his interpretation of events is flawed.

> Anyway, I keep picturing all these little kids playing some game in this big field of rye and all. Thousands of little kids, and nobody's around—nobody big, I mean—except me. And I'm standing on the edge of some crazy cliff. What I have to do, I have to catch everybody if they start to go over the cliff—I mean if they're running and they don't look where they're going I have to come out from somewhere and *catch* them. I'd just be the catcher in the rye. . . .

The irony in the preceding passage comes from our knowledge that the naive narrator, Holden Caulfield, cannot stop children from growing up. Ultimately, they all fall off the "crazy cliff" and mature into adults. His efforts to protect his sister and the other children from the dangers of adulthood are, therefore, doomed from the start.

A naive narrator's background can limit his or her ability to understand a situation. The narrator in Sherwood Anderson's "I'm a Fool," for example, lies to a rich girl he meets at a race track and as a result can never see her again. At the end of the story the boy laments the fact that he lied, believing that if he had not, he could have seen the girl again. The reader knows, however, that the narrator is deceiving himself, and that the social gap that separates the narrator and the girl can never be bridged.

Keep in mind that there is a difference between an unreliable narrator and a narrator whose perspective is limited. All first-person narrators are, by definition, limited because they present a situation as only one person sees it. In "In a Grove," a story by the Japanese writer Ryūnosuke Akutagawa, seven characters give different accounts of a murder. Some of the characters have an incomplete or incorrect understanding of the event, while others seem to be lying or bending the facts to suit their own ends. As readers, you should look for discrepancies between a narrator's view of events and your own sense of what has happened. Discovering that a story has an unreliable narrator enables you not only to question the truth of the narrative but also to recognize the irony inherent in the narrator's version of events. By doing so, you are able to gain a better sense of the story and to recognize something about the writer's purpose.

THIRD-PERSON NARRATOR

In addition to first-person narrators, writers can use **third-person** narrators who are not actually characters in the story. These narrators fall into three categories.

Omniscient Some third-person narrators are **omniscient** (all-knowing) narrators, moving at will from one character's mind to another. By doing so they not only reveal the thoughts of the individual characters, but also present a body of information that no single character could possibly know. One advantage of omniscient narrators is that they are objective and not flawed by the naïveté, dishonesty, gullibility, or mental instability that can characterize first-person narrators. In addition, because omniscient narrators are not characters in the story, their perception is not limited to what any one character can observe or comprehend. As a result, they can present a more effective overview of events and characters than can first-person narrators. Notice how the narrator of Nadine Gordimer's "Once Upon a Time" (p. 64) is able to give such an overview:

> In a house, in a suburb, in a city, there were a man and his wife who loved each other very much and were living happily ever after. They had a little boy, and they loved him very much. They had a cat and a dog that the little boy loved very much. They had a car and a caravan trailer for holidays, and a swimming-pool which was fenced so that the little boy and his playmates would not fall in and drown. They had a housemaid who was absolutely trustworthy and an itinerant gardener who was highly recommended by the neighbours. For when they began to live happily ever after they were warned, by that wise old witch, the husband's mother, not to take anyone off the street.

A certain type of omniscient point of view occurs when narrators not only move in and out of the minds of the characters but also in and out of a persona that speaks in the first person, directly addressing readers. This narrative technique was popular with writers such as Laurence

Sterne and Henry Fielding during the eighteenth century, when the novel was a new literary form. It enabled writers to present themselves as masters of artifice, able to know and control all aspects of experience. Few contemporary writers would give themselves the license that Henry Fielding does in the following passage from *Tom Jones:*

> And true it was that [Mr. Alworthy] did many of these things; but had he done nothing more I should have left him to have recorded his own merit on some fair freestone over the door of that hospital. Matters of a much more extraordinary kind are to be the subject of this history, or I should grossly misspend my time in writing so voluminous a work; and you my sagacious friend, might with equal profit and pleasure travel through some pages which certain droll authors have been facetiously pleased to call *The History of England.*

A contemporary example of this type of omniscient point of view occurs in Ursula K. LeGuin's "The Ones Who Walk Away from Omelas." This story presents a description of a city that in the narrator's words is "like a city in a fairy tale." As the story proceeds, however, the description of Omelas changes, and the narrator's perspective changes as well: "Do you believe? Do you accept the festival, the city, the joy? No? Then let me describe one more thing." In this way the narrator underscores the ironic theme of the story, which suggests the impossibility of ideal societies and the inability of human beings to achieve happiness.

Limited Omniscient Third-person narrators can have **limited omniscience,** focusing on only what a single major or minor character experiences. In other words, events are limited to one character's perspective, and nothing is revealed that the character does not see, hear, feel, or think. Andy in David Michael Kaplan's "Doe Season" (p. 298) is just such a limited-focus character. Limited omniscient narrators, like all third-person narrators, have certain advantages over first-person narrators—for example, greater flexibility. When a writer uses a first-person narrator, the narrator's personality and speech color the story, creating a personal or even idiosyncratic narrative. Also, the narrator's character flaws or lack of knowledge may limit his or her awareness of the significance of events. Limited omniscient narrators take readers into a particular character's mind just as a first-person narrator does, but without the limitations of the first-person narrator's subjectivity, self-deception, or naïveté. In short, because limited omniscient narrators speak from outside a character, they are reliable; they maintain an objective distance from events, giving readers an accurate version of what happened. In the following example from Anne Tyler's "Teenage Wasteland" (p. 504), the limited omniscient narrator presents the story from the point of view of a single character, Daisy:

> Daisy and Matt sat silent, shocked. Matt rubbed his forehead with his fingertips. Imagine, Daisy thought, how they must look to Mr. Lanham: an overweight housewife in a cotton dress and a too-tall, too-thin insurance

> agent in a baggy, frayed suit. Failures, both of them—the kind of people who are hurrying to catch up, missing the point of things that everyone else grasps at once. She wished she'd worn nylons instead of knee socks.

Notice how the narrative point of view in the above example gives readers the impression that they are standing off to the side watching Daisy and her husband Matt. At the same time we get this objective view of the scene, however, we are able to see into the mind of a major character.

Objective Third-person narrators can also use an **objective** (or dramatic) point of view, remaining entirely outside the characters' minds, recording the action as a camera would. With objective narrators, events unfold the way they would in a play or a movie. Narrators tell the story only by reproducing dialogue and by providing descriptions of the action. They do not present the thoughts of characters or offer insight into their actions or motivations. Thus they allow readers to interpret the actions of the characters without any interference. Ernest Hemingway uses the objective point of view in the following passage from his short story "A Clean, Well-Lighted Place" (p. 225):

> The waiter took the brandy bottle and another saucer from the counter inside the café and marched out to the old man's table. He put down the saucer and poured the glass full of brandy.
>
> "You should have killed yourself last week," he said to the deaf man. The old man motioned with his finger. "A little more," he said. The waiter poured on into the glass so that the brandy slopped over and ran down the stem into the top saucer of the pile. "Thank you," the old man said. The waiter took the bottle back inside the café. He sat down at the table with his colleague again.

The narrator of this story is distant, seemingly emotionless. The narrative perspective is consistent with the author's purpose: For Hemingway the attitude of the narrator reflects the stunned, almost anesthetized condition of people in the modern world.

SELECTING AN APPROPRIATE POINT OF VIEW

Because of the limitations of length, writers of short stories often maintain a consistent point of view, but there is no rule that says they must. Although they may maintain one dominant point of view, writers of fiction frequently mix various points of view to achieve complexity and depth. The main criterion that writers use when they decide on a point of view is how the distance they maintain from their material enhances the effect of their narrative. For example, consider this passage from "Doe Season."

Limited Omniscient Point of View

> They were always the same woods, she thought sleepily as they drove through the early morning darkness—deep and immense, covered with

> yesterday's snowfall, which had frozen overnight. They were the same woods that lay behind her house, *and they stretch all the way to here,* she thought, *for miles and miles, longer than I could walk in a day, or a week even, but they are still the same woods.* The thought made her feel good: it was like thinking of God; it was like thinking of the space between here and the moon; it was like thinking of all the foreign countries from her geography book where even now, Andy knew, people were going to bed, while they—she and her father and Charlie Spoon and Mac, Charlie's eleven-year-old son—were driving deeper into the Pennsylvania countryside, to go hunting.
>
> They had risen before dawn. Her mother, yawning and not trying to hide her sleepiness, cooked them eggs and French toast. Her father smoked a cigarette and flicked ashes into his saucer while Andy listened, wondering *Why doesn't he come?* and *Won't he ever come?* until at last a car pulled into the graveled drive and honked. "That will be Charlie Spoon," her father said; he always said "Charlie Spoon," even though his real name was Spreun, because Charlie was, in a sense, shaped like a spoon, with a large head and a narrow waist and chest.

In the preceding passage, David Michael Kaplan uses a third-person limited omniscient narrator to tell the story of Andy, a nine-year-old girl who is going hunting with her father for the first time. This point of view has the advantage of allowing the narrator to give readers information about Andy that she herself is too immature or unsophisticated to know. In addition to presenting the thoughts of the child, the third-person narrator makes connections between ideas and offers a level of language and a degree of insight that readers would not accept from Andy as a first-person narrator. Consider how different the passage would be if it were narrated by Andy.

First-Person Point of View

> "They are always the same woods," I thought sleepily as we drove through the early morning darkness—deep and immense, covered with yesterday's snowfall, which had frozen overnight. "They are the same woods that lie behind my house, and they stretch all the way to here," I thought, "for miles and miles, longer than I could walk in a day, or a week even, but they are still the same woods." It made me feel good: I thought, "It is like thinking of God; it is like thinking of the space between here and the moon; it is like thinking of all the foreign countries from my geography book where even now, I know, people are going to bed, while we—my father and I and Charlie Spoon and Mac, Charlie's eleven-year-old son—are driving deeper into the Pennsylvania countryside, to go hunting."

As a first-person narrator, Andy should be restricted to only those observations that a nine-year-old child could reasonably make. For this reason, the language and scope of the rewritten passage strike us as being too sophisticated for the narrator. Thus a first-person point of view would severely limit Kaplan's ability to develop the central character and the themes of the story. Of course Kaplan could have gotten around this problem by having Andy tell her story as an adult looking back at a childhood experience—James Joyce uses this technique in "Araby" (p. 219), and Alberto Alvaro Rios uses it in "The Secret Lion" (p. 37). The adult could then explore ideas that the child could not be expected to consider or to understand. However, the limited omniscient perspective enables the narrator to maintain some distance while still focusing on the thoughts, motivations, and reactions of the child.

Kaplan had other options as well. For example, he could have used an omniscient narrator to tell his story. In this case, the narrator would be free to reveal and comment on not only Andy's thoughts but also those of her father, and possibly even of her mother and Charlie Spoon. Notice in the following passage how the omniscient narrator interprets the behavior of the characters and tells what each one is thinking.

Omniscient Point of View

They were always the same woods, she thought sleepily as they drove through the early morning darkness—deep and immense, covered with yesterday's snowfall, which had frozen overnight. They were the same woods that lay behind her house, *and they stretch all the way to here,* she thought, *for miles and miles, longer than I could walk in a day, or a week even, but they are still the same woods.*

They had risen before dawn. The mother, yawning and not trying to hide her sleepiness, cooked them eggs and French toast. She looked at her husband and her daughter and wondered if she was doing the right thing by allowing them to go hunting together. "After all," she thought, "he's not the most careful individual. Will he watch her? Make sure that no harm comes to her?"

The father smoked a cigarette and flicked ashes into his saucer. He was listening to the sounds of the early morning. "I know everything will be all right," he thought. "It's about time Andy went hunting. When I was her age. . . ." Andy listened, wondering *Why doesn't he come?* and *Won't he ever come?* until at last a car pulled into the graveled drive and honked. Suddenly the father cocked his head and said, "That will be Charlie Spoon."

Andy thought it was funny that her father called Charlie "Spoon" even though his real name was Spreun, because Charlie was, in a sense, shaped like a spoon, with a large head and a narrow waist and chest.

Certainly the wide scope of this point of view provides a great deal of information about the characters, but it also distracts readers and causes the story to lose its focus.

Finally, Kaplan could have used an objective narrator. This point of view would eliminate all interpretation by the narrator and force readers to make judgments solely on the basis of what the characters say and do. Here is an example of the passage from "Doe Season" presented from this point of view.

Objective Point of View

> Andy sat sleepily staring into her cereal. She played with the dry flakes of bran as they floated in the surface of the milk.
>
> Andy's mother, yawning, cooked them eggs and French toast. She looked at her husband and her daughter, paused for a second, and then went about what she was doing.
>
> Andy's father smoked a cigarette and flicked ashes into his saucer. He looked out the window and said, "I wonder where Charlie Spoon is?"
>
> Andy squirmed restlessly and repeatedly looked up at the clock that hung above the stove.

The main disadvantage of this point of view is that it creates a great deal of distance between the characters and the readers. Instead of gaining the intimate knowledge of Andy—knowledge even greater than she herself has—that the limited third-person account provides, the reader must infer what she thinks and feels without any help from the narrator.

As you can see, the point of view Kaplan uses in "Doe Season" is well suited to his purpose. Ideally, writers choose the point of view that best enables them to achieve their objectives. If they want to create an intimate, subjective portrait of a character, they will employ a first-person narrator. If they want to have a great deal of freedom in telling their story, they will use an omniscient narrator. A limited omniscient narrator enables writers to maintain the focus on a single individual while commenting on the action. And finally, the objective point of view allows writers to remove the narrator from the story and present events in a distant, almost emotionless fashion.

First-Person Narrator *(I or we)*

- *Major character telling his or her own story* "Every morning I lay on the floor in the front parlour watching her door." (James Joyce, "Araby")
- *Minor character as witness or nonparticipant* "And so she died. . . . We did not even know she was sick; we had long since given up trying to get information. . . ." (William Faulkner, "A Rose for Emily")

Third-Person Narrator *(he, she, it, or they)*

- *Omniscient—able to move at will from character to character and comment about them* "In a house, in a suburb, in a city, there were a man and his wife who loved each other very much. . . ." (Nadine Gordimer, "Once Upon a Time")
- *Limited Omniscient—restricts focus to a single character* "The wagon went on. He did not know where they were going." (William Faulkner, "Barn Burning")

- *Objective (Dramatic)—simply reports the dialogue and the actions of characters* "'You'll be drunk,' the waiter said. The old man looked at him. The waiter went away." (Ernest Hemingway, "A Clean, Well-Lighted Place")

A FINAL NOTE

One other option for writers is the **second-person** point of view, the consistent use of *you* and the imperative mood throughout the story. This unusual technique is used by Lorrie Moore in "How to Talk to Your Mother (Notes)" (p. 78):

> You have seen too many Hollywood musicals. You have seen too many people singing in public places and you assume you can do it, too. Practice. Your teacher asks you a question. You warble back: "The answer to number two is twelve." Most of the class laughs at you. . . .

Here Moore uses the second person to address an unspecified audience. The "real" narrator hides behind the protective *you* and gives the appearance of not talking about herself. By using this technique, the narrator attempts to distance herself psychologically from the action and perhaps to abdicate responsibility for what she is saying.

Checklist for Writing about Point of View

- What is the dominant point of view from which the story is told?
- Is the narrator of the story a participant in the story or just a witness?
- Does the story's point of view create irony?
- If the story has a first-person narrator, is the narrator reliable or unreliable? Are there any inconsistencies in the narrator's presentation of the story?
- How do you explain any distortions of fact that you detect? Are these distortions intentional or unintentional?
- If the story has a third-person narrator, is he or she omniscient? Does he or she have limited omniscience? Is he or she objective?
- What are the advantages of the story's point of view? How does the point of view accomplish the author's purpose?
- Is there anything unusual about the point of view?
- Does the point of view remain constant throughout the story, or does it shift? If it does shift, why?
- How might a different point of view change the story?

Edgar Allan Poe (1809–1849) profoundly influenced many corners of the literary world. His tales of psychological terror and the macabre, his hauntingly musical lyric poems, and his writings on the craft of poetry and short-story writing affected the development of symbolic fiction, the modern detective or mystery story, and the gothic horror tale. In most of Poe's horror tales (as in "The Cask of Amontillado"), readers vicariously "live" the story through the first-person narrator who tells the tale.

Poe was born in 1809, the son of a talented English-born actress who, deserted by her actor husband, died of tuberculosis before her son's third birthday. Though raised in material comfort by foster parents in Richmond, Virginia, Poe's life was increasingly uncertain: His foster mother loved him, but her husband became antagonistic. He kept the young Poe so short of money at the University of Virginia (and later at West Point) that Poe gambled to raise money for food and clothing. Then, debt-ridden, he left school altogether.

Poe found work as a magazine editor, gaining recognition as a perceptive (if sometimes vitriolic) literary critic. In 1836, he married his frail, thirteen-year-old cousin, Virginia Clemm. Poe produced many of his most famous stories and poems in the next few years, working feverishly to support his tubercular wife; but although his stories were widely admired, financial success never came. His wife died in 1847. Less than two years later, Poe was found barely conscious in a Baltimore street after a mysterious disappearance; three days later, he was dead at age forty.

Edgar Allan Poe

THE CASK OF AMONTILLADO

(1846)

The thousand injuries of Fortunato I had borne as I best could, but when he ventured upon insult I vowed revenge. You, who so well know the nature of my soul, will not suppose, however, that I gave utterance to a threat. *At length* I would be avenged; this was a point definitely settled—but the very definitiveness with which it was resolved precluded the idea of risk. I must not only punish but punish with impunity. A wrong is unredressed when retribution overtakes its redresser. It is equally unredressed when the avenger fails to make himself felt as such to him who has done the wrong.

It must be understood that neither by word nor deed had I given Fortunato cause to doubt my good will. I continued, as was my wont, to smile in his face, and he did not perceive that my smile *now* was at the thought of his immolation.

He had a weak point—this Fortunato—although in other regards he was a man to be respected and even feared. He prided himself on his connoisseurship in wine. Few Italians have the true virtuoso spirit. For the most part their enthusiasm is adopted to suit the time and opportunity, to practise imposture upon the British and Austrian *millionaires*. In painting and gemmary, Fortunato, like his countrymen, was a quack, but in the matter of old wines he was sincere. In this respect I did not differ from him materially;—I was skillful in the Italian vintages myself, and bought largely whenever I could.

It was about dusk, one evening during the supreme madness of the carnival season, that I encountered my friend. He accosted me with excessive warmth, for he had been drinking much. The man wore motley. He had on a tight-fitting parti-striped dress, and his head was surmounted by the conical cap and bells. I was so pleased to see him that I thought I should never have done wringing his hand.

I said to him—"My dear Fortunato, you are luckily met. How remarkably well you are looking to-day. But I have received a pipe[1] of what passes for Amontillado,[2] and I have my doubts."

"How?" said he. "Amontillado? A pipe? Impossible! And in the middle of the carnival!"

"I have my doubts," I replied; "and I was silly enough to pay the full Amontillado price without consulting you in the matter. You were not to be found, and I was fearful of losing a bargain."

"Amontillado!"

"I have my doubts."

"Amontillado!"

"And I must satisfy them."

"Amontillado!"

"As you are engaged, I am on my way to Luchresi. If any one has a critical turn it is he. He will tell me—"

"Luchresi cannot tell Amontillado from Sherry."

"And yet some fools will have it that his taste is a match for your own."

"Come, let us go."

"Whither?"

"To your vaults."

"My friend, no; I will not impose upon your good nature. I perceive you have an engagement. Luchresi—"

"I have no engagement;—come."

"My friend, no. It is not the engagement, but the severe cold with which I perceive you are afflicted. The vaults are insufferably damp. They are encrusted with nitre."

"Let us go, nevertheless. The cold is merely nothing. Amontillado! You have been imposed upon. And as for Luchresi, he cannot distinguish Sherry from Amontillado."

---

[1] In the United States and England, a cask containing a volume equal to 126 gallons.

[2] A pale, dry sherry; literally, a wine "from Montilla" (Spain).

Thus speaking, Fortunato possessed himself of my arm; and putting on a mask of black silk and drawing a *roquelaire*[3] closely about my person, I suffered him to hurry me to my palazzo.

There were no attendants at home; they had absconded to make merry in honor of the time. I had told them that I should not return until the morning, and had given them explicit orders not to stir from the house. These orders were sufficient, I well knew, to insure their immediate disappearance, one and all, as soon as my back was turned.

I took from their sconces two flambeaux, and giving one to Fortunato, bowed him through several suites of rooms to the archway that led into the vaults. I passed down a long and winding staircase, requesting him to be cautious as he followed. We came at length to the foot of the descent, and stood together upon the damp ground of the catacombs of the Montresors.

The gait of my friend was unsteady, and the bells upon his cap jingled as he strode.

"The pipe," he said.

"It is farther on," said I; "but observe the white web-work which gleams from these cavern walls."

He turned towards me, and looked into my eyes with two filmy orbs that distilled the rheum of intoxication.

"Nitre?" he asked at length.

"Nitre," I replied. "How long have you had that cough?"

"Ugh! ugh! ugh!—ugh! ugh! ugh!—ugh! ugh! ugh!—ugh! ugh! ugh!—ugh! ugh! ugh!"

My poor friend found it impossible to reply for many minutes.

"It is nothing," he said at last.

"Come," I said, with decision, "we will go back; your health is precious. You are rich, respected, admired, beloved; you are happy, as once I was. You are a man to be missed. For me it is no matter. We will go back; you will be ill, and I cannot be responsible. Besides, there is Luchresi—"

"Enough," he said; "the cough is a mere nothing; it will not kill me. I shall not die of a cough."

"True—true," I replied; "and, indeed, I had no intention of alarming you unnecessarily—but you should use all proper caution. A draught of this Medoc[4] will defend us from the damps."

Here I knocked off the neck of a bottle which I drew from a long row of its fellows that lay upon the mould.

"Drink," I said, presenting him the wine.

He raised it to his lips with a leer. He paused and nodded to me familiarly, while his bells jingled.

"I drink," he said, "to the buried that repose around us."

---

[3] A short cloak.

[4] A claret from the Médoc, near Bordeaux, France.

"And I to your long life."

He again took my arm, and we proceeded.

"These vaults," he said, "are extensive."

"The Montresors," I replied, "were a great and numerous family."

"I forget your arms."

"A huge human foot d'or, in a field azure; the foot crushes a serpent rampant whose fangs are imbedded in the heel."

"And the motto?"

"*Nemo me impune lacessit.*"[5]

"Good!" he said.

The wine sparkled in his eyes and the bells jingled. My own fancy grew warm with the Medoc. We had passed through long walls of piled skeletons, with casks and puncheons intermingling, into the inmost recesses of the catacombs. I paused again, and this time I made bold to seize Fortunato by an arm above the elbow.

"The nitre!" I said; "see, it increases. It hangs like moss upon the vaults. We are below the river's bed. The drops of moisture trickle among the bones. Come, we will go back ere it is too late. Your cough—"

"It is nothing," he said; "let us go on. But first, another draught of the Medoc."

I broke and reached him a flagon of De Grâve.[6] He emptied it at a breath. His eyes flashed with a fierce light. He laughed and threw the bottle upwards with a gesticulation I did not understand.

I looked at him in surprise. He repeated the movement—a grotesque one.

"You do not comprehend?" he said.

"Not I," I replied.

"Then you are not of the brotherhood."

"How?"

"You are not of the masons."[7]

"Yes, yes," I said; "yes, yes."

"You? Impossible! A mason?"

"A mason," I replied.

"A sign," he said, "a sign."

"It is this," I answered, producing from beneath the folds of my *roquelaire* a trowel.

"You jest," he exclaimed, recoiling a few paces. "But let us proceed to the Amontillado."

"Be it so," I said, replacing the tool beneath the cloak and again offering him my arm. He leaned upon it heavily. We continued our route in search of the Amontillado. We passed through a range of low arches,

---

[5] "No one insults me with impunity"; this is the legend of the royal arms of Scotland.

[6] Correctly, "Gráves," a light wine from the Bordeaux area.

[7] Freemasons (members of a secret fraternity). The trowel is a symbol of their alleged origin as a guild of stonemasons.

descended, passed on, and descending again, arrived at a deep crypt, in which the foulness of the air caused our flambeaux rather to glow than flame.

At the most remote end of the crypt there appeared another less spacious. Its walls had been lined with human remains, piled to the vault overhead, in the fashion of the great catacombs of Paris. Three sides of this interior crypt were still ornamented in this manner. From the fourth side the bones had been thrown down, and lay promiscuously upon the earth, forming at one point a mound of some size. Within the wall thus exposed by the displacing of the bones, we perceived a still interior crypt or recess, in depth about four feet, in width three, in height six or seven. It seemed to have been constructed for no especial use within itself, but formed merely the interval between two of the colossal supports of the roof of the catacombs, and was backed by one of their circumscribing walls of solid granite.

It was in vain that Fortunato, uplifting his dull torch, endeavored to pry into the depth of the recess. Its termination the feeble light did not enable us to see.

"Proceed," I said; "herein is the Amontillado. As for Luchresi—"

"He is an ignoramus," interrupted my friend, as he stepped unsteadily forward, while I followed immediately at his heels. In an instant he had reached the extremity of the niche, and finding his progress arrested by the rock, stood stupidly bewildered. A moment more and I had fettered him to the granite. In its surface were two iron staples, distant from each other about two feet, horizontally. From one of these depended a short chain, from the other a padlock. Throwing the links about his waist, it was but the work of a few seconds to secure it. He was too much astounded to resist. Withdrawing the key I stepped back from the recess.

"Pass your hand," I said, "over the wall; you cannot help feeling the nitre. Indeed, it is *very* damp. Once more let me *implore* you to return. No? Then I must positively leave you. But I must first render you all the little attentions in my power."

"The Amontillado!" ejaculated my friend, not yet recovered from his astonishment.

"True," I replied; "the Amontillado."

As I said these words I busied myself among the pile of bones of which I have before spoken. Throwing them aside, I soon uncovered a quantity of building stone and mortar. With these materials and with the aid of my trowel, I began vigorously to wall up the entrance of the niche.

I had scarcely laid the first tier of the masonry when I discovered that the intoxication of Fortunato had in a great measure worn off. The earliest indication I had of this was a low moaning cry from the depth of the recess. It was *not* the cry of a drunken man. There was a long and obstinate silence. I laid the second tier, and the third, and the fourth; and then I heard the furious vibrations of the chain. The noise lasted for several minutes, during which, that I might hearken to it with the more satisfaction, I ceased my labors and sat down upon the bones. When at last the clanking subsided, I resumed the trowel, and finished without interruption the fifth, the sixth, and the seventh tier. The wall was now nearly upon a level with my breast. I again paused, and holding the flambeaux over the mason-work, threw a few feeble rays upon the figure within.

A succession of loud and shrill screams, bursting suddenly from the throat of the chained form, seemed to thrust me violently back. For a brief moment I hesitated, I trembled. Unsheathing my rapier, I began to grope with it about the recess; but the thought of an instant reassured me. I placed my hand upon the solid fabric of the catacombs, and felt satisfied. I reapproached the wall; I replied to the yells of him who clamoured. I re-echoed, I aided, I surpassed them in volume and in strength. I did this, and the clamourer grew still.

It was now midnight, and my task was drawing to a close. I had completed the eighth, the ninth and the tenth tier. I had finished a portion of the last and the eleventh; there remained but a single stone to be fitted and plastered in. I struggled with its weight; I placed it partially in its destined position. But now there came from out the niche a low laugh that erected the hairs upon my head. It was succeeded by a sad voice, which I had difficulty in recognizing as that of the noble Fortunato. The voice said—

"Ha! ha! ha!—he! he! he!—a very good joke, indeed—an excellent jest. We will have many a rich laugh about it at the palazzo—he! he! he!—over our wine—he! he! he!"

"The Amontillado!" I said.

"He! he! he!—he! he! he!—yes, the Amontillado. But is it not getting late? Will not they be awaiting us at the palazzo, the Lady Fortunato and the rest? Let us be gone."

"Yes," I said, "let us be gone."

"For the love of God, Montresor!"

"Yes," I said, "for the love of God."

But to these words I hearkened in vain for a reply. I grew impatient. I called aloud—

"Fortunato!"

No answer. I called again—

"Fortunato!"

No answer still. I thrust a torch through the remaining aperture and let it fall within. There came forth in return only a jingling of the bells. My heart grew sick; it was the dampness of the catacombs that made it so. I hastened to make an end of my labour. I forced the last stone into its position; I plastered it up. Against the new masonry I re-erected the old rampart of bones. For the half of a century no mortal has disturbed them. *In pace requiescat!*[8] ◇

---

[8] "May he rest in peace."

READING AND REACTING

1. Montresor cites a "thousand injuries" and an "insult" as his motivation for murdering Fortunato. Given what you learn about the two men during the course of the story, what do you suppose the "injuries" and "insult" might be?
2. Is Montresor a reliable narrator? If not, what makes you distrust his version of events?
3. What is Montresor's concept of honor? Is Montresor's concept of personal honor consistent or inconsistent with the values of contemporary American society? How relevant are the story's ideas about revenge and guilt to our society? Explain.
4. Does Fortunato ever understand why Montresor hates him? What is Fortunato's attitude toward Montresor?
5. What is the significance of Montresor's family coat of arms and motto? What is the significance of Fortunato's costume?
6. In what ways does Montresor manipulate Fortunato? What weaknesses of Fortunato does Montresor exploit?
7. Why does Montresor tell his story fifty years after the murder? To whom do you think he might be telling his story?
8. How does the setting intensify the story's horror?
9. **JOURNAL ENTRY:** Do you think that the use of a first-person point of view makes you more sympathetic toward Montresor than you would be if his story were told by a third-person narrator? Why or why not?

William Faulkner (1897–1962) (See "A Rose for Emily," p. 70, for biographical information.)

"Barn Burning" (1939) marks the first appearance of the Snopes clan in Faulkner's fiction. These crafty and unappealing tenant farmers and traders run roughshod over the aristocratic families of Yoknapatawpha County in three Faulkner novels: *The Hamlet* (1940), *The Town* (1957), and *The Mansion* (1959). According to Ben Wasson in *Count No 'Count,* Faulkner once told a friend that "somebody said I was a genius writer. The only thing I'd claim genius for is thinking up that name *Snopes.*" In Southern literary circles, at least, the name "Snopes" still serves as a shorthand term for the graceless and greedy (but frequently successful) opportunists of the "New South."

William Faulkner

BARN BURNING

(1939)

The store in which the Justice of the Peace's court was sitting smelled of cheese. The boy, crouched on his nail keg at the back of the crowded room, knew he smelled cheese, and more: from where he sat he could see the ranked shelves close-packed with the solid, squat, dynamic shapes of tin cans whose labels his stomach read, not from the lettering which meant nothing to his mind but from the scarlet devils and the silver curve of fish—this, the cheese which he knew he smelled and the hermetic meat[1] which his intestines believed he smelled coming in intermittent gusts momentary and brief between the other constant one, the smell and sense just a little of fear because mostly of despair and grief, the old fierce pull of blood. He could not see the table where the Justice sat and before which his father and his father's enemy (*our enemy* he thought in that despair; *ourn! mine and hisn both! He's my father!*) stood, but he could hear them, the two of them that is, because his father had said no word yet:

"But what proof have you, Mr. Harris?"

"I told you. The hog got into my corn. I caught it up and sent it back to him. He had no fence that would hold it. I told him so, warned him. The next time I put the hog in my pen. When he came to get it I gave him enough wire to patch up his pen. The next time I put the hog up and kept it. I rode down to his house and saw the wire I gave him still rolled on to the spool in his yard. I told him he could have the hog when he paid me a dollar pound fee. That evening a nigger came with the dollar and got the hog. He was a strange nigger. He said, 'He say to tell you wood and hay kin burn.' I said, 'What?' 'That whut he say to tell you,' the nigger said. 'Wood and hay kin burn.' That night my barn burned. I got the stock out but I lost the barn."

"Where is the nigger? Have you got him?"

5 "He was a strange nigger, I tell you. I don't know what became of him."

"But that's not proof. Don't you see that's not proof?"

"Get that boy up here. He knows." For a moment the boy thought too that the man meant his older brother until Harris said, "Not him. The little one. The boy," and, crouching, small for his age, small and wiry like his father, in patched and faded jeans even too small for him, with straight, uncombed, brown hair and eyes gray and wild as storm scud, he saw the men between himself and the table part and become a lane of grim faces, at the end of which he saw the Justice, a shabby, collarless, graying man in spectacles, beckoning him. He felt no floor

[1] Canned meat.

under his bare feet; he seemed to walk beneath the palpable weight of the grim turning faces. His father, stiff in his black Sunday coat donned not for the trial but for the moving, did not even look at him. *He aims for me to lie,* he thought, again with that frantic grief and despair. *And I will have to do hit.*

"What's your name, boy?" the Justice said.

"Colonel Sartoris Snopes," the boy whispered.

"Hey?" the Justice said. "Talk louder. Colonel Sartoris? I reckon anybody named for Colonel Sartoris in this country can't help but tell the truth, can they?" The boy said nothing. *Enemy! Enemy!* he thought; for a moment he could not even see, could not see that the Justice's face was kindly nor discern that his voice was troubled when he spoke to the man named Harris: "Do you want me to question this boy?" But he could hear, and during those subsequent long seconds while there was absolutely no sound in the crowded little room save that of quiet and intent breathing it was as if he had swung outward at the end of a grape vine, over a ravine, and at the top of the swing had been caught in a prolonged instant of mesmerized gravity, weightless in time.

"No!" Harris said violently, explosively. "Damnation! Send him out of here!" Now time, the fluid world, rushed beneath him again, the voices coming to him again through the smell of cheese and sealed meat, the fear and despair and the old grief of blood:

"This case is closed. I can't find against you, Snopes, but I can give you advice. Leave this country and don't come back to it."

His father spoke for the first time, his voice cold and harsh, level, without emphasis: "I aim to. I don't figure to stay in a country among people who . . ." he said something unprintable and vile, addressed to no one.

"That'll do," the Justice said. "Take your wagon and get out of this country before dark. Case dismissed."

His father turned, and he followed the stiff black coat, the wiry figure walking a little stiffly from where a Confederate provost's man's[2] musket ball had taken him in the heel on a stolen horse thirty years ago, followed the two backs now, since his older brother had appeared from somewhere in the crowd, no taller than the father but thicker, chewing tobacco steadily, between the two lines of grim-faced men and out of the store and across the worn gallery and down the sagging steps and among the dogs and half-grown boys in the mild May dust, where as he passed a voice hissed:

"Barn burner!"

Again he could not see, whirling; there was a face in a red haze, moonlike, bigger than the full moon, the owner of it half again his size, he leaping in the red haze toward the face, feeling no blow, feeling no shock when his head struck the earth, scrabbling up and leaping again,

---

[2] Military policeman.

feeling no blow this time either and tasting no blood, scrabbling up to see the other boy in full flight and himself already leaping into pursuit as his father's hand jerked him back, the harsh, cold voice speaking above him: "Go get in the wagon."

It stood in a grove of locusts and mulberries across the road. His two hulking sisters in their Sunday dresses and his mother and her sister in calico and sunbonnets were already in it, sitting on and among the sorry residue of the dozen and more movings which even the boy could remember—the battered stove, the broken beds and chairs, the clock inlaid with mother-of-pearl, which would not run, stopped at some fourteen minutes past two o'clock of a dead and forgotten day and time, which had been his mother's dowry. She was crying, though when she saw him she drew her sleeve across her face and began to descend from the wagon. "Get back," the father said.

"He's hurt. I got to get some water and wash his . . ."

"Get back in the wagon," his father said. He got in too, over the tailgate. His father mounted to the seat where the older brother already sat and struck the gaunt mules two savage blows with the peeled willow, but without heat. It was not even sadistic; it was exactly that same quality which in later years would cause his descendants to overrun the engine before putting a motor car into motion, striking and reining back in the same movement. The wagon went on, the store with its quiet crowd of grimly watching men dropped behind; a curve in the road hid it. *Forever* he thought. *Maybe he's done satisfied now, now that he has* . . . stopping himself, not to say it aloud even to himself. His mother's hand touched his shoulder.

"Does hit hurt?" she said.

"Naw," he said. "Hit don't hurt. Lemme be."

"Can't you wipe some of the blood off before hit dries?"

"I'll wash to-night," he said. "Lemme be, I tell you."

The wagon went on. He did not know where they were going. None of them ever did or ever asked, because it was always somewhere, always a house of sorts waiting for them a day or two days or even three days away. Likely his father had already arranged to make a crop on another farm before he . . . Again he had to stop himself. He (the father) always did. There was something about his wolf-like independence and even courage when the advantage was at least neutral which impressed strangers, as if they got from his latent ravening ferocity not so much a sense of dependability as a feeling that his ferocious conviction in the rightness of his own actions would be of advantage to all whose interest lay with his.

That night they camped, in a grove of oaks and beeches where a spring ran. The nights were still cool and they had a fire against it, of a rail lifted from a nearby fence and cut into lengths—a small fire, neat, niggard almost, a shrewd fire; such fires were his father's habit and custom always, even in freezing weather. Older, the boy might have remarked this and wondered why not a big one; why should not a man who had not only seen the waste and extravagance of war, but who had in his blood an inherent voracious prodigality with material not his own, have burned everything in sight? Then he might have gone a step farther and thought that that was the reason: that niggard blaze was the living fruit of nights passed during those four years in the woods hiding from all men, blue or gray, with his strings of horses (captured horses, he called them). And older still, he might have divined the true reason: that the element of fire spoke to some deep mainspring of his father's being, as the element of steel or of powder spoke to other men, as the one weapon for the preservation of integrity, else breath were not worth the breathing, and hence to be regarded with respect and used with discretion.

But he did not think this now and he had seen those same niggard blazes all his life. He merely ate his supper beside it and was already half asleep over his iron plate when his father called him, and once more he followed the stiff back, the stiff and ruthless limp, up the slope and on to the starlit road where, turning, he could see his father against the stars but without face or depth—a shape black, flat, and bloodless as though cut from tin in the iron folds of the frockcoat which had not been made for him, the voice harsh like tin and without heat like tin:

"You were fixing to tell them. You would have told him." He didn't answer. His father struck him with the flat of his hand on the side of the head, hard but without heat, exactly as he had struck the two mules at the store, exactly as he would strike either of them with any stick in order to kill a horse fly, his voice still without fear or anger: "You're getting to be a man. You got to learn. You got to learn to stick to your own blood or you ain't going to have any blood to stick to you. Do you think either of them, any man there this morning, would? Don't you know all they wanted was a chance to get at me because they knew I had them beat? Eh?" Later, twenty years later, he was to tell himself, "If I had said they wanted only truth, justice, he would have hit me again." But now he said nothing. He was not crying. He just stood there. "Answer me," his father said.

"Yes," he whispered. His father turned.

"Get on to bed. We'll be there tomorrow."

Tomorrow they were there. In the early afternoon the wagon stopped before a paintless two-room house identical almost with the dozen others it had stopped before even in the boy's ten years, and again, as on the other dozen occasions, his mother and aunt got down and began to unload the wagon, although his two sisters and his father and brother had not moved.

"Likely hit ain't fitten for hawgs," one of the sisters said.

"Nevertheless, fit it will and you'll hog it and like it," his father said. "Get out of them chairs and help your Ma unload."

The two sisters got down, big, bovine, in a flutter of cheap ribbons; one of them drew from the jumbled wagon bed a battered lantern, the other a worn broom. His father handed the reins to the older son and began to climb stiffly over the wheel. "When they get unloaded, take the team to the barn and feed them." Then he said, and at first the boy thought he was still speaking to his brother: "Come with me."

"Me?" he said.

"Yes," his father said. "You."

"Abner," his mother said. His father paused and looked back—the harsh level stare beneath the shaggy, graying, irascible brows.

"I reckon I'll have a word with the man that aims to begin tomorrow owning me body and soul for the next eight months."

They went back up the road. A week ago—or before last night, that is—he would have asked where they were going, but not now. His father had struck him before last night but never before had he paused afterward to explain why; it was as if the blow and the following calm, outrageous voice still rang, repercussed, divulging nothing to him save the terrible handicap of being young, the light weight of his few years, just heavy enough to prevent his soaring free of the world as it seemed to be ordered but not heavy enough to keep him footed solid in it, to resist it and try to change the course of its events.

Presently he could see the grove of oaks and cedars and the other flowering trees and shrubs, where the house would be, though not the house yet. They walked beside a fence massed with honeysuckle and Cherokee roses and came to a gate swinging open between two brick pillars, and now, beyond a sweep of drive, he saw the house for the first time and at that instant he forgot his father and the terror and despair both, and even when he remembered his father again (who had not stopped) the terror and despair did not return. Because, for all the twelve movings, they had sojourned until now in a poor country, a land of small farms and fields and houses, and he had never seen a house like this before. *Hit's big as a courthouse* he thought quietly, with a surge of peace and joy whose reason he could not have thought into words, being too young for that: *They are safe from him. People whose lives are a part of this peace and dignity are beyond his touch, he no more to them than a buzzing wasp: capable of stinging for a little moment but that's all; the spell of this peace and dignity rendering even the barns and stable and cribs which belong to it impervious to the puny flames he might contrive* . . . this, the peace and joy, ebbing for an instant as he looked again at the stiff black back, the stiff and implacable limp of the figure which was not dwarfed by the house, for the reason that it had never looked big anywhere and which now, against the serene columned backdrop, had more than ever that impervious quality of something cut ruthlessly from tin, depthless, as though, sidewise to the sun, it would cast no shadow. Watching him, the boy remarked the absolutely undeviating course which his father held and saw the stiff foot come squarely down in a pile of fresh droppings where a horse had stood in the drive and which his father could have avoided by a simple change of stride. But it ebbed only for a moment, though he could not have thought this into words either, walking on in the spell of the house, which he could even want but without envy, without sorrow, certainly never with that ravening and jealous rage which unknown to him walked in the ironlike black coat before him: *Maybe he will feel it too. Maybe it will even change him now from what maybe he couldn't help but be.*

They crossed the portico. Now he could hear his father's stiff foot as it came down on the boards with clocklike finality, a sound out of all proportion to the displacement of the body it bore and which was not dwarfed either by the white door before it, as though it had attained to a sort of vicious and ravening minimum not to be dwarfed by anything—the flat, wide, black hat, the formal coat of broadcloth which had once been black but which had now that friction-glazed greenish cast of the bodies of old house flies, the lifted sleeve which was too large, the lifted hand like a curled claw. The door opened so promptly that the boy knew the Negro must have been watching them all the time, an old man with neat grizzled hair, in a linen jacket, who stood barring the door with his body, saying, "Wipe yo foots, white man, fo you come in here. Major ain't home nohow."

"Get out of my way, nigger," his father said, without heat too, flinging the door back and the Negro also and entering, his hat still on his head. And now the boy saw the prints of the stiff foot on the doorjamb and saw them appear on the pale rug behind the machinelike deliberation of the foot which seemed to bear (or transmit) twice the weight which the body compassed. The Negro was shouting "Miss Lula! Miss Lula!" somewhere behind them, then the boy, deluged as though by a warm wave by a suave turn of carpeted stair and a pendant glitter of chandeliers and a mute gleam of gold frames, heard the swift feet and saw her too, a lady—perhaps he had never seen her like before either—in a gray, smooth gown with lace at the throat and an apron tied at the waist and the sleeves turned back, wiping cake or biscuit dough from her hands with a towel as she came up the hall, looking not at his father at all but at the tracks on the blond rug with an expression of incredulous amazement.

"I tried," the Negro cried, "I tole him to . . ."

"Will you please go away?" she said in a shaking voice. "Major de Spain is not at home. Will you please go away?"

His father had not spoken again. He did not speak again. He did not even look at her. He just stood stiff in the center of the rug, in his hat, the shaggy iron-gray brows twitching slightly above the pebble-colored eyes as he appeared to examine the house with brief deliberation. Then with the same deliberation he turned; the boy watched him pivot on the good leg and saw the stiff foot drag round the arc of the turning, leaving a final long and fading smear. His father never looked at it, he never once looked down at the rug. The Negro held the door. It closed behind them, upon the hysteric and indistinguishable woman-wail. His father stopped at the top of the steps and scraped his boot clean on the edge of it. At the gate he stopped again. He stood for a moment, planted stiffly on the stiff foot, looking back at the house. "Pretty and white, ain't it?" he said. "That's sweat. Nigger sweat. Maybe it ain't white enough yet to suit him. Maybe he wants to mix some white sweat with it."

Two hours later the boy was chopping wood behind the house within which his mother and aunt and the two sisters (the mother and aunt, not the two girls, he knew that; even at this distance and muffled by walls the flat loud voices of the two girls emanated an incorrigible idle inertia) were setting up the stove to prepare a meal, when he heard the hooves and saw the linen-clad man on a fine sorrel mare, whom he recognized even before he saw the rolled rug in front of the Negro youth following on a fat bay carriage horse—a suffused, angry face vanishing, still at full gallop, beyond the corner of the house where his father and brother were sitting in the two tilted chairs; and a moment later, almost before he could have put the axe down, he heard the hooves again and watched the sorrel mare go back out of the yard, already galloping again. Then his father began to shout one of the sisters' names, who presently emerged backward from the kitchen door dragging the rolled rug along the ground by one end while the other sister walked behind it.

"If you ain't going to tote, go on and set up the wash pot," the first said.

"You, Sarty!" the second shouted. "Set up the wash pot!" His father appeared at the door, framed against that shabbiness, as he had been against that other bland perfection, impervious to either, the mother's anxious face at his shoulder.

"Go on," the father said. "Pick it up." The two sisters stooped, broad, lethargic; stooping, they presented an incredible expanse of pale cloth and a flutter of tawdry ribbons.

"If I thought enough of a rug to have to git hit all the way from France I wouldn't keep hit where folks coming in would have to tromp on hit," the first said. They raised the rug.

"Abner," the mother said. "Let me do it."

"You go back and git dinner," his father said. "I'll tend to this."

From the woodpile through the rest of the afternoon the boy watched them, the rug spread flat in the dust beside the bubbling wash-pot, the two sisters stooping over it with that profound and lethargic reluctance, while the father stood over them in turn, implacable and grim, driving them though never raising his voice again. He could smell the harsh homemade lye[3] they were using; he saw his mother come to the door once and look toward them with an expression not anxious now but very like despair; he saw his father turn, and he fell to with the axe and saw from the corner of his eye his father raise from the ground a flattish fragment of field stone and examine it and return to the pot, and this time his mother actually spoke: "Abner. Abner. Please don't. Please, Abner."

Then he was done too. It was dusk; the whippoorwills had already begun. He could smell coffee from the room where they would presently eat the cold food remaining from the mid-afternoon meal, though when he entered the house he realized they were having coffee again probably

---

[3] A soap made from wood ashes and water, unsuitable for washing fine fabrics.

because there was a fire on the hearth, before which the rug now lay spread over the backs of the two chairs. The tracks of his father's foot were gone. Where they had been were now long, water-cloudy scoriations resembling the sporadic course of a Lilliputian mowing machine.

55 It still hung there while they ate the cold food and then went to bed, scattered without order or claim up and down the two rooms, his mother in one bed, where his father would later lie, the older brother in the other, himself, the aunt, and the two sisters on pallets on the floor. But his father was not in bed yet. The last thing the boy remembered was the depthless, harsh silhouette of the hat and coat bending over the rug and it seemed to him that he had not even closed his eyes when the silhouette was standing over him, the fire almost dead behind it, the stiff foot prodding him awake. "Catch up the mule," his father said.

When he returned with the mule his father was standing in the black door, the rolled rug over his shoulder. "Ain't you going to ride?" he said.

"No. Give me your foot."

He bent his knee into his father's hand, the wiry, surprising power flowed smoothly, rising, he rising with it, on to the mule's bare back (they had owned a saddle once; the boy could remember it though not when or where) and with the same effortlessness his father swung the rug up in front of him. Now in the starlight they retraced the afternoon's path, up the dusty road rife with honeysuckle, through the gate and up the black tunnel to the drive to the lightless house, where he sat on the mule and felt the rough warp of the rug drag across his thighs and vanish.

"Don't you want me to help?" he whispered. His father did not answer and now he heard again that stiff foot striking the hollow portico with that wooden and clocklike deliberation, that outrageous overstatement of the weight it carried. The rug, hunched, not flung (the boy could tell that even in the darkness) from his father's shoulder struck the angle of wall and floor with a sound unbelievably loud, thunderous, then the foot again, unhurried and enormous; a light came on in the house and the boy sat, tense, breathing steadily and quietly and just a little fast, though the foot itself did not increase its beat at all, descending the steps now; now the boy could see him.

60 "Don't you want to ride now?" he whispered. "We kin both ride now," the light within the house altering now, flaring up and sinking. *He's coming down the stairs now,* he thought. He had already ridden the mule up beside the horse block; presently his father was up behind him and he doubled the reins over and slashed the mule across the neck, but before the animal could begin to trot the hard, thin arm came round him, the hard, knotted hand jerking the mule back to a walk.

In the first red rays of the sun they were in the lot, putting plow gear on the mules. This time the sorrel mare was in the lot before he heard it at all, the rider collarless and even bareheaded, trembling, speaking in a shaking voice as the woman in the house had done, his father merely looking up once before stooping again to the hame he was buckling, so that the man on the mare spoke to his stooping back:

"You must realize you have ruined that rug. Wasn't there anybody here, any of your women . . ." he ceased, shaking, the boy watching him, the older brother leaning now in the stable door, chewing, blinking slowly and steadily at nothing apparently. "It cost a hundred dollars. But you never had a hundred dollars. You never will. So I'm going to charge you twenty bushels of corn against your crop. I'll add it in your contract and when you come to the commissary you can sign it. That won't keep Mrs. de Spain quiet but maybe it will teach you to wipe your feet off before you enter her house again."

Then he was gone. The boy looked at his father, who still had not spoken or even looked up again, who was now adjusting the loggerhead in the hame.

"Pap," he said. His father looked at him—the inscrutable face, the shaggy brows beneath which the gray eyes glinted coldly. Suddenly the boy went toward him, fast, stopping as suddenly. "You done the best you could!" he cried. "If he wanted hit done different why didn't he wait and tell you how? He won't git no twenty bushels! He won't git none! We'll gether hit and hide hit! I kin watch . . ."

"Did you put the cutter back in that straight stock like I told you?"

"No, sir," he said.

"Then go do it."

That was Wednesday. During the rest of that week he worked steadily, at what was within his scope and some which was beyond it, with an industry that did not need to be driven nor even commanded twice; he had this from his mother, with the difference that some at least of what he did he liked to do, such as splitting wood with the half-size axe which his mother and aunt had earned, or saved money somehow, to present him with at Christmas. In company with the two older women (and on one afternoon, even one of the sisters), he built pens for the shoat and the cow which were a part of his father's contract with the landlord, and one afternoon, his father being absent, gone somewhere on one of the mules, he went to the field.

They were running a middle buster now, his brother holding the plow straight while he handled the reins, and walking beside the straining mule, the rich black soil shearing cool and damp against his bare ankles, he thought *Maybe this is the end of it. Maybe even that twenty bushels that seems hard to have to pay for just a rug will be a cheap price for him to stop forever and always from being what he used to be;* thinking, dreaming now, so that his brother had to speak sharply to him to mind the mule: *Maybe he even won't collect the twenty bushels. Maybe it will all add up and balance and vanish—corn, rug, fire; the terror and grief, the being pulled two ways like between two teams of horses—gone, done with for ever and ever.*

Then it was Saturday; he looked up from beneath the mule he was harnessing and saw his father in the black coat and hat. "Not that," his father said. "The wagon gear." And then, two hours later, sitting in the wagon bed behind his father and brother on the seat, the wagon accomplished a final curve, and he saw the weathered paintless store with its tattered tobacco- and patent-medicine posters and the tethered wagons and saddle animals below the gallery. He mounted the gnawed steps behind his father and brother, and there again was the lane of quiet, watching faces for the three of them to walk through. He saw the man in spectacles sitting at the plank table and he did not need to be told this was a Justice of the Peace; he sent one glare of fierce, exultant, partisan defiance at the man in collar and cravat now, whom he had seen but twice before in his life, and that on a galloping horse, who now wore on his face an expression not of rage but of amazed unbelief which the boy could not have known was at the incredible circumstance of being sued by one of his own tenants, and came and stood against his father and cried at the Justice: "He ain't done it! He ain't burnt . . ."

"Go back to the wagon," his father said.

"Burnt?" the Justice said. "Do I understand this rug was burned too?"

"Does anybody here claim it was?" his father said. "Go back to the wagon." But he did not, he merely retreated to the rear of the room, crowded as that other had been, but not to sit down this time, instead, to stand pressing among the motionless bodies, listening to the voices:

"And you claim twenty bushels of corn is too high for the damage you did to the rug?"

"He brought the rug to me and said he wanted the tracks washed out of it. I washed the tracks out and took the rug back to him."

"But you didn't carry the rug back to him in the same condition it was in before you made the tracks on it."

His father did not answer, and now for perhaps half a minute there was no sound at all save that of breathing, the faint, steady suspiration of complete and intent listening.

"You decline to answer that, Mr. Snopes?" Again his father did not answer. "I'm going to find against you, Mr. Snopes. I'm going to find that you were responsible for the injury to Major de Spain's rug and hold you liable for it. But twenty bushels of corn seems a little high for a man in your circumstances to have to pay. Major de Spain claims it cost a hundred dollars. October corn will be worth about fifty cents. I figure that if Major de Spain can stand a ninety-five dollar loss on something he paid cash for, you can stand a five-dollar loss you haven't earned yet. I hold you in damages to Major de Spain to the amount of ten bushels of corn over and above your contract with him, to be paid to him out of your crop at gathering time. Court adjourned."

It had taken no time hardly, the morning was but half begun. He thought they would return home and perhaps back to the field, since they were late, far behind all other farmers. But instead his father passed on behind the wagon, merely indicating with his hand for the older brother to follow with it, and crossed the road toward the blacksmith shop opposite, pressing on after his father, overtaking him, speaking, whispering up at the harsh, calm face beneath the weathered hat: "He won't git no ten bushels neither. He won't git one. We'll . . ." until his father glanced for an instant down at him, the face absolutely calm, the grizzled eyebrows tangled above the cold eyes, the voice almost pleasant, almost gentle:

"You think so? Well, we'll wait till October anyway."

The matter of the wagon—the setting of a spoke or two and the tightening of the tires—did not take long either, the business of the tires accomplished by driving the wagon into the spring branch behind the shop and letting it stand there, the mules nuzzling into the water from time to time, and the boy on the seat with the idle reins, looking up the slope and through the sooty tunnel of the shed where the slow hammer rang and where his father sat on an upended cypress bolt, easily, either talking or listening, still sitting there when the boy brought the dripping wagon up out of the branch and halted it before the door.

"Take them on to the shade and hitch," his father said. He did so and returned. His father and the smith and a third man squatting on his heels inside the door were talking, about crops and animals; the boy, squatting too in the ammoniac dust and hoof-parings and scales of rust, heard his father tell a long and unhurried story out of the time before the birth of the older brother even when he had been a professional horsetrader. And then his father came up beside him where he stood before a tattered last year's circus poster on the other side of the store, gazing rapt and quiet at the scarlet horses, the incredible poisings and convolutions of tulle and tights and the painted leers of comedians, and said, "It's time to eat."

But not at home. Squatting beside his brother against the front wall, he watched his father emerge from the store and produce from a paper sack a segment of cheese and divide it carefully and deliberately into three with his pocket knife and produce crackers from the same sack. They all three squatted on the gallery and ate, slowly, without talking; then in the store again, they drank from a tin dipper tepid water smelling of the cedar bucket and of living beech trees. And still they did not go home. It was a horse lot this time, a tall rail fence upon and along which men stood and sat and out of which one by one horses were led, to be walked and trotted and then cantered back and forth along the road while the slow swapping and buying went on and the sun began to slant westward, they—the three of them—watching and listening, the older brother with his muddy eyes and his steady, inevitable tobacco, the father commenting now and then on certain of the animals, to no one in particular.

It was after sundown when they reached home. They ate supper by lamplight, then, sitting on the doorstep, the boy watched the night fully accomplish, listening to the whippoorwills and the frogs, when he heard his mother's voice: "Abner! No! No! Oh, God. Oh, God. Abner!" and he rose, whirled, and saw the altered light through the door where a candle stub now burned in a bottle neck on the table and his father, still in the hat and coat, at once formal and burlesque as though dressed carefully for some shabby and ceremonial violence, emptying the reservoir of the lamp back into the five-gallon kerosene can from which it had been filled, while the mother tugged at his arm until he shifted the lamp to the other hand and flung her back, not savagely or viciously, just hard, into the wall, her hands flung out against the wall for balance, her mouth open and in her face the same quality of hopeless despair as had been in her voice. Then his father saw him standing in the door.

"Go to the barn and get that can of oil we were oiling the wagon with," he said. The boy did not move. Then he could speak.

"What . . ." he cried. "What are you . . ."

"Go get that oil," his father said. "Go."

Then he was moving, running, outside the house, toward the stable: this the old habit, the old blood which he had not been permitted to choose for himself, which had been bequeathed him willy nilly and which had run for so long (and who knew where, battening on what of outrage and savagery and lust) before it came to him. *I could keep on,* he thought. *I could run on and on and never look back, never need to see his face again. Only I can't. I can't,* the rusted can in his hand now, the liquid sploshing in it as he ran back to the house and into it, into the sound of his mother's weeping in the next room, and handed the can to his father.

"Ain't you going to even send a nigger?" he cried. "At least you sent a nigger before!"

This time his father didn't strike him. The hand came even faster than the blow had, the same hand which had set the can on the table with almost excruciating care flashing from the can toward him too quick for him to follow it, gripping him by the back of his shirt and on to tiptoe before he had seen it quit the can, the face stooping at him in breathless and frozen ferocity, the cold, dead voice speaking over him to the older brother who leaned against the table, chewing with that steady, curious, sidewise motion of cows:

"Empty the can into the big one and go on. I'll catch up with you."

"Better tie him to the bedpost," the brother said.

"Do like I told you," the father said. Then the boy was moving, his bunched shirt and the hard, bony hand between his shoulderblades, his toes just touching the floor, across the room and into the other one, past the sisters sitting with spread heavy thighs in the two chairs over the cold hearth, and to where his mother and aunt sat side by side on the bed, the aunt's arms about his mother's shoulders.

"Hold him," the father said. The aunt made a startled movement. "Not you," the father said. "Lennie. Take hold of him. I want to see you do it." His mother took him by the wrist. "You'll hold him better than that. If he gets loose don't you know what he is going to do? He will go up yonder." He jerked his head toward the road. "Maybe I'd better tie him."

"I'll hold him," his mother whispered.

"See you do then." Then his father was gone, the stiff foot heavy and measured upon the boards, ceasing at last.

Then he began to struggle. His mother caught him in both arms, he jerking and wrenching at them. He would be stronger in the end, he knew that. But he had no time to wait for it. "Lemme go!" he cried. "I don't want to have to hit you!"

"Let him go!" the aunt said. "If he don't go, before God, I am going up there myself!"

"Don't you see I can't?" his mother cried. "Sarty! Sarty! No! No! Help me, Lizzie!"

Then he was free. His aunt grasped at him but it was too late. He whirled, running, his mother stumbled forward on to her knees behind him, crying to the nearer sister: "Catch him, Net! Catch him!" But that was too late too, the sister (the sisters were twins, born at the same time, yet either of them now gave the impression of being, encompassing as much living meat and volume and weight as any other two of the family) not yet having begun to rise from the chair, her head, face, alone merely turned, presenting to him in the flying instant an astonishing expanse of young female features untroubled by any surprise even, wearing only an expression of bovine interest. Then he was out of the room, out of the house, in the mild dust of the starlit road and the heavy rifeness of honeysuckle, the pale ribbon unspooling with terrific slowness under his running feet, reaching the gate at last and turning in, running, his heart and lungs drumming, on up the drive toward the lighted house, the lighted door. He did not knock, he burst in, sobbing for breath, incapable for the moment of speech; he saw the astonished face of the Negro in the linen jacket without knowing when the Negro had appeared.

"De Spain!" he cried, panted. "Where's . . ." then he saw the white man too emerging from a white door down the hall. "Barn!" he cried. "Barn!"

"What?" the white man said. "Barn?"

"Yes!" the boy cried. "Barn!"

"Catch him!" the white man shouted.

But it was too late this time too. The Negro grasped his shirt, but the entire sleeve, rotten with washing, carried away, and he was out that door too and in the drive again, and had actually never ceased to run even while he was screaming into the white man's face.

Behind him the white man was shouting, "My horse! Fetch my horse!" and he thought for an instant of cutting across the park and climbing the fence into the road, but he did not know the park nor how high the vine-massed fence might be and he dared not risk it. So he ran on down the drive, blood and breath roaring; presently he was in the road again though he could not see it. He could not hear either: the galloping mare was almost upon him before he heard her, and even then he held his course, as if the very urgency of his wild grief and need must in a moment more find him wings, waiting until the ultimate instant to hurl himself aside and into the weed-choked roadside ditch as the horse thundered past and on, for an instant in furious silhouette against the stars, the tranquil early summer night sky which, even before the shape of the horse and rider vanished, stained abruptly and violently upward: a long, swirling roar incredible and soundless, blotting the stars, and he springing up and into the road again, running again, knowing it was too late yet still running even after he heard the shot and, an instant later, two shots, pausing now without knowing he had ceased to run, crying "Pap! Pap!", running again before he knew he had begun to run, stumbling, tripping over something and scrabbling up again without ceasing to run, looking backward over his shoulder at the glare as he got up, running on among the invisible trees, panting, sobbing, "Father! Father!"

At midnight he was sitting on the crest of a hill. He did not know it was midnight and he did not know how far he had come. But there was no glare behind him now and he sat now, his back toward what he had called home for four days anyhow, his face toward the dark woods which he would enter when breath was strong again, small, shaking steadily in the chill darkness, hugging himself into the remainder of his thin, rotten shirt, the grief and despair now no longer terror and fear but just grief and despair. *Father. My father,* he thought. "He was brave!" he cried suddenly, aloud but not loud, no more than a whisper: "He was! He was in the war! He was in Colonel Sartoris' cav'ry!" not knowing that his father had gone to that war a private in the fine old European sense, wearing no uniform, admitting the authority of and giving fidelity to no man or army or flag, going to war as Malbrouck[4] himself did: for booty—it meant nothing and less than nothing to him if it were enemy booty or his own.

The slow constellations wheeled on. It would be dawn and then sun-up after a while and he would be hungry. But that would be tomorrow and now he was only cold, and walking would cure that. His breathing was easier now and he decided to get up and go on, and then he found that he had been asleep because he knew it was almost dawn, the night almost over. He could tell that from the whippoorwills. They were everywhere now among the dark trees below him, constant and inflectioned and ceaseless, so that, as the instant for giving over to the day birds drew nearer and nearer, there was no interval at all between them. He got up. He was a little stiff, but walking would cure that too as it would the cold, and soon there would be the sun. He went on down the hill, toward the dark woods within which the liquid silver voices of the birds called unceasing—the rapid and urgent beating of the urgent and quiring heart of the late spring night. He did not look back.

---

[4] A character in a popular eighteenth-century nursery rhyme about a famous warrior.

READING AND REACTING

1. Is the narrator of "Barn Burning" omniscient, or does he have limited omniscience? Explain.
2. What is the point of view of the italicized passages? What do we learn from them? How would the story have been different without these passages?
3. What are the major conflicts of "Barn Burning"? Which, if any, are resolved in the story? Are the conflicts unavoidable? Explain.
4. What role does the Civil War play in "Barn Burning"? What does Abner Snopes's behavior during the war tell readers about his character?
5. In Books 1 and 2 of Samuel in the Old Testament, Abner was a relative of King Saul and commander in chief of his armies. Abner supported King Saul against David and was killed as a result of his own jealousy and rage. What, if any, significance is there in the fact that Faulkner names Ab Snopes, loyal to no man, fighter "for booty, and father of the Snopes clan" after this mighty biblical leader?
6. Why does Sarty Snopes insist that his father was brave? How does your knowledge of events unknown to the boy affect your reactions to this statement?
7. **JOURNAL ENTRY:** How would the story be different if it were told from Ab's point of view? From Sarty's? From the point of view of a member of a community in which the Snopeses have lived?

Simon J. Ortiz (1941–) is perhaps best known as an important Native American poet whose work tells historical and contemporary stories about Acoma and other Indian pueblos. His collections include *Naked in the Wind* (1970), *Going for the Rain* (1976), *A Good Journey* (1977), *Song, Poetry, Language* (1978), *Fight Back: For the Sake of the People, For the Sake of the Land* (1980), *From Sand Creek* (1981), and *A Poem Is a Journey* (1981). He has also written a children's overview of Native American cultures, *The People Shall Continue,* and edited *Earth Power Coming* (1983), a collection of short stories by thirty Native American authors. His own short stories have been collected in *Howbah Indians* (1978) and *Fightin': New and Collected Stories* (1983).

Ortiz is from Acoma pueblo, which is built on a mesa near Albuquerque and is possibly the oldest continuously inhabited town on the continent. He attended Fort Lewis College in Durango, Colorado (1962–1963), and the University of New Mexico, Albuquerque (1966–1968), spending the intervening years in the U.S. Army. He has taught at several universities, most recently the University of New Mexico. Since 1982 Ortiz has been consultant editor of the Pueblo of Acoma Press. He lives in Albuquerque.

Ortiz's short stories attempt what he sees as an essential task—to preserve Native American traditions by relating them to the lives of contemporary Indians and also by exposing non-Indian readers to the universal qualities of Indian stories. Thus his work attempts to fuse an often bewildering present to a more coherent past by drawing on the oral tradition of songs, stories, and prayers of the Pueblo Indian tribes. "Kaiser and the War" illustrates how the interaction, or collision, of Native American and Anglo-American cultures is further complicated by society's demands on young men in time of war.

Simon J. Ortiz

KAISER AND THE WAR

(1969)

Kaiser got out of the state pen when I was in the fourth grade. I don't know why people called him Kaiser. Some called him Hitler, too, since he was Kaiser, but I don't think he cared at all what they called him. He was probably just glad to get out of the state pen anyway.

Kaiser got into the state pen because he didn't go into the army. That's what my father said anyway, and because he was a crazy nut according to some people, which was probably why he didn't want to go into the army in the first place, which was what my father said also.

The army wanted him anyway, or maybe they didn't know he was crazy or supposed to be. They came for him out at home on the reservation, and he said he wasn't going to go because he didn't speak good English. Kaiser didn't go to school more than just the first or second grade. He said what he said in Indian and his sister said it in English for him. The army men, somebody from the county draft board, said they'd teach him English, don't worry about it, and how to read and write and give him clothes and money when he got out of the army so that he could start regular as any American. Just like anybody else, and they threw in stuff about how it would be good for our tribe and the people of the U.S.A.

Well, Kaiser, who didn't understand that much English anyway, listened quietly to his sister telling him what the army draft-board men were saying. He didn't ask any questions, just once in a while said, "Yes," like he'd been taught to say in the first grade. Maybe some of the interpretation was lost the way his sister was doing it, or maybe he went nuts like some people said he did once in a while because the next thing he did was to bust out the door and start running for Black Mesa.

5 The draft-board men didn't say anything at first and then they got pretty mad. Kaiser's sister cried because she didn't want Kaiser to go into the army but she didn't want him running out just like that either. She had gone to the Indian school in Albuquerque, and she

learned that stuff about patriotism, duty, honor—even if you were said to be crazy.

At about that time, their grandfather, Faustin, cussed in Indian at the draft-board men. Nobody had noticed when he came into the house, but there he was, fierce-looking as hell as usual, although he wasn't fierce at all. Then he got mad at his granddaughter and the men, asked what they were doing in his house, making the women cry and not even sitting down like friendly people did. Old Faustin and the army confronted each other. The army men were confused and getting more and more nervous. The old man told the girl to go out of the room and he'd talk to the army himself, although he didn't speak a word of English except "goddammey" which didn't sound too much like English but he threw it in once in a while anyway.

Those army men tried to get the girl to come back, but the old man wouldn't let her. He told her to get to grinding corn or something useful. They tried sign language and when Faustin figured out what they were waving their hands around for, he laughed out loud. He wouldn't even take the cigarettes offered him, so the army men didn't say anything more. The last thing they did though was give the old man a paper which they didn't try to explain what it was for. They probably hoped it would get read somehow.

Well, after they left, the paper did get read by the girl, and she told Faustin what it was about. The law was going to come and take Kaiser to jail because he wouldn't go into the army by himself. Grandfather Faustin sat down and talked quietly to himself for a while and then he got up to look for Kaiser.

Kaiser was on his way home by then, and his grandfather told him what was going to happen. They sat down by the side of the road and started to make plans. Kaiser would go hide up on Black Mesa and maybe go up all the way to Brushy Mountain if the law really came to poking around seriously. Faustin would take him food and tell him the news once in a while.

10 Everybody in the village knew what was going on pretty soon. Some approved, and some didn't. Some thought it was pretty funny. My father, who couldn't go in the army even if he wanted to because there were too many of us kids, laughed about it for days. The people who approved of it and thought it funny were the ones who knew Kaiser was crazy and that the army must be even crazier. The ones who disapproved were mostly those who were scared of him. A lot of them were the parents or brothers of girls who they must have suspected of liking Kaiser. Kaiser was pretty good-looking and funny in the way he talked for a crazy guy. And he was a hard worker. He worked every day out in the fields or up at the sheep camp for his parents while they were alive and for his sister and nephew and grandfather. These people, who were scared of him and said he should have gone into the army perhaps it'll do him good, didn't want him messing around their daughters or sisters which they said he did from time to time. Mostly these people

were scared he would do something, and there was one too many nuts around in the village anyway, they said.

My old man didn't care though. He was buddies with Kaiser. When there was a corn dance up at the community hall, they would have a whole lot of fun singing and laughing and joking, and once in a while when someone brought around a bottle or two they would really get going and the officers of the tribe would have to warn them to behave themselves.

Kaiser was okay, though. He came around home quite a lot. His own kinfolks didn't care for him too much because he was crazy, and they didn't go out of their way to invite him to eat or spend the night when he dropped by their homes and it happened to get dark before he left. My mother didn't mind him around. When she served him something to eat, she didn't act like he was nuts, or supposed to be; she just served him and fussed over him like he was a kid, which Kaiser acted like a lot of the time. I guess she didn't figure a guy who acted like a kid was crazy.

Right after we finished eating, if it happened to be supper, my own grandfather, who was a medicine man, would talk to him and to all of us kids who were usually paying only half attention. He would tell us advice, about how the world was, how each person, everything, was important. And then he would tell us stories about the olden times. Legends mostly, about the katzina, Spider Woman, where our hano, people, came from. Some of the stories were funny, some sad, and some pretty boring. Kaiser would sit there, not saying anything except "Eheh," which is what you're supposed to say once in a while to show that you're listening to the olden times.

After half of us kids were asleep, grandfather would quit talking, only Kaiser wouldn't want him to quit and he'd ask for more, but grandfather wouldn't tell any more. What Kaiser would do was start telling himself about the olden times. He'd lie on the floor in the dark, or sometimes up on the roof which was where he'd sleep in the summer, talking. And sometimes he'd sing, which is also part of the old times. I would drift off to sleep just listening to him.

15 Well, he didn't come around home after he went up on Black Mesa. He just went up there and stayed there. The law, which was the county sheriff, an officer, and the Indian agent from the Indian Affairs office in Albuquerque, came out to get him, but nobody would tell them where he was. The law had a general idea where he was, but that didn't get them very far because they didn't know the country around Black Mesa. It's rougher than hell up here, just a couple of sheep camps in a lot of country.

The Indian agent had written a letter to the officers of the tribe that they would come up for Kaiser on a certain day. There were a lot of people waiting for them when they drove up to the community meeting hall. The county sheriff had a bulging belly and he had a six-shooter strapped to his hip. When the men standing outside the community hall saw him step out of the government car, they made jokes. Just like the Lone Ranger, someone said. The law didn't know what they were laughing about, and they said, Hello, and paid no attention to what they couldn't understand.

Faustin was among them. But he was silent and he smoked a roll-your-own. The agent stopped before him, and Faustin took a slow drag on his roll-your-own but he didn't look at the man.

"Faustin, my old friend," the agent said. "How are you?"

The old man didn't say anything. He let the tobacco smoke out slowly and looked straight ahead. Someone in the crowd told Faustin what the agent had said, but the old man didn't say anything at all.

The law thought he was praying or that he was a wise man contemplating his answer, the way he was so solemn-like, so they didn't press him. What Faustin was doing was ignoring the law. He didn't want them to talk with him. He turned to a man at his side.

"Tell this man I do not want to talk. I can't understand what they are saying in American anyway. And I don't want anyone to tell me what they say. I'm not interested." He looked at the government then, and he dismissed their presence with his indignation.

"The old man isn't gonna talk to you," someone said.

The agent and sheriff big belly glared at the man. "Who's in charge around here?" the sheriff said.

The Indians laughed. They joked by calling each other big belly. The governor of the tribe and two chiefs soon came. They greeted the law, and then they went into the meeting hall to confer about Kaiser.

"Well, have you brought Kaiser?" the Indian agent asked, although he saw that they hadn't and knew that they wouldn't.

"No," the governor said. And someone interpreted for him. "He will not come."

"Well, why don't you bring him? If he doesn't want to come, why don't you bring him? A bunch of you can bring him," the agent said. He was becoming irritated.

The governor, chiefs and men talked to each other. One old man held the floor a while, until others got tired of him telling about the old times and how it was and how the Americans had said a certain thing and did another and so forth. Someone said, "We can bring him. Kaiser should come by himself anyway. Let's go get him." He was a man who didn't like Kaiser. He looked around carefully when he got through speaking and sat down.

"Tell the Americans that is not the way," one of the chiefs said. "If our son wants to meet these men he will come." And the law was answered with the translation.

"I'll be a son of a bitch," the sheriff said, and the Indians laughed quietly. He glared at them and they stopped. "Let's go get him ourselves," he continued.

The man who had been interpreting said, "He is crazy."

"Who's crazy?" the sheriff yelled, like he was refuting an accusation. "I think you're all crazy."

"Kaiser, I think he is crazy," the interpreter said like he was ashamed of saying so. He stepped back, embarrassed.

Faustin then came to the front. Although he said he didn't want to talk with the law, he shouted, "Go get Kaiser yourself. If he's crazy, I hope he kills you. Go get him."

"Okay," the agent said when the interpreter finished. "We'll go get him ourselves. Where is he?" The agent knew no one would tell him, but he asked it anyway.

Upon that, the Indians assumed the business that the law came to do was over, and that the law had resolved what it came to do in the first place. The Indians began to leave.

"Wait," the agent said. "We need someone to go with us. He's up on Black Mesa, but we need someone to show us where."

The men kept on leaving. "We'll pay you. The government will pay you to go with us. You're deputized," the agent said. "Stop them, Sheriff," he said to the county sheriff, and the sheriff yelled, "Stop, come back here," and put a hand to his six-shooter. When he yelled, some of the Indians looked at him to laugh. He sure looked funny and talked funny. But some of them came back. "All right, you're deputies, you'll get paid," the sheriff said. Some of them knew what that meant, others weren't too sure. Some of them decided they'd come along for the fun of it.

The law and the Indians piled into the government car and a pickup truck which belonged to one of the deputies who was assured that he would get paid more than the others.

Black Mesa is fifteen miles back on the reservation. There are dirt roads up to it, but they aren't very good, nobody uses them except sheep herders and hunters in the fall. Kaiser knew what he was doing when he went up there, and he probably saw them when they were coming. But it wouldn't have made any difference because when the law and the deputies come up to the foot of the mesa, they still weren't getting anywhere. The deputies, who were still Indians too, wouldn't tell or didn't really know where Kaiser was at the moment. So they sat for a couple hours at the foot of the mesa, debating what should be done. The law tried to get the deputies to talk. The sheriff was boiling mad by this time, getting madder too, and he was for persuading one of the deputies into telling where Kaiser was exactly. But he reasoned the deputy wouldn't talk being that he was Indian too, and so he shut up for a while. He had figured out why the Indians laughed so frequently even though it was not as loud as before they were deputized.

Finally, they decided to walk up Black Mesa. It's rough going and when they didn't know which was the best way to go up they found it was even rougher. The real law dropped back one by one to rest on a rock or under a piñon tree until only the deputies were left. They watched the officer from the Indian Affairs office sitting on a fallen log some yards back. He was the last one to keep up so far, and he was unlacing his shoes. The deputies waited patiently for him to start again and for the others to catch up.

"It's sure hot," one of the deputies said.

"Yes, maybe it'll rain soon," another said.

"No, it rained for the last time last month, maybe next year."

"Snow then," another said.

They watched the sheriff and the Indian agent walking toward them half a mile back. One of them limped.

"Maybe the Americans need a rest," someone said. "We walked a long ways."

"Yes, they might be tired," another said. "I'll go tell that one that we're going to stop to rest," he said and walked back to the law sitting on the log. "We gonna stop to rest," he told the law. The law didn't say anything as he massaged his feet. And the deputy walked away to join the others.

They didn't find Kaiser that day or the next day. The deputies said they could walk all over the mesa without finding him for all eternity, but they wouldn't find him. They didn't mind walking, they said. As long as they got paid for their time, their crops were already in, and they'll just hire someone to haul winter wood for them now that they had the money. But they refused to talk. The ones who wanted to tell where Kaiser was, if they knew, didn't say so out loud, but they didn't tell anyway so it didn't make any difference. They were too persuaded by the newly found prosperity of employment.

The sheriff, exhausted by the middle of the second day of walking the mesa, began to sound like he was for going back to Albuquerque. Maybe Kaiser'd come in by himself, he didn't see any sense in looking for some Indian anyway just to get him into the army. Besides, he'd heard the Indian was crazy. When the sheriff had first learned the Indian's name was Kaiser he couldn't believe it, but he was assured that wasn't his real name, just something he was called because he was crazy. But the sheriff didn't feel any better or less tired, and he was getting jumpy about the crazy part.

At the end of the second day, the law decided to leave. Maybe we'll come back, they said; we'll have to talk this over with the Indian Affairs officials, maybe it'll be all right if that Indian didn't have to be in the army after all. And they left. The sheriff, his six-shooter off his hip now, was pretty tired out, and he didn't say anything.

The officials for the Indian Affairs didn't give up though. They sent back some more men. The county sheriff had decided it wasn't worth it, besides he had a whole county to take care of. And the Indians were deputized again. More of them volunteered this time, some had to be turned away. They had figured out how to work it: they wouldn't have to tell, if they knew, where Kaiser was. All they would have to do was walk and say from time to time, "Maybe he's over there by that canyon. Used to be there was some good hiding places back when the Apache and Navaho were raising hell." And some would go over there and some in the other direction, investigating good hiding places. But after camping around Black Mesa for a week this time, the Indian Affairs gave up.

They went by Faustin's house the day they left for Albuquerque and left a message: the government would wait and when Kaiser least expected it, they would get him and he would have to go to jail.

Kaiser decided to volunteer for the army. He had decided to after he had watched the law and the deputies walk all over the mesa. Grandfather Faustin had come to visit him up at one of the sheep camps, and the old man gave him all the news at home and then he told Kaiser the message the government had left.

"Okay," Kaiser said. And he was silent for a while and nodded his head slowly like his grandfather did. "I'll join the army."

"No," his grandfather said. "I don't want you to. I will not allow you."

"Grandfather, I do not have to mind you. If you were my grandfather or uncle on my mother's side, I would listen to you and probably obey you, but you are not, and so I will not obey you."

"You are really crazy then," Grandfather Faustin said. "If that's what you want to do, go ahead." He was angry and he was sad, and he got up and put his hand on his grandson's shoulder and blessed him in the people's way. After that the old man left. It was evening when he left the sheep camp, and he walked for a long time away from Black Mesa before he started to sing.

The next day, Kaiser showed up at home. He ate with us, and after we ate we sat in the living room with my grandfather.

"So you've decided to go into the Americans' army," my grandfather said. None of us kids, nor even my parents, had known he was going but my grandfather had known all along. He probably knew as soon as Kaiser had walked into the house. Maybe even before that.

My grandfather blessed him then, just like Faustin had done, and he talked to him of how a man should behave and what he should expect. Just general things, and grandfather turned sternly toward us kids who are playing around as usual. My father and mother talked with him also, and when they were through, my grandfather put cornmeal in Kaiser's hand for him to pray with. Our parents told us kids to tell Kaiser goodbye and good luck and after we did, he left.

The next thing we heard was that Kaiser was in the state pen.

Later on, some people went to visit him up at the state pen. He was okay and getting fat, they said, and he was getting on okay with everybody and the warden told them. And when someone had asked Kaiser if he was okay, he said he was fine and he guessed he would be American pretty soon being that he was around them so much. The people left Kaiser some home-baked bread and dried meat and came home after being assured by the warden that he'd get out pretty soon, maybe right after the war. Kaiser was a model inmate. When the visitors got home to the reservation, they went and told Faustin his grandson was okay, getting fat and happy as any American. Old Faustin didn't have anything to say about that.

Well, the war was over after a while. Faustin died sometime near the end of it. Nobody had heard him mention Kaiser at all. Kaiser's sister and nephew were the only ones left at their home. Sometimes someone would ask about Kaiser, and his sister and nephew would say, "Oh, he's fine. He'll be home pretty soon, right after the war." But after the war was over, they just said he was fine.

My father and a couple of other guys went down to the Indian Affairs office to see what they could find out about Kaiser. They were told that Kaiser was going to stay in the pen longer now because he had tried to kill somebody. Well, he just went crazy one day, and he made a mistake so he'll just have to stay in for a couple more years or so, the Indian Affairs said. That was the first anybody heard of Kaiser trying to kill somebody, and some people said why the hell didn't they put him in the army for that like they wanted to in the first place. So Kaiser remained in the pen long after the war was over and most of the guys who had gone into the army from the tribe had come home. When he was due to get out, the Indian Affairs sent a letter to the governor and several men from the village went to get him.

65 My father said Kaiser was quiet all the way home on the bus. Some of the guys tried to joke with him, but he just wouldn't laugh or say anything. When they got off the bus at the highway and began to walk home, the guys broke into song, but that didn't bring Kaiser around. He kept walking quiet and reserved in his gray suit. Someone joked that Kaiser probably owned the only suit in the whole tribe.

"You lucky so and so. You look like a rich man," the joker said. The others looked at him sharply and he quit joking, but Kaiser didn't say anything.

When they reached home, his sister and nephew were very happy to see him. They cried and laughed at the same time, but Kaiser didn't do anything except sit at the kitchen table and look around. My father and the other guys gave him advice and welcomed him home again and left.

After that, Kaiser always wore his gray suit. Every time you saw him, he was wearing it. Out in the fields or at the plaza watching the katzina, he wore the suit. He didn't talk much any more, my father said, and he didn't come around home any more either. The suit was getting all beat-up looking, but he just kept on wearing it so that some people began to say that he was showing off.

"That Kaiser," they said, "he's always wearing this suit, just like he was an American or something. Who does he think he is anyway?" And they'd snicker, looking at Kaiser with a sort of envy. Even when the suit was torn and soiled so that it hardly looked anything like a suit, Kaiser wore it. And some people said, "When he dies, Kaiser is going to be wearing his suit." And they said that like they wished they had gotten a suit like Kaiser's.

70 Well, Kaiser died, but without his gray suit. He died up at one of his distant relatives' sheep camps one winter. When someone asked about the suit, they were told by Kaiser's sister that it was rolled up in some newspaper at their home. She said that Kaiser had told her, before he went up to the sheep camp, that she was to send it to the government.

But, she said, she couldn't figure out what he meant, whether Kaiser had meant the law or somebody, maybe the state pen or the Indian Affairs.

The person who asked about the suit wondered about this Kaiser's instructions. He couldn't figure out why Kaiser wanted to send a beat-up suit back. And then he figured, well, maybe that's the way it was when you either went into the state pen or the army and became an American. ○

READING AND REACTING

1. Who is the narrator? Why do you think he decides to tell Kaiser's story? What is his opinion of Kaiser?
2. What are the advantages and disadvantages of the point of view of this story?
3. In what ways do Kaiser's Native American values differ from the values of the draft-board men, the Indian agent, the sheriff, and the warden?
4. In what sense is this story about cultural misunderstanding rather than legal conflict?
5. Why does Kaiser decide to give himself up? Is this action consistent with his behavior until this time? Explain.
6. At one point Kaiser says that he guesses he will become American soon because he is around Americans so much. Do you think Kaiser ever becomes completely "American"?
7. Why does Kaiser wear his gray suit every day? Why does he instruct his sister to send it back to the government after he dies?
8. What role is played in this story by Kaiser's sister? Their grandfather? The Indian school? The narrator's father and grandfather? Black Mesa?
9. **JOURNAL ENTRY:** Throughout the story the narrator tells us that Kaiser is considered "crazy" by many people. Do you think he is "crazy" at the beginning of the story? At the end?

WRITING SUGGESTIONS: POINT OF VIEW

1. How would Poe's "The Cask of Amontillado" be different if it were told by a minor character who observed the events? Rewrite the story from this point of view, or tell the story that precedes the story—explaining the thousand injuries and the insult.
2. Write a letter from Kaiser to the head of the draft board explaining why Kaiser chooses not to be inducted into the army. Relate the events in the story from Kaiser's perspective. Make sure that his

letter has a consistent point of view and that he does not say anything that would be out of character. Keep in mind that Kaiser's letter would have to be transcribed with the aid of an interpreter.

3. Write an essay discussing what would be gained and what would be lost if the story "Barn Burning" were told by Sarty from the point of view of an adult looking back at the story's events.

4. Write an essay in which you consider the reliability of the narrator in "Kaiser and the War." What, if anything, suggests that his version of events may not be entirely accurate?

5. Both "The Cask of Amontillado" and "Barn Burning" deal with crimes that essentially go unpunished, and with the guilt and vengefulness that accompany these crimes. In what sense does each story's point (or points) of view influence its treatment of the crime in question? For instance, how does point of view determine how much readers know about the motives for the crime, the crime's basic circumstances, and the extent to which the crime is justified?

CHAPTER 8

STYLE, TONE, AND LANGUAGE

One of the qualities that gives a work of literature its individual personality is its **style**, the way in which a writer selects and arranges words to express ideas and, ultimately, to communicate a particular theme. Style is a complex entity made up of elements such as word choice; syntax; sentence length and structure; and the presence, frequency, and prominence of imagery and figures of speech. Closely related to style is **tone**, the attitude of the speaker or author of a work toward the subject matter, characters, or audience. Word choice and word order help to create a work's tone, which may be intimate or distant, bitter or affectionate, straightforward or cautious, supportive or critical, respectful or condescending. (Tone may also be ironic; see Chapter 7, Point of View, for a discussion of irony.)

Style offers almost limitless possibilities to a writer. Creative use of language (unusual word choice, word order, or sentence structure, for instance) can enrich a story and add to its overall effect. Sometimes style can reveal a narrator's attitude toward a character or a character's mental state. In other cases, it can help to create an atmosphere that enhances setting or theme. For instance, the breathless, disjointed style of Edgar Allan Poe's "The Tell-Tale Heart" (p. 478) suggests the narrator's increasing emotional instability: "Was it possible they heard not? Almighty God!—no, no! They heard!—they suspected!—they *knew!*—they were making a mockery of my horror!" Ernest Hemingway's clipped sentences and flat, emotionless prose in "Big Two-Hearted River" illustrate still another application of style, revealing his character's alienation and fragility as he struggles to maintain control: "Now things were done. There had been this to do. Now it was done. It had been a hard trip. He was very tired. That was done. He had made his camp. He was settled. Nothing could touch him." Finally, James Joyce's well-known **stream-of-consciousness** style mimics thought, allowing ideas to run into one another as random associations are made, so that readers may follow and participate in the thought processes of the narrator. Here, for example, is a stream-of-consciousness passage from Joyce's experimental novel *Ulysses:*

> frseeeeeeeefronnnng train somewhere whistling the strength those engines have in them like big giants and the water rolling all over and out of them all sides like the end of Loves old sweet sonnnng the poor men

> that have to be out all the night from their wives and families in those roasting engines stifling it was today. . . .

Use of stylistic devices that place emphasis on the sounds and rhythm of words and sentences also enriches works of fiction. Consider the use of such techniques in the following sentence from James Joyce's "Araby" (p. 219):

> The light from the lamp opposite our door caught the white curve of her neck, lit up her hair that rested there and, falling, lit up the hand upon the railing.

The narrator is describing his first conversation with a girl who fascinates him, and the lush, lyrical, almost musical language reflects his enchantment. Note in particular the **alliteration** (light/lamp; caught/curve; hair/hand), the repetition (lit up/lit up), and the rhyme (lit up her *hair*/that rested *there*) and near rhyme (falling/railing); these poetic devices connect the words of the sentence into a smooth, perfect whole. Another example of this emphasis on sound may be found in the measured **parallelism** of this sentence from Nathaniel Hawthorne's "The Birthmark":

> He had left his laboratory to the care of an assistant, cleared his fine countenance from the furnace smoke, washed the stain of acids from his fingers, and persuaded a beautiful woman to become his wife.

The style of the preceding sentence, conveying methodical precision and order, is consistent with the compulsive personality of the character being described.

Although many stylistic options are available to writers, style must be consistent with the writer's purpose and with the effect he or she hopes to create. Just as writers may experiment with point of view or manipulate events to create a complex plot, so they can adjust style to suit particular narrators, characters, settings, or themes. Two elements with which writers frequently experiment are levels of diction, and imagery and figurative language.

LEVELS OF DICTION

The level of diction—how formal or informal a story's language is—can suggest a good deal about those who use the language, thus revealing insights about the story's theme.

Formal Diction Formal diction is characterized by elaborate, complex sentences; a learned vocabulary, which may include **allusions** and **figurative language**; and a serious, objective, detached tone. The speaker avoids contractions, shortened word forms (like *phone*), regional expressions, and slang, and may use *one* or *we* in place of *I*. At its most extreme, formal language may be stiff and stilted, far removed from everyday speech.

Formal diction, whether used by a narrator or by a character, may indicate erudition, a high educational level, a superior social or professional position, or emotional detachment. When one character's language is significantly more formal than others', he or she may seem old-fashioned or stuffy; when language is inappropriately elevated or complex, it may reveal the character to be pompous or ridiculous; when a narrator's language is noticeably more formal than that of the characters, the narrator may seem superior or even condescending. Thus style reveals a good deal about characters and about the narrator's attitude toward them.

The following passage from "The Birthmark" illustrates formal style:

> In the latter part of the last century there lived a man of science, an eminent proficient in every branch of natural philosophy, who not long before our story opens had made experience of a spiritual affinity more attractive than any chemical one. He had left his laboratory to the care of an assistant, cleared his fine countenance from the furnace smoke, washed the stain of acids from his fingers, and persuaded a beautiful woman to become his wife. In those days when the comparatively recent discovery of electricity and other kindred mysteries of Nature seemed to open paths into the region of miracle, it was not unusual for the love of science to rival the love of woman in its depth and absorbing energy. The higher intellect, the imagination, the spirit, and even the heart might all find their congenial aliment in pursuits which, as some of their ardent votaries believed, would ascend from one step of powerful intelligence to another, until the philosopher should lay his hand on the secret of creative force and perhaps make new worlds for himself.

The long, complex sentences, learned vocabulary ("countenance," "aliment," "votaries"), and absence of colloquialisms suit Hawthorne's purpose well, recreating the formal language of the earlier era in which his story is set. The omniscient narrator, despite his use of the first person in "our story," is appropriately aloof and controlled.

Informal Diction Informal diction, consistent with everyday speech, is characterized by slang, contractions, colloquial expressions like *you know* and *I mean,* shortened word forms, incomplete sentences, and a casual, conversational tone. A first-person narrator may use informal style, or characters may speak informally; in either case, informal style tends to narrow the distance between readers and text.

Informal language can range from the straightforward contemporary style of Cal's dialogue in "Teenage Wasteland" ("'I think this kid is hurting. You know?'") to the regionalisms and dialect employed in Flannery O'Connor's "A Good Man Is Hard to Find" ("aloose"; "you all"; "britches"). In "Teenage Wasteland" (p. 504) Cal's self-consciously slangy, conversational style tells readers a good deal about his motives and his method of operating; in "A Good Man Is Hard to Find" (p. 230) the characters' speech patterns and diction reveal their geographic origin and social class. In other stories, a character's use of obscenities may suggest his or her crudeness or adolescent bravado, and use of racial or ethnic slurs suggests that a character is insensitive and bigoted.

The following passages from John Updike's "A&P" (p. 93) illustrates informal style:

> She had sort of oaky hair that the sun and salt had bleached, done up in a bun that was unravelling, and a kind of prim face. Walking into the A&P with your straps down, I suppose it's the only kind of face you *can* have. She held her head so high her neck, coming out of those white shoulders, looked kind of stretched, but I didn't mind. The longer her neck was, the more of her there was.

In the preceding paragraph, the first-person narrator uses a conversational style, including colloquialisms ("sort of," "I suppose," "kind of"), contractions ("it's," "didn't"), and the imprecise, informal *you* ("Walking into the A&P with your straps down. . . ."). The passage includes no elaborate sentences or learned diction.

IMAGERY AND FIGURATIVE LANGUAGE

Imagery Imagery, words and phrases that describe what is seen, heard, smelled, tasted, or touched, can have a significant impact in a story. A pattern of repeated imagery can help to convey a particular impression about a character or situation, or a writer may use such a pattern to communicate or reinforce a story's theme. For example, the theme of newly discovered sexuality can be conveyed through repeated use of words and phrases suggesting blooming or ripening.

In T. Coraghessan Boyle's "Greasy Lake" (p. 341) the narrator's vivid characterization of Greasy Lake itself uses rich visual imagery to evoke a scene. By describing a natural setting with surprising words like "fetid," "murky," and "greasy" and unpleasant images such as the glittering of broken glass, the "ravaged island," and the "charred remains of bonfires," Boyle creates a picture that is completely at odds with the traditional pastoral view of nature. The incongruous images are nevertheless perfectly consistent with the sordid events that unfold at Greasy Lake:

> Through the center of town, up the strip, past the housing developments and shopping malls, street lights giving way to the thin streaming illumination of the headlights, trees crowding the asphalt in a black unbroken wall: that was the way out to Greasy Lake. The Indians had called it Wakan, a reference to the clarity of its waters. Now it was fetid and murky, the mud banks glittering with broken glass and strewn with beer cans and the charred remains of bonfires. There was a single ravaged island a hundred yards from shore, so stripped of vegetation it looked as if the air force had strafed it. We went up to the lake because everyone went there, because we wanted to snuff the rich scent of possibility on the

> breeze, watch a girl take off her clothes and plunge into the festering murk, drink beer, smoke pot, howl at the stars, savor the incongruous full-throated roar of rock and roll against the primeval susurrus of frogs and crickets. This was nature.

Figurative Language Figures of speech—such as *similes, metaphors,* and *personification*—can enrich a story, subtly revealing information about characters, conveying or reinforcing themes, or creating a mood that enhances setting.

Metaphors and **similes**—imaginative comparisons—can convey a writer's or narrator's attitude toward characters and events. For example, Flannery O'Connor's many grotesque similes in "A Good Man Is Hard to Find" help to dehumanize her characters; the children's mother, for instance, has a face "as broad and innocent as a cabbage." In Tillie Olson's "I Stand Here Ironing" (p. 148) an extended metaphor in which a mother compares her daughter to a dress waiting to be ironed conveys the mother's attitude toward her daughter, effectively suggesting to readers the daughter's vulnerability. Similes and metaphors are used freely in Kate Chopin's "The Storm" (p. 143). In a scene of sexual awakening Calixta's skin is "like a creamy lily," her passion is "like a white flame," and her mouth is "a fountain of delight"; these figures of speech add a lushness and sensuality to the scene.

Personification—the attribution of human characteristics to nonhuman entities—is used in "Araby," where houses, "conscious of decent lives within them, gazed at one another with brown imperturbable faces." This use of figurative language expands readers' vision of the story's setting and gives a dreamlike quality to the passage. (Other figures of speech, such as **hyperbole** and **understatement,** can also enrich works of fiction.)

Allusions—references to familiar historical or literary personages or events—may also expand readers' understanding of a work. An allusion widens a work's context by bringing it into the context of a related subject or idea. For instance, Lorrie Moore's frequent references to historical events and popular songs in "How to Talk to Your Mother (Notes)" (p. 78) enhance readers' appreciation of the story's unusual movement backward through time. In addition, readers who recognize the references may gain a deeper understanding of the narrator's position on various political or social issues. Literary or Biblical allusions may be used in much the same way.

The following passage from Alberto Alvaro Rios's story "The Secret Lion" (p. 37) illustrates the power of language to communicate valuable information about a story's characters, setting, and theme.

> We had read the books, after all; we knew about bridges and castles and wildtreacherousraging alligatormouth rivers. We wanted them. So we were going to go out and get them. We went back that morning into that kitchen and we said, "We're going out there, we're going into the hills, we're going away for three days, don't worry." She said, "All right."

> "You know," I said to Sergio, "if we're going to go away for three days, well, we ought to at least pack a lunch."
>
> But we were two young boys with no patience for what we thought at the time was mom-stuff: making sa-and-wiches. My mother didn't offer. So we got out little kid knapsacks that my mother had sewn for us, and into them we put the jar of mustard. A loaf of bread. Knivesforksplates, bottles of Coke, a can opener. This was lunch for the two of us. And we were weighed down, humped over to be strong enough to carry this stuff. But we started walking anyway, into the hills. We were going to eat berries and stuff otherwise. "Goodbye." My mom said that.

The preceding paragraphs are written in an informal, conversational style. Through language, the adult narrator recaptures the bravado of the boys in search of "wildtreacherousraging alligatormouth rivers" even as he suggests to readers that the boys are not going far. The story's use of language is original and inventive: Words are blended together ("getridofit," "knivesforksplates"), linked to form new words ("mom-stuff"), and drawn out ("sa-and-wiches"). These experiments with words show the narrator's willingness to move back into a child's personality and frame of reference while maintaining the advantage of distance. Style is informal: The adult narrator uses sentence fragments ("A loaf of bread."), colloquialisms ("kid," "mom," "stuff"), and contractions. He also includes conversational elements such as *you know* and *well* in the dialogue, accurately recreating the childhood scene at the same time he sees its folly and remains aware of the disillusionment that awaits him. Thus the unique style serves the story's purpose well: It permits the narrator to bring readers with him into the child's world even as he maintains his adult stance ("But we were two young boys with no patience for what we thought at the time was mom-stuff. . . .").

A FINAL NOTE

In analyzing the use of language in a work of fiction, you may occasionally encounter obscure allusions, foreign words and phrases, unusual comparisons, and unfamiliar regional expressions—particularly in works treating cultures and historical periods other than your own. Frequently such language will be clarified by the context, or by explanatory notes in your text; when it is not, you should consult a dictionary, encyclopedia, or other reference work to discover the significance of the unfamiliar words or expressions.

Checklist for Writing about Style, Tone, and Language

- Is the story's tone intimate? Distant? Ironic? How does the tone advance the writer's purpose?
- Does the writer make any unusual creative use of diction, word order, or sentence structure?

- Is the style characterized by poetic features such as alliteration and assonance or repetition and parallelism? What do such techniques add to the story?
- Is the level of diction generally formal, informal, or somewhere in between?
- Is there a difference between the style of the narrator and the style of the characters' speech? If so, what is the effect of this difference?
- Do any of the story's characters use regionalisms, colloquial language, or nonstandard speech? If so, what effect does this language have?
- What do different characters' levels of diction reveal about them?
- What kind of imagery predominates? Where, and why, is imagery used?
- Does the story develop a pattern of imagery? How does this imagery relate to the story's themes?
- Does the story use simile and metaphor? Personification? What is the effect of these figures of speech?
- Does the story make any historical, literary, or Biblical allusions? Why are these allusions appropriate? What do they contribute to the story?
- Do figures of speech reinforce the story's themes? Reveal details about characters? Create a mood that enhances setting?
- What unfamiliar, obscure, or foreign words, phrases, or images are used in the story? What is the effect of these words or expressions?
- Is the story's style consistent with the mood the writer hopes to create? With the ideas the writer wishes to convey?

James Joyce (1884–1941) was born in Dublin but lived his entire adult life in self-imposed exile from his native Ireland. Though his parents sent him to schools that trained young men for the priesthood, Joyce saw himself as a religious and artistic rebel, and he fled to Paris soon after graduation in 1902. Recalled briefly to Dublin by his mother's fatal illness, Joyce returned to the Continent in 1904, taking with him an uneducated Irish country girl named Nora Barnacle, who became his wife in 1931. In dreary quarters in Trieste, Zurich, and Paris, Joyce struggled to support a growing family, sometimes teaching classes in Berlitz language schools.

Though Joyce never again lived in Ireland, he continued to write about Dublin. Publication of *Dubliners* (1914), a collection of short stories including "Araby," was delayed for seven years because the Irish publisher feared libel suits from local citizens who were thinly disguised as characters in the stories. Joyce's autobiographical *Portrait of the Artist as a Young Man* (1916) tells of a young writer's rejection of family, church, and country. *Ulysses* (1922), the comic tale of eighteen hours in the life of a wandering Dublin advertising salesman, was banned when the U.S. Post Office brought charges of obscenity against the book, and it remained banned in the United States and England for more than a decade. In *Ulysses* Joyce begins a revolutionary journey away from traditional techniques of plot and characterization to the interior monologues and stream-of-consciousness style that mark his last great novel, *Finnegans Wake* (1939).

James Joyce

ARABY

(1914)

North Richmond Street, being blind,[1] was a quiet street except at the hour when the Christian Brothers' School set the boys free. An uninhabited house of two storeys stood at the blind end, detached from its neighbours in a square ground. The other houses of the street, conscious of decent lives within them, gazed at one another with brown imperturbable faces.

The former tenant of our house, a priest, had died in the back drawing-room. Air, musty from having been long enclosed, hung in all the rooms, and the waste room behind the kitchen was littered with old useless papers. Among these I found a few paper-covered books, the pages of which were curled and damp: *The Abbot,* by Walter Scott, *The Devout Communicant* and *The Memoirs of Vidocq.*[2] I liked the last best because its leaves were yellow. The wild garden behind the house contained a central apple-tree and a few straggling bushes under one of which I found the late tenant's rusty bicycle-pump. He had been a very charitable priest; in his will he had left all his money to institutions and the furniture of his house to his sister.

When the short days of winter came dusk fell before we had well eaten our dinners. When we met in the street the houses had grown sombre. The space of sky above us was the colour of ever-changing violet and towards it the lamps of the street lifted their feeble lanterns. The cold air stung us and we played till our bodies glowed. Our shouts echoed in the silent street. The career of our play brought us through the dark muddy lanes behind the houses where we ran the gauntlet of the rough tribes from the cottages, to the back doors of the dark dripping gardens where

---

[1] A dead-end street.

[2] Sir Walter Scott (1771–1832)—an English Romantic novelist; *The Devout Communicant* is a variant title for *Pious Meditations,* written by an eighteenth-century English Franciscan friar, Pacifus Baker; *The Memoirs of Vidocq*—an autobiography of François-Jules Vidocq (1775–1857), a French soldier of fortune turned police agent.

odours arose from the ashpits, to the dark odorous stables where a coachman smoothed and combed the horse or shook music from the buckled harness. When we returned to the street light from the kitchen windows had filled the areas. If my uncle was seen turning the corner we hid in the shadow until we had seen him safely housed. Or if Mangan's sister came out on the doorstep to call her brother in to his tea we watched her from our shadow peer up and down the street. We waited to see whether she would remain or go in and, if she remained, we left our shadow and walked up to Mangan's steps resignedly. She was waiting for us, her figure defined by the light from the half-opened door. Her brother always teased her before he obeyed and I stood by the railings looking at her. Her dress swung as she moved her body and the soft rope of her hair tossed from side to side.

Every morning I lay on the floor in the front parlour watching her door. The blind was pulled down to within an inch of the sash so that I could not be seen. When she came out on the doorstep my heart leaped. I ran to the hall, seized my books and followed her. I kept her brown figure always in my eye and, when we came near the point at which our ways diverged, I quickened my pace and passed her. This happened morning after morning. I had never spoken to her, except for a few casual words, and yet her name was like a summons to all my foolish blood.

5 Her image accompanied me even in places the most hostile to romance. On Saturday evenings when my aunt went marketing I had to go to carry some of the parcels. We walked through the flaring streets, jostled by drunken men and bargaining women, amid the curses of labourers, the shrill litanies of shop-boys who stood on guard by the barrels of pigs' cheeks, the nasal chanting of street-singers, who sang a *come-all-you* about O'Donovan Rossa,[3] or a ballad about the troubles in our native land. These noises converged in a single sensation of life for me: I imagined that I bore my chalice safely through a throng of foes. Her name sprang to my lips at moments in strange prayers and praises which I myself did not understand. My eyes were often full of tears (I could not tell why) and at times a flood from my heart seemed to pour itself out into my bosom. I thought little of the future. I did not know whether I would ever speak to her or not or, if I spoke to her, how I could tell her of my confused adoration. But my body was like a harp and her words and gestures were like fingers running upon the wires.

One evening I went into the back drawing-room in which the priest had died. It was a dark rainy evening and there was no sound in the house. Through one of the broken panes I heard the rain impinge upon the earth, the fine incessant needles of water playing in the sodden beds. Some distant lamp or lighted window gleamed below me. I was

---

[3] Any popular song beginning "Come all you gallant Irishmen . . ."; O'Donovan Rossa was an Irish nationalist who was banished in 1870 for advocating violent rebellion against the British.

thankful that I could see so little. All my senses seemed to desire to veil themselves and, feeling that I was about to slip from them, I pressed the palms of my hands together until they trembled, murmuring: "*O love! O love!*" many times.

At last she spoke to me. When she addressed the first words to me I was so confused that I did not know what to answer. She asked me was I going to *Araby*. I forgot whether I answered yes or no. It would be a splendid bazaar, she said she would love to go.

"And why can't you?" I asked.

While she spoke she turned a silver bracelet round and round her wrist. She could not go, she said, because there would be a retreat that week in her convent.[4] Her brother and two other boys were fighting for their caps and I was alone at the railings. She held one of the spikes, bowing her head towards me. The light from the lamp opposite our door caught the white curve of her neck, lit up her hair that rested there and, falling, lit up the hand upon the railing. It fell over one side of her dress and caught the white border of a petticoat, just visible as she stood at ease.

"It's well for you," she said.

"If I go," I said, "I will bring you something."

What innumerable follies laid waste my waking and sleeping thoughts after that evening! I wished to annihilate the tedious intervening days. I chafed against the work of school. At night in my bedroom and by day in the classroom her image came between me and the page I strove to read. The syllables of the word *Araby* were called to me through the silence in which my soul luxuriated and cast an Eastern enchantment over me. I asked for leave to go to the bazaar on Saturday night. My aunt was surprised and hoped it was not some Freemason[5] affair. I answered few questions in class. I watched my master's face pass from amiability to sternness; he hoped I was not beginning to idle. I could not call my wandering thoughts together. I had hardly any patience with the serious work of life which, now that it stood between me and my desire, seemed to me child's play, ugly monotonous child's play.

On Saturday morning I reminded my uncle that I wished to go to the bazaar in the evening. He was fussing at the hallstand, looking for the hatbrush, and answered me curtly:

"Yes, boy, I know."

As he was in the hall I could not go into the front parlour and lie at the window. I left the house in bad humour and walked slowly towards the school. The air was pitilessly raw and already my heart misgave me.

When I came home to dinner my uncle had not yet been home. Still it was early. I sat staring at the clock for some time and, when its ticking began to irritate me, I left the room. I mounted the staircase and gained

---

[4] A week devoted to prayer and meditation in her convent school.

[5] At the time the story takes place, Catholics in Ireland thought the Masonic Order was a threat to the church.

the upper part of the house. The high cold empty gloomy rooms liberated me and I went from room to room singing. From the front window I saw my companions playing below in the street. Their cries reached me weakened and indistinct and, leaning my forehead against the cool glass, I looked over at the dark house where she lived. I may have stood there for an hour, seeing nothing but the brown-clad figure cast by my imagination, touched discreetly by the lamplight at the curved neck, at the hand upon the railings and at the border below the dress.

When I came downstairs again I found Mrs. Mercer sitting at the fire. She was an old garrulous woman, a pawnbroker's widow, who collected used stamps for some pious purpose. I had to endure the gossip of the tea-table. The meal was prolonged beyond an hour and still my uncle did not come. Mrs. Mercer stood up to go: she was sorry she couldn't wait any longer, but it was after eight o'clock and she did not like to be out late, as the night air was bad for her. When she had gone I began to walk up and down the room, clenching my fists. My aunt said:

"I'm afraid you may put off your bazaar for this night of Our Lord."

At nine o'clock I heard my uncle's latchkey in the halldoor. I heard him talking to himself and heard the hallstand rocking when it had received the weight of his overcoat. I could interpret these signs. When he was midway through his dinner I asked him to give me the money to go to the bazaar. He had forgotten.

"The people are in bed and after their first sleep now," he said.

I did not smile. My aunt said to him energetically:

"Can't you give him the money and let him go? You've kept him late enough as it is."

My uncle said he was very sorry he had forgotten. He said he believed in the old saying: "All work and no play makes Jack a dull boy." He asked me where I was going and, when I had told him a second time he asked me did I know *The Arab's Farewell to his Steed.*[6] When I left the kitchen he was about to recite the opening lines of the piece to my aunt.

I held a florin tightly in my hand as I strode down Buckingham Street towards the station. The sight of the streets thronged with buyers and glaring with gas recalled to me the purpose of my journey. I took my seat in a third-class carriage of a deserted train. After an intolerable delay the train moved out of the station slowly. It crept onward among ruinous houses and over the twinkling river. At Westland Row Station a crowd of people pressed to the carriage doors; but the porters moved them back, saying that it was a special train for the bazaar. I remained alone in the bare carriage. In a few minutes the train drew up beside an improvised wooden platform. I passed out on to the road and saw by the lighted dial of a clock that it was ten minutes to ten. In front of me was a large building which displayed the magical name.

---

[6] A sentimental poem by Caroline Norton (1808–1877) that tells the story of a nomad's heartbreak after selling his much-loved horse.

I could not find any sixpenny entrance and, fearing that the bazaar would be closed, I passed in quickly through a turnstile, handing a shilling to a weary-looking man. I found myself in a big hall girdled at half its height by a gallery. Nearly all the stalls were closed and the greater part of the hall was in darkness. I recognised a silence like that which pervades a church after a service. I walked into the centre of the bazaar timidly. A few people were gathered about the stalls which were still open. Before a curtain, over which the words *Café Chantant*[7] were written in coloured lamps, two men were counting money on a salver. I listened to the fall of the coins.

Remembering with difficulty why I had come I went over to one of the stalls and examined porcelain vases and flowered tea-sets. At the door of the stall a young lady was talking and laughing with two young gentlemen. I remarked their English accents and listened vaguely to their conversation.

"O, I never said such a thing!"

"O, but you did!"

"O, but I didn't!"

"Didn't she say that?"

"Yes. I heard her."

"O, there's a . . . fib!"

Observing me the young lady came over and asked me did I wish to buy anything. The tone of her voice was not encouraging; she seemed to have spoken to me out of a sense of duty. I looked humbly at the great jars that stood like eastern guards at either side of the dark entrance to the stall and murmured:

"No, thank you."

The young lady changed the position of one of the vases and went back to the two young men. They began to talk of the same subject. Once or twice the young lady glanced at me over her shoulder.

I lingered before her stall, though I knew my stay was useless, to make my interest in her wares seem the more real. Then I turned away slowly and walked down the middle of the bazaar. I allowed the two pennies to fall against the sixpence in my pocket. I heard a voice call from one end of the gallery that the light was out. The upper part of the hall was now completely dark.

Gazing up into the darkness I saw myself as a creature driven and derided by vanity; and my eyes burned with anguish and anger.

READING AND REACTING

1. How would you characterize the story's level of diction? Is this level appropriate for a story about a young boy's experiences? Explain.
2. In what particular situations or contexts is Joyce most likely to use figurative language? Why?

---

[7] A Paris café featuring musical entertainment.

3. What words and expressions locate this story in a particular time and place?
4. In paragraph 4 the narrator says, "her name was like a summons to all my foolish blood." In the story's last sentence he sees himself as "a creature driven and derided by vanity." What other expressions does he use to describe his feelings?
5. How is language used to emphasize the contrast between the narrator's day-to-day life and the exotic promise of the bazaar?
6. What does each of the italicized words suggest: "We walked through the *flaring* streets" (5); "I heard the rain *impinge* upon the earth" (6); "I *chafed* against the work of school" (11); "I found myself in a big hall *girdled* at half its height by a gallery" (25)? What other examples of unusual word choice can you identify in the story?
7. Explain the significance of the priest's choice of reading matter.
8. Identify words and phrases in the story that suggest religion. What purposes do these references to religion serve?
9. **JOURNAL ENTRY:** What is it about the events in this story that makes the narrator remember them years later? Use your memories of your own childhood to help you respond to this question.

Ernest Hemingway (1898–1961) grew up in Oak Park, Illinois, and after high school graduation began his writing career as a cub reporter on the *Kansas City Star.* As a volunteer ambulance driver in World War I, eighteen-year-old Hemingway was wounded by machine-gun fire while carrying an Italian soldier to safety. In 1922, Hemingway and his first wife (he married four times) moved to Paris, where he taught Ezra Pound how to box, let Gertrude Stein mind the baby, and talked literary shop with expatriate writers F. Scott Fitzgerald and James Joyce. He was, said Joyce, "a big, powerful peasant, as strong as a buffalo . . . and ready to live the life he writes about." In fact, this public image of the "man's man"—the war correspondent, the deep-sea fisherman, the hunter on safari—was one Hemingway carefully created for himself.

Success came early, with publication of the short story collection *In Our Time* (1925) and his first and most acclaimed novel, *The Sun Also Rises* (1926), a portrait of a postwar "lost generation" of Americans adrift in Europe. Hemingway's novels make fiction and art out of the reality of his own life. *A Farewell to Arms* (1929) harks back to his war experiences; *For Whom the Bell Tolls* (1940) emerged out of his experiences as a journalist in Spain during the Spanish Civil War. Late in life, he made his home in Key West, Florida, and then in Cuba, where he wrote *The Old Man and the Sea* (1952). Hemingway's heroes embody the writer's own belief that while life may be followed by *nada,* or nothingness, strong individuals can embrace life and live it with dignity and honor. In 1961, plagued by poor health and mental illness—and perhaps by the difficulty of living up to his own image—Hemingway took his own life.

According to novelist and critic Anthony Burgess, Hemingway changed the sound of English prose by struggling to write a "true simple declarative sentence." His spare, unadorned style "sounds easy now, chiefly because Hemingway has shown us how to do it, but it was not easy at a time when 'literature' still meant fine writing in the Victorian sense. . . ." Hemingway was awarded the 1954 Nobel Prize in literature.

Ernest Hemingway

A CLEAN, WELL-LIGHTED PLACE

(1933)

It was late and every one had left the café except an old man who sat in the shadow the leaves of the tree made against the electric light. In the day time the street was dusty, but at night the dew settled the dust and the old man liked to sit late because he was deaf and now at night it was quiet and he felt the difference. The two waiters inside the café knew that the old man was a little drunk, and while he was a good client they knew that if he became too drunk he would leave without paying, so they kept watch on him.

"Last week he tried to commit suicide," one waiter said.

"Why?"

"He was in despair."

5 "What about?"

"Nothing."

"How do you know it was nothing?"

"He has plenty of money."

They sat together at a table that was close against the wall near the door of the café and looked at the terrace where the tables were all empty except where the old man sat in the shadow of the leaves of the tree that moved slightly in the wind. A girl and a soldier went by in the street. The street light shone on the brass number on his collar. The girl wore no head covering and hurried beside him.

10 "The guard will pick him up," one waiter said.

"What does it matter if he gets what he's after?"

"He had better get off the street now. The guard will get him. They went by five minutes ago."

The old man sitting in the shadow rapped on his saucer with his glass. The younger waiter went over to him.

"What do you want?"

The old man looked at him. "Another brandy," he said.

"You'll be drunk," the waiter said. The old man looked at him. The waiter went away.

"He'll stay all night," he said to his colleague. "I'm sleepy now. I never get into bed before three o'clock. He should have killed himself last week."

The waiter took the brandy bottle and another saucer from the counter inside the café and marched out to the old man's table. He put down the saucer and poured the glass full of brandy.

"You should have killed yourself last week," he said to the deaf man. The old man motioned with his finger. "A little more," he said. The waiter poured on into the glass so that the brandy slopped over and ran down the stem into the top saucer of the pile. "Thank you," the old man said. The waiter took the bottle back inside the café. He sat down at the table with his colleague again.

"He's drunk now," he said.

"He's drunk every night."

"What did he want to kill himself for?"

"How should I know."

"How did he do it?"

"He hung himself with a rope."

"Who cut him down?"

"His niece."

"Why did they do it?"

"Fear for his soul."

"How much money has he got?"

"He's got plenty."

"He must be eighty years old."

"Anyway I should say he was eighty."

"I wish he would go home. I never get to bed before three o'clock. What kind of hour is that to go to bed?"

"He stays up because he likes it."

"He's lonely. I'm not lonely. I have a wife waiting in bed for me."

"He had a wife once too."

"A wife would be no good to him now."

"You can't tell. He might be better with a wife."

"His niece looks after him."

"I know. You said she cut him down."

"I wouldn't want to be that old. An old man is a nasty thing."

"Not always. This old man is clean. He drinks without spilling. Even now, drunk. Look at him."

"I don't want to look at him. I wish he would go home. He has no regard for those who must work."

The old man looked from his glass across the square, then over at the waiters.

"Another brandy," he said, pointing to his glass. The waiter who was in a hurry came over.

"Finished," he said, speaking with that omission of syntax stupid people employ when talking to drunken people or foreigners. "No more tonight. Close now."

"Another," said the old man.

"No. Finished." The waiter wiped the edge of the table with a towel and shook his head.

The old man stood up, slowly counted the saucers, took a leather coin purse from his pocket and paid for the drinks, leaving half a peseta tip.

The waiter watched him go down the street, a very old man walking unsteadily but with dignity.

"Why didn't you let him stay and drink?" the unhurried waiter asked. They were putting up the shutters. "It is not half-past two."

"I want to go home to bed."

"What is an hour?"

"More to me than to him."

"An hour is the same."

"You talk like an old man yourself. He can buy a bottle and drink at home."

"It's not the same."

"No, it is not," agreed the waiter with a wife. He did not wish to be unjust. He was only in a hurry.

"And you? You have no fear of going home before your usual hour?"

"Are you trying to insult me?"

"No, hombre, only to make a joke."

"No," the waiter who was in a hurry said, rising from pulling down the metal shutters. "I have confidence. I am all confidence."

"You have youth, confidence, and a job," the older waiter said. "You have everything."

"And what do you lack?"

"Everything but work."

"You have everything I have."

"No. I have never had confidence and I am not young."

"Come on. Stop talking nonsense and lock up."

"I am of those who like to stay late at the café," the older waiter said. "With all those who do not want to go to bed. With all those who need a light for the night."

"I want to go home and into bed."

"We are of two different kinds," the older waiter said. He was now dressed to go home. "It is not only a question of youth and confidence although those things are very beautiful. Each night I am reluctant to close up because there may be some one who needs the café."

"Hombre, there are bodegas[1] open all night long."

"You do not understand. This is a clean and pleasant café. It is well lighted. The light is very good and also, now, there are shadows of the leaves."

---

[1] Wineshops, sometimes combined with grocery stores.

"Good night," said the younger waiter.

"Good night," the other said. Turning off the electric light he continued the conversation with himself. It is the light of course but it is necessary that the place be clean and pleasant. You do not want music. Certainly you do not want music. Nor can you stand before a bar with dignity although that is all that is provided for these hours. What did he fear? It was not fear or dread. It was a nothing that he knew too well. It was all a nothing and a man was nothing too. It was only that and light was all it needed and a certain cleanness and order. Some lived in it and never felt it but he knew it all was nada y pues nada y nada y pues nada.[2] Our nada who art in nada, nada be thy name thy kingdom nada thy will be nada in nada as it is in nada. Give us this nada our daily nada and nada us our nada as we nada our nadas and nada us not into nada but deliver us from nada; pues nada. Hail nothing full of nothing, nothing is with thee. He smiled and stood before a bar with a shining steam pressure coffee machine.

"What's yours?" asked the barman.

"Nada."

"Otro loco más[3]," said the barman and turned away.

"A little cup," said the waiter.

The barman poured it for him.

"The light is very bright and pleasant but the bar is unpolished," the waiter said.

The barman looked at him but did not answer. It was too late at night for conversation.

"You want another copita[4]?" the barman asked.

"No, thank you," said the waiter and went out. He disliked bars and bodegas. A clean, well-lighted café was a very different thing. Now, without thinking further, he would go home to his room. He would lie in the bed and finally, with daylight, he would go to sleep. After all, he said to himself, it is probably only insomnia. Many must have it.

READING AND REACTING

1. Throughout the story certain words—*nada,* for example—are repeated. Identify as many of these repeated words as you can. What do you think such repetition achieves?
2. The story's dialogue is presented in alternating exchanges of very brief sentences. What is the effect of these clipped exchanges?
3. Characterize the tone of the story.

---

[2] Nothing and then nothing and nothing and then nothing.

[3] Another lunatic.

[4] Little cup.

4. How are the story's style and tone suited to its setting? To its characters?
5. Does the story present the human condition in optimistic or pessimistic terms? In what sense are the story's style and tone well suited to this worldview?
6. Why does Hemingway use Spanish in the story? Would the impact of the prayer be different if it had been spoken in English? Explain.
7. The café is described as "clean" and "pleasant." Why is this description a key element of the story? In what sense is this description ironic?
8. The story's primary point of view is objective. At times, however, a limited omniscient point of view is used. Identify such instances, and explain the reasons for the shift in point of view.
9. Identify any figurative language used in the story. How does the presence (or absence) of such language help to convey the story's theme?
10. **JOURNAL ENTRY:** At the end of the story, the waiter thinks to himself, "it is probably only insomnia. Many must have it." What do you think he means? How do the style and tone of the story influence your reaction to the waiter's conclusion?

(Mary) Flannery O'Connor (1925–1964) was born to a prosperous Catholic family in Savannah, Georgia, and spent most of her adult life on a farm near the town of Milledgeville. She left the South to study writing at the University of Iowa, moving to New York to work on her first novel, *Wise Blood* (1952). On a train going south for Christmas, O'Connor fell desperately ill; she was diagnosed as having lupus, the immune system disease that killed her father and would cause O'Connor's death at age thirty-nine.

While her mother ran the farm, O'Connor spent mornings writing and afternoons wandering the fields with cane or crutches. Her short story collection *A Good Man Is Hard to Find* (1955) and an excellent French translation of *Wise Blood* established her international reputation, which was solidified with publication of a second novel, *The Violent Bear It Away* (1960), and a posthumously published book of short stories, *Everything That Rises Must Converge* (1965).

O'Connor delighted in local reaction to her grotesque, often grisly stories: "Ask her," the men at the hardware store told her uncle, "why she don't write about some nice people." O'Connor, said a friend, believed that an artist "should face all the truth down to the worst of it." Yet however dark, O'Connor's stories are infused with grim humor and a fierce belief in the possibility of spiritual redemption, even for her most tortured characters. A line from her short story "A Good Man Is Hard to Find" says much about what O'Connor perceived about both natural things and her characters: "The trees were full of silver-white sunlight and the meanest of them sparkled." In O'Connor's work, the "meanest" things and people can sparkle, touched by a kind of holy madness and beauty.

Flannery O'Connor

A GOOD MAN IS HARD TO FIND

(1955)

The grandmother didn't want to go to Florida. She wanted to visit some of her connections in east Tennessee and she was seizing at every chance to change Bailey's mind. Bailey was the son she lived with, her only boy. He was sitting on the edge of his chair at the table, bent over the orange sports section of the *Journal*. "Now look here, Bailey," she said, "see here, read this," and she stood with one hand on her thin hip and the other rattling the newspaper at his bald head. "Here this fellow that calls himself The Misfit is aloose from the Federal Pen and headed toward Florida and you read here what it says he did to these people. Just you read it. I wouldn't take my children in any direction with a criminal like that aloose in it. I couldn't answer to my conscience if I did."

Bailey didn't look up from his reading so she wheeled around then and faced the children's mother, a young woman in slacks, whose face was as broad and innocent as a cabbage and was tied around with a green head-kerchief that had two points on the top like a rabbit's ears. She was sitting on the sofa, feeding the baby his apricots out of a jar. "The children have been to Florida before," the old lady said. "You all ought to take them somewhere else for a change so they would see different parts of the world and be broad. They never have been to east Tennessee."

The children's mother didn't seem to hear her but the eight-year-old boy, John Wesley, a stocky child with glasses, said, "If you don't want to go to Florida, why dontcha stay at home?" He and the little girl, June Star, were reading the funny papers on the floor.

"She wouldn't stay at home to be queen for a day," June Star said without raising her yellow head.

5 "Yes and what would you do if this fellow, the Misfit, caught you?" the grandmother asked.

"I'd smack his face," John Wesley said.

"She wouldn't stay at home for a million bucks," June Star said. "Afraid she'd miss something. She has to go everywhere we go."

"All right, Miss," the grandmother said. "Just remember that the next time you want me to curl your hair."

June Star said her hair was naturally curly.

10 The next morning the grandmother was the first one in the car, ready to go. She had her big black valise that looked like the head of a hippopotamus in one corner, and underneath it she was hiding a basket with Pitty Sing, the cat, in it. She didn't intend for the cat to be left alone in the house for three days because he would miss her too much and she was afraid he might brush against one of the gas burners and accidentally asphyxiate himself. Her son, Bailey, didn't like to arrive at a motel with a cat.

She sat in the middle of the back seat with John Wesley and June Star on either side of her. Bailey and the children's mother and the baby sat in front and they left Atlanta at eight forty-five with the mileage on the car at 55890. The grandmother wrote this down because she thought it would be interesting to say how many miles they had been when they got back. It took them twenty minutes to reach the outskirts of the city.

The old lady settled herself comfortably, removing her white cotton gloves and putting them up with her purse on the shelf in front of the back window. The children's mother still had on slacks and still had her head tied up in a green kerchief, but the grandmother had on a navy blue straw sailor hat with a bunch of white violets on the brim and a navy blue dress with a small white dot in the print. Her collars and cuffs were white organdy trimmed with lace and at her neckline she had pinned a purple spray of cloth violets containing a sachet. In case of an accident, anyone seeing her dead on the highway would know at once that she was a lady.

She said she thought it was going to be a good day for driving, neither too hot nor too cold, and she cautioned Bailey that the speed limit was fifty-five miles an hour and that the patrolmen hid themselves behind billboards and small clumps of trees and sped out after you before you had a chance to slow down. She pointed out interesting details of the scenery: Stone Mountain; the blue granite that in some places came up to both sides of the highway; the brilliant red clay banks slightly streaked with purple; and the various crops that made rows of green lace-work on the ground. The trees were full of silver-white sunlight and the meanest of them sparkled. The children were reading comic magazines and their mother had gone back to sleep.

"Let's go through Georgia fast so we won't have to look at it much," John Wesley said.

15 "If I were a little boy," said the grandmother, "I wouldn't talk about my native state that way. Tennessee has the mountains and Georgia has the hills."

"Tennessee is just a hillbilly dumping ground," John Wesley said, "and Georgia is a lousy state too."

"You said it," June Star said.

"In my time," said the grandmother, folding her thin veined fingers, "children were more respectful of their native states and their parents and everything else. People did right then. Oh look at the cute little pickaninny!" she said and pointed to a Negro child standing in the door of a shack. "Wouldn't that make a picture, now?" she asked and they all turned and looked at the little Negro out of the back window. He waved.

"He didn't have any britches on," June Star said.

20 "He probably didn't have any," the grandmother explained. "Little niggers in the country don't have things like we do. If I could paint, I'd paint that picture," she said.

The children exchanged comic books.

The grandmother offered to hold the baby and the children's mother passed him over the front seat to her. She set him on her knee and bounced him and told him about the things they were passing. She rolled her eyes and screwed up her mouth and stuck her leathery thin face into his smooth bland one. Occasionally he gave her a faraway smile. They passed a large cotton field with five or six graves fenced in the middle of it, like a small island. "Look at the graveyard!" the grandmother said, pointing it out. "That was the old family burying ground. That belonged to the plantation."

"Where's the plantation?" John Wesley asked.

"Gone With the Wind," said the grandmother. "Ha. Ha."

25 When the children finished all the comic books they had brought, they opened the lunch and ate it. The grandmother ate a peanut butter sandwich and an olive and would not let the children throw the box and the paper napkins out the window. When there was nothing else to do they played a game by choosing a cloud and making the other two guess what shape it suggested. John Wesley took one the shape of a cow and June Star guessed a cow and John Wesley said, no, an automobile, and June Star said he didn't play fair, and they began to slap each other over the grandmother.

The grandmother said she would tell them a story if they would keep quiet. When she told a story, she rolled her eyes and waved her head and was very dramatic. She said once when she was a maiden lady she had been courted by a Mr. Edgar Atkins Teagarden from Jasper, Georgia. She said he was a very good-looking man and a gentleman and that he brought her a watermelon every Saturday afternoon with his initials cut in it, E. A. T. Well, one Saturday, she said, Mr. Teagarden brought the watermelon and there was nobody at home and he left it on the front porch and returned in his buggy to Jasper, but she never got the watermelon, she said, because a nigger boy ate it when he saw the initials, E. A. T.! This story tickled John Wesley's funny bone and he giggled and giggled but June Star didn't think it was any good. She said she wouldn't marry a man that just brought her a watermelon on Saturday. The grandmother said she would have done well to marry Mr. Teagarden because he was a gentleman and had bought Coca-Cola stock when it first came out and that he died only a few years ago, a very wealthy man.

They stopped at The Tower for barbecued sandwiches. The Tower was a part stucco and part wood filling station and dance hall set in a clearing outside of Timothy. A fat man named Red Sammy Butts ran it and there were signs stuck here and there on the building and for miles up and down the highway saying, TRY RED SAMMY'S FAMOUS BARBECUE. NONE LIKE FAMOUS RED SAMMY'S! RED SAM! THE FAT BOY WITH THE HAPPY LAUGH. A VETERAN! RED SAMMY'S YOUR MAN!

Red Sammy was lying on the bare ground outside The Tower with his head under a truck while a gray monkey about a foot high, chained to a small chinaberry tree, chattered nearby. The monkey sprang back into the tree and got on the highest limb as soon as he saw the children jump out of the car and run toward him.

Inside, The Tower was a long dark room with a counter at one end and tables at the other and dancing space in the middle. They all sat down at a board table next to the nickelodeon and Red Sam's wife, a tall burnt-brown woman with hair and eyes lighter than her skin, came and took their order. The children's mother put a dime in the machine and played "The Tennessee Waltz," and the grandmother said that tune always made her want to dance. She asked Bailey if he would like to dance but he only glared at her. He didn't have a naturally sweet disposition like she did and trips made him nervous. The grandmother's brown eyes were very bright. She swayed her head from side to side and pretended she was dancing in her chair. June Star said play something she could tap to so the children's mother put in another dime and played a fast number and June Star stepped out onto the dance floor and did her tap routine.

"Ain't she cute?" Red Sam's wife said, leaning over the counter. "Would you like to come be my little girl?"

"No I certainly wouldn't," June Star said. "I wouldn't live in a broken-down place like this for a million bucks!" and she ran back to the table.

"Ain't she cute?" the woman repeated, stretching her mouth politely.

"Aren't you ashamed?" hissed the grandmother.

Red Sam came in and told his wife to quit lounging on the counter and hurry up with these people's order. His khaki trousers reached just to his hip bones and his stomach hung over them like a sack of meal swaying under his shirt. He came over and sat down at a table nearby and let out a combination sigh and yodel. "You can't win," he said. "You can't win," and he wiped his sweating red face off with a gray handkerchief. "These days you don't know who to trust," he said. "Ain't that the truth?"

"People are certainly not nice like they used to be," said the grandmother.

"Two fellers come in here last week," Red Sammy said, "driving a Chrysler. It was a old beat-up car but it was a good one and these boys looked all right to me. Said they worked at the mill and you know I let them fellers charge the gas they bought? Now why did I do that?"

"Because you're a good man!" the grandmother said at once.

"Yes'm, I suppose so," Red Sam said as if he were struck with this answer.

His wife brought the orders, carrying the five plates all at once without a tray, two in each hand and one balanced on her arm. "It isn't a soul in this green world of God's that you can trust," she said. "And I don't count nobody out of that, not nobody," she repeated, looking at Red Sammy.

"Did you read about that criminal, The Misfit, that's escaped?" asked the grandmother.

"I wouldn't be a bit surprised if he didn't attact this place right here," said the woman. "If he hears about it being here, I wouldn't be none surprised to see him. If he hears it's two cent in the cash register, I wouldn't be at all surprised if he . . ."

"That'll do," Red Sam said. "Go bring these people their Co'-Colas," and the woman went off to get the rest of the order.

"A good man is hard to find," Red Sammy said. "Everything is getting terrible. I remember the day you could go off and leave your screen door unlatched. Not no more."

He and the grandmother discussed better times. The old lady said that in her opinion Europe was entirely to blame for the way things were now. She said the way Europe acted you would think we were made of money and Red Sam said it was no use talking about it, she was exactly right. The children ran outside into the white sunlight and looked at the monkey in the lacy chinaberry tree. He was busy catching fleas on himself and biting each one carefully between his teeth as if it were a delicacy.

They drove off again into the hot afternoon. The grandmother took cat naps and woke up every few minutes with her own snoring. Outside of Toombsboro she woke up and recalled an old plantation that she had visited in this neighborhood once when she was a young lady. She said the house had six white columns across the front and that there was an avenue of oaks leading up to it and two little wooden trellis arbors on either side in front where you sat down with your suitor after a stroll in the garden. She recalled exactly which road to turn off to get to it. She knew that Bailey would not be willing to lose any time looking at an old house, but the more she talked about it, the more she wanted to see it once again and find out if the little twin arbors were still standing. "There was a secret panel in this house," she said craftily, not telling the truth but wishing that she were, "and the story went that all the family silver was hidden in it when Sherman came through but it was never found . . ."

"Hey!" John Wesley said. "Let's go see it! We'll find it! We'll poke all the woodwork and find it! Who lives there? Where do you turn off at? Hey Pop, can't we turn off there?"

"We never have seen a house with a secret panel!" June Star shrieked. "Let's go to the house with the secret panel! Hey Pop, can't we go see the house with the secret panel!"

"It's not far from here, I know," the grandmother said. "It wouldn't take over twenty minutes."

Bailey was looking straight ahead. His jaw was as rigid as a horseshoe. "No," he said.

The children began to yell and scream that they wanted to see the house with the secret panel. John Wesley kicked the back of the front seat and June Star hung over her mother's shoulder and whined desperately into her ear that they never had any fun even on their vacation, that they could never do what THEY wanted to do. The baby began to scream and John Wesley kicked the back of the seat so hard that his father could feel the blows in his kidney.

"All right!" he shouted and drew the car to a stop at the side of the road. "Will you all shut up? Will you all just shut up for one second? If you don't shut up, we won't go anywhere."

"It would be very educational for them," the grandmother murmured.

"All right," Bailey said, "but get this: this is the only time we're going to stop for anything like this. This is the one and only time."

"The dirt road that you have to turn down is about a mile back," the grandmother directed. "I marked it when we passed."

"A dirt road," Bailey groaned.

After they had turned around and were headed toward the dirt road, the grandmother recalled other points about the house, the beautiful glass over the front doorway and the candle-lamp in the hall. John Wesley said that the secret panel was probably in the fireplace.

"You can't go inside this house," Bailey said. "You don't know who lives there."

"While you all talk to the people in front, I'll run around behind and get in a window," John Wesley suggested.

"We'll all stay in the car," his mother said.

They turned onto the dirt road and the car raced roughly along in a swirl of pink dust. The grandmother recalled the times when there were no paved roads and thirty miles was a day's journey. The dirt road was hilly and there were sudden washes in it and sharp curves on dangerous embankments. All at once they would be on a hill, looking down over the blue tops of trees for miles around, then the next minute, they would be in a red depression with the dust-coated trees looking down on them.

"This place had better turn up in a minute," Bailey said, "or I'm going to turn around."

The road looked as if no one had traveled on it in months.

"It's not much farther," the grandmother said and just as she said it, a horrible thought came to her. The thought was so embarrassing that she turned red in the face and her eyes dilated and her feet jumped up, upsetting her valise in the corner. The instant the valise moved, the newspaper top she had over the basket under it rose with a snarl and Pitty Sing, the cat, sprang onto Bailey's shoulder.

The children were thrown to the floor and their mother, clutching the baby, was thrown out the door onto the ground; the old lady was thrown into the front seat. The car turned over once and landed right-side-up in a gulch off the side of the road. Bailey remained in the driver's seat with the cat—gray-striped with a broad white face and an orange nose—clinging to his neck like a caterpillar.

As soon as the children saw they could move their arms and legs, they scrambled out of the car, shouting, "We've had an ACCIDENT!"

The grandmother was curled up under the dashboard, hoping she was injured so that Bailey's wrath would not come down on her all at once. The horrible thought she had had before the accident was that the house she had remembered so vividly was not in Georgia but in Tennessee.

Bailey removed the cat from his neck with both hands and flung it out the window against the side of a pine tree. Then he got out of the car and started looking for the children's mother. She was sitting against the side of the red gutted ditch, holding the screaming baby, but she only had a cut down her face and a broken shoulder. "We've had an ACCIDENT!" the children screamed in a frenzy of delight.

"But nobody's killed," June Star said with disappointment as the grandmother limped out of the car, her hat still pinned to her head but the broken front brim standing up at a jaunty angle and the violet spray hanging off the side. They all sat down in the ditch, except the children, to recover from the shock. They were all shaking.

"Maybe a car will come along," said the children's mother hoarsely.

"I believe I have injured an organ," said the grandmother, pressing her side, but no one answered her. Bailey's teeth were clattering. He had on a yellow sport shirt with bright blue parrots designed in it and his face was as yellow as the shirt. The grandmother decided that she would not mention that the house was in Tennessee.

The road was about ten feet above and they could see only the tops of the trees on the other side of it. Behind the ditch they were sitting in there were more woods, tall and dark and deep. In a few minutes they saw a car some distance away on top of a hill, coming slowly as if the occupants were watching them. The grandmother stood up and waved both arms dramatically to attract their attention. The car continued to come on slowly, disappeared around a bend and appeared again, moving even slower, on top of the hill they had gone over. It was a big black battered hearse-like automobile. There were three men in it.

It came to a stop just over them and for some minutes, the driver looked down with a steady expressionless gaze to where they were sitting, and didn't speak. Then he turned his head and muttered something to the other two and they got out. One was a fat boy in black trousers and a red sweat shirt with a silver stallion embossed on the front of it. He moved around on the right side of them and stood staring, his mouth partly open in a kind of loose grin. The other had on khaki pants and a blue striped coat and a gray hat pulled down very low, hiding most of his face. He came around slowly on the left side. Neither spoke.

The driver got out of the car and stood by the side of it, looking down at them. He was an older man than the other two. His hair was just beginning to gray and he wore silver-rimmed spectacles that gave him a scholarly look. He had a long creased face and didn't have on any shirt or undershirt. He had on blue jeans that were too tight for him and was holding a black hat and a gun. The two boys also had guns.

"We've had an ACCIDENT!" the children screamed.

The grandmother had the peculiar feeling that the bespectacled man was someone she knew. His face was as familiar to her as if she had known him all her life but she could not recall who he was. He moved away from the car and began to come down the embankment, placing his feet carefully so that he wouldn't slip. He had on tan and white shoes and no socks, and his ankles were red and thin. "Good afternoon," he said. "I see you all had you a little spill."

"We turned over twice!" said the grandmother.

"Oncet," he corrected. "We seen it happen. Try their car and see will it run, Hiram," he said quietly to the boy with the gray hat.

"What you got that gun for?" John Wesley asked. "Watcha gonna do with that gun?"

"Lady," the man said to the children's mother, "would you mind calling them children to sit down by you? Children make me nervous. I want all you all to sit down right together there where you're at."

"What are you telling US what to do for?" June Star asked.

Behind them the line of woods gaped like a dark open mouth. "Come here," said their mother.

"Look here now," Bailey began suddenly, "we're in a predicament! We're in . . ."

The grandmother shrieked. She scrambled to her feet and stood staring. "You're The Misfit!" she said. "I recognized you at once!"

"Yes'm," the man said, smiling slightly as if he were pleased in spite of himself to be known, "but it would have been better for all of you, lady, if you hadn't of reckernized me."

Bailey turned his head sharply and said something to his mother that shocked even the children. The old lady began to cry and The Misfit reddened.

"Lady," he said, "don't you get upset. Sometimes a man says things he don't mean. I don't reckon he meant to talk to you thataway."

"You wouldn't shoot a lady, would you?" the grandmother said and removed a clean handkerchief from her cuff and began to slap at her eyes with it.

The Misfit pointed the toe of his shoe into the ground and made a little hole and then covered it up again. "I would hate to have to," he said.

"Listen," the grandmother almost screamed, "I know you're a good man. You don't look a bit like you have common blood. I know you must come from nice people!"

"Yes mam," he said, "finest people in the world." When he smiled he showed a row of strong white teeth. "God never made a finer woman than my mother and my daddy's heart was pure gold," he said. The boy with the red sweat shirt had come around behind them and was standing with his gun at his hip. The Misfit squatted down on the ground. "Watch them children, Bobby Lee," he said. "You know they make me nervous." He looked at the six of them huddled together in front of him and he seemed to be embarrassed as if he couldn't think of anything to say. "Ain't a cloud in the sky," he remarked, looking up at it. "Don't see no sun but don't see no cloud neither."

"Yes, it's a beautiful day," said the grandmother. "Listen," she said, "you shouldn't call yourself The Misfit because I know you're a good man at heart. I can just look at you and tell."

"Hush!" Bailey yelled. "Hush! Everybody shut up and let me handle this!" He was squatting in the position of a runner about to sprint forward but he didn't move.

"I pre-chate that, lady," The Misfit said and drew a little circle in the ground with the butt of his gun.

"It'll take a half a hour to fix this here car," Hiram called, looking over the raised hood of it.

"Well, first you and Bobby Lee get him and that little boy to step over yonder with you," The Misfit said, pointing to Bailey and John Wesley. "The boys want to ast you something," he said to Bailey. "Would you mind stepping back in them woods there with them?"

"Listen," Bailey began, "we're in a terrible predicament! Nobody realizes what this is," and his voice cracked. His eyes were as blue and intense as the parrots in his shirt and he remained perfectly still.

The grandmother reached up to adjust her hat brim as if she were going to the woods with him but it came off in her hand. She stood staring at it and after a second she let it fall on the ground. Hiram pulled Bailey up by the arm as if he were assisting an old man. John Wesley caught hold of his father's hand and Bobby Lee followed. They went off toward the woods and just as they reached the dark edge, Bailey turned and supporting himself against a gray naked pine trunk, he shouted, "I'll be back in a minute, Mamma, wait on me!"

"Come back this instant!" his mother shrilled but they all disappeared into the woods.

"Bailey Boy!" the grandmother called in a tragic voice but she found she was looking at The Misfit squatting on the ground in front of her. "I just know you're a good man," she said desperately. "You're not a bit common!"

"Nome, I ain't a good man," The Misfit said after a second as if he had considered her statement carefully, "but I ain't the worst in the world neither. My daddy said I was a different breed of dog from my brothers and sisters. 'You know,' Daddy said, 'it's some that can live their whole life out without asking about it and it's others has to know why it is, and this boy is one of the latters. He's going to be into everything!'" He put on his black hat and looked up suddenly and then away deep into the woods as if he were embarrassed again. "I'm sorry I don't have on a shirt before you ladies," he said, hunching his shoulders slightly. "We buried our clothes that we had on when we escaped and we're just making do until we can get better. We borrowed these from some folks we met," he explained.

"That's perfectly all right," the grandmother said. "Maybe Bailey has an extra shirt in his suitcase."

"I'll look and see terrectly," The Misfit said.

"Where are they taking him?" the children's mother screamed.

"Daddy was a card himself," The Misfit said. "You couldn't put anything over on him. He never got in trouble with the Authorities though. Just had the knack of handling them."

"You could be honest too if you'd only try," said the grandmother. "Think how wonderful it would be to settle down and live a comfortable life and not have to think about somebody chasing you all the time."

The Misfit kept scratching in the ground with the butt of his gun as if he were thinking about it. "Yes'm, somebody is always after you," he murmured.

The grandmother noticed how thin his shoulder blades were just behind his hat because she was standing up looking down on him. "Do you ever pray?" she asked.

He shook his head. All she saw was the black hat wiggle between his shoulder blades. "Nome," he said.

There was a pistol shot from the woods, followed closely by another. Then silence. The old lady's head jerked around. She could hear the wind move through the tree tops like a long satisfied insuck of breath. "Bailey Boy!" she called.

"I was a gospel singer for a while," The Misfit said. "I been most everything. Been in the arm service, both land and sea, at home and abroad, been twict married, been an undertaker, been with the railroads, plowed Mother Earth, been in a tornado, seen a man burnt alive oncet," and he looked up at the children's mother and the little girl who were sitting close together, their faces white and their eyes glassy; "I even seen a woman flogged," he said.

"Pray, pray," the grandmother began, "pray, pray . . ."

"I never was a bad boy that I remember of," The Misfit said in an almost dreamy voice, "but somewheres along the line I done something wrong and got sent to the penitentiary. I was buried alive," and he looked up and held her attention to him by a steady stare.

"That's when you should have started to pray," she said. "What did you do to get sent to the penitentiary that first time?"

"Turn to the right, it was a wall," The Misfit said, looking up again at the cloudless sky. "Turn to the left, it was a wall. Look up it was a ceiling, look down it was a floor. I forget what I done, lady. I set there and set there, trying to remember what it was I done and I ain't recalled it to this day. Oncet in a while, I would think it was coming to me, but it never come."

"Maybe they put you in by mistake," the old lady said vaguely.

"Nome," he said. "It wasn't no mistake. They had the papers on me."

"You must have stolen something," she said.

The Misfit sneered slightly. "Nobody had nothing I wanted," he said. "It was a head-doctor at the penitentiary said what I had done was kill my daddy but I known that for a lie. My daddy died in nineteen ought nineteen of the epidemic flu and I never had a thing to do with it. He was buried in the Mount Hopewell Baptist churchyard and you can go there and see for yourself."

"If you would pray," the old lady said, "Jesus would help you."

"That's right," The Misfit said.

"Well then, why don't you pray?" she asked trembling with delight suddenly.

"I don't want no hep," he said. "I'm doing all right by myself."

Bobby Lee and Hiram came ambling back from the woods. Bobby Lee was dragging a yellow shirt with bright blue parrots in it.

"Thow me that shirt, Bobby Lee," The Misfit said. The shirt came flying at him and landed on his shoulder and he put it on. The grandmother couldn't name what the shirt reminded her of. "No, lady," The Misfit said while he was buttoning it up, "I found out the crime don't matter. You can do one thing or you can do another, kill a man or take a tire off his car, because sooner or later you're going to forget what it was you done and just be punished for it."

The children's mother had begun to make heaving noises as if she couldn't get her breath. "Lady," he asked, "would you and that little girl like to step off yonder with Bobby Lee and Hiram and join your husband?"

"Yes, thank you," the mother said faintly. Her left arm dangled helplessly and she was holding the baby, who had gone to sleep, in the other. "Hep that lady up, Hiram," The Misfit said as she struggled to climb out of the ditch, "and Bobby Lee, you hold onto that little girl's hand."

"I don't want to hold hands with him," June Star said. "He reminds me of a pig."

The fat boy blushed and laughed and caught her by the arm and pulled her off into the woods after Hiram and her mother.

Alone with The Misfit, the grandmother found that she had lost her voice. There was not a cloud in the sky nor any sun. There was nothing around her but woods. She wanted to tell him that he must pray. She opened and closed her mouth several times before anything came out. Finally she found herself saying, "Jesus, Jesus," meaning, Jesus will help you, but the way she was saying it, it sounded as if she might be cursing.

"Yes'm," The Misfit said as if he agreed. "Jesus thown everything off balance. It was the same case with Him as with me except He hadn't committed any crime and they could prove I had committed one because they had the papers on me. Of course," he said, "they never shown me my papers. That's why I sign myself now. I said long ago, you get you a signature and sign everything you do and keep a copy of it. Then you'll know what you done and you can hold up the crime to the punishment and see do they match and in the end you'll have something to prove you ain't been treated right. I call myself The Misfit," he said, "because I can't make what all I done wrong fit what all I gone through in punishment."

130 There was a piercing scream from the woods, followed closely by a pistol report. "Does it seem right to you, lady, that one is punished a heap and another ain't punished at all?"

"Jesus!" the old lady cried. "You've got good blood! I know you wouldn't shoot a lady! I know you come from nice people! Pray! Jesus, you ought not to shoot a lady. I'll give you all the money I've got!"

"Lady," The Misfit said, looking beyond her far into the woods, "there never was a body that give the undertaker a tip."

There were two more pistol reports and the grandmother raised her head like a parched old turkey hen crying for water and called, "Bailey Boy, Bailey Boy!" as if her heart would break.

"Jesus was the only One that ever raised the dead," The Misfit continued, "and He shouldn't have done it. He thown everything off balance. If He did what He said, then it's nothing for you to do but thow away everything and follow Him, and if He didn't, then it's nothing for you to do but enjoy the few minutes you got left the best way you can—by killing somebody or burning down his house or doing some other meanness to him. No pleasure but meanness," he said and his voice became almost a snarl.

135 "Maybe He didn't raise the dead," the old lady mumbled, not knowing what she was saying and feeling so dizzy that she sank down in the ditch with her legs twisted under her.

"I wasn't there so I can't say He didn't," The Misfit said. "I wisht I had of been there," he said, hitting the ground with his fist. "It ain't right I wasn't there because if I had of been there I would of known. Listen, lady," he said in a high voice, "if I had of been there I would of known and I wouldn't be like I am now." His voice seemed about to crack and the grandmother's head cleared for an instant. She saw the man's face twisted close to her own as if he were going to cry and she murmured, "Why you're one of my babies. You're one of my own children!" She reached out and touched him on the shoulder. The Misfit sprang back as if a snake had bitten him and shot her three times through the chest. Then he put his gun down on the ground and took off his glasses and began to clean them.

Hiram and Bobby Lee returned from the woods and stood over the ditch, looking down at the grandmother who half sat and half lay in a puddle of blood with her legs crossed under her like a child's and her face smiling up at the cloudless sky.

Without his glasses, The Misfit's eyes were red-rimmed and pale and defenseless-looking. "Take her off and thow her where you thown the others," he said, picking up the cat that was rubbing itself against his leg.

"She was a talker, wasn't she?" Bobby Lee said, sliding down the ditch with a yodel.

140 "She would of been a good woman," The Misfit said, "if it had been somebody there to shoot her every minute of her life."

"Some fun!" Bobby Lee said.

"Shut up, Bobby Lee," The Misfit said. "It's no real pleasure in life."

READING AND REACTING

1. Why are the grandmother and the children's mother referred to by their titles while other family members have names? What other characters remain nameless? Why?
2. How are the style and tone of the narrator's voice different from those of the characters? What, if anything, is the significance of this difference?
3. Figurative language in this story sometimes creates unflattering, even grotesque, pictures of the characters. Find several examples of such negative figures of speech, and explain why the author uses them.
4. What does the grandmother's use of the words *pickaninny* and *nigger* reveal about her? How are readers expected to reconcile this language with her very proper appearance and her preoccupation with manners? How does her use of these words affect your reaction to her?
5. How does The Misfit's dialect characterize him?
6. Explain the irony in this statement: "In case of an accident, anyone seeing her dead on the highway would know at once that she was a lady" (12).
7. What does the allusion to *Gone With the Wind* (24) contribute to the story?
8. How do the style and tone of the two-paragraph description of the three men in the car (71–72) help to prepare readers for the events that follow?
9. When The Misfit tells the grandmother about his life, his language takes on a measured, rhythmic quality: "Been in the arm service, both land and sea, at home and abroad, been twict married, been an undertaker, been with the railroads, plowed Mother Earth, been in a tornado, seen a man burnt alive oncet . . . " (109). Find other examples of parallelism and rhythmic repetition in this character's speech. How is this style consistent with The Misfit's character?
10. **JOURNAL ENTRY:** Why do you think the grandmother tells The Misfit she recognizes him? Why does she fail to realize the danger of her remark?

Tim O'Brien (1946–), sometimes described as a writer whose books are on the short list of essential fiction about the Vietnam War, has built four novels around his experiences as a soldier. His plots focus on danger, violence, courage, endurance, despair, and other topics often associated with war novels, but O'Brien treats these topics with an emphasis on the contemporary dilemmas faced by those who may be unwilling participants in an unpopular war. O'Brien calls *If I Die in a Combat Zone, Box Me Up and Ship Me Home* (1979) a memoir because it relates his war experiences as a naive young college graduate who suddenly finds himself facing bullets and land mines rather than sitting behind a desk. *Northern Lights* (1975) concentrates on the wilderness survival experiences of two brothers, one of whom has just returned from the Vietnam War. A fantastic daydream of an American soldier, *Going After Cacciato* (1978), which has been compared to *Catch 22,* won a National Book Award. *The Things They Carried* (1990) is a quasi-fictional collection of interrelated stories that deal with a single platoon; some stories involve a young soldier named Tim O'Brien, and some a forty-three-year-old writer named Tim O'Brien who writes about his memories.

After graduating summa cum laude from Macalester College in 1968, O'Brien was immediately drafted into the U.S. Army and sent to Vietnam, where he served with the 198th Infantry Brigade. He was promoted to sergeant and awarded a Purple Heart after receiving a shrapnel wound in a battle near My Lai. In 1970, after discharge from the army, he attended Harvard graduate school to study government. He worked as a reporter for the *Washington Post* before pursuing a full-time career as a writer. Currently, O'Brien lives in Cambridge, Massachusetts.

Tim O'Brien

THE THINGS THEY CARRIED

(1986)

First Lieutenant Jimmy Cross carried letters from a girl named Martha, a junior at Mount Sebastian College in New Jersey. They were not love letters, but Lieutenant Cross was hoping, so he kept them folded in plastic at the bottom of his rucksack. In the late afternoon, after a day's march, he would dig his foxhole, wash his hands under a canteen, unwrap the letters, hold them with the tips of his fingers, and spend the last hour of light pretending. He would imagine romantic camping trips into the White Mountains in New Hampshire. He would sometimes taste the envelope flaps, knowing her tongue had been there. More than anything, he wanted Martha to love him as he loved her, but the letters were mostly chatty, elusive on the matter of love. She was a virgin, he was almost sure. She was an English major at Mount Sebastian, and she wrote beautifully about her professors and roommates and midterm exams, about her respect for Chaucer and her great affection for Virginia Woolf. She often quoted lines of poetry; she never mentioned the war, except to say, Jimmy, take care of yourself. The letters weighed ten ounces. They were signed "Love, Martha," but Lieutenant Cross understood that "Love" was only a way of signing and did not mean what he sometimes pretended it meant. At dusk, he would carefully return the letters to his rucksack. Slowly, a bit distracted, he would get up and move among his men, checking the perimeter, then at full dark he would return to his hole and watch the night and wonder if Martha was a virgin.

The things they carried were largely determined by necessity. Among the necessities or near necessities were P-38 can openers, pocket knives, heat tabs, wrist watches, dog tags, mosquito repellent, chewing gum, candy, cigarettes, salt tablets, packets of Kool-Aid, lighters, matches, sewing kits, Military Payment Certificates, C rations, and two or three canteens of water. Together, these items weighed between fifteen and twenty pounds, depending upon a man's habits or rate of metabolism. Henry Dobbins, who was a big man, carried extra rations; he was especially fond of canned peaches in heavy syrup over pound cake. Dave Jensen, who practiced field hygiene, carried a toothbrush, dental floss, and several hotel-size bars of soap he'd stolen on R&R in Sydney, Australia. Ted Lavender, who was scared, carried tranquilizers until he was shot in the head outside the village of Than Khe in mid-April. By necessity, and because it was SOP, they all carried steel helmets that weighed five pounds including the liner and camouflage cover. They carried the standard fatigue jackets and trousers. Very few carried underwear. On their feet they carried jungle boots—2.1 pounds—and Dave Jensen carried three pairs of socks and a can of Dr. Scholl's foot powder as a precaution against trench foot. Until he was shot, Ted Lavender carried six or seven ounces of premium dope, which for him was a necessity. Mitchell Sanders, the RTO, carried condoms. Norman Bowker carried a diary. Rat Kiley carried comic books. Kiowa, a devout Baptist, carried an illustrated New Testament that had been presented to him by his father, who taught Sunday school in Oklahoma City, Oklahoma. As a hedge against bad times, however, Kiowa also carried his grandmother's distrust of the white man, his grandfather's old hunting hatchet. Necessity dictated. Because the land was mined and booby-trapped, it was SOP for each man to carry a steel-centered, nylon-covered flak jacket, which weighed 6.7 pounds, but which on hot days seemed much heavier. Because you could die so quickly, each man carried at least one large compress bandage, usually in the helmet band for easy access. Because the nights were cold, and because the monsoons were wet, each carried a green plastic poncho that could be used as a raincoat or ground sheet or makeshift tent. With its quilted liner, the poncho weighed almost two pounds, but it was worth every ounce. In April, for instance, when Ted Lavender was shot, they used his poncho to wrap him up, then to carry him across the paddy, then to lift him into the chopper that took him away.

They were called legs or grunts.

To carry something was to "hump" it, as when Lieutenant Jimmy Cross humped his love for Martha up the hills and through the swamps.

In its intransitive form, "to hump" meant "to walk," or "to march," but it implied burdens far beyond the intransitive.

5 Almost everyone humped photographs. In his wallet, Lieutenant Cross carried two photographs of Martha. The first was a Kodachrome snapshot signed "Love," though he knew better. She stood against a brick wall. Her eyes were gray and neutral, her lips slightly open as she stared straight-on at the camera. At night, sometimes, Lieutenant Cross wondered who had taken the picture, because he knew she had boyfriends, because he loved her so much, and because he could see the shadow of the picture taker spreading out against the brick wall. The second photograph had been clipped from the 1968 Mount Sebastian yearbook. It was an action shot—women's volleyball—and Martha was bent horizontal to the floor, reaching, the palms of her hands in sharp focus, the tongue taut, the expression frank and competitive. There was no visible sweat. She wore white gym shorts. Her legs, he thought, were almost certainly the legs of a virgin, dry and without hair, the left knee cocked and carrying her entire weight, which was just over one hundred pounds. Lieutenant Cross remembered touching that left knee. A dark theater, he remembered, and the movie was *Bonnie and Clyde,* and Martha wore a tweed skirt, and during the final scene, when he touched her knee, she turned and looked at him in a sad, sober way that made him pull his hand back, but he would always remember the feel of the tweed skirt and the knee beneath it and the sound of the gunfire that killed Bonnie and Clyde, how embarrassing it was, how slow and oppressive. He remembered kissing her good night at the dorm door. Right then, he thought, he should've done something brave. He should've carried her up the stairs to her room and tied her to the bed and touched that left knee all night long. He should've risked it. Whenever he looked at the photographs, he thought of new things he should've done.

What they carried was partly a function of rank, partly of field specialty.

As a first lieutenant and platoon leader, Jimmy Cross carried a compass, maps, code books, binoculars, and a .45-caliber pistol that weighed 2.9 pounds fully loaded. He carried a strobe light and the responsibility for the lives of his men.

As an RTO, Mitchell Sanders carried the PRC-25 radio, a killer, twenty-six pounds with its battery.

As a medic, Rat Kiley carried a canvas satchel filled with morphine and plasma and malaria tablets and surgical tape and comic books and all the things a medic must carry, including M&M's for especially bad wounds, for a total weight of nearly twenty pounds.

10 As a big man, therefore a machine gunner, Henry Dobbins carried the M-60, which weighed twenty-three pounds unloaded, but which was almost always loaded. In addition, Dobbins carried between ten and fifteen pounds of ammunition draped in belts across his chest and shoulders.

As PFCs or Spec 4s, most of them were common grunts and carried the standard M-16 gas-operated assault rifle. The weapon weighed 7.5 pounds unloaded, 8.2 pounds with its full twenty-round magazine. Depending on numerous factors, such as topography and psychology, the riflemen carried anywhere from twelve to twenty magazines, usually in cloth bandoliers, adding on another 8.4 pounds at minimum, fourteen pounds at maximum. When it was available, they also carried M-16 maintenance gear—rods and steel brushes and swabs and tubes of LSA oil—all of which weighed about a pound. Among the grunts, some carried the M-79 grenade launcher, 5.9 pounds unloaded, a reasonably light weapon except for the ammunition, which was heavy. A single round weighed ten ounces. The typical load was twenty-five rounds. But Ted Lavender, who was scared, carried thirty-four rounds when he was shot and killed outside Than Khe, and he went down under an exceptional burden, more than twenty pounds of ammunition, plus the flak jacket and helmet and rations and water and toilet paper and tranquilizers and all the rest, plus the unweighed fear. He was dead weight. There was no twitching or flopping. Kiowa, who saw it happen, said it was like watching a rock fall, or a big sandbag or something—just boom, then down—not like the movies where the dead guy rolls around and does fancy spins and goes ass over teakettle—not like that, Kiowa said, the poor bastard just flat-fuck fell. Boom. Down. Nothing else. It was a bright morning in mid-April. Lieutenant Cross felt the pain. He blamed himself. They stripped off Lavender's canteens and ammo, all the heavy things, and Rat Kiley said the obvious, the guy's dead, and Mitchell Sanders used his radio to report one U.S. KIA and to request a chopper. Then they wrapped Lavender in his poncho. They carried him out to a dry paddy, established security, and sat smoking the dead man's dope until the chopper came. Lieutenant Cross kept to himself. He pictured Martha's smooth young face, thinking he loved her more than anything, more than his men, and now Ted Lavender was dead because he loved her so much and could not stop thinking about her. When the dust-off arrived, they carried Lavender aboard. Afterward they burned Than Khe. They marched until dusk, then dug their holes, and that night Kiowa kept explaining how you had to be there, how fast it was, how the poor guy just dropped like so much concrete. Boom-down, he said. Like cement.

In addition to the three standard weapons—the M-60, M-16, and M-79—they carried whatever presented itself, or whatever seemed appropriate as a means of killing or staying alive. They carried catch-as-catch-can. At various times, in various situations, they carried M-14s and CAR-15s and Swedish Ks and grease guns and captured AK-47s and Chi-Coms and RPGs and Simonov carbines and black-market Uzis and .38-caliber Smith & Wesson handguns and 66 mm LAWs and shotguns and silencers and blackjacks and bayonets and C-4 plastic explosives. Lee Strunk carried a slingshot; a weapon of last resort, he called it. Mitchell Sanders carried brass knuckles. Kiowa carried his grandfather's feathered hatchet. Every third or fourth man carried a Claymore antipersonnel mine—3.5 pounds with its firing device. They all carried fragmentation grenades—fourteen ounces each. They all carried at least one M-18 colored smoke grenade—twenty-four ounces. Some carried CS or tear-gas grenades. Some carried white-phosphorus grenades. They carried all they could bear, and then some, including a silent awe for the terrible power of the things they carried.

In the first week of April, before Lavender died, Lieutenant Jimmy Cross received a good-luck charm from Martha. It was a simple pebble, an ounce at most. Smooth to the touch, it was a milky-white color with flecks of orange and violet, oval-shaped, like a miniature egg. In the accompanying letter, Martha wrote that she had found the pebble on the Jersey shoreline, precisely where the land touched water at high tide, where things came together but also separated. It was this separate-but-together quality, she wrote, that had inspired her to pick up the pebble and to carry it in her breast pocket for several days, where it seemed weightless, and then to send it through the mail, by air, as a token of her truest feelings for him. Lieutenant Cross found this romantic. But he wondered what her truest feelings were, exactly, and what she meant by separate-but-together. He wondered how the tides and waves had come into play on that afternoon along the Jersey shoreline when Martha saw the pebble and bent down to rescue it from geology. He imagined bare feet. Martha was a poet, with the poet's sensibilities, and her feet would be brown and bare, the toenails unpainted, the eyes chilly and somber like the ocean in March, and though it was painful, he wondered who had been with her that afternoon. He imagined a pair of shadows moving along the strip of sand where things came together but also separated. It was phantom jealousy, he knew, but he couldn't help himself. He loved her so much. On the march, through the hot days of early April, he carried the pebble in his mouth, turning it with his tongue, tasting sea salts and moisture. His mind wandered. He had difficulty keeping his attention on the war. On occasion he would yell at his men to spread out the column, to keep their eyes open, but then he would slip away into daydreams, just pretending, walking barefoot along the Jersey shore, with Martha, carrying nothing. He would feel himself rising. Sun and waves and gentle winds, all love and lightness.

What they carried varied by mission.

15 When a mission took them to the mountains, they carried mosquito netting, machetes, canvas tarps, and extra bug juice.

If a mission seemed especially hazardous, or if it involved a place they knew to be bad, they carried everything they could. In certain heavily mined AOs, where the land was dense with Toe Poppers and Bouncing Betties, they took turns humping a twenty-eight-pound mine detector. With its headphones and big sensing plate, the equipment was a stress on the lower back and shoulders, awkward to handle, often useless because of the shrapnel in the earth, but they carried it anyway, partly for safety, partly for the illusion of safety.

On ambush, or other night missions, they carried peculiar little odds and ends. Kiowa always took along his New Testament and a pair of moccasins for silence. Dave Jensen carried night-sight vitamins high in carotin. Lee Strunk carried his slingshot; ammo, he claimed, would never be a problem. Rat Kiley carried brandy and M&M's. Until he was shot, Ted Lavender carried the starlight scope, which weighed 6.3 pounds with its aluminum carrying case. Henry Dobbins carried his girlfriend's pantyhose wrapped around his neck as a comforter. They all carried ghosts. When dark came, they would move out single file across the meadows and paddies to their ambush coordinates, where they would quietly set up the Claymores and lie down and spend the night waiting.

Other missions were more complicated and required special equipment. In mid-April, it was their mission to search out and destroy the elaborate tunnel complexes in the Than Khe area south of Chu Lai. To blow the tunnels, they carried one-pound blocks of pentrite high explosives, four blocks to a man, sixty-eight pounds in all. They carried wiring, detonators, and battery-powered clackers. Dave Jensen carried earplugs. Most often, before blowing the tunnels, they were ordered by higher command to search them, which was considered bad news, but by and large they just shrugged and carried out orders. Because he was a big man, Henry Dobbins was excused from tunnel duty. The others would draw numbers. Before Lavender died there were seventeen men in the platoon, and whoever drew the number seventeen would strip off his gear and crawl in head first with a flashlight and Lieutenant Cross's .45-caliber pistol. The rest of them would fan out as security. They would sit down or kneel, not facing the hole, listening to the ground beneath them, imagining cobwebs and ghosts, whatever was down there—the tunnel walls squeezing in—how the flashlight seemed impossibly heavy in the hand and how it was tunnel vision in the very strictest sense, compression in all ways, even time, and how you had to wiggle in—ass and elbows—a swallowed-up feeling—and how you found yourself worrying about odd things—will your flashlight go dead? Do rats carry rabies? If you screamed, how far would the sound carry? Would your buddies hear it? Would they have the courage to drag you out? In some respects, though not many, the waiting was worse than the tunnel itself. Imagination was a killer.

On April 16, when Lee Strunk drew the number seventeen, he laughed and muttered something and went down quickly. The morning was hot and very still. Not good, Kiowa said. He looked at the tunnel opening, then out across a dry paddy toward the village of Than Khe. Nothing moved. No clouds or birds or people. As they waited, the men smoked and drank Kool-Aid, not talking much, feeling sympathy for Lee Strunk but also feeling the luck of the draw. You win some, you lose some, said Mitchell Sanders, and sometimes you settle for a rain check. It was a tired line and no one laughed.

20 Henry Dobbins ate a tropical chocolate bar. Ted Lavender popped a tranquilizer and went off to pee.

After five minutes, Lieutenant Jimmy Cross moved to the tunnel, leaned down, and examined the darkness. Trouble, he thought—a cave-in maybe. And then suddenly, without willing it, he was thinking about Martha. The stresses and fractures, the quick collapse, the two of them buried alive under all that weight. Dense, crushing love. Kneeling, watching the hole, he tried to concentrate on Lee Strunk and the war, all the dangers, but his love was too much for him, he felt paralyzed, he wanted to sleep inside her lungs and breathe her blood and be smothered. He wanted her to be a virgin and not a virgin, all at once. He wanted to know her. Intimate secrets—why poetry? Why so sad? Why that grayness in her eyes? Why so alone? Not lonely, just alone—riding her bike across campus or sitting off by herself in the cafeteria. Even dancing, she danced alone—and it was the aloneness that filled him with love. He remembered telling her that one evening. How she nodded and looked away. And how, later, when he kissed her, she received the kiss without returning it, her eyes wide open, not afraid, not a virgin's eyes, just flat and uninvolved.

Lieutenant Cross gazed at the tunnel. But he was not there. He was buried with Martha under the white sand at the Jersey shore. They were pressed together, and the pebble in his mouth was her tongue. He was smiling. Vaguely, he was aware of how quiet the day was, the sullen paddies, yet he could not bring himself to worry about matters of security. He was beyond that. He was just a kid at war, in love. He was twenty-two years old. He couldn't help it.

A few moments later Lee Strunk crawled out of the tunnel. He came up grinning, filthy but alive. Lieutenant Cross nodded and closed his eyes while the others clapped Strunk on the back and made jokes about rising from the dead.

Worms, Rat Kiley said. Right out of the grave. Fuckin' zombie.

25 The men laughed. They all felt great relief.

Spook City, said Mitchell Sanders.

Lee Strunk make a funny ghost sound, a kind of moaning, yet very happy, and right then, when Strunk made that high happy moaning sound, when he went *Ahhooooo,* right then Ted Lavender was shot in the head on his way back from peeing. He lay with his mouth open. The teeth were broken. There was a swollen black bruise under his left eye. The cheekbone was gone. Oh shit, Rat Kiley said, the guy's dead. The guy's dead, he kept saying, which seemed profound—the guy's dead. I mean really.

The things they carried were determined to some extent by superstition. Lieutenant Cross carried his good-luck pebble. Dave Jensen carried a rabbit's foot. Norman Bowker, otherwise a very gentle person, carried a thumb that had been presented to him as a gift by Mitchell Sanders. The thumb was dark brown, rubbery to the touch, and weighed four ounces at most. It had been cut from a VC corpse, a boy of fifteen or sixteen. They'd found him at the bottom of an irrigation ditch, badly burned, flies in his mouth and eyes. The boy wore black shorts and sandals. At the time of his death he had been carrying a pouch of rice, a rifle, and three magazines of ammunition.

You want my opinion, Mitchell Sanders said, there's a definite moral here.

30 He put his hand on the dead boy's wrist. He was quiet for a time, as if counting a pulse, then he patted the stomach, almost affectionately, and used Kiowa's hunting hatchet to remove the thumb.

Henry Dobbins asked what the moral was.

Moral?

You know. *Moral.*

Sanders wrapped the thumb in toilet paper and handed it across to Norman Bowker. There was no blood. Smiling, he kicked the boy's head, watched the flies scatter, and said, It's like with that old TV show—Paladin. Have gun, will travel.

35 Henry Dobbins thought about it.

Yeah, well, he finally said. I don't see no moral.

There it *is,* man.

Fuck off.

They carried USO stationery and pencils and pens. They carried Sterno, safety pins, trip flares, signal flares, spools of wire, razor blades, chewing tobacco, liberated joss sticks and statuettes of the smiling Buddha, candles, grease pencils, *The Stars and Stripes,* fingernail clippers, Psy Ops leaflets, bush hats, bolos, and much more. Twice a week, when the resupply choppers came in, they carried hot chow in green Mermite cans and large canvas bags filled with iced beer and soda pop. They carried plastic water containers, each with a two-gallon capacity. Mitchell Sanders carried a set of starched tiger fatigues for special occasions. Henry Dobbins carried Black Flag insecticide. Dave Jensen carried empty sandbags that could be filled at night for added protection. Lee Strunk carried tanning lotion. Some things they carried in common. Taking turns, they carried the big PRC-77 scrambler radio, which weighed thirty pounds with its battery. They shared the weight of memory. They took up what others could no longer bear. Often, they carried each other, the wounded or weak. They carried infections. They carried chess sets, basketballs, Vietnamese-English dictionaries, insignia of rank, Bronze Stars and Purple Hearts, plastic cards imprinted with the Code of Conduct. They carried diseases, among them malaria and dysentery. They carried lice and ringworm and leeches and paddy algae and various rots and molds. They carried the land itself—Vietnam, the place, the soil—a powdery orange-red dust that covered their boots and fatigues and faces. They carried the sky. The whole atmosphere, they carried it, the humidity, the monsoons, the stink of fungus and decay, all of it, they carried gravity. They moved like mules. By daylight they took sniper fire, at night they were mortared, but it was not battle, it was just the endless march, village to village, without purpose, nothing won or lost. They marched for the sake of the march. They plodded along slowly, dumbly, leaning forward against the heat, unthinking, all blood and bone, simple grunts, soldiering with their legs, toiling up the hills and down into the paddies and across the rivers and up again and down, just humping, one step and then the next and then another, but no volition, no will, because it was automatic, it was anatomy, and the war was entirely a matter of posture and carriage, the hump was everything, a kind of inertia, a kind of emptiness, a dullness of desire and intellect and conscience and hope and human sensibility. Their principles were in their feet. Their calculations were biological. They had no sense of strategy or mission. They searched the villages without knowing what to look for, not caring, kicking over jars of rice, frisking children and old men, blowing tunnels, sometimes setting fires and sometimes not, then forming up and moving on to the next village, then other villages, where it would always be the same. They carried their own lives. The pressures were enormous. In the heat of early afternoon, they would remove their helmets and flak jackets, walking bare, which was dangerous but which helped ease the strain. They would often discard things along the route of march. Purely for comfort, they would throw away rations, blow their Claymores and grenades, no matter, because by nightfall the resupply choppers would arrive with more of the same, then a day or two later still more, fresh watermelons and crates of ammunition and sunglasses and woolen sweaters—the resources were stunning—sparklers for the Fourth of July, colored eggs for Easter. It was the great American war chest—the fruits of science, the smokestacks, the canneries, the arsenals at Hartford, the Minnesota forests, the machine shops, the vast fields of corn and wheat—they carried like freight trains; they carried it on their backs and shoulders—and for all the ambiguities of Vietnam, all the mysteries and unknowns, there was at least the single abiding certainty that they would never be at a loss for things to carry.

40 After the chopper took Lavender away, Lieutenant Jimmy Cross led his men into the village of Than Khe. They burned everything. They shot chickens and dogs, they trashed the village well, they called in artillery and watched the wreckage, then they marched for several hours through the hot afternoon, and then at dusk, while Kiowa explained how Lavender died, Lieutenant Cross found himself trembling.

He tried not to cry. With his entrenching tool, which weighed five pounds, he began digging a hole in the earth.

He felt shame. He hated himself. He had loved Martha more than his men, and as a consequence Lavender was now dead, and this was something he would have to carry like a stone in his stomach for the rest of the war.

All he could do was dig. He used his entrenching tool like an ax, slashing, feeling both love and hate, and then later, when it was full dark, he sat at the bottom of his foxhole and wept. It went on for a long while. In part, he was grieving for Ted Lavender, but mostly it was for Martha, and for himself, because she belonged to another world, which was not quite real, and because she was a junior at Mount Sebastian College in New Jersey, a poet and a virgin and uninvolved, and because he realized she did not love him and never would.

Like cement, Kiowa whispered in the dark. I swear to God—boom-down. Not a word.

I've heard this, said Norman Bowker.

A pisser, you know? Still zipping himself up. Zapped while zipping.

All right, fine. That's enough.

Yeah, but you had to see it, the guy just—

I *heard,* man. Cement. So why not shut the fuck *up?*

Kiowa shook his head sadly and glanced over at the hole where Lieutenant Jimmy Cross sat watching the night. The air was thick and wet. A warm, dense fog had settled over the paddies and there was the stillness that precedes rain.

After a time Kiowa sighed.

One thing for sure, he said. The Lieutenant's in some deep hurt. I mean that crying jag—the way he was carrying on—it wasn't fake or anything, it was real heavy-duty hurt. The man cares.

Sure, Norman Bowker said.

Say what you want, the man does care.

We all got problems.

Not Lavender.

No, I guess not, Bowker said. Do me a favor, though.

Shut up?

That's a smart Indian. Shut up.

Shrugging, Kiowa pulled off his boots. He wanted to say more, just to lighten up his sleep, but instead he opened his New Testament and arranged it beneath his head as a pillow. The fog made things seem hollow and unattached. He tried not to think about Ted Lavender, but then he was thinking how fast it was, no drama, down and dead, and how it was hard to feel anything except surprise. It seemed un-Christian. He wished he could find some great sadness, or even anger, but the emotion wasn't there and he couldn't make it happen. Mostly he felt pleased to be alive. He liked the smell of the New Testament under his cheek, the leather and ink and paper and glue, whatever the chemicals were. He liked hearing the sounds of night. Even his fatigue, it felt fine, the stiff muscles and the prickly awareness of his own body, a floating feeling. He enjoyed not being dead. Lying there, Kiowa admired Lieutenant Jimmy Cross's capacity for grief. He wanted to share the man's pain, he wanted to care as Jimmy Cross cared. And yet when he closed his eyes, all he could think was Boom-down, and all he could feel was the pleasure of having his boots off and the fog curling in around him and the damp soil and the Bible smells and the plush comfort of night.

After a moment Norman Bowker sat up in the dark.

What the hell, he said. You want to talk, *talk*. Tell it to me.

Forget it.

No, man, go on. One thing I hate, it's a silent Indian.

For the most part they carried themselves with poise, a kind of dignity. Now and then, however, there were times of panic, when they squealed or wanted to squeal but couldn't, when they twitched and made moaning sounds and covered their heads and said Dear Jesus and flopped around on the earth and fired their weapons blindly and cringed and sobbed and begged for the noise to stop and went wild and made stupid promises to themselves and to God and to their mothers and fathers, hoping not to die. In different ways, it happened to all of them. Afterward, when the firing ended, they would blink and peek up. They would touch their bodies, feeling shame, then quickly hiding it. They would force themselves to stand. As if in slow motion, frame by frame, the world would take on the old logic—absolute silence, then the wind, then sunlight, then voices. It was the burden of being alive. Awkwardly, the men would reassemble themselves, first in private, then in groups, becoming soldiers again. They would repair the leaks in their eyes. They would check for casualties, call in dust-offs, light cigarettes, try to smile, clear their throats and spit and begin cleaning their weapons. After a time someone would shake his head and say, No lie, I almost shit my pants, and someone else would laugh, which meant it was bad, yes, but the guy had obviously not shit his pants, it wasn't that bad, and in any case nobody would ever do such a thing and then go ahead and talk about it. They would squint into the dense, oppressive sunlight. For a few moments, perhaps, they would fall silent, lighting a joint and tracking its passage from man to man, inhaling, holding in the humiliation. Scary stuff, one of them might say. But then someone else would grin or flick his eyebrows and say, Roger-dodger, almost cut me a new asshole, *almost*.

There were numerous such poses. Some carried themselves with a sort of wistful resignation, others with pride or stiff soldierly discipline or good humor or macho zeal. They were afraid of dying but they were even more afraid to show it.

They found jokes to tell.

They used a hard vocabulary to contain the terrible softness. *Greased,* they'd say. *Offed, lit up, zapped while zipping.*[1] It wasn't cruelty, just stage presence. They were actors and the war came at them in 3-D. When someone died, it wasn't quite dying, because in a curious way it seemed scripted, and because they had their lines mostly memorized, irony mixed with tragedy, and because they called it by other names, as if to encyst and destroy the reality of death itself. They kicked corpses. They cut off thumbs. They talked grunt lingo. They told stories about

---

[1] Offed, lit up—killed; zapped while zipping—killed while urinating.

Ted Lavender's supply of tranquilizers, how the poor guy didn't feel a thing, how incredibly tranquil he was.

There's a moral here, said Mitchell Sanders.

They were waiting for Lavender's chopper, smoking the dead man's dope.

The moral's pretty obvious. Sanders said, and winked. Stay away from drugs. No joke, they'll ruin your day every time.

Cute, said Henry Dobbins.

Mind-blower, get it? Talk about wiggy—nothing left, just blood and brains.

They made themselves laugh.

There it is, they'd say, over and over, as if the repetition itself were an act of poise, a balance between crazy and almost crazy, knowing without going. There it is, which meant be cool, let it ride, because oh yeah, man, you can't change what can't be changed, there it is, there it absolutely and positively and fucking well *is*.

They were tough.

They carried all the emotional baggage of men who might die. Grief, terror, love, longing—these were intangibles, but the intangibles had their own mass and specific gravity, they had tangible weight. They carried shameful memories. They carried the common secret of cowardice barely restrained, the instinct to run or freeze or hide, and in many respects this was the heaviest burden of all, for it could never be put down, it required perfect balance and perfect posture. They carried their reputations. They carried the soldier's greatest fear, which was the fear of blushing. Men killed, and died, because they were embarrassed not to. It was what had brought them to the war in the first place, nothing positive, no dreams of glory or honor, just to avoid the blush of dishonor. They died so as not to die of embarrassment. They crawled into tunnels and walked point and advanced under fire. Each morning, despite the unknowns, they made their legs move. They endured. They kept humping. They did not submit to the obvious alternative, which was simply to close the eyes and fall. So easy, really. Go limp and tumble to the ground and let the muscles unwind and not speak and not budge until your buddies picked you up and lifted you into the chopper that would roar and dip its nose and carry you off to the world. A mere matter of falling, yet no one ever fell. It was not courage, exactly; the object was not valor. Rather, they were too frightened to be cowards.

By and large they carried these things inside, maintaining the masks of composure. They sneered at sick call. They spoke bitterly about guys who had found release by shooting off their own toes or fingers. Pussies, they'd say. Candyasses. It was fierce, mocking talk, with only a trace of envy or awe, but even so, the image played itself out behind their eyes.

They imagined the muzzle against flesh. They imagined the quick, sweet pain, then the evacuation to Japan, then a hospital with warm beds and cute geisha nurses.

They dreamed of freedom birds.

At night, on guard, staring into the dark, they were carried away by jumbo jets. They felt the rush of takeoff. *Gone!* they yelled. And then velocity, wings and engines, a smiling stewardess—but it was more than a plane, it was a real bird, a big sleek silver bird with feathers and talons and high screeching. They were flying. The weights fell off, there was nothing to bear. They laughed and held on tight, feeling the cold slap of wind and altitude, soaring, thinking *It's over, I'm gone!*—they were naked, they were light and free—it was all lightness, bright and fast and buoyant, light as light, a helium buzz in the brain, a giddy bubbling in the lungs as they were taken up over the clouds and the war, beyond duty, beyond gravity and mortification and global entanglements—*Sin loi!* they yelled, *I'm sorry, motherfuckers, but I'm out of it, I'm goofed, I'm on a space cruise, I'm gone!*—and it was a restful, disencumbered sensation, just riding the light waves, sailing that big silver freedom bird over the mountains and oceans, over America, over the farms and great sleeping cities and cemeteries and highways and the golden arches of McDonald's. It was flight, a kind of fleeing, a kind of falling, falling higher and higher, spinning off the edge of the earth and beyond the sun and through the vast, silent vacuum where there were no burdens and where everything weighed exactly nothing. *Gone!* they screamed, *I'm sorry but I'm gone!* And so at night, not quite dreaming, they gave themselves over to lightness, they were carried, they were purely borne.

On the morning after Ted Lavender died, First Lieutenant Jimmy Cross crouched at the bottom of his foxhole and burned Martha's letters. Then he burned the two photographs. There was a steady rain falling, which made it difficult, but he used heat tabs and Sterno to build a small fire, screening it with his body, holding the photographs over the tight blue flame with the tips of his fingers.

He realized it was only a gesture. Stupid, he thought. Sentimental, too, but mostly just stupid.

Lavender was dead. You couldn't burn the blame.

Besides, the letters were in his head. And even now, without photographs, Lieutenant Cross could see Martha playing volleyball in her white gym shorts and yellow T-shirt. He could see her moving in the rain.

When the fire died out, Lieutenant Cross pulled his poncho over his shoulders and ate breakfast from a can.

There was no great mystery, he decided.

In those burned letters Martha had never mentioned the war, except to say, Jimmy, take care of yourself. She wasn't involved. She signed the letters "Love," but it wasn't love, and all the fine lines and technicalities did not matter.

The morning came up wet and blurry. Everything seemed part of everything else, the fog and Martha and the deepening rain.

It was a war, after all.

Half smiling, Lieutenant Jimmy Cross took out his maps. He shook his head hard, as if to clear it, then bent forward and began planning the day's march. In ten minutes, or maybe twenty, he would rouse the men and they would pack up and head west, where the maps showed the country to be green and inviting. They would do what they had always done. The rain might add some weight, but otherwise it would be one more day layered upon all the other days.

He was realistic about it. There was that new hardness in his stomach.

No more fantasies, he told himself.

Henceforth, when he thought about Martha, it would be only to think that she belonged elsewhere. He would shut down the daydreams. This was not Mount Sebastian, it was another world, where there were no pretty poems or midterm exams, a place where men died because of carelessness and gross stupidity. Kiowa was right. Boom-down, and you were dead, never partly dead.

95 Briefly, in the rain, Lieutenant Cross saw Martha's gray eyes gazing back at him.

He understood.

It was very sad, he thought. The things men carried inside. The things men did or felt they had to do.

He almost nodded at her, but didn't.

Instead he went back to his maps. He was now determined to perform his duties firmly and without negligence. It wouldn't help Lavender, he knew that, but from this point on he would comport himself as a soldier. He would dispose of his good-luck pebble. Swallow it, maybe, or use Lee Strunk's slingshot, or just drop it along the trail. On the march he would impose strict field discipline. He would be careful to send out flank security, to prevent straggling or bunching up, to keep his troops moving at the proper pace and at the proper interval. He would insist on clean weapons. He would confiscate the remainder of Lavender's dope. Later in the day, perhaps, he would call the men together and speak to them plainly. He would accept the blame for what had happened to Ted Lavender. He would be a man about it. He would look them in the eyes, keeping his chin level, and he would issue the new SOPs in a calm, impersonal tone of voice, an officer's voice, leaving no room for argument or discussion. Commencing immediately, he'd tell them, they would no longer abandon equipment along the route of march. They would police up their acts. They would get their shit together, and keep it together, and maintain it neatly and in good working order.

100 He would not tolerate laxity. He would show strength, distancing himself.

Among the men there would be grumbling, of course, and maybe worse, because their days would seem longer and their loads heavier, but Lieutenant Cross reminded himself that his obligation was not to be loved but to lead. He would dispense with love; it was not now a factor. And if anyone quarreled or complained, he would simply tighten his lips and arrange his shoulders in the correct command posture. He might give a curt little nod. Or he might not. He might just shrug and say Carry on, then they would saddle up and form into a column and move out toward the villages west of Than Khe. ❍

READING AND REACTING

1. Although the setting and the events described in "The Things They Carried" are dramatic and moving, its tone is often curiously flat and emotionless. Why do you think the narrator adopts this kind of tone?
2. Consider the different meanings of the word *carry,* which can refer to burdens abstract or concrete and to things carried physically or emotionally, actively or passively. Give several examples of the different senses in which O'Brien uses the word.
3. One striking characteristic of the story's style is its thorough catalogues of the concrete, tangible "things" the soldiers carry. Why do you suppose such detailed lists are included? What does what each man carries tell you about him? In a less literal, more abstract sense, what else do these men "carry"?
4. How would you characterize the level of formality of the story's diction? Is this level appropriate? Explain.
5. One stylistic technique O'Brien uses is intentional repetition—of phrases ("they carried"); people's names and identifying details (Martha's virginity, for example); and pieces of equipment. What effect do you think O'Brien hopes to achieve through such repetition? Is he successful?
6. Interspersed among long paragraphs crammed with detail are short one- or two-sentence paragraphs. What function do these brief paragraphs serve?
7. What function does Martha serve in the story? Why does Lieutenant Cross burn her letters?
8. In paragraph 68 the narrator says of the soldiers, "They used a hard vocabulary to contain the terrible softness." What do you think he means by this? Do you think this "hard vocabulary" is necessary? How does it affect your reaction to the story?
9. Describing Lieutenant Cross's new sense of purpose in the story's final paragraph, the narrator uses the phrase "Carry on." Do you think this phrase is linked in any way to the story's other uses of the word *carry,* or do you believe it is unrelated? Explain.
10. **JOURNAL ENTRY:** "The Things They Carried" is a story about war. Do you think it is an antiwar story? Why or why not?

WRITING SUGGESTIONS: STYLE, TONE, AND LANGUAGE

1. "A Clean, Well-Lighted Place" does not have a conventional plot in which characters grow and change and conflicts are resolved. For this reason, it might be argued that in this story language takes on more of a central role than it plays in other stories. Write an essay in which you examine this idea.
2. Both "Araby" and "The Things They Carried" deal, at least in part, with infatuation. Compare and contrast the infatuations described in the two stories. How do the kinds of language used by the narrators in the two stories communicate the two men's fascination and subsequent disillusionment?
3. Several of the stories in this chapter present one or more characters who are outsiders or misfits in their social milieus. Choose two or three characters, and explain why each is estranged from others and what efforts, if any, each makes to reconcile himself with society. Be sure to show how language helps to convey each character's alienation.
4. In each of this chapter's stories careful word choice is instrumental in creating a mood or atmosphere. Explain how the use of language creates an appropriate mood in any one of the stories; then explain how that mood helps to communicate the story's central theme.
5. In each of the chapter's four stories, the title communicates a good deal of information in a very few words. Write an essay in which you explain what each title communicates about the story's theme.

CHAPTER 9

SYMBOL AND ALLEGORY

A **symbol** is a person, object, action, place, or event that in addition to its literal or denotative meaning suggests a more complex meaning or range of meanings. **Universal** or **archetypal symbols,** such as the Old Man, the Mother, or the Grim Reaper, are so much a part of human experience that they suggest much the same thing to most people. **Conventional symbols** are likely to suggest the same thing to most people, provided they share common cultural and social assumptions (a rose suggests love, a skull and crossbones denotes poison). Such symbols are often used as a kind of shorthand in films, popular literature, and advertising, where they encourage automatic responses.

Conventional symbols such as the stars and stripes of the American flag can evoke powerful feelings of pride and patriotism in a group of people who share the same orientation toward it, just as the maple leaf and the Union Jack can. Symbols used in works of literature can function in much the same way, enabling writers to convey particular emotions or messages with a high degree of reliability. Thus spring can suggest rebirth and promise; autumn, declining years and powers; summer, youth and beauty. Because a writer can expect a dark forest to evoke fear, or a rainbow to communicate hope, he or she can be quite confident in using such an image to convey a particular idea or mood (provided the audience shares the writer's frame of reference).

Most symbols, however, have the power to suggest different things to different people. (For one thing, different cultures may react differently to the same symbols. In the United States, for example, an owl suggests wisdom; in India it suggests just the opposite.) Thus symbols enrich meaning, expanding the possibilities for interpretation and for reader interaction with the text. It is precisely because they are so potentially rich that symbols have the power to open up a text.

LITERARY SYMBOLS

In addition to having the same associations as conventional symbols, **literary symbols** may derive additional associations through their use in a particular literary work. Often a character, place, action, event, or object is used to suggest multiple meanings in a particular story. For instance, a watch or clock denotes time; as a literary symbol in a particular work, it might seem to suggest just the passing of time, or it might convey anything from a character's inability to recapture the past to the idea of time running out—or, it might suggest more than one of these ideas.

Thinking about an object's possible meanings can suggest a variety of ways to interpret a text. For instance, William Faulkner focuses attention on an unseen watch in a pivotal scene in "A Rose for Emily" (p. 70). The reader's first view of Miss Emily Grierson reveals her as "a small, fat woman in black, with a thin gold chain descending to her waist and vanishing into her belt." Several sentences later the narrator returns to the watch, noting that Miss Emily's visitors "could hear the invisible watch ticking at the end of the gold chain." Like these visitors, readers are drawn to the unseen watch as it ticks away. Because Miss Emily is portrayed as a woman living in the past, readers can assume that the presence of the watch is intended to reinforce the impression that she cannot see that time (the watch) has moved on. The vivid picture of the pale, plump woman in the musty room with the watch invisibly ticking does indeed suggest both that she has been left back in time and that she remains unaware of the progress around her. Thus the symbol enriches both the depiction of character and the story's theme.

In "Barn Burning" (p. 187), another Faulkner story, the clock is a somewhat more complex symbol. The itinerant Snopes family is without financial security and apparently without a future. The clock the mother carries from shack to shack—"The clock inlaid with mother-of-pearl, which would not run, stopped at some fourteen minutes past two o'clock of a dead and forgotten day and time, which had been [Sarty's] mother's dowry"—is their only possession of any value. The fact that the clock no longer works seems at first to suggest that time has run out for the family, and at the same time to reflect their impotence and paralysis. On another level, the clock stands in pathetic contrast to the de Spains' grand home, with its gold and glitter and Oriental rugs. Knowing that the clock was part of the mother's dowry, and that a dowry conventionally suggests a promise, might lead readers to believe that the broken clock symbolizes lost hope; the fact that the mother still clings to the clock, however, could suggest just the opposite.

As you read, you should not concentrate on finding the one true equivalent for a symbol; in fact, this kind of search is very limiting and not very productive. Instead, consider the possibilities, the different meanings a symbol might suggest. Then consider how various interpretations enrich other elements of the story and the work as a whole.

Recognizing Symbols When is a clock just a clock, and when is it also a symbol with a meaning or meanings beyond its literal significance? If a character waiting for a friend once glances at his or her watch to verify the time, there is probably nothing symbolic about the watch or about the act of looking at it. If, however, the watch keeps appearing again and again in the story, at key moments; if the narrator devotes a good deal of time to describing it; if it is placed in a conspicuous physical location; if characters keep noticing it and commenting on its presence; if it is lost (or found) at a critical moment; if its function in some way parallels the development of plot or character (for instance, if it stops as a relationship ends or as a character dies); if the story's opening or closing paragraph focuses on the timepiece; or if the story is called "The Watch"—the watch probably has some symbolic value. In other words, considering how an image is used, how often it is used, and when it appears will help you to determine whether or not it functions as a symbol.

The Purpose of Symbols Symbols expand the possible meanings of a story, thereby heightening interest and involving readers in active participation in the text. In "The Lottery" (p. 276), for example, the mysterious black box has symbolic significance. It is mentioned prominently and repeatedly, and it plays a pivotal role in the story's action. Of course, the black box is important on a purely literal level: It functions as a key component of the lottery. But the box has other associations as well, and it is these associations that suggest what its symbolic value might be.

The black wooden box is very old, a relic of many past lotteries; the narrator observes that it represents tradition. It is also closed and closely guarded, suggesting mystery and uncertainty. It is shabby, "splintered badly along one side . . . and in places faded or stained." This state of disrepair could suggest that the ritual it is part of has also deteriorated, or that tradition itself has deteriorated. The box is also simple in construction and design, suggesting the primitive (and therefore perhaps outdated) nature of the ritual. This symbol encourages readers to probe the story for values and ideas, to consider and weigh the suitability of a variety of interpretations. It serves as a "hot spot" that invites questions and exploration. The answers to these questions reinforce and enrich the story's theme.

ALLEGORY

An **allegory** attempts to communicate a doctrine, message, or moral principle by making it into a narrative in which the characters personify ideas, concepts, qualities, or other abstractions. Thus an allegory is a story with two parallel and consistent levels of meaning—one literal and one figurative. The figurative level, which offers some moral or political lesson, is the story's main concern. The allegorical figures are significant only because they represent something beyond their literal meaning in a rigidly fixed system.

Whereas a symbol has multiple symbolic associations as well as a literal meaning, an **allegorical figure**—a character, object, place, or event in the allegory—has just one meaning within an **allegorical framework**—the ideas that convey the allegory's message. (At the simplest level, for instance, one character can stand for good and another can stand for evil.) For this reason allegorical figures do not open up a text to various interpretations by readers the way symbols do. Because the purpose of allegory is to communicate a particular lesson, readers are not encouraged to speculate about the allegory's possible meanings as they are with other fictional forms; each element must have one equivalent that readers must discover if they are to make sense of the allegorical framework.

Naturally, the better a reader understands the political, religious, and literary assumptions of a writer, the easier it will be to recognize the allegorical significance of his or her work. John Bunyan's *The Pilgrim's Progress,* for example, is a famous seventeenth-century allegory based on the Christian doctrine of salvation. In order to appreciate the complexity of this work, you would have to familiarize yourself with this doctrine—possibly by consulting an encyclopedia or a reference work such as *The Oxford Companion to English Literature.*

One type of allegory, called a **beast fable,** is a short tale, usually including a moral, in which animals assume human characteristics. In one such tale, "The Gentlemen of the Jungle" by the Kenyan writer Jomo Kenyatta, an elephant is allowed to put his trunk inside a man's hut during a rainstorm. Not content with keeping his trunk dry, the elephant pushes his entire body inside the hut, displacing the man. When the man protests, the elephant takes the matter to the lion, who appoints a Commission of Enquiry to settle the matter. Eventually the man is forced not only to abandon his hut to the elephant, but also to build new huts for all the animals on the Commission. Even so, the jealous animals occupy the man's new hut and begin fighting for space; while they are arguing, the man burns down the hut, animals and all. Like the tales told by Aesop, "The Gentlemen of the Jungle" has a moral: "Peace is costly," says the man as he walks away happily, "but it's worth the expense." In order to determine the allegorical significance of each figure in this story, readers would have to know something about government bureaucracies, colonialism in Africa, and possibly a specific historical event in Kenya. The following passage from "The Gentlemen of the Jungle" reveals how the allegorical figures work within the framework of the allegory.

> The elephant, obeying the command of his master (the lion), got busy with the other ministers to appoint a Commission of Enquiry. The following elders of the jungle were appointed to sit on the Commission: (1) Mr. Rhinoceros; (2) Mr. Buffalo; (3) Mr. Alligator; (4) The Rt. Hon. Mr. Fox to act as chairman; and (5) Mr. Leopard to act as Secretary of the Commission. On seeing the personnel, the man protested and asked if it was not necessary to include in this Commission a member from his side. But he was told that it was impossible, since no one from his side was well enough educated to understand the intricacy of jungle law.

From this excerpt we can see how characters represent various ideas. For example, the members of the Commission stand for bureaucratic smugness and inequity and the man stands for the citizens who are victimized by the government.

A work can contain both symbolic elements *and* allegorical elements, as Nathaniel Hawthorne's "Young Goodman Brown" (p. 264) does. The names of both main characters, "Goodman" and "Faith," suggest that they fit within an allegorical system of some sort. Young Goodman Brown, for example, represents a good person who, despite his best efforts, strays from the path of righteousness. His wife, Faith, represents the quality he must hold on to in order to avoid temptation. As characters she and her husband have no significance outside of their allegorical functions. Other elements of the story, however, are not so clear cut. The older man whom Young Goodman Brown meets in the woods carries a staff that has carved on it "the likeness of a great black snake, so curiously wrought, that it might almost be seen to twist and wriggle itself like a living serpent." This staff, carried by a Satanic figure who represents evil and temptation, suggests the snake in the Garden of Eden, an association that neatly fits into the allegorical context of the story. Alternately, however, the staff could suggest the ever-changing nature of sin, the difficulty people have in perceiving sin, or the sexuality that may account for Young Goodman Brown's susceptibility to temptation. This range of possible meanings opens the staff to interpretation and thus suggests it functions as a symbol. Using a symbol in this way, Hawthorne creates a complex image of sin and enriches his allegory.

Other stories work entirely on a symbolic level and contain no allegorical figures. "The Lottery," despite its moral overtones, is not an allegory. For one thing, as has been demonstrated, its symbols do not have easily assignable equivalents. Moreover, the story is not the sum total of a neat system of fixed-value, interlocking characters, events, and objects arranged to serve one rigid, didactic purpose. In fact, many different interpretations have been suggested for this story. When it was first published in June 1948 in *The New Yorker,* some readers believed it to be nonfiction, an accurate representation of an actual custom or ritual. As Shirley Jackson reports in her essay "Biography of a Story," those who recognized it as fiction speculated about its meaning, seeing it as (among other things) an attack on prejudice, a criticism of society's need for a scapegoat, or a treatise on witchcraft, Christian martyrdom, or village gossip. Various critics have argued that "The Lottery" is a story about the evils of violence, capital punishment, mob psychology, or Nazi Germany. The fact is, no single allegorical interpretation will account for every major character, object, and event in the story.

Checklist for Writing about Symbol and Allegory

- Are any universal symbols used in the work? Any conventional symbols? Any literary symbols? What is their function?
- Is any character, place, action, event, or object given unusual prominence or emphasis in the story? If so, does this element seem to have symbolic as well as literal value?
- What possible meanings does each symbol suggest?
- How do symbols help to depict the story's characters?
- How do symbols help to characterize the story's setting?

- How do symbols help to advance the story's plot?
- Are any of the symbols related? Taken together, do they seem to support a common theme?
- Does the story have a moral or didactic purpose? What is the message, idea, or moral principle the story seeks to convey?
- What equivalent may be assigned to each allegorical figure in the story?
- Does the story combine allegorical figures and symbols? What is their function in the story?

Nathaniel Hawthorne (1804–1864) was born in Salem, Massachusetts, the great-great-grandson of a judge who presided over the infamous Salem witch trials. After his sea captain father was killed on a voyage when Hawthorne was four years old, his childhood was one of genteel poverty. An uncle paid for his education at Bowdoin College in Maine, where Hawthorne's friends included a future president of the United States, Franklin Pierce, who in 1853 would appoint him U.S. consul in Liverpool, England. Hawthorne published four novels—*The Scarlet Letter* (1850), *The House of the Seven Gables* (1851), *The Blithedale Romance* (1852), and *The Marble Faun* (1860)—and more than one hundred short stories and sketches.

Hawthorne referred to his own work as *romance.* He used this term to mean not an escape from reality, but a method of confronting "the depths of our common nature" and "the truth of the heart." His stories probe the dark side of human nature and frequently paint a world that is virtuous on the surface but (as Young Goodman Brown comes to believe) "one stain of guilt, one mighty blood spot" beneath. Hawthorne's stories often emphasize the ambiguity of human experience. For example, the reader is left to wonder whether Goodman Brown actually saw a witch's coven or dreamed a dream. For Hawthorne, what is important is Brown's recognition that evil may be found everywhere. "Young Goodman Brown," as Hawthorne's neighbor and friend Herman Melville once said, is a tale "as deep as Dante."

Nathaniel Hawthorne

YOUNG GOODMAN BROWN

(1835)

Young Goodman Brown came forth at sunset, into the street of Salem village, but put his head back, after crossing the threshold, to exchange a parting kiss with his young wife. And Faith, as the wife was aptly named, thrust her own pretty head into the street, letting the wind play with the pink ribbons of her cap, while she called to Goodman Brown.

"Dearest heart," whispered she, softly and rather sadly, when her lips were close to his ear, "prithee, put off your journey until sunrise, and sleep in your own bed to-night. A lone woman is troubled with such dreams and such thoughts, that she's afeard of herself, sometimes. Pray, tarry with me this night, dear husband, of all nights in the year!"

"My love and my Faith," replied young Goodman Brown, "of all nights in the year, this one night must I tarry away from thee. My journey, as thou callest it, forth and back again, must needs be done 'twixt now and sunrise. What, my sweet, pretty wife, dost thou doubt me already, and we but three months married!"

"Then God bless you!" said Faith with the pink ribbons, "and may you find all well, when you come back."

"Amen!" cried Goodman Brown. "Say thy prayers, dear Faith, and go to bed at dusk, and no harm will come to thee."

So they parted; and the young man pursued his way, until, being about to turn the corner by the meeting-house, he looked back and saw the head of Faith still peeping after him, with a melancholy air, in spite of her pink ribbons.

"Poor little Faith!" thought he, for his heart smote him. "What a wretch am I, to leave her on such an errand! She talks of dreams, too. Methought, as she spoke, there was trouble in her face, as if a dream had warned her what work is to be done to-night. But no, no! 't would kill her to think it. Well; she's a blessed angel on earth; and after this one night, I'll cling to her skirts and follow her to Heaven."

With this excellent resolve for the future, Goodman Brown felt himself justified in making more haste on his present evil purpose. He had taken a dreary road, darkened by all the gloomiest trees of the forest, which barely stood aside to let the narrow path creep through, and closed immediately behind. It was as lonely as could be; and there is this peculiarity in such a solitude, that the traveller knows not who may be concealed by the innumerable trunks and the thick boughs overhead; so that, with lonely footsteps, he may yet be passing through an unseen multitude.

"There may be a devilish Indian behind every tree," said Goodman Brown to himself; and he glanced fearfully behind him, as he added, "What if the devil himself should be at my very elbow!"

His head being turned back, he passed a crook of the road, and looking forward again, beheld the figure of a man, in grave and decent attire, seated at the foot of an old tree. He arose at Goodman Brown's approach, and walked onward, side by side with him.

"You are late, Goodman Brown," said he. "The clock of the Old South[1] was striking, as I came through Boston; and that is full fifteen minutes agone."

[1] Old South Church, Boston, renowned meeting place for American patriots during the Revolution.

"Faith kept me back awhile," replied the young man, with a tremor in his voice, caused by the sudden appearance of his companion, though not wholly unexpected.

It was now deep dusk in the forest, and deepest in that part of it where these two were journeying. As nearly as could be discerned, the second traveller was about fifty years old, apparently in the same rank of life as Goodman Brown, and bearing a considerable resemblance to him, though perhaps more in expression than features. Still, they might have been taken for father and son. And yet, though the elder person was as simply clad as the younger, and as simple in manner too, he had an indescribable air of one who knew the world, and would not have felt abashed at the governor's dinner-table, or in King William's court,[2] were it possible that his affairs should call him thither. But the only thing about him that could be fixed upon as remarkable, was his staff, which bore the likeness of a great black snake, so curiously wrought, that it might almost be seen to twist and wriggle itself like a living serpent. This, of course, must have been an ocular deception, assisted by the uncertain light.

"Come, Goodman Brown!" cried his fellow-traveller, "this is a dull pace for the beginning of a journey. Take my staff, if you are so soon weary."

"Friend," said the other, exchanging his slow pace for a full stop, "having kept covenant by meeting thee here, it is my purpose now to return whence I came. I have scruples, touching the matter thou wot'st of."

"Sayest thou so?" replied he of the serpent, smiling apart. "Let us walk on, nevertheless, reasoning as we go, and if I convince thee not, thou shalt turn back. We are but a little way in the forest, yet."

"Too far, too far!" exclaimed the goodman, unconsciously resuming his walk. "My father never went into the woods on such an errand, nor his father before him. We have been a race of honest men and good Christians, since the days of the martyrs. And shall I be the first of the name of Brown that ever took this path and kept—"

"Such company, thou wouldst say," observed the elder person, interrupting his pause. "Well said, Goodman Brown! I have been as well acquainted with your family as with ever a one among the Puritans; and that's no trifle to say. I helped your grandfather, the constable, when he lashed the Quaker woman so smartly through the streets of Salem. And it was I that brought your father a pitch-pine knot, kindled at my own hearth, to set fire to an Indian village, in King Philip's war.[3] They were my good friends, both; and many a pleasant walk have we had along this path, and returned merrily after midnight. I would fain be friends with you, for their sake."

---

[2] William III, king of England from 1689 to 1702.

[3] A war of Indian resistance, led by King Philip, or Metacomet, of the Wampanoags. The war, intended to halt expansion of English settlers in Massachusetts, collapsed after King Philip's death in August 1676.

"If it be as thou sayest," replied Goodman Brown, "I marvel they never spoke of these matters. Or, verily, I marvel not, seeing that the least rumor of the sort would have driven them from New England. We are a people of prayer, and good works to boot, and abide no such wickedness."

"Wickedness or not," said the traveller with the twisted staff, "I have a very general acquaintance here in New England. The deacons of many a church have drunk the communion wine with me; the selectmen, of divers towns, make me their chairman; and a majority of the Great and General Court are firm supporters of my interest. The governor and I, too—but these are state secrets."

"Can this be so!" cried Goodman Brown, with a stare of amazement at his undisturbed companion. "Howbeit, I have nothing to do with the governor and council; they have their own ways, and are no rule for a simple husbandman like me. But, were I to go on with thee, how should I meet the eye of that good old man, our minister, at Salem village? Oh, his voice would make me tremble, both Sabbath-day and lecture-day!"[4]

Thus far, the elder traveller had listened with due gravity, but now burst into a fit of irrepressible mirth, shaking himself so violently, that his snakelike staff actually seemed to wriggle in sympathy.

"Ha, ha, ha!" shouted he, again and again; then composing himself, "Well, go on, Goodman Brown, go on; but, prithee, don't kill me with laughing!"

"Well, then, to end the matter at once," said Goodman Brown, considerably nettled, "there is my wife, Faith. It would break her dear little heart; and I'd rather break my own!"

"Nay, if that be the case," answered the other, "e'en go thy ways, Goodman Brown. I would not, for twenty old women like the one hobbling before us, that Faith should come to any harm."

As he spoke, he pointed his staff at a female figure on the path, in whom Goodman Brown recognized a very pious and exemplary dame, who had taught him his catechism in youth, and was still his moral and spiritual adviser, jointly with the minister and Deacon Gookin.

"A marvel, truly, that Goody[5] Cloyse should be so far in the wilderness, at nightfall!" said he. "But, with your leave, friend, I shall take a cut through the woods, until we have left this Christian woman behind. Being a stranger to you, she might ask whom I was consorting with, and whither I was going."

"Be it so," said his fellow-traveller. "Betake you to the woods, and let me keep the path."

Accordingly, the young man turned aside, but took care to watch his companion, who advanced softly along the road, until he had come

---

[4] The day of the midweek sermon, usually Thursday.

[5] A contraction of "Goodwife," a term of politeness used in addressing a woman of humble station. Goody Cloyse, like Goody Cory and Martha Carrier, who appear later in the story, was one of the Salem "witches" sentenced in 1692.

within a staff's length of the old dame. She, meanwhile, was making the best of her way, with singular speed for so aged a woman, and mumbling some indistinct words, a prayer, doubtless, as she went. The traveller put forth his staff, and touched her withered neck with what seemed the serpent's tail.

"The devil!" screamed the pious old lady.

"Then Goody Cloyse knows her old friend?" observed the traveller, confronting her, and leaning on his writhing stick.

"Ah, forsooth, and is it your worship, indeed?" cried the good dame. "Yea, truly is it, and in the very image of my old gossip, Goodman Brown, the grandfather of the silly fellow that now is. But, would your worship believe it? my broomstick hath strangely disappeared, stolen, as I suspect, by that unhanged witch, Goody Cory, and that, too, when I was all anointed with the juice of smallage and cinque-foil and wolf's bane—"[6]

"Mingled with fine wheat and the fat of a new-born babe," said the shape of old Goodman Brown.

"Ah, your worship knows the recipe," cried the old lady, cackling aloud. "So, as I was saying, being all ready for the meeting, and no horse to ride on, I made up my mind to foot it; for they tell me there is a nice young man to be taken into communion to-night. But now your good worship will lend me your arm, and we shall be there in a twinkling."

"That can hardly be," answered her friend. "I may not spare you my arm, Goody Cloyse, but here is my staff, if you will."

So saying, he threw it down at her feet, where, perhaps, it assumed life, being one of the rods which its owner had formerly lent to the Egyptian Magi. Of this fact, however, Goodman Brown could not take cognizance. He had cast his eyes in astonishment, and looking down again, beheld neither Goody Cloyse nor the serpentine staff, but his fellow-traveller alone, who waited for him as calmly as if nothing had happened.

"That old woman taught me my catechism!" said the young man; and there was a world of meaning in this simple comment.

They continued to walk onward, while the elder traveller exhorted his companion to make good speed and persevere in the path, discoursing so aptly, that his arguments seemed rather to spring up in the bosom of his auditor, than to be suggested by himself. As they went he plucked a branch of maple, to serve for a walking-stick, and began to strip it of the twigs and little boughs, which were wet with evening dew. The moment his fingers touched them, they became strangely withered and dried up, as with a week's sunshine. Thus the pair proceeded, at a good free pace, until suddenly, in a gloomy hollow of the road, Goodman Brown sat himself down on the stump of a tree, and refused to go any farther.

---

[6] All plants believed to have magical powers. "Smallage" is wild celery.

"Friend," said he, stubbornly, "my mind is made up. Not another step will I budge on this errand. What if a wretched old woman do choose to go to the devil, when I thought she was going to Heaven! Is that any reason why I should quit my dear Faith, and go after her?"

"You will think better of this by and by," said his acquaintance, composedly. "Sit here and rest yourself awhile; and when you feel like moving again, there is my staff to help you along."

Without more words, he threw his companion the maple stick, and was as speedily out of sight as if he had vanished into the deepening gloom. The young man sat a few moments by the roadside, applauding himself greatly, and thinking with how clear a conscience he should meet the minister, in his morning walk, nor shrink from the eye of good old Deacon Gookin. And what calm sleep would be his, that very night, which was to have been spent so wickedly, but purely and sweetly now, in the arms of Faith! Amidst these pleasant and praiseworthy meditations, Goodman Brown heard the tramp of horses along the road, and deemed it advisable to conceal himself within the verge of the forest, conscious of the guilty purpose that had brought him thither, though now so happily turned from it.

On came the hoof-tramps and the voices of the riders, two grave old voices, conversing soberly as they drew near. These mingled sounds appeared to pass along the road, within a few yards of the young man's hiding-place; but owing, doubtless, to the depth of the gloom, at that particular spot, neither the travellers nor their steeds were visible. Though their figures brushed the small boughs by the wayside, it could not be seen that they intercepted, even for a moment, the faint gleam from the strip of bright sky, athwart which they must have passed. Goodman Brown alternately crouched and stood on tiptoe, pulling aside the branches, and thrusting forth his head as far as he durst, without discerning so much as a shadow. It vexed him the more, because he could have sworn, were such a thing possible, that he recognized the voices of the minister and Deacon Gookin, jogging along quietly, as they were wont to do, when bound to some ordination or ecclesiastical council. While yet within hearing, one of the riders stopped to pluck a switch.

"Of the two, reverend Sir," said the voice like the deacon's, "I had rather miss an ordination dinner than to-night's meeting. They tell me that some of our community are to be here from Falmouth and beyond, and others from Connecticut and Rhode Island; besides several of the Indian powwows, who, after their fashion, know almost as much deviltry as the best of us. Moreover, there is a goodly young woman to be taken into communion."

"Mighty well, Deacon Gookin!" replied the solemn old tones of the minister. "Spur up, or we shall be late. Nothing can be done, you know, until I get on the ground."

The hoofs clattered again, and the voices, talking so strangely in the empty air, passed on through the forest, where no church had ever been gathered, nor solitary Christian prayed. Whither, then, could these holy men be journeying, so deep into the heathen wilderness? Young Goodman Brown caught hold of a tree, for support, being ready to sink down on the ground, faint and over-burthened with the heavy sickness of his heart. He looked up to the sky, doubting whether there really was a Heaven above him. Yet, there was the blue arch, and the stars brightening in it.

"With Heaven above, and Faith below, I will yet stand firm against the devil!" cried Goodman Brown.

While he still gazed upward, into the deep arch of the firmament, and had lifted his hands to pray, a cloud, though no wind was stirring, hurried across the zenith, and hid the brightening stars. The blue sky was still visible, except directly overhead, where this black mass of cloud was sweeping swiftly northward. Aloft in the air, as if from the depths of the cloud, came a confused and doubtful sound of voices. Once, the listener fancied that he could distinguish the accents of townspeople of his own, men and women, both pious and ungodly, many of whom he had met at the communion-table, and had seen others rioting at the tavern. The next moment, so indistinct were the sounds, he doubted whether he had heard aught but the murmur of the old forest, whispering without a wind. Then came a stronger swell of those familiar tones, heard daily in the sunshine, at Salem village, but never, until now, from a cloud at night. There was one voice, of a young woman, uttering lamentations, yet with an uncertain sorrow, and entreating for some favor, which, perhaps, it would grieve her to obtain. And all the unseen multitude, both saints and sinners, seemed to encourage her onward.

"Faith!" shouted Goodman Brown, in a voice of agony and desperation; and the echoes of the forest mocked him, crying—"Faith! Faith!" as if bewildered wretches were seeking her, all through the wilderness.

The cry of grief, rage, and terror was yet piercing the night, when the unhappy husband held his breath for a response. There was a scream, drowned immediately in a louder murmur of voices fading into far-off laughter, as the dark cloud swept away, leaving the clear and silent sky above Goodman Brown. But something fluttered lightly down through the air, and caught on the branch of a tree. The young man seized it and beheld a pink ribbon.

50 "My Faith is gone!" cried he, after one stupefied moment. "There is no good on earth, and sin is but a name. Come, devil! for to thee is this world given."

And maddened with despair, so that he laughed loud and long, did Goodman Brown grasp his staff and set forth again, at such a rate, that he seemed to fly along the forest path, rather than to walk or run. The road grew wilder and drearier, and more faintly traced, and vanished at length, leaving him in the heart of the dark wilderness, still rushing onward, with the instinct that guides mortal man to evil. The whole forest was peopled with frightful sounds: the creaking of the trees, the howling of wild beasts, and the yell of Indians; while, sometimes, the wind tolled like a distant church bell, and sometimes gave a broad roar around the traveller, as if all Nature was laughing him to scorn. But he was himself the chief horror of the scene, and shrank not from its other horrors.

"Ha! ha! ha!" roared Goodman Brown, when the wind laughed at him. "Let us hear which will laugh loudest! Think not to frighten me with your deviltry! Come witch, come wizard, come Indian powwow, come devil himself! and here comes Goodman Brown. You may as well fear him as he fear you!"

In truth, all through the haunted forest, there could be nothing more frightful than the figure of Goodman Brown. On he flew, among the black pines, brandishing his staff with frenzied gestures, now giving vent to an inspiration of horrid blasphemy, and now shouting forth such laughter, as set all the echoes of the forest laughing like demons around him. The fiend in his own shape is less hideous, than when he rages in the breast of man. Thus sped the demoniac on his course, until, quivering among the trees, he saw a red light before him, as when the felled trunks and branches of a clearing have been set on fire, and throw up their lurid blaze against the sky, at the hour of midnight. He paused, in a lull of the tempest that had driven him onward, and heard the swell of what seemed a hymn, rolling solemnly from a distance, with the weight of many voices. He knew the tune. It was a familiar one in the choir of the village meeting-house. The verse died heavily away, and was lengthened by a chorus, not of human voices, but of all the sounds of the benighted wilderness, pealing in awful harmony together. Goodman Brown cried out; and his cry was lost to his own ear, by its unison with the cry of the desert.

In the interval of silence, he stole forward, until the light glared full upon his eyes. At one extremity of an open space, hemmed in by the dark wall of the forest, arose a rock, bearing some rude, natural resemblance either to an altar or a pulpit, and surrounded by four blazing pines, their tops aflame, their stems untouched, like candles at an evening meeting. The mass of foliage, that had overgrown the summit of the rock, was all on fire, blazing high into the night, and fitfully illuminating the whole field. Each pendent twig and leafy festoon was in a blaze. As the red light arose and fell, a numerous congregation alternately shone forth, then disappeared in shadow, and again grew, as it were, out of the darkness, peopling the heart of the solitary woods at once.

"A grave and dark-clad company!" quoth Goodman Brown.

In truth, they were such. Among them, quivering to-and-fro, between gloom and splendor, appeared faces that would be seen, next day, at the council-board of the province, and others which, Sabbath after Sabbath, looked devoutly heavenward, and benignantly over the crowded pews, from the holiest pulpits in the land. Some affirm, that the lady of the governor was there. At least, there were high dames well known to her, and wives of honored husbands, and widows a great multitude, and ancient maidens, all of excellent repute, and fair young girls, who trembled lest their mothers should espy them. Either the sudden gleams of light, flashing over the obscure field, bedazzled Goodman Brown, or he recognized a score of the church members of Salem village, famous for their especial sanctity. Good old Deacon Gookin had arrived, and waited at the skirts of that venerable saint, his reverend pastor. But, irreverently consorting with these grave, reputable, and pious people, these elders of the church, these chaste dames and dewy virgins, there were men of dissolute lives and women of spotted fame, wretches given over to all mean and filthy vice, and suspected even of horrid crimes. It was strange to see, that the good shrank not from the wicked, nor were the sinners abashed by the saints. Scattered, also, among their pale-faced enemies, were the Indian priests, or powwows, who had often scared their native forest with more hideous incantations than any known to English witchcraft.

"But, where is Faith?" thought Goodman Brown; and, as hope came into his heart, he trembled.

Another verse of the hymn arose, a slow and mournful strain, such as the pious love, but joined to words which expressed all that our nature can conceive of sin, and darkly hinted at far more. Unfathomable to mere mortals is the lore of fiends. Verse after verse was sung, and still the chorus of the desert swelled between, like the deepest tone of a mighty organ. And, with the final peal of that dreadful anthem, there came a sound, as if the roaring wind, the rushing streams, the howling beasts, and every other voice of the unconverted wilderness were mingling and according with the voice of guilty man, in homage to the prince of all. The four blazing pines threw up a loftier flame, and obscurely discovered shapes and visages of horror on the smoke-wreaths, above the impious assembly. At the same moment, the fire on the rock shot redly forth, and formed a glowing arch above its base, where now appeared a figure. With reverence be it spoken, the apparition bore no slight similitude, both in garb and manner, to some grave divine of the New England churches.

"Bring forth the converts!" cried a voice, that echoed through the field and rolled into the forest.

At the word, Goodman Brown stepped forth from the shadow of the trees, and approached the congregation, with whom he felt a loathful brotherhood, by the sympathy of all that was wicked in his heart. He could have well-nigh sworn, that the shape of his own dead father beckoned him to advance, looking downward from a smoke-wreath, while a woman, with dim features of despair, threw out her hand to warn him back. Was it his mother? But he had no power to retreat one step, nor to resist, even in thought, when the minister and good old Deacon Gookin seized his arms, and led him to the blazing rock. Thither came also the slender form of a veiled female, led between Goody Cloyse, that pious teacher of the catechism, and Martha Carrier, who had received the devil's promise to be queen of hell. A rampant hag was she! And there stood the proselytes, beneath the canopy of fire.

"Welcome, my children," said the dark figure, "to the communion of your race! Ye have found, thus young, your nature and your destiny. My children, look behind you!"

They turned; and flashing forth, as it were, in a sheet of flame, the fiend-worshippers were seen; the smile of welcome gleamed darkly on every visage.

"There," resumed the sable form, "are all whom ye have reverenced from youth. Ye deemed them holier than yourselves, and shrank from your own sin, contrasting it with their lives of righteousness and prayerful aspirations heavenward. Yet, here are they all, in my worshipping assembly! This night it shall be granted you to know their secret deeds; how hoary-bearded elders of the church have whispered wanton words to the young maids of their households; how many a woman, eager for widow's weeds, has given her husband a drink at bedtime, and let him sleep his last sleep in her bosom; how beardless youths have made haste to inherit their father's wealth; and how fair damsels—blush not, sweet ones!—have dug little graves in the garden, and bidden me, the sole guest, to an infant's funeral. By the sympathy of your human hearts for sin, ye shall scent out all the places—whether in church, bedchamber, street, field, or forest—where crime has been committed, and shall exult to behold the whole earth one stain of guilt, one mighty blood-spot. Far more than this! It shall be yours to penetrate, in every bosom, the deep mystery of sin, the fountain of all wicked arts, and which inexhaustibly supplies more evil impulses than human power—than my power, at its utmost!—can make manifest in deeds. And now, my children, look upon each other."

They did so; and, by the blaze of the hell-kindled torches, the wretched man beheld his Faith, and the wife her husband, trembling before that unhallowed altar.

"Lo! there ye stand, my children," said the figure, in a deep and solemn tone, almost sad, with its despairing awfulness, as if his once angelic nature could yet mourn for our miserable race. "Depending upon one another's hearts, ye had still hoped that virtue were not all a dream! Now are ye undeceived!—Evil is the nature of mankind. Evil must be your only happiness. Welcome, again, my children, to the communion of your race!"

"Welcome!" repeated the fiend-worshippers, in one cry of despair and triumph.

And there they stood, the only pair, as it seemed, who were yet hesitating on the verge of wickedness, in this dark world. A basin was hollowed, naturally, in the rock. Did it contain water, reddened by the lurid light? or was it blood? or, perchance, a liquid flame? Herein did the Shape of Evil dip his hand, and prepare to lay the mark of baptism upon their foreheads, that they might be partakers of the mystery of sin, more conscious of the secret guilt of others, both in deed and thought, than they could now be of their own. The husband cast one look at his pale wife, and Faith at him. What polluted wretches would the next glance show them to each other, shuddering alike at what they disclosed and what they saw!

"Faith! Faith!" cried the husband. "Look up to Heaven, and resist the Wicked One!"

Whether Faith obeyed, he knew not. Hardly had he spoken, when he found himself amid calm night and solitude, listening to a roar of the wind, which died heavily away through the forest. He staggered against the rock, and felt it chill and damp, while a hanging twig, that had been all on fire, besprinkled his cheek with the coldest dew.

70 The next morning, young Goodman Brown came slowly into the street of Salem village staring around him like a bewildered man. The good old minister was taking a walk along the grave-yard, to get an appetite for breakfast and meditate his sermon, and bestowed a blessing, as he passed, on Goodman Brown. He shrank from the venerable saint, as if to avoid an anathema. Old Deacon Gookin was at domestic worship, and the holy words of his prayer were heard through the open window. "What God doth the wizard pray to?" quoth Goodman Brown. Goody Cloyse, that excellent old Christian, stood in the early sunshine, at her own lattice, catechising a little girl, who had brought her a pint of morning's milk. Goodman Brown snatched away the child, as from the grasp of the fiend himself. Turning the corner by the meeting-house, he spied the head of Faith, with the pink ribbons, gazing anxiously forth, and bursting into such joy at sight of him that she skipt along the street, and almost kissed her husband before the whole village. But Goodman Brown looked sternly and sadly into her face, and passed on without a greeting.

Had Goodman Brown fallen asleep in the forest, and only dreamed a wild dream of a witch-meeting?

Be it so, if you will. But, alas! it was a dream of evil omen for young Goodman Brown. A stern, a sad, a darkly meditative, a distrustful, if not a desperate man did he become, from the night of that fearful dream. On the Sabbath day, when the congregation were singing a holy psalm, he could not listen, because an anthem of sin rushed loudly upon his ear, and drowned all the blessed strain. When the minister spoke from the pulpit, with power and fervid eloquence, and with his hand on the open Bible, of the sacred truths of our religion, and of saint-like lives and triumphant deaths, and of future bliss or misery unutterable, then did Goodman Brown turn pale, dreading lest the roof should thunder down upon the gray blasphemer and his hearers. Often, awaking suddenly at midnight, he shrank from the bosom of Faith, and at morning or eventide, when the family knelt down at prayer, he scowled, and muttered to himself, and gazed sternly at his wife, and turned away. And when he had lived long, and was borne to his grave, a hoary corpse, followed by Faith, an aged woman, and children and grand-children, a goodly procession, besides neighbors not a few, they carved no hopeful verse upon his tombstone; for his dying hour was gloom.

READING AND REACTING

1. Who is the narrator of "Young Goodman Brown"? What advantages does the narrative point of view give the author?
2. What does Young Goodman Brown mean when he says "of all nights in the year, this one must I tarry away from thee" (3)? What is important about *this* night, and why does Young Goodman Brown believe he must journey "twixt now and sunrise"?
3. Is Young Goodman Brown surprised to encounter the second traveler on the road, or does he seem to expect him? What is the significance of their encounter? What reason does Young Goodman Brown give for being late?
4. What sins are the various characters Young Goodman Brown meets in the woods guilty of committing?
5. "Young Goodman Brown" has two distinct settings: Salem and the woods. What are the differences between these settings? How does each contribute to the story?
6. Which figures in the story are allegorical, and which have symbolic significance? On what evidence do you base your conclusions?
7. Explain the change that takes place in Young Goodman Brown at the end of the story. Why can he not listen to the singing of holy psalms or the minister's sermons? What causes him to turn away from Faith and die in gloom?
8. **JOURNAL ENTRY:** At the end of the story the narrator suggests that Goodman Brown might have fallen asleep and imagined his encounter with the witches. Do you think the events are all a dream?

Shirley Jackson (1916–1965) is best known for her restrained tales of horror and the supernatural, most notably her novel *The Haunting of Hill House* (1959) and the short story "The Lottery" (1948). Among her other works are two novels dealing with divided personalities—*The Bird's Nest* (1954) and *We Have Always Lived in the Castle* (1962)—and two collections of comic tales about her children and family life, *Life Among the Savages* (1953) and *Raising Demons* (1957).

Jackson was an intense, self-destructive, contradictory personality: a witty hostess to crowds of literary friends; a self-described witch, clairvoyant, and student of magic; a cookie-baking "Mom" who wrote chilling tales between loads of laundry. With her husband, literary critic Stanley Edgar Hyman, she settled in the small town of Bennington, Vermont, but was never accepted by the townspeople. "The Lottery" is set in much the same kind of small, hidebound town. The story's publication in *The New Yorker* magazine provoked a torrent of letters from enraged and horrified readers. Americans of the post–World War II era saw themselves as "good guys" defending the world against foreign evils. Jackson's story, written scarcely three years after the liberation of Auschwitz, told Americans something they did not want to hear—that the face of human evil could look just like their next-door neighbor. Horror master Stephen King dedicates his book *Firestarter* "to Shirley Jackson, who never had to raise her voice."

Shirley Jackson

THE LOTTERY

(1948)

The morning of June 27th was clear and sunny, with the fresh warmth of a full-summer day; the flowers were blossoming profusely and the grass was richly green. The people of the village began to gather in the square, between the post office and the bank, around ten o'clock; in some towns there were so many people that the lottery took two days and had to be started on June 26th, but in this village, where there were only about three hundred people, the whole lottery took less than two hours, so it could begin at ten o'clock in the morning and still be through in time to allow the villagers to get home for noon dinner.

The children assembled first, of course. School was recently over for the summer, and the feeling of liberty sat uneasily on most of them; they tended to gather together quietly for a while before they broke into boisterous play, and their talk was still of the classroom and the teacher, of books and reprimands. Bobby Martin had already stuffed his pockets full of stones, and the other boys soon followed his example, selecting the smoothest and roundest stones; Bobby and Harry Jones and Dickie Delacroix—the villagers pronounced this name "Dellacroy"—eventually made a great pile of stones in one corner of the square and guarded it against the raids of the other boys. The girls stood aside, talking among themselves, looking over their shoulders at the boys, and the very small children rolled in the dust or clung to the hands of their older brothers or sisters.

Soon the men began to gather, surveying their own children, speaking of planting and rain, tractors and taxes. They stood together, away from the pile of stones in the corner, and their jokes were quiet and they smiled rather than laughed. The women, wearing faded house dresses and sweaters, came shortly after their menfolk. They greeted one another and exchanged bits of gossip as they went to join their husbands. Soon the women, standing by their husbands, began to call to their children, and the children came reluctantly, having to be called four or five times. Bobby Martin ducked under his mother's grasping hand and ran, laughing, back to the pile of stones. His father spoke up sharply, and Bobby came quickly and took his place between his father and his oldest brother.

The lottery was conducted—as were the square dances, the teen-age club, the Halloween program—by Mr. Summers, who had time and energy to devote to civic activities. He was a round-faced, jovial man and he ran the coal business, and people were sorry for him, because he had no children and his wife was a scold. When he arrived in the square, carrying the black wooden box, there was a murmur of conversation among the villagers, and he waved and called, "Little late today, folks." The postmaster, Mr. Graves, followed him, carrying a three-legged stool, and the stool was put in the center of the square and Mr. Summers set the black box down on it. The villagers kept their distance, leaving a space between themselves and the stool, and when Mr. Summers said, "Some of you fellows want to give me a hand?" there was a hesitation before two men, Mr. Martin and his oldest son, Baxter, came forward to hold the box steady on the stool while Mr. Summers stirred up the papers inside it.

5 The original paraphernalia for the lottery had been lost long ago, and the black box now resting on the stool had been put into use even before Old Man Warner, the oldest man in town, was born. Mr. Summers spoke frequently to the villagers about making a new box, but no one liked to upset even as much tradition as was represented by the black box. There was a story that the present box had been made with some pieces of the box that had preceded it, the one that had been constructed when the first people settled down to make a village here. Every year, after the lottery, Mr. Summers began talking again about a new box, but every year the subject was allowed to fade off without anything's being done. The black box grew shabbier each year; by now it was no longer completely black but splintered badly along one side to show the original wood color, and in some places faded or stained.

Mr. Martin and his oldest son, Baxter, held the black box securely on the stool until Mr. Summers had stirred the papers thoroughly with his hand. Because so much of the ritual had been forgotten or discarded, Mr. Summers had been successful in having slips of paper substituted for the chips of wood that had been used for generations. Chips of wood, Mr. Summers had argued, had been all very well when the village was tiny, but now that the population was more than three hundred and likely to keep on growing, it was necessary to use something that would fit more easily into the black box. The night before the lottery, Mr. Summers and Mr. Graves made up the slips of paper and put them in the box, and it was then taken to the safe of Mr. Summers' coal company and locked up until

Mr. Summers was ready to take it to the square next morning. The rest of the year, the box was put away, sometimes one place, sometimes another; it had spent one year in Mr. Graves's barn and another year underfoot in the post office, and sometimes it was set on a shelf in the Martin grocery and left there.

There was a great deal of fussing to be done before Mr. Summers declared the lottery open. There were the lists to make up—of heads of families, heads of households in each family, members of each household in each family. There was the proper swearing-in of Mr. Summers by the postmaster, as the official of the lottery; at one time, some people remembered, there had been a recital of some sort, performed by the official of the lottery, a perfunctory, tuneless chant that had been rattled off duly each year; some people believed that the official of the lottery used to stand just so when he said or sang it, others believed that he was supposed to walk among the people, but years and years ago this part of the ritual had been allowed to lapse. There had been, also, a ritual salute, which the official of the lottery had had to use in addressing each person who came up to draw from the box, but this also had changed with time, until now it was felt necessary only for the official to speak to each person approaching. Mr. Summers was very good at all this; in his clean white shirt and blue jeans, with one hand resting carelessly on the black box, he seemed very proper and important as he talked interminably to Mr. Graves and the Martins.

Just as Mr. Summers finally left off talking and turned to the assembled villagers, Mrs. Hutchinson came hurriedly along the path to the square, her sweater thrown over her shoulders, and slid into place in the back of the crowd. "Clean forgot what day it was," she said to Mrs. Delacroix, who stood next to her, and they both laughed softly. "Thought my old man was out back stacking wood," Mrs. Hutchinson went on, "and then I looked out the window and the kids was gone, and then I remembered it was the twenty-seventh and came a-running." She dried her hands on her apron, and Mrs. Delacroix said, "You're in time, though. They're still talking away up there."

Mrs. Hutchinson craned her neck to see through the crowd and found her husband and children standing near the front. She tapped Mrs. Delacroix on the arm as a farewell and began to make her way through the crowd. The people separated good-humoredly to let her through; two or three people said, in voices just loud enough to be heard across the crowd, "Here comes your Missus, Hutchinson," and "Bill, she made it after all." Mrs. Hutchinson reached her husband, and Mr. Summers, who had been waiting, said cheerfully, "Thought we were going to have to get on without you, Tessie." Mrs. Hutchinson said, grinning, "Wouldn't have me leave m'dishes in the sink, now, would you, Joe?," and soft laughter ran through the crowd as the people stirred back into position after Mrs. Hutchinson's arrival.

10 "Well, now," Mr. Summers said soberly, "guess we better get started, get this over with, so's we can go back to work. Anybody ain't here?"

"Dunbar," several people said. "Dunbar, Dunbar."

Mr. Summers consulted his list. "Clyde Dunbar," he said. "That's right. He's broke his leg, hasn't he? Who's drawing for him?"

"Me, I guess," a woman said, and Mr. Summers turned to look at her. "Wife draws for her husband," Mr. Summers said. "Don't you have a grown boy to do it for you, Janey?" Although Mr. Summers and everyone else in the village knew the answer perfectly well, it was the business of the official of the lottery to ask such questions formally. Mr. Summers waited with an expression of polite interest while Mrs. Dunbar answered.

"Horace's not but sixteen yet," Mrs. Dunbar said regretfully. "Guess I gotta fill in for the old man this year."

"Right," Mr. Summers said. He made a note on the list he was holding. Then he asked, "Watson boy drawing this year?"

A tall boy in the crowd raised his hand. "Here," he said. "I'm drawing for m'mother and me." He blinked his eyes nervously and ducked his head as several voices in the crowd said things like "Good fellow, Jack," and "Glad to see your mother's got a man to do it."

"Well," Mr. Summers said, "guess that's everyone. Old Man Warner make it?"

"Here," a voice said, and Mr. Summers nodded.

A sudden hush fell on the crowd as Mr. Summers cleared his throat and looked at the list. "All ready?" he called. "Now, I'll read the names—heads of families first—and the men come up and take a paper out of the box. Keep the paper folded in your hand without looking at it until everyone has had a turn. Everything clear?"

The people had done it so many times that they only half listened to the directions; most of them were quiet, wetting their lips, not looking around. Then Mr. Summers raised one hand high and said, "Adams." A man disengaged himself from the crowd and came forward. "Hi, Steve," Mr. Summers said, and Mr. Adams said, "Hi, Joe." They grinned at one another humorlessly and nervously. Then Mr. Adams reached into the black box and took out a folded paper. He held it firmly by one corner as he turned and went hastily back to his place in the crowd, where he stood a little apart from his family, not looking down at his hand.

"Allen," Mr. Summers said. "Anderson. . . . Bentham."

"Seems like there's no time at all between lotteries any more," Mrs. Delacroix said to Mrs. Graves in the back row. "Seems like we got through with the last one only last week."

"Time sure goes fast," Mrs. Graves said.

"Clark. . . . Delacroix."

"There goes my old man," Mrs. Delacroix said. She held her breath while her husband went forward.

"Dunbar," Mr. Summers said, and Mrs. Dunbar went steadily to the box while one of the women said, "Go on, Janey," and another said, "There she goes."

"We're next," Mrs. Graves said. She watched while Mr. Graves came around from the side of the box, greeted Mr. Summers gravely, and selected a slip of paper from the box. By now, all through the crowd there were men holding the small folded papers in their large hands, turning them over and over nervously. Mrs. Dunbar and her two sons stood together, Mrs. Dunbar holding the slip of paper.

"Harburt. . . . Hutchinson."

"Get up there, Bill," Mrs. Hutchinson said, and the people near her laughed.

"Jones."

"They do say," Mr. Adams said to Old Man Warner, who stood next to him, "that over in the north village they're talking of giving up the lottery."

Old Man Warner snorted. "Pack of crazy fools," he said. "Listening to the young folks, nothing's good enough for *them.* Next thing you know, they'll be wanting to go back to living in caves, nobody work any more, live *that* way for a while. Used to be a saying about 'Lottery in June, corn be heavy soon.' First thing you know, we'd all be eating stewed chickweed and acorns. There's *always* been a lottery," he added petulantly. "Bad enough to see young Joe Summers up there joking with everybody."

"Some places have already quit lotteries," Mrs. Adams said.

"Nothing but trouble in *that,*" Old Man Warner said stoutly. "Pack of young fools."

"Martin." And Bobby Martin watched his father go forward. "Overdyke. . . . Percy."

"I wish they'd hurry," Mrs. Dunbar said to her older son. "I wish they'd hurry."

"They're almost through," her son said.

"You get ready to run tell Dad," Mrs. Dunbar said.

Mr. Summers called his own name and then stepped forward precisely and selected a slip from the box. Then he called, "Warner."

"Seventy-seventh year I been in the lottery," Old Man Warner said as he went through the crowd. "Seventy-seventh time."

"Watson." The tall boy came awkwardly through the crowd. Someone said, "Don't be nervous, Jack," and Mr. Summers said, "Take your time, son."

"Zanini."

After that, there was a long pause, a breathless pause, until Mr. Summers, holding his slip of paper in the air, said, "All right, fellows." For a minute, no one moved, and then all the slips of paper were opened. Suddenly, all the women began to speak at once, saying, "Who is it?," "Who's got it?," "Is it the Dunbars?," "Is it the Watsons?" Then the voices began to say, 'It's Hutchinson. It's Bill," "Bill Hutchinson's got it."

"Go tell your father," Mrs. Dunbar said to her older son.

People began to look around to see the Hutchinsons. Bill Hutchinson was standing quiet, staring down at the paper in his hand. Suddenly, Tessie Hutchinson shouted to Mr. Summers, "You didn't give him time enough to take any paper he wanted. I saw you. It wasn't fair!"

"Be a good sport, Tessie," Mrs. Delacroix called, and Mrs. Graves said, "All of us took the same chance."

"Shut up, Tessie," Bill Hutchinson said.

"Well, everyone," Mr. Summers said, "that was done pretty fast, and now we've got to be hurrying a little more to get done in time." He consulted his next list. "Bill," he said, "you draw for the Hutchinson family. You got any other households in the Hutchinsons?"

"There's Don and Eva," Mrs. Hutchinson yelled, "Make *them* take their chance!"

"Daughters draw with their husbands' families, Tessie," Mr. Summers said gently. "You know that as well as anyone else."

"It wasn't *fair,*" Tessie said.

"I guess not, Joe," Bill Hutchinson said regretfully. "My daughter draws with her husband's family, that's only fair. And I've got no other family except the kids."

"Then, as far as drawing for families is concerned, it's you," Mr. Summers said in explanation, "and as far as drawing for households is concerned, that's you, too. Right?"

"Right," Bill Hutchinson said.

"How many kids, Bill?" Mr. Summers asked formally.

"Three," Bill Hutchinson said. "There's Bill, Jr., and Nancy, and little Dave. And Tessie and me."

"All right, then," Mr. Summers said. "Harry, you got their tickets back?"

Mr. Graves nodded and held up the slips of paper. "Put them in the box, then," Mr. Summers directed. "Take Bill's and put it in."

"I think we ought to start over," Mrs. Hutchinson said, as quietly as she could. "I tell you it wasn't *fair.* You didn't give him time enough to choose. *Every*body saw that."

Mr. Graves had selected the five slips and put them in the box, and he dropped all the papers but those onto the ground, where the breeze caught them and lifted them off.

"Listen, everybody," Mrs. Hutchinson was saying to the people around her.

"Ready, Bill?" Mr. Summers asked, and Bill Hutchinson, with one quick glance around at his wife and children, nodded.

"Remember," Mr. Summers said, "take the slips and keep them folded until each person has taken one. Harry, you help little Dave." Mr. Graves took the hand of the little boy, who came willingly with him up to the box. "Take a paper out of the box, Davy," Mr. Summers said. Davy put his hand into the box and laughed. "Take just *one* paper," Mr. Summers said. "Harry, you hold it for him." Mr. Graves took the child's hand and removed the folded paper from the tight fist and held it while little Dave stood next to him and looked at him wonderingly.

"Nancy next," Mr. Summers said. Nancy was twelve, and her school friends breathed heavily as she went forward, switching her skirt, and took a slip daintily from the box. "Bill, Jr.," Mr. Summers said, and Billy, his face red and his feet overlarge, nearly knocked the box over as he got a paper out. "Tessie," Mr. Summers said. She hesitated for a minute, looking around defiantly, and then set her lips and went up to the box. She snatched a paper out and held it behind her.

"Bill," Mr. Summers said, and Bill Hutchinson reached into the box and felt around, bringing his hand out at last with the slip of paper in it.

The crowd was quiet. A girl whispered, "I hope it's not Nancy," and the sound of the whisper reached the edges of the crowd.

"It's not the way it used to be," Old Man Warner said clearly. "People ain't the way they used to be."

"All right," Mr. Summers said. "Open the papers. Harry, you open little Dave's."

Mr. Graves opened the slip of paper and there was a general sigh through the crowd as he held it up and everyone could see that it was blank. Nancy and Bill, Jr., opened theirs at the same time, and both beamed and laughed, turning around to the crowd and holding their slips of paper above their heads.

"Tessie," Mr. Summers said. There was a pause, and then Mr. Summers looked at Bill Hutchinson, and Bill unfolded his paper and showed it. It was blank.

"It's Tessie," Mr. Summers said, and his voice was hushed. "Show us her paper, Bill."

Bill Hutchinson went over to his wife and forced the slip of paper out of her hand. It had a black spot on it, the black spot Mr. Summers had made the night before with the heavy pencil in the coal-company office. Bill Hutchinson held it up, and there was a stir in the crowd.

"All right, folks," Mr. Summers said. "Let's finish quickly."

Although the villagers had forgotten the ritual and lost the original black box, they still remembered to use stones. The pile of stones the boys had made earlier was ready; there were stones on the ground with the blowing scraps of paper that had come out of the box. Mrs. Delacroix selected a stone so large she had to pick it up with both hands and turned to Mrs. Dunbar. "Come on," she said. "Hurry up."

Mrs. Dunbar had small stones in both hands, and she said, gasping for breath, "I can't run at all. You'll have to go ahead and I'll catch up with you."

The children had stones already, and someone gave little Davy Hutchinson a few pebbles.

Tessie Hutchinson was in the center of a cleared space by now, and she held her hands out desperately as the villagers moved in on her. "It isn't fair," she said. A stone hit her on the side of the head.

Old Man Warner was saying, "Come on, come on, everyone." Steve Adams was in the front of the crowd of villagers, with Mrs. Graves beside him.

"It isn't fair, it isn't right," Mrs. Hutchinson screamed, and then they were upon her.

READING AND REACTING

1. What possible significance, beyond their literal meaning, might each of these items have: the village square, Mrs. Hutchinson's apron, Old Man Warner, the slips of paper, the black spot.
2. "The Lottery" takes place in June, and summer, a conventional symbol, has a positive connotation. Is summertime in this story just a season, or does it have any symbolic significance? How does the setting enhance the story's overall effect?
3. What, if anything, might the names *Graves, Adams, Summers,* and *Delacroix* signify in the context of this story? Do you think these names are intended to have any special significance? Why or why not?
4. What role do the children play in the ritual? How can you explain their presence in the story? Do they have any symbolic role in the story?
5. What symbolic significance might be found in the way the characters are dressed? In their conversation?
6. In what sense is the story's title ironic?
7. Throughout the story there is a general atmosphere of excitement. What indication is there of nervousness or apprehension?
8. Early in the story, the boys stuff their pockets with stones, foreshadowing the attack in the story's conclusion. What other examples of foreshadowing can you identify?
9. **JOURNAL ENTRY:** How can a ritual like the lottery continue to be held year after year? Why does no one move to end it? Can you think of a modern-day parallel to this lottery—a situation in which people continue to act in ways they know to be wrong rather than challenge the status quo? How can you account for such behavior?

Alice Walker (1944–   ) is an accomplished writer of poetry, fiction, and criticism. Her characters are mainly rural African Americans, often living in her native Georgia, who struggle to survive in hostile environments. Her writing displays a particular sensitivity to the emotions of people who suffer physical or psychological harm in their efforts to assert their own identities.

Walker was the youngest of five boys and three girls born to Willie Lee and Minnie Tallulah Grant Walker, sharefarmers who raised cotton. She left the rural South to attend Atlanta's Spelman College (1961–1963) and Sarah Lawrence College in Bronxville, New York (1963–1965).

In 1967, Walker moved to Mississippi, where she was supported in the writing of her first novel, *The Third Life of Grange Copeland* (1970), by a National Endowment of the Arts grant. Her short story "Everyday Use" was included in *Best American Short Stories* in 1973. Other novels and short story collections followed, including *In Love and Trouble: Stories of Black Women* (1973), *Meridian* (1976), *You Can't Keep a Good Woman Down* (short stories, 1981) and *The Temple of My Familiar* (1989). Walker's third novel, *The Color Purple* (1982) won the American Book Award and a Pulitzer Prize.

In the third year of her marriage, Walker took back her maiden name because she wanted to honor her great-great-great-grandmother who walked, carrying her two children, from Virginia to Georgia. Walker's renaming is consistent with one of her goals in writing, which is to further the process of reconnecting people to their ancestors. She has said that "it is fatal to see yourself as separate," and that if people can reaffirm the past, they can "make a different future."

Alice Walker

EVERYDAY USE

(1973)

for your grandmama

I will wait for her in the yard that Maggie and I made so clean and wavy yesterday afternoon. A yard like this is more comfortable than most people know. It is not just a yard. It is like an extended living room. When the hard clay is swept clean as a floor and the fine sand around the edges lined with tiny, irregular grooves, anyone can come and sit and look up into the elm tree and wait for the breezes that never come inside the house.

Maggie will be nervous until after her sister goes: she will stand hopelessly in corners, homely and ashamed of the burn scars down her arms and legs, eying her sister with a mixture of envy and awe. She thinks her sister has held life always in the palm of one hand, that "no" is a word the world never learned to say to her.

You've no doubt seen those TV shows where the child who has "made it" is confronted, as a surprise, by her own mother and father, tottering in weakly from backstage. (A pleasant surprise, of course: What would they do if parent and child came on the show only to curse out and insult each other?) On TV mother and child embrace and smile into each other's faces. Sometimes the mother and father weep, the child wraps them in her arms and leans across the table to tell how she would not have made it without their help. I have seen these programs.

Sometimes I dream a dream in which Dee and I are suddenly brought together on a TV program of this sort. Out of a dark and soft-seated limousine I am ushered into a bright room filled with many people. There I meet a smiling, gray, sporty man like Johnny Carson who shakes my hand and tells me what a fine girl I have. Then we are on the stage and Dee is embracing me with tears in her eyes. She pins on my dress a large orchid, even though she has told me once that she thinks orchids are tacky flowers.

5 In real life I am a large, big-boned woman with rough, man-working hands. In the winter I wear flannel nightgowns to bed and overalls during the day. I can kill and clean a hog as mercilessly as a man. My fat keeps me hot in zero weather. I can work outside all day, breaking ice to get water for washing; I can eat pork liver cooked over the open fire minutes after it comes steaming from the hog. One winter I knocked a bull calf straight in the brain between the eyes with a sledge hammer and had the meat hung up to chill before nightfall. But of course all this does not show on television. I am the way my daughter would want me to be: a hundred pounds lighter, my skin like an uncooked barley pancake. My hair glistens in the hot bright lights. Johnny Carson has much to do to keep up with my quick and witty tongue.

But that is a mistake. I know even before I wake up. Who ever knew a Johnson with a quick tongue? Who can even imagine me looking a strange white man in the eye? It seems to me I have talked to them always with one foot raised in flight, with my head turned in whichever way is farthest from them. Dee, though. She would always look anyone in the eye. Hesitation was no part of her nature.

"How do I look, Mama?" Maggie says, showing just enough of her thin body enveloped in pink skirt and red blouse for me to know she's there, almost hidden by the door.

"Come out into the yard," I say.

Have you ever seen a lame animal, perhaps a dog run over by some careless person rich enough to own a car, sidle up to someone who is ignorant enough to be kind to him? That is the way my Maggie walks. She has been like this, chin on chest, eyes on ground, feet in shuffle, ever since the fire that burned the other house to the ground.

10 Dee is lighter than Maggie, with nicer hair and a fuller figure. She's a woman now, though sometimes I forget. How long ago was it that the other house burned? Ten, twelve years? Sometimes I can still hear the flames and feel Maggie's arms sticking to me, her hair smoking and her dress falling off her in little black papery flakes. Her eyes seemed stretched open, blazed open by the flames reflected in them. And Dee. I see her standing off under the sweet gum tree she used to dig gum out of; a look of concentration on her face as she watched the last dingy gray board of the house fall in toward the red-hot brick chimney. Why

don't you do a dance around the ashes? I'd wanted to ask her. She had hated the house that much.

I used to think she hated Maggie, too. But that was before we raised the money, the church and me, to send her to Augusta to school. She used to read to us without pity; forcing words, lies, other folks' habits, whole lives upon us two, sitting trapped and ignorant underneath her voice. She washed us in a river of make-believe, burned us with a lot of knowledge we didn't necessarily need to know. Pressed us to her with the serious way she read, to shove us away at just the moment, like dimwits, we seemed about to understand.

Dee wanted nice things. A yellow organdy dress to wear to her graduation from high school; black pumps to match a green suit she'd made from an old suit somebody gave me. She was determined to stare down any disaster in her efforts. Her eyelids would not flicker for minutes at a time. Often I fought off the temptation to shake her. At sixteen she had a style of her own, and knew what style was.

I never had an education myself. After second grade the school was closed down. Don't ask me why: in 1927 colored asked fewer questions than they do now. Sometimes Maggie reads to me. She stumbles along good-naturedly but can't see well. She knows she is not bright. Like good looks and money, quickness passed her by. She will marry John Thomas (who has mossy teeth in an earnest face) and then I'll be free to sit here and I guess just sing church songs to myself. Although I never was a good singer. Never could carry a tune. I was always better at a man's job. I used to love to milk till I was hooked in the side in '49. Cows are soothing and slow and don't bother you, unless you try to milk them the wrong way.

I have deliberately turned my back on the house. It is three rooms, just like the one that burned, except the roof is tin; they don't make shingle roofs any more. There are no real windows, just some holes cut in the sides, like the portholes in a ship, but not round and not square, with rawhide holding the shutters up on the outside. This house is in a pasture, too, like the other one. No doubt when Dee sees it she will want to tear it down. She wrote me once that no matter where we "choose" to live, she will manage to come see us. But she will never bring her friends. Maggie and I thought about this and Maggie asked me, "Mama, when did Dee ever *have* any friends?"

15 She had a few. Furtive boys in pink shirts hanging about on washday after school. Nervous girls who never laughed. Impressed with her they worshiped the well-turned phrase, the cute shape, the scalding humor that erupted like bubbles in lye. She read to them.

When she was courting Jimmy T she didn't have much time to pay to us, but turned all her faultfinding power on him. He *flew* to marry a cheap city girl from a family of ignorant flashy people. She hardly had time to recompose herself.

When she comes I will meet—but there they are!

Maggie attempts to make a dash for the house, in her shuffling way, but I stay her with my hand. "Come back here," I say. And she stops and tries to dig a well in the sand with her toe.

It is hard to see them clearly through the strong sun. But even the first glimpse of leg out of the car tells me it is Dee. Her feet were always neat-looking, as if God himself had shaped them with a certain style. From the other side of the car comes a short, stocky man. Hair is all over his head a foot long and hanging from his chin like a kinky mule tail. I hear Maggie suck in her breath. "Uhnnnh," is what it sounds like. Like when you see the wriggling end of a snake just in front of your foot on the road. "Uhnnnh."

Dee next. A dress down to the ground, in this hot weather. A dress so loud it hurts my eyes. There are yellows and oranges enough to throw back the light of the sun. I feel my whole face warming from the heat waves it throws out. Earrings gold, too, and hanging down to her shoulders. Bracelets dangling and making noises when she moves her arm up to shake the folds of the dress out of her armpits. The dress is loose and flows, and as she walks closer, I like it. I hear Maggie go "Uhnnnh" again. It is her sister's hair. It stands straight up like the wool on a sheep. It is black as night and around the edges are two long pigtails that rope about like small lizards disappearing behind her ears.

"Wa-su-zo-Tean-o!"[1] she says, coming on in that gliding way the dress makes her move. The short stocky fellow with the hair to his navel is all grinning and he follows up with "Asalamalakim,[2] my mother and sister!" He moves to hug Maggie but she falls back, right up against the back of my chair. I feel her trembling there and when I look up I see the perspiration falling off her chin.

"Don't get up," says Dee. Since I am stout it takes something of a push. You can see me trying to move a second or two before I make it. She turns, showing white heels through her sandals, and goes back to the car. Out she peeks next with a Polaroid. She stoops down quickly and lines up picture after picture of me sitting there in front of the house with Maggie cowering behind me. She never takes a shot without making sure the house is included. When a cow comes nibbling around the edge of the yard she snaps it and me and Maggie *and* the house. Then she puts the Polaroid in the back seat of the car, and comes up and kisses me on the forehead.

Meanwhile Asalamalakim is going through motions with Maggie's hand. Maggie's hand is as limp as a fish, and probably as cold, despite the sweat, and she keeps trying to pull it back. It looks like Asalamalakim wants to shake hands but wants to do it fancy. Or maybe he don't know how people shake hands. Anyhow, he soon gives up on Maggie.

---

[1] Greeting in Swahili; Dee sounds it out one syllable at a time.

[2] Greeting in Arabic: "Peace be upon you."

"Well," I say. "Dee."

"No, Mama," she says. "Not 'Dee,' Wangero Leewanika Kemanjo!"

"What happened to 'Dee'?" I wanted to know.

"She's dead," Wangero said. "I couldn't bear it any longer, being named after the people who oppress me."

"You know as well as me you was named after your aunt Dicie," I said. Dicie is my sister. She named Dee. We called her "Big Dee" after Dee was born.

"But who was *she* named after?" asked Wangero.

"I guess after Grandma Dee," I said.

"And who was she named after?" asked Wangero.

"Her mother," I said, and saw Wangero was getting tired. "That's about as far back as I can trace it," I said. Though, in fact, I probably could have carried it back beyond the Civil War through the branches.

"Well," said Asalamalakim, "there you are."

"Uhnnnh," I heard Maggie say.

"There I was not," I said, "before 'Dicie' cropped up in our family, so why should I try to trace it that far back?"

He just stood there grinning, looking down on me like somebody inspecting a Model A car. Every once in a while he and Wangero sent eye signals over my head.

"How do you pronounce this name?" I asked.

"You don't have to call me by it if you don't want to," said Wangero.

"Why shouldn't I?" I asked. "If that's what you want us to call you, we'll call you."

"I know it might sound awkward at first," said Wangero.

"I'll get used to it," I said. "Ream it out again."

Well, soon we got the name out of the way. Asalamalakim had a name twice as long and three times as hard. After I tripped over it two or three times he told me to just call him Hakim-a-barber. I wanted to ask him was he a barber, but I didn't really think he was, so I didn't ask.

"You must belong to those beef-cattle peoples down the road," I said. They said "Asalamalakim" when they met you, too, but they didn't shake hands. Always too busy: feeding the cattle, fixing the fences, putting up salt-lick shelters, throwing down hay. When the white folks poisoned some of the herd the men stayed up all night with rifles in their hands. I walked a mile and a half just to see the sight.

Hakim-a-barber said, "I accept some of their doctrines, but farming and raising cattle is not my style." (They didn't tell me, and I didn't ask, whether Wangero (Dee) had really gone and married him.)

We sat down to eat and right away he said he didn't eat collards and pork was unclean. Wangero, though, went on through the chitlins and corn bread, the greens and everything else. She talked a blue streak over the sweet potatoes. Everything delighted her. Even the fact that we still used the benches her daddy made for the table when we couldn't afford to buy chairs.

"Oh, Mama!" she cried. Then turned to Hakim-a-barber. "I never knew how lovely these benches are. You can feel the rump prints," she said, running her hands underneath her and along the bench. Then she gave a sigh and her hand closed over Grandma Dee's butter dish. "That's it!" she said. "I knew there was something I wanted to ask you if I could have." She jumped up from the table and went over in the corner where the churn stood, the milk in it clabber by now. She looked at the churn and looked at it.

"This churn top is what I need," she said. "Didn't Uncle Buddy whittle it out of a tree you all used to have?"

"Yes," I said.

"Uh huh," she said happily. "And I want the dasher, too."

"Uncle Buddy whittle that, too?" asked the barber.

Dee (Wangero) looked up at me.

"Aunt Dee's first husband whittled the dash," said Maggie so low you almost couldn't hear her. "His name was Henry, but they called him Stash."

"Maggie's brain is like an elephant's," Wangero said, laughing. "I can use the churn top as a centerpiece for the alcove table," she said, sliding a plate over the churn, "and I'll think of something artistic to do with the dasher."

When she finished wrapping the dasher the handle stuck out. I took it for a moment in my hands. You didn't even have to look close to see where hands pushing the dasher up and down to make butter had left a kind of sink in the wood. In fact, there were a lot of small sinks; you could see where thumb and fingers had sunk into the wood. It was beautiful light yellow wood, from a tree that grew in the yard where Big Dee and Stash had lived.

After dinner Dee (Wangero) went to the trunk at the foot of my bed and started rifling through it. Maggie hung back in the kitchen over the dishpan. Out came Wangero with two quilts. They had been pieced by Grandma Dee and then Big Dee and me had hung them on the quilt frames on the front porch and quilted them. One was in the Lone Star pattern. The other was Walk Around the Mountain. In both of them were scraps of dresses Grandma Dee had worn fifty and more years ago. Bits and pieces of Grandpa Jarrell's Paisley shirts. And one teeny faded blue piece, about the size of a penny matchbox, that was from Great Grandpa Ezra's uniform that he wore in the Civil War.

"Mama," Wangero said sweet as a bird. "Can I have these old quilts?"

I heard something fall in the kitchen, and a minute later the kitchen door slammed.

"Why don't you take one or two of the others?" I asked. "These old things was just done by me and Big Dee from some tops your grandma pieced before she died."

"No," said Wangero. "I don't want those. They are stitched around the borders by machine."

"That'll make them last better," I said.

"That's not the point," said Wangero. "These are all pieces of dresses Grandma used to wear. She did all this stitching by hand. Imagine!" She held the quilts securely in her arms, stroking them.

"Some of the pieces, like those lavender ones, come from old clothes her mother handed down to her," I said, moving up to touch the quilts. Dee (Wangero) moved back just enough so that I couldn't reach the quilts. They already belonged to her.

"Imagine!" she breathed again, clutching them closely to her bosom.

"The truth is," I said, "I promised to give them quilts to Maggie, for when she marries John Thomas."

65 She gasped like a bee had stung her.
"Maggie can't appreciate these quilts!" she said. "She'd probably be backward enough to put them to everyday use."

"I reckon she would," I said. "God knows I been saving 'em for long enough with nobody using 'em. I hope she will!" I didn't want to bring up how I had offered Dee (Wangero) a quilt when she went away to college. Then she had told me they were old-fashioned, out of style.

"But, they're *priceless!*" she was saying now, furiously; for she has a temper. "Maggie would put them on the bed and in five years they'd be in rags. Less than that!"

"She can always make some more," I said. "Maggie knows how to quilt."

Dee (Wangero) looked at me with hatred. "You just will not understand. The point is these quilts, *these* quilts!"

70 "Well," I said, stumped. "What would *you* do with them?"

"Hang them," she said. As if that was the only thing you *could* do with quilts.

Maggie by now was standing in the door. I could almost hear the sound her feet made as they scraped over each other.

"She can have them, Mama," she said, like somebody used to never winning anything, or having anything reserved for her. "I can 'member Grandma Dee without the quilts."

I looked at her hard. She had filled her bottom lip with checkerberry snuff and it gave her face a kind of dopey, hangdog look. It was Grandma Dee and Big Dee who taught her how to quilt herself. She stood there with her scarred hands hidden in the folds of her skirt. She looked at her sister with something like fear but she wasn't mad at her. This was Maggie's portion. This was the way she knew God to work.

75 When I looked at her like that something hit me in the top of my head and ran down to the soles of my feet. Just like when I'm in church and the spirit of God touches me and I get happy and shout. I did something I never had done before: hugged Maggie to me, then dragged her on into the room, snatched the quilts out of Miss Wangero's hands and dumped them into Maggie's lap. Maggie just sat there on my bed with her mouth open.

"Take one or two of the others," I said to Dee.

But she turned without a word and went out to Hakim-a-barber.

"You just don't understand," she said, as Maggie and I came out to the car.

"What don't I understand?" I wanted to know.

80 "Your heritage," she said. And then she turned to Maggie, kissed her, and said, "You ought to try to make something of yourself, too, Maggie. It's really a new day for us. But from the way you and Mama still live you'd never know it."

She put on some sunglasses that hid everything above the tip of her nose and her chin.

Maggie smiled; maybe at the sunglasses. But a real smile, not scared. After we watched the car dust settle I asked Maggie to bring me a dip of snuff. And then the two of us sat there just enjoying, until it was time to go in the house and go to bed.

READING AND REACTING

1. What is the conventional symbolic significance of a patchwork quilt in American culture?
2. What is the *literal* meaning of the two quilts to Maggie and her mother? To Dee? Beyond this literal meaning, what symbolic meaning, if any, do they have to Maggie and her mother? Do the quilts have any symbolic meaning to Dee?
3. How does the contrast between the two sisters' appearances, personalities, lifestyles, and feelings about the quilts help to convey the story's theme?
4. What does the name *Wangero* signify to Dee? To her mother and sister? Could the name be considered a symbol? Why or why not?
5. Why do you think Maggie relinquishes the quilts to her sister?
6. When Dee tells her mother and sister that they do not understand their heritage, what does she mean by *heritage?* What do you think *heritage* means to them?
7. What does the story's title suggest to you?
8. What does the narrator's discussion of television shows in paragraphs 3 and 4 contribute to the story?
9. What possible meanings, aside from their literal meanings, might each of the following suggest: the family's yard, Maggie's burn scars, the trunk in which the quilts are kept, Dee's Polaroid camera? What symbolic functions, if any, do these items serve in the story?
10. **JOURNAL ENTRY:** What object has the kind of symbolic value to you that the quilts have to Maggie? What gives it this value?

WRITING SUGGESTIONS: SYMBOL AND ALLEGORY

1. Write an essay in which you discuss how any two symbols from Hawthorne's "Young Goodman Brown" and Jackson's "The Lottery" contribute to the central themes of the respective stories.
2. Select a story that you have read in another chapter of this anthology and discuss its use of symbols.
3. Although not common in contemporary fiction, allegories abound in children's literature. Consider a film version of a children's story such as Walt Disney's *Beauty and the Beast* or *Aladdin,* and write an essay in which you discuss its allegorical elements.
4. Write an essay in which you discuss the conflicts present in "Young Goodman Brown." In your essay show how the allegorical elements in the story reflect and reinforce these conflicts.
5. If Shirley Jackson had wished to write "The Lottery" as an allegory whose purpose was to expose the evils of Nazi Germany, what revisions would she have had to make to convey the dangers of blind obedience to authority? Consider the story's symbols, the characters (and their names), and the setting.

CHAPTER 10

THEME

The **theme** of a work of literature is its central or dominant idea. *Theme* is not the same as *plot* or *subject,* two terms with which it is sometimes confused. A simple *plot summary* of Tadeusz Borowski's "Silence" (p. 321), describing the arrangement and interaction of events in the story, could be "Prisoners are liberated from a concentration camp and, despite the admonitions of the American officer, they kill a captured German guard." The statement "'Silence' is about freed prisoners and a guard" could define the *subject* of the story. A statement of the *theme* of "Silence," however, would have to do more than summarize its plot or identify its subject; it would have to convey the values and ideas expressed by the story. Many effective stories are complex, expressing more than one theme, and "Silence" is no exception. You could say, for example, that "Silence" suggests that human beings have a need for vengeance. You could also say the story demonstrates that silence can mask unspeakable horrors. Although both these themes—and others—are present in the story, one theme seems to dominate: Under extreme conditions the oppressed can become as morally bankrupt as their oppressors.

When writing about theme, be certain you are not merely telling what happens in the story. The theme you identify should be an idea that extends beyond the boundaries of the story, applying to you and to your world. Compare these two statements about Edgar Allan Poe's "The Cask of Amontillado" (p. 180):

> Poe's "The Cask of Amontillado" is about a man who loses his humanity because of his obsessive desire to avenge himself on Fortunato.
>
> Poe's "The Cask of Amontillado" suggests that when the desire for revenge becomes obsessive, it can deprive individuals of all that makes them human.

The first statement merely tells what the story is about; the second identifies its theme. In addition, the first statement restricts the ideas of the story to a specific character, Montresor; the second statement makes a general observation about humanity, giving the story's theme meaning outside the story itself.

Granted, some short works (fairy tales, fables, and some popular fiction, for example) have themes that can be summed up as **clichés**—

overused phrases or expressions—or as morals—lessons dramatized by the work. The fairy tale "Cinderella," for example, expresses the clichéd theme that a virtuous girl who endures misfortune will eventually achieve her just reward; the fable "The Tortoise and the Hare" illustrates the moral "Slow and steady wins the race." Like "The Cask of Amontillado," however, most of the stories in this anthology have themes that require more complex expression than clichés or morals allow.

INTERPRETING THEMES

Contemporary critical theory holds that the theme of a work of fiction is as much the creation of the reader as of the writer. The readers' backgrounds, knowledge, values, and beliefs all determine the theme or themes they will perceive in a work. Most readers, for example, will realize that David Michael Kaplan's story "Doe Season" (p. 298)—in which the main character goes hunting, kills her first deer, and is forced to confront suffering and death—expresses a conventional initiation theme, revealing growing up to be a disillusioning and painful process. Given this interpretation, however, different readers bring different perspectives to the story. In some cases, in fact, they see different themes.

During a classroom discussion of "Doe Season," a student familiar with hunting saw more than his classmates did in the story's conventional initiation theme because he knew that in many states there really is a doe season, which lasts approximately three days. Shorter than the ten-day buck season, it is specifically designed to enable hunters to control the size of the deer herd by killing females. This knowledge enabled the student to conclude that by the end of the story the female child's innocence must inevitably be destroyed, just as the doe must be.

Another student pointed out that Andy is a female who uses a male name. Andy's participation in hunting, a traditional male rite of passage, leads to her killing the deer and to her subsequent disillusionment. It also leads to her decision to abandon her nickname. In this way the story pits Andy's female perspective, expressed by her compassion, against the other characters' male perspective, expressed by killing and death. This interpretation led the student to conclude that the theme of "Doe Season" was that males' and females' different outlooks on life ultimately cannot be reconciled.

Other students did not accept the condemnation of the father and the other male characters implied by the interpretations discussed above. They pointed out that the father is a sympathetic figure who is trying to relate to his daughter. He takes her hunting because he loves her, not because he wants to initiate her into life or to hurt her. One student mentioned that Andy's reaction when she sees the doe, common in children who kill their first deer, is called *buck fever.* In light of this information, several students thought that far from being about irreconcilable male and female perspectives, "Doe Season" makes a statement about a young girl who is hunting for her own identity and who in the process discovers her own mortality. Her father is therefore the agent who enables her to confront the inevitability of death, a fact she must accept if she is going to take her place in the adult world. In this sense the theme of the story is that in order to mature a child must reconcile life with the reality of death.

Different readers may see different themes in a story, but your interpretation of a theme must make sense in light of the various elements of the story. Evidence from the work, not just your own feelings or assumptions, must support your interpretation, and a single symbol or one statement by a character is not enough in itself to reveal a story's theme. Therefore, you must identify a cross section of examples from the text to support your interpretation of the story's theme. If you say that James Joyce's "Araby" (p. 219) implies that an innocent idealist is always doomed to disillusionment, you have to find examples from the text to support your assertion. You could, for example, point to the title and conclude that the word *Araby* suggests the dreams of exotic beauty that the boy tries to find when he goes to the fair. You could reinforce your assertions about the boy's idealism by pointing out that Mangan's sister is a symbol of this beauty that the boy wants so desperately to find. To the boy she is "like a summons to all [his] foolish blood," and her name comes to his lips "at moments in strange prayers. . . ." Finally, you could show how the boy's idealism is ultimately crushed by the society in which he lives. At the end of the story the boy stands alone in the darkness and realizes that his dreams of beauty are false. Although other readers may have different responses to "Araby," if you support your interpretation with enough examples, they should concede that your interpretation is justified.

IDENTIFYING THEMES

Every element of a story can shed light on its themes. As you analyze a short story, look for features that reveal and reinforce what you perceive to be the story's most important ideas.

The *title* of a story can often provide insight into the theme or themes of a story. Franz Kafka's *The Metamorphosis* (p. 393), for example, tells readers that the subject of the story is change—in this case the transformation of the main character, Gregor Samsa, into a gigantic insect. Thus the title suggests a major theme of the story: The isolation and estrangement of the writer in the modern world make him feel degraded and insectlike. The title of an F. Scott Fitzgerald story, "Babylon Revisited," emphasizes a major idea in the story—that Paris of the 1920s is like Babylon, the ancient city the Bible singles out as the epitome of evil and corruption. The story's protagonist, Charlie Wales, comes to realize that no matter how much money he lost after the stock market crash, he lost more—his wife and his daughter—during the boom, when he was in Paris. Charlie's search through his past—his return to "Babylon"—

provides new meaning to his life and offers at least a small bit of hope for the future.

Sometimes a *narrator or character's statement* can lead you to a theme. For example, at the beginning of Alberto Alvaro Rios's "The Secret Lion" (p. 37) the first-person narrator says, "I was twelve and in junior high school and something happened that we didn't have a name for, but it was there nonetheless like a lion, and roaring, roaring that way the biggest things do. Everything changed." Although the narrator does not directly announce the story's theme, he does suggest that the story will communicate the idea that the price children pay for growing up is realizing that everything changes, that nothing stays the way it is.

The *arrangement of events* in a story can suggest a story's theme, as it does in an Ernest Hemingway story, "The Short Happy Life of Francis Macomber." At the beginning of the story the title character is a coward who is stuck in an unhappy marriage. As the story progresses, he gradually learns the nature of courage and, finally, finds it in himself. At the moment of his triumph, however, Francis is killed; his "happy life" is short indeed. The way the events of the story are presented, through foreshadowing and flashbacks, provides insight into the connection between Macomber's marriage and his behavior as a hunter. This connection in turn helps to reveal a possible theme: Sometimes courage can be more important than life itself.

Conflict, a central plot element in short fiction, can offer clues to the themes expressed in a story. In "Araby" the young boy believes that his society neglects art and beauty and glorifies the mundane. This conflict between the boy and his world can help readers to understand why the boy cloisters himself in his room reading books and why he retreats into dreams of idealized love. The theme of the story—that growing up leads to the loss of youthful idealism—is revealed by this central conflict.

Similarly, the main character of "Kaiser and the War" (p. 202), a Native American, is set in opposition to the larger "American" society. At the beginning of the story Kaiser refuses to be inducted into the army. At first he hides from the authorities, but eventually he surrenders and is arrested. The conflicts between Kaiser and "American" society help to communicate the story's central theme: A Native American is always caught between two worlds, the world of his ancestors and the world defined by the "Americans" who live outside the reservation.

The *point of view* of a story can help shed light on theme. For instance, a writer's choice of an innocent or unreliable first-person narrator can reveal a good deal about the theme of a story. For example, Montresor's self-serving first-person account of his crime in "The Cask of Amontillado" provides clues to the theme. The irony in the conversations between Montresor and Fortunato, and Montresor's attempts to justify his actions, enable readers to determine the theme. The voice of a third-person narrator can also help to convey a story's theme. For example, the detachment of the narrator in Stephen Crane's Civil War novel *The Red Badge of Courage* reinforces the theme of the novel: Bravery, cowardice, battle, and even life itself are insignificant when set beside the indifference of the universe.

Quite often a story will give names, places, and objects symbolic significance. These *symbols* can not only enrich the story, but also help to convey a central theme. For example, the rocking horse in D. H. Lawrence's "The Rocking-Horse Winner" (p. 438) can be seen as a symbol of the boy's desperate desire to remain a child. Interpreted in this way, it reinforces the theme that innocence cannot survive when it confronts forces such as greed and selfishness. Similarly, Hawthorne's "Young Goodman Brown" (p. 264) uses symbols such as the walking stick, the woods, sunset and night, and the vague shadows to develop one of its central themes: Evil is everywhere if a person strays from the path of faith.

Finally, *changes in a character* can shed light on the theme or themes of the story. The main character in Ethan Canin's "The Carnival Dog, the Buyer of Diamonds" (p. 349), for example, decides to go to medical school rather than disappoint his father. The change in attitude that precipitates this decision conveys the story's central theme: A person's duty to someone he or she loves may be more important than the pursuit of individual happiness or personal fulfillment. The main character in Charles Baxter's "Gryphon" (p. 123) comes to realize that the "lies" Miss Ferenczi tells may be closer to the truth than the "facts" his teachers present. Thus the narrator's changing attitude toward Miss Ferenczi helps to communicate the story's central theme.

Checklist for Writing about Theme

- What is the central theme of the story?
- What other themes can you identify?
- Does the title of the story suggest a theme?
- Does any character or the narrator make statements that express or imply a theme?
- In what way does the arrangement of events in the story suggest a theme?
- In what way does the central conflict of the story suggest a theme?
- How does the point of view shed light on the story's themes?
- Do any symbols relate to the story's themes?
- Do any characters in the story change in any way? Do these changes reveal the story's themes?
- Can you gather enough evidence to support your interpretation of the story's themes?
- Have you clearly expressed the story's central theme, rather than just summarized the plot or presented a statement of the subject?
- Does your expression of the story's central theme make a general observation that has an application beyond the story itself?

David Michael Kaplan (1946–) is one of a group of American writers who, along with South American writers such as García Márquez of Colombia, are called "magic realists." Magic realists work outside of the "hobbits and wizards" borders of traditional fantasy writing, seamlessly interweaving magical elements and detailed, realistically drawn "everyday" settings. These elements, says a reviewer of Kaplan's work, are invoked "to illuminate and underscore heightened moments of reality." The story "Doe Season," which appears in Kaplan's debut short story collection, *Comfort* (1987), was selected as one of the Best American Short Stories of 1985. Kaplan's first novel, *Skating in the Dark,* was published in 1991.

Interestingly, the stories in *Comfort* break from classic "first-time author" tradition by sidestepping the autobiographical, young-man-comes-of-age theme. Instead, these stories are about young girls or young women—coming to grips with parents (present or absent) and with loss and searching for ways to resolve their ambivalence about becoming women. In "Doe Season" Andy's surreal encounter with the doe may be a dream, but the beauty and horror of their meeting will affect the rest of her life.

David Michael Kaplan

DOE SEASON

(1985)

They were always the same woods, she thought sleepily as they drove through the early morning darkness—deep and immense, covered with yesterday's snowfall, which had frozen overnight. They were the same woods that lay behind her house, *and they stretch all the way to here,* she thought, *for miles and miles, longer than I could walk in a day, or a week even, but they are still the same woods.* The thought made her feel good: it was like thinking of God; it was like thinking of the space between here and the moon; it was like thinking of all the foreign countries from her geography book where even now, Andy knew, people were going to bed, while they—she and her father and Charlie Spoon and Mac, Charlie's eleven-year-old son—were driving deeper into the Pennsylvania countryside, to go hunting.

They had risen long before dawn. Her mother, yawning and not trying to hide her sleepiness, cooked them eggs and French toast. Her father smoked a cigarette and flicked ashes into his saucer while Andy listened, wondering *Why doesn't he come?* and *Won't he ever come?* until at last a car pulled into the graveled drive and honked. "That will be Charlie Spoon," her father said; he always said "Charlie Spoon," even though his real name was Spreun, because Charlie was, in a sense, shaped like a spoon, with a large head and a narrow waist and chest.

Andy's mother kissed her and her father and said, "Well, have a good time" and "Be careful." Soon they were outside in the bitter dark, loading gear by the back-porch light, their breath steaming. The woods behind the house were then only a black streak against the wash of night.

Andy dozed in the car and woke to find that it was half light. Mac—also sleeping—had slid against her. She pushed him away and looked out the window. Her breath clouded the glass, and she was cold; the car's heater didn't work right. They were riding over gentle hills, the woods on both sides now—the same woods, she knew, because she had been watching the whole way, even while she slept. They had been in her dreams, and she had never lost sight of them.

Charlie Spoon was driving. "I don't understand why she's coming," he said to her father. "How old is she anyway—eight?"

"Nine," her father replied. "She's small for her age."

"So—nine. What's the difference? She'll just add to the noise and get tired besides."

"No, she won't," her father said. "She can walk me to death. And she'll bring good luck, you'll see. Animals—I don't know how she does it, but they come right up to her. We go walking in the woods, and we'll spot more raccoons and possums and such than I ever see when I'm alone."

Charlie grunted.

"Besides, she's not a bad little shot, even if she doesn't hunt yet. She shoots the .22 real good."

"Popgun," Charlie said, and snorted. "And target shooting ain't deer hunting."

"Well, she's not gonna be shooting anyway, Charlie," her father said. "Don't worry. She'll be no bother."

"I still don't know why she's coming," Charlie said.

"Because she wants to, and I want her to. Just like you and Mac. No difference."

Charlie turned onto a side road and after a mile or so slowed down. "That's it!" he cried. He stopped, backed up, and entered a narrow dirt road almost hidden by trees. Five hundred yards down, the road ran parallel to a fenced-in field. Charlie parked in a cleared area deeply rutted by frozen tractor tracks. The gate was locked. *In the spring,* Andy thought, *there will be cows here, and a dog that chases them,* but now the field was unmarked and bare.

"This is it," Charlie Spoon declared. "Me and Mac was up here just two weeks ago, scouting it out, and there's deer. Mac saw the tracks."

"That's right," Mac said.

"Well, we'll just see about that," her father said, putting on his gloves. He turned to Andy. "How you doing, honeybun?"

"Just fine," she said.

Andy shivered and stamped as they unloaded: first the rifles, which they unsheathed and checked, sliding the bolts, sighting through scopes, adjusting the slings; then the gear, their food and tents and sleeping bags and stove stored in four backpacks—three big ones for Charlie Spoon and her father and Mac, and a day pack for her.

"That's about your size," Mac said, to tease her.

She reddened and said, "Mac, I can carry a pack big as yours any day." He laughed and pressed his knee against the back of hers, so that her leg buckled. "Cut it out," she said. She wanted to make an iceball and throw it at him, but she knew that her father and Charlie were anxious to get going, and she didn't want to displease them.

Mac slid under the gate, and they handed the packs over to him. Then they slid under and began walking across the field toward the same woods that ran all the way back to her home, where even now her mother was probably rising again to wash their breakfast dishes and make herself a fresh pot of coffee. *She is there, and we are here:* the thought satisfied Andy. There was no place else she would rather be.

Mac came up beside her. "Over there's Canada," he said, nodding toward the woods.

"Huh!" she said. "Not likely."

"I don't mean *right* over there. I mean farther up north. You think I'm dumb?"

Dumb as your father, she thought.

"Look at that," Mac said, pointing to a piece of cow dung lying on a spot scraped bare of snow. "A frozen meadow muffin." He picked it up and sailed it at her. "Catch!"

"Mac!" she yelled. His laugh was as gawky as he was. She walked faster. He seemed different today somehow, bundled in his yellow-and-black-checkered coat, a rifle in hand, his silly floppy hat not quite covering his ears. They all seemed different as she watched them trudge through the snow—Mac and her father and Charlie Spoon—bigger, maybe, as if the cold landscape enlarged rather than diminished them, so that they, the only figures in that landscape, took on size and meaning just by being there. If they weren't there, everything would be quieter, and the woods would be the same as before. *But they are here,* Andy thought, looking behind her at the boot prints in the snow, *and I am too, and so it's all different.*

"We'll go down to the cut where we found those deer tracks," Charlie said as they entered the woods. "Maybe we'll get lucky and get a late one coming through."

The woods descended into a gully. The snow was softer and deeper here, so that often Andy sank to her knees. Charlie and Mac worked the top of the gully while she and her father walked along the base some thirty yards behind them. "If they miss the first shot, we'll get the second," her father said, and she nodded as if she had known this all the time. She listened to the crunch of their boots, their breathing, and the drumming of a distant woodpecker. And the crackling. In winter the woods crackled as if everything were straining, ready to snap like dried chicken bones.

We are hunting, Andy thought. The cold air burned her nostrils.

They stopped to make lunch by a rock outcropping that protected them from the wind. Her father heated the bean soup her mother had made for them, and they ate it with bread already stiff from the cold. He and Charlie took a few pulls from a flask of Jim Beam while she scoured the plates with snow and repacked them. Then they all had coffee with sugar and powdered milk, and her father poured her a cup too. "We won't tell your momma," he said, and Mac laughed. Andy held the cup the way her father did, not by the handle but around the rim. The coffee tasted smoky. She felt a little queasy, but she drank it all.

Charlie Spoon picked his teeth with a fingernail. "Now, you might've noticed one thing," he said.

"What's that?" her father asked.

"You might've noticed you don't hear no rifles. That's because there ain't no other hunters here. We've got the whole damn woods to ourselves. Now, I ask you—do I know how to find 'em?"

"We haven't seen deer yet, neither."

"Oh, we will," Charlie said, "but not for a while now." He leaned back against the rock. "Deer're sleeping, resting up for the evening feed."

"I seen a deer behind our house once, and it was afternoon," Andy said.

"Yeah, honey, but that was *before* deer season," Charlie said, grinning. "They know something now. They're smart that way."

"That's right," Mac said.

Andy looked at her father—had she said something stupid?

"Well, Charlie," he said, "if they know so much, how come so many get themselves shot?"

"Them's the ones that don't *believe* what they know," Charlie replied. The men laughed. Andy hesitated, and then laughed with them.

They moved on, as much to keep warm as to find a deer. The wind became even stronger. Blowing through the treetops, it sounded like the ocean, and once Andy thought she could smell salt air. But that was impossible; the ocean was *hundreds* of miles away, farther than Canada even. She and her parents had gone last summer to stay for a week at a motel on the New Jersey shore. That was the first time she'd seen the ocean, and it frightened her. It was huge and empty, yet always moving. Everything lay hidden. If you walked in it, you couldn't see how deep it was or what might be below; if you swam, something could pull you under and you'd never be seen again. Its musky, rank smell made her think of things dying. Her mother had floated beyond the breakers, calling to her to come in, but Andy wouldn't go farther than a few feet into the surf. Her mother swam and splashed with animal-like delight while her father, smiling shyly, held his white arms above the waist-deep water as if afraid to get them wet. Once a comber rolled over and sent them both tossing, and when her mother tried to stand up, the surf receding behind, Andy saw that her mother's swimsuit top had come off, so that her breasts swayed free, her nipples like two dark eyes. Embarrassed, Andy looked around: except for two women under a yellow umbrella farther up, the beach was empty. Her mother stood up unsteadily, regained her footing. Taking what seemed the longest time, she calmly refixed her top. Andy lay on the beach towel and closed her eyes. The sound of the surf made her head ache.

And now it was winter; the sky was already dimming, not just with the absence of light but with a mist that clung to the hunters' faces like cobwebs. They made camp early. Andy was chilled. When she stood still, she kept wiggling her toes to make sure they were there. Her father rubbed her arms and held her to him briefly, and that felt better. She unpacked the food while the others put up the tents.

"How about rounding us up some firewood, Mac?" Charlie asked.

"I'll do it," Andy said. Charlie looked at her thoughtfully and then handed her the canvas carrier.

There wasn't much wood on the ground, so it took her a while to get a good load. She was about a hundred yards from camp, near a cluster of high, lichen-covered boulders, when she saw through a crack in the rock a buck and two does walking gingerly, almost daintily, through the alder trees. She tried to hush her breathing as they passed not more than twenty yards away. There was nothing she could do. If she yelled, they'd be gone; by the time she got back to camp, they'd be gone. The buck stopped, nostrils quivering, tail up and alert. He looked directly at her. Still she didn't move, not one muscle. He was a beautiful buck, the color of late-turned maple leaves. Unafraid, he lowered his tail, and he and his does silently merged into the trees. Andy walked back to camp and dropped the firewood.

"I saw three deer," she said. "A buck and two does."

"Where?" Charlie Spoon cried, looking behind her as if they might have followed her into camp.

"In the woods yonder. They're gone now."

"Well, hell!" Charlie banged his coffee cup against his knee.

"Didn't I say she could find animals?" her father said, grinning.

"Too late to go after them," Charlie muttered. "It'll be dark in a quarter hour. Damn!"

"Damn," Mac echoed.

"They just walk right up to her," her father said.

"Well, leastwise this proves there's deer here." Charlie began snapping long branches into shorter ones. "You know, I think I'll stick with you," he told Andy, "since you're so good at finding deer and all. How'd that be?"

"Okay, I guess," Andy murmured. She hoped he was kidding; no way did she want to hunt with Charlie Spoon. Still, she was pleased he had said it.

Her father and Charlie took one tent, she and Mac the other. When they were in their sleeping bags, Mac said in the darkness, "I bet you really didn't see no deer, did you?"

She sighed. "I did, Mac. Why would I lie?"

"How big was the buck?"

"Four point. I counted."

Mac snorted.

"You just believe what you want, Mac," she said testily.

"Too bad it ain't buck season," he said. "Well, I got to go pee."

"So pee."

She heard him turn in his bag. "You ever see it?" he asked.

"It? What's 'it'?"

"It. A pecker."

"Sure," she lied.

"Whose? Your father's?"

She was uncomfortable. "No," she said.

"Well, whose then?"

"Oh I don't know! Leave me be, why don't you?"

"Didn't see a deer, didn't see a pecker," Mac said teasingly.

She didn't answer right away. Then she said, "My cousin Lewis. I saw his."

"Well, how old's he?"

"One and a half."

"Ha! A baby! A baby's is like a little worm. It ain't a real one at all."

If he says he'll show me his, she thought, *I'll kick him. I'll just get out of my bag and kick him.*

"I went hunting with my daddy and Versh and Danny Simmons last year in buck season," Mac said, "and we got ourselves one. And we hog-dressed the thing. You know what that is, don't you?"

"No," she said. She was confused. What was he talking about now?

"That's when you cut him open and take out all his guts, so the meat don't spoil. Makes him lighter to pack out, too."

She tried to imagine what the deer's guts might look like, pulled from the gaping hole. "What do you do with them?" she said. "The guts?"

"Oh, just leave 'em for the bears."

She ran her finger like a knife blade along her belly.

"When we left them on the ground," Mac said, "they smoked. Like they were cooking."

"Huh," she said.

"They cut off the deer's pecker, too, you know."

Andy imagined Lewis's pecker and shuddered. "Mac, you're disgusting."

He laughed. "Well, I gotta go pee." She heard him rustle out of his bag. "Broo!" he cried, flapping his arms. "It's cold!"

He makes so much noise, she thought, *just noise and more noise.*

Her father woke them before first light. He warned them to talk softly and said that they were going to the place where Andy had seen the deer, to try to cut them off on their way back from their night feeding. Andy couldn't shake off her sleep. Stuffing her sleeping bag into its sack seemed to take an hour, and tying her boots was the strangest thing she'd ever done. Charlie Spoon made hot chocolate and oatmeal with raisins. Andy closed her eyes and, between beats of her heart, listened to the breathing of the forest. *When I open my eyes, it will be lighter,* she decided.

But when she did, it was still just as dark, except for the swaths of their flashlights and the hissing blue flame of the stove. *There has to be just one moment when it all changes from dark to light,* Andy thought. She had missed it yesterday, in the car; today she would watch more closely.

But when she remembered again, it was already first light and they had moved to the rocks by the deer trail and had set up shooting positions—Mac and Charlie Spoon on the up-trail side, she and her father behind them, some six feet up on a ledge. The day became brighter, the sun piercing the tall pines, raking the hunters, yet providing little warmth. Andy now smelled alder and pine and the slightly rotten odor of rock lichen. She rubbed her hand over the stone and considered that it must be very old, had probably been here before the giant pines, *before anyone was in these woods at all.* A chipmunk sniffed on a nearby branch. She aimed an imaginary rifle and pressed the trigger. The chipmunk froze, then scurried away. Her legs were cramping on the narrow ledge. Her father seemed to doze, one hand in his parka, the other cupped lightly around the rifle. She could smell his scent of old wool and leather. His cheeks were speckled with gray-black whiskers, and he worked his jaws slightly, as if chewing a small piece of gum.

Please let us get a deer, she prayed.

A branch snapped on the other side of the rock face. Her father's hand stiffened on the rifle, startling her—*He hasn't been sleeping at all,* she marveled—and then his jaw relaxed, as did the lines around his eyes, and she heard Charlie Spoon call, "Yo, don't shoot, it's us." He and Mac appeared from around the rock. They stopped beneath the ledge. Charlie solemnly crossed his arms.

"I don't believe we're gonna get any deer here," he said drily.

Andy's father lowered his rifle to Charlie and jumped down from the ledge. Then he reached up for Andy. She dropped into his arms and he set her gently on the ground.

Mac sidled up to her. "I knew you didn't see no deer," he said.

"Just because they don't come when you want 'em to don't mean she didn't see them," her father said.

Still, she felt bad. Her telling about the deer had caused them to spend the morning there, cold and expectant, with nothing to show for it.

They tramped through the woods for another two hours, not caring much about noise. Mac found some deer tracks, and they argued about how old they were. They split up for a while and then rejoined at an old logging road that deer might use, and followed it. The road crossed a stream, which had mostly frozen over but in a few spots still caught leaves and twigs in an icy swirl. They forded it by jumping from rock to rock. The road narrowed after that, and the woods thickened.

They stopped for lunch, heating up Charlie's wife's corn chowder. Andy's father cut squares of applesauce cake with his hunting knife and handed them to her and Mac, who ate his almost daintily. Andy could faintly taste knife oil on the cake. She was tired. She stretched her leg; the muscle that had cramped on the rock still ached.

"Might as well relax," her father said, as if reading her thoughts. "We won't find deer till suppertime."

Charlie Spoon leaned back against his pack and folded his hands across his stomach. "Well, even if we don't get a deer," he said expansively, "it's still great to be out here, breathe some fresh air, clomp around a bit. Get away from the house and the old lady." He winked at Mac, who looked away.

"That's what the woods are all about, anyway," Charlie said. "It's where the women don't want to go." He bowed his head toward Andy. "With your exception, of course, little lady." He helped himself to another piece of applesauce cake.

"She ain't a woman," Mac said.

"Well, she damn well's gonna be," Charlie said. He grinned at her. "Or will you? You're half a boy anyway. You go by a boy's name. What's your real name? Andrea, ain't it?"

"That's right," she said. She hoped that if she didn't look at him, Charlie would stop.

"Well, which do you like? Andy or Andrea?"

"Don't matter," she mumbled. "Either."

"She's always been Andy to me," her father said.

Charlie Spoon was still grinning. "So what are you gonna be, Andrea? A boy or a girl?"

"I'm a girl," she said.

"But you want to go hunting and fishing and everything, huh?"

"She can do whatever she likes," her father said.

"Hell, you might as well have just had a boy and be done with it!" Charlie exclaimed.

"That's funny," her father said, and chuckled. "That's just what her momma tells me."

They were looking at her, and she wanted to get away from them all, even from her father, who chose to joke with them.

"I'm going to walk a bit," she said.

She heard them laughing as she walked down the logging trail. She flapped her arms; she whistled. *I don't care how much noise I make,* she thought. Two grouse flew from the underbrush, startling her. A little farther down, the trail ended in a clearing that enlarged into a frozen meadow; beyond it the woods began again. A few moldering posts were all that was left of a fence that had once enclosed the field. The low afternoon sunlight reflected brightly off the snow, so that Andy's eyes hurt. She squinted hard. A gust of wind blew across the field, stinging her face. And then, as if it had been waiting for her, the doe emerged from the trees opposite and stepped cautiously into the field. Andy watched: it stopped and stood quietly for what seemed a long time and then ambled across. It stopped again about seventy yards away and began to browse in a patch of sugar grass uncovered by the wind. Carefully, slowly, never taking her eyes from the doe, Andy walked backward, trying to step into the boot prints she'd already made. When she was far enough back into the woods, she turned and walked faster, her heart racing. *Please let it stay,* she prayed.

"There's doe in the field yonder," she told them.

They got their rifles and hurried down the trail.

"No use," her father said. "We're making too much noise any way you look at it."

"At least we got us the wind in our favor," Charlie Spoon said, breathing heavily.

But the doe was still there, grazing.

"Good Lord," Charlie whispered. He looked at her father. "Well, whose shot?"

"Andy spotted it," her father said in a low voice. "Let her shoot it."

"What!" Charlie's eyes widened.

Andy couldn't believe what her father had just said. She'd only shot tin cans and targets; she'd never even fired her father's .30-.30, and she'd never killed anything.

"I can't," she whispered.

"That's right, she can't," Charlie Spoon insisted. "She's not old enough and she don't have a license even if she was!"

"Well, who's to tell?" her father said in a low voice. "Nobody's going to know but us." He looked at her. "Do you want to shoot it, punkin?"

Why doesn't it hear us? she wondered. *Why doesn't it run away?* "I don't know," she said.

"Well, I'm sure as hell gonna shoot it," Charlie said. Her father grasped Charlie's rifle barrel and held it. His voice was steady.

"Andy's a good shot. It's her deer. She found it, not you. You'd still be sitting on your ass back in camp." He turned to her again. "Now—do you want to shoot it, Andy? Yes or no."

He was looking at her; they were all looking at her. Suddenly she was angry at the deer, who refused to hear them, who wouldn't run away even when it could. "I'll shoot it," she said. Charlie turned away in disgust.

She lay on the ground and pressed the rifle stock against her shoulder bone. The snow was cold through her parka; she smelled oil and wax and damp earth. She pulled off one glove with her teeth. "It sights just like the .22," her father said gently. "Cartridge's already chambered." As she had done so many times before, she sighted down the scope; now the doe was in the reticle. She moved the barrel until the cross hairs lined up. Her father was breathing beside her.

"Aim where the chest and legs meet, or a little above, punkin," he was saying calmly. "That's the killing shot."

But now, seeing it in the scope, Andy was hesitant. Her finger weakened on the trigger. Still, she nodded at what her father said and sighted again, the cross hairs lining up in exactly the same spot—the doe had hardly moved, its brownish-gray body outlined starkly against the blue-backed snow. *It doesn't know,* Andy thought. *It just doesn't know.* And as she looked, deer and snow and faraway trees flattened within the circular frame to become like a picture on a calendar, not real, and she felt calm, as if she had been dreaming everything—the day, the deer, the hunt itself. And she, finger on trigger, was only a part of that dream.

"Shoot!" Charlie hissed.

Through the scope she saw the deer look up, ears high and straining.

Charlie groaned, and just as he did, and just at the moment when Andy knew—*knew*—the doe would bound away, as if she could feel its haunches tensing and gathering power, she pulled the trigger. Later she would think, *I felt the recoil, I smelled the smoke, but I don't remember pulling the trigger.* Through the scope the deer seemed to shrink into itself, and then slowly knelt, hind legs first, head raised as if to cry out. It trembled, still straining to keep its head high, as if that alone would save it; failing, it collapsed, shuddered, and lay still.

"Whoee!" Mac cried.

"One shot! One shot!" her father yelled, clapping her on the back. Charlie Spoon was shaking his head and smiling dumbly.

"I told you she was a great little shot!" her father said. "I told you!" Mac danced and clapped his hands. She was dazed, not quite understanding what had happened. And then they were crossing the field toward the fallen doe, she walking dreamlike, the men laughing and joking, released now from the tension of silence and anticipation. Suddenly Mac pointed and cried out, "Look at that!"

The doe was rising, legs unsteady. They stared at it, unable to comprehend, and in that moment the doe regained its feet and looked at them, as if it too were trying to understand. Her father whistled softly. Charlie Spoon unslung his rifle and raised it to his shoulder, but the doe was already bounding away. His hurried shot missed, and the deer disappeared into the woods.

"Damn, damn, damn," he moaned.

"I don't believe it," her father said. "That deer was dead."

"Dead, hell!" Charlie yelled. "It was gutshot, that's all. Stunned and gutshot. Clean shot, my ass!"

What have I done? Andy thought.

Her father slung his rifle over his shoulder. "Well, let's go. It can't get too far."

"Hell, I've seen deer run ten miles gutshot," Charlie said. He waved his arms. "We may never find her!"

As they crossed the field, Mac came up to her and said in a low voice, "Gutshoot a deer, you'll go to hell."

"Shut up, Mac," she said, her voice cracking. It was a terrible thing she had done, she knew. She couldn't bear to think of the doe in pain and frightened. *Please let it die,* she prayed.

But though they searched all the last hour of daylight, so that they had to recross the field and go up the logging trail in a twilight made even deeper by thick, smoky clouds, they didn't find the doe. They lost its trail almost immediately in the dense stands of alderberry and larch.

"I am cold, and I am tired," Charlie Spoon declared. "And if you ask me, that deer's in another county already."

"No one's asking you, Charlie," her father said.

They had a supper of hard salami and ham, bread, and the rest of the applesauce cake. It seemed a bother to heat the coffee, so they had cold chocolate instead. Everyone turned in early.

"We'll find it in the morning, honeybun," her father said, as she went to her tent.

"I don't like to think of it suffering." She was almost in tears.

"It's dead already, punkin. Don't even think about it." He kissed her, his breath sour and his beard rough against her cheek.

Andy was sure she wouldn't get to sleep; the image of the doe falling, falling, then rising again, repeated itself whenever she closed her eyes. Then she heard an owl hoot and realized that it had awakened her, so she must have been asleep after all. She hoped the owl would hush, but instead it hooted louder. She wished her father or Charlie Spoon would wake up and do something about it, but no one moved in the other tent, and suddenly she was afraid that they had all decamped, wanting nothing more to do with her. She whispered, "Mac, Mac," to the sleeping bag where he should be, but no one answered. She tried to find the flashlight she always kept by her side, but couldn't, and she cried in panic, "Mac, are you there?" He mumbled something, and immediately she felt foolish and hoped he wouldn't reply.

When she awoke again, everything had changed. The owl was gone, the woods were still, and she sensed light, blue and pale, light where before there had been none. *The moon must have come out,* she thought. And it was warm, too, warmer than it should have been. She got out of her sleeping bag and took off her parka—it was that warm. Mac was asleep, wheezing like an old man. She unzipped the tent and stepped outside.

The woods were more beautiful than she had ever seen them. The moon made everything ice-rimmed glimmer with a crystallized, immanent light, while underneath that ice the branches of trees were as stark as skeletons. She heard a crunching in the snow, the one sound in all that silence, and there, walking down the logging trail into their camp, was the doe. Its body, like everything around her, was silvered with frost and moonlight. It walked past the tent where her father and Charlie Spoon were sleeping and stopped no more than six feet from her. Andy saw that she had shot it, yes, had shot it cleanly, just where she thought she had, the wound a jagged, bloody hole in the doe's chest.

A heart shot, she thought.

The doe stepped closer, so that Andy, if she wished, could have reached out and touched it. It looked at her as if expecting her to do this, and so she did, running her hand, slowly at first, along the rough, matted fur, then down to the edge of the wound, where she stopped. The doe stood still. Hesitantly, Andy felt the edge of the wound. The torn flesh was sticky and warm. The wound parted under her touch. And then, almost without her knowing it, her fingers were within, probing, yet still the doe didn't move. Andy pressed deeper, through flesh and muscle and sinew, until her whole hand and more was inside the wound and she had found the doe's heart, warm and beating. She cupped it gently in her hand. *Alive,* she marveled. *Alive.*

The heart quickened under her touch, becoming warmer and warmer until it was hot enough to burn. In pain, Andy tried to remove her hand, but the wound closed about it and held her fast. Her hand was burning. She cried out in agony, sure they would all hear and come help, but they didn't. And then her hand pulled free, followed by a steaming rush of blood, more blood than she ever could have imagined—it covered her hand and arm, and she saw to her horror that her hand was steaming. She moaned and fell to her knees and plunged her hand into the snow. The doe looked at her gently and then turned and walked back up the trail.

In the morning, when she woke, Andy could still smell the blood, but she felt no pain. She looked at her hand. Even though it appeared unscathed, it felt weak and withered. She couldn't move it freely and was afraid the others would notice. *I will hide it in my jacket pocket,* she decided, *so nobody can see.* She ate the oatmeal that her father cooked and stayed apart from them all.

No one spoke to her, and that suited her. A light snow began to fall. It was the last day of their hunting trip. She wanted to be home.

Her father dumped the dregs of his coffee. "Well, let's go look for her," he said.

Again they crossed the field. Andy lagged behind. She averted her eyes from the spot where the doe had fallen, already filling up with snow. Mac and Charlie entered the woods first, followed by her father. Andy remained in the field and considered the smear of gray sky, the nearby flock of crows pecking at unyielding stubble. *I will stay here,* she thought, *and not move for a long while.* But now someone—Mac—was yelling. Her father appeared at the woods' edge and waved for her to come. She ran and pushed through a brake of alderberry and larch. The thick underbrush scratched her face. For a moment she felt lost and looked wildly about. Then, where the brush thinned, she saw them standing quietly in the falling snow. They were staring down at the dead doe. A film covered its upturned eye, and its body was lightly dusted with snow.

"I told you she wouldn't get too far," Andy's father said triumphantly. "We must've just missed her yesterday. Too blind to see."

"We're just damn lucky no animal got to her last night," Charlie muttered.

Her father lifted the doe's foreleg. The wound was blood-clotted, brown, and caked like frozen mud. "Clean shot," he said to Charlie. He grinned. "My little girl."

Then he pulled out his knife, the blade gray as the morning. Mac whispered to Andy, "Now watch this," while Charlie Spoon lifted the doe from behind by its forelegs so that its head rested between his knees, its underside exposed. Her father's knife sliced thickly from chest to belly to crotch, and Andy was running from them, back to the field and across, scattering the crows who cawed and circled angrily. And now they were all calling to her—Charlie Spoon and Mac and her father—crying *Andy, Andy* (but that wasn't her name, she would no longer be called that); yet louder than any of them was the wind blowing through the treetops, like the ocean where her mother floated in green water, also calling *Come in, come in,* while all around her roared the mocking of the terrible, now inevitable, sea.

READING AND REACTING

1. The initiation of a child into adulthood is a very common literary theme. In this story hunting is presented as an initiation rite. Why is hunting an appropriate coming-of-age ritual?
2. What characters are in conflict in this story? What ideas are in conflict? How do these conflicts help to communicate the story's initiation theme?
3. In the story's opening paragraph and elsewhere, Andy finds comfort and reassurance in the idea that the woods are "always the same"; later in the story, she remembers the ocean, "huge and empty, yet always moving. Everything lay hidden . . ." (45). How does the contrast between the woods and the ocean suggest the transition from childhood to adulthood?
4. How do references to blood suggest the story's initiation theme?
5. Throughout the story references are made to Andy's ability to inspire the trust of animals. As her father says, "I don't know how she does it, but they come right up to her" (8). How does his comment foreshadow later events?
6. Why does Andy pray that she and the others will get a deer? What makes her change her mind? How does the change in Andy's character help to convey the story's theme?
7. Andy's mother is not an active participant in the story's events. Still, her presence is important to the story. *Why* is it important? How does paragraph 45 reveal the importance of the mother's role?
8. What would you say Andy has learned as a result of her experience? What else do you think she has to learn?
9. **JOURNAL ENTRY:** How would the story be different if Andy were a boy?

Amy Tan (1952–) detailed the lives of two generations of Chinese-American women in her first novel, *The Joy Luck Club,* which moves back and forth across the divide between two generations, two continents, and two cultures. Her second novel, *The Kitchen God's Wife* (1991), is an ambitious tale that ranges from China in 1925 to modern-day San Francisco.

Tan's own life experiences have drawn from two cultures and two continents. Her parents emigrated from China to Oakland, California, where Tan was born. Her mother, Daisy Tan, who was descended from a wealthy Shanghai family, left three daughters from a first marriage in China, something she did not reveal until after the death of Tan's father. There are parallels between Tan's upbringing and one of her characters in *The Joy Luck Club,* who feels out of place among Chinese women of her mother's generation who wear "funny Chinese dresses with stiff stand-up collars" and live in houses filled with too many "once fragrant smells" from their cooking. Tan, like the character in her book, found that she did not really know herself until she understood her Chinese heritage and the difficult and often tragic experiences of Chinese people of her parents' generation.

Tan received a bachelor's degree from San Jose State in 1973 and a master's in 1974, and later she did graduate work at the University of California, Berkeley. Her most recent work is a children's book, *The Moon Lady* (1992), which retells one of the stories in *The Joy Luck Club.*

Amy Tan

TWO KINDS

(1989)

My mother believed you could be anything you wanted to be in America. You could open a restaurant. You could work for the government and get good retirement. You could buy a house with almost no money down. You could become rich. You could become instantly famous.

"Of course you can be prodigy, too," my mother told me when I was nine. "You can be best anything. What does Auntie Lindo know? Her daughter, she is only best tricky."

America was where all my mother's hopes lay. She had come here in 1949 after losing everything in China: her mother and father, her family home, her first husband, and two daughters, twin baby girls. But she never looked back with regret. There were so many ways for things to get better.

We didn't immediately pick the right kind of prodigy. At first my mother thought I could be a Chinese Shirley Temple. We'd watch Shirley's old movies on TV as though they were training films. My mother would poke my arm and say, "*Ni kan*"—You watch. And I would see Shirley tapping her feet, or singing a sailor song, or pursing her lips into a very round O while saying, "Oh my goodness."

"*Ni kan,*" said my mother as Shirley's eyes flooded with tears. "You already know how. Don't need talent for crying!"

Soon after my mother got this idea about Shirley Temple, she took me to a beauty training school in the Mission district and put me in the hands of a student who could barely hold the scissors without shaking. Instead of getting big fat curls, I emerged with an uneven mass of crinkly black fuzz. My mother dragged me off to the bathroom and tried to wet down my hair.

"You look like Negro Chinese," she lamented, as if I had done this on purpose.

The instructor of the beauty training school had to lop off these soggy clumps to make my hair even again. "Peter Pan is very popular these days," the instructor assured my mother. I now had hair the length of a boy's, with straight-across bangs that hung at a slant two inches above my eyebrows. I liked the haircut and it made me actually look forward to my future fame.

In fact, in the beginning, I was just as excited as my mother, maybe even more so. I pictured this prodigy part of me as many different images, trying each one on for size. I was a dainty ballerina girl standing by the curtains, waiting to hear the right music that would send me floating on my tiptoes. I was like the Christ child lifted out of the straw manger, crying with holy indignity. I was Cinderella stepping from her pumpkin carriage with sparkly cartoon music filling the air.

In all of my imaginings, I was filled with a sense that I would soon become *perfect.* My mother and father would adore me. I would be beyond reproach. I would never feel the need to sulk for anything.

But sometimes the prodigy in me became impatient. "If you don't hurry up and get me out of here, I'm disappearing for good," it warned. "And then you'll always be nothing."

Every night after dinner, my mother and I would sit at the Formica kitchen table. She would present new tests, taking her examples from stories of amazing children she had read in *Ripley's Believe It or Not,* or *Good Housekeeping, Reader's Digest,* and a dozen other magazines she kept in a pile in our bathroom. My mother got these magazines from people whose houses she cleaned. And since she cleaned many houses each week, we had a great assortment. She would look through them all, searching for stories about remarkable children.

The first night she brought out a story about a three-year-old boy who knew the capitals of all the states and even most of the European countries. A teacher was quoted as saying the little boy could also pronounce the names of the foreign cities correctly.

"What's the capital of Finland?" my mother asked me, looking at the magazine story.

15 All I knew was the capital of California, because Sacramento was the name of the street we lived on in Chinatown. "Nairobi!" I guessed, saying the most foreign word I could think of. She checked to see if that was possibly one way to pronounce "Helsinki" before showing me the answer.

The tests got harder—multiplying numbers in my head, finding the queen of hearts in a deck of cards, trying to stand on my head without using my hands, predicting the daily temperatures in Los Angeles, New York, and London.

One night I had to look at a page from the Bible for three minutes and then report everything I could remember. "Now Jehoshaphat had riches and honor in abundance and . . . that's all I remember, Ma," I said.

And after seeing my mother's disappointed face once again, something inside of me began to die. I hated the tests, the raised hopes and failed expectations. Before going to bed that night, I looked in the mirror above the bathroom sink and when I saw only my face staring back—and that it would always be this ordinary face—I began to cry. Such a sad, ugly girl! I made high-pitched noises like a crazed animal, trying to scratch out the face in the mirror.

And then I saw what seemed to be the prodigy side of me—because I had never seen that face before. I looked at my reflection, blinking so I could see more clearly. The girl staring back at me was angry, powerful. This girl and I were the same. I had new thoughts, willful thoughts, or rather thoughts filled with lots of won'ts. I won't let her change me, I promised myself. I won't be what I'm not.

20 So now on nights when my mother presented her tests, I performed listlessly, my head propped on one arm. I pretended to be bored. And I was. I got so bored I started counting the bellows of the foghorns out on the bay while my mother drilled me in other areas. The sound was comforting and reminded me of the cow jumping over the moon. And the next day, I played a game with myself, seeing if my mother would give up on me before eight bellows. After a while I usually counted only one, maybe two bellows at most. At last she was beginning to give up hope.

Two or three months had gone by without any mention of my being a prodigy again. And then one day my mother was watching *The Ed Sullivan Show* on TV. The TV was old and the sound kept shorting out. Every time my mother got halfway up from the sofa to adjust the set, the sound would go back on and Ed would be talking. As soon as she sat down, Ed would go silent again. She got up, the TV broke into loud piano music. She sat down. Silence. Up and down, back and forth, quiet and loud. It was like a stiff embraceless dance between her and the TV set. Finally she stood by the set with her hand on the sound dial.

She seemed entranced by the music, a little frenzied piano piece with this mesmerizing quality, sort of quick passages and then teasing lilting ones before it returned to the quick playful parts.

"*Ni kan,*" my mother said, calling me over with hurried hand gestures, "Look here."

I could see why my mother was fascinated by the music. It was being pounded out by a little Chinese girl, about nine years old, with a Peter Pan haircut. The girl had the sauciness of a Shirley Temple. She was proudly modest like a proper Chinese child. And she also did this fancy sweep of a curtsy, so that the fluffy skirt of her white dress cascaded slowly to the floor like the petals of a large carnation.

25 In spite of these warning signs, I wasn't worried. Our family had no piano and we couldn't afford to buy one, let alone reams of sheet music and piano lessons. So I could be generous in my comments when my mother bad-mouthed the little girl on TV.

"Play note right, but doesn't sound good! No singing sound," complained my mother.

"What are you picking on her for?" I said carelessly. "She's pretty good. Maybe she's not the best, but she's trying hard." I knew almost immediately I would be sorry I said that.

"Just like you," she said. "Not the best. Because you not trying." She gave a little huff as she let go of the sound dial and sat down on the sofa.

The little Chinese girl sat down also to play an encore of "Anitra's Dance" by Grieg. I remember the song, because later on I had to learn how to play it.

30 Three days after watching *The Ed Sullivan Show,* my mother told me what my schedule would be for piano lessons and piano practice. She had talked to Mr. Chong, who lived on the first floor of our apartment building. Mr. Chong was a retired piano teacher and my mother had traded housecleaning services for weekly lessons and a piano for me to practice on every day, two hours a day, from four until six.

When my mother told me this, I felt as though I had been sent to hell. I whined and then kicked my foot a little when I couldn't stand it anymore.

"Why don't you like me the way I am? I'm *not* a genius! I can't play the piano. And even if I could, I wouldn't go on TV if you paid me a million dollars!" I cried.

My mother slapped me. "Who ask you be genius?" she shouted. "Only ask you be your best. For you sake. You think I want you be genius? Hnnh! What for! Who ask you!"

"So ungrateful," I heard her mutter in Chinese. "If she had as much talent as she has temper, she would be famous now."

35 Mr. Chong, whom I secretly nicknamed Old Chong, was very strange, always tapping his fingers to the silent music of an invisible orchestra. He looked ancient in my eyes. He had lost most of the hair on top of his head and he wore thick glasses and had eyes that always looked tired and sleepy. But he must have been younger than I thought, since he lived with his mother and was not yet married.

I met Old Lady Chong once and that was enough. She had this peculiar smell like a baby that had done something in its pants. And her fingers felt like a dead person's, like an old peach I once found in the back of the refrigerator; the skin just slid off the meat when I picked it up.

I soon found out why Old Chong had retired from teaching piano. He was deaf. "Like Beethoven!" he shouted to me. "We're both listening only in our head!" And he would start to conduct his frantic silent sonatas.

Our lessons went like this. He would open the book and point to different things, explaining their purpose: "Key! Treble! Bass! No sharps or flats! So this is C major! Listen now and play after me!"

And then he would play the C scale a few times, a simple chord, and then, as if inspired by an old, unreachable itch, he gradually added more notes and running trills and a pounding bass until the music was really something quite grand.

I would play after him, the simple scale, the simple chord, and then I just played some nonsense that sounded like a cat running up and down on top of garbage cans. Old Chong smiled and applauded and then said, "Very good! But now you must learn to keep time!"

So that's how I discovered that Old Chong's eyes were too slow to keep up with the wrong notes I was playing. He went through the motions in half-time. To help me keep rhythm, he stood behind me, pushing down on my right shoulder for every beat. He balanced pennies on top of my wrists so I would keep them still as I slowly played scales and arpeggios. He had me curve my hand around an apple and keep that shape when playing chords. He marched stiffly to show me how to make each finger dance up and down, staccato like an obedient little soldier.

He taught me all these things, and that was how I also learned I could be lazy and get away with mistakes, lots of mistakes. If I hit the wrong notes because I hadn't practiced enough, I never corrected myself. I just kept playing in rhythm. And Old Chong kept conducting his own private reverie.

So maybe I never really gave myself a fair chance. I did pick up the basics pretty quickly, and I might have become a good pianist at that young age. But I was so determined not to try, not to be anybody different that I learned to play only the most ear-splitting preludes, the most discordant hymns.

Over the next year, I practiced like this, dutifully in my own way. And then one day I heard my mother and her friend Lindo Jong both talking in a loud bragging tone of voice so others could hear. It was after church, and I was leaning against the brick wall wearing a dress with stiff white petticoats. Auntie Lindo's daughter, Waverly, who was about my age, was standing farther down the wall about five feet away. We had grown up together and shared all the closeness of two sisters squabbling over crayons and dolls. In other words, for the most part, we hated each other. I thought she was snotty. Waverly Jong had gained a certain amount of fame as "Chinatown's Littlest Chinese Chess Champion."

"She bring home too many trophy," lamented Auntie Lindo that Sunday. "All day she play chess. All day I have no time do nothing but dust off her winnings." She threw a scolding look at Waverly, who pretended not to see her.

"You lucky you don't have this problem," said Auntie Lindo with a sigh to my mother.

And my mother squared her shoulders and bragged: "Our problem worser than yours. If we ask Jing-mei wash dish, she hear nothing but music. It's like you can't stop this natural talent."

And right then, I was determined to put a stop to her foolish pride.

A few weeks later, Old Chong and my mother conspired to have me play in a talent show which would be held in the church hall. By then, my parents had saved up enough to buy me a secondhand piano, a black Wurlitzer spinet with a scarred bench. It was the showpiece of our living room.

For the talent show, I was to play a piece called "Pleading Child" from Schumann's *Scenes from Childhood.* It was a simple, moody piece that sounded more difficult than it was. I was supposed to memorize the whole thing, playing the repeat parts twice to make the piece sound longer. But I dawdled over it, playing a few bars and then cheating, looking up to see what notes followed. I never really listened to what I was playing. I daydreamed about being somewhere else, about being someone else.

The part I liked to practice best was the fancy curtsy: right foot out, touch the rose on the carpet with a pointed foot, sweep to the side, left leg bends, look up and smile.

My parents invited all the couples from the Joy Luck Club[1] to witness my debut. Auntie Lindo and Uncle Tin were there. Waverly and her two older brothers had also come. The first two rows were filled with children both younger and older than I was. The little ones got to go first. They recited simple nursery rhymes, squawked out tunes on miniature violins, twirled Hula Hoops, pranced in pink ballet tutus, and when they bowed or curtsied, the audience would sigh in unison, "Awww," and then clap enthusiastically.

When my turn came, I was very confident. I remember my childish excitement. It was as if I knew, without a doubt, that the prodigy side of me really did exist. I had no fear whatsoever, no nervousness. I remember thinking to myself, This is it! This is it! I looked out over the audience, at my mother's blank face, my father's yawn, Auntie Lindo's stiff-lipped smile, Waverly's sulky expression. I had on a white dress layered with sheets of lace, and a pink bow in my Peter Pan haircut. As I sat down I envisioned people jumping to their feet and Ed Sullivan rushing up to introduce me to everyone on TV.

---

[1] A name denoting the mother's circle of friends, all of whom were Chinese immigrants to the United States.

And I started to play. It was so beautiful. I was so caught up in how lovely I looked that at first I didn't worry how I would sound. So it was a surprise to me when I hit the first wrong note and I realized something didn't sound quite right. And then I hit another and another followed that. A chill started at the top of my head and began to trickle down. Yet I couldn't stop playing, as though my hands were bewitched. I kept thinking my fingers would adjust themselves back, like a train switching to the right track. I played this strange jumble through two repeats, the sour notes staying with me all the way to the end.

When I stood up, I discovered my legs were shaking. Maybe I had just been nervous and the audience, like Old Chong, had seen me go through the right motions and had not heard anything wrong at all. I swept my right foot out; went down on my knee, looked up and smiled. The room was quiet, except for Old Chong, who was beaming and shouting, "Bravo! Bravo! Well done!" But then I saw my mother's face, her stricken face. The audience clapped weakly, and as I walked back to my chair, with my whole face quivering as I tried not to cry, I heard a little boy whisper loudly to his mother, "That was awful," and the mother whispered back, "Well, she certainly tried."

And now I realized how many people were in the audience, the whole world it seemed. I was aware of eyes burning into my back. I felt the shame of my mother and father as they sat stiffly throughout the rest of the show.

We could have escaped during intermission. Pride and some strange sense of honor must have anchored my parents to their chairs. And so we watched it all: the eighteen-year-old boy with a fake mustache who did a magic show and juggled flaming hoops while riding a unicycle. The breasted girl with white makeup who sang from *Madama Butterfly* and got honorable mention. And the eleven-year-old boy who won first prize playing a tricky violin song that sounded like a busy bee.

After the show, the Hsus, the Jongs, and the St. Clairs from the Joy Luck Club came up to my mother and father.

"Lots of talented kids," Auntie Lindo said vaguely, smiling broadly.

"That was somethin' else," said my father, and I wondered if he was referring to me in a humorous way, or whether he even remembered what I had done.

Waverly looked at me and shrugged her shoulders. "You aren't a genius like me," she said matter-of-factly. And if I hadn't felt so bad, I would have pulled her braids and punched her stomach.

But my mother's expression was what devastated me: a quiet, blank look that said she had lost everything. I felt the same way, and it seemed as if everybody were now coming up, like gawkers at the scene of an accident, to see what parts were actually missing. When we got on the bus to go home, my father was humming the busy-bee tune and my mother was silent. I kept thinking she wanted to wait until we got home before shouting at me. But when my father unlocked the door to our apartment, my mother walked in and then went to the back, into the bedroom. No accusations. No blame. And in a way, I felt disappointed. I had been waiting for her to start shouting, so I could shout back and cry and blame her for all my misery.

I assumed my talent-show fiasco meant I never had to play the piano again. But two days later, after school, my mother came out of the kitchen and saw me watching TV.

"Four clock," she reminded me as if it were any other day. I was stunned, as though she were asking me to go through the talent-show torture again. I wedged myself more tightly in front of the TV.

"Turn off TV," she called from the kitchen five minutes later.

I didn't budge. And then I decided. I didn't have to do what my mother said anymore. I wasn't her slave. This wasn't China. I had listened to her before and look what happened. She was the stupid one.

She came out from the kitchen and stood in the arched entryway of the living room. "Four clock," she said once again, louder.

"I'm not going to play anymore," I said nonchalantly. "Why should I? I'm not a genius."

She walked over and stood in front of the TV. I saw her chest was heaving up and down in an angry way.

"No!" I said, and I now felt stronger, as if my true self had finally emerged. So this was what had been inside me all along.

"No! I won't!" I screamed.

She yanked me by the arm, pulled me off the floor, snapped off the TV. She was frighteningly strong, half pulling, half carrying me toward the piano as I kicked the throw rugs under my feet. She lifted me up and onto the hard bench. I was sobbing by now, looking at her bitterly. Her chest was heaving even more and her mouth was open, smiling crazily as if she were pleased I was crying.

"You want me to be someone that I'm not!" I sobbed. "I'll never be the kind of daughter you want me to be!"

"Only two kinds of daughters," she shouted in Chinese. "Those who are obedient and those who follow their own mind! Only one kind of daughter can live in this house. Obedient daughter!"

"Then I wish I wasn't your daughter. I wish you weren't my mother," I shouted. As I said these things I got scared. It felt like worms and toads and slimy things crawling out of my chest, but it also felt good, as if this awful side of me had surfaced, at last.

"Too late change this," said my mother shrilly.

And I could sense her anger rising to its breaking point. I wanted to see it spill over. And that's when I remembered the babies she had lost in China, the ones we never talked about. "Then I wish I'd never been born!" I shouted. "I wish I were dead! Like them."

It was as if I had said the magic words. Alakazam!—and her face went blank, her mouth closed, her arms went slack, and she backed out of the room, stunned, as if she were blowing away like a small brown leaf, thin, brittle, lifeless.

It was not the only disappointment my mother felt in me. In the years that followed, I failed her so many times, each time asserting my own will, my right to fall short of expectations. I didn't get straight As. I didn't become class president. I didn't get into Stanford. I dropped out of college.

For unlike my mother, I did not believe I could be anything I wanted to be. I could only be me.

And for all those years, we never talked about the disaster at the recital or my terrible accusations afterward at the piano bench. All that remained unchecked, like a betrayal that was now unspeakable. So I never found a way to ask her why she had hoped for something so large that failure was inevitable.

And even worse, I never asked her what frightened me the most: Why had she given up hope?

For after our struggle at the piano, she never mentioned my playing again. The lessons stopped. The lid to the piano was closed, shutting out the dust, my misery, and her dreams.

So she surprised me. A few years ago, she offered to give me the piano, for my thirtieth birthday. I had not played in all those years. I saw the offer as a sign of forgiveness, a tremendous burden removed.

"Are you sure?" I asked shyly. "I mean, won't you and Dad miss it?"

"No, this your piano," she said firmly. "Always your piano. You only one can play."

"Well, I probably can't play anymore," I said. "It's been years."

"You pick up fast," said my mother, as if she knew this was certain. "You have natural talent. You could been genius if you want to."

"No I couldn't."

"You just not trying," said my mother. And she was neither angry nor sad. She said it as if to announce a fact that could never be disproved. "Take it," she said.

But I didn't at first. It was enough that she had offered it to me. And after that, every time I saw it in my parents' living room, standing in front of the bay windows, it made me feel proud, as if it were a shiny trophy I had won back.

Last week I sent a tuner over to my parents' apartment and had the piano reconditioned, for purely sentimental reasons. My mother had died a few months before and I had been getting things in order for my father, a little bit at a time. I put the jewelry in special silk pouches. The sweaters she had knitted in yellow, pink, bright orange—all the colors I hated—I put those in moth-proof boxes. I found some old Chinese silk dresses, the kind with little slits up the sides. I rubbed the old silk against my skin, then wrapped them in tissue and decided to take them home with me.

After I had the piano tuned, I opened the lid and touched the keys. It sounded even richer than I remembered. Really, it was a very good piano. Inside the bench were the same exercise notes with handwritten scales, the same secondhand music books with their covers held together with yellow tape.

I opened up the Schumann book to the dark little piece I had played at the recital. It was on the left-hand side of the page, "Pleading Child." It looked more difficult than I remembered. I played a few bars, surprised at how easily the notes came back to me.

And for the first time, or so it seemed, I noticed the piece on the right-hand side. It was called "Perfectly Contented." I tried to play this one as well. It had a lighter melody but the same flowing rhythm and turned out to be quite easy. "Pleading Child" was shorter but slower; "Perfectly Contented" was longer, but faster. And after I played them both a few times, I realized they were two halves of the same song.

READING AND REACTING

1. What does the narrator's mother expect of her? Why?
2. Is the mother's strong desire to have her daughter succeed characteristic only of parents who are immigrants, or is this desire universal? What forces motivate the mother to push Jing-mei so hard?
3. Why doesn't the narrator do what her mother wants her to do? Why is she "so determined not to try" (43)?
4. What role do the mother's friends play in the story? The father? Old Chong?
5. How would you interpret the story's title? In what way does it help to communicate the story's themes?
6. How does the narrator's observation that the two Schumann pieces are "two halves of the same song" (95) convey the story's themes?
7. In what sense, if any, does the piano serve as a symbol?
8. **JOURNAL ENTRY:** Do you think the narrator should have tried harder to please her mother? Why or why not?

Tadeusz Borowski (1922–1951), Polish short story writer, poet, essayist, and journalist, was a survivor of the Nazi concentration camps at Auschwitz and Dachau. He is one of a group of European-born writers (including Elie Wiesel and Primo Levi) who drew on their personal experiences to create a unique body of writing sometimes called the "literature of atrocity." Borowski's stories are among the most brutal to come out of the camps, and critics in his lifetime denounced what they saw as his "cynical detachment" in the face of human suffering, notably in his short story collections *Pozegnanie z Maria* [*Farewell to Mary*] (1948) and *Kamienny swiat* (1948) [published in English as *This Way for the Gas, Ladies and Gentlemen, and Other Short Stories,* 1967].

More recent critics, including the well-known Czech writer Jan Kott, have agreed that Borowski's Auschwitz stories are minor masterpieces in which the writer works toward a redefinition of tragedy in light of the Holocaust. "The hero of Borowski's stories is a hero *deprived of all choice,"* writes critic Andrej Wirth. "He finds himself in a situation without choice because every choice is base [evil]." In Borowski's camps, neither victims nor executioners are portrayed as wholly good or evil. Borowski could not even absolve himself of guilt: His frequent use of a first-person narrator who collaborates in the crimes of the camps, writes Kott, "was the moral decision of a prisoner who had lived through Auschwitz [by working for the Nazis as a hospital orderly]—an acceptance of mutual responsibility, mutual participation, and mutual guilt . . . ." The final irony of Borowski's life is that having survived the gas chambers of Auschwitz, he chose to take his own life by asphyxiation when he was just twenty-nine years old.

Tadeusz Borowski

SILENCE

(1959)

Translated by Barbara Vedder

At last they seized him inside the German barracks, just as he was about to climb over the window ledge. In absolute silence they pulled him down to the floor and panting with hate dragged him into a dark alley. Here, closely surrounded by a silent mob, they began tearing at him with greedy hands.

Suddenly from the camp gate a whispered warning was passed from one mouth to another. A company of soldiers, their bodies leaning forward, their rifles on the ready, came running down the camp's main road, weaving between the clusters of men in stripes standing in the way. The crowd scattered and vanished inside the blocks. In the packed, noisy barracks the prisoners were cooking food pilfered during the night from neighbouring farmers. In the bunks and in the passageways between them, they were grinding grain in small flour-mills, slicing meat on heavy slabs of wood, peeling potatoes and throwing the peels on to the floor. They were playing cards for stolen cigars, stirring batter for pancakes, gulping down hot soup, and lazily killing fleas. A stifling odour of sweat hung in the air, mingled with the smell of food, with smoke and with steam that liquified along the ceiling beams and fell on the men, the bunks and the food in large, heavy drops, like autumn rain.

There was a stir at the door. A young American officer with a tin helmet on his head entered the block and looked with curiosity at the bunks and the tables. He wore a freshly pressed uniform; his revolver was hanging down, strapped in an open holster that dangled against his thigh. He was assisted by the translator who wore a yellow band reading "interpreter" on the sleeve of his civilian coat, and by the chairman of the Prisoners' Committee, dressed in a white summer coat, a pair of tuxedo trousers and tennis shoes. The men in the barracks fell silent. Leaning out of their bunks and lifting their eyes from the kettles, bowls and cups, they gazed attentively into the officer's face.

"Gentlemen," said the officer with a friendly smile, taking off his helmet—and the interpreter proceeded at once to translate sentence after sentence—"I know, of course, that after what you have gone through and after what you have seen, you must feel a deep hate for your tormentors. But we, the soldiers of America, and you, the people of Europe, have fought so that law should prevail over lawlessness. We must show our respect for the law. I assure you that the guilty will be punished, in this camp as well as in all the others. You have already seen, for example, that the S.S.[1] men were made to bury the dead."

". . . right, we could use the lot at the back of the hospital. A few of them are still around," whispered one of the men in a bottom bunk.

". . . or one of the pits," whispered another. He sat straddling the bunk, his fingers firmly clutching the blanket.

"Shut up! Can't you wait a little longer? Now listen to what the American has to say," a third man, stretched across the foot of the same bunk, spoke in an angry whisper. The American officer was now hidden from their view behind the thick crowd gathered at the other end of the block.

"Comrades, our new Kommandant gives you his word of honour that all the criminals of the S.S. as well as among the prisoners will be punished," said the translator. The men in the bunks broke into applause and shouts. In smiles and gestures they tried to convey their friendly approval of the young man from across the ocean.

"And so the Kommandant requests," went on the translator, his voice turning somewhat hoarse, "that you try to be patient and do not commit lawless deeds, which may only lead to trouble, and please pass the sons of bitches over to the camp guards. How about it, men?"

The block answered with a prolonged shout. The American thanked the translator and wished the prisoners a good rest and an early reunion with their dear ones. Accompanied by a friendly hum of voices, he left the block and proceeded to the next.

Not until after he had visited all the blocks and returned with the soldiers to his headquarters did we pull our man off the bunk—where covered with blankets and half-smothered with the weight of our bodies he lay gagged, his face buried in the straw mattress—and dragged him on to the cement floor under the stove, where the entire block, grunting and growling with hatred, trampled him to death.

---

[1] The Schutzstaffel (SS) or "Defense Squad" was the elite Nazi military corps. Created in 1925 as Hitler's bodyguards, the SS, or Black Shirts, controlled German security, including the Gestapo (secret state police) and concentration camp guards.

READING AND REACTING

1. What is the narrative point of view of "Silence"? How is this point of view suited to the ideas expressed in the story?
2. In what way does the behavior of the prisoners change when the American officer arrives? How do you account for this change?
3. How do the prisoners react to the American officer's speech? What is their opinion of him? What does he think of them? How do we know?
4. What judgments does the narrator make about the prisoners' treatment of the guard? How accurate do you believe these judgments are?
5. What comment does "Silence" make about the prisoners' need for vengeance? About the Americans' ability to understand the horrors of the concentration camps? Do you believe these observations are accurate?
6. Is this story too short to convey its points effectively? What would be the advantages and disadvantages of a longer format?
7. **JOURNAL ENTRY:** Do you think the prisoners' response is justified? Do you believe such violent actions can ever be justified? If so, under what circumstances?

James Alan McPherson (1943–   ) has been called a master of the short story form. His first collection, *Hue and Cry: Short Stories* (1969), was critically acclaimed for his keen portrayal of human nature as well as for his technical skill; his second, *Elbow Room: Stories* (1977), won a Pulitzer Prize. Unlike many African-American writers, he describes his work as placing the issue of race "far in the background." As he explained in publicity materials for *Hue and Cry,* his work focuses on universal qualities of all kinds of people who have been "used, discarded, and wronged."

McPherson credits his upbringing in the culturally rich multiracial and multinational city of Savannah, Georgia, with giving him a viewpoint that transcends racial barriers. Educated in segregated public schools at the height of the civil rights movement, McPherson graduated from Morris Brown College in 1965. That same year his short story "Gold Coast" won first prize in a contest sponsored by *The Atlantic Monthly,* for which he is now a contributing editor. He received an LL.B. degree from Harvard Law School in 1968 and a master's of fine arts from the University of Iowa in 1969, the year his first collection of short stories was published. Since 1981 McPherson has been a professor at the University of Iowa Writer's Workshop. He lives in Iowa City.

James Alan McPherson

A LOAF OF BREAD

(1977)

It was one of those obscene situations, pedestrian to most people, but invested with meaning for a few poor folk whose lives are usually spent outside the imaginations of their fellow citizens. A grocer named Harold Green was caught red-handed selling to one group of people the very same goods he sold at lower prices at similar outlets in better neighborhoods. He had been doing this for many years, and at first he could not understand the outrage heaped upon him. He acted only from habit, he insisted, and had nothing personal against the people whom he served. They were his neighbors. Many of them he had carried on the cuff during hard times. Yet, through some mysterious access to a television station, the poor folk were now empowered to make grand denunciations of the grocer. Green's children now saw their father's business being picketed on the Monday evening news.

No one could question the fact that the grocer had been overcharging the people. On the news even the reporter grimaced distastefully while reading the statistics. His expression said, "It is my job to report the news, but sometimes even I must disassociate myself from it to protect my honor." This, at least, was the impression the grocer's children seemed to bring away from the television. Their father's name had not been mentioned, but there was a close-up of his store with angry black people, and a few outraged whites, marching in groups of three in front of it. There was also a close-up of his name. After seeing this, they were in no mood to watch cartoons. At the dinner table, disturbed by his children's silence, Harold Green felt compelled to say, "I am not a dishonest man." Then he felt ashamed. The children, a boy and his older sister, immediately left the table, leaving Green alone with his wife. "Ruth, I am not dishonest," he repeated to her.

Ruth Green did not say anything. She knew, and her husband did not, that the outraged people had also picketed the school attended by their children. They had threatened to return each day until Green lowered his prices. When they called her at home to report this, she had promised she would talk with him. Since she could not tell him this, she waited for an opening. She looked at her husband across the table.

"I did not make the world," Green began, recognizing at once the seriousness in her stare. "My father came to this country with nothing but his shirt. He was exploited for as long as he couldn't help himself. He did not protest or picket. He put himself in a position to play by the rules he had learned." He waited for his wife to answer, and when she did not, he tried again. "I did not make this world," he repeated. "I only make my way in it. Such people as these, they do not know enough to not be exploited. If not me, there would be a Greek, a Chinaman, maybe an Arab or a smart one of their own kind. Believe me, I deal with them.

There is something in their style that lacks the patience to run a concern such as mine. If I closed down, take my word on it, someone else would do what has to be done."

But Ruth Green was not thinking of his leaving. Her mind was on other matters. Her children had cried when they came home early from school. She had no special feeling for the people who picketed, but she did not like to see her children cry. She had kissed them generously, then sworn them to silence. "One day this week," she told her husband, "you will give free, for eight hours, anything your customers come in to buy. There will be no publicity, except what they spread by word of mouth. No matter what they say to you, no matter what they take, you will remain silent." She stared deeply into him for what she knew was there. "If you refuse, you have seen the last of your children and myself."

Her husband grunted. Then he leaned toward her. "I will not knuckle under," he said. "I will *not* give!"

"We shall see," his wife told him.

The black pickets, for the most part, had at first been frightened by the audacity of their undertaking. They were peasants whose minds had long before become resigned to their fate as victims. None of them, before now, had thought to challenge this. But now, when they watched themselves on television, they hardly recognized the faces they saw beneath the hoisted banners and placards. Instead of reflecting the meekness they all felt, the faces looked angry. The close-ups looked especially intimidating. Several of the first pickets, maids who worked in the suburbs, reported that their employers, seeing the activity on the afternoon news, had begun treating them with new respect. One woman, midway through the weather report, called around the neighborhood to disclose that her employer had that very day given her a new china plate for her meals. The paper plates, on which all previous meals had been served, had been thrown into the wastebasket. One recipient of this call, a middle-aged woman known for her bashfulness and humility, rejoined that her husband, a sheet-metal worker, had only a few hours before been called "Mister" by his supervisor, a white man with a passionate hatred of color. She added the tale of a neighbor down the street, a widow-woman named Murphy, who had at first been reluctant to join the picket; this woman now was insisting it should be made a daily event. Such talk as this circulated among the people who had been instrumental in raising the issue. As news of their victory leaked into the ears of others who had not participated, they received all through the night calls from strangers requesting verification, offering advice, and vowing support. Such strangers listened, and then volunteered stories about indignities inflicted on them by city officials, policemen, other grocers. In this way, over a period of hours, the community became even more incensed and restless than it had been at the time of the initial picket.

Soon, the man who had set events in motion found himself a hero. His name was Nelson Reed, and all his adult life he had been employed as an assembly-line worker. He was a steady husband, the father of three children, and a deacon in the Baptist church. All his life he had trusted in God and gotten along. But now something in him capitulated to the reality that came suddenly into focus. "I was wrong," he told people who called him. "The onliest thing that matters in this world is *money*. And when was the last time you seen a picture of Jesus on a dollar bill?" This line, which he repeated over and over, caused a few callers to laugh nervously, but not without some affirmation that this was indeed the way things were. Many said they had known it all along. Others argued that although it was certainly true, it was one thing to live without money and quite another to live without faith. But still most callers laughed and said, "You right. You *know* I know you right. Ain't it the truth, though?" Only a few people, among them Nelson Reed's wife, said nothing and looked very sad.

10 Why they looked sad, however, they would not communicate. And anyone observing their troubled faces would have to trust his own intuition. It is known that Reed's wife, Betty, measured all events against the fullness of her own experience. She was skeptical of everything. Brought to the church after a number of years of living openly with a jazz musician, she had embraced religion when she married Nelson Reed. But though she no longer believed completely in the world, she nonetheless had not fully embraced God. There was something in the nature of Christ's swift rise that had always bothered her, and something in the blood and vengeance of the Old Testament that was mellowing and refreshing. But she had never communicated these thoughts to anyone, especially her husband. Instead, she smiled vacantly while others professed leaps of faith, remained silent when friends spoke fiercely of their convictions. The presence of this vacuum in her contributed to her personal mystery; people said she was beautiful, although she was not outwardly so. Perhaps it was because she wished to protect this inner beauty that she did not smile now, and looked extremely sad, listening to her husband on the telephone.

Nelson Reed had no reason to be sad. He seemed to grow more energized and talkative as the days passed. He was invited by an alderman, on the Tuesday after the initial picket, to tell his story on a local television talk show. He sweated heavily under the hot white lights and attempted to be philosophical. "I notice," the host said to him, "that you are not angry at this exploitative treatment. What, Mr. Reed, is the source of your calm?" The assembly-line worker looked unabashedly into the camera and said, "I have always believed in *Justice* with a capital *J*. I was raised up from a baby believin' that God ain't gonna let nobody go *too* far. See, in *my* mind God is in charge of *all* the capital letters in the alphabet of this world. It say in the Scripture He is Alpha and Omega, the first and the last. He is just about the *onliest* capitalizer they is." Both Reed and the alderman laughed. "Now, when *men* start to capitalize, they gets *greedy*. They put a little *j* in *joy* and a littler one in *justice*. They raise up a big *G* in *Greed* and a big *E* in *Evil*. Well, soon as they commence to put a little *g* in *god,* you can expect some kind of reaction. The Savior will just raise up the *H* in *Hell* and go on from there. And that's just what I'm doin', giving these sharpies *HELL* with a big *H.*"

The talk show host laughed along with Nelson Reed and the alderman. After the taping they drank coffee in the back room of the studio and talked about the sad shape of the world.

Three days before he was to comply with his wife's request, Green, the grocer, saw this talk show on television while at home. The words of Nelson Reed sent a chill through him. Though Reed had attempted to be philosophical, Green did not perceive the statement in this light. Instead, he saw a vindictive-looking black man seated between an ambitious alderman and a smug talk-show host. He saw them chatting comfortably about the nature of evil. The cameraman had shot mostly close-ups, and Green could see the set in Nelson Reed's jaw. The color of Reed's face was maddening. When his children came into the den, the grocer was in a sweat. Before he could think, he had shouted at them and struck the button turning off the set. The two children rushed from the room screaming. Ruth Green ran in from the kitchen. She knew why he was upset because she had received a call about the show; but she said nothing and pretended ignorance. Her children's school had been picketed that day, as it had the day before. But both children were still forbidden to speak of this to their father.

"Where do they get so much power?" Green said to his wife. "Two days ago, nobody would have cared. Now, everywhere, even in my home, I am condemned as a rascal. And what do I own? An airline? A multinational? Half of South America? *No!* I own three stores, one of which happens to be in a certain neighborhood inhabited by people who cost me money to run it." He sighed and sat upright on the sofa, his chubby legs spread wide. "A cab driver has a meter that clicks as he goes along. I pay extra for insurance, iron bars, pilfering by customers and employees. Nothing clicks. But when I add a little overhead to my prices, suddenly everything clicks. But for someone else. When was there such a world?" He pressed the palms of both hands to his temples, suggesting a bombardment of brain-stinging sounds.

This gesture evoked no response from Ruth Green. She remained standing by the door, looking steadily at him. She said, "To protect yourself, I would not stock any more fresh cuts of meat in the store until after the giveaway on Saturday. Also, I would not tell it to the employees until after the first customer of the day has begun to check out. But I would urge you to hire several security guards to close the door promptly at seven-thirty, as is usual." She wanted to say much more than this, but did not. Instead she watched him. He was looking at the blank gray television screen, his palms still pressed against his ears. "In case you need to hear again," she continued in a weighty tone of voice, "I said two days ago, and I say again now, that if you fail to do this you will not see your children again for many years."

15 He twisted his head and looked up at her. "What is the color of these people?" he asked.

"Black," his wife said.

"And what is the name of my children?"

"Green."

The grocer smiled. "There is your answer," he told his wife. "Green is the only color I am interested in."

20 His wife did not smile. "Insufficient," she said.

"The world is mad!" he moaned. "But it is a point of sanity with me to not bend. I will not bend." He crossed his legs and pressed one hand firmly atop his knee. *"I will not bend,"* he said.

"We will see," his wife said.

Nelson Reed, after the television interview, became the acknowledged leader of the disgruntled neighbors. At first a number of them met in the kitchen at his house; then, as space was lacking for curious newcomers, a mass meeting was held on Thursday in an abandoned theater. His wife and three children sat in the front row. Behind them sat the widow Murphy, Lloyd Dukes, Tyrone Brown, Les Jones—those who had joined him on the first picket line. Behind these sat people who bought occasionally at the store, people who lived on the fringes of the neighborhood, people from other neighborhoods come to investigate the problem, and the merely curious. The middle rows were occupied by a few people from the suburbs, those who had seen the talk show and whose outrage at the grocer proved much more powerful than their fear of black people. In the rear of the theater crowded aging, old-style leftists, somber students, cynical young black men with angry grudges to explain with inarticulate gestures. Leaning against the walls, and huddled near the doors at the rear, tape-recorder-bearing social scientists looked as detached and serene as bookies at the track. Here and there, in this diverse crowd, a politician stationed himself, pumping hands vigorously and pressing his palms gently against the shoulders of elderly people. Other visitors passed out leaflets, buttons, glossy color prints of men who promoted causes, the familiar and obscure. There was a hubbub of voices, a blend of the strident and the playful, the outraged and the reverent, lending an undercurrent of ominous energy to the assembly.

Nelson Reed spoke from a platform on the stage, standing before a yellowed, shredded screen that had once reflected the images of matinee idols. "I don't mind sayin' that I have always been a sucker," he told the crowd. "All my life I have been a sucker for the words of Jesus. Being a natural-born fool, I just ain't never had the *sense* to learn no better. Even right today, while the whole world is sayin' wrong is right and up is down, I'm so dumb I'm *still* steady believin' what is wrote in the Good Book . . ."

25 From the audience, especially the front rows, came a chorus singing, "Preach!"

"I have no doubt," he continued in a low baritone, "that it's true what is writ in the Good Book: 'The last shall be first and the first shall be last.' I don't know about y'all, but I have *always* been the last. I never wanted to be the first, but sometimes it look like the world get so bad that them that's holdin' onto the tree of life is the onliest ones left when God commence to blowin' dead leafs off the branches."

"Now you preaching," someone called.

In the rear of the theater a white student shouted an awkward "Amen."

Nelson Reed began walking across the stage to occupy the major part of his nervous energy. But to those in the audience, who now hung on his every word, it looked as though he strutted. "All my life," he said, "I have claimed to be a man without earnin' the right to call myself that. You know, the *average* man ain't really a man. The average man is a *book-licker.* In fact, the *average* man would *run away* if he found hisself standing alone facin' down a adversary. I have done that *too many a time* in my life! But *not no more.* Better to be *once* was than *never* was a man. I will tell you tonight, there is somethin' *wrong* in being average. *I intend to stand up!* Now, if your average man that ain't really a man stand up, two things gonna happen: *One,* he g'on bust through all the weights that been place on his head, and, *two,* he g'on feel a lot of pain. But that same hurt is what make things fall in place. That, and gettin' your hands on one of these slick four-flushers tight enough so's you can squeeze him and say, *'No more!'* You do that, you g'on hurt some, but *you won't be average no more . . .*"

"No more!" a few people in the front rows repeated.

"I say *no more!"* Nelson Reed shouted.

"No more! No more! No more!" The chant rustled through the crowd like the rhythm of an autumn wind against a shedding tree.

Then people laughed and chattered in celebration.

As for the grocer, from the evening of the television interview he had begun to make plans. Unknown to his wife, he cloistered himself several times with his brother-in-law, an insurance salesman, and plotted a course. He had no intention of tossing steaks to the crowd. "And why should I, Tommy?" he asked his wife's brother, a lean, bald-headed man named Thomas. "I don't cheat anyone. I have never cheated anyone. The businesses I run are always on the up-and-up. So why should I pay?"

"Quite so," the brother-in-law said, chewing an unlit cigarillo. "The world has gone crazy. Next they will say that people in my business are responsible for prolonging life. I have found that people who refuse to believe in death refuse also to believe in the harshness of life. I sell well by saying that death is a long happiness. I show people the realities of life and compare this to a funeral with dignity, *and* the promise of a bundle for every loved one salted away. When they look around hard at life, they usually buy."

"So?" asked Green. Thomas was a college graduate with a penchant for philosophy.

"So," Thomas answered. "You must fight to show these people the reality of both your situation and theirs. How would it be if you visited one of their meetings and chalked out, on a blackboard, the dollars and cents of your operation? Explain your overhead, your security fees, all the additional expenses. If you treat them with respect, they might understand."

Green frowned. "That I would never do," he said. "It would be admission of a certain guilt."

The brother-in-law smiled, but only with one corner of his mouth. "Then you have something to feel guilty about?" he asked.

The grocer frowned at him. *"Nothing!"* he said with great emphasis.

"So?" Thomas said.

This first meeting between the grocer and his brother-in-law took place on Thursday, in a crowded barroom.

At the second meeting, in a luncheonette, it was agreed that the grocer should speak privately with the leader of the group, Nelson Reed. The meeting at which this was agreed took place on Friday afternoon. After accepting this advice from Thomas, the grocer resigned himself to explain to Reed, in as finite detail as possible, the economic structure of his operation. He vowed to suppress no information. He would explain everything: inventories, markups, sale items, inflation, balance sheets, specialty items, overhead, and that mysterious item called profit. This last item, promising to be the most difficult to explain, Green and his brother-in-law debated over for several hours. They agreed first of all that a man should not work for free, then they agreed that it was unethical to ruthlessly exploit. From these parameters, they staked out an area between fifteen and forty percent, and agreed that someplace between these two borders lay an amount of return that could be called fair. This was easy, but then Thomas introduced the factor of circumstance. He questioned whether the fact that one serviced a risky area justified the earning of profits closer to the forty-percent edge of the scale. Green was unsure. Thomas smiled. "Here is a case that will point out an analogy," he said, licking a cigarillo. "I read in the papers that a family wants to sell an electric stove. I call the home and the man says fifty dollars. I ask to come out and inspect the merchandise. When I arrive I see they are poor, have already bought a new stove that is connected, and are selling the old one for fifty dollars because they want it out of the place. The electric stove is in good condition, worth much more than fifty. But because I see what I see I offer forty-five."

Green, for some reason, wrote down this figure on the back of the sales slip for the coffee they were drinking.

The brother-in-law smiled. He chewed his cigarillo. "The man agrees to take forty-five dollars, saying he has had no other calls. I look at the stove again and see a spot of rust. I say I will give him forty dollars. He agrees to this, on condition that I myself haul it away. I say I will haul it away if he comes down to thirty. You, of course, see where I am going."

The grocer nodded. "The circumstances of his situation, his need to get rid of the stove quickly, placed him in a position where he has little room to bargain?"

"Yes," Thomas answered. "So? Is it ethical, Harry?"

Harold Green frowned. He had never liked his brother-in-law, and now he thought the insurance agent was being crafty. "But," he answered, "this man does not *have* to sell! It is his choice whether to wait for other calls. It is not the fault of the buyer that the seller is in a hurry. It is the right of the buyer to get what he wants at the lowest price possible. That is the rule. That has *always* been the rule. And the reverse of it applies to the seller as well."

"Yes," Thomas said, sipping coffee from the Styrofoam cup. "But suppose that in addition to his hurry to sell, the owner was also of a weak soul. There are, after all, many such people." He smiled. "Suppose he placed no value on the money?"

"Then," Green answered, "your example is academic. Here we are not talking about real life. One man lives by the code, one man does not. Who is there free enough to make a judgment?" He laughed. "Now you see," he told his brother-in-law. "Much more than a few dollars are at stake. If this one buyer is to be condemned, then so are most people in the history of the world. An examination of history provides the only answer to your question. This code will be here tomorrow, long after the ones who do not honor it are not."

They argued fiercely late into the afternoon, the brother-in-law leaning heavily on his readings. When they parted, a little before 5:00 P.M., nothing had been resolved.

Neither was much resolved during the meeting between Green and Nelson Reed. Reached at home by the grocer in the early evening, the leader of the group spoke coldly at first, but consented finally to meet his adversary at a nearby drugstore for coffee and a talk. They met at the lunch counter, shook hands awkwardly, and sat for a few minutes discussing the weather. Then the grocer pulled two gray ledgers from his briefcase. "You have for years come into my place," he told the man. "In my memory I have always treated you well. Now our relationship has come to this." He slid the books along the counter until they touched Nelson Reed's arm.

Reed opened the top book and flipped the thick green pages with his thumb. He did not examine the figures. "All I know," he said, "is over at your place a can of soup cost me fifty-five cents, and two miles away at your other store for white folks you chargin' thirty-nine cents." He said this with the calm authority of an outraged soul. A quality of condescension tinged with pity crept into his gaze.

The grocer drummed his fingers on the counter top. He twisted his head and looked away, toward shelves containing cosmetics, laxatives, toothpaste. His eyes lingered on a poster of a woman's apple red lips and milk white teeth. The rest of the face was missing.

55 "Ain't no use to hide," Nelson Reed said, as to a child. "*I* know you wrong, *you* know you wrong, and before I finish, *everybody in this city* g'on know you wrong. God don't *like* ugly." He closed his eyes and gripped the cup of coffee. Then he swung his head suddenly and faced the grocer again. "Man, why you want to *do* people that way?" he asked. "We human, same as you."

"Before *God!*" Green exclaimed, looking squarely into the face of Nelson Reed. "Before God!" he said again. *"I am not an evil man!"* These last words sounded more like a moan as he tightened the muscles in his throat to lower the sound of his voice. He tossed his left shoulder as if adjusting the sleeve of his coat, or as if throwing off some unwanted weight. Then he peered along the counter top. No one was watching. At the end of the counter the waitress was scrubbing the coffee urn. "Look at these figures, please," he said to Reed.

The man did not drop his gaze. His eyes remained fixed on the grocer's face.

"All right," Green said. "Don't look. I'll tell you what is in these books, believe me if you want. I work twelve hours a day, one day off per week, running my business in three stores. I am not a wealthy person. In one place, in the area you call white, I get by barely by smiling lustily at old ladies, stocking gourmet stuff on the chance I will build a reputation as a quality store. The two clerks there cheat me; there is nothing I can do. In this business you must be friendly with everybody. The second place is on the other side of town, in a neighborhood as poor as this one. I get out there seldom. The profits are not worth the gas. I use the loss there as a write-off against some other properties." He paused. "Do you understand write-off?" he asked Nelson Reed.

"Naw," the man said.

60 Harold Green laughed. "What does it matter?" he said in a tone of voice intended for himself alone. "In this area I will admit I make a profit, but it is not so much as you think. But I do not make a profit here because the people are black. I make a profit because a profit is here to be made. I invest more here in window bars, theft losses, insurance, spoilage; I deserve to make more here than at the other places." He looked, almost imploringly, at the man seated next to him. "You don't accept this as the right of a man in business?"

Reed grunted. "Did the bear shit in the woods?" he said.

Again Green laughed. He gulped his coffee awkwardly, as if eager to go. Yet his motions slowed once he had set the coffee cup down on the blue plastic saucer. "Place yourself in *my* situation," he said, his voice high and tentative. "If *you* were running my store in this neighborhood, what would be *your* position? Say on a profit scale of fifteen to forty percent, at what point in between would you draw the line?"

Nelson Reed thought. He sipped his coffee and seemed to chew the liquid. "Fifteen to forty?" he repeated.

"Yes."

"I'm a churchgoin' man," he said. "Closer to fifteen than to forty."

"How close?"

Nelson thought. "In church you tithe ten percent."

"In restaurants you tip fifteen," the grocer said quickly.

"All right," Reed said. "Over fifteen."

"How much over?"

Nelson Reed thought.

"Twenty, thirty, thirty-five?" Green chanted, leaning closer to Reed.

Still the man thought.

"Forty? Maybe even forty-five or fifty?" the grocer breathed in Reed's ear. "In the supermarkets, you know, they have more subtle ways of accomplishing such feats."

Reed slapped his coffee cup with the back of his right hand. The brown liquid swirled across the counter top, wetting the books. *"Damn this!"* he shouted.

Startled, Green rose from his stool.

Nelson Reed was trembling. "I ain't *you,"* he said in a deep baritone. "I ain't the *supermarket* neither. All I is is a poor man that works *too* hard to see his pay slip through his fingers like rainwater. All I know is you done *cheat* me, you done *cheat* everybody in the neighborhood, and we organized now to get some of it *back!"* Then he stood and faced the grocer. "My daddy sharecropped down in Mississippi and bought in the company store. He owed them twenty-three years when he died. I paid off five of them years and then run away to up here. Now, I'm a deacon in the Baptist church. I raised my kids the way my daddy raise me and don't bother nobody. Now come to find out, after all my runnin', they done lift that *same company store* up out of Mississippi and slip it down on us here! Well, my daddy was a *fighter,* and if he hadn't owed all them years he would of raise him some hell. Me, I'm steady my daddy's child, plus I got seniority in my union. I'm a free man. Buddy, don't you know *I'm gonna raise me some hell!"*

Harold Green reached for a paper napkin to sop the coffee soaking into his books.

Nelson Reed threw a dollar on top of the books and walked away.

"I *will not* do it!" Harold Green said to his wife that same evening. They were in the bathroom of their home. Bending over the face bowl, she was washing her hair with a towel draped around her neck. The grocer stood by the door, looking in at her. "I will not bankrupt myself tomorrow," he said.

"I've been thinking about it, too," Ruth Green said, shaking her wet hair. "You'll do it, Harry."

"Why should I?" he asked. "You won't leave. You know it was a bluff. I've waited this long for you to calm down. Tomorrow is Saturday. This week has been a hard one. Tonight let's be realistic."

"Of course you'll do it," Ruth Green said. She said it the way she would say "Have some toast." She said, "You'll do it because you want to see your children grow up."

"And for what other reason?" he asked.

85 She pulled the towel tighter around her neck. "Because you are at heart a moral man."

He grinned painfully. "If I am, why should I have to prove it to *them?*"

"Not them," Ruth Green said, freezing her movements and looking in the mirror. "Certainly not them. By no means them. They have absolutely nothing to do with this."

"Who, then?" he asked, moving from the door into the room. "Who else should I prove something to?"

His wife was crying. But her entire face was wet. The tears moved secretly down her face.

90 "Who else?" Harold Green asked.

It was almost 11:00 P.M. and the children were in bed. They had also cried when they came home from school. Ruth Green said, "For yourself, Harry. For the love that lives inside your heart."

All night the grocer thought about this.

Nelson Reed also slept little that Friday night. When he returned home from the drugstore, he reported to his wife as much of the conversation as he could remember. At first he had joked about the exchange between himself and the grocer, but as more details returned to his conscious mind he grew solemn and then bitter. "He ask me to put myself in *his* place," Reed told his wife. "Can you imagine that kind of gumption? I never cheated nobody in my life. All my life I have lived on Bible principles. I am a deacon in the church. I have work all my life for other folks and I don't even own the house I live in." He paced up and down the kitchen, his big arms flapping loosely at his sides. Betty Reed sat at the table, watching. "This here's a low-down, ass-kicking world," he said. "I swear to God it is! All my life I have lived on principle and I ain't got a dime in the bank. Betty," he turned suddenly toward her, "don't you think I'm a fool?"

"Mr. Reed," she said. "Let's go on to bed."

95 But he would not go to bed. Instead, he took the fifth of bourbon from the cabinet under the sink and poured himself a shot. His wife refused to join him. Reed drained the glass of whiskey, and then another, while he resumed pacing the kitchen floor. He slapped his hands against his sides. "*I* think I'm a fool," he said. "Ain't got a dime in the bank, ain't got a pot to *pee* in or a wall to pitch it over, and that there *cheat* ask me to put myself inside *his* shoes. Hell, I can't even *afford* the kind of shoes he wears." He stopped pacing and looked at his wife.

"Mr. Reed," she whispered, "tomorrow ain't a work day. Let's go to bed."

Nelson Reed laughed, the bitterness in his voice rattling his wife. "The *hell* I will!" he said.

He strode to the yellow telephone on the wall beside the sink and began to dial. The first call was to Lloyd Dukes, a neighbor two blocks away and a lieutenant in the organization. Dukes was not at home. The second call was to McElroy's Bar on the corner of 65th and Carroll, where Stanley Harper, another of the lieutenants, worked as a bartender. It was Harper who spread the word, among those men at the bar, that the organization would picket the grocer's store the following morning. And all through the night, in the bedroom of their house, Betty Reed was awakened by telephone calls coming from Lester Jones, Nat Lucas, Mrs. Tyrone Brown, the widow-woman named Murphy, all coordinating the time when they would march in a group against the store owned by Harold Green. Betty Reed's heart beat loudly beneath the covers as she listened to the bitterness and rage in her husband's voice. On several occasions, hearing him declare himself a fool, she pressed the pillow against her eyes and cried.

The grocer opened later than usual this Saturday morning, but still it was early enough to make him one of the first walkers in the neighborhood. He parked his car one block from the store and strolled to work. There were no birds singing. The sky in this area was not blue. It was smog-smutted and gray, seeming on the verge of a light rain. The street, as always, was littered with cans, papers, bits of broken glass. As always the garbage cans overflowed. The morning breeze plastered a sheet of newspaper playfully around the sides of a rusted garbage can. For some reason, using his right foot, he loosened the paper and stood watching it slide into the street and down the block. The movement made him feel good. He whistled while unlocking the bars shielding the windows and door of his store. When he had unlocked the main door he stepped in quickly and threw a switch to the right of the jamb, before the shrill sound of the alarm could shatter his mood. Then he switched on the lights. Everything was as it had been the night before. He had already telephoned his two employees and given them the day off. He busied himself doing the usual things—hauling milk and vegetables from the cooler, putting cash in the till—not thinking about the silence of his wife, or the look in her eyes, only an hour before when he left home. He had determined, at some point while driving through the city, that today it would be business as usual. But he expected very few customers.

The first customer of the day was Mrs. Nelson Reed. She came in around 9:30 A.M. and wandered about the store. He watched her from the checkout counter. She seemed uncertain of what she wanted to buy. She kept glancing at him down the center aisle. His suspicions aroused, he said finally, "Yes, may I help you, Mrs. Reed?" His words caused her to jerk, as if some devious thought had been perceived going through her mind. She reached over quickly and lifted a loaf of whole wheat bread from the rack and walked with it to the counter. She looked at him and smiled. The smile was a broad, shy one, that rare kind of smile one sees on virgin girls when they first confess love to themselves. Betty Reed was a woman of about forty-five. For some reason he could not comprehend, this gesture touched him. When she pulled a dollar from her purse and laid it on the counter, an impulse, from no place he could locate with his mind, seized control of his tongue. "Free," he told Betty Reed. She paused, then pushed the dollar toward him with a firm and determined thrust of her arm. "Free," he heard himself saying strongly, his right palm spread and meeting her thrust with absolute force. She clutched the loaf of bread and walked out of his store.

The next customer, a little girl, arriving well after 10:30 A.M., selected a candy bar from the rack beside the counter. "Free," Green said cheerfully. The little girl left the candy on the counter and ran out of the store.

At 11:15 A.M. a wino came in looking desperate enough to sell his soul. The grocer watched him only for an instant. Then he went to the wine counter and selected a half-gallon of medium-grade red wine. He shoved the jug into the belly of the wino, the man's sour breath bathing his face. "Free," the grocer said. "But you must not drink it in here."

He felt good about the entire world, watching the wino through the window gulping the wine and looking guiltily around.

At 11:25 A.M. the pickets arrived.

Two dozen people, men and women, young and old, crowded the pavement in front of his store. Their signs, placards, and voices denounced him as a parasite. The grocer laughed inside himself. He felt lighthearted and wild, like a man drugged. He rushed to the meat counter and pulled a long roll of brown wrapping paper from the rack, tearing it neatly with a quick shift of his body resembling a dance step practiced fervently in his youth. He laid the paper on the chopping block and with the black-inked, felt-tipped marker scrawled, in giant letters, the word FREE. This he took to the window and pasted in place with many strands of Scotch tape. He was laughing wildly. "Free!" he shouted from behind the brown paper. "Free! Free! Free! Free! Free! Free!" He rushed to the door, pushed his head out, and screamed to the confused crowd, *"Free!"* Then he ran back to the counter and stood behind it, like a soldier at attention.

They came in slowly.

Nelson Reed entered first, working his right foot across the dirty tile as if tracking a squiggling worm. The other followed: Lloyd Dukes dragging a placard, Mr. and Mrs. Tyrone Brown, Stanley Harper walking with his fists clenched. Lester Jones with three of his children, Nat Lucas looking sheepish and detached, a clutch of winos, several bashful nuns, ironic-smiling teenagers and a few students. Bringing up the rear was a bearded social scientist holding a tape recorder to his chest. "Free!" the grocer screamed. He threw up his arms in a gesture that embraced, or dismissed, the entire store. *"All free!"* he shouted. He was grinning with the grace of a madman.

The winos began grabbing first. They stripped the shelf of wine in a matter of seconds. Then they fled, dropping bottles on the tile in their wake. The others, stepping quickly through this liquid, soon congealed it into a sticky, blood-like consistency. The young men went for the cigarettes and luncheon meats and beer. One of them had the prescience to grab a sack from the counter, while the others loaded their arms swiftly, hugging cartons and packages of cold cuts like long-lost friends. The students joined them, less for greed than for the thrill of the experience. The two nuns backed toward the door. As for the older people, men and women, they stood at first as if stuck to the wine-smeared floor. Then Stanley Harper, the bartender, shouted, "The man said *free,* y'all heard him." He paused. "Didn't you say *free* now?" he called to the grocer.

"I said free," Harold Green answered, his temples pounding.

A cheer went up. The older people began grabbing, as if the secret lusts of a lifetime had suddenly seized command of their arms and eyes. They grabbed toilet tissue, cold cuts, pickles, sardines, boxes of raisins, boxes of starch, cans of soup, tins of tuna fish and salmon, bottles of spices, cans of boned chicken, slippery cans of olive oil. Here a man, Lester Jones, burdened himself with several heads of lettuce, while his wife, in another aisle, shouted for him to drop those small items and concentrate on the gourmet section. She herself took imported sardines, wheat crackers, bottles of candied pickles, herring, anchovies, imported olives, French wafers, an ancient, half-rusted can of paté, stocked, by mistake, from the inventory of another store. Others packed their arms with detergents, hams, chocolate-coated cereal, whole chickens with hanging asses, wedges of bologna and salami like squashed footballs, chunks of cheeses, yellow and white, shriveled onions, and green peppers. Mrs. Tyrone Brown hung a curve of pepperoni around her neck and seemed to take on instant dignity, much like a person of noble birth in possession now of a long sought-after gem. Another woman, the widow Murphy, stuffed tomatoes into her bosom, holding a half-chewed lemon in her mouth. The more enterprising fought desperately over the three rusted shopping carts, and the victors wheeled these along the narrow aisles, sweeping into them bulk items—beer in six-packs, sacks of sugar, flour, glass bottles of syrup, toilet cleanser, sugar cookies, prune, apple and tomato juices—while others endeavored to snatch the carts from them. There were several fistfights and much cursing. The grocer, standing behind the counter, hummed and rang his cash register like a madman.

Nelson Reed, the first into the store, followed the nuns out, empty-handed.

In less than half an hour the others had stripped the store and vanished in many directions up and down the block. But still more people came, those late in hearing the news. And when they saw the shelves were bare, they cursed soberly and chased those stragglers still bearing away goods. Soon only the grocer and the social scientist remained, the latter stationed at the door with his tape recorder sucking in leftover sounds. Then he too slipped away up the block.

By 12:10 P.M. the grocer was leaning against the counter, trying to make his mind slow down. Not a man given to drink during work hours, he nonetheless took a swallow from a bottle of wine, a dusty bottle from beneath the wine shelf, somehow overlooked by the winos. Somewhat recovered, he was preparing to remember what he should do next when he glanced toward a figure at the door. Nelson Reed was standing there, watching him.

"All gone," Harold Green said. "My friend, Mr. Reed, there is no more." Still the man stood in the doorway, peering into the store.

The grocer waved his arms about the empty room. Not a display case had a single item standing. "All gone," he said again, as if addressing a stupid child. "There is nothing left to get. You, my friend, have come back too late for a second load. I am cleaned out."

Nelson Reed stepped into the store and strode toward the counter. He moved through wine-stained flour, lettuce leaves, red, green, and blue labels, bits and pieces of broken glass. He walked toward the counter.

"All day," the grocer laughed, not quite hysterically now, "all day long I have not made a single cent of profit. The entire day was a loss. This store, like the others, is *bleeding* me." He waved his arms about the room in a magnificent gesture of uncaring loss. "Now do you understand?" he said. "Now will you put yourself in my shoes? I have nothing here. Come, now, Mr. Reed, would it not be so bad a thing to walk in my shoes?"

"Mr. Green," Nelson Reed said coldly. "My wife bought a loaf of bread in here this mornin'. She forgot to pay you. I, myself, have come here to pay you your money."

"Oh," the grocer said.

"I think it was brown bread. Don't that cost more than white?"

The two men looked away from each other, but not at anything in the store.

"In my store, yes," Harold Green said. He rang the register with the most casual movement of his finger. The register read fifty-five cents.

Nelson Reed held out a dollar.

"And two cents tax," the grocer said.

The man held out the dollar.

"After all," Harold Green said. "We are all, after all, Mr. Reed, in debt to the government."

He rang the register again. It read fifty-seven cents.

Nelson Reed held out a dollar.

READING AND REACTING

1. Considering the gravity of the situation he describes, why do you think McPherson chooses the simple title "A Loaf of Bread"?

2. Is the grocer presented as a stereotype or as a three-dimensional character? Explain.
3. In paragraph 1 the narrator says, "through some mysterious access to a television station, the poor folk were now empowered to make denunciations of the grocer." Is the narrator denying the legitimacy of the people's complaints, or is he making some other point? Explain.
4. Several times in the story Harold Green says, "I did not make this world. . . . I only make my way in it" (4). How justifiable is this position in light of recent events in some American cities? Do you agree with Green when he says that if he closed his store, someone else would come in and do the same thing he did?
5. The grocer's position is opposed by his wife, Ruth, and by the leader of the picketers, Nelson Reed. In what way do their contrasting stands suggest a theme of the story?
6. To what degree are the characters in the story in control of events? To what degree are they swept along by events that have gotten out of control?
7. In the middle of the story, Harold Green attempts unsuccessfully to explain his position to Nelson Reed. At the end of the story, after he has given away all his merchandise, Green asks Nelson, "Now do you understand? . . . Now will you put yourself in my shoes?" Do these characters ever come to understand each other's situations, or are there some things they never understand?
8. **JOURNAL ENTRY:** Is the dispute between Harold Green and Nelson Reed about overpricing, or is it really about something else? Explain.

WRITING SUGGESTIONS: THEME

1. The major characters in both "Doe Season" and "Two Kinds" learn a hard lesson. Write an essay in which you compare the lessons that Andy and Jing-mei learn and discuss what effect their knowledge has on them.
2. In "Silence" Tadeusz Borowski writes about prisoners who have just been liberated from a Nazi concentration camp and who have knowledge they are unable to put into words. Write an essay in which you discuss how the prisoners' silence reinforces a major theme of the story.
3. Both "Two Kinds" and "A Loaf of Bread" are about struggles between two strong-willed people. How are the struggles alike? How are they different?

4. Both "Doe Season" and "Silence" deal with violence. How do the two stories' treatments of this subject differ?

5. Like "Doe Season," the poem "Rainbow" by Robert Huff (printed below) also focuses on a child's experience with hunting. How is its central theme different from the central theme of "Doe Season"?

RAINBOW

After the shot the driven feathers rock
In the air and are by sunlight trapped.
Their moment of descent is eloquent.
It is the rainbow echo of a bird
Whose thunder, stopped, puts in my daughter's eyes
A question mark. She does not see the rainbow,
And the folding bird-fall was for her too quick.
It is about the stillness of the bird
Her eyes are asking. She is three years old;
Has cut her fingers; found blood tastes of salt;
But she has never witnessed quiet blood,
Nor ever seen before the peace of death.
I say: "The feathers—Look!" but she is torn
And wretched and draws back. And I am glad
That I have wounded her, have winged her heart,
And that she goes beyond my fathering.

STORIES

FOR FURTHER READING

T. Coraghessan Boyle
(1948–)

GREASY LAKE
(1985)

It's about a mile down on the dark side of Route 88.
Bruce Springsteen

There was a time when courtesy and winning ways went out of style, when it was good to be bad, when you cultivated decadence like a taste. We were all dangerous characters then. We wore torn-up leather jackets, slouched around with toothpicks in our mouths, sniffed glue and ether and what somebody claimed was cocaine. When we wheeled our parents' whining station wagons out into the street we left a patch of rubber half a block long. We drank gin and grape juice, Tango, Thunderbird, and Bali Hai. We were nineteen. We were bad. We read André Gide[1] and struck elaborate poses to show that we didn't give a shit about anything. At night, we went up to Greasy Lake.

Through the center of town, up the strip, past the housing developments and shopping malls, street lights giving way to the thin streaming illumination of the headlights, trees crowding the asphalt in a black unbroken wall: that was the way out to Greasy Lake. The Indians had called it Wakan, a reference to the clarity of its waters. Now it was fetid and murky, the mud banks glittering with broken glass and strewn with beer cans and the charred remains of bonfires. There was a single ravaged island a hundred yards from shore, so stripped of vegetation it looked as if the air force had strafed it. We went up to the lake because everyone went there, because we wanted to snuff the rich scent of possibility on the breeze, watch a girl take off her clothes and plunge into the festering murk, drink beer, smoke pot, howl at the stars, savor the incongruous

---

[1] André Gide (1869–1951). French novelist and critic whose work—much of it semiautobiographical—examines the conflict between desire and discipline and shows individuals battling conventional morality.

full-throated roar of rock and roll against the primeval susurrus of frogs and crickets. This was nature.

I was there one night, late, in the company of two dangerous characters. Digby wore a gold star in his right ear and allowed his father to pay his tuition at Cornell; Jeff was thinking of quitting school to become a painter/musician/head-shop proprietor. They were both expert in the social graces, quick with a sneer, able to manage a Ford with lousy shocks over a rutted and gutted blacktop road at eighty-five while rolling a joint as compact as a Tootsie Roll Pop stick. They could lounge against a bank of booming speakers and trade "man"s with the best of them or roll out across the dance floor as if their joints worked on bearings. They were slick and quick and they wore their mirror shades at breakfast and dinner, in the shower, in closets and caves. In short, they were bad.

I drove. Digby pounded the dashboard and shouted along with Toots & the Maytals while Jeff hung his head out the window and streaked the side of my mother's Bel Air with vomit. It was early June, the air soft as a hand on your cheek, the third night of summer vacation. The first two nights we'd been out till dawn, looking for something we never found. On this, the third night, we'd cruised the strip sixty-seven times, been in and out of every bar and club we could think of in a twenty-mile radius, stopped twice for bucket chicken and forty-cent hamburgers, debated going to a party at the house of a girl Jeff's sister knew, and chucked two dozen raw eggs at mailboxes and hitchhikers. It was 2:00 A.M.; the bars were closing. There was nothing to do but take a bottle of lemon-flavored gin up to Greasy Lake.

5 The taillights of a single car winked at us as we swung into the dirt lot with its tufts of weed and washboard corrugations; '57 Chevy, mint, metallic blue. On the far side of the lot, like the exoskeleton of some gaunt chrome insect, a chopper leaned against its kickstand. And that was it for excitement: some junkie half-wit biker and a car freak pumping his girlfriend. Whatever it was we were looking for, we weren't about to find it at Greasy Lake. Not that night.

But then all of a sudden Digby was fighting for the wheel. "Hey, that's Tony Lovett's car! Hey!" he shouted, while I stabbed at the brake pedal and the Bel Air nosed up to the gleaming bumper of the parked Chevy. Digby leaned on the horn, laughing, and instructed me to put my brights on. I flicked on the brights. This was hilarious. A joke. Tony would experience premature withdrawal and expect to be confronted by grim-looking state troopers with flashlights. We hit the horn, strobed the lights, and then jumped out of the car to press our witty faces to Tony's windows; for all we knew we might even catch a glimpse of some little fox's tit, and then we could slap backs with red-faced Tony, roughhouse a little, and go on to new heights of adventure and daring.

The first mistake, the one that opened the whole floodgate, was losing my grip on the keys. In the excitement, leaping from the car with the gin in one hand and a roach clip in the other, I spilled them in the grass—in the dark, rank, mysterious nighttime grass of Greasy Lake. This was a tactical error, as damaging and irreversible in its way as Westmoreland's decision to dig in at Khe Sanh.[2] I felt it like a jab of intuition, and I stopped there by the open door, peering vaguely into the night that puddled up round my feet.

The second mistake—and this was inextricably bound up with the first—was identifying the car as Tony Lovett's. Even before the very bad character in greasy jeans and engineer boots ripped out of the driver's door, I began to realize that this chrome blue was much lighter than the robin's-egg of Tony's car, and that Tony's car didn't have rear-mounted speakers. Judging from their expressions, Digby and Jeff were privately groping toward the same inevitable and unsettling conclusion as I was.

In any case, there was no reasoning with this bad greasy character—clearly he was a man of action. The first lusty Rockette[3] kick of his steel-toed boot caught me under the chin, chipped my favorite tooth, and left me sprawled in the dirt. Like a fool, I'd gone down on one knee to comb the stiff hacked grass for the keys, my mind making connections in the most dragged-out, testudineous way, knowing that things had gone wrong, that I was in a lot of trouble, and that the lost ignition key was my grail and my salvation. The three or four succeeding blows were mainly absorbed by my right buttock and the tough piece of bone at the base of my spine.

10 Meanwhile, Digby vaulted the kissing bumpers and delivered a savage kung-fu blow to the greasy character's collarbone. Digby had just finished a course in martial arts for phys-ed credit and had spent the better part of the past two nights telling us apocryphal tales of Bruce Lee types and of the raw power invested in lightning blows shot from coiled wrists, ankles, and elbows. The greasy character was unimpressed. He merely backed off a step, his face like a Toltec mask, and laid Digby out with a single whistling roundhouse blow . . . but by now Jeff had got into the act, and I was beginning to extricate myself from the dirt, a tinny compound of shock, rage, and impotence wadded in my throat.

Jeff was on the guy's back, biting at his ear. Digby was on the ground, cursing. I went for the tire iron I kept under the driver's seat. I kept it there because bad characters always keep tire irons under the driver's seat, for just such an occasion as this. Never mind that I hadn't been involved in a fight since sixth grade, when a kid with a sleepy eye

---

[2] In late 1967 North Vietnamese and Viet Cong forces mounted a strong attack against American troops at Khe Sanh, thereby causing General William C. Westmoreland, commander of U.S. forces in Vietnam, to "dig in" to defend an area of relatively little tactical importance.

[3] Famed dancing troupe at New York's Radio City Music Hall, noted for their precision and can-can-like high kicks.

and two streams of mucus depending from his nostrils hit me in the knee with a Louisville slugger,[4] never mind that I'd touched the tire iron exactly twice before, to change tires: it was there. And I went for it.

I was terrified. Blood was beating in my ears, my hands were shaking, my heart turning over like a dirtbike in the wrong gear. My antagonist was shirtless, and a single cord of muscle flashed across his chest as he bent forward to peel Jeff from his back like a wet overcoat. "Motherfucker," he spat, over and over, and I was aware in that instant that all four of us—Digby, Jeff, and myself included—were chanting "motherfucker, motherfucker," as if it were a battle cry. (What happened next? the detective asks the murderer from beneath the turned-down brim of his porkpie hat. I don't know, the murderer says, something came over me. Exactly.)

Digby poked the flat of his hand in the bad character's face and I came at him like a kamikaze, mindless, raging, stung with humiliation—the whole thing, from the initial boot in the chin to this murderous primal instant involving no more than sixty hyperventilating, gland-flooding seconds—I came at him and brought the tire iron down across his ear. The effect was instantaneous, astonishing. He was a stunt man and this was Hollywood, he was a big grimacing toothy balloon and I was a man with a straight pin. He collapsed. Wet his pants. Went loose in his boots.

A single second, big as a zeppelin, floated by. We were standing over him in a circle, gritting our teeth, jerking our necks, our limbs and hands and feet twitching with glandular discharges. No one said anything. We just stared down at the guy, the car freak, the lover, the bad greasy character laid low. Digby looked at me; so did Jeff. I was still holding the tire iron, a tuft of hair clinging to the crook like dandelion fluff, like down. Rattled, I dropped it in the dirt, already envisioning the headlines, the pitted faces of the police inquisitors, the gleam of handcuffs, clank of bars, the big black shadows rising from the back of the cell . . . when suddenly a raw torn shriek cut through me like all the juice in all the electric chairs in the country.

15 It was the fox. She was short, barefoot, dressed in panties and a man's shirt. "Animals!" she screamed, running at us with her fists clenched and wisps of blow-dried hair in her face. There was a silver chain round her ankle, and her toenails flashed in the glare of the headlights. I think it was the toenails that did it. Sure, the gin and the cannabis and even the Kentucky Fried may have had a hand in it, but it was the sight of those flaming toes that set us off—the toad emerging from the loaf in *Virgin Spring,*[5] lipstick smeared on a child: she was already tainted. We were on her like Bergman's deranged brothers—see no evil, hear none, speak none—panting, wheezing, tearing at her clothes, grabbing for flesh. We

---

[4] A popular brand of baseball bat.

[5] Film by Swedish director Ingmar Bergman.

were bad characters, and we were scared and hot and three steps over the line—anything could have happened.

It didn't.

Before we could pin her to the hood of the car, our eyes masked with lust and greed and the purest primal badness, a pair of headlights swung into the lot. There we were, dirty, bloody, guilty, dissociated from humanity and civilization, the first of the Ur-crimes behind us, the second in progress, shreds of nylon panty and spandex brassiere dangling from our fingers, our flies open, lips licked—there we were, caught in the spotlight. Nailed.

We bolted. First for the car, and then, realizing we had no way of starting it, for the woods. I thought nothing. I thought escape. The headlights came at me like accusing fingers. I was gone.

Ram-bam-bam, across the parking lot, past the chopper and into the feculent undergrowth at the lake's edge, insects flying up in my face, weeds whipping, frogs and snakes and red-eyed turtles splashing off into the night: I was already ankle-deep in muck and tepid water and still going strong. Behind me, the girl's screams rose in intensity, disconsolate, incriminating, the screams of the Sabine women,[6] the Christian martyrs, Anne Frank[7] dragged from the garret. I kept going, pursued by those cries, imagining cops and bloodhounds. The water was up to my knees when I realized what I was doing: I was going to swim for it. Swim the breadth of Greasy Lake and hide myself in the thick clot of woods on the far side. They'd never find me there.

20 I was breathing in sobs, in gasps. The water lapped at my waist as I looked out over the moon-burnished ripples, the mats of algae that clung to the surface like scabs. Digby and Jeff had vanished. I paused. Listened. The girl was quieter now, screams tapering to sobs, but there were male voices, angry, excited, and the high-pitched ticking of the second car's engine. I waded deeper, stealthy, hunted, the ooze sucking at my sneakers. As I was about to take the plunge—at the very instant I dropped my shoulder for the first slashing stroke—I blundered into something. Something unspeakable, obscene, something soft, wet, moss-grown. A patch of weed? A log? When I reached out to touch it, it gave like a rubber duck, it gave like flesh.

In one of those nasty little epiphanies for which we are prepared by films and TV and childhood visits to the funeral home to ponder the shrunken painted forms of dead grandparents, I understood what it was

---

[6] According to legend, members of an ancient Italian tribe abducted by Romans who took them for wives. The "Rape of the Sabine Women" has been depicted by various artists, most notably by seventeenth-century French painter Nicolas Poussin.

[7] Anne Frank (1929–1945). German Jewish girl whose family was forced to hide in an attic in Amsterdam during the Nazi occupation of the Netherlands. Frank, who along with her family was discovered by storm troopers and sent to die at the concentration camp at Belsen, is famous for her diary, which recounts her days in hiding.

that bobbed there so inadmissibly in the dark. Understood, and stumbled back in horror and revulsion, my mind yanked in six different directions (I was nineteen, a mere child, an infant, and here in the space of five minutes I'd struck down one greasy character and blundered into the waterlogged carcass of a second), thinking, The keys, the keys, why did I have to go and lose the keys? I stumbled back, but the muck took hold of my feet—a sneaker snagged, balance lost—and suddenly I was pitching face forward into the buoyant black mass, throwing out my hands in desperation while simultaneously conjuring the image of reeking frogs and muskrats revolving in slicks of their own deliquescing juices. AAAAArrrgh! I shot from the water like a torpedo, the dead man rotating to expose a mossy beard and eyes cold as the moon. I must have shouted out, thrashing around in the weeds, because the voices behind me suddenly became animated.

"What was that?"

"It's them, it's them: they tried to, tried to . . . *rape* me!" Sobs.

A man's voice, flat Midwestern accent. "You sons a bitches, we'll kill you!"

Frogs, crickets.

Then another voice, harsh, *r*-less, Lower East Side: "Motherfucker!" I recognized the verbal virtuosity of the bad greasy character in the engineer boots. Tooth chipped, sneakers gone, coated in mud and slime and worse, crouching breathless in the weeds waiting to have my ass thoroughly and definitively kicked and fresh from the hideous stinking embrace of a three-days-dead-corpse, I suddenly felt a rush of joy and vindication: the son of a bitch was alive! Just as quickly, my bowels turned to ice. "Come on out of there, you pansy mothers!" the bad greasy character was screaming. He shouted curses till he was out of breath.

The crickets started up again, then the frogs. I held my breath. All at once there was a sound in the reeds, a swishing, a splash: thunk-a-thunk. They were throwing rocks. The frogs fell silent. I cradled my head. Swish, swish, thunk-a-thunk. A wedge of feldspar the size of a cue ball glanced off my knee. I bit my finger.

It was then that they turned to the car. I heard a door slam, a curse, and then the sound of the headlights shattering—almost a good-natured sound, celebratory, like corks popping from the necks of bottles. This was succeeded by the dull booming of the fenders, metal on metal, and then the icy crash of the windshield. I inched forward, elbows and knees, my belly pressed to the muck, thinking of guerrillas and commandos and *The Naked and the Dead*.[8] I parted the weeds and squinted the length of the parking lot.

The second car—it was a Trans-Am—was still running, its high beams washing the scene in a lurid stagy light. Tire iron flailing, the greasy bad character was laying into the side of my mother's Bel Air like

[8] A popular and critically successful 1948 novel by Norman Mailer, depicting U.S. Army life during World War II.

an avenging demon, his shadow riding up the trunks of the trees. Whomp. Whomp. Whomp-whomp. The other two guys—blond types, in fraternity jackets—were helping out with tree branches and skull-sized boulders. One of them was gathering up bottles, rocks, muck, candy wrappers, used condoms, pop-tops, and other refuse and pitching it through the window on the driver's side. I could see the fox, a white bulb behind the windshield of the '57 Chevy. "Bobbie," she whined over the thumping, "come *on.*" The greasy character paused a moment, took one good swipe at the left taillight, and then heaved the tire iron halfway across the lake. Then he fired up the '57 and was gone.

30 Blond head nodded at blond head. One said something to the other, too low for me to catch. They were no doubt thinking that in helping to annihilate my mother's car they'd committed a fairly rash act, and thinking too that there were three bad characters connected with that very car watching them from the woods. Perhaps other possibilities occurred to them as well—police, jail cells, justices of the peace, reparations, lawyers, irate parents, fraternal censure. Whatever they were thinking, they suddenly dropped branches, bottles, and rocks and sprang for their car in unison, as if they'd choreographed it. Five seconds. That's all it took. The engine shrieked, the tires squealed, a cloud of dust rose from the rutted lot and then settled back on darkness.

I don't know how long I lay there, the bad breath of decay all around me, my jacket heavy as a bear, the primordial ooze subtly reconstituting itself to accommodate my upper thighs and testicles. My jaws ached, my knee throbbed, my coccyx was on fire. I contemplated suicide, wondered if I'd need bridgework, scraped the recesses of my brain for some sort of excuse to give my parents—a tree had fallen on the car, I was blindsided by a bread truck, hit and run, vandals had got to it while we were playing chess at Digby's. Then I thought of the dead man. He was probably the only person on the planet worse off than I was. I thought about him, fog on the lake, insects chirring eerily, and felt the tug of fear, felt the darkness opening up inside me like a set of jaws. Who was he, I wondered, this victim of time and circumstance bobbing sorrowfully in the lake at my back. The owner of the chopper, no doubt, a bad older character come to this. Shot during a murky drug deal, drowned while drunkenly frolicking in the lake. Another headline. My car was wrecked; he was dead.

When the eastern half of the sky went from black to cobalt and the trees began to separate themselves from the shadows, I pushed myself up from the mud and stepped out into the open. By now the birds had begun to take over for the crickets, and dew lay slick on the leaves. There was a smell in the air, raw and sweet at the same time, the smell of the sun firing buds and opening blossoms. I contemplated the car. It lay there like a wreck along the highway, like a steel sculpture left over from a vanished civilization. Everything was still. This was nature.

I was circling the car, as dazed and bedraggled as the sole survivor of an air blitz, when Digby and Jeff emerged from the trees behind me.

Digby's face was crosshatched with smears of dirt; Jeff's jacket was gone and his shirt was torn across the shoulder. They slouched across the lot, looking sheepish, and silently came up beside me to gape at the ravaged automobile. No one said a word. After a while Jeff swung open the driver's door and began to scoop the broken glass and garbage off the seat. I looked at Digby. He shrugged. "At least they didn't slash the tires," he said.

It was true: the tires were intact. There was no windshield, the headlights were staved in, and the body looked as if it had been sledgehammered for a quarter a shot at the county fair, but the tires were inflated to regulation pressure. The car was drivable. In silence, all three of us bent to scrape the mud and shattered glass from the interior. I said nothing about the biker. When we were finished, I reached in my pocket for the keys, experienced a nasty stab of recollection, cursed myself, and turned to search the grass. I spotted them almost immediately, no more than five feet from the open door, glinting like jewels in the first tapering shaft of sunlight. There was no reason to get philosophical about it: I eased into the seat and turned the engine over.

35 It was at that precise moment that the silver Mustang with the flame decals rumbled into the lot. All three of us froze; then Digby and Jeff slid into the car and slammed the door. We watched as the Mustang rocked and bobbed across the ruts and finally jerked to a halt beside the forlorn chopper at the far end of the lot. "Let's go," Digby said. I hesitated, the Bel Air wheezing beneath me.

Two girls emerged from the Mustang. Tight jeans, stiletto heels, hair like frozen fur. They bent over the motorcycle, paced back and forth aimlessly, glanced once or twice at us, and then ambled over to where the reeds sprang up in a green fence round the perimeter of the lake. One of them cupped her hands to her mouth. "Al," she called, "Hey, Al!"

"Come on," Digby hissed. "Let's get out of here."

But it was too late. The second girl was picking her way across the lot, unsteady on her heels, looking up at us and then away. She was older—twenty-five or -six—and as she came closer we could see there was something wrong with her: she was stoned or drunk, lurching now and waving her arms for balance. I gripped the steering wheel as if it were the ejection lever of a flaming jet, and Digby spat out my name, twice, terse and impatient.

"Hi," the girl said.

40 We looked at her like zombies, like war veterans, like deaf-and-dumb pencil peddlers.

She smiled, her lips cracked and dry. "Listen," she said, bending from the waist to look in the window, "you guys seen Al?" Her pupils were pinpoints, her eyes glass. She jerked her neck. "That's his bike over there—Al's. You seen him?"

Al. I didn't know what to say. I wanted to get out of the car and retch, I wanted to go home to my parents' house and crawl into bed. Digby poked me in the ribs. "We haven't seen anybody," I said.

The girl seemed to consider this, reaching out a slim veiny arm to brace herself against the car. "No matter," she said, slurring the *t*'s, "he'll turn up." And then, as if she'd just taken stock of the whole scene—the ravaged car and our battered faces, the desolation of the place—she said: "Hey, you guys look like some pretty bad characters—been fightin', huh?" We stared straight ahead, rigid as catatonics. She was fumbling in her pocket and muttering something. Finally she held out a handful of tablets in glassine wrappers: "Hey, you want to party, you want to do some of these with me and Sarah?"

I just looked at her. I thought I was going to cry. Digby broke the silence. "No, thanks," he said, leaning over me. "Some other time."

45 I put the car in gear and it inched forward with a groan, shaking off pellets of glass like an old dog shedding water after a bath, heaving over the ruts on its worn springs, creeping toward the highway. There was a sheen of sun on the lake. I looked back. The girl was still standing there, watching us, her shoulders slumped, hand outstretched.

Ethan Canin
(1960–)

THE CARNIVAL DOG, THE BUYER OF DIAMONDS
(1988)

What's the one thing you should never do? Quit? Depends on who you talk to. Steal? Cheat? Eat food from a dented can? Myron Lufkin's father, Abe, once told him never get your temperature taken at the hospital. Bring your own thermometer, he said; you should see how they wash theirs. He ought to have known; when he was at Yeshiva University he worked as an orderly in the hospital, slid patients around on gurneys, cleaned steelware. Myron knows all his father's hospital stories and all his rules. On the other hand, there are things you *should* do. Always eat sitting down. Wear a hat in the rain. What else? Never let the other guy start the fight. Certain inviolable commandments. In thirty-two years Myron Lufkin had never seen his father without an answer.

That is, until the day five years ago when Myron called home from Albert Einstein College of Medicine and told his father he had had enough, was quitting, leaving, *kaput,* he said. Now, Myron, living in Boston, sometime Jew, member of the public gym where he plays basketball and swims in the steamy pool after rounds, still calls home every other week. The phone calls, if he catches his father asleep, remind him of the day five years ago when he called to say that he was not, after all, going to be a doctor.

It was not the kind of thing you told Abe Lufkin. Abe Lufkin, a man who once on Election Day put three twelve-pound chains across his chest and dove into San Francisco Bay at Aquatic Park, to swim most of the mile and three-quarters across to Marin. As it turned out they had to pull him from the frothy cold water before he made the beach—but to give him credit, he was not a young man. In the *Chronicle* the next day there he was on an inside page, sputtering and shaking on the sand, steam rising off his body. Rachel, Myron's mother, is next to him in a sweater and baggy wool pants. Myron still has the newspaper clipping in one of his old butterfly display cases wrapped in tissue paper in a drawer in Boston.

On the day Myron called home from Albert Einstein to say that three years of studying and money, three years of his life, had been a waste, he could imagine the blood-rush in his father's head. But he knew what to expect. He kept firm, though he could feel the pulse in his own neck. Itzhak, his roommate at medical school, had stood behind him with his hand on Myron's shoulder, smoking a cigarette. But Abe simply did not believe it.

5 Myron didn't expect him to believe it: Abe, after all, didn't understand quitting. If his father had been a sea captain, Myron thought, he would have gone down with his ship—singing, boasting, denying the ocean that closed over his head—and this was not, in Myron's view, a glorious death. It just showed stubbornness. His father was stubborn about everything. When he was young, for example, when stickball was what you did in the Bronx, Abe played basketball. Almost nobody else played. In those days, Abe told Myron, you went to the Yankee games when Detroit was in town and rooted for Hank Greenberg to hit one out, and when he did you talked about it and said how the *goyishe* umpires would have ruled it foul if they could have, if it hadn't been to center field. In Abe's day, baseball was played by men named McCarthy, Murphy, and Burdock, and basketball wasn't really played at all, except by the very very tall, awkward kids. But not Abe Lufkin. He was built like a road-show wrestler and he kept a basketball under his bed. It was his love for the game, maybe, that many years later made him decide to have a kid. When Myron was born, Abe nailed a backboard to the garage. This is my boy, he said, my *mensch*. He began playing basketball with his son when Myron was nine. But really, what they did was not playing. By the time Myron was in the fifth grade Abe had visions in his already balding pharmacist's head. He sat in the aluminum lawn furniture before dinner and counted out the one hundred lay-ups Myron had to do from each side of the basket. One hundred from the left. One hundred from the right. No misses.

But it paid off. At Woodrow Wilson High, Myron was the star. Myron hitting a twenty-foot bank shot. Myron slipping a blind pass inside, stealing opponents' dribbles so their hands continued down, never realizing the ball was gone. Myron blocking the last-second shot. It was a show. Before the games he stood alone under the basket, holding his toes and stretching loose the muscles in his thighs. He knew Abe was sitting in the stands. His father always got there before the teams even came upstairs to the gym. He took the front-row seat at one corner and made Rachel take the one at the opposite corner. Then at halftime they switched. This way Abe could always see the basket his son was shooting at. After the games Abe waited in the car for Myron. Rachel sat in the back, and when Myron got in, Abe talked about the game until the windows steamed or Rachel finally said that it was unhealthy to sit like this in the cold. Then Abe wiped the windows and started the car, and they drove home with the heater blasting up warm air between the seats.

Abe had always believed the essence of the body was in the lungs, and sometimes, to keep Myron in shape for basketball, he challenged him to breath-holding contests. They sat facing each other across the kitchen table without breathing while an egg timer ran down between them. Myron could never beat his father, though; Abe held his breath like a blowfish at low tide. Myron's eyes teared, his heart pounded in his head, his lungs swelled to combustion, while all the time his father just stared at him, winking. He made Myron admit defeat out loud. "Do you give?" Abe whispered when half the sand had run down through the timer. Myron swallowed, pressed his lips together, stared at the sand falling through the narrow neck. A few seconds later, Abe said it again: "Do you give?" Myron squeezed his legs together, held his hands over his mouth, stood up, sat down, and finally let his breath explode out. "I give," he said, then sat there until the egg timer ran down and Abe exhaled.

There was always this obsession in the Lufkin family, this holiness about the affairs of the body. What were wars or political speeches next to the importance of body heat, expansive lungs, or leg muscles that could take you up the stairs instead of the elevator? Abe told hospital stories because to him there was no more basic truth than keeping your bronchial tubes cleared, or drying between your toes. Any questions of the body were settled quickly and finally when Abe showed Myron the smelly fungus between his own toes, or opened the *Encyclopaedia Britannica* to pictures of stomach worms, syphilis, or skin rash.

Any religious fervor in the family went instead into this worship of the body. Rachel did not light candles on Friday nights, and Myron was never *bar-mitzvahed*. Instead there was health to be zealous about. It was Abe's way. But at times he wavered, and these were nearly the only times Myron ever saw him unsure—in the evenings when he read the newspaper and talked about the state of Israel, or on Friday nights sometimes when he stood in the living room with the lights off, staring out at the sidewalk as the congregation filtered by in wool coats and *yarmulkes*. It put Abe into a mood. The spring after Myron's fifteenth birthday he told Myron he was sending him to a Judaism camp in the mountains for the month of July. They were outside on the porch when Abe told him.

10 "What? A Judaism camp? I don't believe it."

"What don't you believe?"

"I'm not going to a Judaism camp."

"What's this? Yes, you're going. You've got no more religion than *goyim.* I've already sent the money."

"How much money?"

15 "Fifty dollars."

Then Abe went in from the porch, and that was the end of the argument. Myron knew he would have to go off in the hot, bright month of July. That was how Abe argued. He wasn't wordy. If you wanted to change his mind you didn't argue, you fought him with your fists or your knees. This was what he expected from the world, and this was what he taught his son. Once, when Myron was fourteen, Abe had taken him to a bar, and when the bouncer hadn't wanted to let him in Abe said, "This is my *mensch;* he's not going to drink," and had pushed Myron in front of him through the door. Later, when they stood in line to pee away their drinks, Abe told him you can do what you want with strangers because they don't want to fight. "Remember that," he said.

But the day after he told Myron about the Judaism camp, Abe came out on the porch and said, "Myron, you're a man now and we're going to decide about camp like men."

"What?"

"We're going to decide like men. We're going to have a race."

20 "We can't race."

"What do you mean, we can't race? We sure can. A footrace, from here to the end of the block. I win, you go to camp."

"I don't want to do it."

"What, do you want it longer? We can do what you want. We can make it two times to the corner."

Then Abe went into the house, and Myron sat on the porch. He didn't want to learn religion during the hottest month of the year, but also, he knew, there was something in beating his father that was like the toppling of an ancient king. What was it for him to race an old man? He walked down to the street, stretched the muscles in his legs, and sprinted up to the corner. He sprinted back down to the house, sat down on the steps, and decided it wasn't so bad to go to the mountains in July. That afternoon Abe came out of the house in long pants and black, rubber-soled shoes, and he and Myron lined up on one of the sidewalk lines and raced, and Abe won going away. The sound of Abe's fierce breathing and his hard shoes pounding the cement hid the calmness of Myron's own breath. That July Myron packed Abe's old black cloth traveling bag and got on the bus to the mountains.

25 But what Abe taught Myron was more than just competition; it was everything. It was the way he got to work every day for thirty-seven years without being late, the way he treated Rachel, his bride of uncountable years, who sewed, cooked, cleaned for him, in return for what? For Sunday night dinners out every single week, a ritual so ancient that Myron couldn't break it even after he moved out of the house. For Sunday dinners out, and a new diamond each year. It was a

point of honor, an expectation. Obviously on a pharmacist's salary Abe couldn't afford it. He bought her rings, necklaces, bracelets, brooches, hairpins, earrings, lockets—one gift at the end of each year for, what is it, almost forty years? One year Rachel was sick with mild hepatitis and spent the holidays in the hospital. On the first evening of Chanukah Abe took Myron with him to visit her, and in the hospital room he pulled out a small bracelet strung with a diamond and gave it to her, his wife, as she lay in the bed. But what is the value of a diamond, he later asked Myron in the car, next to the health of the body?

It was two years later that Abe tried the swim across San Francisco Bay. But there were other things before that. At the age of fifty-four he fought in a bar over politics. Yes, fought. He came home with his knuckles wrapped in a handkerchief. On his cheek there was a purple bruise that even over the years never disappeared, only gradually settled down the side of his face and formed a black blotch underneath his jaw. That was when he told Myron never to let the other guy start the fight. Always get the first punch, he said. Myron was sixteen then, sitting in the kitchen watching his father rub iodine into the split skin behind his knuckles. The smell stayed in the kitchen for days, the smell of hospitals that later came to be the smell of all his father's clothes, and of his closet. Maybe Myron had just never noticed it before, but on that day his father began to smell old.

Myron was startled. Even then he had been concerned with life. He was a preserver, a collector of butterflies that he caught on the driving trips the family took in the summers. The shelves in his bedroom were lined with swallowtails and monarchs pressed against glass panes, the crystal dust still on their wings. Later, in college, he had studied biology, zoology, entomology, looking inside things, looking at life. Once, on a driving trip through Colorado when Myron was young, Abe had stopped the car near the lip of a deep gorge. Across from where they got out and stood, the cliffs extended down a quarter of a mile, colored with clinging green brush, wildflowers, shafts of red clay, and, at the bottom, a turquoise river. But there were no animals on the sheer faces, no movement anywhere in the gorge. Abe said that life could survive anywhere, even on cliffs like these, and that this was a miracle. But Myron said nothing. To him, anything that couldn't move, that couldn't fly or swim or run, was not really alive. Real life interested him. His father interested him, with his smells and exertions, with the shifting bruise on his jaw.

Years later, on his first day at Albert Einstein medical school, the thing Myron noticed was the smell, the pungency of the antiseptics, like the iodine Abe had once rubbed into his knuckles. On that first day when a whole class of new medical students listened to an address by the dean of the medical college, the only thing Myron noticed was that the room smelled like his father.

* * *

Medical school was a mountain of facts, a giant granite peak full of outcroppings and hidden crevices. Physiology. Anatomy. Histology. More facts than he could ever hope to remember. To know the twenty-eight bones of the hand seemed to Myron a rare and privileged knowledge, but then there were the arms and shoulders with their bones and tendons and opposing muscles, then the whole intricate, extravagant cavity of the chest, and then the head and the abdomen and the legs. Myron never really tried to learn it all. It wasn't the volume of knowledge so much as it was the place where he had to be in order to learn it. The anatomy labs reeked of formaldehyde, the hospitals of a mixture of cleanliness and death. All of it reminded Myron of men getting old, and that is why in three years of medical school he made the minuscule but conscious effort not to study enough. He let the knowledge collect around him, in notebooks, binders, pads, on napkins and checks, everywhere except in his brain. His room was strewn with notes he never studied. Once in a letter home he said learning medicine was like trying to drink water from a fire hose.

But that was something Abe would want to hear. Once on a driving trip through the Florida deltas, Abe came upon three men trying to lift an abandoned car from a sludge pit with a rope they had looped around it. Only the roof and the tops of the windows were showing above the mud, but Abe got out anyway and helped the men pull. His face turned red and the muscles in his belly shook so much Myron could see them through his shirt. Myron didn't understand the futility of his father's effort, or even know why he helped save a useless car for men he didn't know, until years later. Abe did things like that; he loved doing things like that.

Myron, on the other hand, just didn't want to study. His weren't the usual reasons for quitting medical school. It wasn't the hours, and really, it wasn't the studying and the studying. It was something smaller, harder, that in a vague way he knew had to do with Abe. Perhaps he saw his own father in the coughing middled-aged men whose hearts he watched flutter across oscilloscope screens. But it was not Abe's death that he feared. Heart stoppage or brain tumors or sudden clots of blood were reactions of the body, and thus, he had always believed, they were good. Death, when it was a fast action, didn't bother him. The fatty cadavers in anatomy labs were no more than objects to Myron, and it meant nothing to him that they were dead. The only time in his life that he had had to really think about death was in his childhood, when the phone rang in the middle of the night to tell Abe about his aunt in Miami Beach. The next morning Myron had found his father downstairs drinking coffee. "Life is for the living," Abe had said, and even then Myron could weigh the seriousness in his voice. It was plain that death meant only a little if you still had the good muscles in your own heart, and that people's bodies, once underground, were not to be mourned. And besides, there really was no blood in the medical school anatomy classes. The cadavers were gray, no different when you cut them than the cooked leg of a turkey. They had none of the pliable fleshiness, none of the pink, none of the smells and secretions that told you of life.

No, it wasn't death that bothered Myron; it was the downhill plunge of the living body—the muscles that stretched off the bones into folds, the powdery flesh odors of middle-aged men. He longed for some octogenarian to stand up suddenly from a wheelchair and run the length of a corridor. Once, a drugged coronary patient, a sixty-year-old man, had unhooked an IV cart and caromed on it through the corridor until Myron cornered him. When Myron looked at the blood spots that were in the old man's eyes, he wanted to take him in his own arms then and there, in his triumph. That was why Myron wanted to quit medical school. He hated the demise of the spirit.

So he let the work pile up around him. In his third year he felt the walls of the lecture halls and the sponged hospital floors to be somehow holding him against his will. Fifty-year-old men who could no longer walk, or whose intestines bled and collapsed, Myron felt, were betrayers of the human race. He was convinced of the mind's control over the flesh.

In the winter of his third year he started jogging. First two, three miles a day, then, later, long six-mile runs into the hills and neighborhoods around the medical school. He left in the early mornings and ran in the frozen air so that he could feel the chill in his lungs. He ran every morning through November and December, and then January after the holidays, until one morning in February, when the grass was still breaking like needles underneath his feet, he realized he could run forever. That morning he just kept running. He imagined Itzhak sitting with two cups of coffee at the table, but he ran to the top of a hill and watched the streets below him fill with morning traffic. Then onward he went, amidst the distant bleating of car horns and the whistling wind. He thought of the hospital, of the arriving interns, sleepless, pale, and of the third-year students following doctors from room to room. He ran on the balls of his feet and never got tired.

When he returned to the apartment Itzhak was at the table eating lunch. Myron took a carton of milk from the refrigerator and drank standing up, without a glass.

"You ever think about passing infection that way?"

Myron put down the carton and looked at the muscles twitching in his thighs. Itzhak lit a cigarette.

"You're a real one," Itzhak said. "Where the hell were you?"

"Hypoxia. No oxygen to the brain. You know how easy it is to forget what time it is."

"Watch it," Itzhak said. "You'll get into trouble."

The next day Myron went to classes and to rounds, but that night he ran again, stumbling in the unlit paths, and after that, over the next weeks of frozen, windless days, he ran through his morning assignments and spent the afternoons in a park near his apartment. There was a basketball hoop there, a metal backboard with a chain net, and sometimes he shot with a group of kids or joined their half-court games. Afterward, he always ran again. He loved to sweat when the air was cold enough to turn the grass brittle, when a breath of air felt like a gulp of cold water. After a while, Itzhak began to ignore his disappearances. One day when Myron returned from running, Itzhak took his pulse. "Damn, Myron," he said, "you *are* running." His professors tried to take him aside, and Myron could see them looking into his pupils when they spoke. But he ignored them. One night he returned late from running, still dripping sweat, picked up the telephone and dialed, and heard his father's sleepy voice on the other end of the line. "Pa," he said, "it's *kaput* here."

So why the quitting now? Why the phone call at ten-thirty on a Thursday night when Abe and Rachel were just going into their dream sleep? Myron could hear the surprise, the speechlessness. He heard Rachel over the line telling Abe to calm himself, to give her the phone. He imagined the blood rushing to Abe's face, the breathing starting again the way he breathed the morning they pulled him from the frothy water in San Francisco Bay. Rachel took the phone and spoke, and Myron, because he had lived with his father for most of his life, knew Abe was taking black socks from the drawer and stretching them over his feet.

The next morning at seven Myron opened the apartment door and Abe was sitting there in a chair with the black cloth traveling bag on his lap. He was wide awake, blocking the passage out of the apartment.

"For crying out loud!"

"Who else did you expect? Am I supposed to let you throw away everything?"

"Pa, I didn't expect *anybody.*"

"Well, I came, and I'm here, and I spent like a madman to get a flight. You think I don't have the lungs to argue with my son?"

"I was about to go running."

"I'll come along. We're going to settle this thing."

"Okay," Myron said, "come," and in his sweatsuit, hooded and wrapped against the cold, he led Abe down through the corridors of the building and out into the street. The ground outside was frozen from the night, the morning icy cold and without wind. Abe held the black traveling bag at his side as they stood under the entrance awning.

"I was planning to run."

"It won't hurt you to walk a few blocks."

It was cold, so they walked quickly. Abe was wearing what he always wore in the winter, a black hat, gloves, galoshes, an overcoat that smelled of rain. Myron watched him out of the side of his vision. He tried to look at his father without turning around—at the face, at the black bruise under the jaw, at the shoulders. He tried to see the body beneath the clothing. Abe's arm swung with the weight of the traveling bag, and for the first time, as he watched through the corner of his eye, Myron noticed the faint spherical outline inside the cloth.

They walked wordlessly, Myron watching Abe's breath come out in clouds. By now the streets had begun to move with traffic, and the ice patches, black and treacherous, crackled underneath their feet. The streetlamps had gone off and in the distance dogs barked. They came to the park where Myron played basketball in the afternoons.

"So you brought the ball," Myron said.

"Maybe you want some shooting to calm you."

"You're not thinking of any games, are you?"

"I just brought it in case you wanted to shoot."

Abe unzipped the bag and pulled out the basketball. They went into the court. He bounced the ball on the icy pavement, then handed it to Myron. Myron spun it on his finger, dribbled it off the ice. He was watching Abe. He couldn't see beneath the overcoat, but Abe's face seemed drawn down, the cheeks puffier, the dark bruise lax on his jaw.

"Pa, why don't you shoot some? It would make you warm."

"You think you have to keep me warm? Look at this." He took off the overcoat. "Give me the ball."

Myron threw it to him, and Abe dribbled it in his gloved hands. Abe was standing near the free-throw line, and he turned then, brought the ball to his hip, and shot it, and as his back was turned to watch the shot, Myron did an incredible thing—he crouched, took three lunging steps, and dove into the back of his father's thin, tendoned knees. Abe tumbled backward over him. What could have possessed Myron to do such a thing? A medical student, almost a doctor—what the hell was he doing? But Myron knew his father. Abe was a prizefighter, a carnival dog. Myron knew he would protect the exposed part of his skull, that he would roll and take the weight on his shoulders, that he would be up instantly, crouched and ready to go at it. But Myron had slid on the ice after the impact and when he scrambled back up and turned around, his father was on his back on the icy pavement. He was flat out.

"Pa!"

Abe was as stiff and extended as Myron had ever seen a human being. He was like a man who had laid out his own body.

"What kind of crazy man are you?" Abe said hoarsely. "I think it's broken."

"What? What's broken?"

"My back. You broke your old man's back."

"Oh no, Pa, I couldn't have! Can you move your toes?"

But the old man couldn't. He lay on the ground staring up at Myron like a beached sea animal. Oh, Pa. Myron could see the unnatural stiffness in his body, in the squat legs and the hard, protruding belly.

"Look," Myron said, "don't move." Then he turned and started back to get his father's coat, and he had taken one step when Abe—Abe the carnival dog, the buyer of diamonds and the man of endurance—hooked his hand around Myron's ankles and sent him tumbling onto the ice. Bastard! Pretender! He scrambled up and pinned Myron's shoulders against the pavement. "Faker!" Myron cried. He grappled with the old man, butted him with his head and tried to topple his balance, but Abe clung viciously and set the weight of his chest against Myron's shoulders. "Fraud!" shouted Myron. "Cheat!" He shifted his weight and tried to roll Abe over, but his father's legs were spread wide and he had pinned Myron's hands. "Coward," Myron said. Abe's wrists pressed into Myron's arms. His knees dug into Myron's thighs. "Thief," Myron whispered. "Scoundrel." Cold water was spreading upward through Myron's clothes and Abe was panting hoarse clouds of steam into his face when Myron realized his father was leaning down and speaking into his ear.

"Do you give?"

"What?"

"Do you give?"

"You mean, will I go back to school?"

"That's what I mean."

"Look," Myron said, "you're crazy."

"Give me your answer."

Myron thought about this. While his father leaned down over him, pressed into him with his knees and elbows, breathed steam into his face, he thought about it. As he lay there he thought about other things too: This is my father, he thought. Then: This is my life. For a while, as the cold water spread through his clothes, he lay there and remembered things—the thousands and thousands of lay-ups, the smell of a cadaver, the footrace on a bright afternoon in April. Then he thought: What can you do? These are clouds above us, and below us there is ice and the earth. He said, "I give."

Stephen Crane
(1871–1900)

THE BLUE HOTEL
(1898)

I

The Palace Hotel at Fort Romper was painted a light blue, a shade that is on the legs of a kind of heron, causing the bird to declare its position against any background. The Palace Hotel, then, was always screaming and howling in a way that made the dazzling winter landscape of Nebraska seem only a grey swampish hush. It stood alone on the prairie, and when the snow was falling the town two hundred yards away was not visible. But when the traveller lighted at the railway station he was obliged to pass the Palace Hotel before he could come upon the company of low clapboard houses which composed Fort Romper, and it was not to be thought that any traveller could pass the Palace Hotel without looking at it. Pat Scully, the proprietor, had proved himself a master of strategy when he chose his paints. It is true that on clear days, when the great transcontinental expresses, long lines of swaying Pullmans, swept through Fort Romper, passengers were overcome at the sight and the cult that knows the brown-reds and the subdivisions of the dark greens of the East expressed shame, pity, horror, in a laugh. But to the citizens of this prairie town and to the people who would naturally stop there, Pat Scully had performed a feat. With this opulence and splendour, these creeds, classes, egotisms, that streamed through Romper on the rails day after day, they had no colour in common.

As if the displayed delights of such a blue hotel were not sufficiently enticing, it was Scully's habit to go every morning and evening to meet the leisurely trains that stopped at Romper and work his seductions upon any man that he might see wavering, gripsack in hand.

One morning, when a snow-crusted engine dragged its long string of freight cars and its one passenger coach to the station, Scully performed the marvel of catching three men. One was a shaky and quick-eyed Swede, with a great shining cheap valise; one was a tall bronzed cowboy, who was on his way to a ranch near the Dakota line; one was a little silent man from the East, who didn't look it, and didn't announce it. Scully practically made them prisoners. He was so nimble and merry and kindly that each probably felt it would be the height of brutality to try to escape. They trudged off over the creaking board sidewalks in the wake of the eager little Irishman. He wore a heavy fur cap squeezed tightly down on his head. It caused his two red ears to stick out stiffly, as if they were made of tin.

At last, Scully, elaborately, with boisterous hospitality, conducted them through the portals of the blue hotel. The room which they entered was small. It seemed to be merely a proper temple for an enormous stove, which, in the centre, was humming with godlike violence. At various points on its surface the iron had become luminous and glowed yellow from the heat. Beside the stove Scully's son Johnnie was playing High-Five[1] with an old farmer who had whiskers both grey and sandy. They were quarreling. Frequently the old farmer turned his face toward a box of sawdust—coloured brown from tobacco juice—that was behind the stove, and spat with an air of great impatience and irritation. With a loud flourish of words Scully destroyed the game of cards, and bustled his son upstairs with part of the baggage of the new guests. He himself conducted them to three basins of the coldest water in the world. The cowboy and the Easterner burnished themselves fiery red with this water, until it seemed to be some kind of metal-polish. The Swede, however, merely dipped his fingers gingerly and with trepidation. It was notable that throughout this series of small ceremonies the three travellers were made to feel that Scully was very benevolent. He was conferring great favors upon them. He handed the towel from one to another with an air of philanthropic impulse.

5 Afterward they went to the first room, and, sitting about the stove, listened to Scully's officious clamour at his daughters, who were

---

[1] A popular card game.

preparing the midday meal. They reflected in the silence of experienced men who tread carefully amid new people. Nevertheless, the old farmer, stationary, invincible in his chair near the warmest part of the stove, turned his face from the sawdust-box frequently and addressed a glowing commonplace to the strangers. Usually he was answered in short but adequate sentences by either the cowboy or the Easterner. The Swede said nothing. He seemed to be occupied in making furtive estimates of each man in the room. One might have thought that he had the sense of silly suspicion which comes to guilt. He resembled a badly frightened man.

Later, at dinner, he spoke a little, addressing his conversation entirely to Scully. He volunteered that he had come from New York, where for ten years he had worked as a tailor. These facts seemed to strike Scully as fascinating, and afterward he volunteered that he had lived at Romper for fourteen years.[2] The Swede asked about the crops and the price of labour. He seemed barely to listen to Scully's extended replies. His eyes continued to rove from man to man.

Finally, with a laugh and a wink, he said that some of these Western communities were very dangerous; and after his statement he straightened his legs under the table, tilted his head, and laughed again, loudly. It was plain that the demonstration had no meaning to the others. They looked at him wondering and in silence.

II

As the men trooped heavily back into the front room, the two little windows presented views of a turmoiling sea of snow. The huge arms of the wind were making attempts—mighty, circular, futile—to embrace the flakes as they sped. A gate-post like a still man with a blanched face stood aghast amid this profligate fury. In a hearty voice Scully announced the presence of a blizzard. The guests of the blue hotel, lighting their pipes, assented with grunts of lazy masculine contentment. No island of the sea could be exempt in the degree of this little room with its humming stove. Johnnie, son of Scully, in a tone which defined his opinion of his ability as a card-player, challenged the old farmer of both grey and sandy whiskers to a game of High-Five. The farmer agreed with a contemptuous and bitter scoff. They sat close to the stove, and squared their knees under a wide board. The cowboy and the Easterner watched the game with interest. The Swede remained near the window, aloof, but with a countenance that showed signs of an inexplicable excitement.

The play of Johnnie and the grey-beard was suddenly ended by another quarrel. The old man arose while casting a look of heated scorn at his adversary. He slowly buttoned his coat, and then stalked with fabulous dignity from the room. In the discreet silence of all other men the Swede laughed. His laughter rang somehow childish. Men by this time

---

[2] The "he" is Scully.

had begun to look at him askance, as if they wished to inquire what ailed him.

A new game was formed jocosely. The cowboy volunteered to become the partner of Johnnie, and they all then turned to ask the Swede to throw in his lot with the little Easterner. He asked some questions about the game, and, learning that it wore many names, and that he had played it when it was under an alias, he accepted the invitation. He strode toward the men nervously, as if he expected to be assaulted. Finally, seated, he gazed from face to face and laughed shrilly. This laugh was so strange that the Easterner looked up quickly, the cowboy sat intent and with his mouth open, and Johnnie paused, holding the cards with still fingers.

Afterward there was a short silence. Then Johnnie said, "Well, let's get at it. Come on now!" They pulled their chairs forward until their knees were bunched under the board. They began to play, and their interest in the game caused the others to forget the manner of the Swede.

The cowboy was a board-whacker. Each time that he held superior cards he whanged them, one by one, with exceeding force, down upon the improvised table, and took the tricks with a glowing air of prowess and pride that sent thrills of indignation into the hearts of his opponents. A game with a board-whacker in it is sure to become intense. The countenances of the Easterner and the Swede were miserable whenever the cowboy thundered down his aces and kings, while Johnnie, his eyes gleaming with joy, chuckled and chuckled.

Because of the absorbing play none considered the strange ways of the Swede. They paid strict heed to the game. Finally, during a lull caused by a new deal, the Swede suddenly addressed Johnnie: "I suppose there have been a good many men killed in this room." The jaws of the others dropped and they looked at him.

"What in hell are you talking about?" said Johnnie.

The Swede laughed again his blatant laugh, full of a kind of false courage and defiance. "Oh, you know what I mean all right," he answered.

"I'm a liar if I do!" Johnnie protested. The card was halted, and the men stared at the Swede. Johnnie evidently felt that as the son of the proprietor he should make a direct inquiry. "Now, what might you be drivin' at, mister?" he asked. The Swede winked at him. It was a wink full of cunning. His fingers shook on the edge of the board. "Oh, maybe you think I have been to nowheres. Maybe you think I'm a tenderfoot?"

"I don't know nothin' about you," answered Johnnie, "and I don't give a damn where you've been. All I got to say is that I don't know what you're driving at. There hain't never been nobody killed in this room."

The cowboy, who had been steadily gazing at the Swede, then spoke. "What's wrong with you, mister?"

Apparently it seemed to the Swede that he was formidably menaced. He shivered and turned white near the corners of his mouth. He sent an appealing glance in the direction of the little Easterner. During these moments he did not forget to wear his air of advanced pot-valour. "They say they don't know what I mean," he remarked mockingly to the Easterner.

20 The latter answered after prolonged and cautious reflection. "I don't understand you," he said, impassively.

The Swede made a movement then which announced that he thought he had encountered treachery from the only quarter where he had expected sympathy, if not help. "Oh, I see you are all against me. I see—"

The cowboy was in a state of deep stupefaction. "Say," he cried, as he tumbled the deck violently down upon the board, "say, what are you gittin' at, hey?"

The Swede sprang up with the celerity of a man escaping from a snake on the floor. "I don't want to fight!" he shouted, "I don't want to fight!"

The cowboy stretched his long legs indolently and deliberately. His hands were in his pockets. He spat into the sawdust-box. "Well, who the hell thought you did?" he inquired.

25 The Swede backed rapidly toward a corner of the room. His hands were out protectingly in front of his chest, but he was making an obvious struggle to control his fright. "Gentlemen," he quavered. "I suppose I am going to be killed before I can leave this house! I suppose I am going to be killed before I can leave this house!" In his eyes was the dying-swan[3] look. Through the windows could be seen the snow turning blue in the shadow of dusk. The wind tore at the house, and some loose thing beat regularly against the clapboards like a spirit tapping.

A door opened, and Scully himself entered. He paused in surprise as he noted the tragic attitude of the Swede. Then he said, "What's the matter here?"

The Swede answered him swiftly and eagerly: "These men are going to kill me."

"Kill you!" ejaculated Scully. "Kill you! What are you talkin'?"

The Swede made the gesture of a martyr.

30 Scully wheeled sternly upon his son. "What is this, Johnnie?"

The lad had grown sullen. "Damned if I know," he answered. "I can't make no sense of it." He began to shuffle the cards, fluttering them together with an angry snap. "He says a good many men have been killed in this room, or something like that. And he says he's going' to be killed here too. I don't know what ails him. He's crazy, I shouldn't wonder."

Scully then looked for explanation to the cowboy, but the cowboy simply shrugged his shoulders.

"Kill you?" said Scully again to the Swede. "Kill you? Man, you're off your nut."

---

[3] The proverbial swan that sings (or talks) beautifully before dying.

"Oh, I know," burst out the Swede. "I know what will happen. Yes, I'm crazy—yes. Yes, of course, I'm crazy—yes. But I know one thing—" There was a sort of sweat of misery and terror upon his face. "I know I won't get out of here alive."

The cowboy drew a deep breath, as if his mind was passing into the last stages of dissolution. "Well, I'm doggoned," he whispered to himself.

Scully wheeled suddenly and faced his son. "You've been troublin' this man!"

Johnnie's voice was loud with its burden of grievance. "Why, good Gawd, I ain't done nothin' to 'im."

The Swede broke in. "Gentlemen, do not disturb yourselves. I will leave this house. I will go away, because"—he accused them dramatically with his glance—"because I do not want to be killed."

Scully was furious with his son. "Will you tell me what is the matter, you young divil? What's the matter, anyhow? Speak out!"

"Blame it!" cried Johnnie in despair, "don't I tell you I don't know? He—he says we want to kill him, and that's all I know. I can't tell what ails him."

The Swede continued to repeat: "Never mind, Mr. Scully; never mind. I will leave this house. I will go away, because I do not wish to be killed. Yes, of course, I am crazy—yes. But I know one thing! I will go away. I will leave this house. Never mind, Mr. Scully; never mind, I will go away."

"You will not go 'way," said Scully. "You will not go 'way until I hear the reason of this business. If anybody has troubled you I will take care of him. This is my house. You are under my roof, and I will not allow any peaceable man to be troubled here." He cast a terrible eye upon Johnnie, the cowboy, and the Easterner.

"Never mind, Mr. Scully; never mind. I will go away. I do not wish to be killed." The Swede moved toward the door which opened upon the stairs. It was evidently his intention to go at once for his baggage.

"No, no," shouted Scully peremptorily; but the white-faced man slid by him and disappeared. "Now," said Scully severely, "what does this mane?"[4]

Johnnie and the cowboy cried together: "Why, we didn't do nothin' to 'im!"

Scully's eyes were cold. "No," he said, "you didn't?"

Johnnie swore a deep oath. "Why, this is the wildest loon I ever see. We didn't do nothin' at all. We were just sittin' here playin cards, and he—"

The father suddenly spoke to the Easterner. "Mr. Blanc," he asked, "what has these boys been doin'?"

The Easterner reflected again. "I didn't see anything wrong at all," he said at last, slowly.

---

[4] Mean, spoken with an Irish brogue.

Scully began to howl, "But what does it mane?" He stared ferociously at his son. "I have a mind to lather you for this, me boy."

Johnnie was frantic. "Well, what have I done?" he bawled at his father.

III

"I think you are tongue-tied," said Scully finally to his son, the cowboy, and the Easterner; and at the end of this scornful sentence he left the room.

Upstairs the Swede was swiftly fastening the straps of his great valise. Once his back happened to be half turned toward the door, and, hearing a noise there, he wheeled and sprang up, uttering a loud cry. Scully's wrinkled visage showed grimly in the light of the small lamp he carried. This yellow effulgence, streaming upward, coloured only his prominent features, and left his eyes, for instance, in mysterious shadow. He resembled a murderer.

"Man! man!" he exclaimed, "have you gone daffy?"

"Oh, no! Oh, no!" rejoined the other. "There are people in this world who know pretty nearly as much as you do—understand?"

For a moment they stood gazing at each other. Upon the Swede's deathly pale cheeks were two spots brightly crimson and sharply edged, as if they had been carefully painted. Scully placed the light on the table and sat himself on the edge of the bed. He spoke ruminatively. "By cracky, I never heard of such a thing in my life. It's a complete muddle. I can't, for the soul of me, think how you ever got this idea into your head." Presently he lifted his eyes and asked: "And did you sure think they were going to kill you?"

The Swede scanned the old man as if he wished to see into his mind. "I did," he said at last. He obviously suspected that this answer might precipitate an outbreak. As he pulled on a strap his whole arm shook, the elbow wavering like a bit of paper.

Scully banged his hand impressively on the footboard of the bed. "Why, man, we're goin' to have a line of ilictric street-cars in this town next spring."

"'A line of electric street-cars,'" repeated the Swede, stupidly.

"And," said Scully, "there's a new railroad goin' to be built down from Broken Arm to here. Not to mintion the four churches and the smashin' big brick schoolhouse. Then there's the big factory, too. Why, in two years Romper'll be a met-tro-*pol*-is."

Having finished the preparation of his baggage, the Swede straightened himself. "Mr. Scully" he said, with sudden hardihood, "how much do I owe you?"

"You don't owe me anythin'," said the old man, angrily.

"Yes, I do," retorted the Swede. He took seventy-five cents from his pocket and tendered it to Scully; but the latter snapped his fingers in disdainful refusal. However, it happened that they both stood gazing in a strange fashion at three silver pieces on the Swede's open palm.

"I'll not take your money," said Scully at last. "Not after what's been goin' on here." Then a plan seemed to strike him. "Here," he cried, picking up his lamp and moving toward the door. "Here! Come with me a minute."

65 "No," said the Swede, in overwhelming alarm.

"Yes," urged the old man. "Come on! I want you to come and see a picter—just across the hall—in my room."

The Swede must have concluded that his hour was come. His jaw dropped and his teeth showed like a dead man's. He ultimately followed Scully across the corridor, but he had the step of one hung in chains.

Scully flashed the light high on the wall of his own chamber. There was revealed a ridiculous photograph of a little girl. She was leaning against a balustrade of gorgeous decoration, and the formidable bang to her hair was prominent. The figure was as graceful as an upright sled-stake, and, withal, it was of the hue of lead. "There," said Scully, tenderly, "that's the picter of my little girl that died. Her name was Carrie. She had the purtiest hair you even saw! I was that fond of her, she—"

Turning then, he saw that the Swede was not contemplating the picture at all, but, instead, was keeping keen watch on the gloom in the rear.

70 "Look, man!" cried Scully, heartily. "That's the picter of my little gal that died. Her name was Carrie. And then here's the picter of my oldest boy, Michael. He's a lawyer in Lincoln, an' doin' well. I gave that boy a grand eddication, and I'm glad for it now. He's a fine boy. Look at 'im now. Ain't he bold as blazes, him there in Lincoln, an honoured an' respicted gintleman! An honoured and respicted gintleman," concluded Scully with a flourish. And, so saying, he smote the Swede jovially on the back.

The Swede faintly smiled.

"Now," said the old man, "there's only one more thing." He dropped suddenly to the floor and thrust his head beneath the bed. The Swede could hear his muffled voice. "I'd keep it under me piller if it wasn't for that boy Johnnie. Then there's the old woman—Where is it now? I never put it twice in the same place. Ah, now come out with you!"

Presently he backed clumsily from under the bed, dragging with him an old coat rolled into a bundle. "I've fetched him," he muttered. Kneeling on the floor, he unrolled the coat and extracted from its heart a large yellow-brown whiskey-bottle.

His first maneuver was to hold the bottle up to the light. Reassured, apparently, that nobody had been tampering with it, he thrust it with a generous movement toward the Swede.

75 The weak-kneed Swede was about to eagerly clutch this element of strength, but he suddenly jerked his hand away and cast a look of horror upon Scully.

"Drink," said the old man affectionately. He had risen to his feet, and now stood facing the Swede.

There was a silence. Then again Scully said: "Drink!"

The Swede laughed wildly. He grabbed the bottle, put it to his mouth; and as his lips curled absurdly around the opening and his throat worked, he kept his glance, burning with hatred, upon the old man's face.

IV

After the departure of Scully the three men, with the card-board still upon their knees, preserved for a long time an astounded silence. Then Johnnie said: "That's the dod-dangedest Swede I ever see."

"He ain't no Swede," said the cowboy, scornfully.

"Well, what is he then?" cried Johnnie. "What is he then?"

"It's my opinion," replied the cowboy deliberately, "he's some kind of a Dutchman." It was a venerable custom of the country to entitle as Swedes all light-haired men who spoke with a heavy tongue. In consequence the idea of the cowboy was not without its daring. "Yes, sir," he repeated. "It's my opinion this feller is some kind of Dutchman."

"Well, he says he's a Swede, anyhow," muttered Johnnie, sulkily. He turned to the Easterner: "What do you think, Mr. Blanc?"

"Oh, I don't know," replied the Easterner.

"Well, what do you think makes him act that way?" asked the cowboy.

"Why, he's frightened." The Easterner knocked his pipe against the rim of the stove. "He's clear frightened out of his boots."

"What at?" cried Johnnie and the cowboy together.

The Easterner reflected over his answer.

"What at?" cried the others again.

"Oh, I don't know, but it seems to me this man has been reading dime novels, and he thinks he's right out in the middle of it—the shootin' and stabbin' and all."

"But," said the cowboy, deeply scandalized, "this ain't Wyoming, ner none of them places. This is Nebrasker."

"Yes," added Johnnie, "an' why don't he wait till he gits *out West?"*

The travelled Easterner laughed. "It isn't different there even—not in these days. But he thinks he's right in the middle of hell."

Johnnie and the cowboy mused long.

"It's awful funny," remarked Johnnie at last.

"Yes," said the cowboy. "This is a queer game. I hope we don't git snowed in, because then we'd have to stand this here man bein' around with us all the time. That wouldn't be no good."

"I wish pop would throw him out," said Johnnie.

Presently they heard a loud stamping on the stairs, accompanied by ringing jokes in the voice of old Scully, and laughter, evidently from the Swede. The men around the stove stared vacantly at each other. "Gosh!" said the cowboy. The door flew open, and old Scully, flushed and anecdotal, came into the room. He was jabbering at the Swede, who followed him, laughing bravely. It was the entry of two roisterers from a banquet hall.

"Come now," said Scully sharply to the three seated men, "move up and give us a chance at the stove." The cowboy and the Easterner obediently sidled their chairs to make room for the new-comers. Johnnie, however, simply arranged himself in a more indolent attitude, and then remained motionless.

"Come! Git over, there," said Scully.

"Plenty of room on the other side of the stove," said Johnnie.

"Do you think we want to sit in the draught?" roared the father.

But the Swede here interposed with a grandeur of confidence. "No, no. Let the boy sit where he likes," he cried in a bullying voice to the father.

"All right! All right!" said Scully, deferentially. The cowboy and the Easterner exchanged glances of wonder.

The five chairs were formed in a crescent about one side of the stove. The Swede began to talk; he talked arrogantly, profanely, angrily. Johnnie, the cowboy, and the Easterner maintained a morose silence, while old Scully appeared to be receptive and eager, breaking in constantly with sympathetic ejaculations.

Finally the Swede announced that he was thirsty. He moved in his chair, and said that he would go for a drink of water.

"I'll git it for you," cried Scully at once.

"No," said the Swede contemptuously. "I'll get it for myself." He arose and stalked with the air of an owner off into the executive parts of the hotel.

As soon as the Swede was out of hearing Scully sprang to his feet and whispered intensely to the others: "Upstairs he thought I was tryin' to poison 'im."

"Say," said Johnnie, "this makes me sick. Why don't you throw 'im out in the snow?"

"Why, he's all right now," declared Scully. "It was only that he was from the East, and he thought this was a tough place. That's all. He's all right now."

The cowboy looked with admiration upon the Easterner. "You were straight," he said. "You were on to that there Dutchman."

"Well," said Johnnie to his father, "he may be all right now, but I don't see it. Other time he was scared, but now he's too fresh."

Scully's speech was always a combination of Irish brogue and idiom, Western twang and idiom, and scraps of curiously formal diction taken from the storybooks and newspapers. He now hurled a strange mass of language at the head of his son. "What do I keep? What do I keep? What do I keep?" he demanded, in a voice of thunder. He slapped his knee impressively, to indicate that he himself was going to make reply, and that all should heed. "I keep a hotel," he shouted. "A hotel, do you mind? A guest under my roof has sacred privileges. He is to be intimidated by none. Not one word shall he hear that would prijudice him in favor of goin' away. I'll not have it. There's no place in this here town where they can say they iver took in a guest of mine because he was afraid to stay here." He wheeled suddenly upon the cowboy and the Easterner. "Am I right?"

"Yes, Mr. Scully," said the cowboy, "I think you're right."

"Yes, Mr. Scully," said the Easterner, "I think you're right."

V

At six-o'clock supper, the Swede fizzed like a fire-wheel. He sometimes seemed on the point of bursting into riotous song, and in all his madness, he was encouraged by old Scully. The Easterner was encased in reserve; the cowboy sat in wide-mouthed amazement, forgetting to eat, while Johnnie wrathily demolished great plates of food. The daughters of the house, when they were obliged to replenish the biscuits, approached as warily as Indians, and, having succeeded in their purpose, fled with ill-concealed trepidation. The Swede domineered the whole feast, and he gave it the appearance of a cruel bacchanal. He seemed to have grown suddenly taller; he gazed, brutally disdainful, into every face. His voice rang through the room. Once when he jabbed out harpoon-fashion with his fork to pinion a biscuit, the weapon nearly impaled the hand of the Easterner, which had been stretched quietly out for the same biscuit.

After supper, as the men filed toward the other room, the Swede smote Scully ruthlessly on the shoulder. "Well, old boy, that was a good, square meal." Johnnie looked hopefully at his father; he knew that shoulder was tender from an old fall; and, indeed, it appeared for a moment as if Scully was going to flame out over the matter, but in the end he smiled a sickly smile and remained silent. The others understood from his manner that he was admitting his responsibility for the Swede's new view-point.

Johnnie, however, addressed his parent in an aside. "Why don't you license somebody to kick you downstairs?" Scully scowled darkly by way of reply.

When they were gathered about the stove, the Swede insisted on another game of High-Five. Scully gently deprecated the plan at first, but the Swede turned a wolfish glare upon him. The old man subsided, and the Swede canvassed the others. In his tone there was always a great threat. The cowboy and the Easterner both remarked indifferently that they would play. Scully said that he would presently have to go to meet the 6.58 train, and so the Swede turned menacingly upon Johnnie. For a moment their glances crossed like blades, and then Johnnie smiled and said, "Yes, I'll play."

They formed a square, with the little board on their knees. The Easterner and the Swede were again partners. As the play went on, it was noticeable that the cowboy was not board-whacking as usual. Meanwhile, Scully, near the lamp, had put on his spectacles and, with an appearance curiously like an old priest, was reading a newspaper. In time he went out to meet the 6.58 train, and, despite his precautions, a gust of polar wind whirled into the room as he opened the door. Besides scattering the cards, it chilled the players to the marrow. The Swede cursed frightfully. When Scully returned, his entrance disturbed a cosy and friendly scene. The Swede again cursed. But presently they were once more intent, their heads bent forward and their hands moving swiftly. The Swede had adopted the fashion of board-whacking.

Scully took up his paper and for a long time remained immersed in matters which were extraordinarily remote from him. The lamp burned badly, and once he stopped to adjust the wick. The newspaper, as he turned from page to page, rustled with a slow and comfortable sound. Then suddenly he heard three terrible words: "You are cheatin'!"

Such scenes often prove that there can be little of dramatic import in environment. Any room can present a tragic front: any room can be comic. This little den was now hideous as a torture-chamber. The new faces of the men themselves had changed it upon the instant. The Swede held a huge fist in front of Johnnie's face, while the latter looked steadily over it into the blazing orbs of his accuser. The Easterner had grown pallid: the cowboy's jaw had dropped in that expression of bovine amazement which was one of his important mannerisms. After the three words, the first sound in the room was made by Scully's paper as it floated forgotten to his feet. His spectacles had also fallen from his nose, but by a clutch he had saved them in air. His hand, grasping the spectacles, now remained poised awkwardly and near his shoulder. He stared at the card-players.

Probably the silence was while a second elapsed. Then, if the floor had been suddenly twitched out from under the men they could not have moved quicker. The five had projected themselves headlong toward a common point. It happened that Johnnie, in rising to hurl himself upon the Swede, had stumbled slightly because of his curiously instinctive care for the cards and the board. The loss of the moment allowed time for the arrival of Scully, and also allowed the cowboy time to give the Swede a great push which sent him staggering back. The men found tongue together, and hoarse shouts of rage, appeal, or fear burst from every throat. The cowboy pushed and jostled feverishly at the Swede, and the Easterner and Scully clung wildly to Johnnie; but through the smoky air, above the swaying bodies of the peace-compellers, the eyes of the two warriors ever sought each other in glances of challenge that were at once hot and steely.

125 Of course the board had been overturned, and now the whole company of cards was scattered over the floor, where the boots of the men trampled the fat and painted kings and queens as they gazed with their silly eyes at the war that was waging above them.

Scully's voice was dominating the yells. "Stop now! Stop, I say! Stop, now—"

Johnnie, as he struggled to burst through the rank formed by Scully and the Easterner, was crying, "Well, he says I cheated! He says I cheated! I won't allow no man to say I cheated! If he says I cheated, he's a—!"

The cowboy was telling the Swede, "Quit, now! Quit, d'ye hear—"

The screams of the Swede never ceased: "He did cheat! I saw him! I saw him—"

As for the Easterner, he was importuning in a voice that was not heeded: "Wait a moment, can't you? Oh, wait a moment. What's the good of a fight over a game of cards? Wait a moment—"

In this tumult no complete sentences were clear. "Cheat"—"Quit"—"He says"—these fragments pierced the uproar and rang out sharply. It was remarkable that, whereas Scully undoubtedly made the most noise, he was the least heard of any of the riotous band.

Then suddenly there was a great cessation. It was as if each man had paused for breath; and although the room was still lighted with the anger of men, it could be seen that there was no danger of immediate conflict, and at once Johnnie, shouldering his way forward, almost succeeded in confronting the Swede. "What did you say I cheated for? What did you say I cheated for? I don't cheat, and I won't let no man say I do!"

The Swede said, "I saw you! I saw you!"

"Well," cried Johnnie, "I'll fight any man what says I cheat!"

"No, you won't," said the cowboy. "Not here."

"Ah, be still, can't you?" said Scully, coming between them.

The quiet was sufficient to allow the Easterner's voice to be heard. He was repeating, "Oh, wait a moment, can't you? What's the good of a fight over a game of cards? Wait a moment!"

Johnnie, his red face appearing above his father's shoulder, hailed the Swede again. "Did you say I cheated?"

The Swede showed his teeth. "Yes."

"Then," said Johnnie, "we must fight."

"Yes, fight," roared the Swede. He was like a demoniac. "Yes, fight! I'll show you what kind of a man I am! I'll show you who you want to fight! Maybe you think I can't fight! Maybe you think I can't! I'll show you, you skin, you card-sharp! Yes, you cheated! You cheated!"

"Well, let's go at it, then, mister," said Johnnie coolly.

The cowboy's brow was beaded with sweat from his efforts in intercepting all sorts of raids. He turned in despair to Scully. "What are you goin' to do now?"

A change had come over the Celtic visage of the old man. He now seemed all eagerness; his eyes glowed.

"We'll let them fight," he answered stalwartly. "I can't put up with it any longer. I've stood this damned Swede till I'm sick. We'll let them fight."

VI

The men prepared to go out of doors. The Easterner was so nervous that he had great difficulty in getting his arms into the sleeves of his new leather coat. As the cowboy drew his fur cap down over his ears his hands trembled. In fact, Johnnie and old Scully were the only ones who displayed no agitation. These preliminaries were conducted without words.

Scully threw open the door. "Well, come on," he said. Instantly a terrific wind caused the flame of the lamp to struggle at its wick, while a puff of black smoke sprang from the chimney-top. The stove was in mid-current of the blast, and its voice swelled to equal the roar of the storm. Some of the scarred and bedabbled cards were caught up from the floor and dashed helplessly against the farther wall. The men lowered their heads and plunged into the tempest as into a sea.

No snow was falling, but great whirls and clouds of flakes, swept up from the ground by the frantic winds, were streaming southward with the speed of bullets. The covered land was blue with the sheen of an unearthly satin, and there was no other hue save where, at the low, black railway station—which seemed incredibly distant—one light gleamed like a tiny jewel. As the men floundered into a thigh-deep drift, it was known that the Swede was bawling out something. Scully went to him, put a hand on his shoulder, and projected an ear. "What's that you say?" he shouted.

"I say," bawled the Swede again. "I won't stand much show against this gang, I know you'll all pitch on me."

150 Scully smote him reproachfully on the arm. "Tut, man!" he yelled. The wind tore the words from Scully's lips and scattered them far alee.

"You are all a gang of—" boomed the Swede, but the storm also seized the remainder of this sentence.

Immediately turning their backs upon the wind, the men had swung around a corner to the sheltered side of the hotel. It was the function of the little house to preserve here, amid this great devastation of snow, an irregular V-shape of heavily encrusted grass, which crackled beneath the feet. One could imagine the great drifts piled against the windward side. When the party reached the comparative peace of this spot it was found that the Swede was still bellowing.

"Oh, I know what kind of a thing this is! I know you'll all pitch on me. I can't lick you all!"

Scully turned upon him panther-fashion. "You'll not have to whip all of us. You'll have to whip my son Johnnie. An' the man what troubles you durin' that time will have me to dale with."

155 The arrangements were swiftly made. The two men faced each other, obedient to the harsh commands of Scully, whose face, in the subtly luminous gloom, could be seen set in the austere impersonal lines that are pictured on the countenances of the Roman veterans. The Easterner's teeth were chattering, and he was hopping up and down like a mechanical toy. The cowboy stood rock-like.

The contestants had not stripped off any clothing. Each was in his ordinary attire. Their fists were up, and they eyed each other in a calm that had the elements of leonine cruelty in it.

During this pause, the Easterner's mind, like a film, took lasting impressions of three men—the iron-nerved master of the ceremony; the Swede, pale, motionless, terrible; and Johnnie, serene yet ferocious, brutish yet heroic. The entire prelude had in it a tragedy greater than the tragedy of action, and this aspect was accentuated by the long, mellow cry of the blizzard, as it sped the tumbling and wailing flakes into the black abyss of the south.

"Now!" said Scully.

The two combatants leaped forward and crashed together like bullocks. There was heard the cushioned sound of blows, and of a curse squeezing out from between the tight teeth of one.

160 As for the spectators, the Easterner's pent-up breath exploded from him with a pop of relief, absolute relief from the tension of the preliminaries. The cowboy bounded into the air with a yowl. Scully was immovable as from supreme amazement and fear at the fury of the fight which he himself had permitted and arranged.

For a time the encounter in the darkness was such a perplexity of flying arms that it presented no more detail than would a swiftly revolving wheel. Occasionally a face, as if illumined by a flash of light, would shine out, ghastly and marked with pink spots. A moment later, the men might have been known as shadows, if it were not for the involuntary utterance of oaths that came from them in whispers.

Suddenly a holocaust of warlike desire caught the cowboy, and he bolted forward with the speed of a broncho. "Go it, Johnnie! go it! Kill him! Kill him!"

Scully confronted him. "Kape back," he said; and by his glance the cowboy could tell that this man was Johnnie's father.

To the Easterner there was a monotony of unchangeable fighting that was an abomination. This confused mingling was eternal to his sense, which was concentrated in a longing for the end, the priceless end. Once the fighters lurched near him, and as he scrambled hastily backward he heard them breathe like men on the rack.

165 "Kill him, Johnnie! Kill him! Kill him! Kill him!" The cowboy's face was contorted like one of those agony masks in museums.

"Keep still," said Scully, icily.

Then there was a sudden loud grunt, incomplete, cut short, and Johnnie's body swung away from the Swede and fell with sickening heaviness to the grass. The cowboy was barely in time to prevent the mad Swede from flinging himself upon his prone adversary. "No, you don't," said the cowboy, interposing an arm. "Wait a second."

Scully was at his son's side. "Johnnie! Johnnie, me boy!" His voice had a quality of melancholy tenderness. "Johnnie! Can you go on with it?" He looked anxiously down into the bloody, pulpy face of his son.

There was a moment of silence, and then Johnnie answered in his ordinary voice, "Yes, I—it—yes."

170 Assisted by his father he struggled to his feet. "Wait a bit now till you git your wind," said the old man.

A few paces away the cowboy was lecturing the Swede. "No, you don't! Wait a second!"

The Easterner was plucking at Scully's sleeve. "Oh, this is enough," he pleaded. "This is enough! Let it go as it stands. This is enough!"

"Bill," said Scully, "git out of the road." The cowboy stepped aside. "Now." The combatants were actuated by a new caution as they advanced toward collision. They glared at each other, and then the Swede aimed a lightning blow that carried with it his entire weight. Johnnie was evidently half stupid from weakness, but he miraculously dodged, and his fist sent the over-balanced Swede sprawling.

The cowboy, Scully, and the Easterner burst into a cheer that was like a chorus of triumphant soldiery, but before its conclusion the Swede has scuffed agilely to his feet and come in berserk abandon at his foe. There was another perplexity of flying arms, and Johnnie's body again swung away and fell, even as a bundle might fall from a roof. The Swede instantly staggered to a little wind-waved tree and leaned upon it, breathing like an engine, while his savage and flamelit eyes roamed from face to face as the men bent over Johnnie. There was a splendour of isolation in his situation at this time which the Easterner felt once when, lifting his eyes from the man on the ground, he beheld that mysterious and lonely figure, waiting.

"Are you any good yet, Johnnie?" asked Scully in a broken voice.

The son gasped and opened his eyes languidly. After a moment he answered, "No—I ain't—any good—any—more." Then, from shame, and bodily ill, he began to weep, the tears furrowing down through the bloodstains on his face. "He was too—too—too heavy for me."

Scully straightened and addressed the waiting figure.

"Stranger," he said, evenly, "it's all up with our side." Then his voice changed into that vibrant huskiness which is commonly the tone of the most simple and deadly announcements. "Johnnie is whipped."

Without replying, the victor moved off on the route to the front door of the hotel.

The cowboy was formulating new and unspellable blasphemies. The Easterner was startled to find that they were out in a wind that seemed to come direct from the shadowed arctic floes. He heard again the wail of the snow as it was flung to its grave in the south. He knew now that all this time the cold had been sinking into him deeper and deeper, and he wondered that he had not perished. He felt indifferent to the condition of the vanquished man.

"Johnnie, can you walk?" asked Scully.

"Did I hurt—hurt him any?" asked the son.

"Can you walk, boy? Can you walk?"

Johnnie's voice was suddenly strong. There was a robust impatience in it. "I asked you whether I hurt him any!"

"Yes, yes, Johnnie," answered the cowboy, consolingly; "he's hurt a good deal."

They raised him from the ground, and as soon as he was on his feet he went tottering off, rebuffing all attempts at assistance. When the party rounded the corner they were fairly blinded by the pelting of the snow. It burned their faces like fire. The cowboy carried Johnnie through the drift to the door. As they entered, some cards again rose from the floor and beat against the wall.

The Easterner rushed to the stove. He was so profoundly chilled that he almost dared to embrace the glowing iron. The Swede was not in the room. Johnnie sank into a chair and, folding his arms on his knees, buried his face in them. Scully, warming one foot and then the other at a rim of the stove, muttered to himself with Celtic mournfulness. The cowboy had removed his fur cap, and with a dazed and rueful air he was running one hand through his tousled locks. From overhead they could hear the creaking of boards, as the Swede tramped here and there in his room.

The sad quiet was broken by the sudden flinging open of a door that led toward the kitchen. It was instantly followed by an inrush of women. They precipitated themselves upon Johnnie amid a chorus of lamentation. Before they carried their prey off to the kitchen, there to be bathed and harangued with that mixture of sympathy and abuse which is a feat of their sex, the mother straightened herself and fixed old Scully with an eye of stern reproach, "Shame be upon you, Patrick Scully!" she cried, "Your own son, too. Shame be upon you!"

"There, now! Be quiet, now!" said the old man, weakly.

"Shame be upon you, Patrick Scully!" The girls, rallying to this slogan, sniffed disdainfully in the direction of those trembling accomplices, the cowboy and the Easterner. Presently they bore Johnnie away, and left the three men to dismal reflection.

VII

"I'd like to fight this here Dutchman myself," said the cowboy, breaking a long silence.

Scully wagged his head sadly. "No, that wouldn't do. It wouldn't be right. It wouldn't be right."

"Well, why wouldn't it?" argued the cowboy. "I don't see no harm in it."

"No," answered Scully, with mournful heroism. "It wouldn't be right. It was Johnnie's fight, and now we mustn't whip the man just because he whipped Johnnie."

"Yes, that's true enough," said the cowboy; "but—he better not get fresh with me, because I couldn't stand no more of it."

"You'll not say a word to him," commanded Scully, and even then they heard the tread of the Swede on the stairs. His entrance was made theatric. He swept the door back with a bang and swaggered to the middle of the room. No one looked at him. "Well," he cried, insolently, at Scully, "I s'pose you'll tell me now how much I owe you?"

The old man remained stolid. "You don't owe me nothin'."

"Huh!" said the Swede, "huh! Don't owe 'im nothin'."

The cowboy addressed the Swede. "Stranger, I don't see how you come to be so gay around here."

Old Scully was instantly alert. "Stop!" he shouted, holding his hand forth, fingers upward. "Bill, you shut up!"

The cowboy spat carelessly into the sawdust-box. "I didn't say a word, did I?" he asked.

"Mr. Scully," called the Swede, "how much do I owe you?" It was seen that he was attired for departure, and that he had his valise in his hand.

"You don't owe me nothin'," repeated Scully in the same imperturbable way.

"Huh!" said the Swede. "I guess you're right. I guess if it was any way at all, you'd owe me somethin'. That's what I guess." He turned to the cowboy. "'Kill him! Kill him! Kill him!'" he mimicked, and then guffawed victoriously. "'Kill him!'" He was convulsed with ironical humour.

But he might have been jeering the dead. The three men were immovable and silent, staring with glassy eyes at the stove.

The Swede opened the door and passed into the storm, giving one derisive glance backward at the still group.

As soon as the door was closed, Scully and the cowboy leaped to their feet and began to curse. They trampled to and fro, waving their arms and smashing into the air with their fists. "Oh, but that was a hard minute!" wailed Scully. "That was a hard minute! Him there leerin' and scoffin'! One bang at his nose was worth forty dollars to me that minute! How did you stand it, Bill?"

"How did I stand it?" cried the cowboy in a quivering voice. "How did I stand it? Oh!"

The old man burst into sudden brogue. "I'd loike to take that Swade," he wailed, "and hould 'im down on a shtone flure and bate 'im to a jelly wid a shtick!"

The cowboy groaned in sympathy. "I'd like to git him by the neck and hammer him"—he brought his hand down on a chair with a noise like a pistol-shot—"hammer that there Dutchman until he couldn't tell himself from a dead coyote!"

"I'd bate 'im until he—"

"I'd show *him* some things—"

And then together they raised a yearning, fanatic cry—"Oh-o-oh! if we only could—"

"Yes!"

"Yes!"

"And then I'd—"

"O-o-oh!"

VIII

The Swede, tightly gripping his valise, tacked across the face of the storm as if he carried sails. He was following a line of little naked, gasping trees which, he knew, must mark the way of the road. His face, fresh from the pounding of Johnnie's fists, felt more pleasure than pain in the wind and the driving snow. A number of square shapes loomed upon him finally, and he knew them as the houses of the main body of the town. He found a street and made travel along it, leaning heavily upon the wind whenever, at a corner, a terrific blast caught him.

He might have been in a deserted village. We picture the world as thick with conquering and elate humanity, but here, with the bugles of the tempest pealing, it was hard to imagine a peopled earth. One viewed the existence of man then as marvel, and conceded a glamour of wonder to these lice which were caused to cling to a whirling, fire-smitten, ice-locked, disease-stricken, space-lost bulb. The conceit of man was explained by this storm to be the very engine of life. One was a coxcomb not to die in it. However, the Swede found a saloon.

220 In front of it an indomitable red light was burning, and the snow-flakes were made blood-colour as they flew through the circumscribed territory of the lamp's shining. The Swede pushed open the door of the saloon and entered. A sanded expanse was before him, and at the end of it four men sat about a table drinking. Down one side of the room extended a radiant bar, and its guardian was leaning upon his elbows listening to the talk of the men at the table. The Swede dropped his valise upon the floor and, smiling fraternally upon the barkeeper, said, "Gimme some whisky, will you?" The man placed a bottle, a whisky-glass, and a glass of ice-thick water upon the bar. The Swede poured himself an abnormal portion of whisky and drank it in three gulps. "Pretty bad night," remarked the bartender, indifferently. He was making the pretension of blindness which is usually a distinction of his class; but it could have been seen that he was furtively studying the half-erased blood-stains on the face of the Swede. "Bad night," he said again.

"Oh, it's good enough for me," replied the Swede, hardily, as he poured himself some more whisky. The barkeeper took his coin and manoeuvred it through its reception by the highly nickelled cash-machine. A bell rang; a card labelled "20 cts." had appeared.

"No," continued the Swede, "this isn't too bad weather. It's good enough for me."

"So?" murmured the barkeeper, languidly.

The copious drams made the Swede's eyes swim, and he breathed a trifle heavier. "Yes, I like this weather. I like it. It suits me." It was apparently his design to impart a deep significance to these words.

225 "So?" murmured the bartender again. He turned to gaze dreamily at the scroll-like birds and bird-like scrolls which had been drawn with soap upon the mirrors in back of the bar.

"Well, I guess I'll take another drink," said the Swede, presently. "Have something?"

"No, thanks; I'm not drinkin'," answered the bartender. Afterward he asked, "How did you hurt your face?"

The Swede immediately began to boast loudly. "Why, in a fight. I thumped the soul out of a man down here at Scully's hotel."

The interest of the four men at the table was at last aroused.

230 "Who was it?" said one.

"Johnnie Scully," blustered the Swede. "Son of the man what runs it. He will be pretty near dead for some weeks, I can tell you. I made a nice thing of him. I did. He couldn't get up. They carried him in the house. Have a drink?"

Instantly the men in some subtle way encased themselves in reserve. "No, thanks," said one. The group was of curious formation. Two were prominent local business men; one was the district attorney; and one was a professional gambler of the kind known as "square." But a scrutiny of the group would not have enabled an observer to pick the gambler from the men of more reputable pursuits. He was, in fact, a man so delicate in manner, when among people of fair class, and so judicious in his choice of victims, that in the strictly masculine part of the town's life he had come to be explicitly trusted and admired. People called him a thoroughbred. The fear and contempt with which his craft was regarded were undoubtedly the reason why his quiet dignity shone conspicuous above the quiet dignity of men who might be merely hatters, billiard-markers, or grocery clerks. Beyond an occasional unwary traveller who came by rail, this gambler was supposed to prey solely upon reckless and senile farmers, who, when flush with good crops, drove into town in all the pride and confidence of an absolutely invulnerable stupidity. Hearing at times in circuitous fashion of the despoilment of such a farmer, the important men of Romper invariably laughed in contempt of the victim, and if they thought of the wolf at all, it was with a kind of pride at the knowledge that he would never dare think of attacking their wisdom and courage. Besides, it was popular that this gambler had a real wife and two real children in a neat cottage in a suburb, where he led an exemplary home life; and when any one even suggested a discrepancy in his character, the crowd immediately vociferated descriptions of this virtuous family circle. Then men who led exemplary home lives, and men who did not lead exemplary home lives, all subsided in a bunch, remarking that there was nothing more to be said.

However, when a restriction was placed upon him—as, for instance, when a strong clique of members of the new Pollywog Club refused to permit him, even as a spectator, to appear in the rooms of the organization—the candour and gentleness with which he accepted the judgment disarmed many of his foes and made his friends more desperately partisan. He invariably distinguished between himself and a respectable Romper man so quickly and frankly that his manner actually appeared to be a continual broadcast compliment.

And one must not forget to declare the fundamental fact of his entire position in Romper. It is irrefutable that in all affairs outside his business, in all matters that occur eternally and commonly between man and man, this thieving cardplayer was so generous, so just, so moral, that, in a contest, he could have put to flight the consciences of nine tenths of the citizens of Romper.

235 And so it happened that he was seated in this saloon with the two prominent local merchants and the district attorney.

The Swede continued to drink raw whisky, meanwhile babbling at the barkeeper and trying to induce him to indulge in potations. "Come on.

Have a drink. Come on. What—no? Well, have a little one, then. By gawd, I've whipped a man to-night, and I want to celebrate. I whipped him good, too. Gentlemen," the Swede cried to the men at the table, "have a drink?"

"Ssh!" said the barkeeper.

The group at the table, although furtively attentive, had been pretending to be deep in talk, but now a man lifted his eyes toward the Swede and said, shortly, "Thanks. We don't want any more."

At this reply the Swede ruffled out his chest like a rooster. "Well," he exploded, "it seems I can't get anybody to drink with me in this town. Seems so, don't it? Well!"

"Ssh!" said the barkeeper.

"Say," snarled the Swede, "don't you try to shut me up. I won't have it. I'm a gentleman, and I want people to drink with me. And I want 'em to drink with me now. *Now*—do you understand?" He rapped the bar with his knuckles.

Years of experience had calloused the bartender. He merely grew sulky. "I hear you," he answered.

"Well," cried the Swede, "listen hard then. See those men over there? Well, they're going to drink with me, and don't you forget it. Now you watch."

"Hi!" yelled the barkeeper, "this won't do!"

"Why won't it?" demanded the Swede. He stalked over to the table, and by chance laid his hand upon the shoulder of the gambler. "How about this?" he asked wrathfully. "I asked you to drink with me."

The gambler simply twisted his head and spoke over his shoulder. "My friend, I don't know you."

"Oh, hell!" answered the Swede, "come and have a drink."

"Now, my boy," advised the gambler, kindly, "take your hand off my shoulder and go 'way and mind your own business." He was a little, slim man, and it seemed strange to hear him use this tone of heroic patronage to the burly Swede. The other men at the table said nothing.

"What! You won't drink with me, you little dude? I'll make you, then! I'll make you!" The Swede had grasped the gambler frenziedly at the throat, and was dragging him from his chair. The other men sprang up. The barkeeper dashed around the corner of his bar. There was a great tumult, and then was seen a long blade in the hand of the gambler. It shot forward, and a human body, this citadel of virtue, wisdom, power, was pierced as easily as if it had been a melon. The Swede fell with a cry of supreme astonishment.

The prominent merchants and the district attorney must have at once tumbled out of the place backward. The bartender found himself hanging limply to the arm of a chair and gazing into the eyes of a murderer.

"Henry," said the latter, as he wiped his knife on one of the towels that hung beneath the bar rail, "you tell 'em where to find me. I'll be home, waiting for 'em." Then he vanished. A moment afterward the barkeeper was in the street dinning through the storm for help and, moreover, companionship.

The corpse of the Swede, alone in the saloon, had its eyes fixed upon a dreadful legend that dwelt atop the cash-machine: "This registers the amount of your purchase."

IX

Months later, the cowboy was frying pork over the stove of a little ranch near the Dakota line, when there was a quick thud of hoofs outside, and presently the Easterner entered with the letters and the papers.

"Well," said the Easterner at once, "the chap that killed the Swede has got three years. Wasn't much, was it?"

"He has? Three years?" The cowboy poised his pan of pork, while he ruminated upon the news. "Three years. That ain't much."

"No. It was a light sentence," replied the Easterner as he unbuckled his spurs. "Seems there was a good deal of sympathy for him in Romper."

"If the bartender had been any good," observed the cowboy, thoughtfully, "he would have gone in and cracked that there Dutchman on the head with a bottle in the beginnin' of it and stopped all this here murderin'."

"Yes, a thousand things might have happened," said the Easterner, tartly.

The cowboy returned his pan of pork to the fire, but his philosophy continued. "It's funny, ain't it? If he hadn't said Johnnie was cheatin' he'd be alive this minute. He was an awful fool. Game played for fun, too. Not for money. I believe he was crazy."

"I feel sorry for that gambler," said the Easterner.

"Oh, so do I," said the cowboy. "He don't deserve none of it for killin' who he did."

"The Swede might not have been killed if everything had been square."

"Might not have been killed?" exclaimed the cowboy. "Everythin' square? Why, when he said that Johnnie was cheatin' and acted like such a jackass? And then in the saloon he fairly walked up to git hurt?" With these arguments the cowboy browbeat the Easterner and reduced him to rage.

"You're a fool!" cried the Easterner, viciously. "You're a bigger jackass than the Swede by a million majority. Now let me tell you one thing. Let me tell you something. Listen! Johnnie *was* cheating!"

"'Johnnie,'" said the cowboy, blankly. There was a minute of silence, and then he said, robustly, "Why, no. The game was only for fun."

"Fun or not," said the Easterner, "Johnnie was cheating. I saw him. I know it. I saw him. And I refused to stand up and be a man. I let the Swede fight it out alone. And you—you were simply puffing around the place wanting to fight. And then old Scully himself! We are all in it! This poor gambler isn't even a noun. He is a kind of an adverb. Every sin is the result of collaboration. We, five of us, have collaborated in the murder of this Swede. Usually there are from a dozen to forty women really involved in every murder, but in this case it seems to be only five men—you, I, Johnnie, old Scully; and that fool of an unfortunate gambler came merely as a culmination, the apex of a human movement, and gets all the punishment."

The cowboy, injured and rebellious, cried out blindly into this fog of mysterious theory: "Well, I didn't do anythin', did I?"

Isabel Huggan
(1943–)

CELIA BEHIND ME
(1984)

There was a little girl with large smooth cheeks and very thick glasses who lived up the street when I was in public school. Her name was Celia. It was far too rare and grownup a name, so we always laughed at it. And we laughed at her because she was a chubby, diabetic child, made peevish by our teasing.

My mother always said, "You must be nice to Celia, she won't live forever," and even as early as seven I could see the unfairness of that position. Everybody died sooner or later, I'd die too, but that didn't mean everybody was nice to me or to each other. I already knew about mortality and was prepared to go to heaven with my two aunts who had died together in a car crash with their heads smashed like overripe melons. I overheard the bit about the melons when my mother was on the telephone, repeating that phrase and sobbing. I used to think about it often, repeating the words to myself as I did other things so that I got a nice rhythm: "Their heads smashed like melons, like melons, like melons." I imagined the pulpy insides of muskmelons and watermelons all over the road.

I often thought about the melons when I saw Celia because her head was so round and she seemed so bland and stupid and fruitlike. All rosy and vulnerable at the same time as being the most *awful* pain. She'd follow us home from school, whining if we walked faster than she did. Everybody always walked faster than Celia because her short little legs wouldn't keep up. And she was bundled in long stockings and heavy underwear, summer and winter, so that even her clothes held her back from our sturdy, leaping pace over and under hedges and across backyards and, when it was dry, or when it was frozen, down the stream bed and through the drainage pipe beneath the bridge on Church Street.

Celia, by the year I turned nine in December, had failed once and was behind us in school, which was a relief because at least in class there wasn't someone telling you to be nice to Celia. But she'd always be in the playground at recess, her pleading eyes magnified behind those ugly lenses so that you couldn't look at her when you told her she couldn't play skipping unless she was an ender. "Because you can't skip worth a fart," we'd whisper in her ear. "Fart, fart, fart," and watch her round pink face crumple as she stood there, turning, turning, turning the rope over and over.

5 As the fall turned to winter, the five of us who lived on Brubacher Street and went back and forth to school together got meaner and meaner to Celia. And, after the brief diversions of Christmas, we returned with a vengeance to our running and hiding and scaring games that kept Celia in a state of terror all the way home.

My mother said, one day when I'd come into the kitchen and she'd just turned away from the window so I could see she'd been watching us coming down the street, "You'll be sorry, Elizabeth. I see how you're treating that poor child, and it makes me sick. You wait, young lady. Some day you'll see how it feels yourself. Now you be nice to her, d'you hear?"

"But it's not just me," I protested. "I'm nicer to her than anybody else, and I don't see why I have to be. She's nobody special, she's just a pain. She's really dumb and she can't do anything. Why can't I just play with the other kids like everybody else?"

"You just remember I'm watching," she said, ignoring every word I'd said. "And if I see one more snowball thrown in her direction, by you or by anybody else, I'm coming right out there and spanking you in front of them all. Now you remember that!"

I knew my mother, and knew this was no idle threat. The awesome responsibility of now making sure the other kids stopped snowballing Celia made me weep with rage and despair, and I was locked in my room after supper to "think things over."

10 I thought things over. I hated Celia with a dreadful and absolute passion. Her round guileless face floated in the air above me as I finally fell asleep, taunting me: "You have to be nice to me because I'm going to die."

I did as my mother bid me, out of fear and the thought of the shame that a public spanking would bring. I imagined my mother could see much farther up the street than she really could, and it prevented me from throwing snowballs or teasing Celia for the last four blocks of our homeward journey. And then came the stomach-wrenching task of making the others quit.

"You'd better stop," I'd say. "If my mother sees you she's going to thrash us all."

Terror of terrors that they wouldn't be sufficiently scared of her strap-wielding hand; gut-knotting fear that they'd find out or guess what she'd really said and throw millions of snowballs just for the joy of seeing me whipped, pants down in the snowbank, screaming. I visualized that scene all winter, and felt a shock of relief when March brought such a cold spell that the snow was too crisp for packing. It meant a temporary safety for Celia, and respite for me. For I knew, deep in my wretched heart, that were it not for Celia I was next in line for humiliation. I was kind of chunky and wore glasses too, and had sucked my thumb so openly in kindergarten that "Sucky" had stuck with me all the way to Grade 3 where I now balanced at a hazardous point, nearly accepted by the amorphous Other Kids and always at the brink of being laughed at, ignored or teased. I cried very easily, and prayed during those years—not to become pretty or smart or popular, all aims too far out of my or God's reach, but simply to be strong enough not to cry when I got called Sucky.

During that cold snap, we were all bundled up by our mothers as much as poor Celia ever was. Our comings and goings were hampered by layers of flannel bloomers and undershirts and ribbed stockings and itchy wool against us no matter which way we turned; mitts, sweaters, scarves and hats, heavy and wet-smelling when the snot from our dripping noses mixed with the melting snow on our collars and we wiped, in frigid resignation, our sore red faces with rough sleeves knobbed over with icy pellets.

Trudging, turgid little beasts we were, making our way along slippery streets, breaking the crusts on those few front yards we'd not yet stepped all over in glee to hear the glorious snapping sound of boot through hard snow. Celia, her glasses steamed up even worse than mine, would scuffle and trip a few yards behind us, and I walked along wishing that some time I'd look back and she wouldn't be there. But she always was, and I was always conscious of the abiding hatred that had built up during the winter, in conflict with other emotions that gave me no peace at all. I felt pity, and a rising urge within me to cry as hard as I could so that Celia would cry too, and somehow realize how bad she made me feel, and ask my forgiveness.

It was the last day before the thaw when the tension broke, like northern lights exploding in the frozen air. We were all a little wingy after days of switching between the extremes of bitter cold outdoors and the heat of our homes and school. Thermostats had been turned up in a desperate attempt to combat the arctic air, so that we children suffered scratchy, tingly torment in our faces, hands and feet as the blood in our bodies roared in confusion, first freezing, then boiling. At school we had to go outside at recess—only an act of God would have ever prevented recess, the teachers had to have their cigarettes and tea—and in bad weather we huddled in a shed where the bicycles and the janitor's outdoor equipment were stored.

During the afternoon recess of the day I'm remembering, at the end of the shed where the girls stood, a sudden commotion broke out when Sandra, a rich big girl from Grade 4, brought forth a huge milk-chocolate bar from her pocket. It was brittle in the icy air, and snapped into little bits in its foil wrapper, to be divided among the chosen. I made my way cautiously to the fringe of her group, where many of my classmates were receiving their smidgens of sweet chocolate, letting it melt on their tongues like dark communion wafers. Behind me hung Celia, who had mistaken my earlier cries of "Stop throwing snowballs at Celia!" for kindness. She'd been mooning behind me for days, it seemed to me, as I stepped a little farther forward to see that there were only a few pieces left. Happily, though, most mouths were full and the air hummed with the murmuring sound of chocolate being pressed between tongue and palate.

Made bold by cold and desire, I spoke up. "Could I have a bit, Sandra?" She turned to where Celia and I stood, holding the precious foil in her mittened hand. Wrapping it in a ball, she pushed it over at Celia. Act of kindness, act of spite, vicious bitch or richness seeking expiation? She gave the chocolate to Celia and smiled at her. "This last bit is for Celia," she said to me.

"But I can't eat it," whispered Celia, her round red face aflame with the sensation of being singled out for a gift. "I've got di-a-beet-is." The word. Said so carefully. As if it were a talisman, a charm to protect her against our rough healthiness.

I knew it was a trick. I knew she was watching me out of the corner of her eye, that Sandra, but I was driven. "Then could I have it, eh?" The duress under which I acted prompted my chin to quiver and a tear to start down my cheek before I could wipe it away.

"No, no, no!" jeered Sandra then. "Suckybabies can't have sweets either. Di-a-beet-ics and Suck-y-ba-bies can't eat chocolate. Give it back, you little fart, Celia! That's the last time I ever give you anything!"

Wild, appreciative laughter from the chocolate-tongued mob, and they turned their backs on us, Celia and me, and waited while Sandra crushed the remaining bits into minuscule slivers. They had to take off their mitts and lick their fingers to pick up the last fragments from the foil. I stood there and prayed: "Dear God and Jesus, I would please like very much not to cry. Please help me. Amen." And with that the clanging recess bell clanked through the playground noise, and we all lined up, girls and boys in straight, straight rows, to go inside.

After school there was the usual bunch of us walking home and, of course, Celia trailing behind us. The cold of the past few days had been making us hurry, taking the shortest routes on our way to steaming cups of Ovaltine and cocoa. But this day we were all full of that peculiar energy that swells up before a turn in the weather and, as one body, we turned down the street that meant the long way home. Past the feed store where the Mennonites tied their horses, out the back of the town hall parking-lot and then down a ridge to the ice-covered stream and through the Church Street culvert to come out in the unused field behind the Front Street stores; the forbidden adventure we indulged in as a gesture of defiance against the parental "come right home."

We slid down the snowy slope at the mouth of the pipe that seemed immense then but was really only five feet in diameter. Part of its attraction was the tremendous racket you could make by scraping a stick along the corrugated sides as you went through. It was also long enough to echo very nicely if you made good booming noises, and we occasionally titillated each other by saying bad words at one end that grew as they bounced along the pipe and became wonderfully shocking in their magnitude . . . poopy, Poopy, POOpy, POOOOPy, POOOOPPYYY!

25 I was last because I had dropped my schoolbag in the snow and stopped to brush it off. And when I looked up, down at the far end, where the white plate of daylight lay stark in the darkness, the figures of my four friends were silhouetted as they emerged into the brightness. As I started making great sliding steps to catch up, I heard Celia behind me, and her plaintive, high voice: "Elizabeth! Wait for me, okay? I'm scared to go through alone. Elizabeth?"

And of course I slid faster and faster, unable to stand the thought of being the only one in the culvert with Celia. Then we would come out together and we'd really be paired up. What if they always ran on ahead and left us to walk together? What would I ever do? And behind me I heard the rising call of Celia, who had ventured as far as a few yards into the pipe, calling my name to come back and walk with her. I got right to the end, when I heard another noise and looked up. There they all were, on the bridge looking down, and as soon as they saw my face began to chant, "Better wait for Celia, Sucky. Better get Celia, Sucky."

The sky was very pale and lifeless, and I looked up in the air at my breath curling in spirals and felt, I remember this very well, an exhilarating, clear-headed instant of understanding. And with that, raced back into the tunnel where Celia stood whimpering half-way along.

"You little fart!" I screamed at her, my voice breaking and tearing at the words. "You little diabetic fart! I hate you! I hate you! Stop it, stop crying, I hate you! I could bash your head in I hate you so much, you fart, you fart! I'll smash your head like a melon! And it'll go in pieces all over and you'll die. You'll die, you diabetic. You're going to die!" Shaking her, shaking her and banging her against the cold, ribbed metal, crying and sobbing for grief and gasping with the exertion of pure hatred. And then there were the others, pulling at me, yanking me away, and in the moral tones of those who don't actually take part, warning me that they were going to tell, that Celia probably was going to die now, that I was really evil, they would tell what I said.

And there, slumped in a little heap, was Celia, her round head in its furry bonnet all dirty at the back where it had hit against the pipe, and she was hiccupping with fear. And for a wild, terrible moment I thought I had killed her, that the movements and noises her body made were part of dying.

30 I ran.

I ran as fast as I could back out the way we had come, and all the way back to the schoolyard. I didn't think about where I was going, it simply seemed the only bulwark to turn to when I knew I couldn't go home. There were a few kids still in the yard but they were older and ignored me as I tried the handle of the side door and found it open. I'd never been in the school after hours, and was stricken with another kind of terror that it might be a strappable offence. But no-one saw me, even the janitor was blessedly in another part of the building, so I was able to creep down to the girls' washroom and quickly hide in one of the cubicles. Furtive, criminal, condemned.

I was so filled with horror I couldn't even cry. I just sat on the toilet seat, reading all the things that were written in pencil on the green, wooden walls. *G.R. loves M.H.* and *Y.F. hates W.S. for double double sure. Mr. Becker wears ladies pants.* Thinking that I might die myself, die right here, and then it wouldn't matter if they told on me that I had killed Celia.

But the inevitable footsteps of retribution came down the stone steps before I had been there very long. I heard the janitor's voice explaining he hadn't seen any children come in and then my father's voice saying that the others were sure this is where Elizabeth would be. And they called my name, and then came in, and I guess saw my boots beneath the door because I suddenly thought it was too late to scrunch them up on the seat and my father was looking down at me and grabbed my arm, hurting it, pulling me, saying "Get in the car, Elizabeth."

Both my mother and my father spanked me that night. At first I tried not to cry, and tried to defend myself against their diatribe, tried to tell them when they asked, "But whatever possessed you to do such a terrible thing?" But whatever I said seemed to make them more angry and they became so soured by their own shame that they slapped my stinging buttocks for personal revenge as much as for any rehabilitative purposes.

"I'll never be able to lift my head on this street again!" my mother cried, and it struck me then, as it still does now, as a marvellous turn of phrase. I thought about her head on the street as she hit me, and wondered what Celia's head looked like, and if I had dented it at all.

Celia hadn't died, of course. She'd been half-carried, half-dragged home by the heroic others, and given pills and attention and love, and the doctor had come to look at her head but she didn't have so much as a bruise. She had a dirty hat, and a bad case of hiccups all night, but she survived.

Celia forgave me, all too soon. Within weeks her mother allowed her to walk back and forth to school with me again. But, in all the years before she finally died at seventeen, I was never able to forgive her. She made me discover a darkness far more frightening than the echoing culvert, far more enduring than her smooth, pink face.

Cynthia Kadohata*

JACK'S GIRL

(1987)

I talked to a ghost once, but he didn't talk back. I asked the ghost questions and then I told him I hated him. The ghost was my father, who had died a month earlier. We sat on a curb and ate candy bars together.

---

* Birth date is not available.

I ate the real thing; he ate candy that you couldn't exactly see through but that wavered whenever the wind blew. By the time we parted, I no longer hated him. Or I realized it wasn't as simple as that. He was standing next to his rose-colored convertible—he'd always liked racy cars. The top was open. It was a lovely night—hazy, but the sort of haze that makes the air itself seem to be all different colors.

This happened in Arizona about ten years ago, when I was twenty. My father—whom I called Jack—had died in Barstow, California. That's where he'd been living, with his wife and kids, when he met my mother, the year before I was born. I lived only a few hours' drive away, in Los Angeles, but Jack and I hardly ever saw each other.

When my father was alive, he was "in vending machines," as my mother used to say, when she said anything about him at all. He owned and serviced a vending-machine route, and when he died his wife, whom I knew even less well, asked me to take over the route until she could sell it. A vending-machine route had to be kept alive, she said. If the machines stayed empty too long, the customers—gas stations, bus stops, offices, and schools—might let new venders move in. Even if that didn't happen, the route would shrivel and die without constant servicing. Jack and his wife had two sons, but neither of them could get away just then, and his wife was in bad health. For helping her, she promised me a very small percentage of the profits from the sale of the business. The route was in California, Arizona, and Nevada, and it was while I was servicing it that I saw the ghost. The last time I'd seen Jack alive was five years earlier. I'd always lived with my mother and stepfather—whom I called Dad—and my three younger brothers.

A year before Jack died, I left college and moved in with a boy I loved. Of course, my parents wanted me to stay in school, and it felt strange to go against their wishes about something so important. But it also felt good. My boyfriend and I lived in a stucco apartment house near downtown Los Angeles. Music ruled that building, in an insane sort of way. The man in the adjoining apartment used to practice throwing knives into the wall while listening to loud classical music. He was a former child movie star.

5 Below our apartment lived a girl who couldn't have been more than eighteen years old, and she played disco music constantly. She didn't always close the curtains, so if you were outside you could see into her place. She would be sitting in front of her tape player and turntable changing songs. She'd play a song from an album and just as it was ending she would start a tape. On weekends she would play disk jockey like that for hours, from when she woke up to when she went to bed.

Jack's wife sent all of his business papers, maps, keys, and files to me in Los Angeles, and I tried to figure everything out. Jack used codes that I couldn't always understand for the machines' keys. I'd planned to organize for a couple of days before I left to service the route, but it took me nearly a week. As I sat at my desk and started decoding, I felt surreptitious and secretive, like a spy, but that illusion was destroyed by the din of the disco from below and the knives thumping alongside.

I had written my mother about all this, and she called me one night while I was decoding. "Honey, your dad says he would be glad to go with you on the route," she said.

I could hear his voice in the background saying, "Tell her things aren't that busy at work for me right now." He owned a garage, a good one, and I had never known him not to be busy.

"I can do it myself," I said. Actually, I had some doubts about that, but I didn't want to admit them to my parents.

I heard my dad, closer to the phone now, saying, "What did she say?"

My mother said, "Well, your dad just thought maybe you wouldn't want to be alone."

I asked whether he would come just until I felt comfortable, and he agreed. I didn't doubt that he wanted to help me, but I also thought he was curious about the man he had perceived as a rival: when he married my mother, she still loved Jack. She had married my dad because she was pregnant with me, and though she later claimed that she loved him, I was never really sure. The first time my mother saw me with my boyfriend, she'd kept staring at us in a funny way. Later, when I asked her what had made her stare, she said we'd both had the same look on our faces, as if we'd been washed over with the same water. I used to try to picture her with Jack, both of them washed over with the same water.

My dad and I left Los Angeles on one of those hot, ashy days when the surrounding hills are burning with brushfires and a feeling of siege has settled on the whole city. The fires filled me with languor and restlessness, so it was a good time to leave.

Since the time I went to college, when I was eighteen, I had seen little of my family; it took me by surprise how naturally and quickly new people covered the surface of my life. My dad and I didn't talk much on the phone, and though my mother and I wrote, my dad and I never did any more. We had at first, but one of my brothers told me that whenever my dad received a letter from me he got a weary look on his face, the way he did when he had to do a chore like filling out tax forms. He always wrote me back, but I knew it was a burden. "It's almost as bad as having to read a book," my brother told me he'd said.

I had worked out a logical route, to cover the territory in the most efficient way. The first day our stops were mainly gas stations, plus a couple of offices. Mostly small stuff. Our last stop, in the evening, was a Chinese-Italian restaurant. The restaurant had live entertainment—a man in a bow tie singing ballads. Signs hanging inside and out said that if you bought two entrées you'd get the second free.

"Let's eat here," said my dad. "A free meal." Bargains always delighted him in ways that were embarrassing or that seemed to me out of proportion to the amount of money saved. Once when I was younger, my dad took us over to the house of a friend of his to pick up some spare car parts for his garage. Our own car was being fixed at the time. On our way back, we walked through town, one of my brothers carrying a carburetor, another brother, my father, and I carrying a blue car door, and my youngest brother carrying two hubcaps that he kept trying to balance on his head.

"It's not really a free meal," I said. He mumbled something I couldn't quite make out, but it sounded like "Killjoy." "Oh, all right," I said.

My dad ordered sweet-and-sour pork with spaghetti for twelve ninety-five, and I wanted to order a vegetable plate.

"That's only five ninety-five," said my dad. "Besides, didn't you tell me when you were in high school that eating too many vegetables would make your complexion orange?"

"It's what I feel like eating."

"You had a date with that Scott guy, or Trott, or whatever his name was, and you wouldn't eat any carrots all week."

The waitress came and I asked for the vegetable plate. My dad looked crestfallen: "Don't you feel like shrimp? Look, here's some great shrimp for fourteen ninety-five." His face, always changeable, looked hopeful now. I gave in, which didn't seem to surprise him.

The shrimp was supposed to be marinated in ginger sauce; it arrived bathed in ketchup, but my dad didn't want me to return it. "We got a free meal!" he said.

When we were finished, we went into the foyer, where I had to climb on the cigarette machine to reach the lock on the candy machine. I smiled to myself when I realized that Jack must have done the same thing. "Can you hand me a screwdriver?" I said. "The lock is stuck." My dad didn't answer and when I looked down he was staring glassy-eyed out a window into the parking lot.

"You know, sometimes I have thoughts so big they scare me," he said.

A couple of customers walked by and gave each other a look on the way out. "The screwdriver?" I said. My dad kept staring. "What was the big thought?"

"I don't know. I can't explain it. It's gone now anyway."

"About Mom?"

"Maybe."

My dad handed me the screwdriver. "So have you thought any more about going back to school?" he said. He spoke tentatively, as if he were afraid I would lose my temper and say once again that it was *my* life. "No" was all I said.

His face took on a sad aspect and I wondered whether he was having a different kind of thought now—a practical, unhappy one. He had never finished high school himself, and I think he felt that going to college would guarantee me my place in the world. Maybe he worried I might end up unhappy, the way he thought my mother was.

Many of the machines we filled were in small towns, clusters of one-story buildings surrounded by yellowed weeds. The buildings had cracked stucco walls of pale pink, pale yellow, or white, and nearly all the windows in all the buildings were open, the curtains behind them shivering in the breeze. The children I saw always appeared to me tan and curious without being either healthy or alert, and the houses, as if they were organic, seemed to blend into the fields. In the background there were water towers, silver globes protecting the towns from the surrounding desert. At night the scenery was bare but not barren. There were no lights along the highway, and sometimes it was hard to tell we were in a real car, because the scenery on either side changed hardly at all. It was like one of those pretend cars in arcades, where you have a seat and a steering wheel and the road moves on a screen in front of the wheel. When trucks passed us, their emblems hung surreally in the blackness between the headlights.

One day in the car my dad said that he'd already stayed away from the garage longer than he'd planned to. But he quickly added that he would be glad to continue the route with me. Who knows what he really wanted to do? I told him I thought I could handle things by myself now. There was a machine in an Arizona bus-stop restaurant that we'd reach in a few more hours, and my dad decided to catch a bus back to his home from there. When we got to the restaurant's address, I asked a passerby where the place was, and he pointed to a white frame house and said, "Second floor." I hesitated, because there was no sign anywhere, and he said again, this time irritably, "Second floor." We followed his directions and found a small, quiet, dark restaurant up a flight of squeaky stairs. A young girl served us. She lingered at our table, eager to talk. She wanted to know where we were from and what we did. Ordinarily my dad was the talkative one, but this time I answered. He had been looking more tired each day.

"So you're only halfway done with the route," he said, after the girl left. "Think you can hold out?"

"I'm fine. I kind of like it." And in fact I did—I realized it was the first time I'd ever had any genuine responsibility.

My dad was quiet again. A little boy at the next table dropped a container of milk and knocked over his chair as he caught it. His mother told him to sit still, and he smiled at me, sly and angelic.

When the bus came we went downstairs. My dad idly leaned over and knocked on one of the wheels of the bus. He examined the tread, nodded approvingly, then got that glassy-eyed look again.

"What are you thinking about?" I said.

"To tell the truth, I was thinking did you know your mother had an affair once?"

I hesitated, then said, "I know."

"Did you know I almost had one, too, a couple of years ago?"

I shook my head, though his back was to me now. I felt sick and sad inside to hear this, and I was glad he didn't turn to look at me.

He shrugged. "It doesn't matter. We went out to dinner a couple of times. See, I wanted to tell you because nothing happened. See, your mother told me once how she ended with Jack. She said he took her to his house one day and on the wall was this thing called a Wish List. It had writing all over it, like 'toy truck' and 'stuffed animal' and Jack's wife had written 'a new couch for my birthday.' Your mother was about seventeen years old. A few weeks later he took her there again and a new couch was sitting in the living room. His wife had wanted this thing for the house and he'd gotten it for her, and that made your mother see for the first time the way his wife was connected to him and the way he was connected to her. She and Jack went into the bedroom then, but the whole time she just lay there feeling sad. So I kept thinking about that when I met this other lady, and somehow that stuff your mother had told me meant more to me than the other things, the things she did to me." He turned to me and became energized for the first time in days. "It's wrong!" he said. "Two people get married! They get married. Period."

There had always been something primitive about his morality; it was as if his need for a moral order were as strong as the need for food and water. When I was growing up, I'd always felt sheltered by his convictions, and by his belief that all his children would grow up "good." Whenever we did something "bad" or "wrong," he wasn't so much disappointed as confused and disbelieving.

As my dad was about to get on the bus, he reached into his wallet and took out all the money in there: twelve dollars. "Here, you might need some cash."

"Dad, I'm grown up, I work, I have money—remember?" I said. "Plus, I've got all the change from the machines."

"Don't worry, I have credit cards," he said, handing me the bills. As he was going up the bus steps, he paused and turned and said plaintively, "Now, don't you write me." Then he took his seat.

After the bus left, I walked back upstairs to the restaurant. I felt greasy and ragged, and I noticed spots on my blouse, and bruises on my hands from working.

The girl from the restaurant talked with me while I filled the candy machines. She said her town was bigger than it looked, maybe ten thousand people. She said she was fifteen, then seemed to be studying my face to see whether I believed her. Before I left I gave her a bottle of clear nail polish and she gave me a few breakfast rolls she sneaked out of the kitchen.

Work grew less complex as time passed, because the more machines I serviced the fewer keys remained that I hadn't matched with a machine. I worked harder, but I also felt relaxed. I would sit on the car in the sun eating candy bars and figuring things out—working on adjustments to my route, computing how much money I'd spent. Jack's wife was going to reimburse me for my expenses. Using Jack's notebooks, I saw that his neat handwriting had changed over time, the slant moving from left to right. Occasionally, there was a note in the margins: "Need new lock for C-24. . . . New man trying to take over territory, A-5." I wondered what *he* had written on the Wish List.

I knew I didn't have to service all the machines. I had originally planned to leave some, doing only enough to keep the route salable. But then I decided to do them all anyway, just for the obsession of it. A couple of the most out-of-the-way places were tiny offices for which Jack had simply laid out candy on shelves, with no machines, and the office workers paid on the honor system. He'd gotten to know the people in those offices better than the people at his more profitable locations. I thought maybe he'd told some of those smaller customers about me, maybe showed them pictures if he had any. In any case, "Jack's girl" is what a couple of them called me.

I saw my father's ghost when I was almost finished with the route, at one of those out-of-the-way places I had considered not servicing. Earlier that night someone had been tailgating me, though the road was empty and he could easily have passed. I slowed, he slowed, I pulled over, and he stopped rather than pass. Finally, I turned onto a side road and he sped on.

It was very late, but I had only two more stops for the night. The next-to-last one was a gas station; it had two machines, one with snacks like potato chips and cookies, and one with candy bars and gum. I was testing keys when I suddenly noticed Jack standing next to me, at a third vending machine that had appeared out of nowhere. I think I screamed and ran a few steps toward my car, but something made me stop and turn. Jack was shaking his keys, but I heard no jingling. "Jack?" I called. I walked back. His image was not quite right. I realized he was a ghost when the wind came up but didn't muss his hair, just made his whole body flow to the side and back. His personality seemed to flow back and forth as well: at first, with his cagey glances to one side, he reminded me of a weasel; then he smiled to himself and seemed almost innocent. I looked around and behind me and saw nothing, no one. I had that same relaxed feeling I'd had a lot lately, a hypnotized feeling. "Do you always come out here to service this machine, even though it's so out of the way?" I said. Like me, he had probably been tempted to skip it. But I bet he never did. He needed to be diligent for a business like this to work, I realized. I'd never thought about that before. The first time I remember seeing him, he was driving a convertible, and I guessed he didn't need to worry much about money. It had probably been important for him to appear that way to people.

He began putting coins into the machine and checking each candy slot to make sure nothing was out of order. Before he put his key into the lock he studied the key, blew on the metal, shined it with his shirt. He paused for a split second, and I realized it was to see whether he could catch a piece of his reflection in the key.

"I see your car over there," I said. "You were following me earlier." My voice sounded the way it always did, but it also sounded strange, because I was basically talking to myself. We worked silently together.

When he was finished, he sat on the gas-station curb, and I joined him. Across the road the ground was so flat it exhilarated me, the way it went on and on. We both tore open a candy-bar wrapper. I had never eaten so much candy in my life. For the last couple of weeks, I'd been living mostly on candy bars and milk.

Jack ate appreciatively, as if chocolate were his favorite food. I reached out and ran my hand through him, only it didn't go through, exactly, it just stretched him out in the middle, as if he were elastic. I asked him about my mother, what she had been like and how much he had loved her, and when he didn't answer I told him I hated him for putting a curse on my dad's life. He tore the wrapper on his candy bar lower and wiped his mouth with his shirt. It seemed like such a lonely life suddenly—before he died he had sat out here in the middle of this nowhere or another again and again for twenty years.

"Well, if you're just going to be sitting there we ought to talk," I said. "Do you have any questions? Shall I tell you about my brothers? Do you want to hear about my boyfriend?"

He nodded at an appropriate moment, but I guess it was just coincidence. "My boyfriend's name is Andy Chin. He's twenty, like me. He's moody, but I wouldn't say he has a bad temper. Sometimes we talk about having a baby and about what kind of house we'd like. But the thing is, we'd rather get a really nice apartment than a house. A condo is more our ideal." Jack sneezed soundlessly. "Bless you," I said. "Did I ever show you any pictures of my brothers? Walker's really quiet, but he's not really shy, the way he used to be. He just doesn't like to talk to people if they don't interest him. Ben's the opposite. He has too many friends. Walker and Ben are in high school. Peter's in grammar school. He skipped a grade because he's so smart." I couldn't help adding, "I bet neither of your sons skipped a grade."

I took a breath. I noticed for the first time that Jack was quite young, maybe about my age or a few years older. He was younger than I could remember ever having seen him. That meant he'd probably just bought the candy route. I think he met my mother around that time. But perhaps that was still in the future for him, a few months or years away. I hadn't been born yet as he sat there. When my mother fell in love with Jack, she must have realized how young they were and that things wouldn't turn out well.

Jack got up and went to his car, brushed it with his hand, admired it. He took out a small notebook and started writing. I wondered where he was going now. Down the highway past the gas station sat a couple of small signs, the back of a billboard, another gas station, and then the highway curved into the night. In the other direction there were no signs and no buildings, just the highway cutting through the fields of yellowed grass. The grass was so pale with dryness it looked almost snow-covered.

Jack started scribbling in a bigger notebook, probably one that I later read. I got angry again, because he wouldn't or couldn't pay attention to me. "If it weren't for you, maybe my mother would have loved my dad more," I said. But that didn't quite make sense. I tried to figure why not: I was at Max's Texaco, but Jack wasn't, although in a way he was, and I wouldn't be there if it weren't for him, even though he . . . What time was it? I was getting sleepy. The dry air smelled faintly of gasoline. I still had another stop, and for a moment I began to worry about my work and forgot about Jack. I tried to calculate from the night sky what time it was, but then I gave up. It didn't matter; it was high time I left.

Franz Kafka
(1883–1924)

THE METAMORPHOSIS
(1915)

I

As Gregor Samsa awoke one morning from uneasy dreams he found himself transformed in his bed into a gigantic insect. He was lying on his hard, as it were armor-plated, back and when he lifted his head a little he could see his dome-like brown belly divided into stiff arched segments on top of which the bed quilt could hardly keep in position and was about to slide off completely. His numerous legs, which were pitifully thin compared to the rest of his bulk, waved helplessly before his eyes.

What has happened to me? he thought. It was no dream. His room, a regular human bedroom, only rather too small, lay quiet between the four familiar walls. Above the table on which a collection of cloth samples was unpacked and spread out—Samsa was a commercial traveler—hung the picture which he had recently cut out of an illustrated magazine and put into a pretty gilt frame. It showed a lady, with a fur cap on and a fur stole, sitting upright and holding out to the spectator a huge fur muff into which the whole of her forearm had vanished!

Gregor's eyes turned next to the window, and the overcast sky—one could hear rain drops beating on the window gutter—made him quite melancholy. What about sleeping a little longer and forgetting all this nonsense, he thought, but it could not be done, for he was accustomed to sleep on his right side and in his present condition he could not turn himself over. However violently he forced himself towards his right side he always rolled on to his back again. He tried it at least a hundred times, shutting his eyes to keep from seeing his struggling legs, and only desisted when he began to feel in his side a faint dull ache he had never experienced before.

Oh God, he thought, what an exhausting job I've picked on! Traveling about day in, day out. It's much more irritating work than doing the actual business in the office, and on top of that there's the trouble of constant traveling, of worrying about train connections, the bed and irregular meals, casual acquaintances that are always new and never become intimate friends. The devil take it all! He felt a slight itching up on his belly; slowly pushed himself on his back nearer to the top of the bed so that he could lift his head more easily; identified the itching place which was surrounded by many small white spots the nature of which he could not understand and made to touch it with a leg, but drew the leg back immediately, for the contact made a cold shiver run through him.

He slid down again into his former position. This getting up early, he thought, makes one quite stupid. A man needs his sleep. Other commercials live like harem women. For instance, when I come back to the hotel of a morning to write up the orders I've got, these others are only sitting down to breakfast. Let me just try that with my chief; I'd be sacked on the spot. Anyhow, that might be quite a good thing for me, who can tell? If I didn't have to hold my hand because of my parents I'd have given notice long ago, I'd have gone to the chief and told him exactly what I think of him. That would knock him endways from his desk! It's a queer way of doing, too, this sitting on high at a desk and talking down to employees, especially when they have to come quite near because the chief is hard of hearing. Well, there's still hope; once I've saved enough money to pay back my parents' debts to him—that should take another five or six years—I'll do it without fail. I'll cut myself completely loose then. For the moment, though, I'd better get up, since my train goes at five.

He looked at the alarm clock ticking on the chest. Heavenly Father! he thought. It was half-past six o'clock and the hands were quietly moving on, it was even past the half-hour, it was getting on toward a quarter to seven. Had the alarm clock not gone off? From the bed one could see that it had been properly set for four o'clock; of course it must have gone off. Yes, but was it possible to sleep quietly through that ear-splitting noise? Well, he had not slept quietly, yet apparently all the more soundly for that. But what was he to do now? The next train went at seven o'clock; to catch that he would need to hurry like mad and his samples weren't even packed up, and he himself wasn't feeling particularly fresh and active. And even if he did catch the train he wouldn't avoid a row with the chief, since the firm's porter would have been waiting for the five o'clock train and would have long since reported his failure to turn up. The porter was a creature of the chief's, spineless and stupid. Well, supposing he were to say he was sick? But that would be most unpleasant and would look suspicious, since during his five years' employment he had not been ill once. The chief himself would be sure to come with the sick-insurance doctor, would reproach his parents with their son's laziness and would cut all excuses short by referring to the insurance doctor, who of course regarded all mankind as perfectly healthy malingerers. And would he be so far wrong on this occasion? Gregor really felt quite well, apart from a drowsiness that was utterly superfluous after such a long sleep, and he was even unusually hungry.

As all this was running through his mind at top speed without his being able to decide to leave his bed—the alarm clock had just struck a quarter to seven—there came a cautious tap at the door behind the head of his bed. "Gregor," said a voice—it was his mother's—"it's a quarter to seven. Hadn't you a train to catch?" That gentle voice! Gregor had a shock as he heard his own voice answering hers, unmistakably his own voice, it was true, but with a persistent horrible twittering squeak behind it like an undertone, that left the words in their clear shape only for the first moment and then rose up reverberating round them to destroy their sense, so that one could not be sure one had heard them rightly. Gregor wanted to answer at length and explain everything, but in the circumstances he confined himself to saying: "Yes, yes, thank you, Mother, I'm getting up now." The wooden door between them must have kept the change in his voice from being noticeable outside, for his mother contented herself with this statement and shuffled away. Yet this brief exchange of words had made the other members of the family aware that Gregor was still in the house, as they had not expected, and at one of the side doors his father was already knocking, gently, yet with his fist. "Gregor, Gregor," he called, "what's the matter with you?" And after a little while he called again in a deeper voice: "Gregor! Gregor!" At the other side door his sister was saying in a low, plaintive tone: "Gregor? Aren't you well? Are you needing anything?" He answered them both at once: "I'm just ready," and did his best to make his voice sound as normal as possible by enunciating the words very clearly and leaving long pauses between them. So his father went back to his breakfast, but his sister whispered: "Gregor, open the door, do." However, he was not thinking of opening the door, and felt thankful for the prudent habit he had acquired in traveling of locking all doors during the night, even at home.

His immediate intention was to get up quietly without being disturbed, to put on his clothes and above all eat his breakfast, and only then to consider what else was to be done, since in bed, he was well aware, his meditations would come to no sensible conclusion. He remembered that often enough in bed he had felt small aches and pains, probably caused by awkward postures, which had proved purely imaginary once he got up, and he looked forward eagerly to seeing this morning's delusions gradually fall away. That the change in his voice was nothing but the precursor of a severe chill, a standing ailment of commercial travelers, he had not the least possible doubt.

To get rid of the quilt was quite easy; he had only to inflate himself a little and it fell off by itself. But the next move was difficult, especially because he was so uncommonly broad. He would have needed arms and hands to hoist himself up; instead he had only the numerous little legs which never stopped waving in all directions and which he could not control in the least. When he tried to bend one of them it was the first to stretch itself straight; and did he succeed at last in making it do what he wanted, all the other legs meanwhile waved the more wildly in a high degree of unpleasant agitation. "But what's the use of lying idle in bed," said Gregor to himself.

He thought that he might get out of bed with the lower part of his body first, but this lower part, which he had not yet seen and of which he could form no clear conception, proved too difficult to move; it shifted so slowly; and when finally, almost wild with annoyance, he gathered his forces together and thrust out recklessly, he had miscalculated the direction and bumped heavily against the lower end of the bed, and the stinging pain he felt informed him that precisely this lower part of his body was at the moment probably the most sensitive.

So he tried to get the top part of himself out first, and cautiously moved his head towards the edge of the bed. That proved easy enough, and despite its breadth and mass the bulk of his body at last slowly followed the movement of his head. Still, when he finally got his head free over the edge of the bed he felt too scared to go on advancing, for after all if he let himself fall in this way it would take a miracle to keep his head from being injured. And at all costs he must not lose consciousness now, precisely now; he would rather stay in bed.

But when after a repetition of the same efforts he lay in his former position again, sighing, and watched his little legs struggling against each other more wildly than ever, if that were possible, and saw no way of bringing any order into this arbitrary confusion, he told himself again that it was impossible to stay in bed and that the most sensible course was to risk everything for the smallest hope of getting away from it. At the same time he did not forget meanwhile to remind himself that cool reflection, the coolest possible, was much better than desperate resolves. In such moments he focused his eyes as sharply as possible on the window, but, unfortunately, the prospect of the morning fog, which muffled even the other side of the narrow street, brought him little encouragement and comfort. "Seven o'clock already," he said to himself when the alarm clock chimed again, "seven o'clock already and still such a thick fog." And for a little while he lay quiet, breathing lightly, as if perhaps expecting such complete repose to restore all things to their real and normal condition.

But then he said to himself: "Before it strikes a quarter past seven I must be quite out of this bed, without fail. Anyhow, by that time someone will have come from the office to ask for me, since it opens before seven." And he set himself to rocking his whole body at once in a regular rhythm, with the idea of swinging it out of the bed. If he tipped himself out in that way he could keep his head from injury by lifting it at an acute angle when he fell. His back seemed to be hard and was not likely to suffer from a fall on the carpet. His biggest worry was the loud crash he would not be able to help making, which would probably cause anxiety, if not terror, behind all the doors. Still, he must take the risk.

When he was already half out of the bed—the new method was more a game than an effort, for he needed only to hitch himself across by rocking to and fro—it struck him how simple it would be if he could get help. Two strong people—he thought of his father and the servant girl—would be amply sufficient; they would only have to thrust their arms under his convex back, lever him out of the bed, bend down with their burden and then be patient enough to let him turn himself right over on to the floor, where it was to be hoped his legs would then find their proper function. Well, ignoring the fact that the doors were all locked, ought he really to call for help? In spite of his misery he could not suppress a smile at the very idea of it.

He had got so far that he could barely keep his equilibrium when he rocked himself strongly, and he would have to nerve himself very soon for the final decision since in five minutes' time it would be a quarter past seven—when the front door bell rang. "That's someone from the office," he said to himself, and grew almost rigid, while his little legs only jigged about all the faster. For a moment everything stayed quiet. "They're not going to open the door," said Gregor to himself, catching at some kind of irrational hope. But then of course the servant girl went as usual to the door with her heavy tread and opened it. Gregor needed only to hear the first good morning of the visitor to know immediately who it was—the chief clerk himself. What a fate, to be condemned to work for a firm where the smallest omission at once gave rise to the gravest suspicion! Were all employees in a body nothing but scoundrels, was there not among them one single loyal devoted man who, had he wasted only an hour or so of the firm's time in a morning, was so tormented by conscience as to be driven out of his mind and actually incapable of leaving his bed? Wouldn't it really have been sufficient to send an apprentice to inquire—if any inquiry were necessary at all—did the chief clerk himself have to come and thus indicate to the entire family, an innocent family, that this suspicious circumstance could be investigated by no one less versed in affairs than himself? And more through the agitation caused by these reflections than through any act of will Gregor swung himself out of bed with all his strength. There was a loud thump, but it was not really a crash. His fall was broken to some extent by the carpet, his back, too, was less stiff than he thought, and so there was merely a dull thud, not so very startling. Only he had not lifted his head carefully enough and had hit it; he turned it and rubbed it on the carpet in pain and irritation.

"That was something falling down in there," said the chief clerk in the next room to the left. Gregor tried to suppose to himself that something like what had happened to him today might some day happen to the chief clerk; one really could not deny that it was possible. But as if in brusque reply to this supposition the chief clerk took a couple of firm steps in the next-door room and his patent leather boots creaked. From the right-hand room his sister was whispering to inform him of the situation: "Gregor, the chief clerk's here." "I know," muttered Gregor to himself; but he didn't dare to make his voice loud enough for his sister to hear it.

"Gregor," said his father now from the left-hand room, "the chief clerk has come and wants to know why you didn't catch the early train. We don't know what to say to him. Besides, he wants to talk to you in person. So open the door, please. He will be good enough to excuse the untidiness of your room." "Good morning, Mr. Samsa," the chief clerk was calling amiably meanwhile. "He's not well," said his mother to the visitor, while his father was still speaking through the door, "he's not well, sir, believe me. What else would make him miss a train! The boy thinks about nothing but his work. It makes me almost cross the way he never goes out in the evenings; he's been here the last eight days and has stayed at home every single evening. He just sits there quietly at the table reading a newspaper or looking through railway timetables. The only amusement he gets is doing fretwork. For instance, he spent two or three evenings cutting out a little picture frame; you would be surprised to see how pretty it is; it's hanging in his room; you'll see it in a minute when Gregor opens the door. I must say I'm glad you've come, sir; we should never have got him to unlock the door by ourselves; he's so obstinate; and I'm sure he's unwell, though he wouldn't have it to be so this morning." "I'm just coming," said Gregor slowly and carefully, not moving an inch for fear of losing one word of the conversation. "I can't think of any other explanation, madam," said the chief clerk, "I hope it's nothing serious. Although on the other hand I must say that we men of business—fortunately or unfortunately—very often simply have to ignore any slight indisposition, since business must be attended to." "Well, can the chief clerk come in now?" asked Gregor's father impatiently, again knocking on the door. "No," said Gregor. In the left-hand room a painful silence followed this refusal, in the right-hand room his sister began to sob.

Why didn't his sister join the others? She was probably newly out of bed and hadn't even begun to put on her clothes yet. Well, why was she crying? Because he wouldn't get up and let the chief clerk in, because he was in danger of losing his job, and because the chief would begin dunning his parents again for the old debts? Surely these were things one didn't need to worry about for the present. Gregor was still at home and not in the least thinking of deserting the family. At the moment, true, he was lying on the carpet and no one who knew the condition he was in could seriously expect him to admit the chief clerk. But for such a small discourtesy, which could plausibly be explained away somehow later on, Gregor could hardly be dismissed on the spot. And it seemed to Gregor that it would be much more sensible to leave him in peace for the present than to trouble him with tears and entreaties. Still, of course, their uncertainty bewildered them all and excused their behavior.

"Mr. Samsa," the chief clerk called now in a louder voice, "what's the matter with you? Here you are, barricading yourself in your room, giving only 'yes' and 'no' for answers, causing your parents a lot of unnecessary trouble and neglecting—I mention this only in passing—neglecting your business duties in an incredible fashion. I am speaking here in the name of your parents and of your chief, and I beg you quite seriously to give me an immediate and precise explanation. You amaze me, you amaze me. I thought you were a quiet, dependable person, and now all at once you seem bent on making a disgraceful exhibition of yourself. The chief did hint to me early this morning a possible explanation for your disappearance—with reference to the cash payments that were entrusted to you recently—but I almost pledged my solemn word of honor that this could not be so. But now that I see how incredibly obstinate you are, I no longer have the slightest desire to take your part at all. And your position in the firm is not so unassailable. I came with the intention of telling you all this in private, but since you are wasting my time so needlessly I don't see why your parents shouldn't hear it too. For some time past your work has been most unsatisfactory; this is not the season of the year for a business boom, of course, we admit that, but a season of the year for doing no business at all, that does not exist, Mr. Samsa, must not exist."

"But, sir," cried Gregor, beside himself and in his agitation forgetting everything else, "I'm just going to open the door this very minute. A slight illness, an attack of giddiness, has kept me from getting up. I'm still lying in bed. But I feel all right again. I'm getting out of bed now. Just give me a moment or two longer! I'm not quite so well as I thought. But I'm all right, really. How a thing like that can suddenly strike one down! Only last night I was quite well, my parents can tell you, or rather I did have a slight presentiment. I must have showed some sign of it. Why didn't I report it at the office! But one always thinks that an indisposition can be got over without staying in the house. Oh sir, do spare my parents! All that you're reproaching me with now has no foundation; no one has ever said a word to me about it. Perhaps you haven't looked at the last orders I sent in. Anyhow, I can still catch the eight o'clock train, I'm much the better for my few hours' rest. Don't let me detain you here, sir; I'll be attending to business very soon, and do be good enough to tell the chief so and to make my excuses to him!"

And while all this was tumbling out pell-mell and Gregor hardly knew what he was saying, he had reached the chest quite easily, perhaps because of the practice he had had in bed, and was now trying to lever himself upright by means of it. He meant actually to open the door, actually to show himself and speak to the chief clerk; he was eager to find out what the others, after all their insistence, would say at the sight of him. If they were horrified then the responsibility was no longer his and he could stay quiet. But if they took it calmly, then he had no reason either to be upset, and could really get to the station for the eight o'clock train if he hurried. At first he slipped down a few times from the polished surface of the chest, but at length with a last heave he stood upright; he paid no more attention to the pains in the lower part of his body, however they smarted. Then he let himself fall against the back of a near-by chair, and clung with his little legs to the edges of it. That brought him into control of himself again and he stopped speaking, for now he could listen to what the chief clerk was saying.

"Did you understand a word of it?" the chief clerk was asking; "surely he can't be trying to make fools of us?" "Oh dear," cried his mother, in tears, "perhaps he's terribly ill and we're tormenting him. Grete! Grete!" she called out then. "Yes Mother?" called his sister from the other side. They were calling to each other across Gregor's room. "You must go this minute for the doctor. Gregor is ill. Go for the doctor, quick. Did you hear how he was speaking?" "That was no human voice," said the chief clerk in a voice noticeably low beside the shrillness of the mother's. "Anna! Anna!" his father was calling through the hall to the kitchen, clapping his hands, "get a locksmith at once!" And the two girls were already running through the hall with a swish of skirts—how could his sister have got dressed so quickly?—and were tearing the front door open. There was no sound of its closing again; they had evidently left it open, as one does in houses where some great misfortune has happened.

But Gregor was now much calmer. The words he uttered were no longer understandable, apparently, although they seemed clear enough to him, even clearer than before, perhaps because his ear had grown accustomed to the sound of them. Yet at any rate people now believed that something was wrong with him, and were ready to help him. The positive certainty with which these first measures had been taken comforted him. He felt himself drawn once more into the human circle and hoped for great and remarkable results from both the doctor and the locksmith, without really distinguishing precisely between them. To make his voice as clear as possible for the decisive conversation that was now imminent he coughed a little, as quietly as he could, of course, since this noise too might not sound like a human cough for all he was able to judge. In the next room meanwhile there was complete silence. Perhaps his parents were sitting at the table with the chief clerk, whispering, perhaps they were all leaning against the door and listening.

Slowly Gregor pushed the chair towards the door, then let go of it, caught hold of the door for support—the soles at the end of his little legs were somewhat sticky—and rested against it for a moment after his efforts. Then he set himself to turning the key in the lock with his mouth. It seemed, unhappily, that he hadn't really any teeth—what could he grip the key with?—but on the other hand his jaws were certainly very strong; with their help he did manage to set the key in motion, heedless of the fact that he was undoubtedly damaging them somewhere, since a brown fluid issued from his mouth, flowed over the key and dripped on the floor. "Just listen to that," said the chief clerk next door; "he's turning the key." That was a great encouragement to Gregor; but they should all have shouted encouragement to him, his father and mother too: "Go on, Gregor," they should have called out, "keep going, hold on to that key!" And in the belief that they were all following his efforts intently, he clenched his jaws recklessly on the key with all the force at his command. As the turning of the key progressed he circled round the lock, holding on now only with his mouth, pushing on the key, as required, or pulling it down again with all the weight of his body. The louder click of the finally yielding lock literally quickened Gregor. With a deep breath of relief he said to himself: "So I didn't need the locksmith," and laid his head on the handle to open the door wide.

Since he had to pull the door towards him, he was still invisible when it was really wide open. He had to edge himself slowly round the near half of the double door, and to do it very carefully if he was not to fall plump upon his back just on the threshold. He was still carrying out this difficult manoeuvre, with no time to observe anything else, when he heard the chief clerk utter a loud "Oh!"—it sounded like a gust of wind—and how he could see the man, standing as he was nearest to the door, clapping one hand before his open mouth and slowly backing away as if driven by some invisible steady pressure. His mother—in spite of the chief clerk's being there her hair was still undone and sticking up in all directions—first clasped her hands and looked at his father, then took two steps towards Gregor and fell on the floor among her outspread skirts, her face quite hidden on her breast. His father knotted his fist with a fierce expression on his face as if he meant to knock Gregor back into his room, then looked uncertainly round the living room, covered his eyes with his hands and wept till his great chest heaved.

Gregor did not go now into the living room, but leaned against the inside of the firmly shut wing of the door, so that only half his body was visible and his head above it bending sideways to look at the others. The light had meanwhile strengthened; on the other side of the street one could see clearly a section of the endlessly long, dark gray building opposite—it was a hospital—abruptly punctuated by its row of regular windows; the rain was still falling, but only in large singly discernible and literally singly splashing drops. The breakfast dishes were set out on the table lavishly, for breakfast was the most important meal of the day to Gregor's father, who lingered it out for hours over various newspapers. Right opposite Gregor on the wall hung a photograph of himself on military service, as a lieutenant, hand on sword, a carefree smile on his face, inviting one to respect his uniform and military bearing. The door leading to the hall was open, and one could see that the front door stood open too, showing the landing beyond and the beginning of the stairs going down.

"Well," said Gregor, knowing perfectly that he was the only one who had retained any composure, "I'll put my clothes on at once, pack up my samples and start off. Will you only let me go? You see, sir, I'm not obstinate, and I'm willing to work; traveling is a hard life, but I couldn't live without it. Where are you going, sir? To the office? Yes? Will you give a true account of all this? One can be temporarily incapacitated, but that's just the moment for remembering former services and bearing in mind that later on, when the incapacity has been got over, one will certainly work with all the more industry and concentration. I'm loyally bound to serve the chief, you know that very well. Besides, I have to provide for my parents and my sister. I'm in great difficulties, but I'll get out of them again. Don't make things any worse for me than they are. Stand up for me in the firm. Travelers are not popular there, I know. People think they earn sacks of money and just have a good time. A prejudice there's no particular reason for revising. But you, sir, have a more comprehensive view of affairs than the rest of the staff, yes, let me tell you in confidence, a more comprehensive view than the chief himself, who, being the owner, lets his judgment easily be swayed against one of his employees. And you know very well that the traveler, who is never seen in the office almost the whole year round, can so easily fall a victim to gossip and ill luck and unfounded complaints, which he mostly knows nothing about, except when he comes back exhausted from his rounds, and only then suffers in person from their evil consequences, which he can no longer trace back to the original causes. Sir, sir, don't go away without a word to me to show that you think me in the right at least to some extent!"

But at Gregor's very first words the chief clerk had already backed away and only stared at him with parted lips over one twitching shoulder. And while Gregor was speaking he did not stand still one moment but stole away towards the door, without taking his eyes off Gregor, yet only an inch at a time, as if obeying some secret injunction to leave the room. He was already at the hall, and the suddenness with which he took his last step out of the living room would have made one believe he had burned the sole of his foot. Once in the hall he stretched his right arm before him towards the staircase, as if some supernatural power were waiting there to deliver him.

Gregor perceived that the chief clerk must on no account be allowed to go away in this frame of mind if his position in the firm were not to be endangered to the utmost. His parents did not understand this so well; they had convinced themselves in the course of years that Gregor was settled for life in this firm, and besides they were so occupied with their immediate troubles that all foresight had forsaken them. Yet Gregor had this foresight. The chief clerk must be detained, soothed, persuaded and finally won over; the whole future of Gregor and his family depended on it! If only his sister had been there! She was intelligent; she had begun to cry while Gregor was still lying quietly on his back. And no doubt the chief clerk, so partial to ladies, would have been guided by her; she would have shut the door of the flat and in the hall talked him out of his horror. But she was not there, and Gregor would have to handle the situation himself. And without remembering that he was still unaware what powers of movement he possessed, without even remembering that his words in all possibility, indeed in all likelihood, would again be unintelligible, he let go the wing of the door, pushed himself through the opening, started to walk towards the chief clerk, who was already ridiculously clinging with both hands to the railing on the landing; but immediately, as he was feeling for a support, he fell down with a little cry upon all his numerous legs. Hardly was he down when he experienced for the first time this morning a sense of physical comfort; his legs had firm ground under them; they were completely obedient, as he noted with joy; they even strove to carry him forward in whatever direction he chose; and he was inclined to believe that a final relief from all his sufferings was at hand. But in the same moment as he found himself on the floor, rocking with suppressed eagerness to move, not far from his mother, indeed just in front of her, she, who had seemed so completely crushed, sprang all at once to her feet, her arms and fingers outspread, cried: "Help, for God's sake, help!" bent her head down as if to see Gregor better, yet on the contrary kept backing senselessly away; had quite forgotten that the laden table stood behind her; sat upon it hastily, as if in absence of mind, when she bumped into it; and seemed altogether unaware that the big coffee pot beside her was upset and pouring coffee in a flood over the carpet.

"Mother, Mother," said Gregor in a low voice, and looked up at her. The chief clerk, for the moment, had quite slipped from his mind; instead, he could not resist snapping his jaws together at the sight of the streaming coffee. That made his mother scream again, she fled from the table and fell into the arms of his father, who hastened to catch her. But Gregor had now no time to spare for his parents; the chief clerk was already on the stairs; with his chin on the banisters he was taking one last backward look. Gregor made a spring, to be as sure as possible of overtaking him; the chief clerk must have divined his intention, for he leaped down several steps and vanished; he was still yelling "Ugh!" and it echoed through the whole staircase.

Unfortunately, the flight of the chief clerk seemed completely to upset Gregor's father, who had remained relatively calm until now, for instead of running after the man himself, or at least not hindering Gregor in his pursuit, he seized in his right hand the walking stick which the chief clerk had left behind on a chair, together with a hat and greatcoat, snatched in his left hand a large newspaper from the table and began stamping his feet and flourishing the stick and the newspaper to drive Gregor back into his room. No entreaty of Gregor's availed, indeed no entreaty was even understood, however humbly he bent his head his father only stamped on the floor the more loudly. Behind his father his mother had torn open a window, despite the cold weather, and was leaning far out of it with her face in her hands. A strong draught set in from the street to the staircase, the window curtains blew in, the newspapers on the table fluttered, stray pages whisked over the floor. Pitilessly Gregor's father drove him back, hissing and crying "Shoo!" like a savage. But Gregor was quite unpracticed in walking backwards, it really was a slow business. If he only had a chance to turn around he could get back to his room at once, but he was afraid of exasperating his father by the slowness of such a rotation and at any moment the stick in his father's hand might hit him a fatal blow on the back or on the head. In the end, however, nothing else was left for him to do since to his horror he observed that in moving backwards he could not even control the direction he took; and so, keeping an anxious eye on his father all the time over his shoulder, he began to turn round as quickly as he could, which was in reality very slowly. Perhaps his father noted his good intentions, for he did not interfere except every now and then to help him in the manoeuvre from a distance with the point of the stick. If only he would have stopped making that unbearable hissing noise! It made Gregor quite lose his head. He had turned almost completely round when the hissing noise so distracted him that he even turned a little the wrong way again. But when at last his head was fortunately right in front of the doorway, it appeared that his body was too broad simply to get through the opening. His father, of course, in his present mood was far from thinking of such a thing as opening the other half of the door, to let Gregor have enough space. He had merely the fixed idea of driving Gregor back into his room as quickly as possible. He would never have suffered Gregor to make the circumstantial preparations for standing up on end and perhaps slipping his way through the door. Maybe he was now making more noise than ever to urge Gregor forward, as if no obstacle impeded him; to Gregor, anyhow, the noise in his rear sounded no longer like the voice of one single father; this was really no joke, and Gregor thrust himself—come what might—into the doorway. One side of his body rose up, he was tilted at an angle in the doorway, his flank was quite bruised, horrid blotches stained the white door, soon he was stuck fast and, left to himself, could not have moved at all, his legs on one side fluttered trembling to the air, those on the other were crushed painfully to the floor—when from behind his father gave him a strong push which was literally a deliverance and he flew far into the room, bleeding freely. The door was slammed behind him with the stick, and then at last there was silence.

II

Not until it was twilight did Gregor awake out of a deep sleep, more like a swoon than a sleep. He would certainly have waked up of his own accord not much later, for he felt himself sufficiently rested and well-slept, but it seemed to him as if a fleeting step and a cautious shutting of the door leading into the hall had aroused him. The electric lights in the street cast a pale sheen here and there on the ceiling and the upper surfaces of the furniture, but down below, where he lay, it was dark. Slowly, awkwardly trying out his feelers, which he now first learned to appreciate, he pushed his way to the door to see what had been happening there. His left side felt like one single long, unpleasantly tense scar, and he had actually to limp on his two rows of legs. One little leg, moreover, had been severely damaged in the course of that morning's events—it was almost a miracle that only one had been damaged—and trailed uselessly behind him.

He had reached the door before he discovered what had really drawn him to it: the smell of food. For there stood a basin filled with fresh milk in which floated little sops of white bread. He could almost have laughed with joy, since he was now still hungrier than in the morning, and he dipped his head almost over the eyes straight into the milk. But soon in disappointment he withdrew it again; not only did he find it difficult to feed because of his tender left side—and he could only feed with the palpitating collaboration of his whole body—he did not like the milk either, although milk had been his favorite drink and that was certainly why his sister had set it there for him, indeed it was almost with repulsion that he turned away from the basin and crawled back to the middle of the room.

He could see through the crack of the door that the gas was turned on in the living room, but while usually at this time his father made a habit of reading the afternoon newspaper in a loud voice to his mother and occasionally to his sister as well, not a sound was now to be heard. Well, perhaps his father had recently given up this habit of reading aloud, which his sister had mentioned so often in conversation and in her letters. But there was the same silence all around, although the flat was certainly not empty of occupants. "What a quiet life our family has been leading," said Gregor to himself, and as he sat there motionless staring into the darkness he felt great pride in the fact that he had been able to provide such a life for his parents and sister in such a fine flat. But what if all the quiet, the comfort, the contentment were now to end in horror? To keep himself from being lost in such thoughts Gregor took refuge in movement and crawled up and down the room.

Once during the long evening one of the side doors was opened a little and quickly shut again, later the other side door too; someone had apparently wanted to come in and then thought better of it. Gregor now stationed himself immediately before the living room door, determined to persuade any hesitating visitor to come in or at least to discover who it might be; but the door was not opened again and he waited in vain. In the early morning, when the doors were locked, they had all wanted to come in, now that he had opened one door and the other had apparently been opened during the day, no one came in and even the keys were on the other side of the doors.

It was late at night before the gas went out in the living room, and Gregor could easily tell that his parents and his sister had all stayed awake until then, for he could clearly hear the three of them stealing away on tiptoe. No one was likely to visit him, not until the morning, that was certain; so he had plenty of time to meditate at his leisure on how he was to arrange his life afresh. But the lofty, empty room in which he had to lie flat on the floor filled him with an apprehension he could not account for, since it had been his very own room for the past five years—and with a half-unconscious action, not without a slight feeling of shame, he scuttled under the sofa, where he felt comfortable at once, although his back was a little cramped and he could not lift his head up, and his only regret was that his body was too broad to get the whole of it under the sofa.

He stayed there all night, spending the time partly in a light slumber, from which his hunger kept waking him up with a start, and partly in worrying and sketching vague hopes, which all led to the same conclusion, that he must lie low for the present and, by exercising patience and the utmost consideration, help the family to bear the inconvenience he was bound to cause them in his present condition.

Very early in the morning, it was still almost night, Gregor had the chance to test the strength of his new resolutions, for his sister, nearly fully dressed, opened the door from the hall and peered in. She did not see him at once, yet when she caught sight of him under the sofa—well, he had to be somewhere, he couldn't have flown away, could he?—she was so startled that without being able to help it she slammed the door shut again. But as if regretting her behavior she opened the door again immediately and came in on tiptoe, as if she were visiting an invalid or even a stranger. Gregor had pushed his head forward to the very edge of the sofa and watched her. Would she notice that he had left the milk standing, and not for lack of hunger, and would she bring in some other kind of food more to his taste? If she did not do it of her own accord, he would rather starve than draw her attention to the fact, although he felt a wild impulse to dart out from under the sofa, throw himself at her feet and beg her for something to eat. But his sister at once noticed, with surprise, that the basin was still full, except for a little milk that had been spilt all around it, she lifted it immediately, not with her bare hands, true, but with a cloth and carried it away. Gregor was wildly curious to know what she would bring instead, and made various speculations about it. Yet what she actually did next, in the goodness of her heart, he could never have guessed at. To find out what he liked she brought him a whole selection of food, all set out on an old newspaper. There were old, half-decayed vegetables, bones from last night's supper covered with a white sauce that had thickened; some raisins and almonds; a piece of cheese that Gregor would have called uneatable two days ago; a dry roll of bread, a buttered roll, and a roll both buttered and salted. Besides all that, she set down again the same basin, into which she had poured some water, and which was apparently to be reserved for his exclusive use. And with fine tact, knowing that Gregor would not eat in her presence, she withdrew quickly and even turned the key, to let him understand that he could take his ease as much as he liked. Gregor's legs all whizzed towards the food. His wounds must have healed completely, moreover, for he felt no disability, which amazed him and made him reflect how more than a month ago he had cut one finger a little with a knife and had still suffered pain from the wound only the day before yesterday. Am I less sensitive now? he thought, and sucked greedily at the cheese, which above all the other edibles attracted him at once and strongly. One after another and with tears of satisfaction in his eyes he quickly devoured the cheese, the vegetables and the sauce; the fresh food, on the other hand, had no charms for him, he could not even stand the smell of it and actually dragged away to some little distance the things he could eat. He had long finished his meal and was only lying lazily on the same spot when his sister turned the key slowly as a sign for him to retreat. That roused him at once, although he was nearly asleep, and he hurried under the sofa again. But it took considerable self-control for him to stay under the sofa, even for the short time his sister was in the room, since the large meal had swollen his body somewhat and he was so cramped he could hardly breathe. Slight attacks of breathlessness afflicted him and his eyes were starting a little out of his head as he watched his unsuspecting sister sweeping together with a broom not only the remains of what he had eaten but even the things he had not touched, as if these were now of no use to anyone, and hastily shoveling it all into a bucket, which she covered with a wooden lid and carried away. Hardly had she turned her back when Gregor came from under the sofa and stretched and puffed himself out.

In this manner Gregor was fed, once in the early morning while his parents and the servant girl were still asleep, and a second time after they had all had their midday dinner, for then his parents took a short nap and the servant girl could be sent out on some errand or other by his sister. Not that they would have wanted him to starve, of course, but perhaps they could not have borne to know more about his feeding than from hearsay, perhaps too his sister wanted to spare them such little anxieties wherever possible, since they had quite enough to bear as it was.

Under what pretext the doctor and the locksmith had been got rid of on that first morning Gregor could not discover, for since what he said was not understood by the others it never struck any of them, not even his sister, that he could understand what they said, and so whenever his sister came into his room he had to content himself with hearing her utter only a sigh now and then and an occasional appeal to the saints. Later on, when she had got a little used to the situation—of course she could never get completely used to it—she sometimes threw out a remark which was kindly meant or could be so interpreted. "Well, he liked his dinner today," she would say when Gregor had made a good clearance of his food; and when he had not eaten, which gradually happened more and more often, she would say almost sadly: "Everything's been left standing again."

But although Gregor could get no news directly, he overheard a lot from the neighboring rooms, and as soon as voices were audible, he would run to the door of the room concerned and press his whole body against it. In the first few days especially there was no conversation that did not refer to him somehow, even if only indirectly. For two whole days there were family consultations at every mealtime about what should be done; but also between meals the same subject was discussed, for there were always at least two members of the family at home, since no one wanted to be alone in the flat and to leave it quite empty was unthinkable. And on the very first of these days the household cook—it was not quite clear what and how much she knew of the situation—went down on her knees to his mother and begged leave to go, and when she departed, a quarter of an hour later, gave thanks for her dismissal with tears in her eyes as if for the greatest benefit that could have been conferred on her, and without any prompting swore a solemn oath that she would never say a single word to anyone about what had happened.

Now Gregor's sister had to cook too, helping her mother; true, the cooking did not amount to much, for they ate scarcely anything. Gregor was always hearing one of the family vainly urging another to eat and getting no answer but: "Thanks, I've had all I want," or something similar. Perhaps they drank nothing either. Time and again his sister kept asking his father if he wouldn't like some beer and offered kindly to go and fetch it herself, and when he made no answer suggested that she could ask the concierge to fetch it, so that he need feel no sense of obligation, but then a round "No" came from his father and no more was said about it.

In the course of that very first day Gregor's father explained the family's financial position and prospects to both his mother and his sister. Now and then he rose from the table to get some voucher or memorandum out of the small safe he had rescued from the collapse of his business five years earlier. One could hear him opening the complicated lock and rustling papers out and shutting it again. This statement made by his father was the first cheerful information Gregor had heard since his imprisonment. He had been of the opinion that nothing at all was left over from his father's business, at least his father had never said anything to the contrary, and of course he had not asked him directly. At that time Gregor's sole desire was to do his utmost to help the family to forget as soon as possible the catastrophe which had overwhelmed the business and thrown them all into a state of complete despair. And so he had set to work with unusual ardor and almost overnight had become a commercial traveler instead of a little clerk, with of course much greater chances of earning money, and his success was immediately translated into good round coin which he could lay on the table for his amazed and happy family. These had been fine times, and they had never recurred, at least not with the same sense of glory, although later on Gregor had earned so much money that he was able to meet the expenses of the whole household and did so. They had simply got used to it, both the family and Gregor; the money was gratefully accepted and gladly given, but there was no special uprush of warm feeling. With his sister alone had he remained intimate, and it was a secret plan of his that she, who loved music, unlike himself, and could play movingly on the violin, should be sent next year to study at the Conservatorium, despite the great expense that would entail, which must be made up in some other way. During his brief visits home the Conservatorium was often mentioned in the talks he had with his sister, but always merely as a beautiful dream which could never come true, and his parents discouraged even these innocent references to it; yet Gregor had made up his mind firmly about it and meant to announce the fact with due solemnity on Christmas Day.

Such were the thoughts, completely futile in his present condition, that went through his head as he stood clinging upright to the door and listening. Sometimes out of sheer weariness he had to give up listening and let his head fall negligently against the door, but he always had to pull himself together again at once, for even the slight sound his head made was audible next door and brought all conversation to a stop. "What can he be doing now?" his father would say after a while, obviously turning towards the door, and only then would the interrupted conversation gradually be set going again.

Gregor was now informed as amply as he could wish—for his father tended to repeat himself in his explanations, partly because it was a long time since he had handled such matters and partly because his mother could not always grasp things at once—that a certain amount of investments, a very small amount it was true, had survived the wreck of their fortunes and had even increased a little because the dividends had not been touched meanwhile. And besides that, the money Gregor brought home every month—he had kept only a few dollars for himself—had never been quite used up and now amounted to a small capital sum. Behind the door Gregor nodded his head eagerly, rejoiced at this evidence of unexpected thrift and foresight. True, he could really have paid off some more of his father's debts to the chief with his extra money, and so brought much nearer the day on which he could quit his job, but doubtless it was better the way his father had arranged it.

Yet this capital was by no means sufficient to let the family live on the interest of it; for one year, perhaps, or at the most two, they could live on the principal, that was all. It was simply a sum that ought not to be touched and should be kept for a rainy day; money for living expenses would have to be earned. Now his father was still hale enough but an old man, and he had done no work for the past five years and could not be expected to do much; during these five years, the first years of leisure in his laborious though unsuccessful life, he had grown rather fat and become sluggish. And Gregor's old mother, how was she to earn a living with her asthma, which troubled her even when she walked through the flat and kept her lying on a sofa every other day panting for breath beside an open window? And was his sister to earn her bread, she who was still a child of seventeen and whose life hitherto had been so pleasant, consisting as it did in dressing herself nicely, sleeping long, helping in the housekeeping, going out to a few modest entertainments and above all playing the violin? At first whenever the need for earning money was mentioned Gregor let go his hold on the door and threw himself down on the cool leather sofa beside it, he felt so hot with shame and grief.

Often he just lay there the long nights through without sleeping at all, scrabbling for hours on the leather. Or he nerved himself to the great effort of pushing an armchair to the window, then crawled up over the window sill and, braced against the chair, leaned against the window panes, obviously in some recollection of the sense of freedom that looking out of a window always used to give him. For in reality day by day things that were even a little way off were growing dimmer to his sight; the hospital across the street, which he used to execrate for being all too often before his eyes, was now quite beyond his range of vision, and if he had not known that he lived in Charlotte Street, a quiet street but still a city street, he might have believed that his window gave on a desert waste where gray sky and gray land blended indistinguishably into each other. His quick-witted sister only needed to observe twice that the armchair stood by the window; after that whenever she had tidied the room she always pushed the chair back to the same place at the window and even left the inner casements open.

If he could have spoken to her and thanked her for all she had to do for him, he could have borne her ministrations better; as it was, they oppressed him. She certainly tried to make as light as possible of whatever was disagreeable in her task, and as time went on she succeeded, of course, more and more, but time brought more enlightenment to Gregor too. The very way she came in distressed him. Hardly was she in the room when she rushed to the window, without even taking time to shut the door, careful as she was usually to shield the sight of Gregor's room from the others, and as if she were almost suffocating tore the casements open with hasty fingers, standing then in the open draught for a while even in the bitterest cold and drawing deep breaths. This noisy scurry of hers upset Gregor twice a day; he would crouch trembling under the sofa all the time, knowing quite well that she would certainly have spared him such a disturbance had she found it at all possible to stay in his presence without opening a window.

On one occasion, about a month after Gregor's metamorphosis, when there was surely no reason for her to be still startled at his appearance, she came a little earlier than usual and found him gazing out of the window, quite motionless, and thus well placed to look like a bogey. Gregor would not have been surprised had she not come in at all, for she could not immediately open the window while he was there, but not only did she retreat, she jumped back as if in alarm and banged the door shut; a stranger might well have thought that he had been lying in wait for her there meaning to bite her. Of course he hid himself under the sofa at once, but he had to wait until midday before she came again, and she seemed more ill at ease than usual. This made him realize how repulsive the sight of him still was to her, and that it was bound to go on being repulsive, and what an effort it must cost her not to run away even from the sight of the small portion of his body that stuck out from under the sofa. In order to spare her that, therefore, one day he carried a sheet on his back to the sofa—it cost him four hours' labor—and arranged it there in such a way as to hide him completely, so that even if she were to bend down she could not see him. Had she considered the sheet unnecessary, she would certainly have stripped it off the sofa again, for it was clear enough that this curtaining and confining of himself was not likely to conduce Gregor's comfort, but she left it where it was, and Gregor even fancied that he caught a thankful glance from her eye when he lifted the sheet carefully a very little with his head to see how she was taking the new arrangement.

50 For the first fortnight his parents could not bring themselves to the point of entering his room, and he often heard them expressing their appreciation of his sister's activities, whereas formerly they had frequently scolded her for being as they thought a somewhat useless daughter. But

now, both of them often waited outside the door, his father and his mother, while his sister tidied his room, and as soon as she came out she had to tell them exactly how things were in the room, what Gregor had eaten, how he had conducted himself this time and whether there was not perhaps some slight improvement in his condition. His mother, moreover, began relatively soon to want to visit him, but his father and sister dissuaded her at first with arguments which Gregor listened to very attentively and altogether approved. Later, however, she had to be held back by main force, and when she cried out: "Do let me in to Gregor, he is my unfortunate son! Can't you understand that I must go to him?" Gregor thought it might be well to have her come in, not every day, of course, but perhaps once a week; she understood things, after all, much better than his sister, who was only a child despite the efforts she was making and had perhaps taken on so difficult a task merely out of childish thoughtlessness.

Gregor's desire to see his mother was soon fulfilled. During the daytime he did not want to show himself at the window, out of consideration for his parents, but he could not crawl very far around the few square yards of floor space he had, nor could he bear lying quietly at rest all during the night, while he was fast losing any interest he had ever taken in food, so that for mere recreation he had formed the habit of crawling crisscross over the walls and ceiling. He especially enjoyed hanging suspended from the ceiling; it was much better than lying on the floor; one could breathe more freely; one's body swung and rocked lightly; and in the almost blissful absorption induced by this suspension it could happen to his own surprise that he let go and fell plump on the floor. Yet he now had his body much better under control than formerly, and even such a big fall did him no harm. His sister at once remarked the new distraction Gregor had found for himself—he left traces behind him of the sticky stuff on his soles wherever he crawled—and she got the idea in her head of giving him as wide a field as possible to crawl in and of removing the pieces of furniture that hindered him, above all the chest of drawers and the writing desk. But that was more than she could manage all by herself; she did not dare ask her father to help her; and as for the servant girl, a young creature of sixteen who had had the courage to stay on after the cook's departure, she could not be asked to help, for she had begged as an especial favor that she might keep the kitchen door locked and open it only on a definite summons; so there was nothing left but to apply to her mother at an hour when her father was out. And the old lady did come, with exclamations of joyful eagerness, which, however, died away at the door of Gregor's room. Gregor's sister, of course, went in first, to see that everything was in order before letting his mother enter. In great haste Gregor pulled the sheet lower and rucked it more in folds so that it really looked as if it had been thrown accidentally over the sofa. And this time he did not peer out from under it; he renounced the pleasure of seeing his mother on this occasion and was only glad that she had come at all. "Come in, he's out of sight," said his sister, obviously leading her mother in by the hand. Gregor could now hear the two women struggling to shift the heavy old chest from its place, and his sister claiming the greater part of the labor for herself, without listening to the admonitions of her mother who feared she might overstrain herself. It took a long time. After at least a quarter of an hour's tugging his mother objected that the chest had better be left where it was, for in the first place it was too heavy and could never be got out before his father came home, and standing in the middle of the room like that it would only hamper Gregor's movements, while in the second place it was not at all certain that removing the furniture would be doing a service to Gregor. She was inclined to think to the contrary; the sight of the naked walls made her own heart heavy, and why shouldn't Gregor have the same feeling, considering that he had been used to his furniture for so long and might feel forlorn without it. "And doesn't it look," she concluded in a low voice—in fact she had been almost whispering all the time as if to avoid letting Gregor, whose exact whereabouts she did not know, hear even the tones of her voice, for she was convinced that he could not understand her words—"doesn't it look as if we were showing him, by taking away his furniture, that we have given up hope of his ever getting better and are just leaving him coldly to himself? I think it would be best to keep his room exactly as it has always been, so that when he comes back to us he will find everything unchanged and be able all the more easily to forget what has happened in between."

On hearing these words from his mother Gregor realized that the lack of all direct human speech for the past two months together with the monotony of family life must have confused his mind, otherwise he could not account for the fact that he had quite earnestly looked forward to having his room emptied of furnishing. Did he really want his warm room, so comfortably fitted with old family furniture, to be turned into a naked den in which he would certainly be able to crawl unhampered in all directions but at the price of shedding simultaneously all recollection of his human background? He had indeed been so near the brink of forgetfulness that only the voice of his mother, which he had not heard for so long, had drawn him back from it. Nothing should be taken out of his room; everything must stay as it was; he could not dispense with the good influence of the furniture on his state of mind; and even if the furniture did hamper him in his senseless crawling round and round, that was no drawback but a great advantage.

Unfortunately his sister was of the contrary opinion; she had grown accustomed, and not without reason, to consider herself an expert in Gregor's affairs as against her parents, and so her mother's advice was now enough to make her determined on the removal not only of the chest and the writing desk, which had been her first intention, but of all the furniture except the indispensable sofa. This determination was not, of course, merely the outcome of childish recalcitrance and of the self-confidence she had recently developed so unexpectedly and at such cost;

she had in fact perceived that Gregor needed a lot of space to crawl about in, while on the other hand he never used the furniture at all, so far as could be seen. Another factor might have been also the enthusiastic temperament of an adolescent girl, which seeks to indulge itself on every opportunity and which now tempted Grete to exaggerate the horror of her brother's circumstances in order that she might do all the more for him. In a room where Gregor lorded it all alone over empty walls no one save herself was likely ever to set foot.

And so she was not to be moved from her resolve by her mother who seemed moreover to be ill at ease in Gregor's room and therefore unsure of herself, was soon reduced to silence and helped her daughter as best she could to push the chest outside. Now, Gregor could do without the chest, if need be, but the writing desk he must retain. As soon as the two women had got the chest out of his room, groaning as they pushed it, Gregor stuck his head out from under the sofa to see how he might intervene as kindly and cautiously as possible. But as bad luck would have it, his mother was the first to return, leaving Grete clasping the chest in the room next door where she was trying to shift it all by herself, without of course moving it from the spot. His mother however was not accustomed to the sight of him, it might sicken her and so in alarm Gregor backed quickly to the other end of the sofa, yet could not prevent the sheet from swaying a little in front. That was enough to put her on the alert. She paused, stood still for a moment and then went back to Grete.

Although Gregor kept reassuring himself that nothing out of the way was happening, but only a few bits of furniture were being changed round, he soon had to admit that all this trotting to and fro of the two women, their little ejaculations and the scraping of furniture along the floor affected him like a vast disturbance coming from all sides at once, and however much he tucked in his head and legs and cowered to the very floor he was bound to confess that he would not be able to stand it for long. They were clearing his room out; taking away everything he loved; the chest in which he kept his fret saw and other tools was already dragged off; they were now loosening the writing desk which had almost sunk into the floor, the desk at which he had done all his homework when he was at the commercial academy, at the grammar school before that, and, yes, even at the primary school—he had no more time to waste in weighing the good intentions of the two women, whose existence he had by now almost forgotten, for they were so exhausted that they were laboring in silence and nothing could be heard but the heavy scuffling of their feet.

And so he rushed out—the women were just leaning against the writing desk in the next room to give themselves a breather—and four times changed his direction, since he really did not know what to rescue first, then on the wall opposite, which was already otherwise cleared, he was struck by the picture of the lady muffled in so much fur and quickly crawled up to it and pressed himself to the glass, which was a good surface to hold on to and comforted his hot belly. This picture at least, which was entirely hidden beneath him, was going to be removed by nobody. He turned his head towards the door of the living room so as to observe the women when they came back.

They had not allowed themselves much of a rest and were already coming; Grete had twined her arm round her mother and was almost supporting her. "Well, what shall we take now?" said Grete, looking round. Her eyes met Gregor's from the wall. She kept her composure, presumably because of her mother, bent her head down to her mother, to keep her from looking up, and said, although in a fluttering, unpremeditated voice: "Come, hadn't we better go back to the living room for a moment?" Her intentions were clear enough to Gregor, she wanted to bestow her mother in safety and then chase him down from the wall. Well, just let her try it! He clung to his picture and would not give it up. He would rather fly in Grete's face.

But Grete's words had succeeded in disquieting her mother, who took a step to one side, caught sight of the huge brown mass on the flowered wallpaper, and before she was really conscious that what she saw was Gregor screamed in a loud, hoarse voice: "Oh God, oh God!" fell with outspread arms over the sofa as if giving up and did not move. "Gregor!" cried his sister, shaking her fist and glaring at him. This was the first time she had directly addressed him since his metamorphosis. She ran into the next room for some aromatic essence with which to rouse her mother from her fainting fit. Gregor wanted to help too—there was still time to rescue the picture—but he was stuck fast to the glass and had to tear himself loose; he then ran after his sister into the next room as if he could advise her, as he used to do; but then had to stand helplessly behind her; she meanwhile searched among various small bottles and when she turned round started in alarm at the sight of him; one bottle fell on the floor and broke; a splinter of glass cut Gregor's face and some kind of corrosive medicine splashed him; without pausing a moment longer Grete gathered up all the bottles she could carry and ran to her mother with them; she banged the door shut with her foot. Gregor was now cut off from his mother, who was perhaps nearly dying because of him; he dared not open the door for fear of frightening away his sister, who had to stay with her mother; there was nothing he could do but wait; and harassed by self-reproach and worry he began now to crawl to and fro, over everything, walls, furniture and ceiling, and finally in his despair, when the whole room seemed to be reeling round him, fell down on to the middle of the big table.

A little while elapsed, Gregor was still lying there feebly and all around was quiet, perhaps that was a good omen. Then the doorbell rang. The servant girl was of course locked in her kitchen, and Grete would have to open the door. It was his father. "What's been happening?" were his first words; Grete's face must have told him everything. Grete answered in a muffled voice, apparently hiding her head on his breast: "Mother has been fainting, but she's better now. Gregor's broken loose." "Just what I expected," said his father, "just what I've been telling you, but you women would never listen." It was clear to Gregor that his father had taken the worst interpretation of Grete's all too brief statement and was assuming that Gregor had been guilty of some violent act. Therefore Gregor must now try to propitiate his father, since he had neither time nor means for an explanation. And so he fled to the door of his own room and crouched against it, to let his father see as soon as he came in from the hall that his son had the good intention of getting back into his room immediately and that it was not necessary to drive him there, but that if only the door were opened he would disappear at once.

60 Yet his father was not in the mood to perceive such fine distinctions. "Ah!" he cried as soon as he appeared, in a tone which sounded at once angry and exultant. Gregor drew his head back from the door and lifted it to look at his father. Truly, this was not the father he had imagined to himself; admittedly he had been too absorbed of late in his new recreation of crawling over the ceiling to take the same interest as before in what was happening elsewhere in the flat, and he ought really to be prepared for some changes. And yet, and yet, could that be his father? The man who used to lie wearily sunk in bed whenever Gregor set out on a business journey; who welcomed him back of an evening lying in a long chair in a dressing gown; who could not really rise to his feet but only lifted his arms in greeting, and on the rare occasions when he did go out with his family, on one or two Sundays a year and on high holidays, walked between Gregor and his mother, who were slow walkers anyhow, even more slowly than they did, muffled in his old greatcoat, shuffling laboriously forward with the help of his crookhandled stick which he set down most cautiously at every step and, whenever he wanted to say anything, nearly always came to a full stop and gathered his escort around him? Now he was standing there in fine shape; dressed in a smart blue uniform with gold buttons, such as bank messengers wear; his strong double chin bulged over the stiff high collar of his jacket; from under his bushy eyebrows his black eyes darted fresh and penetrating glances; his onetime tangled white hair had been combed flat on either side of a shining and carefully exact parting. He pitched his cap, which bore a gold monogram, probably the badge of some bank, in a wide sweep across the whole room on to a sofa and with the tail-ends of his jacket thrown back, his hands in his trouser pockets, advanced with a grim visage towards Gregor. Likely enough he did not himself know what he meant to do; at any rate he lifted his feet uncommonly high, and Gregor was dumbfounded at the enormous size of his shoe soles. But Gregor could not risk standing up to him, aware as he had been from the very first day of his new life that his father believed only the severest measures suitable for dealing with him. And so he ran before his father, stopping when he stopped and scuttling forward again when his father made any kind of move. In this way they circled the room several times without anything decisive happening; indeed the whole operation did not even look like a pursuit because it was

carried out so slowly. And so Gregor did not leave the floor, for he feared that his father might take as a piece of peculiar wickedness any excursion of his over the walls or the ceiling. All the same, he could not stay this course much longer, for while his father took one step he had to carry out a whole series of movements. He was already beginning to feel breathless, just as in his former life his lungs had not been very dependable. As he was staggering along, trying to concentrate his energy on running, hardly keeping his eyes open; in his dazed state never even thinking of any other escape than simply going forward; and having almost forgotten that the walls were free to him, which in this room were well provided with finely carved pieces of furniture full of knobs and crevices—suddenly something lightly flung landed close behind him and rolled before him. It was an apple; a second apple followed immediately; Gregor came to a stop in alarm; there was no point in running on, for his father was determined to bombard him. He had filled his pockets with fruit from the dish on the sideboard and was now shying apple after apple, without taking particularly good aim for the moment. The small red apples rolled about the floor as if magnetized and cannoned into each other. An apple thrown without much force grazed Gregor's back and glanced off harmlessly. But another following immediately landed right on his back and sank in; Gregor wanted to drag himself forward, as if this startling, incredible pain could be left behind him: but he felt as if nailed to the spot and flattened himself out in a complete derangement of all his senses. With his last conscious look he saw the door of his room being torn open and his mother rushing out ahead of his screaming sister, in her underbodice, for her daughter had loosened her clothing to let her breathe more freely and recover from her swoon, he saw his mother rushing towards his father, leaving one after another behind her on the floor her loosened petticoats, stumbling over her petticoats straight to his father and embracing him, in complete union with him—but here Gregor's sight began to fail—with her hands clasped round his father's neck as she begged for her son's life.

III

The serious injury done to Gregor, which disabled him for more than a month—the apple went on sticking in his body as a visible reminder, since no one ventured to remove it—seemed to have made even his father recollect that Gregor was a member of the family, despite his present unfortunate and repulsive shape, and ought not to be treated as an enemy, that, on the contrary, family duty required the suppression of disgust and the exercise of patience, nothing but patience.

And although his injury had impaired, probably for ever, his power of movement, and for the time being it took him long, long minutes to creep across his room like an old invalid—there was no question now of crawling up the wall—yet in his own opinion he was sufficiently compensated for this worsening of his condition by the fact that towards evening the living-room door, which he used to watch intently for an hour or two beforehand, was always thrown open, so that lying in the darkness of his room, invisible to the family, he could see them all at the lamp-lit table and listen to their talk, by general consent as it were, very different from his earlier eavesdropping.

True, their intercourse lacked the lively character of former times, which he had always called to mind with a certain wistfulness in the small hotel bedrooms where he had been wont to throw himself down, tired out, on damp bedding. They were now mostly very silent. Soon after supper his father would fall asleep in his armchair; his mother and sister would admonish each other to be silent; his mother, bending low over the lamp, stitched at fine sewing for an underwear firm; his sister, who had taken a job as a salesgirl, was learning shorthand and French in the evenings on the chance of bettering herself. Sometimes his father woke up, and as if quite unaware that he had been sleeping said to his mother: "What a lot of sewing you're doing today!" and at once fell asleep again, while the two women exchanged a tired smile.

With a kind of mulishness his father persisted in keeping his uniform on even in the house; his dressing gown hung uselessly on its peg and he slept fully dressed where he sat, as if he were ready for service at any moment and even here only at the beck and call of his superior. As a result, his uniform, which was not brand-new to start with, began to look dirty, despite all the loving care of the mother and sister to keep it clean, and Gregor often spent whole evenings gazing at the many greasy spots on the garment, gleaming with gold buttons always in a high state of polish, in which the old man sat sleeping in extreme discomfort and yet quite peacefully.

65 As soon as the clock struck ten his mother tried to rouse his father with gentle words and to persuade him after that to get into bed, for sitting there he could not have a proper sleep and that was what he needed most, since he had to go to duty at six. But with the mulishness that had obsessed him since he became a bank messenger he always insisted on staying longer at the table, although he regularly fell asleep again and in the end only with the greatest trouble could be got out of his armchair and into his bed. However insistently Gregor's mother and sister kept urging him with gentle reminders, he would go on slowly shaking his head for a quarter of an hour, keeping his eyes shut, and refuse to get to his feet. The mother plucked at his sleeve, whispering endearments in his ear, the sister left her lessons to come to her mother's help, but Gregor's father was not to be caught. He would only sink down deeper in his chair. Not until the two women hoisted him up by the armpits did he open his eyes and look at them both, one after the other, usually with the remark: "This is a life. This is the peace and quiet of my old age." And leaning on the two of them he would heave himself up, with difficulty, as if he were a great burden to himself, suffer them to lead him as far as the door and then wave them off and go on alone, while the mother abandoned her needlework and the sister her pen in order to run after him and help him farther.

Who could find time, in this overworked and tired-out family, to bother about Gregor more than was absolutely needful? The household was reduced more and more; the servant girl was turned off; a gigantic bony charwoman with white hair flying round her head came in morning and evening to do the rough work; everything else was done by Gregor's mother, as well as great piles of sewing. Even various family ornaments, which his mother and sister used to wear with pride at parties and celebrations, had to be sold, as Gregor discovered of an evening from hearing them all discuss the prices obtained. But what they lamented most was the fact that they could not leave the flat which was much too big for their present circumstances, because they could not think of any way to shift Gregor. Yet Gregor saw well enough that consideration for him was not the main difficulty preventing the removal, for they could have easily shifted him in some suitable box with a few air holes in it; what really kept them from moving into another flat was rather their own complete hopelessness and the belief that they had been singled out for a misfortune such as had never happened to any of their relations or acquaintances. They fulfilled to the uttermost all that the world demands of poor people, the father fetched breakfast for the small clerks in the bank, the mother devoted her energy to making underwear for strangers, the sister trotted to and fro behind the counter at the behest of customers, but more than this they had not the strength to do. And the wound in Gregor's back began to nag at him afresh when his mother and sister, after getting his father into bed came back again, left their work lying, drew close to each other and sat cheek by cheek; when his mother, pointing towards his room, said: "Shut that door now, Grete," and he was left again in darkness, while next door the women mingled their tears or perhaps sat dry-eyed staring at the table.

Gregor hardly slept at all by night or by day. He was often haunted by the idea that next time the door opened he would take the family's affairs in hand again just as he used to do; once more, after this long interval, there appeared in his thoughts the figures of the chief and the chief clerk, the commercial travelers and the apprentices, the porter who was so dull-witted, two or three friends in other firms, a chambermaid in one of the rural hotels, a sweet and fleeting memory, a cashier in a milliner's shop, whom he had wooed earnestly but too slowly—they all appeared, together with strangers or people he had quite forgotten, but instead of helping him and his family they were one and all unapproachable and he was glad when they vanished. At other times he would not be in the mood to bother about his family, he was only filled with rage at the way they were neglecting him, and although he had no clear idea of what he might care to eat he would make plans for getting into the larder to take the food that was after all his due, even if he were not hungry. His sister no longer took thought to bring him what might especially please him, but in the morning and at noon before she went to business hurriedly pushed into his room with her foot any food that was available, and in the evening cleared it out again with one sweep of the broom, heedless of whether it had been merely tasted, or—as most frequently happened—

left untouched. The cleaning of his room, which she now did always in the evenings, could not have been more hastily done. Streaks of dirt stretched along the walls, here and there lay balls of dust and filth. At first Gregor used to station himself in some particularly filthy corner when his sister arrived, in order to reproach her with it, so to speak. But he could have sat there for weeks without getting her to make any improvements; she could see the dirt as well as he did, but she had simply made up her mind to leave it alone. And yet, with a touchiness that was new to her, which seemed anyhow to have infected the whole family, she jealously guarded her claim to be the sole caretaker of Gregor's room. His mother once subjected his room to a thorough cleaning, which was achieved only by means of several buckets of water—all this dampness of course upset Gregor too and he lay widespread, sulky and motionless on the sofa—but she was well punished for it. Hardly had his sister noticed the changed aspect of his room that evening than she rushed in high dudgeon into the living room and, despite the imploringly raised hands of her mother, burst into a storm of weeping, while her parents—her father had of course been startled out of his chair—looked on at first in helpless amazement; then they too began to go into action; the father reproached the mother on his right for not having left the cleaning of Gregor's room to his sister; shrieked at the sister on his left that never again was she to be allowed to clean Gregor's room; while the mother tried to pull the father into his bedroom, since he was beyond himself with agitation; the sister, shaken with sobs, then beat upon the table with her small fists; and Gregor hissed loudly with rage because not one of them thought of shutting the door to spare him such a spectacle and so much noise.

Still, even if the sister, exhausted by her daily work, had grown tired of looking after Gregor as she did formerly, there was no need for his mother's intervention or for Gregor's being neglected at all. The charwoman was there. This old widow, whose strong bony frame had enabled her to survive the worst a long life could offer, by no means recoiled from Gregor. Without being in the least curious she had once by chance opened the door of his room and at the sight of Gregor, who, taken by surprise, began to rush to and fro although no one was chasing him, merely stood there with her arms folded. From that time she never failed to open his door a little for a moment, morning and evening, to have a look at him. At first she even used to call him to her, with words which apparently she took to be friendly, such as: "Come along, then, you old dung beetle!" or "Look at the old dung beetle, then!" To such allocutions Gregor made no answer, but stayed motionless where he was, as if the door had never been opened. Instead of being allowed to disturb him so senselessly whenever the whim took her, she should rather have been ordered to clean out his room daily, that charwoman! Once, early in the morning—heavy rain was lashing on the windowpanes, perhaps a sign that spring was on the way—Gregor was so exasperated when she began addressing him again that he ran at her, as if to attack her, although slowly and feebly enough. But the charwoman instead of showing fright merely lifted high a chair that happened to be beside the door, and as she stood there with her mouth wide open it was clear that she meant to shut it only when she brought the chair down on Gregor's back. "So you're not coming any nearer?" she asked, as Gregor turned away again, and quietly put the chair back into the corner.

Gregor was now eating hardly anything. Only when he happened to pass the food laid out for him did he take a bit of something in his mouth as a pastime, kept it there for an hour at a time and usually spat it out again. At first he thought it was chagrin over the state of his room that prevented him from eating, yet he soon got used to the various changes in his room. It had become a habit in the family to push into his room things there was no room for elsewhere, and there were plenty of these now, since one of the rooms had been let to three lodgers. These serious gentlemen—all three of them with full beards, as Gregor once observed through a crack in the door—had a passion for order, not only in their own room but, since they were now members of the household, in all its arrangements, especially in the kitchen. Superfluous, not to say dirty, objects they could not bear. Besides, they had brought with them most of the furnishings they needed. For this reason many things could be dispensed with that it was no use trying to sell but that should not be thrown away either. All of them found their way into Gregor's room. The ash can likewise and the kitchen garbage can. Anything that was not needed for the moment was simply flung into Gregor's room by the charwoman, who did everything in a hurry; fortunately Gregor usually saw only the object, whatever it was, and the hand that held it. Perhaps she intended to take the things away again as time and opportunity offered, or to collect them until she could throw them all out in a heap, but in fact they just lay wherever she happened to throw them, except when Gregor pushed his way through the junk heap and shifted it somewhat, at first out of necessity, because he had not room enough to crawl, but later with increasing enjoyment, although after such excursions, being sad and weary to death, he would lie motionless for hours. And since the lodgers often ate their supper at home in the common living room, the living-room door stayed shut many an evening, yet Gregor reconciled himself quite easily to the shutting of the door, for often enough on evenings when it was opened he had disregarded it entirely and lain in the darkest corner of his room, quite unnoticed by the family. But on one occasion the charwoman left the door open a little and it stayed ajar even when the lodgers came in for supper and the lamp was lit. They set themselves at the top end of the table where formerly Gregor and his father and mother had eaten their meals, unfolded their napkins and took knife and fork in hand. At once his mother appeared in the other doorway with a dish of meat and close behind her his sister with a dish of potatoes piled high. The food steamed with a thick vapor. The lodgers bent over the food set before them as if to scrutinize it before eating, in fact the man in the middle, who seemed to pass for an authority with the other two, cut a piece of meat as it lay on the dish, obviously to discover if it were tender or should be sent back to the kitchen. He showed satisfaction, and Gregor's mother and sister, who had been watching anxiously, breathed freely and began to smile.

The family itself took its meals in the kitchen. Nonetheless, Gregor's father came into the living room before going into the kitchen and with one prolonged bow, cap in hand, made a round of the table. The lodgers all stood up and murmured something in their beards. When they were alone again they ate their food in almost complete silence. It seemed remarkable to Gregor that among the various noises coming from the table he could always distinguish the sound of their masticating teeth, as if this were a sign to Gregor that one needed teeth in order to eat, and that with toothless jaws even of the finest make one could no nothing. "I'm hungry enough," said Gregor sadly to himself, "But not for that kind of food. How these lodgers are stuffing themselves, and here am I dying of starvation!"

On that very evening—during the whole of his time there Gregor could not remember ever having heard the violin—the sound of violin-playing came from the kitchen. The lodgers had already finished their supper, the one in the middle had brought out a newspaper and given the other two a page apiece, and now they were leaning back at ease reading and smoking. When the violin began to play they pricked up their ears, got to their feet, and went on tiptoe to the hall door where they stood huddled together. Their movements must have been heard in the kitchen, for Gregor's father called out: "Is the violin-playing disturbing you, gentlemen? It can be stopped at once." "On the contrary," said the middle lodger, "could not Fräulein Samsa come and play in this room, beside us, where it is much more convenient and comfortable?" "Oh certainly," cried Gregor's father, as if he were the violin-player. The lodgers came back into the living room and waited. Presently Gregor's father arrived with the music stand, his mother carrying the music and his sister with the violin. His sister quietly made everything ready to start playing; his parents, who had never let rooms before and so had an exaggerated idea of the courtesy due to lodgers, did not venture to sit down on their own chairs; his father leaned against the door, the right hand thrust between two buttons of his livery coat, which was formally buttoned up; but his mother was offered a chair by one of the lodgers and, since she left the chair just where he had happened to put it, sat down in a corner to one side.

Gregor's sister began to play; the father and mother, from either side, intently watched the movements of her hands. Gregor, attracted by the playing, ventured to move forward a little until his head was actually inside the living room. He felt hardly any surprise at his growing lack of consideration for the others; there had been a time when he prided himself on being considerate. And yet just on this occasion he had more reason than ever to hide himself, since owing to the amount of dust which lay thick in his room and rose into the air at the slightest movement, he too was covered with dust; fluff and hair and remnants of food trailed with him, caught on his back and along his sides; his indifference to everything was much too great for him to turn on his back and scrape himself clean on the carpet, as once he had done several times a day. And in spite of his condition, no shame deterred him from advancing a little over the spotless floor of the living room.

To be sure, no one was aware of him. The family was entirely absorbed in the violin-playing; the lodgers, however, who first of all had stationed themselves, hands in pockets, much too close behind the music stand so that they could all have read the music, which must have bothered his sister, had soon retreated to the window, half-whispering with downbent heads, and stayed there while his father turned an anxious eye on them. Indeed, they were making it more than obvious that they had been disappointed in their expectation of hearing good or enjoyable violin-playing, that they had had more than enough of the performance and only out of courtesy suffered a continued disturbance of their peace. From the way they all kept blowing the smoke of their cigars high in the air through nose and mouth one could divine their irritation. And yet Gregor's sister was playing so beautifully. Her face leaned sideways, intently and sadly her eyes followed the notes of music. Gregor crawled a little farther forward and lowered his head to the ground so that it might be possible for his eyes to meet hers. Was he an animal, that music had such an effect upon him? He felt as if the way were opening before him to the unknown nourishment he craved. He was determined to push forward till he reached his sister, to pull at her skirt and so let her know that she was to come into his room with her violin, for no one here appreciated her playing as he would appreciate it. He would never let her out of his room, at least, not so long as he lived; his frightful appearance would become, for the first time, useful to him; he would watch all the doors of his room at once and spit at intruders; but his sister should need no constraint, she should stay with him of her own free will; she should sit beside him on the sofa, bend down her ear to him and hear him confide that he had had the firm intention of sending her to the Conservatorium, and that, but for his mishap, last Christmas—surely Christmas was long past?—he would have announced it to everybody without allowing a single objection. After this confession his sister would be so touched that she would burst into tears, and Gregor would then raise himself to her shoulder and kiss her on the neck, which, now that she went to business, she kept free of any ribbon or collar.

"Mr. Samsa!" cried the middle lodger, to Gregor's father, and pointed, without wasting any more words, at Gregor, now working himself slowly forwards. The violin fell silent, the middle lodger first smiled to his friends with a shake of the head and then looked at Gregor again. Instead of driving Gregor out, his father seemed to think it more needful to begin by soothing down the lodgers, although they were not at all agitated and apparently found Gregor more entertaining than the violin-playing. He hurried toward them and, spreading out his arms, tried to urge them back into their own room and at the same time to block their view of Gregor.

They now began to be really a little angry, one could not tell whether because of the old man's behavior or because it had just dawned on them that all unwittingly they had such a neighbor as Gregor next door. They demanded explanations of his father, they waved their arms like him, tugged uneasily at their beards, and only with reluctance backed towards their room. Meanwhile Gregor's sister, who stood there as if lost when her playing was so abruptly broken off, came to life again, pulled herself together all at once after standing for a while holding violin and bow in nervelessly hanging hands and staring at her music, pushed her violin into the lap of her mother, who was still sitting in her chair fighting asthmatically for breath, and ran into the lodgers' room to which they were now being shepherded by her father rather more quickly than before. One could see the pillows and blankets on the beds flying under her accustomed fingers and being laid in order. Before the lodgers had actually reached their room she had finished making the beds and slipped out.

The old man seemed once more to be so possessed by his mulish self-assertiveness that he was forgetting all the respect he should show to his lodgers. He kept driving them on and driving them on until in the very door of the bedroom the middle lodger stamped his foot loudly on the floor and so brought him to a halt. "I beg to announce," said the lodger, lifting one hand and looking also at Gregor's mother and sister, "that because of the disgusting conditions prevailing in this household and family"—here he spat on the floor with emphatic brevity—"I give you notice on the spot. Naturally I won't pay you a penny for the days I have lived here, on the contrary I shall consider bringing an action for damages against you, based on claims—believe me—that will be easily susceptible of proof." He ceased and stared straight in front of him, as if he expected something. In fact his two friends at once rushed into the breach with these words: "And we too give notice on the spot." On that he seized the door-handle and shut the door with a slam.

Gregor's father, groping with his hands, staggered forward and fell into his chair; it looked as if he were stretching himself there for his ordinary evening nap, but the marked jerkings of his head, which was as if uncontrollable, showed that he was far from asleep. Gregor had simply stayed quietly all the time on the spot where the lodgers had espied him. Disappointment at the failure of his plan, perhaps also the weakness arising from extreme hunger, made it impossible for him to move. He feared, with a fair degree of certainty, that at any moment the general tension would discharge itself in a combined attack upon him, and he lay waiting. He did not react even to the noise made by the violin as it fell off his mother's lap from under her trembling fingers and gave out a resonant note.

"My dear parents," said his sister, slapping her hand on the table by way of introduction, "things can't go on like this. Perhaps you don't realize that, but I do. I won't utter my brother's name in the presence of this creature, and so all I say is: we must try to get rid of it. We've tried to look after it and to put up with it as far as is humanly possible, and I don't think anyone could reproach us in the slightest."

"She is more than right," said Gregor's father to himself. His mother, who was still choking for lack of breath, began to cough hollowly into her hand with a wild look in her eyes.

His sister rushed over to her and held her forehead. His father's thoughts seemed to have lost their vagueness at Grete's words, he sat more upright, fingering his service cap that lay among the plates still lying on the table from the lodgers' supper, and from time to time looked at the still form of Gregor.

"We must try to get rid of it," his sister now said explicitly to her father, since her mother was coughing too much to hear a word, "it will be the death of both of you, I can see that coming. When one has to work as hard as we do, all of us, one can't stand this continual torment at home on top of it. At least I can't stand it any longer." And she burst into such a passion of sobbing that her tears dropped on her mother's face, where she wiped them off mechanically.

"My dear," said the old man sympathetically, and with evident understanding, "but what can we do?"

Gregor's sister merely shrugged her shoulders to indicate the feeling of helplessness that had now overmastered her during her weeping fit, in contrast to her former confidence.

"If he could understand us," said her father, half questioningly; Grete, still sobbing, vehemently waved a hand to show how unthinkable that was.

"If he could understand us," repeated the old man, shutting his eyes to consider his daughter's conviction that understanding was impossible, "then perhaps we might come to some agreement with him. But as it is—"

"He must go," cried Gregor's sister, "That's the only solution, Father. You must try to get rid of the idea that this is Gregor. The fact that we've believed it for so long is the root of all our trouble. But how can it be Gregor? If this were Gregor, he would have realized long ago that human beings can't live with such a creature, and he'd have gone away on his own accord. Then we wouldn't have any brother, but we'd be able to go on living and keep his memory in honor. As it is, this creature persecutes us, drives away our lodgers, obviously wants the whole apartment to himself and would have us all sleep in the gutter. Just look, Father," she shrieked all at once, "he's at it again!" And in an access of panic that was quite incomprehensible to Gregor she even quitted her mother, literally thrusting the chair from her as if she would rather sacrifice her mother than stay so near to Gregor, and rushed behind her father, who also rose up, being simply upset by her agitation, and half-spread his arms out as if to protect her.

Yet Gregor had not the slightest intention of frightening anyone, far less his sister. He had only begun to turn round in order to crawl back to his room, but it was certainly a startling operation to watch, since because of his disabled condition he could not execute the difficult turning movements except by lifting his head and then bracing it against the floor over and over again. He paused and looked round. His good intentions seemed to have been recognized; the alarm had only been momentary. Now they were all watching him in melancholy silence. His mother lay in her chair, her legs stiffly outstretched and pressed together, her eyes almost closing for sheer weariness; his father and his sister were sitting beside each other, his sister's arm around the old man's neck.

Perhaps I can go on turning round now, thought Gregor, and began his labors again. He could not stop himself from panting with the effort, and had to pause now and then to take breath. Nor did anyone harass him, he was left entirely to himself. When he had completed the turn-round he began at once to crawl straight back. He was amazed at the distance separating him from his room and could not understand how in his weak state he had managed to accomplish the same journey so recently, almost without remarking it. Intent on crawling as fast as possible, he barely noticed that not a single word, not an ejaculation from his family, interfered with his progress. Only when he was already in the doorway did he turn his head round, not completely, for his neck muscles were getting stiff, but enough to see that nothing had changed behind him except that his sister had risen to her feet. His last glance fell on his mother, who was not quite overcome by sleep.

Hardly was he well inside his room when the door was hastily pushed shut, bolted and locked. The sudden noise in his rear startled him so much that his little legs gave beneath him. It was his sister who had shown such haste. She had been standing ready waiting and made a light spring forward, Gregor had not even heard her coming, and she cried "At last!" to her parents as she turned the key in the lock.

"And what now?" said Gregor to himself, looking round in the darkness. Soon he made the discovery that he was now unable to stir a limb. This did not surprise him, rather it seemed unnatural that he should ever actually have been able to move on these feeble little legs. Otherwise he felt relatively comfortable. True, his whole body was aching, but it seemed that the pain was gradually growing less and would finally pass away. The rotting apple in his back and the inflamed area around it, all covered with soft dust, already hardly troubled him. He thought of his family with tenderness and love. The decision that he must disappear was one that he held to even more strongly than his sister, if that were possible. In this state of vacant and peaceful meditation he remained until the tower clock struck three in the morning. The first broadening of light in the world outside the window entered his consciousness once more. Then his head sank to the floor of its own accord and from his nostrils came the last faint flicker of his breath.

90 When the charwoman arrived early in the morning—what between her strength and her impatience she slammed all the doors so loudly, never mind how often she had been begged not to do so, that no one in the whole apartment could enjoy any quiet sleep after her arrival—she

noticed nothing unusual as she took her customary peep into Gregor's room. She thought he was lying motionless on purpose, pretending to be in the sulks; she credited him with every kind of intelligence. Since she happened to have the longhanded broom in her hand she tried to tickle him up with it from the doorway. When that too produced no reaction she felt provoked and poked at him a little harder, and only when she had pushed him along the floor without meeting any resistance was her attention aroused. It did not take her long to establish the truth of the matter, and her eyes widened, she let out a whistle, yet did not waste much time over it but tore open the door of the Samsas' bedroom and yelled into the darkness at the top of her voice: "Just look at this, it's dead; it's lying here dead and done for!"

Mr. and Mrs. Samsa started up in their double bed and before they realized the nature of the charwoman's announcement had some difficulty in overcoming the shock of it. But then they got out of bed quickly, one on either side, Mr. Samsa throwing a blanket over his shoulders, Mrs. Samsa in nothing but her nightgown; in this array they entered Gregor's room. Meanwhile the door of the living room opened, too, where Grete had been sleeping since the advent of the lodgers; she was completely dressed as if she had not been to bed, which seemed to be confirmed also by the paleness of her face. "Dead?" said Mrs. Samsa, looking questioningly at the charwoman, although she could have investigated for herself, and the fact was obvious enough without investigation. "I should say so," said the charwoman, proving her words by pushing Gregor's corpse a long way to one side with her broomstick. Mrs. Samsa made a movement as if to stop her, but checked it. "Well," said Mr. Samsa, "now thanks be to God." He crossed himself, and the three women followed his example. Grete, whose eyes never left the corpse, said: "Just see how thin he was. It's such a long time since he's eaten anything. The food came out again just as it went in." Indeed, Gregor's body was completely flat and dry, as could only now be seen when it was no longer supported by the legs and nothing prevented one from looking closely at it.

"Come in beside us, Grete, for a little while," said Mrs. Samsa with a tremulous smile, and Grete, not without looking back at the corpse, followed her parents into their bedroom. The charwoman shut the door and opened the window wide. Although it was so early in the morning a certain softness was perceptible in the fresh air. After all, it was already the end of March.

The three lodgers emerged from their room and were surprised to see no breakfast; they had been forgotten. "Where's our breakfast?" said the middle lodger peevishly to the charwoman. But she put her finger to her lips and hastily, without a word, indicated by gestures that they should go into Gregor's room. They did so and stood, their hands in the pockets of their somewhat shabby coats, around Gregor's corpse in the room where it was now fully light.

At that the door of the Samsas' bedroom opened and Mr. Samsa appeared in his uniform, his wife on one arm, his daughter on the other.

They all looked a little as if they had been crying; from time to time Grete hid her face on her father's arm.

"Leave my house at once!" said Mr. Samsa, and pointed to the door without disengaging himself from the women. "What do you mean by that?" said the middle lodger, taken somewhat aback, with a feeble smile. The two others put their hands behind them and kept rubbing them together, as if in gleeful expectation of a fine set-to in which they were bound to come off the winners. "I mean just what I say," answered Mr. Samsa, and advanced in a straight line with his two companions towards the lodger. He stood his ground at first quietly, looking at the floor as if his thoughts were taking a new pattern in his head. "Then let us go, by all means," he said, and looked up at Mr. Samsa as if in a sudden access of humility he were expecting some renewed sanction for this decision. Mr. Samsa merely nodded briefly once or twice with meaning eyes. Upon that the lodger really did go with long strides into the hall, his two friends had been listening and had quite stopped rubbing their hands for some moments and now went scuttling after him as if afraid that Mr. Samsa might get into the hall before them and cut them off from their leader. In the hall they all three took their hats from the rack, their sticks from the umbrella stand, bowed in silence and quitted the apartment. With a suspiciousness which proved quite unfounded Mr. Samsa and the two women followed them out to the landing; leaning over the banister they watched the three figures slowly but surely going down the long stairs, vanishing from sight at a certain turn of the staircase on every floor and coming into view again after a moment or so; the more they dwindled, the more the Samsa family's interest in them dwindled, and when a butcher's boy met them and passed them on the stairs coming up proudly with a tray on his head, Mr. Samsa and the two women soon left the landing and as if a burden had been lifted from them went back into their apartment.

They decided to spend this day in resting and going for a stroll; they had not only deserved such a respite from work, but absolutely needed it. And so they sat down at the table and wrote three notes of excuse, Mr. Samsa to his board of management, Mrs. Samsa to her employer and Grete to the head of her firm. While they were writing, the charwoman came in to say that she was going now, since her morning's work was finished. At first they only nodded without looking up, but as she kept hovering there they eyed her irritably. "Well?" said Mr. Samsa. The charwoman stood grinning in the doorway as if she had good news to impart to the family but meant not to say a word unless properly questioned. The small ostrich feather standing upright on her hat, which had annoyed Mr. Samsa ever since she was engaged, was waving gaily in all directions. "Well, what is it then?" asked Mrs. Samsa, who obtained more respect from the charwoman than the others. "Oh," said the charwoman, giggling so amiably that she could not at once continue, "just this, you don't need to bother about how to get rid of the thing next door. It's been seen to already." Mrs. Samsa and Grete bent over their letters again, as if preoccupied; Mr. Samsa, who perceived that she was eager to begin describing it all in detail, stopped her with a decisive hand. But since she was not allowed to tell her story, she remembered the great hurry she was in, being obviously deeply huffed: "Bye, everybody," she said, whirling off violently, and departed with a frightful slamming of doors.

"She'll be given notice tonight," said Mr. Samsa, but neither from his wife nor his daughter did he get any answer, for the charwoman seemed to have shattered again the composure they had barely achieved. They rose, went to the window and stayed there, clasping each other tight. Mr. Samsa turned to his chair to look at them and quietly observed them for a little. Then he called out: "Come along, now, do. Let bygones be bygones. And you might have some consideration for me." The two of them complied at once, hastened to him, caressed him and quickly finished their letters.

Then they all three left the apartment together, which was more than they had done for months, and went by tram into the open country outside the town. The tram, in which they were the only passengers, was filled with warm sunshine. Leaning comfortably back in their seats they canvassed their prospects for the future, and it appeared on closer inspection that these were not at all bad, for the jobs they had got, which so far they had never really discussed with each other, were all three admirable and likely to lead to better things later on. The greatest immediate improvement in their condition would of course arise from moving to another house; they wanted to take a smaller and cheaper but also better situated and more easily run apartment than the one they had, which Gregor had selected. While they were thus conversing, it struck both Mr. and Mrs. Samsa, almost at the same moment, as they became aware of their daughter's increasing vivacity, that in spite of all the sorrow of recent times, which had made her cheeks pale, she had bloomed into a pretty girl with a good figure. They grew quieter and half unconsciously exchanged glances of complete agreement, having come to the conclusion that it would soon be time to find a good husband for her. And it was like a confirmation of their new dreams and excellent intentions that at the end of their journey their daughter sprang to her feet first and stretched her young body.

Jamaica Kincaid
(1949–)

GIRL
(1984)

Wash the white clothes on Monday and put them on the stone heap; wash the color clothes on Tuesday and put them on the clothesline to dry; don't walk barehead in the hot sun; cook pumpkin fritters in very hot sweet oil; soak your little clothes right after you take them off; when buying cotton to make yourself a nice blouse, be sure that it doesn't have gum on it, because that way it won't hold up well after a wash; soak salt fish overnight before you cook it; is it true that you sing benna in Sunday School?; always eat your food in such a way that it won't turn someone else's stomach; on Sundays try to walk like a lady and not like the slut you are so bent on becoming; don't sing benna in Sunday School; you mustn't speak to wharf-rat boys, not even to give directions; don't eat fruits on the street—flies will follow you; *but I don't sing benna on Sundays at all and never in Sunday school;* this is how to sew on a button; this is how to make a buttonhole for the button you have just sewed on; this is how to hem a dress when you see the hem coming down and so to prevent yourself from looking like the slut I know you are so bent on becoming; this is how you iron your father's khaki shirt so that it doesn't have a crease; this is how you iron your father's khaki pants so that they don't have a crease; this is how you grow okra—far from the house, because okra tree harbors red ants; when you are growing dasheen, make sure it gets plenty of water or else it makes your throat itch when you are eating it; this is how you sweep a corner; this is how you sweep a whole house; this is how you sweep a yard; this is how you smile to someone you don't like too much; this is how you smile to someone you don't like at all; this is how you smile to someone you like completely; this is how you set a table for tea; this is how you set a table for dinner; this is how you set a table for dinner with an important guest; this is how you set a table for lunch; this is how you set a table for breakfast; this is how to behave in the presence of men who don't know you very well, and this way they won't recognize immediately the slut I have warned you against becoming; be sure to wash every day, even if it is with your own spit; don't squat down to play marbles—you are not a boy, you know; don't pick people's flowers—you might catch something; don't throw stones at blackbirds, because it might not be a blackbird at all; this is how to make a bread pudding; this is how to make doukona; this is how to make pepper pot; this is how to make a good medicine for a cold; this is how to make a good medicine to throw away a child before it even becomes a child; this is how to catch a fish; this is how to throw back a fish you don't like, and that way something bad won't fall on you; this is how to bully a man; this is how a man bullies you; this is how to love a man, and if this doesn't work there are other ways, and if they don't work don't feel too bad about giving up; this is how to spit up in the air if you feel like it, and this is how to move quick so that it doesn't fall on you; this is how to make ends meet; always squeeze bread to make sure it's fresh; *but what if the baker won't let me feel the bread?;* you mean to say that after all you are really going to be the kind of woman who the baker won't let near the bread?

Salvatore LaPuma
(1929–)

GRAVESEND BAY
(1987)

"You all know this one," said Carmine as the orchestra struck up "Do I Love You?" Applause rose in anticipiation. Melting girls were thinking that his singing, tainted with longing, could be the history of love.

"He's singing that for me," said Julia Albanesi, who sat with Tonino.

"I leave him in the dust," said Tonino, Carmine's rival on the track in 1940.

Carmine Carmellini, eighteen, hadn't studied voice as urged by his father, Mario, who slaved over his viola. Music had always come easily to Carmine; his voice served him well. He'd been pampered with applause since he was five.

5 From his mother, Carmine had inherited the looks of the eleventh-century Norman invaders of Sicily, Viking eyes and hair which made blue and yellow sparks in the bold Arab eyes of New Utrecht High's Sicilian girls. These girls were taught by their mothers to act like virgins with downcast glances, but whenever Carmine was singing or running or just passing by, they forgot.

"Did fifty laps," said Carmine, collapsing on the bench.

"Don't sit. Cool down slow," said Tonino, dragging Carmine to walk on the grass.

Both were about six feet tall. Carmine's legs, longer than Tonino's, knit yards together over cross-country distances, but before a finish line, his sap depleted, Carmine always unraveled and Tonino always won.

"I'm building up," said Carmine.

10 "Moving your arms is a waste. You ain't singing," said Tonino.

"I'll beat you next time," said Carmine.

"You're an old lady," said Tonino.

"Edward G. Robinson starts tonight," said Julia.

Julia's mother, Agnese Albanesi, sewed dresses in the storefront factory on 16th Avenue when orders came in. In the first year of her marriage to Rudy he claimed to have asthma in their tiny cavelike apartment downstairs in the rear of a four-family house. One day Rudy didn't stop his produce truck at the market at three in the morning, but kept going. In a pileup in Detroit he was killed the week before Julia was born.

15 "Robinson acts Sicilian," said Carmine.

Carmine liked Julia's heart-shaped face and bow mouth. She was one of the prettiest girls in school, didn't giggle, and looked sad, which got his sympathy.

"You can't tell between Jewish and us," said Julia, serving him her provolone sandwich. "We even look alike. Except *you're* different."

"I'm not inside," said Carmine. They were sitting on the grass oval inside the cinder track. "I get a kiss for dessert?"

"Mom's cookies," said Julia.

Julia made Carmine's lunch every school day, knitted his pullover, wrote him notes, and in her morning and evening prayers asked for Carmine's love.

"Let's go under the stairs," said Carmine.

Julia gave him her saucy red kisses, but he resisted the cookies under her clothes. He wanted to be in the chorus of angels eventually, and not a roasting chestnut, having gotten his religion, like his eyes and hair, from his mother.

Carmine and Julia went to the Hollywood once a week, held hands in the dark, then went for ice cream sundaes. If the weather was warm and the night late, he'd sing an Italian ballad in the school yard, and Julia would think his voice was the fallen angel's leading her into temptation. She would even put his picture on her dresser in place of the Sacred Heart, though over that blasphemous thought she chewed her nails.

Other boys jostled to sniff Julia's neck and rub against her hip, but she was so absorbed in Carmine she couldn't see anyone else. She kept his kisses in her diary, and some days lived only remembering them, especially as he was now running during lunch. Then she didn't eat lunch at all, and was soon swimming in her dress, and one day Carmine noticed her raw and bloody wrists. Skin from each wrist was missing like an absent watchband.

"Jesus. What happened?"

"I bite my wrists."

"That's crazy."

"The doctor says I'm nervous."

"About what?"

"It's a secret."

"Look, Julia. Everything works out. You don't have to be nervous."

"I'm really not," she said. "I'm biting them for a reason."

"Don't you have bandages?"

"I took them off."

"You have to stop."

"You can't make me."

"We won't go to the show."

"Then I'll kill myself."

"Quit it for me, Julia."

"That's the reason I'm doing it, Carmine."

"You could sing Verdi at the Met," said first violinist Patricia Schneck, her rosy face in the long vase of her neck.

Carmine and Patricia eyed each other like forbidden fruit. Sicilian students mixed agreeably with Jewish students who were in the majority at New Utrecht. The other's culture was approved of at home, but falling for it would bring their families' wrath, if not God's, down on their heads.

"I'd take voice if you taught it," said Carmine.

Patricia always seemed about to be captured by the crowd or another boy, so Carmine sought her out and he didn't let her get away. Sometimes he was in near panic, his lips drying and face flushing as if he'd run ten miles. He focused on no one else, phoning every night as if he didn't see her every day. That he was wild about her was infecting her with a wonderful illness of becoming wild about him, and they often laughed together like maniacs.

"You can't walk me home," she said as they left the April Festival.

Carmine stayed at her side in the crowd going up 79th Street. Ahead was the BMT elevated train and in the street below it the trolley car that she would take. Some of the guys stopped off at the candy store for "looseys," Camels and Chesterfields at a penny each, but Carmine was saving his breath for running and singing.

"Let's go down to the bay," he said. "They're making a new beach."

"I'm sorry," said Patricia. "I've French to read."

"Me too," he said.

"Gentiles should be with Gentiles. I'm not."

"Who cares?"

"Doesn't your father?

"He doesn't.""

"Your mother, then?"

"I'm not some kid does what his mother says."

The next afternoon and the next, Carmine asked her again to go to Gravesend Bay. Then Patricia stopped hearing the objection her father would make, and went. It was what she wanted to do all along. Steered by muscled men, the tractors coughed like old smokers as they pushed the bay back into the Atlantic by dumping in sand castles and boulders at the water's edge, turning on steel ribbon feet behind a fresh load. Tasting the salty air, Carmine carrying their books, they slogged through sand, holding hands. Midway on the new beach, laughing from exhaustion, they dropped, entertained by the whitecaps. Their kiss was small and fragile, as if breakable in two at any moment, but they were careful with it.

"Don't see anyone else," said Carmine.

"You have Julia."

"We stopped going out."

"We couldn't ever go to each other's house," said Patricia.

"It's not impossible," he said.

"You shouldn't break up with Julia. She's sick over you."

Patricia wanted to obey her father, Herbert Schneck, a decent man who gave all his work, play, and prayers to his family. But a woman was growing in Patricia, pink when she was with Carmine, absent of color when she wasn't. In the following weeks, if he didn't find her, she searched for him. They went often to Gravesend Bay, and stayed late after school.

Despite her husband's ridicule that God couldn't exist where stars were as plentiful as unanswered prayers, Anna Carmellini, believing the impossible sometimes comes true, went daily to the 8:00 A.M. Mass. On Sundays Mario kept her company at the high 11:15, where Anna always took communion, but Mario never did. Saturday evenings Anna also made her weekly confession at St. Finbar's, where afterward she said her penance.

"You have nothing to confess," said her husband when Anna returned late one Saturday night.

"You know my sins?" she said, almost as if she'd tell them, but then covered her mouth.

"True, you burn the pots, but I forgive you," he said, but Anna wasn't amused.

"Sin's in the heart," she said.

"Yours must be a lump of coal. I think you're never coming back from confession. Go to another priest."

"Father Hartigan's very pious," she said.

"What's an Irishman know about Sicilian sins?"

"I try to be a good wife, Mario."

"Tell me your sins, Anna. I forgive you better than the priest."

"Only God forgives. I want to offer my hair as a sacrifice."

"Your beautiful hair?" he said, shaking his head. "If there's a God, He'll cry like a baby."

"For the feast of Santa Lucia," she said. "And carry a candle and walk on my knees."

"That's for witches. Let's go to bed. I kiss your belly. Wherever you feel sin."

"We can't two more days. The cycle," she said. "But play your viola. I want to hear. While I say the rosary."

His viola, two violins, and a cello were in a string quartet. Their musica da camera made them famous on Manhattan's Upper East Side, but infrequent performances earned them little. Still, day and night, Mario crossed catgut with horsehair.

Haydn's Opus 33 rose from Mario's viola as from the bottom of the sea. He nodded to his instrument, caught in the ebb and flow of the music as Anna wished she could be caught up in religion.

Alone in their bedroom, Anna heard Mario's viola in the parlor, clever, graceful, and imaginative, but distant too, touching only her ears. Instead of his music, she preferred Carmine's singing, especially her favorite song at a family celebration, "La Donne è Mobile," which brought tears to her eyes.

Father Hartigan said God would give her peace, she should pray and make small sacrifices, though not her hair. "God forbid," he said.

After Mass one Thursday morning Anna met Father Hartigan in the school yard. Lined-up children were waiting to go in. Anna and the priest buttoned up jackets, tied shoelaces, dabbed away tears, and replaced lost or stolen lunch money as if the children were theirs. Anna's library opened at noon, and the priest was pleased she could substitute half a day for the sick nun. Her reading delighted the children.

It could be misunderstood why Anna and Father Hartigan were always together, but the nuns and other priests seemed not to notice. Anna noticed and so did he, but instead of their friendship ending, it grew. In his confessional Anna kneeled for hours whispering with him about God and what He must be like, and of sinners to be forgiven, and in the code known only to themselves, they were talking about themselves.

One hot June Saturday night after confession the priest suggested they go for iced tea. Beside him in his Dodge, Anna was uneasy. Only rarely had she been alone with a man not her husband or a relative. Yet she wanted to be there. He was more than her priest, he was the man she should've had. The priest drove out of Bensonhurst and through strange streets, he and Anna wordless. When they returned to the neighborhood, he parked at Gravesend's dark and lonely beach, and still they didn't speak.

In green shorts and a sleeveless white shirt, the school colors, Carmine ran before classes, breathing with his mouth open.

Marty Katz gave him lung and leg exercises, but his speed and endurance didn't improve. Running also took place in the mind, where Carmine fell down, thought Marty, but Marty didn't care that Carmine didn't win. Marty had Tonino for that. To sweat was reward enough. Those who had to win eventually did.

"Suppose your girl's waiting," said Marty. "She's a little fickle. Just might give it to any guy comes in first. Wouldn't you run harder?"

"If it was Patricia."

"She goes for you."

"Maybe I should convert to Jewish."

"You have to ask yourself. At your age, if you'd give up a piece of your dick."

"Would I have to?"

"Marry one of my daughters in six, seven years. I married an Italian."

A spring rain fell during the night. It wouldn't have mattered on the school track banked to drain and lift, but the cross-country was taking place at six in the morning on Prospect Park's pathways. Puddles like black glass had collected on the asphalt, and Carmine often didn't jump soon enough and splashed in the water. His wet feet slowed him down even more than usual.

Carmine began too fast, thinking he was inexhaustible. Singing, he was. But even with his desire for things out of reach, even believing, despite Tonino's jeering, that he could beat Tonino, Carmine was running out of gas.

Orange arrows on trees pointed to paths. Through the trees Carmine glimpsed the lake still and gray. The park was chosen for the absence of people going to the zoo or rowing at this early hour. By the boathouse were the few spectators from participating schools. Julia's red blouse caught his eye, then her blurred pretty face. Her wave boosted him on. His team had come on the school bus, but Julia had gotten up very early to take the BMT in the dark. Carmine wished he could give her the cup. She deserved it, but she also made him feel a little guilty.

Out of breath, dripping as if from a dozen faucets, bites itching, mouth cracking, Carmine was unable to live up to his standard and hated himself. Runner after runner was passing him by as he chugged on. Under the leafing maple, coaches in whites were clumped like toadstools on the damp earth. "Carmine, your girl's at the finish," called Marty. "Run like hell." Carmine couldn't believe in the illusion. Patricia was staying home this Saturday to practice Mozart.

Jobs were scarce that summer, and many girls who graduated with Julia had to stay at home crocheting tablecloths for their trousseaus. But Julia, then eighteen, was hired by Alfonso, the pastryman, for his 16th Avenue shop. With her triangular face, she was just too pretty to be sent away. Customers would be attracted by her for gelato and ices in the heat. Alfonso was right. Sad-eyed, naturally blushed, and figure ripe, she made boys whistle and want to draw her out. If she smiled they won something that showed they'd soon be men. Alfonso, near forty and married to a young woman, looked at Julia, yearning for a still younger bride.

Hiding her healing wrists in long-sleeved blouses, Julia seemed as happy or as unhappy as always, keeping her misery as she had her joy between the covers of her diary. She read newspapers and listened to the radio with her mother, and went to the movies with her friend Bianca whenever Bianca's Ernesto worked late or went downtown to study automotive mechanics.

When she came home from the movies one moonless night, time turning invisibly, her mother asleep in her room, Julia went into the kitchen and closed the door and windows. Turning on all the jets in the dark, she put her head in the oven. She despised heaven's mysterious design excluding men from her life. Her father had run away and died. Her mother's brother, their family adviser, had become senile and was taken away when she was fourteen. Now Carmine, at the show with Patricia, was also gone from her life. Julia knew all along he wanted Patricia, but she waited patiently, hoping their religions would clash like cymbals. It could still happen, but seeing them together tore Julia's heart out. To rid herself of heartache and the memory of Carmine, she breathed in the gas.

The heavy thud she made when she fell awakened her mother, and Agnese Albanesi rushed in and began screaming from her gut. Since they didn't own a phone, the landlord upstairs called the ambulance.

Old women in black, putting their heads together, whispered and stared as Carmine went by. Fearing him, they directed their pointer and pinkie devil-horns at him to ward off the evil he could bring into their lives. A week passed before he got up his nerve and went to the hospital. Julia was pale. Her ruffled nightgown was opaque in the second layer and sheer in the first. Seeing her he loved her, but not as he should. He never dreamed of Julia without her clothes.

Tonino, at Julia's bedside, had brought flowers, unlike Carmine. Awkward at the foot of the bed, his hands in and out of his pockets, Carmine knew he should kiss Julia, apologize, offer to kill himself instead, but he did none of that.

105 "That was dumb," said Carmine.

"Are you smart?" said Julia.

Getting up, Tonino said, "I'll come back," but was delayed by Julia's extended hand.

"You're sweet. The flowers," she said.

"Next time you get ice cream," said Tonino, and then went out.

110 "He steals things," said Carmine.

"He's taking the fireman's test," said Julia. "He's brave to be a fireman."

Still a little jealous, Carmine said, "Don't let him swipe your heart."

"You going to marry that girl?" asked Julia.

For a while after graduation Carmine didn't know what to do with himself. He'd discuss with his father summer jobs he should look for, but he'd do nothing about getting them. The one thing he knew how to do of course was sing, so finally he applied to The Glass Hat in Sheepshead Bay, and was hired after a fifteen-minute audition in which he sang, "The Very Thought of You," "All the Things You Are," and "Wishing."

115 Carmine would be going to Brooklyn College, Patricia to Massachusetts, she wouldn't say where exactly. She came to The Glass Hat often, the headwaiter seating her close to the mike so Carmine could sing to her, and she and the patrons loved it. After two weeks a talent agent said, "You could be rich and famous, kid."

Carmine and Patricia were seeing each other a few times a day, made love at night on the new beach, and called each other hourly, often with nothing to say, as if their voices hid messages. They also made many promises. That midsummer their love was still perfectly whole, a china cup without the small chips that come after years of use. The passing season and the impossibility of their love made them cling to it as something precious about to slip through their fingers.

Neither family knew. Carmine and Patricia were protecting themselves from parents who would break them up, and protecting their parents from the misery of knowing. And besides, posting the news of a love about to end seemed pointless.

On a warm Monday night when the nightclub was closed Carmine and Patricia went to their place on the sand and uncovered something they tried to bury: they couldn't ever leave each other. A first love has no history of failure, no knowledge that a broken heart survives, and they thought if their love ended so too would their lives.

"I'll take morning classes. Sing at night," Carmine said.

"I'll take the same classes and work at night too."

"Your father will be sore."

"I might be miserable, Carmine. And your mother?"

"She'll say novenas."

"I'll never give up being Jewish."

"Marrying at city hall, I'll be excommunicated."

"Will you be hurt?"

"You can touch it where it hurts," he said.

Anna and Father Hartigan grew comfortable riding around mornings, and in the afternoons she called in sick. They carelessly had egg creams in the Bay Parkway Cafeteria. They fumbled chopsticks over chow mein at Fat Choy's on 86th Street. Finally, Anna took the wheel, learning to drive within Bensonhurst, and sometimes the priest was recognized. One young woman shopping for shoes, a former nun, Cristina, saw them and phoned his pastor.

Like mannequins, they hadn't touched, kissed, or spoken a word about love. They yearned for something not even allowed into thought, were driven to be together as if they were whispered to by the same Holy Ghost who had visited Mary.

"You have to leave the parish," said Monsignor Kerry, bent and sprouting warts, avoiding the obvious questions, almost as if the same thing had happened to him once.

"It was nothing," said Father Hartigan. "But I'm ashamed."

"The nun will tell a hundred people, and each will tell another hundred," said the monsignor. "You don't stand a chance. You're one of them now. The sinners expect us to be their saints."

"Where will I be sent?"

"I'll recommend as far as possible. It's up to the bishop."

"How soon?"

"I'll call Monday. He'll need two, three days. Figure the end of next week. Next time, try the bottle, father. Won't get you in as much trouble."

Late Saturday night Mario called the church and the housekeeper fetched the monsignor. The monsignor couldn't remember having seen Anna at confession. She was at church so often she was almost another plaster statue. Surely he had seen her, but he was sleepy or drunk or feigning, and hung up on Mario before the conversation ended.

Wading fearfully into the early hours, Mario in his sleepless anguish thought of running to the church to tear down its doors. But Anna wouldn't be sleeping in a pew. Maybe she had been struck down by a careless driver. He called the police, but Anna hadn't been in an accident. They took her description and told him they would look for her in the morning.

They didn't have to. Someone found the priest's Dodge on the beach, a garden hose from the exhaust pipe run through an inch of rear-window space. The police told Mario and he woke Carmine. It was Carmine's last night in their apartment.

Carmine ran as never before, swift, at ease, without hungering for breath, without stretching for extra inches. He was the gazelle, running the miles to where police cars, ambulances, and people littered the sand.

The mask on Anna's face forced in oxygen.

"It's weak, but beating," said the man with the stethoscope.

The seat behind the wheel was vacant. Carmine heard the priest's name.

The priest had parked his car at night and they said the rosary until passing out. It was a miracle made by a mistake, as many of man's are: he'd neglected to fill his tank, and the engine had run out of gas before they could die. Father Hartigan was assigned to New Mexico's Pueblo Indians.

When Anna came home from the hospital, she shaved off her golden hair. As it grew back slowly, she seemed to be coming to her senses again and kissed Mario and took him between her legs, though she hardly said a word. Mario played his viola for her.

Forgiven by Mario, Anna then had to forgive Carmine for marrying a Jewish girl. They were invited for the first time two years later. After dinner Mario bounced their baby on his knee and asked Carmine to sing for his mother, but Carmine declined.

"He doesn't sing anymore. Not for a long time," said Patricia. "Now he runs fast. He's even faster than Tonino in their fireman's training."

D. H. Lawrence
(1885–1930)

THE ROCKING-HORSE WINNER
(1920)

There was a woman who was beautiful, who started with all the advantages, yet she had no luck. She married for love, and the love turned to dust. She had bonny children, yet she felt they had been thrust upon her, and she could not love them. They looked at her coldly, as if they were finding fault with her. And hurriedly she felt she must cover up some fault in herself. Yet what it was that she must cover up she never knew. Nevertheless, when her children were present, she always felt the centre of her heart go hard. This troubled her, and in her manner she was all the more gentle and anxious for her children, as if she loved them very much. Only she herself knew that at the centre of her heart was a hard little place that could not feel love, no, not for anybody. Everybody else said of her: "She is such a good mother. She adores her children." Only she herself, and her children themselves, knew it was not so. They read it in each other's eyes.

There were a boy and two little girls. They lived in a pleasant house, with a garden, and they had discreet servants, and felt themselves superior to anyone in the neighbourhood.

Although they lived in style, they felt always an anxiety in the house. There was never enough money. The mother had a small income, and the father had a small income, but not nearly enough for the social position which they had to keep up. The father went into town to some office. But though he had good prospects, these prospects never materialised. There was always the grinding sense of the shortage of money, though the style was always kept up.

At last the mother said: "I will see if *I* can't make something." But she did not know where to begin. She racked her brains, and tried this thing and the other, but could not find anything successful. The failure made deep lines come into her face. Her children were growing up, they would have to go to school. There must be more money, there must be more money. The father, who was always very handsome and expensive in his tastes, seemed as if he never *would* be able to do anything worth doing. And the mother, who had a great belief in herself, did not succeed any better, and her tastes were just as expensive.

And so the house came to be haunted by the unspoken phrase: *There must be more money! There must be more money!* The children could hear it all the time, though nobody said it aloud. They heard it at Christmas, when the expensive and splendid toys filled the nursery. Behind the shining modern rocking-horse, behind the smart doll's house, a voice would start whispering: "There *must* be more money! There *must* be more money!" And the children would stop playing, to listen for a moment. They would look into each other's eyes, to see if they had all heard. And each one saw in the eyes of the other two that they too had heard. "There *must* be more money! There *must* be more money!"

It came whispering from the springs of the still-swaying rocking-horse, and even the horse, bending his wooden, champing head, heard it. The big doll, sitting so pink and smirking in her new pram, could hear it quite plainly, and seemed to be smirking all the more self-consciously because of it. The foolish puppy, too, that took the place of the teddybear, he was looking so extraordinarily foolish for no other reason but that he heard the secret whisper all over the house: "There *must* be more money!"

Yet nobody ever said it aloud. The whisper was everywhere, and therefore no one spoke it. Just as no one ever says: "We are breathing!" in spite of the fact that breath is coming and going all the time.

"Mother," said the boy Paul one day, "why don't we keep a car of our own? Why do we always use uncle's, or else a taxi?"

"Because we're the poor members of the family," said the mother.

"But why *are* we, mother?"

"Well—I suppose," she said slowly and bitterly, "it's because your father has no luck."

The boy was silent for some time.

"Is luck money, mother?" he asked, rather timidly.

"No, Paul. Not quite. It's what causes you to have money."

"Oh!" said Paul vaguely. "I thought when Uncle Oscar said *filthy lucker,* it meant money."

"*Filthy lucre* does mean money," said the mother. "But it's lucre, not luck."

"Oh!" said the boy. "Then what *is* luck, mother?"

"It's what causes you to have money. If you're lucky you have money. That's why it's better to be born lucky than rich. If you're rich, you may lose your money. But if you're lucky, you will always get more money."

"Oh! Will you? And is father not lucky?"

"Very unlucky, I should say," she said bitterly.

The boy watched her with unsure eyes.

"Why?" he asked.

"I don't know. Nobody ever knows why one person is lucky and another unlucky."

"Don't they? Nobody at all? Does *nobody* know?"

"Perhaps God. But He never tells."

"He ought to, then. And aren't you lucky either, mother?"

"I can't be, if I married an unlucky husband."

"But by yourself, aren't you?"

"I used to think I was, before I married. Now I think I am very unlucky indeed."

"Why?"

"Well—never mind! Perhaps I'm not really," she said.

The child looked at her to see if she meant it. But he saw, by the lines of her mouth, that she was only trying to hide something from him.

"Well, anyhow," he said stoutly, "I'm a lucky person."

"Why?" said his mother, with a sudden laugh.

He stared at her. He didn't even know why he had said it.

"God told me," he asserted, brazening it out.

"I hope He did, dear!" she said, again with a laugh, but rather bitter.

"He did, mother!"

"Excellent!" said the mother, using one of her husband's exclamations.

The boy saw she did not believe him; or rather, that she paid no attention to his assertion. This angered him somewhat, and made him want to compel her attention.

He went off by himself, vaguely, in a childish way, seeking for the clue to "luck." Absorbed, taking no heed of other people, he went about with a sort of stealth, seeking inwardly for luck. He wanted luck, he wanted it, he wanted it. When the two girls were playing dolls in the nursery, he would sit on his big rocking-horse, charging madly into space, with a frenzy that made the little girls peer at him uneasily. Wildly the horse careered, the waving dark hair of the boy tossed, his eyes had a strange glare in them. The little girls dared not speak to him.

When he had ridden to the end of his mad little journey, he climbed down and stood in front of his rocking-horse, staring fixedly into its lowered face. Its red mouth was slightly open, its big eye was wide and glassy-bright.

"Now!" he would silently command the snorting steed. "Now, take me to where there is luck! Now take me!"

And he would slash the horse on the neck with the little whip he had asked Uncle Oscar for. He *knew* the horse could take him to where there was luck, if only he forced it. So he would mount again and start on his furious ride, hoping at last to get there. He knew he could get there.

"You'll break your horse, Paul!" said the nurse.

"He's always riding like that! I wish he'd leave off!" said his elder sister Joan.

But he only glared down on them in silence. Nurse gave him up. She could make nothing of him. Anyhow, he was growing beyond her.

One day his mother and his Uncle Oscar came in when he was on one of his furious rides. He did not speak to them.

"Hallo, you young jockey! Riding a winner?" said his uncle.

"Aren't you growing too big for a rocking-horse? You're not a very little boy any longer, you know," said his mother.

But Paul only gave a blue glare from his big, rather close-set eyes. He would speak to nobody when he was in full tilt. His mother watched him with an anxious expression on her face.

At last he suddenly stopped forcing his horse into the mechanical gallop and slid down.

"Well, I got there!" he announced fiercely, his blue eyes still flaring, and his sturdy long legs straddling apart.

"Where did you get to?" asked his mother.

"Where I wanted to go," he flared back at her.

"That's right, son!" said Uncle Oscar. "Don't you stop till you get there. What's the horse's name?"

"He doesn't have a name," said the boy.

"Gets on without all right?" asked the uncle.

"Well, he has different names. He was called Sansovino last week."

"Sansovino, eh? Won the Ascot.[1] How did you know this name?"

"He always talks about horse-races with Bassett," said Joan.

The uncle was delighted to find that his small nephew was posted with all the racing news. Bassett, the young gardener, who had been wounded in the left foot in the war and had got his present job through Oscar Cresswell, whose batman he had been, was a perfect

---

[1] The annual horse race at Ascot Heath in England.

blade of the "turf." He lived in the racing events, and the small boy lived with him.

Oscar Cresswell got it all from Bassett.

"Master Paul comes and asks me, so I can't do more than tell him, sir," said Bassett, his face terribly serious, as if he were speaking of religious matters.

"And does he ever put anything on a horse he fancies?"

"Well—I don't want to give him away—he's a young sport, a fine sport, sir. Would you mind asking him himself? He sort of takes a pleasure in it, and perhaps he'd feel I was giving him away, sir, if you don't mind."

Bassett was serious as a church.

The uncle went back to his nephew and took him off for a ride in the car.

"Say, Paul, old man, do you ever put anything on a horse?" the uncle asked.

The boy watched the handsome man closely.

"Why, do you think I oughtn't to?" he parried.

"Not a bit of it! I thought perhaps you might give me a tip for the Lincoln."[2]

The car sped on into the country, going down to Uncle Oscar's place in Hampshire.

"Honour bright?" said the nephew.

"Honour bright, son!" said the uncle.

"Well, then, Daffodil."

"Daffodil! I doubt it, sonny. What about Mirza?"

"I only know the winner," said the boy. "That's Daffodil."

"Daffodil, eh?"

There was a pause. Daffodil was an obscure horse comparatively.

"Uncle!"

"Yes, son?"

"You won't let it go any further, will you? I promised Bassett."

"Bassett be damned, old man! What's he got to do with it?"

"We're partners. We've been partners from the first. Uncle, he lent me my first five shillings, which I lost. I promised him, honour bright, it was only between me and him; only you gave me that ten-shilling note I started winning with, so I thought you were lucky. You won't let it go any further, will you?"

The boy gazed at his uncle from those big, hot, blue eyes, set rather close together. The uncle stirred and laughed uneasily.

"Right you are, son! I'll keep your tip private. Daffodil, eh? How much are you putting on him?"

"All except twenty pounds," said the boy. "I keep that in reserve."

The uncle thought it a good joke.

---

[2] The Lincolnshire Handicap.

"You keep twenty pounds in reserve, do you, you young romancer? What are you betting, then?"

"I'm betting three hundred," said the boy gravely. "But it's between you and me, Uncle Oscar! Honour bright?"

The uncle burst into a roar of laughter.

"It's between you and me all right, you young Nat Gould,"[3] he said, laughing. "But where's your three hundred?"

"Bassett keeps it for me. We're partners."

"You are, are you! And what is Bassett putting on Daffodil?"

"He won't go quite as high as I do, I expect. Perhaps he'll go a hundred and fifty."

"What, pennies?" laughed the uncle.

"Pounds," said the child, with a surprised look at his uncle. "Bassett keeps a bigger reserve than I do."

Between wonder and amusement Uncle Oscar was silent. He pursued the matter no further, but he determined to take his nephew with him to the Lincoln races.

"Now, son," he said, "I'm putting twenty on Mirza, and I'll put five on for you on any horse you fancy. What's your pick?"

"Daffodil, uncle."

"No, not the fiver on Daffodil!"

"I should if it was my own fiver," said the child.

"Good! Good! Right you are! A fiver for me and a fiver for you on Daffodil."

The child had never been to a race-meeting before, and his eyes were blue fire. He pursed his mouth tight and watched. A Frenchman just in front had put his money on Lancelot. Wild with excitement, he flayed his arms up and down, yelling *"Lancelot! Lancelot!"* in his French accent.

Daffodil came in first, Lancelot second, Mirza third. The child, flushed and with eyes blazing, was curiously serene. His uncle brought him four five-pound notes, four to one.

"What am I to do with these?" he cried, waving them before the boy's eyes.

"I suppose we'll talk to Bassett," said the boy. "I expect I have fifteen hundred now; and twenty in reserve; and this twenty."

His uncle studied him for some moments.

"Look here, son!" he said. "You're not serious about Bassett and that fifteen hundred, are you?"

"Yes, I am. But it's between you and me, uncle. Honour bright?"

"Honour bright all right, son! But I must talk to Bassett."

"If you'd like to be a partner, uncle, with Bassett and me, we could all be partners. Only, you'd have to promise, honour bright, uncle, not

---

[3] Nathaniel Gould (1857–1919). British journalist and writer known for his stories about horse racing.

to let it go beyond us three. Bassett and I are lucky, and you must be lucky, because it was your ten shillings I started winning with. . . ."

Uncle Oscar took both Bassett and Paul into Richmond Park for an afternoon, and there they talked.

"It's like this, you see, sir," Bassett said. "Master Paul would get me talking about racing events, spinning yarns, you know, sir. And he was always keen on knowing if I'd made or if I'd lost. It's about a year since, now, that I put five shillings on Blush of Dawn for him: and we lost. Then the luck turned, with that ten shillings he had from you: that we put on Singhalese. And since that time, it's been pretty steady, all things considering. What do you say, Master Paul?"

"We're all right when we're sure," said Paul. "It's when we're not quite sure that we go down."

"Oh, but we're careful then," said Bassett.

"But when are you *sure?*" smiled Uncle Oscar.

"It's Master Paul, sir," said Bassett in a secret, religious voice. "It's as if he had it from heaven. Like Daffodil, now, for the Lincoln. That was as sure as eggs."

"Did you put anything on Daffodil?" asked Oscar Cresswell.

"Yes, sir. I made my bit."

"And my nephew?"

Bassett was obstinately silent, looking at Paul.

"I made twelve hundred, didn't I, Bassett? I told uncle I was putting three hundred on Daffodil."

"That's right," said Bassett, nodding.

"But where's the money?" asked the uncle.

"I keep it safe locked up, sir. Master Paul can have it any minute he likes to ask for it."

"What, fifteen hundred pounds?"

"And twenty! And *forty,* that is, with the twenty he made on the course."

"It's amazing!" said the uncle.

"If Master Paul offers you to be partners, sir, I would, if I were you: if you'll excuse me," said Bassett.

Oscar Cresswell thought about it.

"I'll see the money," he said.

They drove home again, and, sure enough, Bassett came round to the garden-house with fifteen hundred pounds in notes. The twenty pounds reserve was left with Joe Glee, in the Turf Commission deposit.

"You see, it's all right, uncle, when I'm *sure!* Then we go strong, for all we're worth. Don't we, Bassett?"

"We do that, Master Paul."

"And when are you sure?" said the uncle, laughing.

"Oh, well, sometimes I'm *absolutely* sure, like about Daffodil," said the boy; "and sometimes I have an idea; and sometimes I haven't even an idea, have I, Bassett? Then we're careful, because we mostly go down."

"You do, do you! And when you're sure, like about Daffodil, what makes you sure, sonny?"

"Oh, well, I don't know," said the boy uneasily. "I'm sure, you know, uncle; that's all."

"It's as if he had it from heaven, sir," Bassett reiterated.

"I should say so!" said the uncle.

But he became a partner. And when the Leger[4] was coming on Paul was "sure" about Lively Spark, which was a quite inconsiderable horse. The boy insisted on putting a thousand on the horse, Bassett went for five hundred, and Oscar Cresswell two hundred. Lively Spark came in first, and the betting had been ten to one against him. Paul had made ten thousand.

"You see," he said, "I was absolutely sure of him."

Even Oscar Cresswell had cleared two thousand.

"Look here, son," he said, "this sort of thing makes me nervous."

"It needn't, uncle! Perhaps I shan't be sure again for a long time."

"But what are you going to do with your money?" asked the uncle.

"Of course," said the boy, "I started it for mother. She said she had no luck, because father is unlucky, so I thought if *I* was lucky, it might stop whispering."

"What might stop whispering?"

"Our house. I *hate* our house for whispering."

"What does it whisper?"

"Why—why"—the boy fidgeted—"why, I don't know. But it's always short of money, you know, uncle."

"I know it, son, I know it."

"You know people send mother writs,[5] don't you, uncle?"

"I'm afraid I do," said the uncle.

"And then the house whispers, like people laughing at you behind your back. It's awful, that is! I thought if I was lucky ______"

"You might stop it," added the uncle.

The boy watched him with big blue eyes, that had an uncanny cold fire in them, and he said never a word.

"Well, then!" said the uncle. "What are we doing?"

"I shouldn't like mother to know I was lucky," said the boy.

"Why not, son?"

"She'd stop me."

"I don't think she would."

"Oh!"—and the boy writhed in an odd way—"I *don't* want her to know, uncle."

"All right, son! We'll manage it without her knowing."

They managed it very easily. Paul, at the other's suggestion, handed over five thousand pounds to his uncle, who deposited it with the family

---

[4] The St. Leger Stakes.

[5] Letters from creditors requesting payment.

lawyer, who was then to inform Paul's mother that a relative had put five thousand pounds into his hands, which sum was to be paid out a thousand pounds at a time, on the mother's birthday, for the next five years.

"So she'll have a birthday present of a thousand pounds for five successive years," said Uncle Oscar. "I hope it won't make it all the harder for her later."

Paul's mother had her birthday in November. The house had been 'whispering' worse than ever lately, and, even in spite of his luck, Paul could not bear up against it. He was very anxious to see the effect of the birthday letter, telling his mother about the thousand pounds.

When there were no visitors, Paul now took his meals with his parents, as he was beyond the nursery control. His mother went into town nearly every day. She had discovered that she had an odd knack of sketching furs and dress materials, so she worked secretly in the studio of a friend who was the chief 'artist' for the leading drapers. She drew the figures of ladies in furs and ladies in silk and sequins for the newspaper advertisements. This young woman artist earned several thousand pounds a year, but Paul's mother only made several hundreds, and she was again dissatisfied. She so wanted to be first in something, and she did not succeed, even in making sketches for drapery advertisements.

She was down to breakfast on the morning of her birthday. Paul watched her face as she read her letters. He knew the lawyer's letter. As his mother read it, her face hardened and became more expressionless. Then a cold, determined look came on her mouth. She hid the letter under the pile of others, and said not a word about it.

"Didn't you have anything nice in the post for your birthday, mother?" said Paul.

"Quite moderately nice," she said, her voice cold and absent.

She went away to town without saying more.

But in the afternoon Uncle Oscar appeared. He said Paul's mother had had a long interview with the lawyer, asking if the whole five thousand could not be advanced at once, as she was in debt.

"What do you think, uncle?" asked the boy.

"I leave it to you, son."

"Oh, let her have it, then! We can get some more with the other," said the boy.

"A bird in the hand is worth two in the bush, laddie!" said Uncle Oscar.

"But I'm sure to *know* for the Grand National; or the Lincolnshire; or else the Derby.[6] I'm sure to know for *one* of them," said Paul.

So Uncle Oscar signed the agreement, and Paul's mother touched the whole five thousand. Then something very curious happened. The voices in the house suddenly went mad, like a chorus of frogs on a

---

[6] Famous British horse races. The Grand National is run at Aintree, the Derby at Epsom Downs.

spring evening. There was certain new furnishings, and Paul had a tutor. He was *really* going to Eton, his father's school, in the following autumn. There were flowers in the winter, and a blossoming of the luxury Paul's mother had been used to. And yet the voices in the house, behind the sprays of mimosa and almond-blossom, and from under the piles of iridescent cushions, simply trilled and screamed in a sort of ecstasy: "There *must* be more money! Oh-h-h; there *must* be more money. Oh, now, now-w! Now-w-w—there *must* be more money!—more than ever! More than ever!"

It frightened Paul terribly. He studied away at his Latin and Greek with his tutor. But his intense hours were spent with Bassett. The Grand National had gone by: he had not "known," and had lost a hundred pounds. Summer was at hand. He was in agony for the Lincoln. But even for the Lincoln he didn't "know," and he lost fifty pounds. He became wild-eyed and strange, as if something were going to explode in him.

"Let it alone, son! Don't you bother about it!" urged Uncle Oscar. But it was as if the boy couldn't really hear what his uncle was saying.

"I've got to know for the Derby! I've got to know for the Derby!" the child reiterated, his big blue eyes blazing with a sort of madness.

His mother noticed how overwrought he was.

"You'd better go to the seaside. Wouldn't you like to go now to the seaside, instead of waiting? I think you'd better," she said, looking down at him anxiously, her heart curiously heavy because of him.

But the child lifted his uncanny blue eyes.

"I couldn't possibly go before the Derby, mother!" he said. "I couldn't possibly!"

"Why not?" she said, her voice becoming heavy when she was opposed. "Why not? You can still go from the seaside to see the Derby with your Uncle Oscar, if that's what you wish. No need for you to wait here. Besides, I think you care too much about these races. It's a bad sign. My family has been a gambling family, and you won't know till you grow up how much damage it has done. But it has done damage. I shall have to send Bassett away, and ask Uncle Oscar not to talk racing to you, unless you promise to be reasonable about it: go away to the seaside and forget it. You're all nerves!"

"I'll do what you like, mother, so long as you don't send me away till after the Derby," the boy said.

"Send you away from where? Just from this house?"

"Yes," he said, gazing at her.

"Why, you curious child, what makes you care about this house so much, suddenly? I never knew you loved it."

He gazed at her without speaking. He had a secret within a secret, something he had not divulged, even to Bassett or to his Uncle Oscar.

But his mother, after standing undecided and a little bit sullen for some moments, said:

"Very well, then! Don't go to the seaside till after the Derby, if you don't wish it. But promise me you won't let your nerves go to pieces.

Promise you won't think so much about horse-racing and *events,* as you call them!"

"Oh no," said the boy casually. "I won't think much about them, mother. You needn't worry. I wouldn't worry, mother, if I were you."

"If you were me and I were you," said his mother, "I wonder what we *should* do!"

"But you know you needn't worry, mother, don't you?" the boy repeated.

"I should be awfully glad to know it," she said wearily.

"Oh, well, you *can,* you know. I mean, you *ought* to know you needn't worry," he insisted.

"Ought I? Then I'll see about it," she said.

Paul's secret of secrets was his wooden horse, that which had no name. Since he was emancipated from a nurse and a nursery-governess, he had had his rocking-horse removed to his own bedroom at the top of the house.

"Surely you're too big for a rocking-horse!" his mother had remonstrated.

"Well, you see, mother, till I can have a *real* horse, I like to have *some* sort of animal about," had been his quaint answer.

"Do you feel he keeps you company?" she laughed.

"Oh yes! He's very good, he always keeps me company, when I'm there," said Paul.

So the horse, rather shabby, stood in an arrested prance in the boy's bedroom.

The Derby was drawing near, and the boy grew more and more tense. He hardly heard what was spoken to him, he was very frail, and his eyes were really uncanny. His mother had sudden strange seizures of uneasiness about him. Sometimes, for half an hour, she would feel a sudden anxiety about him that was almost anguish. She wanted to rush to him at once, and know he was safe.

Two nights before the Derby, she was at a big party in town, when one of her rushes of anxiety about her boy, her firstborn, gripped her heart till she could hardly speak. She fought with the feeling, might and main, for she believed in common sense. But it was too strong. She had to leave the dance and go downstairs to telephone to the country. The children's nursery-governess was terribly surprised and startled at being rung up in the night.

"Are the children all right, Miss Wilmot?"

"Oh yes, they are quite all right."

"Master Paul? Is he all right?"

"He went to bed as right as a trivet. Shall I run up and look at him?"

"No," said Paul's mother reluctantly. "No! Don't trouble. It's all right. Don't sit up. We shall be home fairly soon." She did not want her son's privacy intruded upon.

"Very good," said the governess.

It was about one o'clock when Paul's mother and father drove up to their house. All was still. Paul's mother went to her room and slipped off her white fur cloak. She had told her maid not to wait up for her. She heard her husband downstairs, mixing a whisky and soda.

And then, because of the strange anxiety at her heart, she stole upstairs to her son's room. Noiselessly she went along the upper corridor. Was there a faint noise? What was it?

She stood, with arrested muscles, outside his door, listening. There was a strange, heavy, and yet not loud noise. Her heart stood still. It was a soundless noise, yet rushing and powerful. Something huge, in violent, hushed motion. What was it? What in God's name was it? She ought to know. She felt that she knew the noise. She knew what it was.

Yet she could not place it. She couldn't say what it was. And on and on it went, like a madness.

Softly, frozen with anxiety and fear, she turned the door-handle.

The room was dark. Yet in the space near the window, she heard and saw something plunging to and fro. She gazed in fear and amazement.

Then suddenly she switched on the light, and saw her son, in his green pyjamas, madly surging on the rocking-horse. The blaze of light suddenly lit him up, as he urged the wooden horse, and lit her up, as she stood, blonde, in her dress of pale green and crystal, in the doorway.

"Paul!" she cried. "Whatever are you doing?"

"It's Malabar!" he screamed in a powerful, strange voice. "It's Malabar!"

His eyes blazed at her for one strange and senseless second, as he ceased urging his wooden horse. Then he fell with a crash to the ground, and she, all her tormented motherhood flooding upon her, rushed to gather him up.

But he was unconscious, and unconscious he remained, with some brain-fever. He talked and tossed, and his mother sat stonily by his side.

"Malabar! It's Malabar! Bassett, Bassett, I *know!* It's Malabar!"

So the child cried, trying to get up and urge the rocking-horse that gave him his inspiration.

"What does he mean by Malabar?" asked the heart-frozen mother.

"I don't know," said the father stonily.

"What does he mean by Malabar?" she asked her brother Oscar.

"It's one of the horses running for the Derby," was the answer.

And, in spite of himself, Oscar Cresswell spoke to Bassett, and himself put a thousand on Malabar: at fourteen to one.

The third day of the illness was critical: they were waiting for a change. The boy, with his rather long, curly hair, was tossing ceaselessly on the pillow. He neither slept nor regained consciousness, and his eyes were like blue stones. His mother sat, feeling her heart had gone, turned actually into a stone.

In the evening, Oscar Cresswell did not come, but Bassett sent a message, saying could he come up for one moment, just one moment?

Paul's mother was very angry at the intrusion, but on second thoughts she agreed. The boy was the same. Perhaps Bassett might bring him to consciousness.

The gardener, a shortish fellow with a little brown moustache and sharp little brown eyes, tiptoed into the room, touched his imaginary cap to Paul's mother, and stole to the bedside, staring with glittering, smallish eyes at the tossing, dying child.

"Master Paul!" he whispered. "Master Paul! Malabar came in first all right, a clean win. I did as you told me. You've made over seventy thousand pounds, you have; you've got over eighty thousand. Malabar came in all right, Master Paul."

"Malabar! Malabar! Did I say Malabar, mother? Did I say Malabar? Do you think I'm lucky, mother? I knew Malabar, didn't I? Over eighty thousand pounds! I call that lucky, don't you, mother? Over eighty thousand pounds! I knew, didn't I know I knew? Malabar came in all right. If I ride my horse till I'm sure, then I tell you, Bassett, you can go as high as you like. Did you go for all you were worth, Bassett?"

"I went a thousand on it, Master Paul."

"I never told you, mother, that if I can ride my horse, and *get there,* then I'm absolutely sure—oh, absolutely! Mother, did I ever tell you? I *am* lucky!"

"No, you never did," said his mother.

But the boy died in the night.

And even as he lay dead, his mother heard her brother's voice saying to her: "My God, Hester, you're eighty-odd thousand to the good, and a poor devil of a son to the bad. But, poor devil, poor devil, he's best gone out of a life where he rides his rocking-horse to find a winner."

Doris Lessing
(1919–)

A WOMAN ON A ROOF
(1963)

It was during the week of hot sun, that June.

Three men were at work on the roof, where the leads got so hot they had the idea of throwing water on to cool them. But the water steamed, then sizzled; and they made jokes about getting an egg from some woman in the flats under them, to poach it for their dinner. By two it was not possible to touch the guttering they were replacing, and they speculated about what workmen did in regularly hot countries. Perhaps they should borrow kitchen gloves with the egg? They were all a bit dizzy, not used to the heat; and they shed their coats and stood side by side squeezing themselves into a foot-wide patch of shade against a chimney, careful to keep their feet in the thick socks and boots out of the sun. There was a fine view across several acres of roofs. Not far off a man sat in a deck chair reading the newspapers. Then they saw her, between chimneys, about fifty yards away. She lay face down on a brown blanket. They could see the top part of her: black hair, a flushed solid back, arms spread out.

"She's stark naked," said Stanley, sounding annoyed.

Harry, the oldest, a man of about forty-five, said: "Looks like it."

Young Tom, seventeen, said nothing, but he was excited and grinning.

Stanley said: "Someone'll report her if she doesn't watch out."

"She thinks no one can see," said Tom, craning his head all ways to see more.

At this point the woman, still lying prone, brought her two hands up behind her shoulders with the ends of a scarf in them, tied it behind her back, and sat up. She wore a red scarf tied around her breasts and brief red bikini pants. This being the first day of the sun she was white, flushing red. She sat smoking, and did not look up when Stanley let out a wolf whistle. Harry said: "Small things amuse small minds," leading the way back to their part of the roof, but it was scorching. Harry said: "Wait, I'm going to rig up some shade," and disappeared down the skylight into the building. Now that he'd gone, Stanley and Tom went to the farthest point they could to peer at the woman. She had moved, and all they could see were two pink legs stretched on the blanket. They whistled and shouted but the legs did not move. Harry came back with a blanket and shouted: "Come on, then." He sounded irritated with them. They clambered back to him and he said to Stanley: "What about your missus?" Stanley was newly married, about three months. Stanley said, jeering: "What about my missus?"—preserving his independence. Tom said nothing, but his mind was full of the nearly naked woman. Harry slung the blanket, which he had borrowed from a friendly woman downstairs, from the stem of a television aerial to a row of chimney-pots. This shade fell across the piece of gutter they had to replace. But the shade kept moving, they had to adjust the blanket, and not much progress was made. At last some of the heat left the roof, and they worked fast, making up for lost time. First Stanley, then Tom, made a trip to the end of the roof to see the woman. "She's on her back," Stanley said, adding a jest which made Tom snicker, and the older man smile tolerantly. Tom's report was that she hadn't moved, but it was a lie. He wanted to keep what he had seen to himself: he had caught her in the act of rolling down the little red pants over her hips, till they were no more than a small triangle. She was on her back, fully visible, glistening with oil.

Next morning, as soon as they came up, they went to look. She was already there, face down, arms spread out, naked except for the little red pants. She had turned brown in the night. Yesterday she was a scarlet-and-white woman, today she was a brown woman. Stanley let out a whistle. She lifted her head, startled, as if she'd been asleep, and looked straight over at them. The sun was in her eyes, she blinked and stared, then she dropped her head again. At this gesture of indifference, they all three, Stanley, Tom and old Harry, let out whistles and yells. Harry was doing it in parody of the younger men, making fun of them, but he was also angry. They were all angry because of her utter indifference to the three men watching her.

"Bitch," said Stanley.

"She should ask us over," said Tom, snickering.

Harry recovered himself and reminded Stanley: "If she's married, her old man wouldn't like that."

"Christ," said Stanley virtuously, "if my wife lay about like that, for everyone to see, I'd soon stop her."

Harry said, smiling: "How do you know, perhaps she's sunning herself at this very moment?"

"Not a chance, not on our roof." The safety of his wife put Stanley into a good humor, and they went to work. But today it was hotter than yesterday; and several times one or the other suggested they should tell Matthew, the foreman, and ask to leave the roof until the heat wave was over. But they didn't. There was work to be done in the basement of the big block of flats, but up here they felt free, on a different level from ordinary humanity shut in the streets or the buildings. A lot more people came out on to the roofs that day, for an hour at midday. Some married couples sat side by side in deck chairs, the women's legs stockingless and scarlet, the men in vests with reddening shoulders.

The woman stayed on her blanket, turning herself over and over. She ignored them, no matter what they did. When Harry went off to fetch more screws, Stanley said: "Come on." Her roof belonged to a different system of roofs, separated from theirs at one point by about twenty feet. It meant a scrambling climb from one level to another, edging along parapets, clinging to chimneys, while their big boots slipped and slithered, but at last they stood on a small square projecting roof looking straight down at her, close. She sat smoking, reading a book. Tom thought she looked like a poster, or a magazine cover, with the blue sky behind her and her legs stretched out. Behind her a great crane at work on a new building in Oxford Street swung its black arm across roofs in a great arc. Tom imagined himself at work on the crane, adjusting the arm to swing over and pick her up and swing her back across the sky to drop her near him.

They whistled. She looked up at them, cool and remote, then went on reading. Again, they were furious. Or, rather, Stanley was. His sun-heated face was screwed into a rage as he whistled again and again, trying to make her look up. Young Tom stopped whistling. He stood beside Stanley, excited, grinning; but he felt as if he were saying to the woman: Don't associate me with *him,* for his grin was apologetic. Last night he had thought of the unknown woman before he slept, and she had been tender with him. This tenderness he was remembering as he shifted his feet by the jeering, whistling Stanley, and watched the indifferent, healthy brown woman a few feet off, with the gap that plunged to the street between them. Tom thought it was romantic, it was like being high on two hilltops. But there was a shout from Harry, and they clambered back. Stanley's face was hard, really angry. The boy kept looking at him and wondered why he hated the woman so much, for by now he loved her.

They played their little games with the blanket, trying to trap shade to work under; but again it was not until nearly four that they could work seriously, and they were exhausted, all three of them. They were grumbling about the weather by now. Stanley was in a thoroughly bad humor. When they made their routine trip to see the woman before they packed up for the day, she was apparently asleep, face down, her back all naked save for the scarlet triangle on her buttocks. "I've got a good mind to report her to the police," said Stanley, and Harry said: "What's eating you? What harm's she doing?"

"I tell you, if she was my wife!"

"But she isn't, is she?" Tom knew that Harry, like himself, was uneasy at Stanley's reaction. He was normally a sharp young man, quick at his work, making a lot of jokes, good company.

"Perhaps it will be cooler tomorrow," said Harry.

But it wasn't; it was hotter, if anything, and the weather forecast said the good weather would last. As soon as they were on the roof, Harry went over to see if the woman was there, and Tom knew it was to prevent Stanley going, to put off his bad humor. Harry had grownup children, a boy the same age as Tom, and the youth trusted and looked up to him.

Harry came back and said: "She's not there."

"I bet her old man has put his foot down," said Stanley, and Harry and Tom caught each other's eyes and smiled behind the young married man's back.

Harry suggested they should get permission to work in the basement, and they did, that day. But before packing up Stanley said: "Let's have a breath of fresh air." Again Harry and Tom smiled at each other as they followed Stanley up to the roof. Tom in the devout conviction that he was there to protect the woman from Stanley. It was about five-thirty, and a calm, full sunlight lay over the roofs. The great crane still swung its black arm from Oxford Street to above their heads. She was not there. Then there was a flutter of white from behind a parapet, and she stood up, in a belted, white dressing-gown. She had been there all day, probably, but on a different patch of roof, to hide from them. Stanley did not whistle; he said nothing, but watched the woman bend to collect papers, books, cigarettes, then fold the blanket over her arm. Tom was thinking: If they weren't here, I'd go over and say . . . what? But he knew from his nightly dreams of her that she was kind and friendly. Perhaps she would ask him down to her flat? Perhaps . . . He stood watching her disappear down the skylight. As she went, Stanley let out a shrill derisive yell; she started, and it seemed as if she nearly fell. She clutched to save herself, they could hear things falling. She looked straight at them, angry. Harry said, facetiously: "Better be careful on those slippery ladders, love." Tom knew he said it to save her from Stanley, but she could not know it. She vanished, frowning. Tom was full of a secret delight, because he knew her anger was for the others, not for him.

"Roll on some rain," said Stanley, bitter, looking at the blue evening sky.

Next day was cloudless, and they decided to finish the work in the basement. They felt excluded, shut in the grey cement basement fitting pipes, from the holiday atmosphere of London in a heat wave. At lunchtime they came up for some air, but while the married couples, and the men in shirtsleeves or vests, were there, she was not there, either on her usual patch of roof or where she had been yesterday. They all, even Harry, clambered about, between chimney-pots, over parapets, the hot leads stinging their fingers. There was not a sign of her. They took off their shirts and vests and exposed their chests, feeling their feet sweaty and hot. They did not mention the woman. But Tom felt alone again. Last night she had him into her flat: it was big and had fitted white carpets and a bed with a padded white leather headboard. She wore a black filmy negligée and her kindness to Tom thickened his throat as he remembered it. He felt she had betrayed him by not being there.

And again after work they climbed up, but still there was nothing to be seen of her. Stanley kept repeating that if it was as hot as this tomorrow he wasn't going to work and that's all there was to it. But they were all there next day. By ten the temperature was in the middle seventies, and it was eighty long before noon. Harry went to the foreman to say it was impossible to work on the leads in that heat; but the foreman said there was nothing else he could put them on, and they'd have to. At midday they stood, silent, watching the skylight on her roof open, and then she slowly emerged in her white gown, holding a bundle of blanket. She looked at them, gravely, then went to the part of the roof where she was hidden from them. Tom was pleased. He felt she was more his when the other men couldn't see her. They had taken off their shirts and vests, but now they put them back again, for they felt the sun bruising their flesh. "She must have the hide of a rhino," said Stanley, tugging at guttering and swearing. They stopped work, and sat in the shade, moving around behind chimney stacks. A woman came to water a yellow window box opposite them. She was middleaged, wearing a flowered summer dress. Stanley said to her: "We need a drink more than them." She smiled and said: "Better drop down to the pub quick, it'll be closing in a minute." They exchanged pleasantries, and she left them with a smile and a wave.

"Not like Lady Godiva,"[1] said Stanley. "She can give us a bit of a chat and a smile."

"You didn't whistle at *her,*" said Tom, reproving.

"Listen to him," said Stanley, "you didn't whistle, then?"

But the boy felt as if he hadn't whistled, as if only Harry and Stanley had. He was making plans, when it was time to knock off work, to get left

[1] According to legend, Lady Godiva rode naked through the streets of Coventry in an effort to win relief for the townspeople from an exorbitant tax.

behind and somehow make his way over to the woman. The weather report said the hot spell was due to break, so he had to move quickly. But there was no chance of being left. The other two decided to knock off work at four, because they were exhausted. As they went down, Tom quickly climbed a parapet and hoisted himself higher by pulling his weight up a chimney. He caught a glimpse of her lying on her back, her knees up, eyes closed, a brown woman lolling in the sun. He slipped and clattered down, as Stanley looked for information: "She's gone down," he said. He felt as if he had protected her from Stanley, and that she must be grateful to him. He could feel the bond between the woman and himself.

Next day, they stood around on the landing below the roof, reluctant to climb up into the heat. The woman who had lent Harry the blanket came out and offered them a cup of tea. They accepted gratefully, and sat around Mrs. Pritchett's kitchen an hour or so, chatting. She was married to an airline pilot. A smart blonde, of about thirty, she had an eye for the handsome sharp-faced Stanley; and the two teased each other while Harry sat in a corner, watching, indulgent, though his expression reminded Stanley that he was married. And young Tom felt envious of Stanley's ease in badinage;[2] felt, too, that Stanley's getting off with Mrs. Pritchett left his romance with the woman on the roof safe and intact.

"I thought they said the heat wave'd break," said Stanley, sullen, as the time approached when they really would have to climb up into the sunlight.

"You don't like it, then?" asked Mrs. Pritchett.

"All right for some," said Stanley. "Nothing to do but lie about as if it was a beach up there. Do you ever go up?"

"Went up once," said Mrs. Pritchett. "But it's a dirty place up there, and it's too hot."

"Quite right too," said Stanley.

Then they went up, leaving the cool neat little flat and the friendly Mrs. Pritchett.

As soon as they were up they saw her. The three men looked at her, resentful at her ease in this punishing sun. Then Harry said, because of the expression on Stanley's face: "Come on, we've got to pretend to work, at least."

They had to wrench another length of guttering that ran beside a parapet out of its bed, so that they could replace it. Stanley took it in his two hands, tugged, swore, stood up. "Fuck it," he said, and sat down under a chimney. He lit a cigarette. "Fuck them," he said. "What do they think we are, lizards? I've got blisters all over my hands." Then he jumped up and climbed over the roofs and stood with his back to them. He put his fingers either side of his mouth and let out a shrill whistle. Tom and Harry squatted, not looking at each other, watching him. They could just see the woman's head, the beginnings of her brown shoulders.

---

[2] Playful banter.

Stanley whistled again. Then he began stamping with his feet, and whistled and yelled and screamed at the woman, his face getting scarlet. He seemed quite mad, as he stamped and whistled, while the woman did not move, she did not move a muscle.

"Barmy," said Tom.

"Yes," said Harry, disapproving.

Suddenly the older man came to a decision. It was, Tom knew, to save some sort of scandal or real trouble over the woman. Harry stood up and began packing tools into a length of oily cloth. "Stanley," he said, commanding. At first Stanley took no notice, but Harry said: "Stanley, we're packing it in, I'll tell Matthew."

Stanley came back, cheeks mottled, eyes glaring.

"Can't go on like this," said Harry. "It'll break in a day or so. I'm going to tell Matthew we've got sunstroke, and if he doesn't like it, it's too bad." Even Harry sounded aggrieved, Tom noted. The small, competent man, the family man with his grey hair, who was never at a loss, sounded really off balance. "Come on," he said, angry. He fitted himself into the open square in the roof, and went down, watching his feet on the ladder. Then Stanley went, with not a glance at the woman. Then Tom, who, his throat beating with excitement, silently promised her on a backward glance: Wait for me, wait, I'm coming.

On the pavement Stanley said: "I'm going home." He looked white now, so perhaps he really did have sunstroke. Harry went off to find the foreman, who was at work on the plumbing of some flats down the street. Tom slipped back, not into the building they had been working on, but the building on whose roof the woman lay. He went straight up, no one stopping him. The skylight stood open, with an iron ladder leading up. He emerged on to the roof a couple of yards from her. She sat up, pushing back her black hair with both hands. The scarf across her breasts bound them tight, and brown flesh bulged around it. Her legs were brown and smooth. She stared at him in silence. The boy stood grinning, foolish, claiming the tenderness he expected from her.

"What do you want?" she asked.

"I . . . I came to . . . make your acquaintance," he stammered, grinning, pleading with her.

They looked at each other, the slight, scarlet-faced excited boy, and the serious, nearly naked woman. Then, without a word, she lay down on her brown blanket, ignoring him.

"You like the sun, do you?" he enquired of her glistening back.

Not a word. He felt panic, thinking of how she had held him in her arms, stroked his hair, brought him where he sat, lordly, in her bed, a glass of some exhilarating liquor he had never tasted in life. He felt that if he knelt down, stroked her shoulders, her hair, she would turn and clasp him in her arms.

He said: "The sun's all right for you, isn't it?"

She raised her head, set her chin on two small fists. "Go away," she said. He did not move. "Listen," she said, in a slow reasonable voice, where anger was kept in check, though with difficulty; looking at him, her face weary with anger, "if you get a kick out of seeing women in bikinis, why don't you take a sixpenny bus ride to the Lido?[3] You'd see dozens of them, without all this mountaineering."

She hadn't understood him. He felt her unfairness pale him. He stammered: "But I like you, I've been watching you and . . ."

"Thanks," she said, and dropped her face again, turned away from him.

She lay there. He stood there. She said nothing. She had simply shut him out. He stood, saying nothing at all, for some minutes. He thought: She'll have to say something if I stay. But the minutes went past, with no sign of them in her, except in the tension of her back, her thighs, her arms—the tension of waiting for him to go.

He looked up at the sky, where the sun seemed to spin in heat; and over the roofs where he and his mates had been earlier. He could see the heat quivering where they had worked. And they expect us to work in these conditions! he thought, filled with righteous indignation. The woman hadn't moved. A bit of hot wind blew her black hair softly; it shone, and was iridescent. He remembered how he had stroked it last night.

Resentment of her at last moved him off and away down the ladder, through the building, into the street. He got drunk then, in hatred of her.

Next day when he woke the sky was grey. He looked at the wet grey and thought, vicious: Well, that's fixed you, hasn't it now? That's fixed you good and proper.

The three men were at work early on the cool leads, surrounded by damp drizzling roofs where no one came to sun themselves, black roofs, slimy with rain. Because it was cool now, they would finish the job that day, if they hurried.

Gabriel Garcia Márquez
(1928–)

THE HANDSOMEST DROWNED MAN IN THE WORLD

A TALE FOR CHILDREN

(1955)

Translated by Gregory Rabassa

The first children who saw the dark and slinky bulge approaching through the sea let themselves think it was an empty ship. Then they

---

[3] A bathing area in London's Hyde Park.

saw it had no flags or masts and they thought it was a whale. But when it washed up on the beach, they removed the clumps of seaweed, the jellyfish tentacles, and the remains of fish and flotsam, and only then did they see that it was a drowned man.

They had been playing with him all afternoon, burying him in the sand and digging him up again, when someone chanced to see them and spread the alarm in the village. The men who carried him to the nearest house noticed that he weighed more than any dead man they had ever known, almost as much as a horse, and they said to each other that maybe he'd been floating too long and the water had got into his bones. When they laid him on the floor they said he'd been taller than all other men because there was barely enough room for him in the house, but they thought that maybe the ability to keep on growing after death was part of the nature of certain drowned men. He had the smell of the sea about him and only his shape gave one to suppose that it was the corpse of a human being, because the skin was covered with a crust of mud and scales.

They did not even have to clean off his face to know that the dead man was a stranger. The village was made up of only twenty-odd wooden houses that had stone courtyards with no flowers and which were spread about on the end of a desertlike cape. There was so little land that mothers always went about with the fear that the wind would carry off their children and the few dead that the years had caused among them had to be thrown off the cliffs. But the sea was calm and bountiful and all the men fit into seven boats. So when they found the drowned man they simply had to look at one another to see that they were all there.

That night they did not go out to work at sea. While the men went to find out if anyone was missing in neighboring villages, the women stayed behind to care for the drowned man. They took the mud off with grass swabs, they removed the underwater stones entangled in his hair, and they scraped the crust off with tools used for scaling fish. As they were doing that they noticed that the vegetation on him came from faraway oceans and deep water and that his clothes were in tatters, as if he had sailed through labyrinths of coral. They noticed too that he bore his death with pride, for he did not have the lonely look of other drowned men who came out of the sea or that haggard, needy look of men who drowned in rivers. But only when they finished cleaning him off did they become aware of the kind of man he was and it left them breathless. Not only was he the tallest, strongest, most virile, and best built man they had ever seen, but even though they were looking at him there was no room for him in their imagination.

5 They could not find a bed in the village large enough to lay him on nor was there a table solid enough to use for his wake. The tallest men's holiday pants would not fit him, nor the fattest ones' Sunday shirts, nor the shoes of the one with the biggest feet. Fascinated by his huge size and his beauty, the women then decided to make him some pants from

a large piece of sail and a shirt from some bridal Brabant linen so that he could continue through his death with dignity. As they sewed, sitting in a circle and gazing at the corpse between stitches, it seemed to them that the wind had never been so steady nor the sea so restless as on that night and they supposed that the change had something to do with the dead man. They thought that if that magnificent man had lived in the village, his house would have had the widest doors, and highest ceiling, and the strongest floor; his bedstead would have been made from a midship frame held together by iron bolts, and his wife would have been the happiest woman. They thought that he would have had so much authority that he could have drawn fish out of the sea simply by calling their names and that he would have put so much work into his land that springs would have burst forth from among the rocks so that he would have been able to plant flowers on the cliffs. They secretly compared him to their own men, thinking that for all their lives theirs were incapable of doing what he could do in one night, and they ended up dismissing them deep in their hearts as the weakest, meanest, and most useless creatures on earth. They were wandering through that maze of fantasy when the oldest woman, who as the oldest had looked upon the drowned man with more compassion than passion, sighed:

"He has the face of someone called Esteban."

It was true. Most of them had only to take another look at him to see that he could not have any other name. The more stubborn among them, who were the youngest, still lived for a few hours with the illusion that when they put his clothes on and he lay among the flowers in patent leather shoes his name might be Lautaro. But it was a vain illusion. There had not been enough canvas, the poorly cut and worse sewn pants were too tight, and the hidden strength of his heart popped the buttons on his shirt. After midnight the whistling of the wind died down and the sea fell into its Wednesday drowsiness. The silence put an end to any last doubts: he was Esteban. The women who had dressed him, who had combed his hair, had cut his nails and shaved him were unable to hold back a shudder of pity when they had to resign themselves to his being dragged along the ground. It was then that they understood how unhappy he must have been with that huge body since it bothered him even after death. They could see him in life, condemned to going through doors sideways cracking his head on crossbeams, remaining on his feet during visits, not knowing what to do with his soft pink, sealion hands while the lady of the house looked for her most resistant chair and begged him, frightened to death, sit here, Esteban, please, and he, leaning against the wall, smiling, don't bother, ma'am, I'm fine where I am, his heels raw and his back roasted from having done the same thing so many times whenever he paid a visit, don't bother, ma'am, I'm fine where I am to avoid the embarrassment of breaking up the chair, and never knowing perhaps that the one who said don't go, Esteban, at least wait till the coffee's ready, were the ones who later on would whisper the big boob finally left, how nice, the handsome fool has gone. That was what the women were thinking beside the body a little before dawn. Later, when they covered his face with a handkerchief so that the light would not bother him, he looked so forever dead, so defenseless, so much like their men that the first furrows of tears opened in their hearts. It was one of the younger ones who began the weeping. The others, coming to, went from sighs to wails, and the more they sobbed the more they felt like weeping, because the drowned man was becoming all the more Esteban for them, and so they wept so much, for he was the most destitute, most peaceful, and most obliging man on earth, poor Esteban. So when the men returned with the news that the drowned man was not from the neighboring villages either, the women felt an opening of jubilation in the midst of their tears.

"Praise the Lord," they sighed, "he's ours!"

The men thought the fuss was only womanish frivolity. Fatigued because of the difficult nighttime inquiries, all they wanted was to get rid of the bother of the newcomer once and for all before the sun grew strong on that arid, windless day. They improvised a litter with the remains of foremasts and gaffs, tying it together with rigging so that it would bear the weight of the body until they reached the cliffs. They wanted to tie the anchor from a cargo ship to him so that he would sink easily into the deepest waves, where the fish are blind and divers die of nostalgia, and bad currents would not bring him back to shore, as had happened with other bodies. But the more they hurried, the more the women thought of ways to waste time. They walked about like startled hens, pecking with the sea charms on their breasts, some interfering on one side to put a scapular of the good wind on the drowned man, some on the other side to put a wrist compass on him, and after a great deal of *get away from there, woman, stay out of the way, look, you almost made me fall on top of the dead man,* the men began to feel mistrust in their livers and started grumbling about why so many main-altar decorations for a stranger, because no matter how many nails and holywater jars he had on him, the sharks would chew him all the same, but the women kept on piling on their junk relics, running back and forth, stumbling, while they released in sighs what they did not in tears, so that the men finally exploded with *since when has there ever been such a fuss over a drifting corpse, a drowned nobody, a piece of cold Wednesday meat.* One of the women, mortified by so much lack of care, then removed the handkerchief from the dead man's face and the men were left breathless too.

10 He was Esteban. It was not necessary to repeat it for them to recognize him. If they had been told Sir Walter Raleigh, even they might have been impressed with his gringo accent, the macaw on his shoulder, his cannibal-killing blunderbuss, but there could be only one Esteban in the world and there he was, stretched out like a sperm whale, shoeless, wearing the pants of an undersized child, and with those stony nails that had to be cut with a knife. They had only to take the handkerchief off his face to see that he was ashamed, that it was not his fault that he was so big or so heavy or so handsome, and if he had known that this was going to happen, he would have looked for a more discreet place to

drown in; seriously, I even would have tied the anchor off a galleon around my neck and staggered off a cliff like someone who doesn't like things in order not to be upsetting people now with this Wednesday dead body, as you people say, in order not to be bothering anyone with this filthy piece of cold meat that doesn't have anything to do with me. There was so much truth in his manner that even the most mistrustful men, the ones who felt the bitterness of endless nights at sea fearing that their women would tire of dreaming about them and begin to dream of drowned men, even they and others who were harder still shuddered in the marrow of their bones at Esteban's sincerity.

That was how they came to hold the most splendid funeral they could conceive of for an abandoned drowned man. Some women who had gone to get flowers in the neighboring villages returned with other women who could not believe what they had been told, and those women went back for more flowers when they saw the dead man, and they brought more and more until there were so many flowers and so many people that it was hard to walk about. At the final moment it pained them to return him to the waters as an orphan and they chose a father and mother from among the best people, and aunts and uncles and cousins, so that through him all the inhabitants of the village became kinsmen. Some sailors who heard the weeping from a distance went off course, and people heard of one who had himself tied to the mainmast, remembering ancient fables about sirens. While they fought for the privilege of carrying him on their shoulders along the steep escarpment by the cliffs, men and women became aware for the first time of the desolation of their streets, the dryness of their courtyards, the narrowness of their dreams as they faced the splendor and beauty of their drowned man. They let him go without an anchor so that he could come back if he wished and whenever he wished, and they all held their breath for the fraction of centuries the body took to fall into the abyss. They did not need to look to one another to realize that they were no longer all present, that they would never be. But they also knew that everything would be different from then on, that their houses would have wider doors, higher ceilings, and stronger floors so that Esteban's memory could go everywhere without bumping into beams and so that no one in the future would dare whisper the big boob finally died, too bad, the handsome fool has finally died, because they were going to paint their house fronts gay colors to make Esteban's memory eternal and they were going to break their backs digging for springs among the stones and planting flowers on the cliffs so that in future years at dawn the passengers on great liners would awaken, suffocated by the smell of gardens on the high seas, and the captain would have to come down from the bridge in his dress uniform, with his astrolabe, his pole star, and his row of war medals and, pointing to the promontory of roses on the horizon, he would say in fourteen languages, look there, where the wind is so peaceful now that it's gone to sleep beneath the beds, over there, where the sun's so bright that the sunflowers don't know which way to turn, yes, over there, that's Esteban's village.

Alice Munro
(1931–)

BOYS AND GIRLS
(1968)

My father was a fox farmer. That is, he raised silver foxes, in pens; and in the fall and early winter, when their fur was prime, he killed them and skinned them and sold their pelts to the Hudson's Bay Company or the Montreal Fur Traders. These companies supplied us with heroic calendars to hang, one on each side of the kitchen door. Against a background of cold blue sky and black pine forests and treacherous northern rivers, plumed adventurers planted the flags of England or of France; magnificent savages bent their backs to the portage.[1]

For several weeks before Christmas, my father worked after supper in the cellar of our house. The cellar was whitewashed, and lit by a hundred-watt bulb over the worktable. My brother Laird and I sat on the top step and watched. My father removed the pelt inside-out from the body of the fox, which looked surprisingly small, mean and rat-like, deprived of its arrogant weight of fur. The naked, slippery bodies were collected in a sack and buried at the dump. One time the hired man, Henry Bailey, had taken a swipe at me with this sack, saying, "Christmas present!" My mother thought that was not funny. In fact she disliked the whole pelting operation—that was what the killing, skinning, and preparation of the furs was called—and wished it did not have to take place in the house. There was the smell. After the pelt had been stretched inside-out on a long board my father scraped away delicately, removing the little clotted webs of blood vessels, the bubbles of fat; the smell of blood and animal fat, with the strong primitive odour of the fox itself, penetrated all parts of the house. I found it reassuringly seasonal, like the smell of oranges and pine needles.

Henry Bailey suffered from bronchial troubles. He would cough and cough until his narrow face turned scarlet, and his light blue, derisive eyes filled up with tears; then he took the lid off the stove, and, standing well back, shot out a great clot of phlegm—hsss—straight into the heart of the flames. We admired him for his performance and for his ability to make his stomach growl at will, and for his laugher, which was full of high whistlings and gurglings and involved the whole faulty machinery of his chest. It was sometimes hard to tell what he was laughing at, and always possible that it might be us.

After we had been sent to bed we could still smell fox and still hear Henry's laugh, but these things, reminders of the warm, safe, brightly

---

[1] Carrying boats or goods overland from one body of water to another or around an obstacle such as rapids.

lit downstairs world, seemed lost and diminished, floating on the stale cold air upstairs. We were afraid at night in the winter. We were not afraid of *outside* though this was the time of year when snowdrifts curled around our house like sleeping whales and the wind harassed us all night, coming up from the buried fields, the frozen swamp, with its old bugbear chorus of threats and misery. We were afraid of *inside,* the room where we slept. At this time the upstairs of our house was not finished. A brick chimney went up one wall. In the middle of the floor was a square hole, with a wooden railing around it; that was where the stairs came up. On the other side of the stairwell were the things that nobody had any use for any more—a soldiery roll of linoleum, standing on end, a wicker baby carriage, a fern basket, china jugs and basins with cracks in them, a picture of the Battle of Balaclava, very sad to look at. I had told Laird, as soon as he was old enough to understand such things, that bats and skeletons lived over there; whenever a man escaped from the county jail, twenty miles away, I imagined that he had somehow let himself in the window and was hiding behind the linoleum. But we had rules to keep us safe. When the light was on, we were safe as long as we did not step off the square of worn carpet which defined our bedroom-space; when the light was off no place was safe but the beds themselves. I had to turn out the light kneeling on the end of my bed, and stretching as far as I could to reach the cord.

5 In the dark we lay on our beds, our narrow life rafts, and fixed our eyes on the faint light coming up the stairwell, and sang songs. Laird sang "Jingle Bells," which he would sing any time, whether it was Christmas or not, and I sang "Danny Boy." I love the sound of my own voice, frail and supplicating, rising in the dark. We could make out the tall frosted shapes of the windows now, gloomy and white. When I came to the part, *When I am dead, as dead I well may be*—a fit of shivering caused not by the cold sheets but by pleasurable emotion almost silenced me. *You'll kneel and say, an Ave there above me*—What was an Ave? Every day I forgot to find out.

Laird went straight from singing to sleep. I could hear his long, satisfied, bubbly breaths. Now for the time that remained to me, the most perfectly private and perhaps the best time of the whole day, I arranged myself tightly under the covers and went on with one of the stories I was telling myself from night to night. These stories were about myself, when I had grown a little older; they took place in a world that was recognizably mine, yet one that presented opportunities for courage, boldness and self-sacrifice, as mine never did. I rescued people from a bombed building (it discouraged me that the real war had gone on so far away from Jubilee). I shot two rabid wolves who were menacing the schoolyard (the teachers cowered terrified at my back). I rode a fine horse spiritedly down the main street of Jubilee, acknowledging the towns-people's gratitude for some yet-to-be-worked-out piece of heroism (nobody ever rode a horse there, except King Billy in the Orangemen's Day parade). There was always riding and shooting in these stories, though I had only been on a horse twice—bareback because we did not own a saddle—and the second time I had slid right around and dropped under the horse's feet; it had stepped placidly over me. I really was learning to shoot, but I could not hit anything yet, not even tin cans on fence posts.

Alive, the foxes inhabited a world my father made for them. It was surrounded by a high guard fence, like a medieval town, with a gate that was padlocked at night. Along the streets of this town were ranged large, sturdy pens. Each of them had a real door that a man could go through, a wooden ramp along the wire, for the foxes to run up and down on, and a kennel—something like a clothes chest with airholes—where they slept and stayed in winter and had their young. There were feeding and watering dishes attached to the wire in such a way that they could be emptied and cleaned from the outside. The dishes were made of old tin cans, and the ramps and kennels of odds and ends of old lumber. Everything was tidy and ingenious; my father was tirelessly inventive and his favourite book in the world was Robinson Crusoe. He had fitted a tin drum on a wheelbarrow, for bringing water down to the pens. This was my job in summer, when the foxes had to have water twice a day. Between nine and ten o'clock in the morning, and again after supper, I filled the drum at the pump and trundled it down through the barnyard to the pens, where I parked it, and filled my watering can and went along the streets. Laird came too, with his little cream and green gardening can, filled too full and knocking against his legs and slopping water on his canvas shoes. I had the real watering can, my father's, though I could only carry it three-quarters full.

The foxes all had names, which were printed on a tin plate and hung beside their doors. They were not named when they were born, but when they survived the first year's pelting and were added to the breeding stock. Those my father had named were called names like Prince, Bob, Wally and Betty. Those I had named were called Star or Turk, or Maureen or Diana. Laird named one Maud after a hired girl we had when he was little, one Harold after a boy at school, and one Mexico, he did not say why.

Naming them did not make pets out of them, or anything like it. Nobody but my father ever went into the pens, and he had twice had blood-poisoning from bites. When I was bringing them their water they prowled up and down on the paths they had made inside their pens, barking seldom—they saved that for nighttime, when they might get up a chorus of community frenzy—but always watching me, their eyes burning, clear gold, in their pointed, malevolent faces. They were beautiful for their delicate legs and heavy, aristocratic tails and the bright fur sprinkled on dark down their backs—which gave them their name—but especially for their faces, drawn exquisitely sharp in pure hostility, and their golden eyes.

10 Besides carrying water I helped my father when he cut the long grass, and the lamb's quarter and flowering money-musk, that grew between the pens. He cut with the scythe and I raked into piles. Then he took a pitchfork and threw fresh-cut grass all over the top of the pens, to keep the foxes cooler and shade their coats, which were browned by too much sun. My father did not talk to me unless it was about the job we were doing. In this he was quite different from my mother, who, if she was feeling cheerful, would tell me all sorts of things—the name of a dog she had had when she was a little girl, the names of boys she had gone out with later on when she was grown up, and what certain dresses of hers had looked like—she could not imagine now what had become of them. Whatever thoughts and stories my father had were private, and I was shy of him and would never ask him questions. Nevertheless I worked willingly under his eyes, and with a feeling of pride. One time a feed salesman came down into the pens to talk to him and my father said, "Like to have you meet my new hired man." I turned away and raked furiously, red in the face with pleasure.

"Could of fooled me," said the salesman. "I thought it was only a girl."

After the grass was cut, it seemed suddenly much later in the year. I walked on stubble in the earlier evening, aware of the reddening skies, the entering silences, of fall. When I wheeled the tank out of the gate and put the padlock on, it was almost dark. One night at this time I saw my mother and father standing talking on the little rise of ground we called the gangway, in front of the barn. My father had just come from the meathouse; he had his stiff bloody apron on, and a pail of cut-up meat in his hand.

It was an odd thing to see my mother down at the barn. She did not often come out of the house unless it was to do something—hang out the wash or dig potatoes in the garden. She looked out of place, with her bare lumpy legs, not touched by the sun, her apron still on and damp across the stomach from the supper dishes. Her hair was tied up in a kerchief, wisps of it falling out. She would tie her hair up like this in the morning, saying she did not have time to do it properly, and it would stay tied up all day. It was true, too; she really did not have time. These days our back porch was piled with baskets of peaches and grapes and pears, bought in town, and onions and tomatoes and cucumbers grown at home, all waiting to be made into jelly and jam and preserves, pickles and chili sauce. In the kitchen there was a fire in the stove all day, jars clinked in boiling water, sometimes a cheesecloth bag was strung on a pole between two chairs, straining blue-black grape pulp for jelly. I was given jobs to do and I would sit at the table peeling peaches that had been soaked in the hot water, or cutting up onions, my eyes smarting and streaming. As soon as I was done I ran out of the house, trying to get out of earshot before my mother thought of what she wanted me to do next. I hated the hot dark kitchen in summer, the green blinds and the flypapers, the same old oilcloth table and wavy mirror and bumpy linoleum. My mother was too tired and preoccupied to talk to me, she had no heart to tell about the Normal School Graduation Dance; sweat trickled over her face and she was always counting under her breath, pointing at jars, dumping cups of sugar. It seemed to me that work in the house was endless, dreary and peculiarly depressing; work done out of doors, and in my father's service, was ritualistically important.

I wheeled the tank up to the barn, where it was kept, and I heard my mother saying, "Wait till Laird gets a little bigger, then you'll have a real help."

What my father said I did not hear. I was pleased by the way he stood listening, politely as he would to a salesman or a stranger, but with an air of wanting to get on with his real work. I felt my mother had no business down here and I wanted him to feel the same way. What did she mean about Laird? He was no help to anybody. Where was he now? Swinging himself sick on the swing, going around in circles, or trying to catch caterpillars. He never once stayed with me till I was finished.

"And then I can use her more in the house," I heard my mother say. She had a dead-quiet, regretful way of talking about me that always made me uneasy. "I just get my back turned and she runs off. It's not like I had a girl in the family at all."

I went and sat on a feedbag in the corner of the barn, not wanting to appear when this conversation was going on. My mother, I felt, was not to be trusted. She was kinder than my father and more easily fooled, but you could not depend on her, and the real reasons for the things she said and did were not to be known. She loved me, and she sat up late at night making a dress of the difficult style I wanted, for me to wear when school started, but she was also my enemy. She was always plotting. She was plotting now to get me to stay in the house more, although she knew I hated it (*because* she knew I hated it) and keep me from working for my father. It seemed to me she would do this simply out of perversity, and to try her power. It did not occur to me that she could be lonely, or jealous. No grown-up could be; they were too fortunate. I sat and kicked my heels monotonously against a feedbag, raising dust, and did not come out till she was gone.

At any rate, I did not expect my father to pay any attention to what she said. Who could imagine Laird doing my work—Laird remembering the padlock and cleaning out the watering-dishes with a leaf on the end of a stick, or even wheeling the tank without it tumbling over? It showed how little my mother knew about the way things really were.

I have forgotten to say what the foxes were fed. My father's bloody apron reminded me. They were fed horsemeat. At this time most farmers still kept horses, and when a horse got too old to work, or broke a leg or got down and would not get up, as they sometimes did, the owner would call my father, and he and Henry went out to the farm in the truck. Usually they shot and butchered the horse there, paying the farmer from five to twelve dollars. If they had already too much meat on hand, they would bring the horse back alive, and keep it for a few days or weeks in our stable, until the meat was needed. After the war the farmers were buying tractors and gradually getting rid of horses altogether, so it sometimes happened that we got a good healthy horse, that there was just no use for any more. If this happened in the winter we might keep the horse in our stable till spring, for we had plenty of hay and if there was a lot of snow—and the plow did not always get our road cleared—it was convenient to be able to go to town with a horse and cutter.

The winter I was eleven years old we had two horses in the stable. We did not know what names they had had before, so we called them Mack and Flora. Mack was an old black workhorse, sooty and indifferent. Flora was a sorrel mare, a driver. We took them both out in the cutter. Mack was slow and easy to handle. Flora was given to fits of violent alarm, veering at cars and even at other horses, but we loved her speed and high-stepping, her general air of gallantry and abandon. On Saturdays we went down to the stable and as soon as we opened the door on its cosy, animal-smelling darkness Flora threw up her head, rolled her eyes, whinnied despairingly and pulled herself through a crisis of nerves on the spot. It was not safe to go into her stall; she would kick.

This winter also I began to hear a great deal more on the theme my mother had sounded when she had been talking in front of the barn. I no longer felt safe. It seemed that in the minds of the people around me there was a steady undercurrent of thought, not to be deflected, on this one subject. The word *girl* had formerly seemed to me innocent and unburdened, like the word *child;* now it appeared that it was no such thing. A girl was not, as I had supposed, simply what I was; it was what I had to become. It was a definition, always touched with emphasis, with reproach and disappointment. Also it was a joke on me. Once Laird and I were fighting, and for the first time ever I had to use all my strength against him; even so, he caught and pinned my arm for a moment, really hurting me. Henry saw this, and laughed, saying, "Oh, that there Laird's gonna show you, one of these days!" Laird was getting a lot bigger. But I was getting bigger too.

My grandmother came to stay with us for a few weeks and I heard other things. "Girls don't slam doors like that." "Girls keep their knees together when they sit down." And worse still, when I asked some questions, "That's none of girls' business." I continued to slam the doors and sit as awkwardly as possible, thinking that by such measures I kept myself free.

When spring came, the horses were let out in the barnyard. Mack stood against the barn wall trying to scratch his neck and haunches, but Flora trotted up and down and reared at the fences, clattering her hooves against the rails. Snow drifts dwindled quickly, revealing the hard grey and brown earth, the familiar rise and fall of the ground, plain and bare after the fantastic landscape of winter. There was a great feeling of opening-out, of release. We just wore rubbers now, over our shoes; our feet felt ridiculously light. One Saturday we went out to the stable and found all the doors open, letting in the unaccustomed sunlight and fresh air. Henry was there, just idling around looking at his collection of calendars which were tacked up behind the stalls in a part of the stable my mother had probably never seen.

"Come to say goodbye to your old friend Mack?" Henry said. "Here, you give him a taste of oats." He poured some oats into Laird's cupped hands and Laird went to feed Mack. Mack's teeth were in bad shape. He ate very slowly, patiently shifting the oats around in his mouth, trying to find a stump of a molar to grind it on. "Poor old Mack," said Henry mournfully. "When a horse's teeth's gone, he's gone. That's about the way."

"Are you going to shoot him today?" I said. Mack and Flora had been in the stable so long I had almost forgotten they were going to be shot.

Henry didn't answer me. Instead he started to sing in a high, trembly, mocking-sorrowful voice, *Oh, there's no more work, for poor Uncle Ned, he's gone where the good darkies go.* Mack's thick, blackish tongue worked diligently at Laird's hand. I went out before the song was ended and sat down on the gangway.

I had never seen them shoot a horse, but I knew where it was done. Last summer Laird and I had come upon a horse's entrails before they were buried. We had thought it was a big black snake, coiled up in the sun. That was around in the field that ran up beside the barn. I thought that if we went inside the barn, and found a wide crack or a knothole to look through, we would be able to see them do it. It was not something I wanted to see; just the same, if a thing really happened, it was better to see it, and know.

My father came down from the house, carrying the gun.

"What are you doing here?" he said.

"Nothing."

"Go on up and play around the house."

He sent Laird out of the stable. I said to Laird, "Do you want to see them shoot Mack?" and without waiting for an answer led him around to the front door of the barn, opened it carefully, and went in. "Be quiet or they'll hear us," I said. We could hear Henry and my father talking in the stable, then the heavy, shuffling steps of Mack being backed out of his stall.

In the loft it was cold and dark. Thin, crisscrossed beams of sunlight fell through the cracks. The hay was low. It was a rolling country, hills and hollows, slipping under our feet. About four feet up was a beam going around the walls. We piled hay up in one corner and I boosted Laird up and hoisted myself. The beam was not very wide; we crept along it with our hands flat on the barn walls. There were plenty of knotholes, and I found one that gave me the view I wanted—a corner of the barnyard, the gate, part of the field. Laird did not have a knothole and began to complain.

I showed him a widened crack between two boards. "Be quiet and wait. If they hear you you'll get us in trouble."

35 My father came in sight carrying the gun. Henry was leading Mack by the halter. He dropped it and took out his cigarette papers and tobacco; he rolled cigarettes for my father and himself. While this was going on Mack nosed around in the old, dead grass along the fence. Then my father opened the gate and they took Mack through. Henry led Mack away from the path to a patch of ground and they talked together, not loud enough for us to hear. Mack again began searching for a mouthful of fresh grass, which was not to be found. My father walked away in a straight line, and stopped short at a distance which seemed to suit him. Henry was walking away from Mack too, but sideways, still negligently holding on to the halter. My father raised the gun and Mack looked up as if he had noticed something and my father shot him.

Mack did not collapse at once but swayed, lurched sideways and fell, first on his side; then he rolled over on his back and, amazingly, kicked his legs for a few seconds in the air. At this Henry laughed, as if Mack had done a trick for him. Laird, who had drawn a long, groaning breath of surprise when the shot was fired, said out loud, "He's not dead." And it seemed to me it might be true. But his legs stopped, he rolled on his side again, his muscles quivered and sank. The two men walked over and looked at him in a businesslike way; they bent down and examined his forehead where the bullet had gone in, and now I saw his blood on the brown grass.

"Now they just skin him and cut him up," I said. "Let's go." My legs were a little shaky and I jumped gratefully down into the hay. "Now you've seen how they shoot a horse," I said in a congratulatory way, as if I had seen it many times before. "Let's see if any barn cat's had kittens in the hay." Laird jumped. He seemed young and obedient again. Suddenly I remembered how, when he was little, I had brought him into the barn and told him to climb the ladder to the top beam. That was in the spring, too, when the hay was low. I had done it out of a need for excitement, a desire for something to happen so that I could tell about it. He was wearing a little bulky brown and white checked coat, made down from one of mine. He went all the way up, just as I told him, and sat down on the top beam with the hay far below him on one side, and the barn floor and some old machinery on the other. Then I ran screaming to my father, "Laird's up on the top beam!" My father came, my mother came, my father went up the ladder talking very quietly and brought Laird down under his arm, at which my mother leaned against the ladder and began to cry. They said to me, "Why weren't you watching him?" but nobody ever knew the truth. Laird did not know enough to tell. But whenever I saw the brown and white checked coat hanging in the closet, or at the bottom of the rag bag, which was where it ended up, I felt a weight in my stomach, the sadness of unexorcized guilt.

I looked at Laird who did not even remember this, and I did not like the look on his thin, winter-pale face. His expression was not frightened or upset, but remote, concentrating. "Listen," I said, in an unusually bright and friendly voice, "you aren't going to tell, are you?"

"No," he said absently.

40 "Promise."

"Promise," he said. I grabbed the hand behind his back to make sure he was not crossing his fingers. Even so, he might have a nightmare; it might come out that way. I decided I had better work hard to get all thoughts of what he had seen out of his mind—which, it seemed to me, could not hold very many things at a time. I got some money I had saved and that afternoon we went into Jubilee and saw a show, with Judy Canova, at which we both laughed a great deal. After that I thought it would be all right.

Two weeks later I knew they were going to shoot Flora. I knew from the night before, when I heard my mother ask if the hay was holding out all right, and my father said, "Well, after to-morrow there'll just be the cow, and we should be able to put her out to grass in another week." So I knew it was Flora's turn in the morning.

This time I didn't think of watching it. That was something to see just one time. I had not thought about it very often since, but sometimes when I was busy, working at school, or standing in front of the mirror combing my hair and wondering if I would be pretty when I grew up, the whole scene would flash into my mind: I would see the easy, practised way my father raised the gun, and hear Henry laughing when Mack kicked his legs in the air. I did not have any great feeling of horror and opposition, such as a city child might have had; I was too used to seeing the death of animals as a necessity by which we lived. Yet I felt a little ashamed, and there was a new wariness, a sense of holding-off, in my attitude to my father and his work.

It was a fine day, and we were going around the yard picking up tree branches that had been torn off in winter storms. This was something we had been told to do, and also we wanted to use them to make a teepee. We heard Flora whinny, and then my father's voice and Henry's shouting, and we ran down to the barnyard to see what was going on.

45 The stable door was open. Henry had just brought Flora out, and she had broken away from him. She was running free in the barnyard, from one end to the other. We climbed up on the fence. It was exciting to see her running, whinnying, going up on her hind legs, prancing and threatening like a horse in a Western movie, an unbroken ranch horse, though she was just an old driver, an old sorrel mare. My father and Henry ran after her and tried to grab the dangling halter. They tried to work her into a corner, and they had almost succeeded when she made a run between them, wild-eyed, and disappeared around the corner of the barn. We heard the rails clatter down as she got over the fence, and Henry yelled, "She's into the field now!"

That meant she was in the long L-shaped field that ran up by the house. If she got around the center, heading towards the lane, the gate was open; the truck had been driven into the field this morning. My father shouted to me, because I was on the other side of the fence, nearest the lane, "Go shut the gate!"

I could run very fast. I ran across the garden, past the tree where our swing was hung, and jumped across a ditch into the lane. There was the open gate. She had not got out, I could not see her up on the road; she must have run to the other end of the field. The gate was heavy. I lifted it out of the gravel and carried it across the roadway. I had it half-way across when she came in sight, galloping straight towards me. There was just time to get the chain on. Laird came scrambling through the ditch to help me.

Instead of shutting the gate, I opened it as wide as I could. I did not make any decision to do this, it was just what I did. Flora never slowed down; she galloped straight past me, and Laird jumped up and down, yelling, "Shut it, shut it!" even after it was too late. My father and Henry appeared in the field a moment too late to see what I had done. They only saw Flora heading for the township road. They would think I had not got there in time.

They did not waste any time asking about it. They went back to the barn and got the gun and the knives they used, and put these in the truck; then they turned the truck around and came bouncing up the field toward us. Laird called to them, "Let me go too, let me go too!" and Henry stopped the truck and they took him in. I shut the gate after they were all gone.

50 I supposed Laird would tell. I wondered what would happen to me. I had never disobeyed my father before, and I could not understand why I had done it. Flora would not really get away. They would catch up with her in the truck. Or if they did not catch her this morning somebody would see her and telephone us this afternoon or tomorrow. There was no wild country here for her to run to, only farms. What was more, my father had paid for her, we needed the meat to feed the foxes, we needed the foxes to make our living. All I had done was make more work for my father who worked hard enough already. And when my father found out about it he was not going to trust me any more; he would know that I was not entirely on his side. I was on Flora's side, and that made me no use to anybody, not even to her. Just the same, I did not regret it; when she came running at me and I held the gate open, that was the only thing I could do.

I went back to the house, and my mother said, "What's all the commotion?" I told her that Flora had kicked down the fence and got away. "Your poor father," she said, "now he'll have to go chasing over the countryside. Well, there isn't any use planning dinner before one." She put up the ironing board. I wanted to tell her, but thought better of it and went upstairs and sat on my bed.

Lately I had been trying to make my part of the room fancy, spreading the bed with old lace curtains, and fixing myself a dressing-table with some leftovers of cretonne for a skirt. I planned to put up some kind of barricade between my bed and Laird's, to keep my section separate from his. In the sunlight, the lace curtains were just dusty rags. We did not sing at night any more. One night when I was singing Laird said, "You sound silly," and I went right on but the next night I did not start. There was not so much need to anyway, we were no longer afraid. We knew it was just old furniture over there, old jumble and confusion. We did not keep to the rules. I still stayed awake after Laird was asleep and told myself stories, but even in these stories something different was happening, mysterious alterations took place. A story might start off in the old way, with a spectacular danger, a fire or wild animals, and for a while I might rescue people; then things would change around, and instead, somebody would be rescuing me. It might be a boy from our class at school, or even Mr. Campbell, our teacher, who tickled girls under the arms. And at this point the story concerned itself at great length with what I looked like—how long my hair was, and what kind of dress I had on; by the time I had these details worked out the real excitement of the story was lost.

It was later than one o'clock when the truck came back. The tarpaulin was over the back, which meant there was meat in it. My mother had to heat dinner up all over again. Henry and my father had changed from their bloody overalls into ordinary working overalls in the barn, and they washed their arms and necks and faces at the sink, and splashed water on their hair and combed it. Laird lifted his arm to show off a streak of blood. "We shot old Flora," he said, "and cut her up in fifty pieces."

"Well, I don't want to hear about it," my mother said. "And don't come to my table like that."

My family made him go and wash the blood off.

We sat down and my father said grace and Henry pasted his chewing-gum on the end of his fork, the way he always did; when he took it off he would have us admire the pattern. We began to pass the bowls of steaming, overcooked vegetables. Laird looked across the table at me and said proudly, distinctly, "Anyway it was her fault Flora got away."

"What?" my father said.

"She could of shut the gate and she didn't. She just open' it up and Flora run out."

"Is that right?" my father said.

Everybody at the table was looking at me. I nodded, swallowing food with great difficulty. To my shame, tears flooded my eyes.

My father made a curt sound of disgust. "What did you do that for?"

I did not answer. I put down my fork and waited to be sent from the table, still not looking up.

But this did not happen. For some time nobody said anything, then Laird said matter-of-factly, "She's crying."

"Never mind," my father said. He spoke with resignation, even good humour, the words which absolved and dismissed me for good. "She's only a girl," he said.

I didn't protest that, even in my heart. Maybe it was true.

V. S. Naipaul
(1932–)

B. WORDSWORTH
(1959)

Three beggars called punctually every day at the hospitable houses in Miguel Street. At about ten an Indian came in his dhoti and white jacket, and we poured a tin of rice into the sack he carried on his back. At twelve an old woman smoking a clay pipe came and she got a cent. At two a blind man led by a boy called for his penny.

Sometimes we had a rogue. One day a man called and said he was hungry. We gave him a meal. He asked for a cigarette and wouldn't go until we had lit it for him. That man never came again.

The strangest caller came one afternoon at about four o'clock. I had come back from school and was in my home-clothes. The man said to me, "Sonny, may I come inside your yard?"

He was a small man and he was tidily dressed. He wore a hat, a white shirt and black trousers.

I asked, "What you want?"

He said, "I want to watch your bees."

We had four small gru-gru palm trees and they were full of uninvited bees.

I ran up the steps and shouted, "Ma, it have a man outside here. He say he want to watch the bees."

My mother came out, looked at the man and asked in an unfriendly way, "What you want?"

The man said, "I want to watch your bees."

His English was so good, it didn't sound natural, and I could see my mother was worried.

She said to me, "Stay here and watch him while he watch the bees."

The man said, "Thank you, Madam. You have done a good deed today."

He spoke very slowly and very correctly as though every word was costing him money.

We watched the bees, this man and I, for about an hour, squatting near the palm trees.

The man said, "I like watching bees. Sonny, do you like watching bees?"

I said, "I ain't have the time."

He shook his head sadly. He said, "That's what I do, I just watch. I can watch ants for days. Have you ever watched ants? And scorpions, and centipedes, and *congorees*—have you watched those?"

I shook my head.

I said, "What you does do, mister?"

He got up and said, "I am a poet."

I said, "A good poet?"

He said, "The greatest in the world."

"What your name, mister?"

"B. Wordsworth."

"B for Bill?"

"Black. Black Wordsworth. White Wordsworth was my brother. We share one heart. I can watch a small flower like the morning glory and cry."

I said, "Why you does cry?"

"Why, boy? Why? You will know when you grow up. You're a poet, too, you know. And when you're a poet you can cry for everything."

I couldn't laugh.

He said, "You like your mother?"

"When she not beating me."

He pulled out a printed sheet from his hip-pocket and said, "On this paper is the greatest poem about mothers and I'm going to sell it to you at a bargain price. For four cents."

I went inside and I said, "Ma, you want to buy a poetry for four cents?"

My mother said, "Tell that blasted man to haul his tail away from my yard, you hear."

I said to B. Wordsworth, "My mother say she ain't have four cents."

B. Wordsworth said, "It is the poet's tragedy."

And he put the paper back in his pocket. He didn't seem to mind.

I said, "Is a funny way to go round selling poetry like that. Only calypsonians do that sort of thing. A lot of people does buy?"

He said, "No one has yet bought a single copy."

"But why you does keep on going round, then?"

He said, "In this way I watch many things, and I always hope to meet poets."

I said, "You really think I is a poet?"

"You're as good as me," he said.

And when B. Wordsworth left, I prayed I would see him again.

About a week later, coming back from school one afternoon, I met him at the corner of Miguel Street.

He said, "I have been waiting for you a long time."

I said, "You sell any poetry yet?"

He shook his head.

He said, "In my yard I have the best mango tree in Port of Spain. And now the mangoes are ripe and red and very sweet and juicy. I have waited here for you to tell you this and to invite you to come and eat some of my mangoes."

He lived in Alberto Street in a one-roomed hut placed right in the centre of the lot. The yard seemed all green. There was the big mango tree. There was a coconut tree and there was a plum tree. The place looked wild, as though it wasn't in the city at all. You couldn't see all the big concrete houses in the street.

He was right. The mangoes were sweet and juicy. I ate about six, and the yellow mango juice ran down my arms to my elbows and down my mouth to my chin and my shirt was stained.

My mother said when I got home, "Where you was? You think you is a man now and could go all over the place? Go cut a whip for me."

She beat me rather badly, and I ran out of the house swearing that I would never come back. I went to B. Wordsworth's house. I was so angry, my nose was bleeding.

B. Wordsworth said, "Stop crying, and we will go for a walk."

I stopped crying, but I was breathing short. We went for a walk. We walked down St. Clair Avenue to the Savannah and we walked to the race-course.

B. Wordsworth said, "Now, let us lie on the grass and look up at the sky, and I want you to think how far those stars are from us."

I did as he told me, and I saw what he meant. I felt like nothing, and at the same time I had never felt so big and great in all my life. I forgot all my anger and all my tears and all the blows.

When I said I was better, he began telling me the names of the stars, and I particularly remembered the constellation of Orion the Hunter, though I don't really know why. I can spot Orion even today, but I have forgotten the rest.

Then a light was flashed into our faces, and we saw a policeman. We got up from the grass.

The policeman said, "What you doing here?"

B. Wordsworth said, "I have been asking myself the same question for forty years."

We became friends, B. Wordsworth and I. He told me, "You must never tell anybody about me and about the mango tree and the coconut tree and the plum tree. You must keep that a secret. If you tell anybody, I will know, because I am a poet."

I gave him my word and I kept it.

I liked his little room. It had no more furniture than George's front room, but it looked cleaner and healthier. But it also looked lonely.

One day I asked him, "Mister Wordsworth, why you does keep all this bush in your yard? Ain't it does make the place damp?"

He said, "Listen, and I will tell you a story. Once upon a time a boy and girl met each other and they fell in love. They loved each other so much they got married. They were both poets. He loved words. She loved grass and flowers and trees. They lived happily in a single room, and then one day, the girl poet said to the boy poet, "We are going to have another poet in the family." But this poet was never born, because the girl died, and the young poet died with her, inside her. And the girl's husband was very sad, and he said he would never touch a thing in the girl's garden. And so the garden remained, and grew high and wild."

I looked at B. Wordsworth, and as he told me this lovely story, he seemed to grow older. I understood his story.

We went for long walks together. We went to the Botanical Gardens and the Rock Gardens. We climbed Chancellor Hill in the late afternoon and watched the darkness fall on Port of Spain, and watched the lights go on in the city and on the ships in the harbour.

He did everything as though he were doing it for the first time in his life. He did everything as though he were doing some church rite.

He would say to me, "Now, how about having some ice-cream?"

And when I said, yes, he would grow very serious and say, "Now, which café shall we patronize?" As though it were a very important thing. He would think for some time about it, and finally say, "I think I will go and negotiate the purchase with that shop."

The world became a most exciting place.

One day, when I was in his yard, he said to me, "I have a great secret which I am now going to tell you."

I said, "It really secret?"

"At the moment, yes."

I looked at him, and he looked at me. He said, "This is just between you and me, remember. I am writing a poem."

"Oh." I was disappointed.

He said, "But this is a different sort of poem. This is the greatest poem in the world."

I whistled.

He said, "I have been working on it for more than five years now. I will finish it in about twenty-two years from now, that is, if I keep on writing at the present rate."

"You does write a lot, then?"

He said, "Not any more. I just write one line a month. But I make sure it is a good line."

I asked, "What was last month's good line?"

He looked up at the sky, and said, *"The past is deep."*

I said, "It is a beautiful line."

B. Wordsworth said, "I hope to distil the experiences of a whole month into that single line of poetry. So, in twenty-two years, I shall have written a poem that will sing to all humanity."

I was filled with wonder.

Our walks continued. We walked along the sea-wall at Docksite one day, and I said, "Mr Wordsworth, if I drop this pin in the water, you think it will float?"

He said, "This is a strange world. Drop your pin, and let us see what will happen."

The pin sank.

I said, "How is the poem this month?"

But he never told me any other line. He merely said. "Oh, it comes, you know. It comes."

Or we would sit on the sea-wall and watch the liners come into the harbour.

But of the greatest poem in the world I heard no more.

I felt he was growing older.

"How you does live, Mr Wordsworth?" I asked him one day.

He said, "You mean how I get money?"

When I nodded, he laughed in a crooked way.

He said, "I sing calypsoes in the calypso season."

"And that last you the rest of the year?"

"It is enough."

"But you will be the richest man in the world when you write the greatest poem?"

He didn't reply.

One day when I went to see him in his little house, I found him lying on his little bed. He looked so old and so weak, that I found myself wanting to cry.

He said, "The poem is not going well."

He wasn't looking at me. He was looking through the window at the coconut tree, and he was speaking as though I wasn't there. He said, "When I was twenty I felt the power within myself." Then, almost in front of my eyes, I could see his face growing older and more tired. He said, "But that—that was a long time ago."

And then—I felt it so keenly, it was as though I had been slapped by my mother. I could see it clearly on his face. It was there for everyone to see. Death on the shrinking face.

He looked at me, and saw my tears and sat up.

He said, "Come." I went and sat on his knees.

He looked into my eyes, and he said, "Oh, you can see it, too. I always knew you had the poet's eye."

He didn't even look sad, and that made me burst out crying loudly.

He pulled me to his thin chest, and said, "Do you want me to tell you a funny story?" and he smiled encouragingly at me.

But I couldn't reply.

He said, "When I have finished this story, I want you to promise that you will go away and never come back to see me. Do you promise?"

I nodded.

He said, "Good. Well, listen. That story I told you about the boy poet and the girl poet, do you remember that? That wasn't true. It was something I just made up. All this talk about poetry and the greatest poem in the world, that wasn't true, either. Isn't that the funniest thing you have heard?"

But his voice broke.

I left the house, and ran home crying, like a poet, for everything I saw.

I walked along Alberto Street a year later, but I could find no sign of the poet's house. It hadn't vanished, just like that. It had been pulled down, and a big, two-storeyed building had taken its place. The mango tree and the plum tree and the coconut tree had all been cut down, and there was brick and concrete everywhere.

It was just as though B. Wordsworth had never existed.

Edgar Allan Poe
(1809–1849)

THE TELL-TALE HEART
(1850)

True!—nervous—very, very dreadfully nervous I had been and am; but why *will* you say that I am mad? The disease had sharpened my senses—not destroyed—not dulled them. Above all was the sense of hearing acute. I heard all things in the heaven and in the earth. I heard many things in hell. How, then, am I mad? Hearken! and observe how healthily—how calmly I can tell you the whole story.

It is impossible to say how first the idea entered my brain; but once conceived, it haunted me day and night. Object there was none. Passion there was none. I loved the old man. He had never wronged me. He had never given me insult. For his gold I had no desire. I think it was his eye! yes, it was this! One of his eyes resembled that of a vulture—a pale blue eye, with a film over it. Whenever it fell upon me, my blood ran cold; and so by degrees—very gradually—I made up my mind to take the life of the old man, and thus rid myself of the eye for ever.

Now this is the point. You fancy me mad. Madmen know nothing. But you should have seen *me*. You should have seen how wisely I proceeded—with what caution—with what foresight—with what dissimulation I went to work! I was never kinder to the old man than during the whole week before I killed him. And every night, about midnight, I turned the latch of his door and opened it—oh, so gently! And then, when I had made an opening sufficient for my head, I put in a dark lantern, all closed, closed, so that no light shone out, and then I thrust in my head. Oh, you would have laughed to see how cunningly I thrust it in! I moved it slowly—very, very slowly, so that I might not disturb the old man's sleep. It took me an hour to place my whole head within the opening so far that I could see him as he lay upon his bed. Ha!—would a madman have been so wise as this? And then, when my head was well in the room, I undid the lantern cautiously—oh, so cautiously—cautiously (for the hinges creaked)—I undid it just so much that a single thin ray fell upon the vulture eye. And this I did for seven long nights—every night just at midnight—but I found the eye always closed; and so it was impossible to do the work; for it was not the old man who vexed me, but his Evil Eye. And every morning, when the day broke, I went boldly into the chamber, and spoke courageously to him, calling him by name in a hearty tone, and inquiring how he had passed the night. So you see he would have been a very profound old man, indeed, to suspect that every night, just at twelve, I looked in upon him while he slept.

Upon the eighth night I was more than usually cautious in opening the door. A watch's minute hand moves more quickly than did mine. Never before that night had I *felt* the extent of my own powers—of my sagacity. I could scarcely contain my feelings of triumph. To think that there I was, opening the door, little by little, and he not even to dream of my secret deeds or thoughts. I fairly chuckled at the idea; and perhaps he heard me; for he moved on the bed suddenly, as if startled. Now you may think that I drew back—but no. His room was as black as pitch with the thick darkness (for the shutters were close fastened, through fear of robbers), and so I knew that he could not see the opening of the door, and I kept pushing it on steadily, steadily.

5 I had my head in, and was about to open the lantern, when my thumb slipped upon the tin fastening, and the old man sprang up in the bed, crying out—"Who's there?"

I kept quite still and said nothing. For a whole hour I did not move a muscle, and in the meantime I did not hear him lie down. He was still sitting up in the bed listening;—just as I have done, night after night, hearkening to the death watches[1] in the wall.

Presently I heard a slight groan, and I knew it was the groan of mortal terror. It was not a groan of pain or of grief—oh, no!—it was the low stifled sound that arises from the bottom of the soul when overcharged with awe. I knew the sound well. Many a night, just at midnight, when all the world slept, it has welled up from my own bosom, deepening, with its dreadful echo, the terrors that distracted me. I say I knew it well. I knew what the old man felt, and pitied him, although I chuckled at heart. I knew that he had been lying awake ever since the first slight noise, when he had turned in the bed. His fears had been ever since growing upon him. He had been trying to fancy them causeless, but could not. He had been saying to himself—"It is nothing but the wind in the chimney—it is only a mouse crossing the floor," or "it is merely a cricket which has made a single chirp." Yes, he had been trying to comfort himself with these suppositions; but he had found all in vain. *All in vain;* because Death, in approaching him, had stalked with his black shadow before him, and enveloped the victim. And it was the mournful influence of the unperceived shadow that caused him to feel—although he neither saw nor heard—to *feel* the presence of my head within the room.

---

[1] Beetles that infest timbers. Their clicking sound was thought to be an omen of death.

When I had waited a long time, very patiently, without hearing him lie down, I resolved to open a little—a very, very little crevice in the lantern. So I opened it—you cannot imagine how stealthily, stealthily—until, at length, a single dim ray, like the thread of the spider, shot from out the crevice and full upon the vulture eye.

It was open—wide, wide open—and I grew furious as I gazed upon it. I saw it with perfect distinctness—all a dull blue, with a hideous veil over it that chilled the very marrow in my bones; but I could see nothing else of the old man's face or person: for I had directed the ray as if by instinct, precisely upon the damned spot.

10 And now have I not told you that what you mistake for madness is but over-acuteness of the senses?—now, I say, there came to my ears a low, dull, quick sound, such as a watch makes when enveloped in cotton. I knew *that* sound well too. It was the beating of the old man's heart. It increased my fury, as the beating of a drum stimulates the soldier into courage.

But even yet I refrained and kept still. I scarcely breathed. I held the lantern motionless. I tried how steadily I could maintain the ray upon the eye. Meantime the hellish tattoo of the heart increased. It grew quicker and quicker, and louder and louder every instant. The old man's terror *must* have been extreme! It grew louder, I say, louder every moment!—do you mark me well? I have told you that I am nervous: so I am. And now at the dead hour of the night, amid the dreadful silence of that old house, so strange a noise as this excited me to uncontrollable terror. Yet, for some minutes longer I refrained and stood still. But the beating grew louder, louder! I thought the heart must burst. And now a new anxiety seized me—the sound would be heard by a neighbor! The old man's hour had come! With a loud yell, I threw open the lantern and leaped into the room. He shrieked once—once only. In an instant I dragged him to the floor, and pulled the heavy bed over him. I then smiled gaily, to find the deed so far done. But, for many minutes, the heart beat on with a muffled sound. This, however, did not vex me; it would not be heard through the wall. At length it ceased. The old man was dead. I removed the bed and examined the corpse. Yes, he was stone, stone dead. I placed my hand upon the heart and held it there many minutes. There was no pulsation. He was stone dead. His eye would trouble me no more.

If still you think me mad, you will think so no longer when I describe the wise precautions I took for the concealment of the body. The night waned, and I worked hastily, but in silence. First of all I dismembered the corpse. I cut off the head and the arms and the legs.

I then took up three planks from the flooring of the chamber, and deposited all between the scantlings. I then replaced the boards so cleverly, so cunningly, that no human eye—not even *his*—could have detected anything wrong. There was nothing to wash out—no stain of any kind—no blood-spot whatever. I had been too wary for that. A tub had caught all—ha! ha!

When I had made an end of these labors, it was four o'clock—still dark as midnight. As the bell sounded the hour, there came a knocking at the street door. I went down to open it with a light heart,—for what had I *now* to fear? There entered three men, who introduced themselves, with perfect suavity, as officers of the police. A shriek had been heard by a neighbor during the night; suspicion of foul play had been aroused; information had been lodged at the police office, and they (the officers) had been deputed to search the premises.

I smiled,—for *what* had I to fear? I bade the gentlemen welcome. The shriek, I said, was my own in a dream. The old man, I mentioned, was absent in the country. I took my visitors all over the house. I bade them search—search *well*. I led them, at length, to *his* chamber. I showed them his treasures, secure, undisturbed. In the enthusiasm of my confidence, I brought chairs into the room, and desired them *here* to rest from their fatigues, while I myself, in the wild audacity of my perfect triumph, placed my own seat upon the very spot beneath which reposed the corpse of the victim.

The officers were satisfied. My *manner* had convinced them. I was singularly at ease. They sat, and while I answered cheerily, they chatted familiar things. But, ere long, I felt myself getting pale and wished them gone. My head ached, and I fancied a ringing in my ears: but still they sat and still chatted. The ringing became more distinct:—it continued and became more distinct: I talked more freely to get rid of the feeling: but it continued and gained definitiveness—until, at length, I found that the noise was *not* within my ears.

No doubt I now grew *very* pale:—but I talked more fluently, and with a heightened voice. Yet the sound increased—and what could I do? It was *a low, dull, quick sound—much such a sound as a watch makes when enveloped in cotton.* I gasped for breath—and yet the officers heard it not. I talked more quickly—more vehemently; but the noise steadily increased. I arose and argued about trifles, in a high key and with violent gesticulations, but the noise steadily increased. Why *would* they not be gone? I paced the floor to and fro with heavy strides, as if excited to fury by the observation of the men—but the noise steadily increased. On God! what *could* I do? I foamed—I raved—I swore! I swung the chair upon which I had been sitting, and grated it upon the boards, but the noise arose over all and continually increased. It grew louder—louder—*louder!* And still the men chatted pleasantly, and smiled. Was it possible they heard not? Almighty God!—no, no! They heard!—they suspected!—they *knew!*—they were making a mockery of my horror!—this I thought, and this I think. But any thing was better than this agony! Any thing was more tolerable than this derision! I could bear those hypocritical smiles no longer! I felt that I must scream or die!—and now—again!—hark! louder! louder! louder! *louder*!—

"Villains!" I shrieked, "dissemble no more! I admit the deed!—tear up the planks!—here, here!—it is the beating of his hideous heart!"

Katherine Anne Porter
(1890–1980)

THE JILTING OF GRANNY WEATHERALL
(1930)

She flicked her wrist neatly out of Doctor Harry's pudgy careful fingers and pulled the sheet up to her chin. The brat ought to be in knee breeches. Doctoring around the country with spectacles on his nose! "Get along now, take your schoolbooks and go. There's nothing wrong with me."

Doctor Harry spread a warm paw like a cushion on her forehead where the forked green vein danced and made her eyelids twitch. "Now, now, be a good girl, and we'll have you up in no time."

"That's no way to speak to a woman nearly eighty years old just because she's down. I'd have you respect your elders, young man."

"Well, Missy, excuse me." Doctor Harry patted her cheek. "But I've got to warn you, haven't I? You're a marvel, but you must be careful or you're going to be good and sorry."

5 "Don't tell me what I'm going to be. I'm on my feet now, morally speaking. It's Cornelia. I had to go to bed to get rid of her."

Her bones felt loose, and floated around in her skin, and Doctor Harry floated like a balloon around the foot of the bed. He floated and pulled down his waistcoat and swung his glasses on a cord. "Well, stay where you are, it certainly can't hurt you."

"Get along and doctor your sick," said Granny Weatherall. "Leave a well woman alone. I'll call for you when I want you. . . . Where were you forty years ago when I pulled through milk-leg and double pneumonia? You weren't even born. Don't let Cornelia lead you on," she shouted, because Doctor Harry appeared to float up to the ceiling and out. "I pay my own bills, and I don't throw my money away on nonsense!"

She meant to wave good-by, but it was too much trouble. Her eyes closed of themselves, it was like a dark curtain drawn around the bed. The pillow rose and floated under her, pleasant as a hammock in a light wind. She listened to the leaves rustling outside the window. No, somebody was swishing newspapers: no, Cornelia and Doctor Harry were whispering together. She leaped broad awake, thinking they whispered in her ear.

"She was never like this, *never* like this!" "Well, what can we expect?" "Yes, eighty years old. . . ."

10 Well, and what if she was? She still had ears. It was like Cornelia to whisper around doors. She always kept things secret in such a public way. She was always being tactful and kind. Cornelia was dutiful; that was the trouble with her. Dutiful and good: "So good and dutiful," said Granny, "that I'd like to spank her." She saw herself spanking Cornelia and making a fine job of it.

"What'd you say, Mother?"

Granny felt her face tying up in hard knots.

"Can't a body think, I'd like to know?"

"I thought you might want something."

"I do. I want a lot of things. First off, go away and don't whisper."

She lay and drowsed, hoping in her sleep that the children would keep out and let her rest a minute. It had been a long day. Not that she was tired. It was always pleasant to snatch a minute now and then. There was always so much to be done, let me see: tomorrow.

Tomorrow was far away and there was nothing to trouble about. Things were finished somehow when the time came; thank God there was always a little margin over for peace: then a person could spread out the plan of life and tuck in the edges orderly. It was good to have everything clean and folded away, with the hair brushes and tonic bottles sitting straight on the white embroidered linen: the day started without fuss and the pantry shelves laid out with rows of jelly glasses and brown jugs and white stone-china jars with blue whirligigs and words painted on them: coffee, tea, sugar, ginger, cinnamon, allspice: and the bronze clock with the lion on top nicely dusted off. The dust that lion could collect in twenty-four hours! The box in the attic with all those letters tied up, well, she'd have to go through that tomorrow. All those letters—George's letters and John's letters and her letters to them both—lying around for the children to find afterwards made her uneasy. Yes, that would be tomorrow's business. No use to let them know how silly she had been once.

While she was rummaging around she found death in her mind and it felt clammy and unfamiliar. She had spent so much time preparing for death there was no need for bringing it up again. Let it take care of itself now. When she was sixty she had felt very old, finished, and went around making farewell trips to see her children and grandchildren, with a secret in her mind: This is the very last of your mother, children! Then she made her will and came down with a long fever. That was all just a notion like a lot of other things, but it was lucky too, for she had once and for all got over the idea of dying for a long time. Now she couldn't be worried. She hoped she had better sense now. Her father had lived to be one hundred and two years old and had drunk a noggin of strong hot toddy on his last birthday. He told the reporters it was his daily habit, and he owed his long life to that. He had made quite a scandal and was very pleased about it. She believed she'd just plague Cornelia a little.

"Cornelia! Cornelia!" No footsteps, but a sudden hand on her cheek. "Bless you, where have you been?"

"Here, Mother."

"Well, Cornelia, I want a noggin of hot toddy."

"Are you cold, darling?"

"I'm chilly, Cornelia. Lying in bed stops the circulation. I must have told you that a thousand times."

Well, she could just hear Cornelia telling her husband that Mother was getting a little childish and they'd have to humor her. The thing that most annoyed her was that Cornelia thought she was deaf, dumb, and blind. Little hasty glances and tiny gestures tossed around her and over her head saying, "Don't cross her, let her have her way, she's eighty years old," and she sitting there as if she lived in a thin glass cage. Sometimes Granny almost made up her mind to pack up and move back to her own house where nobody could remind her every minute that she was old. Wait, wait, Cornelia, till your own children whisper behind your back!

In her day she had kept a better house and had got more work done. She wasn't too old yet for Lydia to be driving eighty miles for advice when one of the children jumped the track, and Jimmy still dropped in and talked things over: "Now, Mammy, you've a good business head, I want to know what you think of this? . . ." Old. Cornelia couldn't change the furniture around without asking. Little things, little things! They had been so sweet when they were little. Granny wished the old days were back again with the children young and everything to be done over. It had been a hard pull, but not too much for her. When she thought of all the food she had cooked, and all the clothes she had cut and sewed, and all the gardens she had made—well, the children showed it. There they were, made out of her, and they couldn't get away from that. Sometimes she wanted to see John again and point to them and say, Well, I didn't do so badly, did I? But that would have to wait. That was for tomorrow. She used to think of him as a man, but now all the children were older than their father, and he would be a child beside her if she saw him now. It seemed strange and there was something wrong in the idea. Why, he couldn't possibly recognize her. She had fenced in a hundred acres once, digging the post holes herself and clamping the wires with just a negro boy to help. That changed a woman. John would be looking for a young woman with the peaked Spanish comb in her hair and the painted fan. Digging post holes changed a woman. Riding country roads in the winter when women had their babies was another thing: sitting up nights with sick horses and sick negroes and sick children and hardly ever losing one. John, I hardly ever lost one of them! John would see that in a minute, that would be something he could understand, she wouldn't have to explain anything!

It made her feel like rolling up her sleeves and putting the whole place to rights again. No matter if Cornelia was determined to be everywhere at once, there were a great many things left undone on this place. She would start tomorrow and do them. It was good to be strong enough for everything, even if all you made melted and changed and slipped under your hands, so that by the time you finished you almost forgot what you were working for. What was it I set out to do? she asked herself intently, but she could not remember. A fog rose over the valley, she saw it marching across the creek swallowing the trees and moving up the hill like an army of ghosts. Soon it would be at the near edge of the orchard, and then it was time to go in and light the lamps. Come in, children, don't stay out in the night air.

Lighting the lamps had been beautiful. The children huddled up to her and breathed like little calves waiting at the bars in the twilight. Their eyes followed the match and watched the flame rise and settle in a blue curve, then they moved away from her. The lamp was lit, they didn't have to be scared and hang on to mother any more. Never, never, never more. God, for all my life I thank Thee. Without Thee, my God, I could never have done it. Hail, Mary, full of grace.

I want you to pick all the fruit this year and see that nothing is wasted. There's always someone who can use it. Don't let good things rot for want of using. You waste life when you waste good food. Don't let things get lost. It's bitter to lose things. Now, don't let me get to thinking, not when I am tired and taking a little nap before supper. . . .

The pillow rose about her shoulders and pressed against her heart and the memory was being squeezed out of it: oh, push down the pillow, somebody: it would smother her if she tried to hold it. Such a fresh breeze blowing and such a green day with no threats in it. But he had not come, just the same. What does a woman do when she has put on the white veil and set out the white cake for a man and he doesn't come? She tried to remember. No, I swear he never harmed me but in that. He never harmed me but in that . . . and what if he did? There was the day, the day, but a whirl of dark smoke rose and covered it, crept up and over into the bright field where everything was planted so carefully in orderly rows. That was hell, she knew hell when she saw it. For sixty years she had prayed against remembering him and against losing her soul in the deep pit of hell, and now the two things were mingled in one and the thought of him was a smoky cloud from hell that moved and crept in her head when she had just got rid of Doctor Harry and was trying to rest a minute. Wounded vanity, Ellen, said a sharp voice in the top of her mind. Don't let your wounded vanity get the upper hand of you. Plenty of girls get jilted. You were jilted, weren't you? Then stand up to it. Her eyelids wavered and let in streamers of blue-gray light like tissue paper over her eyes. She must get up and pull the shades down or she'd never sleep. She was in bed again and the shades were not down. How could that happen? Better turn over, hide from the light, sleeping in the light gave you nightmares. "Mother, how do you feel now?" and a stinging wetness on her forehead. But I don't like having my face washed in cold water!

Hapsy? George? Lydia? Jimmy? No, Cornelia, and her features were swollen and full of little puddles. "They're coming, darling, they'll all be here soon." Go wash your face, child, you look funny.

Instead of obeying, Cornelia knelt down and put her head on the pillow. She seemed to be talking but there was no sound. "Well, are you tongue-tied? Whose birthday is it? Are you going to give a party?"

Cornelia's mouth moved urgently in strange shapes. "Don't do that, you bother me, daughter."

"O, no, Mother. Oh, no. . . ."

Nonsense. It was strange about children. They disputed your every word. "No what, Cornelia?"

"Here's Doctor Harry."

"I won't see that boy again. He just left five minutes ago."

"That was this morning, Mother. It's night now. Here's the nurse."

"This is Doctor Harry, Mrs. Weatherall. I never saw you look so young and happy!"

"Ah, I'll never be young again—but I'd be happy if they'd let me lie in peace and get rested."

40 She thought she spoke up loudly, but no one answered. A warm weight on her forehead, a warm bracelet on her wrist, and a breeze went on whispering, trying to tell her something. A shuffle of leaves in the everlasting hand of God. He blew on them and they danced and rattled. "Mother, don't mind, we're going to give you a little hypodermic." "Look here, daughter, how do ants get in this bed? I saw sugar ants yesterday." Did you send for Hapsy too?

It was Hapsy she really wanted. She had to go a long way back through a great many rooms to find Hapsy standing with a baby on her arm. She seemed to herself to be Hapsy also, and the baby on Hapsy's arm was Hapsy and himself and herself, all at once, and there was no surprise in the meeting. Then Hapsy melted from within and turned flimsy as gray gauze and the baby was a gauzy shadow, and Hapsy came up close and said, "I thought you'd never come," and looked at her very searchingly and said, "You haven't changed a bit!" They leaned forward to kiss, when Cornelia began whispering from a long way off, "Oh, is there anything you want to tell me? Is there anything I can do for you?"

Yes, she had changed her mind after sixty years and she would like to see George. I want you to find George. Find him and be sure to tell him I forgot him. I want him to know I had my husband just the same and my children and my house like any other woman. A good house too and a good husband that I loved and fine children out of him. Better than I hoped for even. Tell him I was given back everything he took away and more. Oh, no, oh, God, no, there was something else besides the house and the man and the children. Oh, surely they were not all? What was it? Something not given back. . . . Her breath crowded down under her ribs and grew into a monstrous frightening shape with cutting edges; it bored up into her head, and the agony was unbelievable: Yes, John, get the Doctor now, no more talk, my time has come.

When this one was born it should be the last. The last. It should have been born first, for it was the one she had truly wanted. Everything came in good time. Nothing left out, left over. She was strong, in three days she would be as well as ever. Better. A woman needed milk in her to have her full health.

"Mother, do you hear me?"

45 "I've been telling you—"

"Mother, Father Connolly's here."

"I went to Holy Communion last week. Tell him I'm not so sinful as all that."

"Father just wants to speak to you."

He could speak as much as he pleased. It was like him to drop in and inquire about her soul as if it were a teething baby, and then stay on for a cup of tea and a round of cards and gossip. He always had a funny story of some sort, usually about an Irishman who made his little mistakes and confessed them, and the point lay in some absurd thing he would blurt out in the confessional showing his struggles between native piety and original sin. Granny felt easy about her soul. Cornelia, where are your manners? Give Father Connolly a chair. She had her secret comfortable understanding with a few favorite saints who cleared a straight road to God for her. All as surely signed and sealed as the papers for the new Forty Acres. Forever . . . heirs and assigns forever. Since the day the wedding cake was not cut, but thrown out and wasted. The whole bottom dropped out of the world, and there she was blind and sweating with nothing under her feet and the walls falling away. His hand had caught her under the breast, she had not fallen, there was the freshly polished floor with the green rug on it, just as before. He had cursed like a sailor's parrot and said, "I'll kill him for you." Don't lay a hand on him, for my sake leave something to God. "Now, Ellen, you must believe what I tell you. . . ."

So there was nothing, nothing to worry about any more, except sometimes in the night one of the children screamed in a nightmare, and they both hustled out shaking and hunting for the matches and calling, "There, wait a minute, here we are!" John, get the doctor now, Hapsy's time has come. But there was Hapsy standing by the bed in a white cap. "Cornelia, tell Hapsy to take off her cap. I can't see her plain."

Her eyes opened very wide and the room stood out like a picture she had seen somewhere. Dark colors with the shadows rising towards the ceiling in long angles. The tall black dresser gleamed with nothing on it but John's picture, enlarged from a little one, with John's eyes very black when they should have been blue. You never saw him, so how do you know how he looked? But the man insisted the copy was perfect, it was very rich and handsome. For a picture, yes, but it's not my husband. The table by the bed had a linen cover and a candle and a crucifix. The light was blue from Cornelia's silk lampshades. No sort of light at all, just frippery. You had to live forty years with kerosene lamps to appreciate honest electricity. She felt very strong and she saw Doctor Harry with a rosy nimbus around him.

"You look like a saint, Doctor Harry, and I vow that's as near as you'll ever come to it."

"She's saying something."

"I heard you, Cornelia. What's all this carrying-on?"

"Father Connolly's saying—"

Cornelia's voice staggered and bumped like a cart in a bad road. It rounded corners and turned back again and arrived nowhere. Granny stepped up in the cart very lightly and reached for the reins, but a man sat beside her and she knew him by his hands, driving the cart. She did not look in his face, for she knew without seeing, but looked instead down the road where the trees leaned over and bowed to each other and a thousand birds were singing a Mass. She felt like singing too, but she put her hand in the bosom of her dress and pulled out a rosary, and Father Connolly murmured Latin in a very solemn voice and tickled her feet. My God, will you stop that nonsense? I'm a married woman. What if he did run away and leave me to face the priest by myself? I found another a whole world better. I wouldn't have exchanged my husband for anybody except St. Michael himself, and you may tell him that for me with a thank you in the bargain.

Light flashed on her closed eyelids, and a deep roaring shook her. Cornelia, is that lightning? I hear thunder. There's going to be a storm. Close all the windows. Call the children in. . . . "Mother, here we are, all of us." "Is that you, Hapsy?" "Oh, no, I'm Lydia. We drove as fast as we could." Their faces drifted above her, drifted away. The rosary fell out of her hands and Lydia put it back. Jimmy tried to help, their hands fumbled together, and Granny closed two fingers around Jimmy's thumb. Beads wouldn't do, it must be something alive. She was so amazed her thoughts ran round and round. So, my dear Lord, this is my death and I wasn't even thinking about it. My children have come to see me die. But I can't, it's not time. Oh, I always hated surprises. I wanted to give Cornelia the amethyst set—Cornelia, you're to have the amethyst set, but Hapsy's to wear it when she wants, and, Doctor Harry, do shut up. Nobody sent for you. Oh, my dear Lord, do wait a minute. I meant to do something about the Forty Acres, Jimmy doesn't need it and Lydia will later on, with that worthless husband of hers. I meant to finish the altar cloth and send six bottles of wine to Sister Borgia for her dyspepsia. I want to send six bottles of wine to Sister Borgia, Father Connolly, now don't let me forget.

Cornelia's voice made short turns and tilted over and crashed. "Oh, Mother, oh, Mother, oh, Mother. . . ."

"I'm not going, Cornelia. I'm taken by surprise. I can't go."

You'll see Hapsy again. What about her? "I thought you'd never come." Granny made a long journey outward, looking for Hapsy. What if I don't find her? What then? Her heart sank down and down, there was no bottom to death, she couldn't come to the end of it. The blue light from Cornelia's lampshade drew into a tiny point in the center of her brain, it flickered and winked like an eye, quietly it fluttered and dwindled. Granny lay curled down within herself, amazed and watchful, staring at the point of light that was herself; her body was now only a deeper mass of shadow in an endless darkness and this darkness would curl around the light and swallow it up. God, give a sign!

For the second time there was no sign. Again no bridegroom and the priest in the house. She could not remember any other sorrow because this grief wiped them all away. Oh, no, there's nothing more cruel than this—I'll never forgive it. She stretched herself with a deep breath and blew out the light.

John Steinbeck
(1902–1968)

THE CHRYSANTHEMUMS
(1937)

The high grey-flannel fog of winter closed off the Salinas Valley from the sky and from all the rest of the world. On every side it sat like a lid on the mountains and made of the great valley a closed pot. On the broad, level land floor the gang plows bit deep and left the black earth shining like metal where the shares had cut. On the foothill ranches across the Salinas River, the yellow stubble fields seemed to be bathed in pale cold sunshine, but there was no sunshine in the valley now in December. The thick willow scrub along the river flamed with sharp and positive yellow leaves.

It was a game of quiet and of waiting. The air was cold and tender. A light wind blew up from the southwest so that the farmers were mildly hopeful of a good rain before long; but fog and rain do not go together.

Across the river, on Henry Allen's foothill ranch there was little work to be done, for the hay was cut and stored and the orchards were plowed up to receive the rain deeply when it should come. The cattle on the higher slopes were becoming shaggy and rough-coated.

Elisa Allen, working in her flower garden, looked down across the yard and saw Henry, her husband, talking to two men in business suits. The three of them stood by the tractor shed, each man with one foot on the side of the little Fordson. They smoked cigarettes and studied the machine as they talked.

5 Elisa watched them for a moment and then went back to her work. She was thirty-five. Her face was lean and strong and her eyes were as clear as water. Her figure looked blocked and heavy in her gardening costume, a man's black hat pulled low down over her eyes, clod-hopper shoes, a figured print dress almost completely covered by a big corduroy apron with four big pockets to hold the snips, the trowel and scratcher, the seeds and the knife she worked with. She wore heavy leather gloves to protect her hands while she worked.

She was cutting down the old year's chrysanthemum stalks with a pair of short and powerful scissors. She looked down toward the men by the tractor shed now and then. Her face was eager and mature and handsome; even her work with the scissors was over-eager, over-powerful. The chrysanthemum stems seemed too small and easy for her energy.

She brushed a cloud of hair out of her eyes with the back of her glove, and left a smudge of earth on her cheek in doing it. Behind her stood the neat white farm house with red geraniums close-banked around it as high as the windows. It was a hard-swept looking little house with hard-polished windows, and a clean mud-mat on the front steps.

Elisa cast another glance toward the tractor shed. The strangers were getting into their Ford coupe. She took off a glove and put her strong fingers down into the forest of new green chrysanthemum sprouts that were growing around the old roots. She spread the leaves and looked down among the close-growing stems. No aphids were there, no sowbugs or snails or cutworms. Her terrier fingers destroyed such pests before they could get started.

Elisa started at the sound of her husband's voice. He had come near quietly, and he leaned over the wire fence that protected her flower garden from cattle and dogs and chickens.

"At it again," he said. "You've got a strong new crop coming."

Elisa straightened her back and pulled on the gardening glove again. "Yes. They'll be strong this coming year." In her tone and on her face there was a little smugness.

"You've got a gift with things," Henry observed. "Some of those yellow chrysanthemums you had this year were ten inches across. I wish you'd work out in the orchard and raise some apples that big."

Her eyes sharpened. "Maybe I could do it, too. I've a gift with things, all right. My mother had it. She could stick anything in the ground and make it grow. She said it was having planters' hands that knew how to do it."

"Well, it sure works with flowers," he said.

"Henry, who were those men you were talking to?"

"Why, sure, that's what I came to tell you. They were from the Western Meat Company. I sold those thirty head of three-year-old steers. Got nearly my own price, too."

"Good," she said. "Good for you."

"And I thought," he continued, "I thought how it's Saturday afternoon, and we might go into Salinas for dinner at a restaurant, and then to a picture show—to celebrate, you see."

"Good," she repeated. "Oh, yes. That will be good."

Henry put on his joking tone. "There's fights tonight. How'd you like to go to the fights?"

"Oh, no," she said breathlessly. "No, I wouldn't like fights."

"Just fooling, Elisa. We'll go to a movie. Let's see. It's two now. I'm going to take Scotty and bring down those steers from the hill. It'll take us maybe two hours. We'll go in town about five and have dinner at the Cominos Hotel. Like that?"

"Of course I'll like it. It's good to eat away from home."

"All right, then. I'll go get up a couple of horses."

She said, "I'll have plenty of time to transplant some of these sets, I guess."

She heard her husband calling Scotty down by the barn. And a little later she saw the two men ride up the pale yellow hillside in search of the steers.

There was a little square sandy bed kept for rooting the chrysanthemums. With her trowel she turned the soil over and over, and smoothed it and patted it firm. Then she dug ten parallel trenches to receive the sets.

Back at the chrysanthemum bed she pulled out the little crisp shoots, trimmed off the leaves of each one with her scissors and laid it on a small orderly pile.

A squeak of wheels and plod of hoofs came from the road. Elisa looked up. The country road ran along the dense bank of willows and cottonwoods that bordered the river, and up this road came a curious vehicle, curiously drawn. It was an old spring-wagon, with a round canvas top on it like the cover of a prairie schooner. It was drawn by an old bay horse and a little grey-and-white burro. A big stubble-bearded man sat between the cover flaps and drove the crawling team. Underneath the wagon, between the hind wheels, a lean and rangy mongrel dog walked sedately. Words were painted on the canvas, in clumsy, crooked letters. "Pots, pans, knives, sisors, lawn mores, Fixed." Two rows of articles, and the triumphantly definitive "Fixed" below. The black paint had run down in little sharp points beneath each letter.

Elisa, squatting on the ground, watched to see the crazy, loose-jointed wagon pass by. But it didn't pass. It turned into the farm road in front of her house, crooked old wheels skirling and squeaking. The rangy dog darted from between the wheels and ran ahead. Instantly the two ranch shepherds flew out at him. Then all three stopped, and with stiff and quivering tails, with taut straight legs, with ambassadorial dignity, they slowly circled, sniffing daintily. The caravan pulled up to Elisa's wire fence and stopped. Now the newcomer dog, feeling outnumbered, lowered his tail and retired under the wagon with raised hackles and bared teeth.

The man on the wagon seat called out, "That's a bad dog in a fight when he gets started."

Elisa laughed. "I see he is. How soon does he generally get started?"

The man caught up her laughter and echoed it heartily. "Sometimes not for weeks and weeks," he said. He climbed stiffly down, over the wheel. The horse and the donkey drooped like unwatered flowers.

Elisa saw that he was a very big man. Although his hair and beard were greying, he did not look old. His worn black suit was wrinkled and spotted with grease. The laughter had disappeared from his face and eyes the moment his laughing voice ceased. His eyes were dark, and they were full of the brooding that gets in the eyes of teamsters and of sailors. The calloused hands he rested on the wire fence were cracked, and every crack was a black line. He took off his battered hat.

"I'm off my general road, ma'am," he said. "Does this dirt road cut over across the river to the Los Angeles highway?"

Elisa stood up and shoved the thick scissors in her apron pocket. "Well, yes, it does, but it winds around and then fords the river. I don't think your team could pull through the sand."

He replied with some asperity. "It might surprise you what them beasts can pull through."

"When they get started?" she asked.

He smiled for a second. "Yes. When they get started."

"Well," said Elisa, "I think you'll save time if you go back to the Salinas road and pick up the highway there."

He drew a big finger down the chicken wire and made it sing. "I ain't in any hurry, ma'am. I go from Seattle to San Diego and back every year. Takes all my time. About six months each way. I aim to follow nice weather."

Elisa took off her gloves and stuffed them in the apron pocket with the scissors. She touched the under edge of her man's hat, searching for fugitive hairs. "That sounds like a nice kind of a way to live," she said.

He leaned confidentially over the fence. "Maybe you noticed the writing on my wagon. I mend pots and sharpen knives and scissors. You got any of them things to do?"

"Oh, no," she said quickly. "Nothing like that." Her eyes hardened with resistance.

"Scissors is the worst thing," he explained. "Most people just ruin scissors trying to sharpen 'em, but I know how. I got a special tool. It's a little bobbit kind of thing, and patented. But it sure does the trick."

"No. My scissors are all sharp."

"All right, then. Take a pot," he continued earnestly, "a bent pot, or a pot with a hole. I can make it like new so you don't have to buy no new ones. That's a saving for you."

"No," she said shortly. "I tell you I have nothing like that for you to do."

His face fell to an exaggerated sadness. His voice took on a whining undertone. "I ain't had a thing to do today. Maybe I won't have no supper tonight. You see I'm off my regular road. I know folks on the highway clear from Seattle to San Diego. They save their things for me to sharpen up because they know I do it so good and save them money."

"I'm sorry," Elisa said irritably. "I haven't anything for you to do."

His eyes left her face and fell to searching the ground. They roamed about until they came to the chrysanthemum bed where she had been working. "What's them plants, ma'am?"

The irritation and resistance melted from Elisa's face. "Oh, those are chrysanthemums, giant whites and yellows. I raise them every year, bigger than anybody around here."

"Kind of a long-stemmed flower? Looks like a quick puff of colored smoke?" he asked.

"That's it. What a nice way to describe them."

"They smell kind of nasty till you get used to them," he said.

"It's a good bitter smell," she retorted, "not nasty at all."

He changed his tone quickly. "I like the smell myself."

"I had ten-inch blooms this year," she said.

The man leaned farther over the fence. "Look. I know a lady down the road a piece, has got the nicest garden you ever seen. Got nearly every kind of flower but no chrysanthemums. Last time I was mending a copper-bottom washtub for her (that's a hard job but I do it good), she said to me, 'If you ever run acrost some nice chrysanthemums I wish you'd try to get me a few seeds.' That's what she told me."

Elisa's eyes grew alert and eager. "She couldn't have known much about chrysanthemums. You *can* raise them from seed, but it's much easier to root the little sprouts you see there."

"Oh," he said. "I s'pose I can't take none to her, then."

"Why yes you can," Elisa cried. "I can put some in damp sand, and you can carry them right along with you. They'll take root in the pot if you keep them damp. And then she can transplant them."

"She'd sure like to have some, ma'am. You say they're nice ones?"

"Beautiful," she said. "Oh, beautiful." Her eyes shone. She tore off the battered hat and shook out her dark pretty hair. "I'll put them in a flower pot, and you can take them right with you. Come into the yard."

While the man came through the picket gate Elisa ran excitedly along the geranium-bordered path to the back of the house. And she returned carrying a big red flower pot. The gloves were forgotten now. She kneeled on the ground by the starting bed and dug up the sandy soil with her fingers and scooped it into the bright new flower pot. Then she picked up the little pile of shoots she had prepared. With her strong fingers she pressed them into the sand and tamped around them with her knuckles. The man stood over her. "I'll tell you what to do," she said. "You remember so you can tell the lady."

"Yes, I'll try to remember."

"Well, look. These will take root in about a month. Then she must set them out, about a foot apart in good rich earth like this, see?" She lifted a handful of dark soil for him to look at. "They'll grow fast and tall. Now remember this: In July tell her to cut them down, about eight inches from the ground."

"Before they bloom?" he asked.

"Yes, before they bloom." Her face was tight with eagerness. "They'll grow right up again. About the last of September the buds will start."

She stopped and seemed perplexed. "It's the budding that takes the most care," she said hesitantly. "I don't know how to tell you." She looked deep into his eyes, searchingly. Her mouth opened a little, and she seemed to be listening. "I'll try to tell you," she said. "Did you ever hear of planting hands?"

"Can't say I have, ma'am."

"Well, I can only tell you what it feels like. It's when you're picking off the buds you don't want. Everything goes right down into your fingertips. You watch your fingers work. They do it themselves. You can feel how it is. They pick and pick the buds. They never make a mistake. They're with the plant. Do you see? Your fingers and the plant. You can feel that, right up your arm. They know. They never make a mistake. You can feel it. When you're like that you can't do anything wrong. Do you see that? Can you understand that?"

She was kneeling on the ground looking up at him. Her breast swelled passionately.

The man's eyes narrowed. He looked away self-consciously. "Maybe I know," he said. "Sometimes in the night in the wagon there—"

Elisa's voice grew husky. She broke in on him, "I've never lived as you do, but I know what you mean. When the night is dark—why, the stars are sharp-pointed, and there's quiet. Why, you rise up and up! Every pointed star gets driven into your body. It's like that. Hot and sharp and—lovely."

Kneeling there, her hand went out toward his legs in the greasy black trousers. Her hesitant fingers almost touched the cloth. Then her hand dropped to the ground. She crouched low like a fawning dog.

He said, "It's nice, just like you say. Only when you don't have no dinner, it ain't."

She stood up then, very straight, and her face was ashamed. She held the flower pot out to him and placed it gently in his arms. "Here. Put it in your wagon, on the seat, where you can watch it. Maybe I can find something for you to do."

At the back of the house she dug in the can pile and found two old and battered aluminum saucepans. She carried them back and gave them to him. "Here, maybe you can fix these."

His manner changed. He became professional. "Good as new I can fix them." At the back of his wagon he set a little anvil, and out of an oily tool box dug a small machine hammer. Elisa came through the gate to watch him while he pounded out the dents in the kettles. His mouth grew sure and knowing. At a difficult part of the work he sucked his under-lip.

"You sleep right in the wagon?" Elisa asked.

"Right in the wagon, ma'am. Rain or shine I'm dry as a cow in there."

"It must be nice," she said. "It must be very nice. I wish women could do such things."

"It ain't the right kind of a life for a woman."

Her upper lip raised a little, showing her teeth. "How do you know? How can you tell?" she said.

"I don't know, ma'am," he protested. "Of course I don't know. Now here's your kettles, done. You don't have to buy no new ones."

"How much?"

"Oh, fifty cents'll do. I keep my prices down and my work good. That's why I have all them satisfied customers up and down the highway."

Elisa brought him a fifty-cent piece from the house and dropped it in his hand. "You might be surprised to have a rival some time. I can sharpen scissors, too. And I can beat the dents out of little pots. I could show you what a woman might do."

He put his hammer back in the oily box and shoved the little anvil out of sight. "It would be a lonely life for a woman, ma'am, and a scarey life, too, with animals creeping under the wagon all night." He climbed over the singletree, steadying himself with a hand on the burro's white rump. He settled himself in the seat, picked up the lines. "Thank you kindly, ma'am," he said. "I'll do like you told me; I'll go back and catch the Salinas road."

90 "Mind," she called, "if you're long in getting there, keep the sand damp."

"Sand, ma'am? . . . Sand? Oh, sure. You mean around the chrysanthemums. Sure I will." He clucked his tongue. The beasts leaned luxuriously into their collars. The mongrel dog took his place between the back wheels. The wagon turned and crawled out the entrance road and back the way it had come, along the river.

Elisa stood in front of her wire fence watching the slow progress of the caravan. Her shoulders were straight, her head thrown back, her eyes half-closed, so that the scene came vaguely into them. Her lips moved silently, forming the words "Good-bye—good-bye." Then she whispered, "That's a bright direction. There's a glowing there." The sound of her whisper startled her. She shook herself free and looked about to see whether anyone had been listening. Only the dogs had heard. They lifted their heads toward her from their sleeping in the dust, and then stretched out their chins and settled asleep again. Elisa turned and ran hurriedly into the house.

In the kitchen she reached behind the stove and felt the water tank. It was full of hot water from the noonday cooking. In the bathroom she tore off her soiled clothes and flung them into the corner. And then she scrubbed herself with a little block of pumice, legs and thighs, loins and chest and arms, until her skin was scratched and red. When she had dried herself she stood in front of a mirror in her bedroom and looked at her body. She tightened her stomach and threw out her chest. She turned and looked over her shoulder at her back.

After a while she began to dress, slowly. She put on her newest underclothing and her nicest stockings and the dress which was the symbol of her prettiness. She worked carefully on her hair, penciled her eyebrows and rouged her lips.

95 Before she was finished she heard the little thunder of hoofs and the shouts of Henry and his helper as they drove the red steers into the corral. She heard the gate bang shut and set herself for Henry's arrival.

His step sounded on the porch. He entered the house calling, "Elisa, where are you?"

"In my room, dressing. I'm not ready. There's hot water for your bath. Hurry up. It's getting late."

When she heard him splashing in the tub, Elisa laid his dark suit on the bed, and shirt and socks and tie beside it. She stood his polished shoes on the floor beside the bed. Then she went to the porch and sat primly and stiffly down. She looked toward the river road where the willow-line was still yellow with frosted leaves so that under the high grey fog they seemed a thin band of sunshine. This was the only color in the grey afternoon. She sat unmoving for a long time. Her eyes blinked rarely.

Henry came banging out of the door, shoving his tie inside his vest as he came. Elisa stiffened and her face grew tight. Henry stopped short and looked at her. "Why—why, Elisa. You look so nice!"

100 "Nice? You think I look nice? What do you mean by 'nice'?"

Henry blundered on. "I don't know. I mean you look different, strong and happy."

"I am strong? Yes, strong. What do you mean 'strong'?"

He looked bewildered. "You're playing some kind of a game," he said helplessly. "It's a kind of a play. You look strong enough to break a calf over your knee, happy enough to eat it like a watermelon."

For a second she lost her rigidity. "Henry! Don't talk like that. You didn't know what you said." She grew complete again. "I'm strong," she boasted. "I never knew before how strong."

105 Henry looked down toward the tractor shed, and when he brought his eyes back to her, they were his own again. "I'll get out the car. You can put on your coat while I'm starting."

Elisa went into the house. She heard him drive to the gate and idle down his motor, and then she took a long time to put on her hat. She pulled it here and pressed it there. When Henry turned the motor off she slipped into her coat and went out.

The little roadster bounced along on the dirt road by the river, raising the birds and driving the rabbits into the brush. Two cranes flapped heavily over the willow-line and dropped into the river-bed.

Far ahead on the road Elisa saw a dark speck. She knew.

She tried not to look as they passed it, but her eyes would not obey. She whispered to herself sadly, "He might have thrown them off the road. That wouldn't have been much trouble, not very much. But he kept the pot," she explained. "He had to keep the pot. That's why he couldn't get them off the road."

110 The roadster turned a bend and she saw the caravan ahead. She swung full around toward her husband so she could not see the little covered wagon and the mismatched team as the car passed them.

In a moment it was over. The thing was done. She did not look back.

She said loudly, to be heard above the motor, "It will be good, tonight, a good dinner."

"Now you're changed again," Henry complained. He took one hand from the wheel and patted her knee. "I ought to take you in to dinner oftener. It would be good for both of us. We get so heavy out on the ranch."

"Henry," she asked, "could we have wine at dinner?"

115 "Sure we could. Say! That will be fine."

She was silent for a while; then she said, "Henry, at those prize fights, do the men hurt each other very much?"

"Sometimes a little, not often. Why?"

"Well, I've read how they break noses, and blood runs down their chests. I've read how the fighting gloves get heavy and soggy with blood."

He looked around at her. "What's the matter, Elisa? I didn't know you read things like that." He brought the car to a stop, then turned to the right over the Salinas River bridge.

"Do any women ever go to the fights?" she asked.

"Oh, sure, some. What's the matter, Elisa? Do you want to go? I don't think you'd like it, but I'll take you if you really want to go."

She relaxed limply in the seat. "Oh, no. No. I don't want to go. I'm sure I don't." Her face was turned away from him. "It will be enough if we can have wine. It will be plenty." She turned up her coat collar so he could not see that she was crying weakly—like an old woman.

James Thurber
(1894–1961)

THE CATBIRD SEAT
(1943)

Mr. Martin bought the pack of Camels on Monday night in the most crowded cigar store on Broadway. It was theater time and seven or eight men were buying cigarettes. The clerk didn't even glance at Mr. Martin, who put the pack in his overcoat pocket and went out. If any of the staff at F & S had seen him buy the cigarettes, they would have been astonished, for it was generally known that Mr. Martin did not smoke, and never had. No one saw him.

It was just a week to the day since Mr. Martin had decided to rub out Mrs. Ulgine Barrows. The term "rub out" pleased him because it suggested nothing more than the correction of an error—in this case an error of Mr. Fitweiler. Mr. Martin had spent each night of the past week working out his plan and examining it. As he walked home now he went over it again. For the hundredth time he resented the element of imprecision, the margin of guesswork that entered into the business. The project as he had worked it out was casual and bold, the risks were considerable. Something might go wrong anywhere along the line. And therein lay the cunning of his scheme. No one would ever see in it the cautious, painstaking hand of Erwin Martin, head of the filing department at F & S, of whom Mr. Fitweiler had once said, "Man is fallible but Martin isn't." No one would see his hand, that is, unless it were caught in the act.

Sitting in his apartment, drinking a glass of milk, Mr. Martin reviewed his case against Mrs. Ulgine Barrows, as he had every night for seven nights. He began at the beginning. Her quacking voice and braying laugh had first profaned the halls of F & S on March 7, 1941 (Mr. Martin had a head for dates). Old Roberts, the personnel chief, had introduced her as the newly appointed special adviser to the president of the firm, Mr. Fitweiler. The woman had appalled Mr. Martin instantly, but he hadn't shown it. He had given her his dry hand, a look of studious concentration, and a faint smile. "Well," she had said, looking at the papers on his desk, "are you lifting the oxcart out of the ditch?" As Mr. Martin recalled that moment, over his milk, he squirmed slightly. He must keep his mind on her crimes as a special adviser, not on her peccadillos as a personality. This he found difficult to do, in spite of entering an objection and sustaining it. The faults of the woman as a woman kept chattering on in his mind like an unruly witness. She had, for almost two years now, baited him. In the halls, in the elevator, even in his own office, into which she romped now and then like a circus horse, she was constantly shouting these silly questions at him. "Are you lifting the oxcart out of the ditch? Are you tearing up the pea patch? Are you hollering down the rain barrel? Are you scraping around the bottom of the pickle barrel? Are you sitting in the catbird seat?"

It was Joey Hart, one of Mr. Martin's two assistants, who had explained what the gibberish meant. "She must be a Dodger fan," he had said. "Red Barber announces the Dodger games over the radio and he uses those expressions—picked 'em up down South." Joey had gone on to explain one or two. "Tearing up the pea patch" meant going on a rampage; "sitting in the catbird seat" meant sitting pretty, like a batter with three balls and no strikes on him. Mr. Martin dismissed all this with an effort. It had been annoying, it had driven him near to distraction, but he was too solid a man to be moved to murder by anything so childish. It was fortunate, he reflected as he passed on to the important charges against Mrs. Barrows, that he had stood up under it so well. He had maintained always an outward appearance of polite tolerance. "Why, I even believe you like the woman," Miss Paird, his other assistant, had once said to him. He had simply smiled.

5 A gavel rapped in Mr. Martin's mind and the case proper was resumed. Mrs. Ulgine Barrows stood charged with willful, blatant, and persistent attempts to destroy the efficiency and system of F & S. It was competent, material, and relevant to review her advent and rise to power. Mr. Martin had got the story from Miss Paird, who seemed always able to find things out. According to her, Mrs. Barrows had met Mr. Fitweiler at a party, where she had rescued him from the embraces of a powerfully built drunken man who had mistaken the president of F & S for a famous retired Middle Western football coach. She had led him to a sofa and somehow worked upon him a monstrous magic. The aging gentleman had jumped to the conclusion there and then that this was a woman of singular attainments, equipped to bring out the best in him and in the firm. A week later he had introduced her into F & S as his special adviser. On that day confusion got its foot in the door. After Miss Tyson, Mr. Brundage, and Mr. Bartlett had been fired and Mr. Munson had taken his hat and stalked out, mailing in his resignation later, old Roberts had been emboldened to speak to Mr. Fitweiler. He mentioned that Mr. Munson's department had been "a little disrupted" and hadn't they perhaps better resume the old system there?

Mr. Fitweiler had said certainly not. He had the greatest faith in Mrs. Barrow's ideas. "They require a little seasoning, a little seasoning, is all," he had added. Mr. Roberts had given it up. Mr. Martin reviewed in detail all the changes wrought by Mrs. Barrows. She had begun chipping at the cornices of the firm's edifice and now she was swinging at the foundation stones with a pickaxe.

Mr. Martin came now, in his summing up, to the afternoon of Monday, November 2, 1942—just one week ago. On that day, at 3 P.M., Mrs. Barrows had bounced into his office. "Boo!" she had yelled. "Are you scraping around the bottom of the pickle barrel?" Mr. Martin had looked at her from under his green eyeshade, saying nothing. She had begun to wander about the office, taking it in with her great, popping eyes. "Do you really need *all* these filing cabinets?" she had demanded suddenly. Mr. Martin's heart had jumped. "Each of these files," he had said, keeping his voice even, "plays an indispensable part in the system of F & S." She had brayed at him, "Well, don't tear up the pea patch!" and gone to the door. From there she had bawled, "But you sure have got a lot of fine scrap in here!" Mr. Martin could no longer doubt that the finger was on his beloved department. Her pickaxe was on the upswing, poised for the first blow. It had not come yet; he had received no blue memo from the enchanted Mr. Fitweiler bearing nonsensical instructions deriving from the obscene woman. But there was no doubt in Mr. Martin's mind that one would be forthcoming. He must act quickly. Already a precious week had gone by. Mr. Martin stood up in his living room, still holding his milk glass. "Gentlemen of the jury," he said to himself, "I demand the death penalty for this horrible person."

The next day Mr. Martin followed his routine, as usual. He polished his glasses more often and once sharpened an already sharp pencil, but not even Miss Paird noticed. Only once did he catch sight of his victim; she swept past him in the hall with a patronizing "Hi!" At five-thirty he walked home, as usual, and had a glass of milk, as usual. He had never drunk anything stronger in his life—unless you could count ginger ale. The late Sam Schlosser, the S of F & S, had praised Mr. Martin at a staff meeting several years before for his temperate habits. "Our most efficient worker neither drinks nor smokes," he had said. "The results speak for themselves." Mr. Fitweiler had sat by, nodding approval.

Mr. Martin was still thinking about that red-letter day as he walked over to the Schrafft's on Fifth Avenue near Forty-sixth Street. He got there, as he always did, at eight o'clock. He finished his dinner and the financial page of the *Sun* at a quarter to nine, as he always did. It was his custom after dinner to take a walk. This time he walked down Fifth Avenue at a casual pace. His gloved hands felt moist and warm, his forehead cold. He transferred the Camels from his overcoat to a jacket pocket. He wondered, as he did so, if they did not represent an unnecessary note of strain. Mrs. Barrows smoked only Luckies. It was his idea to puff a few puffs on a Camel (after the rubbing-out), stub it out in the ashtray holding her lipstick-stained Luckies, and thus drag a small red herring across the trail. Perhaps it was not a good idea. It would take time. He might even choke, too loudly.

Mr. Martin had never seen the house on West Twelfth Street where Mrs. Barrows lived, but he had a clear enough picture of it. Fortunately, she had bragged to everybody about her ducky first-floor apartment in the perfectly darling three-story red-brick. There would be no doorman or other attendants; just the tenants of the second and third floors. As he walked along, Mr. Martin realized that he would get there before nine-thirty. He had considered walking north on Fifth Avenue from Schrafft's to a point from which it would take him until ten o'clock to reach the house. At that hour people were less likely to be coming in or going out. But the procedure would have made an awkward loop in the straight thread of his casualness, and he had abandoned it. It was impossible to figure when people would be entering or leaving the house, anyway. There was a great risk at any hour. If he ran into anybody, he would simply have to place the rubbing-out of Ulgine Barrows in the inactive file forever. The same thing would hold true if there were someone in her apartment. In that case he would just say that he had been passing by, recognized her charming house and thought to drop in.

10 It was eighteen minutes after nine when Mr. Martin turned into Twelfth Street. A man passed him, and a man and a woman talking. There was no one within fifty paces when he came to the house, halfway down the block. He was up the steps and in the small vestibule in no time, pressing the bell under the card that said "Mrs. Ulgine Barrows." When the clicking in the lock started, he jumped forward against the door. He got inside fast, closing the door behind him. A bulb in a lantern hung from the hall ceiling on a chain seemed to give a monstrously bright light. There was nobody on the stair, which went up ahead of him along the left wall. A door opened down the hall in the wall on the right. He went toward it swiftly, on tiptoe.

"Well, for God's sake, look who's here!" bawled Mrs. Barrows, and her braying laugh rang out like the report of a shotgun. He rushed past her like a football tackle, bumping her. "Hey, quit shoving!" she said, closing the door behind them. They were in her living room, which seemed to Mr. Martin to be lighted by a hundred lamps. "What's after you?" she said. "You're as jumpy as a goat." He found he was unable to speak. His heart was wheezing in his throat. "I—yes," he finally brought out. She was jabbering and laughing as she started to help him off with his coat. "No, no," he said. "I'll put it here." He took it off and put it on a chair near the door. "Your hat and gloves, too," she said. "You're in a lady's house." He put his hat on top of the coat. Mrs. Barrows seemed larger than he had thought. He kept his gloves on. "I was passing by," he said. "I recognized—is there anyone here?" She laughed louder than ever. "No," she said, "we're all alone. You're as white as a sheet, you funny man. Whatever *has* come over you? I'll mix you a toddy." She started toward a door across the room. "Scotch-and-soda be all right? But say, you don't drink, do you?" She turned and gave him her amused look. Mr. Martin pulled himself together. "Scotch-and-soda will be all right," he heard himself say. He could hear her laughing in the kitchen.

Mr. Martin looked quickly around the living room for the weapon. He had counted on finding one there. There were andirons and a poker and something in a corner that looked like an Indian club. None of them would do. It couldn't be that way. He began to pace around. He came to a desk. On it lay a metal paper knife with an ornate handle. Would it be sharp enough? He reached for it and knocked over a small brass jar. Stamps spilled out of it and it fell to the floor with a clatter. "Hey," Mrs. Barrows yelled from the kitchen, "are you tearing up the pea patch?" Mr. Martin gave a strange laugh. Picking up the knife, he tried its point against his left wrist. It was blunt. It wouldn't do.

When Mrs. Barrows reappeared, carrying two highballs, Mr. Martin, standing there with his gloves on, became acutely conscious of the fantasy he had wrought. Cigarettes in his pocket, a drink prepared for him—it was all too grossly improbable. It was more than that; it was impossible. Somewhere in the back of his mind a vague idea stirred, sprouted. "For heaven's sake, take off those gloves," said Mrs. Barrows. "I always wear them in the house," said Mr. Martin. The idea began to bloom, strange and wonderful. She put the glasses on a coffee table in front of a sofa and sat on the sofa. "Come over here, you odd little man," she said. Mr. Martin went over and sat beside her. It was difficult getting a cigarette out of the pack of Camels, but he managed it. She held a match for him, laughing. "Well," she said, handing him his drink, "this is perfectly marvelous. You with a drink and a cigarette."

Mr. Martin puffed, not too awkwardly, and took a gulp of the highball. "I drink and smoke all the time," he said. He clinked his glass against hers. "Here's nuts to that old windbag, Fitweiler," he said, and gulped again. The stuff tasted awful, but he made no grimace. "Really, Mr. Martin," she said, her voice and posture changing, "you are insulting our employer." Mrs. Barrows was now all special adviser to the president. "I am preparing a bomb," said Mr. Martin, "which will blow the old goat higher than hell." He had only had a little of the drink, which was not strong. It couldn't be that. "Do you take dope or something?" Mrs. Barrows asked coldly. "Heroin," said Mr. Martin. "I'll be coked to the gills when I bump that old buzzard off." "Mr. Martin!" she shouted, getting to her feet. "That will be all of that. You must go at once." Mr. Martin took another swallow of his drink. He tapped his cigarette out in the ashtray and put the pack of Camels on the coffee table. Then he got up. She stood glaring at him. He walked over and put on his hat and coat. "Not a word about this," he said, and laid an index finger against his lips. All Mrs. Barrows could bring out was "Really!" Mr. Martin put his hand on the doorknob. "I'm sitting in the catbird seat," he said. He stuck his tongue out at her and left. Nobody saw him go.

15 Mr. Martin got to his apartment, walking, well before eleven. No one saw him go in. He had two glasses of milk after brushing his teeth, and he felt elated. It wasn't tipsiness, because he hadn't been tipsy. Anyway, the walk had worn off all effects of the whisky. He got in bed and read a magazine for a while. He was asleep before midnight.

Mr. Martin got to the office at eight-thirty the next morning, as usual. At a quarter to nine, Ulgine Barrows, who had never before arrived at work before ten, swept into his office. "I'm reporting to Mr. Fitweiler now!" she shouted. "If he turns you over to the police, it's no more than you deserve!" Mr. Martin gave her a look of shocked surprise. "I beg your pardon?" he said. Mrs. Barrows snorted and bounced out of the room, leaving Miss Paird and Joey Hart staring after her. "What's the matter with that old devil now?" asked Miss Paird. "I have no idea," said Mr. Martin, resuming his work. The other two looked at him and then at each other. Miss Paird got up and went out. She walked slowly past the closed door of Mr. Fitweiler's office. Mrs. Barrows was yelling inside, but she was not braying. Miss Paird could not hear what the woman was saying. She went back to her desk.

Forty-five minutes later, Mrs. Barrows left the president's office and went into her own, shutting the door. It wasn't until half an hour later that Mr. Fitweiler sent for Mr. Martin. The head of the filing department, neat, quiet, attentive, stood in front of the old man's desk. Mr. Fitweiler was pale and nervous. He took his glasses off and twiddled them. He made a small, bruffing sound in his throat. "Martin," he said, "you have been with us more than twenty years." "Twenty-two, sir," said Mr. Martin. "In that time," pursued the president, "your work and your—uh—manner have been exemplary." "I trust so, sir," said Mr. Martin. "I have understood, Martin," said Mr. Fitweiler, "that you have never taken a drink or smoked." "That is correct, sir," said Mr. Martin. "Ah, yes." Mr. Fitweiler polished his glasses. "You may describe what you did after leaving the office yesterday, Martin," he said. Mr. Martin allowed less than a second for his bewildered pause. "Certainly, sir," he said. "I walked home. Then I went to Schrafft's for dinner. Afterward I walked home again. I went to bed early, sir, and read a magazine for a while. I was asleep before eleven." "Ah, yes," said Mr. Fitweiler again. He was silent for a moment, searching for the proper words to say to the head of the filing department. "Mrs. Barrows," he said finally, "Mrs. Barrows has worked hard, Martin, very hard. It grieves me to report that she has suffered a severe breakdown. It has taken the form of a persecution complex accompanied by distressing hallucinations." "I am very sorry, sir," said Mr. Martin. "Mrs. Barrows is under the delusion," continued Mr. Fitweiler, "that you visited her last evening and behaved yourself in an—uh—unseemly manner." He raised his hand to silence Mr. Martin's little pained outcry. "It is the nature of these psychological diseases," Mr. Fitweiler said, "to fix upon the least likely and most innocent party as the—uh—source of persecution. These matters are not for the lay mind to grasp, Martin. I've just had my psychiatrist, Dr. Fitch, on the phone. He would not, of course, commit himself, but he made enough generalizations to substantiate my suspicions. I suggested to Mrs. Barrows when she had completed her—uh—story to me this morning, that she visit Dr. Fitch, for I suspected a condition at once. She flew, I regret to say, into a rage, and demanded—uh—requested that I call you on the carpet. You may not know, Martin, but Mrs. Barrows had planned a reorganization of your department—subject to my approval, of course, subject to my approval. This brought you, rather than anyone else, to her mind—but again that is a phenomenon for Dr. Fitch and not for us. So, Martin, I am afraid Mrs. Barrows' usefulness here is at an end." "I am dreadfully sorry, sir," said Mr. Martin.

It was at this point that the door to the office blew open with the suddenness of a gas-main explosion and Mrs. Barrows catapulted through it. "Is the little rat denying it?" she screamed. "He can't get away with that!" Mr. Martin got up and moved discreetly to a point beside Mr. Fitweiler's chair. "You drank and smoked at my apartment," she bawled at Mr. Martin, "and you know it! You called Mr. Fitweiler an old windbag and said you were going to blow him up when you got coked to the gills on your heroin!" She stopped yelling to catch her breath and a new glint came into her popping eyes. "If you weren't such a drab, ordinary little man," she said, "I'd think you'd planned it all. Sticking your tongue out at me, saying you were sitting in the catbird seat, because you thought no one would believe me when I told it! My God, it's really too perfect!" She brayed loudly and hysterically, and the fury was on her again. She glared at Mr. Fitweiler. "Can't you see how he has tricked us, you old fool? Can't you see his little game?" But Mr. Fitweiler had been surreptitiously pressing all the buttons under the top of his desk and employees of F & S began pouring into the room. "Stockton," said Mr. Fitweiler, "you and Fishbein will take Mrs. Barrows to her home. Mrs. Powell, you will go with them." Stockton, who had played a little football in high school, blocked Mrs. Barrows as she made for Mr. Martin. It took him and Fishbein together to force her out of the door into the hall, crowded with stenographers and office boys. She was still screaming imprecations at Mr. Martin, tangled and contradictory imprecations. The hubbub finally died out down the corridor.

"I regret that this has happened," said Mr. Fitweiler. "I shall ask you to dismiss it from your mind, Martin." "Yes, sir," said Mr. Martin, anticipating his chief's "That will be all" by moving to the door. "I will dismiss it." He went out and shut the door, and his step was light and quick in the hall. When he entered his department he had slowed down to his customary gait, and he walked quietly across the room to the W20 file, wearing a look of studious concentration.

Anne Tyler
(1941–)

TEENAGE WASTELAND
(1984)

He used to have very blond hair—almost white—cut shorter than other children's so that on his crown a little cowlick always stood up to catch the light. But this was when he was small. As he grew older, his hair grew darker, and he wore it longer—past his collar even. It hung in lank, taffy-colored ropes around his face, which was still an endearing face, fine-featured, the eyes an unusual aqua blue. But his cheeks, of course, were no longer round, and a sharp new Adam's apple jogged in his throat when he talked.

In October, they called from the private school he attended to request a conference with his parents. Daisy went alone; her husband was at work. Clutching her purse, she sat on the principal's couch and learned that Donny was noisy, lazy, and disruptive; always fooling around with his friends, and he wouldn't respond in class.

In the past, before her children were born, Daisy had been a fourth-grade teacher. It shamed her now to sit before this principal as a parent, a delinquent parent, a parent who struck Mr. Lanham, no doubt, as unseeing or uncaring. "It isn't that we're not concerned," she said. "Both of us are. And we've done what we could, whatever we could think of. We don't let him watch TV on school nights. We don't let him talk on the phone till he's finished his homework. But he tells us he doesn't *have* any homework or he did it all in study hall. How are we to know what to believe?"

From early October through November, at Mr. Lanham's suggestion, Daisy checked Donny's assignments every day. She sat next to him as he worked, trying to be encouraging, sagging inwardly as she saw the poor quality of everything he did—the sloppy mistakes in math, the illogical leaps in his English themes, the history questions left blank if they required any research.

5 Daisy was often late starting supper, and she couldn't give as much attention to Donny's younger sister. "You'll never guess what happened at . . ." Amanda would begin, and Daisy would have to tell her, "Not now, honey."

By the time her husband, Matt, came home, she'd be snappish. She would recite the day's hardships—the fuzzy instructions in English, the botched history map, the morass of unsolvable algebra equations. Matt would look surprised and confused, and Daisy would gradually wind down. There was no way, really, to convey how exhausting all this was.

In December, the school called again. This time, they wanted Matt to come as well. She and Matt had to sit on Mr. Lanham's couch like two bad children and listen to the news: Donny had improved only slightly, raising a D in history to a C, and a C in algebra to a B-minus. What was worse, he had developed new problems. He had cut classes on at least three occasions. Smoked in the furnace room. Helped Sonny Barnett break into a freshman's locker. And last week, during athletics, he and three friends had been seen off the school grounds; when they returned, the coach had smelled beer on their breath.

Daisy and Matt sat silent, shocked. Matt rubbed his forehead with his fingertips. Imagine, Daisy thought, how they must look to Mr. Lanham: an overweight housewife in a cotton dress and a too-tall, too-thin insurance agent in a baggy, frayed suit. Failures, both of them—the kind of people who are always hurrying to catch up, missing the point of things that everyone else grasps at once. She wished she'd worn nylons instead of knee socks.

It was arranged that Donny would visit a psychologist for testing. Mr. Lanham knew just the person. He would set this boy straight, he said.

10 When they stood to leave, Daisy held her stomach in and gave Mr. Lanham a firm, responsible handshake.

Donny said the psychologist was a jackass and the tests were really dumb; but he kept all three of his appointments, and when it was time for the follow-up conference with the psychologist and both parents, Donny combed his hair and seemed unusually sober and subdued. The psychologist said Donny had no serious emotional problems. He was merely going through a difficult period in his life. He required some academic help and a better sense of self-worth. For this reason, he was suggesting a man named Calvin Beadle, a tutor with considerable psychological training.

In the car going home, Donny said he'd be damned if he'd let them drag him to some stupid fairy tutor. His father told him to watch his language in front of his mother.

That night, Daisy lay awake pondering the term "self-worth." She had always been free with her praise. She had always told Donny he had talent, was smart, was good with his hands. She had made a big to-do over every little gift he gave her. In fact, maybe she had gone too far, although, Lord knows, she had meant every word. Was that his trouble?

She remembered when Amanda was born. Donny had acted lost and bewildered. Daisy had been alert to that, of course, but still, a new baby keeps you so busy. Had she really done all she could have? She longed—she ached—for a time machine. Given one more chance, she'd do it perfectly—hug him more, praise him more, or perhaps praise him less. Oh, who can say . . .

15 The tutor told Donny to call him Cal. All his kids did, he said. Daisy thought for a second that he meant his own children, then realized her mistake. He seemed too young, anyhow, to be a family man. He wore a heavy brown handlebar mustache. His hair was as long and stringy as Donny's, and his jeans as faded. Wire-rimmed spectacles slid down his nose. He lounged in a canvas director's chair with his fingers laced across his chest, and he casually, amiably questioned Donny, who sat upright and glaring in an armchair.

"So they're getting on your back at school," said Cal. "Making a big deal about anything you do wrong."

"Right," said Donny.

"Any idea why that would be?"

"Oh, well, you know, stuff like homework and all," Donny said.

"You don't do your homework?"

"Oh, well, I might do it sometimes but not just exactly like they want it." Donny sat forward and said, "It's like a prison there, you know? You've got to go to every class, you can never step off the school grounds."

"You cut classes sometimes?"

"Sometimes," Donny said, with a glance at his parents.

Cal didn't seem perturbed. "Well," he said, "I'll tell you what. Let's you and me try working together three nights a week. Think you can handle that? We'll see if we can show that school of yours a thing or two. Give it a month; then if you don't like it, we'll stop. If *I* don't like it, we'll stop. I mean, sometimes people just don't get along, right? What do you say to that?"

"Okay," Donny said. He seemed pleased.

"Make it seven o'clock till eight, Monday, Wednesday, and Friday," Cal told Matt and Daisy. They nodded. Cal shambled to his feet, gave them a little salute, and showed them to the door.

This was where he lived as well as worked, evidently. The interview had taken place in the dining room, which had been transformed into a kind of office. Passing the living room, Daisy winced at the rock music she had been hearing, without registering it, ever since she had entered the house. She looked in and saw a boy about Donny's age lying on a sofa with a book. Another boy and a girl were playing Ping-Pong in front of the fireplace. "You have several here together?" Daisy asked Cal.

"Oh, sometimes they stay on after their sessions, just to rap. They're a pretty sociable group, all in all. Plenty of goof-offs like young Donny here."

He cuffed Donny's shoulder playfully. Donny flushed and grinned.

Climbing into the car, Daisy asked Donny, "Well? What do you think?"

But Donny had returned to his old evasive self. He jerked his chin toward the garage. "Look," he said. "He's got a basketball net."

Now on Mondays, Wednesdays, and Fridays, they had supper early—the instant Matt came home. Sometimes, they had to leave before they were really finished. Amanda would still be eating her dessert. "Bye, honey. Sorry," Daisy would tell her.

Cal's first bill sent a flutter of panic through Daisy's chest, but it was worth it, of course. Just look at Donny's face when they picked him up: alight and full of interest. The principal telephoned Daisy to tell her how Donny had improved. "Of course, it hasn't shown up in his grades yet, but several of the teachers have noticed how his attitude's changed. Yes, sir, I think we're onto something here."

At home, Donny didn't act much different. He still seemed to have a low opinion of his parents. But Daisy supposed that was unavoidable—

part of being fifteen. He said his parents were too "controlling"—a word that made Daisy give him a sudden look. He said they acted like wardens. On weekends, they enforced a curfew. And any time he went to a party, they always telephoned first to see if adults would be supervising. "For God's sake!" he said. "Don't you trust me?"

"It isn't a matter of trust, honey . . ." But there was no explaining to him.

His tutor called one afternoon. "I get the sense," he said, "that this kid's feeling . . . underestimated, you know? Like you folks expect the worst of him. I'm thinking we ought to give him more rope."

"But see, he's still so suggestible," Daisy said. "When his friends suggest some mischief—smoking or drinking or such—why, he just finds it hard not to go along with them."

"Mrs. Coble," the tutor said, "I think this kid is hurting. You know? Here's a serious, sensitive kid, telling you he'd like to take on some grown-up challenges, and you're giving him the message that he can't be trusted. Don't you understand how that hurts?"

"Oh," said Daisy.

"It undermines his self-esteem—don't you realize that?"

"Well, I guess you're right," said Daisy. She saw Donny suddenly from a whole new angle: his pathetically poor posture, that slouch so forlorn that his shoulders seemed about to meet his chin . . . oh, wasn't it awful being young? She'd had a miserable adolescence herself and had always sworn no child of hers would ever be that unhappy.

They let Donny stay out later, they didn't call ahead to see if the parties were supervised, and they were careful not to grill him about his evening. The tutor had set down so many rules! They were not allowed any questions at all about any aspect of school, nor were they to speak with his teachers. If a teacher had some complaint, she should phone Cal. Only one teacher disobeyed—the history teacher, Miss Evans. She called one morning in February. "I'm a little concerned about Donny, Mrs. Coble."

"Oh, I'm sorry, Miss Evans, but Donny's tutor handles these things now . . ."

"I always deal directly with the parents. You are the parent," Miss Evans said, speaking very slowly and distinctly. "Now, here is the problem. Back when you were helping Donny with his homework, his grades rose from a D to a C, but now they've slipped back, and they're closer to an F."

"They are?"

"I think you should start overseeing his homework again."

"But Donny's tutor says . . ."

"It's nice that Donny has a tutor, but you should still be in charge of his homework. With you, he learned it. Then he passed his tests. With the tutor, well, it seems the tutor is more of a crutch. 'Donny,' I say, 'a quiz is coming up on Friday. Hadn't you better be listening instead of talking?' 'That's okay, Miss Evans,' he says. 'I have a tutor now.' Like a talisman! I really think you ought to take over, Mrs. Coble."

"I see," said Daisy. "Well, I'll think about that. Thank you for calling."

Hanging up, she felt a rush of anger at Donny. A talisman! For a talisman, she'd given up all luxuries, all that time with her daughter, her evenings at home!

She dialed Cal's number. He sounded muzzy. "I'm sorry if I woke you," she told him, "but Donny's history teacher just called. She says he isn't doing well."

"She should have dealt with me."

"She wants me to start supervising his homework again. His grades are slipping."

"Yes," said the tutor, "but you and I both know there's more to it than mere grades, don't we? I care about the *whole* child—his happiness, his self-esteem. The grades will come. Just give them time."

When she hung up, it was Miss Evans she was angry at. What a narrow woman!

It was Cal this, Cal that, Cal says this, Cal and I did that. Cal lent Donny an album by the Who. He took Donny and two other pupils to a rock concert. In March, when Donny began to talk endlessly on the phone with a girl named Miriam, Cal even let Miriam come to one of the tutoring sessions. Daisy was touched that Cal would grow so involved in Donny's life, but she was also a little hurt, because she had offered to have Miriam to dinner and Donny had refused. Now he asked them to drive her to Cal's house without a qualm.

This Miriam was an unappealing girl with blurry lipstick and masses of rough red hair. She wore a short, bulky jacket that would not have been out of place on a motorcycle. During the trip to Cal's she was silent, but coming back, she was more talkative. "What a neat guy, and what a house! All those kids hanging out, like a club. And the stereo playing rock . . . gosh, he's not like a grown-up at all! Married and divorced and everything, but you'd think he was our own age."

"Mr. Beadle was married?" Daisy asked.

"Yeah, to this really controlling lady. She didn't understand him a bit."

"No, I guess not," Daisy said.

Spring came, and the students who hung around at Cal's drifted out to the basketball net above the garage. Sometimes, when Daisy and Matt arrived to pick up Donny, they'd find him there with the others—spiky and excited, jittering on his toes beneath the backboard. It was staying light much longer now, and the neighboring fence cast narrow bars across the bright grass. Loud music would be spilling from Cal's windows. Once it was the Who, which Daisy recognized from the time that Donny had borrowed the album. "*Teenage Wasteland,*"[1] she said aloud,

[1] The song is actually "Baba O'Riley," from the band's *Who's Next* album.

identifying the song, and Matt gave a short, dry laugh. "It certainly is," he said. He'd misunderstood; he thought she was commenting on the scene spread before them. In fact, she might have been. The players looked like hoodlums, even her son. Why, one of Cal's students had recently been knifed in a tavern. One had been shipped off to boarding school in midterm; two had been withdrawn by their parents. On the other hand, Donny had mentioned someone who'd been studying with Cal for five years. "Five years!" said Daisy. "Doesn't anyone ever stop needing him?"

Donny looked at her. Lately, whatever she said about Cal was read as criticism. "You're just feeling competitive," he said. "And controlling."

She bit her lip and said no more.

In April, the principal called to tell her that Donny had been expelled. There had been a locker check, and in Donny's locker they found five cans of beer and half a pack of cigarettes. With Donny's previous record, his offense meant expulsion.

Daisy gripped the receiver tightly and said, "Well, where is he now?"

"We've sent him home," said Mr. Lanham. "He's packed up all his belongings, and he's coming home on foot."

Daisy wondered what she would say to him. She felt him looming closer and closer, bringing this brand-new situation that no one had prepared her to handle. What other place would take him? Could they enter him in public school? What were the rules? She stood at the living room window, waiting for him to show up. Gradually, she realized that he was taking too long. She checked the clock. She stared up the street again.

When an hour had passed, she phoned the school. Mr. Lanham's secretary answered and told her in a grave, sympathetic voice that yes, Donny Coble had most definitely gone home. Daisy called her husband. He was out of the office. She went back to the window and thought awhile, and then she called Donny's tutor.

"Donny's been expelled from school," she said, "and now I don't know where he's gone. I wonder if you've heard from him?"

There was a long silence. "Donny's with me, Mrs. Coble," he finally said.

"With you? How'd he get there?"

"He hailed a cab, and I paid the driver."

"Could I speak to him, please?"

There was another silence. "Maybe it'd be better if we had a conference," Cal said.

"I don't *want* a conference. I've been standing at the window picturing him dead or kidnapped or something, and now you tell me you want a—"

"Donny is very, very upset. Understandably so," said Cal. "Believe me, Mrs. Coble, this is not what it seems. Have you asked Donny's side of the story?"

"Well, of course not, how could I? He went running off to you instead."

"Because he didn't feel he'd be listened to."

"But I haven't even—"

"Why don't you come out and talk? The three of us," said Cal, "will try to get this thing in perspective."

"Well, all right," Daisy said. But she wasn't as reluctant as she sounded. Already, she felt soothed by the calm way Cal was taking this.

Cal answered the doorbell at once. He said, "Hi, there," and led her into the dining room. Donny sat slumped in a chair, chewing the knuckle of one thumb. "Hello, Donny," Daisy said. He flicked his eyes in her direction.

"Sit here, Mrs. Coble," said Cal, placing her opposite Donny. He himself remained standing, restlessly pacing. "So," he said.

Daisy stole a look at Donny. His lips were swollen, as if he'd been crying.

"You know," Cal told Daisy, "I kind of expected something like this. That's a very punitive school you've got him in—you realize that. And any half-decent lawyer will tell you they've violated his civil rights. Locker checks! Where's their search warrant?"

"But if the rule is—" Daisy said.

"Well, anyhow, let him tell you his side."

She looked at Donny. He said, "It wasn't my fault. I promise."

"They said your locker was full of beer."

"It was a put-up job! See, there's this guy that doesn't like me. He put all these beers in my locker and started a rumor going, so Mr. Lanham ordered a locker check."

"What was the boy's name?" Daisy asked.

"Huh?"

"Mrs. Coble, take my word, the situation is not so unusual," Cal said. "You can't imagine how vindictive kids can be sometimes."

"What was the boy's *name,*" said Daisy, "so that I can ask Mr. Lanham if that's who suggested he run a locker check."

"You don't believe me," Donny said.

"And how'd this boy get your combination in the first place?"

"Frankly," said Cal, "I wouldn't be surprised to learn the school was in on it. Any kid that marches to a different drummer, why, they'd just love an excuse to get rid of him. The school is where I lay the blame."

"Doesn't *Donny* ever get blamed?"

"Now, Mrs. Coble, you heard what he—"

"Forget it," Donny told Cal. "You can see she doesn't trust me."

Daisy drew in a breath to say that of course she trusted him—a reflex. But she knew that bold-faced, wide-eyed look of Donny's. He had worn that look when he was small, denying some petty misdeed with the evidence plain as day all around him. Still, it was hard for her to accuse him outright. She temporized and said, "The only thing I'm sure of is that they've kicked you out of school, and now I don't know what we're going to do."

"We'll fight it," said Cal.

"We can't. Even you must see we can't."

"I could apply to Brantly," Donny said.

105 Cal stopped his pacing to beam down at him. "Brantly! Yes. They're really onto where a kid is coming from, at Brantly. Why, *I* could get you into Brantly. I work with a lot of their students."

Daisy had never heard of Brantly, but already she didn't like it. And she didn't like Cal's smile, which struck her now as feverish and avid—a smile of hunger.

On the fifteenth of April, they entered Donny in a public school, and they stopped his tutoring sessions. Donny fought both decisions bitterly. Cal, surprisingly enough, did not object. He admitted he'd made no headway with Donny and said it was because Donny was emotionally disturbed.

Donny went to his new school every morning, plodding off alone with his head down. He did his assignments, and he earned average grades, but he gathered no friends, joined no clubs. There was something exhausted and defeated about him.

The first week in June, during final exams, Donny vanished. He simply didn't come home one afternoon, and no one at school remembered seeing him. The police were reassuring, and for the first few days, they worked hard. They combed Donny's sad, messy room for clues; they visited Miriam and Cal. But then they started talking about the number of kids who ran away every year. Hundreds, just in this city. "He'll show up, if he wants to," they said. "If he doesn't, he won't."

110 Evidently, Donny didn't want to.

It's been three months now and still no word. Matt and Daisy still look for him in every crowd of awkward, heartbreaking teenage boys. Every time the phone rings, they imagine it might by Donny. Both parents have aged. Donny's sister seems to be staying away from home as much as possible.

At night, Daisy lies awake and goes over Donny's life. She is trying to figure out what went wrong, where they made their first mistake. Often, she finds herself blaming Cal, although she knows he didn't begin it. Then at other times she excuses him, for without him, Donny might have left earlier. Who really knows? In the end, she can only sigh and search for a cooler spot on the pillow. As she falls asleep, she occasionally glimpses something in the corner of her vision. It's something fleet and round, a ball—a basketball. It flies up, it sinks through the hoop, descends, lands in a yard littered with last year's leaves and striped with bars of sunlight as white as bones, bleached and parched and cleanly picked.

Ed Vega*

THE BARBOSA EXPRESS

(1987)

Several years ago, at the tail end of a big snowstorm, I was in Florindo's Bar on 110th Street and Lexington Avenue when Chu Chu Barbosa walked in cursing and threatening to join the FALN[1] and bomb the hell out of somebody or other. Barbosa's name is *Jesús* but nobody likes being called Gee Zoos or Hay Siouxs, so it's convenient that the nickname for *Jesús* is Chu or Chuíto because Barbosa was a motorman for the last seventeen years with the New York City Transit Authority.

Barbosa is your typical working class stiff, bitter on the outside but full of stubborn optimism on the inside. He has gone through the same kind of immigrant nonsense everyone else has to go through and has come out of it in great shape. In spite of ups and downs he has remained married to the same woman twenty-two years, has never found reason to be unfaithful to her, put one kid through college and has four more heading in the same direction. He owns a two-family home in Brooklyn and on weekends during the summer, he takes Bobby and Mike, his two sons, fishing on his outboard, "Mercedes," named after the children's mother.

Usually even tempered and singularly civic minded, he lists among his responsibilities his serving as treasurer of the "Roberto Clemente Little League of Brooklyn," vice-president of the "Sons of Cacimar Puerto Rican Day Parade Organizing Committee," Den Father for the Boy Scouts of America Troop 641, Secretary of the "Wilfredo Santiago American Legion Post 387," and member of the Courtelyou Street Block Association.

That night Barbosa was out of his mind with anger. At first I thought it was the weather. The snowstorm was wreaking havoc with the city and it seemed conceivable Barbosa was stranded in Manhattan and could not get back to his family in Brooklyn. Knocking the snow off his coat and stamping his feet, Barbosa walked up to the bar and ordered a boilermaker. He downed the whiskey, chugalugged the beer and ordered another one. I was right next to him but he didn't recognize me until he had finished his second beer and ordered another. Halfway through his third beer he suddenly looked at me and shook his head as if there were no reason for trying anymore.

5 "This does it, Mendoza," he said, still shaking his head. "It makes no sense, man. The whole town is sinking."

"Yeah, the snow is pretty bad," I said, but it was as if I hadn't even spoken.

---

* Birth date is not available.

[1] FALN—Fuerzas Armadas de Liberación Nacional Puertorriqueña (Armed Forces of Puerto Rican Liberation).

"The friggin capital of the world," he went on. "And it's going down the d-r-a-drain. I mean, who am I kidding? I put on a uniform in the morning, step into my little moving phone booth and off I go. From Coney Island to 205th in the B-r-o-Bronx. Fifteen years I've been on the run. I mean, you gotta be born to the job, Mendoza. And listen, I take pride in what I do. It isn't just a job with me. I still get my kicks outta pushing my ten car rig. Brooklyn, Manhattan and the Bronx. I run through those boroughs four times a shift, picking up passengers, letting them off. School kids going up to Bronx Science, people going to work in midtown Manhattan, in the summertime the crowds going up to Yankee Stadium. And that run from 125th Street to 59th Street and Columbus Circle when I let her out and race through that tunnel at sixty miles an hour. Did you know that was the longest run of any express train between stops?"

"No, I didn't," I said.

"It is," he said. "Sixty-six b-l-o-blocks."

"No kidding," I said, suddenly hopeful that Barbosa was pulling out of his dark mood. "That's amazing."

"You're damn right it's amazing," he replied, his face angry once more. "And I love it, but it's getting to me. How can they friggin do this? I mean it's their trains. Don't they know that, Mendoza? They don't have to shove it down my throat. But who the hell am I, right? I'm the little guy. Just put him in that moving closet and forget about him. Jerónimo Anónimo, that's me. I don't care what anybody thinks. For me it's like I'm pulling the Super Chief on a transcontinental run, or maybe the old Texas Hummingbird from Chicago to San Antonio along all that flat land, eighty, ninety miles an hour. I give 'em an honest day's work. It's 'cause I'm Puerto Rican, man. It's nothing but discrimination."

I could certainly sympathize with Barbosa on that account. I had met severe discrimination in the publishing world and had been forced to write nothing but lies about the people. I was curious to find out what had taken place to make Barbosa so angry.

"I know how you feel, Chu Chu," I said.

"I mean you're a writer and it might sound strange, Mendoza. But I'm not a stupid man. I've read, so I know about words. When I'm in my rig going along the tracks and making my stops, it feels like I'm inside the veins of the city down in those tunnels. It's like my train is the blood and the people the food for this city. Sometimes there is a mugging or worse down there, but I say to myself, hell, so the system ate a stale *alcapurria* or some bad chittlins or maybe an old knish. Do you understand what I'm saying?"

"Of course I do," I said. "Subway travel as a metaphor of the lifeblood of the city."

"Right. It's the people, the little people that keep the city going. Not the big shots."

"Exactly."

"Then how can they do it? The trains belong to them."

"The graffiti's getting to you," I said, sympathetically.

"No, that's a pain in the ass but you get used to it. Those kids are harmless. I got a nephew that's into that whole thing. I wish the hell they'd find someplace else to do their thing, but they're nothing compared to the creeps that are running the system these days. Nothing but prejudice against our people, Mendoza."

I asked Barbosa exactly what had happened and he told me that nearly a thousand new cars had arrived. "They're beautiful," he said. "Not a spot on them. Stainless steel, colorful plastic seats and a big orange D in front of them for my line. Oh, and they also have this bell that signals that the doors are gonna close. Have you seen 'em yet?" I told him I had not since I avoid subway travel as much as possible, which he doesn't know nor would I tell him for fear of hurting his feelings. He then went on to tell me that even though he had seniority on other motormen, they didn't assign a new train to him.

"Why not?" I said.

"Discrimination," he said. "'Cause I'm Puerto Rican. That's the only reason, Mendoza. Just plain discrimination. Even *morenos* with less time than me got new rigs and I got stuck with my old messed up train. I'm not saying black people are not entitled to a break. You know me. I ain't got a prejudiced bone in my body. Man, I even told them I'd be willing to take an evening trick just to handle one of the new trains, but they said no. I'm burnt up, Mendoza. I feel like blowing up the whole damn system is how I feel."

I immediately counseled Barbosa to calm down and not be hasty in his response. I said that there were legal avenues that he could explore. Perhaps he could file a grievance with his union, but he just kept shaking his head and pounding his fist into his hand, muttering and ordering one beer after the other. At the end of an hour he began laughing real loud and saying that he had the perfect solution to the problem. He patted me on the back and said goodbye.

Of course I worried about Chu Chu for three or four days because you couldn't find a nicer guy and I was worried that he would do something crazy. Every time I stopped by Florindo's Bar I'd ask for him, but no one had seen him around. Once, one of the bartenders said he had seen him in Brooklyn and that he was still working for the Transit Authority. I asked if he had gotten a new train, but the bartender didn't know. I didn't hear from Barbosa or see him again for the next six months and then I wished I hadn't.

About a week before the Fourth of July I received a call from Barbosa. He was no longer angry. In fact he sounded euphoric. This made me immediately suspicious. Perhaps he had taken up drugs as a relief from his anger.

"How you doing, Mendoza?" he said. "How's the writing going?"

"It's going, but just barely," I said. "My caboose is dragging," I added, throwing in a little railroad humor.

He let loose a big roaring belly laugh and, speaking away from the telephone, told his wife, Mercedes, what I'd said. In the background I heard his wife say, "that's nice," and I could tell she wasn't too pleased with Barbosa's condition.

"Your caboose, huh?" he said. "Well, I got just the right maintenance for that. Something to get your engine going again and stoke up that boiler with fresh fuel."

"What did you have in mind?" I said, fighting my suspicion.

"A party, Mendoza. A Fourth of July party. We're gonna celebrate our independence."

This didn't sound too strange since Barbosa believed in the American Way of Life. He was a Puerto Rican, but he loved the United States and he wasn't ashamed to admit it. He didn't go around spouting island independence and reaping the fruits of the system. His philosophy was simple. His kids spoke English, were studying here and there were more opportunities for a career in the U.S. Whatever they wanted to do on the island was their business. "I don't pay no taxes there," he'd say. "I don't live there, I don't own property there, so why should I have anything to say about what goes on. Don't get me wrong. I love the island and nobody's ever gonna let me forget I'm from P.R., but it don't make no sense for me to be a phony about where I earn my rice and beans." I personally thought it was an irresponsible political stand, but I don't meddle in how people think or feel, I simply report on what I see.

"What kind of party?" I said.

"That's a surprise, but it's gonna be a party to end all parties. Music. Food. Drink. Entertainment. Fire works. You name it, we're gonna have it."

"At your house in Brooklyn?"

"Naw, too small. Up in the Bronx. Ralph, my nephew, can come pick you up."

"I don't know," I said. "I got a backlog of stuff and I'm not too good at celebrating the independence of this country," I found myself saying, even though I like to keep politics out of my conversations. He knew that and sensed that I was simply trying to get out of it.

"Aw, com'on, Mendoza," he said. "It's gonna be great. I wouldn't be inviting you if I didn't think you'd enjoy it. I know how hard you work and what your feelings are about this whole American and Puerto Rican thing, okay? Trust me. You'll never forget this. You're gonna be proud of me. Everybody's coming. The whole clan. You never seen my family together. I don't mean just my wife and the kids, but my eight brothers and five sisters and their husbands and wives and their kids and my aunts and uncles and my parents and grandparents. And Mercedes' side of the family which is not as big but they're great. You gotta come."

I couldn't help myself asking the next question.

"Where are you holding this party, Yankee Stadium?"

"That's funny," he said, and again laughed so loud my ear hurt. "No, nothing like that. You gotta come. My niece, Zoraida, can't wait to meet you. She's a big fan of yours. She's doing her, what do you call it, to become a doctor, but not a doctor."

"Her PhD? Her doctorate."

"That's it. She's doing it on your books. She's just starting out, so she wants to talk to you and get to know you."

All of a sudden I felt flattered, even though most of what I've written doesn't amount to much. I felt myself swayed by the upcoming adulation, but I truly wish I hadn't participated in what took place between early evening on the Fourth of July and some time around four o'clock in the morning when all hell broke loose on the elevated tracks near Coney Island.

"Where is she studying?" I said.

"Some college in Michigan," Barbosa answered. "I don't know. You can ask her yourself. Ralph'll pick you up about 6:30 on July 4th, okay?"

"All right," I said, suddenly experiencing a strange feeling of foreboding about the entire matter. "But I can't stay long."

"Don't worry," Barbosa said. "Once you get up there and the party starts you can decide that."

"What does that mean?"

Barbosa laughed and said he'd see me on the Fourth.

So on the Fourth of July I got ready. I put on white pants, polished my white shoes, got out one of my *guayaberas* and my panama hat and at 6:30 that afternoon Ralph Barbosa knocked on the door and down I went to one of my infrequent social activities.

I got into the car and off we went across the Willis Avenue Bridge into the Bronx. I asked him where we were going and he replied that his uncle had told him to keep it a surprise, but that it was up near Lehman College. I relaxed for a while, but still felt that feeling that something not quite right was about to take place. Some twenty minutes later we drove under the Woodlawn Avenue elevated line tracks and into the campus of Herbert H. Lehman College. Ralph parked the car, we got out and walked to a grassy area where a number of people were seated on blankets. Around them were boxes of food and drink, ice coolers, paper plates and cups, coffee urns and several other items that indicated we were to have a picnic.

I felt relaxed at once and as I was introduced to different members of the family I noticed that there were very few men. Out of the over 100 people gathered around several trees, most of them were women and children. I asked Ralph where I could find his uncle and I was informed that Barbosa was making final preparations. I was offered a beer, which I accepted gladly, was offered a beach chair which I also accepted, and then was introduced to Zoraida Barbosa, the PhD student, a lovely, articulate young woman with a keen intellect and, unfortunately, a genuine interest in my work. So enraptured and flattered was I by her attention that more than an hour and a half passed. I then realized that the sun was going down and Barbosa still had not shown up. I once again began to worry.

Another half hour passed and now we were sitting in the dark and some of the younger children began to get restless. And then the word came that we were ready to move. "Move where?" I inquired. "It's all right, Mr. Mendoza," Zoraida said, taking my hand. "Just follow me." Such was her persuasiveness and her interest in me that I allowed her to take my hand and followed her as we crossed the grassy field. We walked for nearly a half mile until we were at the train yards. At that point I knew I was heading for a major catastrophe, but there did not seem to be any way of turning back.

I soon found out why the men had not been in attendance. I saw the plan clearly now. We were to descend into the train yards, a rather hazardous undertaking from the place where our crowd had stopped. The men, however, had constructed a staircase, complete with sturdy banisters. This staircase went up over the wall and down some fifty feet into the floor of the train yard. I followed Zoraida and as we went I looked down on the nearly forty rails below, most of them with trains on them. This was the terminal of the Independent Subway System or IND as it is popularly known, a place where trains came to be cleaned and repaired or to lay up when they were not in use. Down we went and then guided by young men with flash-lights we walked along, seemingly dangerously close to the ever present third rails until we arrived at an enclosure where a train had been parked. I suspected this was where trains were washed.

Again, utilizing a makeshift staircase I followed Zoraida as we climbed up into a train. Although the light of the flashlights being employed by the young men was sufficient for us to find our way, it was impossible to see what I had walked into. I was directed to a place on the train and asked to sit down. Expecting to find a hard surface when I sat down, I was surprised to find myself sinking into a plush armchair. Moments later I recognized Barbosa's voice asking if everyone were on board. Word came back that everyone indeed had boarded the train. Then quite suddenly the motors in the car were activated. I heard doors close and lights came on. I found myself in a typical New York Puerto Rican living room, complete with sofas, armchairs with covers, little tables with figurines, lamps, linoleum on the floor and curtains in the windows. I thought I would have a heart attack and began to get up from my chair, but at that moment the train began moving slowly out and a loud cheer went up.

I turned to Zoraida sitting on the arm of my chair and she patted my shoulder and said I shouldn't worry. A few moments later we were moving at fairly rapid rate and then the music came on, at first faintly but then as the volume was adjusted it was quite clear: Salsa, I don't know who, Machito, Tito Puente, Charlie Palmieri. I didn't care. This was outrageous. Moments later Barbosa came into our car and smiling from ear to ear greeted me.

"How do you like it?" he said, after I explained to him that my heart was nearly at the point of quitting. "It's pretty good, right? My nephew,

Ernest, he's the interior decorator, did the whole thing. Wait till you see the rest of it. It's not a new train, but it'll do."

60 I wanted to tell him that I had seen enough, but was too much in shock to protest. With an escort of his two brothers who, to my great surprise, were members of the police department undercover detective squad, we went forward as the train began picking up speed. I asked who was driving and Barbosa informed me that he had another nephew who was a motorman on the IRT Seventh Avenue line and he was doing the driving. From the living room car we moved forward into the next car, which was a control center laid out with tables, maps and computers. I was introduced to another nephew, a computer whiz working on his PhD in electrical engineering. Several young people were busily working away plotting and programming, all of it very efficient. The next car, the lead one, was laid out as an executive office with a switchboard connecting the other cars by phone. There also were several television sets and radios, all tuned to the major channels and radio station. "We're gonna monitor everything that happens," Barbosa said, and introduced me to yet another nephew, an executive from AT&T, dressed in a business suit, seated at a big desk with wood paneling on the walls around him. Off to the side a young woman was transcribing from dictaphone onto an IBM Selectric. My shock was indescribable.

We retraced our steps through the train until we came out of the living room car into the bar car. How they had managed to get a thirty foot oak bar with matching wall length mirror on the train is beyond me, but there it was, stools riveted into the floor. I was introduced all around to the men and women at the bar, all of them relatives of Barbosa and all of them grinning from ear to ear about this adventure.

"I hope you're doing the right thing," I said.

"Don't worry, Mendoza," he said. "Everything's under control."

The next car was a kitchen with six different stoves, four refrigerators, two meat lockers, cutting boards, kitchen cabinets. Here I was introduced to Monsieur Pierre Barbosa, the chef for the Lancaster Hotel, on leave especially for this occasion. Dressed in white and wearing a tall chef's hat, he greeted me warmly and invited me to taste one of his sauces. I did so and found it quite agreeable, if somewhat tart. "Too tart?" he said. I nodded and he spoke rapidly in French to one of his assistants, another Barbosa nephew who moved directly to the sauce with several condiments.

65 In the next car there was a nursery with cribs and beds for the children and a medical staff headed by Dr. Elizabeth Barbosa, a niece who was a pediatrician in Philadelphia. There were also bathrooms for ladies and gentlemen in the next car. Two cars were devoted to dining tables with linen and candlesticks, each with its own piano. The last car was the most magnificent and modern dance establishment I've ever seen. The floor gleamed and there were lights beneath it and on the ceiling colored lights were going on and off and young people were dancing. "Our disco," Barbosa said, proudly. "With D.J. Mike, my son." His oldest son

waved and Barbosa laughed. "I hope you know what you're doing," I said. "But I have to hand it to you. How did you do it?"

"This is a family, Mendoza," Barbosa said. "We'd do anything for each other."

Ten subway cars decked out for partying were moving through the Bronx, making stops but not letting anyone on, the Latin music blaring from loud speakers above four of the central cars. Every stop we made, people laughed and slapped their thighs and began dancing and very few people seemed angry that they couldn't board the train. All of them pointed at the train. I asked Barbosa why they were pointing and he explained that the train was painted. He described it but it wasn't until the following morning when the escapade came to an abrupt end that I truly was able to see what he was talking about. Each of the cars had been sprayed a different color: orange, red, yellow, pink, green, several blues, white (I think that was the nursery) and the disco which was black and even had a neon sign with the letters *El Son de Barbosa.* All along the cars in huge graffiti letters each car said *The Barbosa Express* and each one, rather than having the Transit Authority seal had BTA or Barbosa Transit Authority on it. All of them were decorated with beautiful graffiti "pieces," as I learned these expressions were called when I was introduced to Tac 121, the master "writer," as these young men and women are called. Tac 121 was in reality Victor Barbosa, another nephew, studying graphic design at Boston University.

The party began in full and we kept moving through Manhattan and then into Brooklyn and the elevated tracks. Everyone had eaten by now and it was then that all hell began to break loose. It was now close to midnight. At this point one of the dining rooms was cleared and converted into a launching pad for a tremendous fire works display. I was introduced to yet another nephew, Larry Barbosa, who was a mechanical engineer. He had managed to restructure the roof of the car so that it folded and opened, allowing his brother Bill, a member of Special Forces during the Vietnam War and a demolitions expert, to set up shop and begin firing colored rockets from the car so that as we made a wide turn before coming into the Coney Island terminal I could see the sky being lit up as the train made its way. The music was blaring and the rockets were going off in different directions so that one could see the beaches and the water in the light from the explosions.

I was exhausted and fell asleep while Zoraida was explaining her project and asking me very intricate questions about my work, details which I had forgotten with the passage of time. Two hours or so must have passed when I woke up to a great deal of shouting. I got up and went to the control car where Barbosa, dressed in his motorman's uniform, and some of his relatives were listening to news of the hijacking of a train, the announcers insinuating that the thieves had gotten the idea from the film "The Taking of Pelham 123." One of the television stations was maintaining continuous coverage with interviews of high officials of the Transit Authority, the Mayor, pedestrians, the police and sundry experts, who put forth a number of theories on why the people had commandeered the train. They even interviewed an art professor, a specialist on the graffiti culture, who explained that the creation of art on trains was an expression of youths' dissatisfaction with the rapid rate at which information was disseminated and how difficult it was to keep up with changing developments. "Using a mode of transportation to display their art," he said, "obviously keeps that art moving forward at all times and ahead of change."

In another corner a couple of young men and women were monitoring the communications from the Transit Authority.

"We gotta clear channel, Uncle Chu Chu," said one of the girls. "They wanna talk to somebody."

Barbosa sat down and spoke to some high official. I was surprised when the official asked Barbosa to identify himself and Barbosa did so, giving his name and his badge number. When they asked him what was happening, he explained how the hijackers had come to his house and kidnapped him, took him down to the train yards and forced him to drive the train or they would kill him.

"What do they want?" said the official.

"They wanna a clear track from here to the Bronx," Barbosa said. "And they want no cops around, otherwise they're gonna shoot everybody. They grabbed some women and children on the way and they look like they mean business."

"Can you identify them?"

"The women and children?"

"No, the perpetrators."

"Are you crazy or what!" shouted Barbosa, winking at me and the rest of the members of the family around him, most of whom were holding their sides to keep from laughing. "Whatta you wanna do, get me killed, or what? There's a guy holding a gun to my head and you want me to identify him?"

"Okay, okay," said the official. "I understand. Just keep your cool and do as they say. The Mayor wants to avoid any bloodshed. Do as they say. Where are you now?"

"Kings Highway," Barbosa said.

I was amazed. The train had gone to Coney Island, backed up, turned around and had made another trip to the end of the Bronx and back to Brooklyn. I looked above and saw news and police helicopters, following the train as it moved.

"Okay, we'll clear the tracks and no police," said the official. "Over and out."

"Roger, over and out," said Barbosa, clicking off the radio. He raised his hand and his nephew, leaning out of the motorman's compartment, waved and ducked back in, let go with three powerful blasts from the train whistle and then we were moving down the tracks at top speed with the music playing and the rockets going off and people dancing in every car.

"We did it, Mendoza," Barbosa said. "Son of a gun! We d-i-d-did it."

I was so tired I didn't care. All I wanted to do was go home and go to sleep. I went back in to the living room car and sat down again. When I woke up we were in the Bronx and Barbosa's relatives were streaming out of the cars carrying all their boxes and coolers with them. There were no policemen around. Zoraida Barbosa helped me out of the train and minutes later we were in Ralph's car. A half hour later I was in my apartment.

The next day there were pictures of Barbosa dressed in his uniform on the front pages of all the newspapers. The official story as it turned out was that graffiti artists had worked on the old train over a period of three or four weeks and then had kidnapped Barbosa to drive the train. Why they chose him was never revealed, but he emerged as a hero.

Unofficially, several people at the Transit Authority were convinced that Barbosa had had something to do with the "train hijacking."

A month later I was in Florindo's Bar and in walked Barbosa, happy as a lark. He bought me a beer and informed me that shortly after the train incident they had assigned him a new train and that in a year or so he was retiring. I congratulated him and told him that his niece had written again and that her dissertation on my work was going quite well. One thing still bothered me and I needed to find out.

"It doesn't matter," I said. "But who thought up the whole thing?"

"I thought up the idea, but it was my nephew Kevin, my oldest brother Joaquin's kid, who worked out the strategy and brought in all the electronic gear to tap into the MTA circuits and communication lines. He works for the Pentagon."

"He does what?" I said, looking around me to make sure no one was listening.

"The Pentagon in Washington," Barbosa repeated.

"You're kidding?" I said.

"Nope," Barbosa said. "You wanna another beer?"

"See you in the subway," said Barbosa and laughed.

"I don't think so," I said. "I gotta be going."

I walked out into the late summer evening trying to understand what it all meant. By the time I reached my apartment I knew one thing for certain. I knew that the United States of America would have to pay for passing the Jones Act in 1917,[2] giving the people automatic U.S. citizenship and allowing so many of them to enter their country.

As they say on the street: "What goes around, comes around."

---

[2] The Jones Act of 1917 granted political autonomy and American citizenship to the people of Puerto Rico, which is now a commonwealth of the United States.

Eudora Welty
(1909–   )

A WORN PATH
(1940)

It was December—a bright frozen day in the early morning. Far out in the country there was an old Negro woman with her head tied in a red rag, coming along a path through the pinewoods. Her name was Phoenix Jackson. She was very old and small and she walked slowly in the dark pine shadows, moving a little from side to side in her steps, with the balanced heaviness and lightness of a pendulum in a grandfather clock. She carried a thin, small cane made from an umbrella, and with this she kept tapping the frozen earth in front of her. This made a grave and persistent noise in the still air, that seemed meditative like the chirping of a solitary little bird.

She wore a dark striped dress reaching down to her shoe tops, and an equally long apron of bleached sugar sacks, with a full pocket: all neat and tidy, but every time she took a step she might have fallen over her shoelaces, which dragged from her unlaced shoes. She looked straight ahead. Her eyes were blue with age. Her skin had a pattern all its own of numberless branching wrinkles and as though a whole little tree stood in the middle of her forehead, but a golden color ran underneath, and the two knobs of her cheeks were illumined by a yellow burning under the dark. Under the red rag her hair came down on her neck in the frailest of ringlets, still black, and with an odor like copper.

Now and then there was a quivering in the thicket. Old Phoenix said, "Out of my way, all you foxes, owls, beetles, jack rabbits, coons and wild animals! . . . Keep out from under these feet, little bob-whites. . . . Keep the big wild hogs out of my path. Don't let none of those come running my direction. I got a long way." Under her small black-freckled hand her cane, limber as a buggy whip, would switch at the brush as if to rouse up any hiding things.

On she went. The woods were deep and still. The sun made the pine needles almost too bright to look at, up where the wind rocked. The cones dropped as light as feathers. Down in the hollow was the mourning dove—it was not too late for him.

5 The path ran up a hill. "Seem like there is chains about my feet, time I get this far," she said, in the voice of argument old people keep to use with themselves. "Something always take a hold of me on this hill—pleads I should stay."

After she got to the top she turned and gave a full, severe look behind her where she had come. "Up through pines," she said at length. "Now down through oaks."

Her eyes opened their widest, and she started down gently. But before she got to the bottom of the hill a bush caught her dress.

Her fingers were busy and intent, but her skirts were full and long, so that before she could pull them free in one place they were caught in another. It was not possible to allow the dress to tear. "I in the thorny bush," she said. "Thorns, you doing your appointed work. Never want to let folks pass, no sir. Old eyes thought you was a pretty little *green* bush."

Finally, trembling all over, she stood free, and after a moment dared to stoop for her cane.

"Sun so high!" she cried, leaning back and looking, while the thick tears went over her eyes. "The time getting all gone here."

At the foot of this hill was a place where a log was laid across the creek.

"Now comes the trial," said Phoenix.

Putting her right foot out, she mounted the log and shut her eyes. Lifting her skirt, leveling her cane fiercely before her, like a festival figure in some parade, she began to march across. Then she opened her eyes and she was safe on the other side.

"I wasn't as old as I thought," she said.

But she sat down to rest. She spread her skirts on the bank around her and folded her hands over her knees. Up above her was a tree in a pearly cloud of mistletoe. She did not dare to close her eyes, and when a little boy brought her a plate with a slice of marble-cake on it she spoke to him. "That would be acceptable," she said. But when she went to take it there was just her own hand in the air.

So she left that tree, and had to go through a barbed-wire fence. There she had to creep and crawl, spreading her knees and stretching her fingers like a baby trying to climb the steps. But she talked loudly to herself: she could not let her dress be torn now, so late in the day, and she could not pay for having her arm or her leg sawed off if she got caught fast where she was.

At last she was safe through the fence and risen up out in the clearing. Big dead trees, like black men with one arm, were standing in the purple stalks of the withered cotton field. There sat a buzzard.

"Who you watching?"

In the furrow she made her way along.

"Glad this not the season for bulls," she said, looking sideways, "and the good Lord made his snakes to curl up and sleep in the winter. A pleasure I don't see no two-headed snake coming around that tree, where it come once. It took a while to get by him, back in the summer."

She passed through the old cotton and went into a field of dead corn. It whispered and shook and was taller than her head. "Through the maze now," she said, for there was no path.

Then there was something tall, black, and skinny there, moving before her.

At first she took it for a man. It could have been a man dancing in the field. But she stood still and listened, and it did not make a sound. It was as silent as a ghost.

"Ghost," she said sharply, "who be you the ghost of? For I have heard of nary death close by."

But there was no answer—only the ragged dancing in the wind.

She shut her eyes, reached out her hand, and touched a sleeve. She found a coat and inside that an emptiness, cold as ice.

"You scarecrow," she said. Her face lighted. "I ought to be shut up for good," she said with laughter. "My senses is gone. I too old. I the oldest people I ever know. Dance, old scarecrow," she said, "while I dancing with you."

She kicked her foot over the furrow, and with mouth drawn down, shook her head once or twice in a little strutting way. Some husks blew down and whirled in streamers about her skirts.

Then she went on, parting her way from side to side with the cane, through the whispering field. At last she came to the end, to a wagon track where the silver grass blew between the red ruts. The quail were walking around like pullets, seeming all dainty and unseen.

"Walk pretty," she said. "This is the easy place. This the easy going."

She followed the track, swaying through the quiet bare fields, through the little strings of trees silver in their dead leaves, past cabins silver from weather, with the doors and windows boarded shut, all like old women under a spell sitting there. "I walking in their sleep," she said, nodding her head vigorously.

In a ravine she went where a spring was silently flowing through a hollow log. Old Phoenix bent and drank. "Sweet-gum makes the water sweet," she said, and drank more. "Nobody know who made this well, for it was here when I was born."

The track crossed a swampy part where the moss hung as white as lace from every limb. "Sleep on, alligators, and blow your bubbles." Then the track went into the road.

Deep, deep the road went down between the high green-colored banks. Overhead the live-oaks met, and it was as dark as a cave.

A black dog with a lolling tongue came up out of the weeds by the ditch. She was meditating, and not ready, and when he came at her she only hit him a little with her cane. Over she went in the ditch, like a little puff of milkweed.

Down there, her senses drifted away. A dream visited her, and she reached her hand up, but nothing reached down and gave her a pull. So she lay there and presently went to talking. "Old woman," she said to herself, "that black dog come up out of the weeds to stall you off, and now there he sitting on his fine tail, smiling at you."

A white man finally came along and found her—a hunter, a young man, with his dog on a chain.

"Well, Granny!" he laughed. "What are you doing there?"

"Lying on my back like a June-bug waiting to be turned over, mister," she said, reaching up her hand.

He lifted her up, gave her a swing in the air, and set her down. "Anything broken, Granny?"

"No sir, them old dead weeds is springy enough," said Phoenix, when she had got her breath. "I thank you for your trouble."

"Where do you live, Granny?" he asked, while the two dogs were growling at each other.

"Away back yonder, sir, behind the ridge. You can't even see it from here."

"On your way home?"

"No sir, I going to town."

"Why, that's too far! That's as far as I walk when I come out myself, and I get something for my trouble." He patted the stuffed bag he carried, and there hung down a little closed claw. It was one of the bob-whites, with its beak hooked bitterly to show it was dead. "Now you go on home, Granny!"

"I bound to go to town, mister," said Phoenix. "The time come around."

He gave another laugh, filling the whole landscape. "I know you old colored people! Wouldn't miss going to town to see Santa Claus!"

But something held old Phoenix very still. The deep lines in her face went into a fierce and different radiation. Without warning, she had seen with her own eyes a flashing nickel fall out of the man's pocket onto the ground.

"How old are you, Granny?" he was saying.

"There is no telling, mister," she said, "no telling."

Then she gave a little cry and clapped her hands and said, "Git on away from here, dog! Look! Look at that dog!" She laughed as if in admiration. "He ain't scared of nobody. He a big black dog." She whispered, "Sic him!"

"Watch me get rid of that cur," said the man. "Sic him, Pete! Sic him!"

Phoenix heard the dogs fighting, and heard the man running and throwing sticks. She even heard a gunshot. But she was slowly bending forward by that time, further and further forward, the lid stretched down over her eyes, as if she were doing this in her sleep. Her chin was lowered almost to her knees. The yellow palm of her hand came out from the fold of her apron. Her fingers slid down and along the ground under the piece of money with the grace and care they would have in lifting an egg from under a setting hen. Then she slowly straightened up, she stood erect, and the nickel was in her apron pocket. A bird flew by. Her lips moved. "God watching me the whole time. I come to stealing."

The man came back, and his own dog panted about them. "Well, I scared him off that time," he said, and then he laughed and lifted his gun and pointed it at Phoenix.

She stood straight and faced him.

"Doesn't the gun scare you?" he said, still pointing it.

"No, sir, I seen plenty go off closer by, in my day, and for less than what I done," she said, holding utterly still.

He smiled, and shouldered the gun. "Well, Granny," he said, "you must be a hundred years old, and scared of nothing. I'd give you a dime if I had any money with me. But you take my advice and stay home, and nothing will happen to you."

"I bound to go on my way, mister," said Phoenix. She inclined her head in the red rag. Then they went in different directions, but she could hear the gun shooting again and again over the hill.

She walked on. The shadows hung from the oak trees to the road like curtains. Then she smelled wood-smoke, and smelled the river, and she saw a steeple and the cabins on their steep steps. Dozens of little black children whirled around her. There ahead was Natchez shining. Bells were ringing. She walked on.

In the paved city it was Christmas time. There were red and green electric lights strung and crisscrossed everywhere, and all turned on in the daytime. Old Phoenix would have been lost if she had not distrusted her eyesight and depended on her feet to know where to take her.

She paused quietly on the sidewalk where people were passing by. A lady came along in the crowd, carrying an armful of red-, green- and silver-wrapped presents; she gave off perfume like the red roses in hot summer, and Phoenix stopped her.

"Please, missy, will you lace up my shoe?" She held up her foot.

"What do you want, Grandma?"

"See my shoe," said Phoenix. "Do all right for out in the country, but wouldn't look right to go in a big building."

"Stand still then, Grandma," said the lady. She put her packages down on the sidewalk beside her and laced and tied both shoes tightly.

"Can't lace 'em with a cane," said Phoenix. "Thank you, missy. I doesn't mind asking a nice lady to tie up my shoe, when I gets out on the street."

Moving slowly and from side to side, she went into the big building, and into a tower of steps, where she walked up and around and around until her feet knew to stop.

She entered a door, and there she saw nailed up on the wall the document that had been stamped with the gold seal and framed in the gold frame, which matched the dream that was hung up in her head.

"Here I be," she said. There was a fixed and ceremonial stiffness over her body.

"A charity case, I suppose," said an attendant who sat at the desk before her.

But Phoenix only looked above her head. There was sweat on her face, the wrinkles in her face shone like a bright net.

"Speak up, Grandma," the woman said. "What's your name? We must have your history, you know. Have you been here before? What seems to be the trouble with you?"

Old Phoenix only gave a twitch to her face as if a fly were bothering her.

"Are you deaf?" cried the attendant.

But then the nurse came in.

"Oh, that's just old Aunt Phoenix," she said. "She doesn't come for herself—she has a little grandson. She makes these trips just as regular as clockwork. She lives away back off the Old Natchez Trace." She bent down. "Well, Aunt Phoenix, why don't you just take a seat? We won't keep you standing after your long trip." She pointed.

The old woman sat down, bolt upright in the chair.

"Now, how is the boy?" asked the nurse.

Old Phoenix did not speak.

"I said, how is the boy?"

But Phoenix only waited and stared straight ahead, her face very solemn and withdrawn into rigidity.

"Is his throat any better?" asked the nurse. "Aunt Phoenix, don't you hear me? Is your grandson's throat any better since the last time you came for the medicine?"

With her hands on her knees, the old woman waited, silent, erect and motionless, just as if she were in armor.

"You mustn't take up our time this way, Aunt Phoenix," the nurse said. "Tell us quickly about your grandson, and get it over. He isn't dead, is he?"

At last there came a flicker and then a flame of comprehension across her face, and she spoke.

"My grandson. It was my memory had left me. There I sat and forgot why I made my long trip."

"Forgot?" The nurse frowned. "After you came so far?"

Then Phoenix was like an old woman begging a dignified forgiveness for waking up frightened in the night. "I never did go to school, I was too old at the Surrender,"[1] she said in a soft voice. "I'm an old woman without an education. It was my memory fail me. My little grandson, he is just the same, and I forgot it in the coming."

"Throat never heals, does it?" said the nurse, speaking in a loud, sure voice to old Phoenix. By now she had a card with something written on it, a little list. "Yes. Swallowed lye. When was it?—January—two-three years ago—"

Phoenix spoke unasked now. "No, missy, he not dead, he just the same. Every little while his throat begin to close up again, and he not able to swallow. He not get his breath. He not able to help himself. So the time come around, and I go on another trip for the soothing medicine."

"All right. The doctor said as long as you came to get it, you could have it," said the nurse. "But it's an obstinate case."

"My little grandson, he sit up there in the house all wrapped up, waiting by himself," Phoenix went on. "We is the only two left in the world. He suffer and it don't seem to put him back at all. He got a sweet

[1] Of General Robert E. Lee to General Ulysses S. Grant at the end of the Civil War, April 9, 1865.

look. He going to last. He wear a little patch quilt and peep out holding his mouth open like a little bird. I remembers so plain now. I not going to forget him again, no, the whole enduring time. I could tell him from all the others in creation."

"All right." The nurse was trying to hush her now. She brought her a bottle of medicine. "Charity," she said, making a check mark in a book.

Old Phoenix held the bottle close to her eyes, and then carefully put it into her pocket.

"I thank you," she said.

"It's Christmas time, Grandma," said the attendant. "Could I give you a few pennies out of my purse?"

"Five pennies is a nickel," said Phoenix stiffly.

"Here's a nickel," said the attendant.

Phoenix rose carefully and held out her hand. She received the nickel and then fished the other nickel out of her pocket and laid it beside the new one. She stared at her palm closely, with her head on one side.

Then she gave a tap with her cane on the floor.

"This is what come to me to do," she said. "I going to the store and buy my child a little windmill they sells, made out of paper. He going to find it hard to believe there such a thing in the world. I'll march myself back where he waiting, holding it straight up in this hand."

She lifted her free hand, gave a little nod, turned around, and walked out of the doctor's office. Then her slow step began on the stairs, going down.

FICTION CASEBOOK

This section contains the 1966 short story "Where Are You Going, Where Have You Been?" by Joyce Carol Oates, an American writer born in 1938, and the following source materials.[1]

- Oates, Joyce Carol. "When Characters from the Page Are Made Flesh on the Screen." *New York Times* 23 Mar. 1986, sec. 2:1+. An article by the author in which she discusses her feelings about the film *Smooth Talk,* based on her story.
- Schulz, Gretchen, and R. J. R. Rockwood. "In Fairyland, without a Map: Connie's Exploration Inward in Joyce Carol Oates' 'Where Are You Going, Where Have You Been?'" *Literature and Psychology* 30 (1980): 155–67. A psychological interpretation of the story from a scholarly journal.
- Tierce, Mike, and John Michael Crafton. "Connie's Tambourine Man: A New Reading of Arnold Friend." *Studies in Short Fiction* 22 (1985): 219–24. A critical interpretation of the character of Arnold Friend.
- Dylan, Bob. "It's All Over Now, Baby Blue." Los Angeles: Warner Bros., 1965. Lyrics from a popular folk song, which, according to Oates, inspired the story. (This and other Dylan songs are discussed in Tierce and Crafton's article.)
- Wegs, Joyce M. "'Don't You Know Who I Am?' The Grotesque in Oates's 'Where Are You Going, Where Have You Been?'" *Journal of Narrative Technique* 5 (1975): 66–72. An examination of the cultural context of Oates's story.

Each of these sources provides insights (sometimes contradictory ones) into the short story "Where Are You Going, Where Have You Been?" Other kinds of sources can also enrich your understanding of the work—for instance, other stories by Oates, biographical data about the author, or stories by other writers dealing with similar themes.In addition, non-print sources—such as the film *Smooth Talk*— can provide additional suggestions about how to approach the story. Although no analytical or biographical source—not even the author's comments—can give you the magical key that will unlock a story's secrets, such sources can enhance

[1] Note that some of the critical articles in this casebook were written before the current MLA documentation style was adopted. See Appendix A for current MLA format. Page references to specific editions of the Oates story have been deleted to avoid confusion.

your enjoyment and aid your understanding of a work; they can also suggest topics to explore in writing.

In preparation for writing an essay on a topic of your choice about the story "Where Are You Going, Where Have You Been?" read the story and the accompanying source materials carefully. Then consider the questions at the end of this casebook in light of what you have read. These questions are *not* presented as writing assignments but rather as springboards to a topic you can develop in a three- to five-page essay. For guidelines on evaluating literary criticism, see p. 14; for guidelines on using source materials, see Appendix A. Be sure to document any words or ideas borrowed from the story or from another source, and remember to place any words that are not your own in quotation marks.

A complete student paper, "Mesmerizing Men and Vulnerable Teens: Power Relationships in 'Where Are You Going, Where Have You Been?' and 'Teenage Wasteland,'" based on the source materials in this casebook, begins on p. 576.

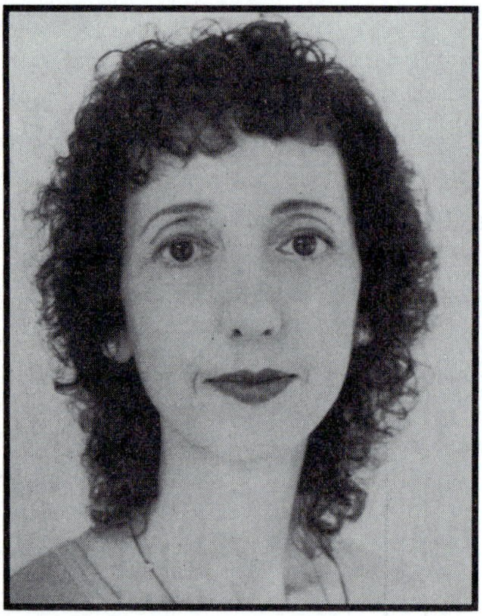

Joyce Carol Oates (1938–   ) is one of contemporary America's most prolific novelists and short story writers. Born and raised in rural Erie County, New York, Oates first gained prominence in the 1960s with publication of *A Garden of Earthly Delights* (1967), *Expensive People* (1968), and *them* (1969), which won the National Book Award. In these and other works, Oates began to explore the multilayered nature of American society—writing of urban slums, decaying rural communities, and exclusive suburbs in a dense and compellingly realistic prose style. In some of her more recent novels, including *Bellefleur* (1980) and *Mysteries of Winterthurn* (1984), Oates reveals her deep fascination with the traditions of nineteenth-century gothic writers—Edgar Allan Poe, Fyodor Dostoevski, Mary Shelley, and others. Oates's recent works include *Lock My Door upon Myself* (1990), *The Rise of Life on Earth* (1991), *Black Water* (1992), and *Foxfire* (1993).

Oates, wrote *Washington Post* critic Susan Wood, "attempts more than most of our writers . . . to explore the profound issues of evil and innocence, betrayal and revenge and atonement, as they are manifest in contemporary American experience. . . ." Although Oates frequently centers her novels around larger issues and moral questions, she can also focus on the purely personal and private worlds of her characters, as in *Black Water* (1992).

Critics responding to Oates's work have called it violent, lurid, even depraved. Yet, asks Laura Z. Hobson in a review of Oates's 1981 novel, *Angel of Light,* "Would there be such a hullabaloo about the violence in her books if they had been written by a man? From her earliest books onward, reviewers too often struck an insulting tone of surprise: *What's a nice girl like you going in a place like this?* . . . [Oates] replies that in these violent times only tales of violence have reality. Well, maybe. But the critics' preoccupation with a single facet of her work ignores everything else: her inventiveness, her insider's knowledge of college life, her evocations of nature . . . her ability to tell a story, to write a spellbinder. . . ."

Joyce Carol Oates

WHERE ARE YOU GOING, WHERE HAVE YOU BEEN?

(1966)

For Bob Dylan

Her name was Connie. She was fifteen and she had a quick nervous giggling habit of craning her neck to glance into mirrors, or checking other people's faces to make sure her own was all right. Her mother, who noticed everything and knew everything and who hadn't much reason any longer to look at her own face, always scolded Connie about it. "Stop gawking at yourself, who are you? You think you're so pretty?" she would say. Connie would raise her eyebrows at these familiar complaints and look right through her mother, into a shadowy vision of herself as she was right at that moment: she knew she was pretty and that was everything. Her mother had been pretty once too, if you could believe those old snapshots in the album, but now her looks were gone and that was why she was always after Connie.

"Why don't you keep your room clean like your sister? How've you got your hair fixed—what the hell stinks? Hair spray? You don't see your sister using that junk."

Her sister June was twenty-four and still lived at home. She was a secretary in the high school Connie attended, and if that wasn't bad enough—with her in the same building—she was so plain and chunky and steady that Connie had to hear her praised all the time by her mother and her mother's sisters. June did this, June did that, she saved money and helped clean the house and cooked and Connie couldn't do a thing, her mind was all filled with trashy daydreams. Their father was away at work most of the time and when he came home he wanted supper and he read the newspaper at supper and after supper he went to bed. He didn't bother talking much to them, but around his bent head Connie's mother kept picking at her until Connie wished her mother was dead and she herself was dead and it was all over. "She makes me want to throw up sometimes," she complained to her friends. She had a high, breathless, amused voice which made everything she said sound a little forced, whether it was sincere or not.

There was one good thing: June went places with girl friends of hers, girls who were just as plain and steady as she, and so when Connie wanted to do that her mother had no objections. The father of Connie's best girl friend drove the girls the three miles to town and left them off at a shopping plaza, so that they could walk through the stores or go to a movie, and when he came to pick them up again at eleven he never bothered to ask what they had done.

5 They must have been familiar sights, walking around that shopping plaza in their shorts and flat ballerina slippers that always scuffed the sidewalk, with charm bracelets jingling on their thin wrists; they would lean together to whisper and laugh secretly if someone passed by who amused or interested them. Connie had long dark blond hair that drew anyone's eye to it, and she wore part of it pulled up on her head and puffed out and the rest of it she let fall down her back. She wore a pull-over jersey blouse that looked one way when she was at home and another way when she was away from home. Everything about her had two sides to it, one for home and one for anywhere that was not home: her walk that could be childlike and bobbing, or languid enough to make anyone think she was hearing music in her head, her mouth which was pale and smirking most of the time, but bright and pink on these evenings out, her laugh which was cynical and drawling at home—"Ha, ha, very funny"—but high-pitched and nervous anywhere else, like the jingling of the charms on her bracelet.

Sometimes they did go shopping or to a movie, but sometimes they went across the highway, ducking fast across the busy road, to a drive-in restaurant where older kids hung out. The restaurant was shaped like a big bottle, though squatter than a real bottle, and on its cap was a revolving figure of a grinning boy who held a hamburger aloft. One night in mid-summer they ran across, breathless with daring, and right away someone leaned out a car window and invited them over, but it was just a boy from high school they didn't like. It made them feel good to be able to ignore him. They went up through the maze of parked and cruising cars to the bright-lit, fly-infested restaurant, their faces pleased and expectant as if they were entering a sacred building that loomed out of the night to give them what haven and what blessing they yearned for. They sat at the counter and crossed their legs at the ankles, their thin shoulders rigid with excitement, and listened to the music that made everything so good: the music was always in the background like music at a church service, it was something to depend upon.

A boy named Eddie came in to talk with them. He sat backwards on his stool, turning himself jerkily around in semi-circles and then stopping and turning again, and after a while he asked Connie if she would like something to eat. She said she did and so she tapped her friend's arm on her way out—her friend pulled her face up into a brave droll look—and Connie said she would meet her at eleven, across the way. "I just hate to leave her like that," Connie said earnestly, but the boy said that she wouldn't be alone for long. So they went out to his car and on the way Connie couldn't help but let her eyes wander over the windshields and faces all around her, her face gleaming with a joy that had nothing to do with Eddie or even this place; it might have been the music. She drew her shoulders up and sucked in her breath with the pure pleasure of being alive, and just at that moment she happened to glance at a face just a few feet from hers. It was a boy with shaggy black hair, in a convertible jalopy painted gold. He stared at her and then his lips widened into a grin. Connie slit her eyes at him and turned away, but she couldn't help glancing back and there he was still watching her. He wagged a finger and laughed and said, "Gonna get you, baby," and Connie turned away again without Eddie noticing anything.

She spent three hours with him, at the restaurant where they ate hamburgers and drank Cokes in wax cups that were always sweating, and then down an alley a mile or so away, and when he left her off at five to eleven only the movie house was still open at the plaza. Her girl friend was there, talking with a boy. When Connie came up the two girls smiled at each other and Connie said, "How was the movie?" and the girl said, "*You* should know." They rode off with the girl's father, sleepy and pleased, and Connie couldn't help but look at the darkened shopping plaza with its big empty parking lot and its signs that were faded and ghostly now, and over at the drive-in restaurant where cars were still circling tirelessly. She couldn't hear the music at this distance.

Next morning June asked her how the movie was and Connie said, "So-so."

10 She and that girl and occasionally another girl went out several times a week that way, and the rest of the time Connie spent around the house—it was summer vacation—getting in her mother's way and thinking, dreaming, about the boys she met. But all the boys fell back and dissolved into a single face that was not even a face, but an idea, a feeling, mixed up with the urgent insistent pounding of the music and the humid night air of July. Connie's mother kept dragging her back to the daylight by finding things for her to do or saying, suddenly, "What's this about the Pettinger girl?"

And Connie would say nervously, "Oh, her. That dope." She always drew thick clear lines between herself and such girls, and her mother was simple and kindly enough to believe her. Her mother was so simple, Connie thought, that it was maybe cruel to fool her so much. Her mother went scuffling around the house in old bedroom slippers and complained over the telephone to one sister about the other, then the other called up and the two of them complained about the third one. If June's name was mentioned her mother's tone was approving, and if Connie's name was mentioned it was disapproving. This did not really mean she disliked Connie and actually Connie thought that her mother preferred her to June because she was prettier, but the two of them kept up a pretense of exasperation, a sense that they were tugging and struggling over something of little value to either of them. Sometimes, over coffee, they were almost friends, but something would come up—some vexation that was like a fly buzzing suddenly around their heads—and their faces went hard with contempt.

One Sunday Connie got up at eleven—none of them bothered with church—and washed her hair so that it could dry all day long, in the sun. Her parents and sister were going to a barbecue at an aunt's house and Connie said no, she wasn't interested, rolling her eyes to let her mother know just what she thought of it. "Stay home alone then," her mother said sharply. Connie sat out back in a lawn chair and watched them drive away, her father quiet and bald, hunched around so that he could back the car out, her mother with a look that was still angry and not at all softened through the windshield, and in the back seat poor old June all dressed up as if she didn't know what a barbecue was, with all the running yelling kids and the flies. Connie sat with her eyes closed in the sun, dreaming and dazed with the warmth about her as if this were a kind of love, the caresses of love, and her mind slipped over onto thoughts of the boy she had been with the night before and how nice he had been, how sweet it always was, not the way someone like June would suppose but sweet, gentle, the way it was in movies and promised in songs; and when she opened her eyes she hardly knew where she was, the back yard ran off into weeds and a fence-line of trees and behind it the sky was perfectly blue and still. The asbestos "ranch house" that was now three years old startled her—it looked small. She shook her head as if to get awake.

It was too hot. She went inside the house and turned on the radio to drown out the quiet. She sat on the edge of her bed, barefoot, and listened for an hour and a half to a program called *XYZ* Sunday Jamboree, record after record of hard, fast, shrieking songs she sang along with, interspersed by exclamations from "Bobby King": "An' look here you girls at Napoleon's—Son and Charley want you to pay real close attention to this song coming up!"

And Connie paid close attention herself, bathed in a glow of slow-pulsed joy that seemed to rise mysteriously out of the music itself and lay languidly about the airless little room, breathed in and breathed out with each gentle rise and fall of her chest.

15 After a while she heard a car coming up the drive. She sat up at once, startled, because it couldn't be her father so soon. The gravel kept crunching all the way in from the road—the driveway was long—and Connie ran to the window. It was a car she didn't know. It was an open jalopy, painted a bright gold that caught the sunlight opaquely. Her heart began to pound and her fingers snatched at her hair, checking it, and she whispered "Christ. Christ," wondering how bad she looked. The car came to a stop at the side door and the horn sounded four short taps as if this were a signal Connie knew.

She went into the kitchen and approached the door slowly, then hung out the screen door, her bare toes curling down off the step. There were two boys in the car and now she recognized the driver: he had shaggy, shabby black hair that looked crazy as a wig and he was grinning at her.

"I ain't late, am I?" he said.

"Who the hell do you think you are?" Connie said.

"Toldja I'd be out, didn't I?"

20 "I don't even know who you are."

She spoke sullenly, careful to show no interest or pleasure, and he spoke in a fast bright monotone. Connie looked past him to the other boy, taking her time. He had fair brown hair, with a lock that fell onto his forehead. His sideburns gave him a fierce, embarrassed look, but so far he hadn't even bothered to glance at her. Both boys wore sunglasses. The driver's glasses were metallic and mirrored everything in miniature.

"You wanta come for a ride?" he said.

Connie smirked and let her hair fall loose over one shoulder.

"Don'tcha like my car? New paint job," he said. "Hey."

25 "What?"

"You're cute."

She pretended to fidget, chasing flies away from the door.

"Don'tcha believe me, or what?" he said.

"Look, I don't even know who you are," Connie said in disgust.

30 "Hey, Ellie's got a radio, see. Mine's broke down." He lifted his friend's arm and showed her the little transistor the boy was holding, and now Connie began to hear the music. It was the same program that was playing inside the house.

"Bobby King?" she said.

"I listen to him all the time. I think he's great."

"He's kind of great," Connie said reluctantly.

"Listen, that guy's *great*. He knows where the action is."

35 Connie blushed a little, because the glasses made it impossible for her to see just what this boy was looking at. She couldn't decide if she liked him or if he was just a jerk, and so she dawdled in the doorway and wouldn't come down or go back inside. She said, "What's all that stuff painted on your car?"

"Can'tcha read it?" He opened the door very carefully, as if he was afraid it might fall off. He slid out just as carefully, planting his feet firmly on the ground, the tiny metallic world in his glasses slowing down like gelatine hardening and in the midst of it Connie's bright green blouse. "This here is my name, to begin with," he said. ARNOLD FRIEND was written in tarlike black letters on the side, with a drawing of a round grinning face that reminded Connie of a pumpkin, except it wore sunglasses. "I wanta introduce myself, I'm Arnold Friend and that's my real name and I'm gonna be your friend, honey, and inside the car's Ellie Oscar, he's kinda shy." Ellie brought his transistor radio up to his shoulder and balanced it there. "Now these numbers are a secret code, honey," Arnold Friend explained. He read off the numbers 33, 19, 17 and raised his eyebrows at her to see what she thought of that, but she didn't think much of it. The left rear fender had been smashed and around it was written, on the gleaming gold background: DONE BY CRAZY WOMAN DRIVER. Connie had to laugh at that. Arnold Friend was pleased at her laughter and looked up at her. "Around the other side's a lot more—you wanta come and see them?"

"No."

"Why not?"

"Why should I?"

"Don'tcha wanta see what's on the car? Don'tcha wanta go for a ride?"

"I don't know."

"Why not?"

"I got things to do."

"Like what?"

"Things."

He laughed as if she had said something funny. He slapped his thighs. He was standing in a strange way, leaning back against the car as if he were balancing himself. He wasn't tall, only an inch or so taller than she would be if she came down to him. Connie liked the way he was dressed, which was the way all of them dressed: tight faded jeans stuffed into black, scuffed boots, a belt that pulled his waist in and showed how lean he was, and a white pull-over shirt that was a little soiled and showed the hard small muscles of his arms and shoulders. He looked as if he probably did hard work, lifting and carrying things. Even his neck looked muscular. And his face was a familiar face, somehow: the jaw and chin and cheeks slightly darkened, because he hadn't shaved for a day or two, and the nose long and hawk-like, sniffing as if she were a treat he was going to gobble up and it was all a joke.

"Connie, you ain't telling the truth. This is your day set aside for a ride with me and you know it," he said, still laughing. The way he straightened and recovered from his fit of laughing showed that it had been all fake.

"How do you know what my name is?" she said suspiciously.

"It's Connie."

"Maybe and maybe not."

"I know my Connie," he said, wagging his finger. Now she remembered him even better, back at the restaurant, and her cheeks warmed at the thought of how she sucked in her breath just at the moment she passed him—how she must have looked to him. And he had remembered her. "Ellie and I come out here especially for you," he said. "Ellie can sit in back. How about it?"

"Where?"

"Where what?"

"Where're we going?"

He looked at her. He took off the sunglasses and she saw how pale the skin around his eyes was, like holes that were not in shadow but instead in light. His eyes were chips of broken glass that catch the light in an amiable way. He smiled. It was as if the idea of going for a ride somewhere, to some place, was a new idea to him.

"Just for a ride, Connie sweetheart."

"I never said my name was Connie," she said.

"But I know what it is. I know your name and all about you, lots of things," Arnold Friend said. He had not moved yet but stood still leaning back against the side of his jalopy. "I took a special interest in you, such a pretty girl, and found out all about you like I know your parents and sister are gone somewheres and I know where and how long they're going to be gone, and I know who you were with last night, and your best girl friend's name is Betty. Right?"

He spoke in a simple lilting voice, exactly as if he were reciting the words to a song. His smile assured her that everything was fine. In the car Ellie turned up the volume on his radio and did not bother to look around at them.

"Ellie can sit in the back seat," Arnold Friend said. He indicated his friend with a casual jerk of his chin, as if Ellie did not count and she should not bother with him.

"How'd you find out all that stuff?" Connie said.

"Listen: Betty Schultz and Tony Fitch and Jimmy Pettinger and Nancy Pettinger," he said, in a chant. "Raymond Stanley and Bob Hutter—"

"Do you know all those kids?"

"I know everybody."

"Look, you're kidding. You're not from around here."

"Sure."

"But—how come we never saw you before?"

"Sure you saw me before," he said. He looked down at his boots, as if he were a little offended. "You just don't remember."

"I guess I'd remember you," Connie said.

"Yeah?" He looked up at this, beaming. He was pleased. He began to mark time with the music from Ellie's radio, tapping his fists lightly together. Connie looked away from his smile to the car, which was painted so bright it almost hurt her eyes to look at it. She looked at that name, ARNOLD FRIEND. And up at the front fender was an expression that was familiar—MAN THE FLYING SAUCERS. It was an expression kids had used the year before, but didn't use this year. She looked at it for a while as if the words meant something to her that she did not yet know.

"What're you thinking about? Huh?" Arnold Friend demanded. "Not worried about your hair blowing around in the car, are you?"

"No."

"Think I maybe can't drive good?"

"How do I know?"

"You're a hard girl to handle. How come?" he said. "Don't you know I'm your friend? Didn't you see me put my sign in the air when you walked by?"

"What sign?"

"My sign." And he drew an X in the air, leaning out toward her. They were maybe ten feet apart. After his hand fell back to his side the X was still in the air, almost visible. Connie let the screen door close and stood perfectly still inside it, listening to the music from her radio and the boy's blend together. She stared at Arnold Friend. He stood there so stiffly relaxed, pretending to be relaxed, with one hand idly on the door handle as if he were keeping himself up that way and had no intention of ever moving again. She recognized most things about him, the tight jeans that showed his thighs and buttocks and the greasy leather boots and the tight shirt, and even that slippery friendly smile of his, that sleepy dreamy smile that all the boys used to get across ideas they didn't want to put into words. She recognized all this and also the singsong way he talked, slightly mocking, kidding, but serious and a little melancholy, and she recognized the way he tapped one fist against the other in homage to the perpetual music behind him. But all these things did not come together.

She said suddenly, "Hey, how old are you?"

His smile faded. She could see then that he wasn't a kid, he was much older—thirty, maybe more. At this knowledge her heart began to pound faster.

80 "That's a crazy thing to ask. Can'tcha see I'm your own age?"

"Like hell you are."

"Or maybe a coupla years older, I'm eighteen."

"Eighteen?" she said doubtfully.

He grinned to reassure her and lines appeared at the corners of his mouth. His teeth were big and white. He grinned so broadly his eyes became slits and she saw how thick the lashes were, thick and black as if painted with a black tarlike material. Then he seemed to become embarrassed, abruptly, and looked over his shoulder at Ellie. "*Him,* he's crazy," he said. "Ain't he a riot, he's a nut, a real character." Ellie was still listening to the music. His sunglasses told nothing about what he was thinking. He wore a bright orange shirt unbuttoned halfway to show his chest, which was a pale, bluish chest and not muscular like Arnold Friend's. His shirt collar was turned up all around and the very tips of the collar pointed out past his chin as if they were protecting him. He was pressing the transistor radio up against his ear and sat there in a kind of daze, right in the sun.

85 "He's kinda strange," Connie said.

"Hey, she says you're kinda strange! Kinda strange!" Arnold Friend cried. He pounded on the car to get Ellie's attention. Ellie turned for the first time and Connie saw with shock that he wasn't a kid either—he had a fair, hairless face, cheeks reddened slightly as if the veins grew too close to the surface of his skin, the face of a forty-year-old baby. Connie felt a wave of dizziness rise in her at this sight and she stared at him as if waiting for something to change the shock of the moment, make it all right again. Ellie's lips kept shaping words, mumbling along with the words blasting in his ear.

"Maybe you two better go away," Connie said faintly.

"What? How come?" Arnold Friend cried. "We come out here to take you for a ride. It's Sunday." He had the voice of the man on the radio now. It was the same voice, Connie thought. "Don'tcha know it's Sunday all day and honey, no matter who you were with last night today you're with Arnold Friend and don't you forget it!—Maybe you better step out here," he said, and this last was in a different voice. It was a little flatter, as if the heat was finally getting to him.

"No. I got things to do."

90 "Hey."

"You two better leave."

"We ain't leaving until you come with us."

"Like hell I am—"

"Connie, don't fool around with me. I mean, I mean, don't fool *around,*" he said, shaking his head. He laughed incredulously. He placed his sunglasses on top of his head, carefully, as if he were indeed wearing a wig, and brought the stems down behind his ears. Connie stared at him, another wave of dizziness and fear rising in her so that for a moment he wasn't even in focus but was just a blur, standing there against his gold car, and she had the idea that he had driven up the driveway all right but had come from nowhere before that and belonged nowhere and that everything about him and even about the music that was so familiar to her was only half real.

95 "If my father comes and sees you—"

"He ain't coming. He's at a barbecue."

"How do you know that?"

"Aunt Tillie's. Right now they're—uh—they're drinking. Sitting around," he said vaguely, squinting as if he were staring all the way to town and over to Aunt Tillie's backyard. Then the vision seemed to get clear and he nodded energetically. "Yeah. Sitting around. There's your sister in a blue dress, huh? And high heels, the poor sad bitch—nothing like you sweetheart! And your mother's helping some fat woman with the corn, they're cleaning the corn—husking the corn—"

"What fat woman?" Connie cried.

100 "How do I know what fat woman. I don't know every goddam fat woman in the world!" Arnold Friend laughed.

"Oh, that's Mrs. Hornby. . . . Who invited her?" Connie said. She felt a little light-headed. Her breath was coming quickly.

"She's too fat. I don't like them fat. I like them the way you are, honey," he said, smiling sleepily at her. They stared at each other for a while, through the screen door. He said softly, "Now what you're going to do is this: you're going to come out that door. You're going to sit up front with me and Ellie's going to sit in the back, the hell with Ellie, right? This isn't Ellie's date. You're my date. I'm your lover, honey."

"What? You're crazy—"

"Yes, I'm your lover. You don't know what that is but you will," he said. "I know that too. I know all about you. But look: it's real nice and you couldn't ask for nobody better than me, or more polite. I always keep my word. I'll tell you how it is, I'm always nice at first, the first time. I'll hold you so tight you won't think you have to try to get away or pretend anything because you'll know you can't. And I'll come inside you where it's all secret and you'll give in to me and you'll love me—"

105 "Shut up! You're crazy!" Connie said. She backed away from the door. She put her hands against her ears as if she'd heard something terrible, something not meant for her. "People don't talk like that, you're crazy," she muttered. Her heart was almost too big now for her chest and its pumping made sweat break out all over her. She looked out to see Arnold Friend pause and then take a step toward the porch lurching. He almost fell. But, like a clever drunken man, he managed to catch his balance. He wobbled in his high boots and grabbed hold of one of the porch posts.

"Honey?" he said. "You still listening?"

"Get the hell out of here!"

"Be nice, honey. Listen."

"I'm going to call the police—"

110 He wobbled again and out of the side of his mouth came a fast spat curse, an aside not meant for her to hear. But even this "Christ!" sounded forced. Then he began to smile again. She watched this smile come, awkward as if he were smiling from inside a mask. His whole face was a mask, she thought wildly, tanned down onto his throat but then running out as if he had plastered make-up on his face but had forgotten about his throat.

"Honey—? Listen, here's how it is. I always tell the truth and I promise you this: I ain't coming in that house after you."

"You better not! I'm going to call the police if you—if you don't—"

"Honey," he said, talking right through her voice, "honey, I'm not coming in there but you are coming out here. You know why?"

She was panting. The kitchen looked like a place she had never seen before, some room she had run inside but which wasn't good enough, wasn't going to help her. The kitchen window had never had a curtain, after three years, and there were dishes in the sink for her to do—probably—and if you ran your hand across the table you'd probably feel something sticky there.

115 "You listening, honey? Hey?"

"—going to call the police—"

"Soon as you touch the phone I don't need to keep my promise and can come inside. You won't want that."

She rushed forward and tried to lock the door. Her fingers were shaking. "But why lock it," Arnold Friend said gently, talking right into her face. "It's just a screen door. It's just nothing." One of his boots was at a strange angle, as if his foot wasn't in it. It pointed out to the left, bent at the ankle. "I mean, anybody can break through a screen door and glass and wood and iron or anything else if he needs to, anybody at all and specially Arnold Friend. If the place got lit up with a fire honey you'd come running out into my arms, right into my arms and safe at home—like you knew I was your lover and'd stopped fooling around. I don't mind a nice shy girl but I don't like no fooling around." Part of those words were spoken with a slight rhythmic lilt, and Connie somehow recognized them—the echo of a song from last year, about a girl rushing into her boy friend's arms and coming home again—

Connie stood barefoot on the linoleum floor, staring at him. "What do you want?" she whispered.

120 "I want you," he said.

"What?"

"Seen you that night and thought, that's the one, yes sir. I never needed to look any more."

"But my father's coming back. He's coming to get me. I had to wash my hair first—" She spoke in a dry, rapid voice, hardly raising it for him to hear.

"No, your daddy is not coming and yes, you had to wash your hair and you washed it for me. It's nice and shining and all for me, I thank you, sweetheart," he said, with a mock bow, but again he almost lost his balance. He had to bend and adjust his boots. Evidently his feet did not go all the way down; the boots must have been stuffed with something so that he would seem taller. Connie stared out at him and behind him Ellie in the car, who seemed to be looking off toward Connie's right, into nothing. This Ellie said, pulling the words out of the air one after another as if he were just discovering them, "You want me to pull out the phone?"

125 "Shut your mouth and keep it shut," Arnold Friend said, his face red from bending over or maybe from embarrassment because Connie had seen his boots. "This ain't none of your business."

"What—what are you doing? What do you want?" Connie said. "If I call the police they'll get you, they'll arrest you—"

"Promise was not to come in unless you touch that phone, and I'll keep that promise," he said. He resumed his erect position and tried to force his shoulders back. He sounded like a hero in a movie, declaring something important. He spoke too loudly and it was as if he were speaking to someone behind Connie. "I ain't made plans for coming in that house where I don't belong but just for you to come out to me, the way you should. Don't you know who I am?"

"You're crazy," she whispered. She backed away from the door but did not want to go into another part of the house, as if this would give him permission to come through the door. "What do you. . . . You're crazy, you . . ."

"Huh? What're you saying, honey?"

130 Her eyes darted everywhere in the kitchen. She could not remember what it was, this room.

"This is how it is, honey: you come out and we'll drive away, have a nice ride. But if you don't come out we're gonna wait till your people come home and then they're all going to get it."

"You want that telephone pulled out?" Ellie said. He held the radio away from his ear and grimaced, as if without the radio the air was too much for him.

"I toldja shut up, Ellie," Arnold Friend said, "you're deaf, get a hearing aid, right? Fix yourself up. This little girl's no trouble and's gonna be nice to me, so Ellie keep to yourself, this ain't your date—right? Don't hem in on me. Don't hog. Don't crush. Don't bird dog. Don't trail me," he said in a rapid meaningless voice, as if he were running through all the expressions he'd learned but was no longer sure which one of them was in style, then rushing on to new ones, making them up with his eyes closed, "Don't crawl under my fence, don't squeeze in my chipmunk hole, don't sniff my glue, suck my popsicle, keep your own greasy fingers on yourself!" He shaded his eyes and peered in at Connie, who was backed against the kitchen table. "Don't mind him honey he's just a creep. He's a dope. Right? I'm the boy for you and like I said you come out here nice like a lady and give me your hand, and nobody else gets hurt, I mean, your nice old bald-headed daddy and your mummy and your sister in her high heels. Because listen: why bring them in this?"

"Leave me alone," Connie whispered.

135 "Hey, you know that old woman down the road, the one with the chickens and stuff—you know her?"

"She's dead!"

"Dead? What? You know her?" Arnold Friend said.

"She's dead—"

"Don't you like her?"

140 "She's dead—she's—she isn't here any more—"

"But don't you like her, I mean, you got something against her? Some grudge or something?" Then his voice dipped as if he were conscious of a rudeness. He touched the sunglasses perched on top of his head as if to make sure they were still there. "Now you be a good girl."

"What are you going to do?"

"Just two things, or maybe three," Arnold Friend said. "But I promise it won't last long and you'll like me that way you get to like people you're close to. You will. It's all over for you here, so come on out. You don't want your people in any trouble, do you?"

She turned and bumped against a chair or something, hurting her leg, but she ran into the back room and picked up the telephone. Something roared in her ear, a tiny roaring, and she was so sick with fear that she could do nothing but listen to it—the telephone was clammy and very heavy and her fingers groped down to the dial but were too weak to touch it. She began to scream into the phone, into the roaring. She cried out, she cried for her mother, she felt her breath start jerking back and forth in her lungs as if it were something Arnold Friend were stabbing her with again and again with no tenderness. A noisy sorrowful wailing rose all about her and she was locked inside it the way she was locked inside the house.

145 After a while she could hear again. She was sitting on the floor with her wet back against the wall.

Arnold Friend was saying from the door, "That's a good girl. Put the phone back."

She kicked the phone away from her.

"No, honey. Pick it up. Put it back right."

She picked it up and put it back. The dial tone stopped.

150 "That's a good girl. Now you come outside."

She was hollow with what had been fear, but what was now just an emptiness. All that screaming had blasted it out of her. She sat, one leg cramped under her, and deep inside her brain was something like a pinpoint of light that kept going and would not let her relax. She thought, I'm not going to see my mother again. She thought, I'm not going to sleep in my bed again. Her bright green blouse was all wet.

Arnold Friend said, in a gentle-loud voice that was like a stage voice, "The place where you came from ain't there any more, and where you had in mind to go is cancelled out. This place you are now—inside your daddy's house—is nothing but a cardboard box I can knock down any time. You know that and always did know it. You hear me?"

She thought, I have got to think. I have to know what to do.

"We'll go out to a nice field, out in the country here where it smells so nice and it's sunny," Arnold Friend said. "I'll have my arms around you so you won't need to try to get away and I'll show you what love is like, what it does. The hell with this house! It looks solid all right," he said. He ran a fingernail down the screen and the noise did not make Connie shiver, as it would have the day before. "Now put your hand on your heart, honey. Feel that? That feels solid too but we know better, be nice to me, be sweet like you can because what else is there for a girl like you but to be sweet and pretty and give in?—and get away before her people come back?"

155 She felt her pounding heart. Her hand seemed to enclose it. She thought for the first time in her life that it was nothing that was hers, that belonged to her, but just a pounding, living thing inside this body that wasn't really hers either.

"You don't want them to get hurt," Arnold Friend went on. "Now get up, honey. Get up all by yourself."

She stood.

"Now turn this way. That's right. Come over here to me—Ellie, put that away, didn't I tell you? You dope. You miserable creepy dope," Arnold Friend said. His words were not angry but only part of an incantation. The incantation was kindly. "Now come out through the kitchen to me honey and let's see a smile, try it, you're a brave sweet little girl and now they're eating corn and hotdogs cooked to bursting over an outdoor fire, and they don't know one thing about you and never did and honey you're better than them because not a one of them would have done this for you."

Connie felt the linoleum under her feet; it was cool. She brushed her hair back out of her eyes. Arnold Friend let go of the post tentatively and opened his arms for her, his elbows pointing in toward each other and his wrists limp, to show that this was an embarrassed embrace and a little mocking, he didn't want to make her self-conscious.

160 She put out her hand against the screen. She watched herself push the door slowly open as if she were safe back somewhere in the other doorway, watching this body and this head of long hair moving out into the sunlight where Arnold Friend waited.

"My sweet little blue-eyed girl," he said, in a half-sung sigh that had nothing to do with her brown eyes but was taken up just the same by the vast sunlit reaches of the land behind him and on all sides of him, so much land that Connie had never seen before and did not recognize except to know that she was going to it.

When Characters from the Page Are Made Flesh on the Screen

By Joyce Carol Oates

Some years ago in the American Southwest there surfaced a tabloid psychopath known as "The Pied Piper of Tucson." I have forgotten his name but his specialty was the seduction and occasional murder of teen-age girls. He may or may not have had actual accomplices, but his bizarre activities were known among a circle of teenagers in the Tucson area; for some reason they kept his secrets, deliberately did not inform parents or police. It was this fact, not the fact of the mass murderer himself, that struck me at the time. And this was a pre-Manson time, this was early or mid-1960's.

The "Pied Piper" mimicked teen-agers in their talk, dress and behavior, but he was not a teen-ager—he was a man in his early 30's. Rather short, he stuffed rags in his leather boots to give himself height. (And sometimes walked unsteadily as a consequence: did none among his admiring constituency notice?) He charmed his victims, to the bewilderment of others who fancy themselves free of all lunatic attractions. "The Pied Piper of Tucson": a trashy dream, a tabloid archetype, sheer artifice, comedy, cartoon—surrounded, however improbably, and finally tragically, by real people. You think that, if you look twice, he won't be there. But there he is.

I don't remember any longer where I first read about "The Pied Piper"—very likely in *Life* magazine. I do recall deliberately not reading the full article because I didn't want to be distracted by too much detail. It was not after all the mass murderer himself who intrigued me, but the disturbing fact that a number of teen-agers—from "good" families—aided and abetted his crimes. This is the sort of thing authorities and responsible citizens invariably call "inexplicable" because they can't find explanations for it. *They* would not have fallen under this maniac's spell, after all.

An early draft of my short story "Where Are You Going, Where Have You Been?"—from which the current film "Smooth Talk" has been adapted by Joyce Chopra and Tom Cole—had the rather too explicit title "Death and the Maiden." It was cast in a mode of fiction to which I am still partial—indeed, every third or fourth story of mine is probably in this mode—"realistic allegory," it might be called. It is Hawthornian, romantic, shading into parable. Like the medieval German engraving from which my title was taken the story was minutely detailed yet clearly an allegory of the fatal attractions of death (or the devil). An innocent young girl is seduced by way of her own vanity; she mistakes death for erotic romance of a particularly American/trashy sort.

In subsequent drafts the story changed its tone, its focus, its language, its title. It became "Where Are You Going, Where Have You Been?" Written at a time when the author was intrigued by the music of Bob Dylan, particularly the hauntingly elegiac song "It's All Over Now, Baby Blue," it was dedicated to Bob Dylan. The charismatic mass murderer drops into the background and his innocent victim, a 15-year-old, moves into the foreground. She becomes the true protagonist of the tale, courting and being courted by her fate, a self-styled 1950's pop figure, alternately absurd and winning.

There is no suggestion in the published story that "Arnold Friend" has seduced and murdered other young girls, or even that he necessarily intends to murder Connie. Is his interest "merely" sexual? (Nor is there anything about the complicity of other teen-agers. I saved that yet more provocative note for a current story,

"Testimony.") Connie is shallow, vain, silly, hopeful, doomed—perhaps as I saw, and still see, myself?—but capable nonetheless of an unexpected gesture of heroism at the story's end.

Her smooth-talking seducer, who cannot lie, promises her that her family will be unharmed if she gives herself to him; and so she does. The story ends abruptly at the point of her "crossing over." We don't know the nature of her sacrifice, only that she is generous enough to make it.

In adapting a narrative so spare and thematically foreshortened as "Where Are You Going, Where Have You Been?" film director Joyce Chopra and screenwriter Tom Cole were required to do a good deal of filling in, expanding, inventing. Connie's story becomes lavishly, and lovingly, textured; she is not an allegorical figure so much as a "typical" teen-age girl (if Laura Dern, spectacularly good-looking, can be so defined).

Joyce Chopra, who has done documentary films on contemporary teen-age culture, and, yet more authoritatively, has an adolescent daughter of her own, creates in "Smooth Talk" a believable world for Connie to inhabit. Or worlds: as in the original story there is Connie-at-home, and there is Connie-with-her-friends. Two 15-year-old girls, two finely honed styles, two voices, sometimes but not often overlapping. It is one of the marvelous visual features of the film that we *see* Connie and her friends transform themselves, once they are safely free of parental observation. What freedom, what joy! The girls claim their true identities in the neighborhood shopping mall!

"Smooth Talk" is, in a way, as much Connie's mother's story as it is Connie's; its center of gravity, its emotional nexus, is frequently with the mother—played by Mary Kay Place. (Though the mother's sexual jealousy of her daughter is slighted in the film.) Connie's ambiguous relationship with her affable, somewhat mysterious father (played by Levon Helm) is an excellent touch: I had thought, subsequent to the story's publication, that I should have built up the father, suggesting, as subtly as I could, an attraction there paralleling the attraction Connie feels for her seducer Arnold Friend.

Treat Williams impersonates Arnold Friend as Arnold Friend impersonates—is it James Dean? James Dean regarding himself in mirrors, doing James Dean impersonations? Laura Dern is so right as "my" Connie that I may come to think I modeled the fictitious girl on her, in the way that writers frequently delude themselves about notions of causality.

My difficulties with "Smooth Talk" have primarily to do with my chronic hesitation—a justifiable shyness, I'm sure—about seeing/hearing work of mine abstracted from its contexture of language. All writers know that language is their subject; quirky word choices, patterns of rhythm, enigmatic pauses, punctuation marks. Where the quick-scanner sees "quick" writing, the writer conceals nine-tenths of his iceberg.

Of course we all have "real" subjects, and we will fight to the death to defend these subjects, but beneath the tale-telling it is the tale-telling that grips us so very fiercely: "the soul at the *white heat*" in Emily Dickinson's words. Because of this it is always an eerie experience for me, as a writer, to hear "my" dialogue floating back to me from the external world; particularly when it is surrounded, as of course it must be, by "other" dialogue I seem not to recall having written. Perhaps a panic reaction sets in—perhaps I worry that I might be responsible for knowing what "I" meant, in writing things "I" didn't write? Like a student who has handed in work not entirely his own, and dreads interrogation from his teacher?

It is startling too to *see* fictitious characters inhabiting, with such seeming aplomb, roles that until now seemed private, flat on the page. (I don't, like many of my writing colleagues, feel affronted, thinking, "*That* isn't how he/she looks!" I think instead, guiltily, "Is *that* how he/she really looks?")

I have also had a number of plays produced and so characteristically doubtful am I about intruding into my directors' territories that I nearly always abrogate my authority to them. The writer works in a single dimension, the director works in three. I assume that they are professionals to their fingertips; authorities in their medium as I am an authority (if I am) in mine. I would fiercely defend the placement of a semicolon in one of my novels, but I would probably have deferred fairly quickly to Joyce Chopra's decision to reverse the story's ending, turn it upside-down, in a sense, so that the film ends not with death, not with a sleepwalker's crossing-over to her fate, but upon a sense of reconciliation, rejuvenation. Laura Dern's Connie is no longer "my" Connie at the film's conclusion; she is very much alive, assertive, strong-willed—a girl, perhaps, of the mid-1980's, and not of the mid-1960's.

A girl's loss of virginity, bittersweet but not necessarily tragic. Not today. A girl's coming of age that involves her succumbing to, but then rejecting, the "trashy dreams" of her pop teenage culture. "Where Are You Going, Where Have You Been?" deliberately betrays itself as allegorical in its conclusion: Death and Death's chariot (a funky souped-up convertible) have come for the Maiden. Awakening is, in the story's final lines, moving out into the sunlight where Arnold Friend waits:

"My sweet little blue-eyed girl," he said in a half-sung sigh that had nothing to do with (Connie's) brown eyes but was taken up just the same by the vast sunlit reaches of the land behind him and on all sides of him—so much land that Connie had never seen before and did not recognize except to know that she was going to it.

I quite understand that this is an unfilmable conclusion, and "Where Are You Going, Where Have You Been?" is in fact an unfilmable short story. But Joyce Chopra's "Smooth Talk" is an accomplished and sophisticated movie that attempts to do just that.

In Fairyland, without a Map: Connie's Exploration Inward in Joyce Carol Oates' "Where Are You Going, Where Have You Been?"

Gretchen Schulz
R. J. R. Rockwood

Joyce Carol Oates has stated that her prize-winning story *Where Are You Going, Where Have You Been?* (Fall, 1966) came to her "more or less in a piece" after hearing Bob Dylan's song *It's All Over Now, Baby Blue,* and then reading about a "killer in some Southwestern state," and thinking about "the old legends and folk songs of Death and the Maiden."[1] The "killer" that Miss Oates had in mind, the one on whom her character Arnold Friend is modeled, was twenty-three-year-old Charles Schmid of Tucson, Arizona. Schmid had been charged with the murders of three teen-age girls, and was the subject of a lengthy article in the March 4, 1966, issue of *Life* magazine. It is not surprising that this account should have generated mythic musings in Miss Oates—musings that culminated in a short story which has depths as mythic as any of the "old legends and folk songs." The *Life* reporter, Don Moser, himself had found in this raw material such an abundance of the reality which is the stuff of myth, that he entitled his article "The Pied Piper of Tucson."

The article states that Schmid—or "Smitty," as he was called—had sought deliberately "to create an exalted, heroic image of himself." To the teen-agers in Smitty's crowd, who "had little to do but look each other over," their leader was a "folk hero . . . more dramatic, more theatrical, more *interesting* than anyone else in their lives," and seemed to embody the very lyrics of a then popular song: "Hey, c'mon babe, follow me,/ I'm the Pied Piper, follow me,/ I'm the Pied Piper,/ And I'll show you where it's at." With a face which was "his own creation: the hair dyed raven black, the skin darkened to a deep tan with pancake make-up, the lips whitened, the whole effect heightened by a mole he had painted on one cheek," Smitty would cruise "in a golden car," haunting "all the teen-age hangouts," looking for pretty girls, especially ones with long blond hair. Because he was only five-foot-three, Smitty "habitually stuffed three or four inches of old rags and tin cans into the bottoms of his high-topped boots to make himself taller," even though the price he paid for that extra height was an awkward, stumbling walk that made people think he had "wooden feet."[2]

In his transformation into the Arnold Friend of *Where Are You Going, Where Have You Been?,* Smitty underwent the kind of apotheosis[3] which he had tried, by means of bizarre theatrics, to achieve in actuality, for Arnold is the exact transpersonal[4] counterpart of the real-life "Pied Piper of Tucson." Thus, although Arnold is a "realistic" figure, drawn from the life of a specific psychopathic killer, that superficial realism is only incidental to the more essential realism of the mythic characteristics—the archetypal qualities—he shares with the man who was his model. Asked to comment on Arnold, Miss Oates reveals that, to her, the character is *truly* mythological. No longer quite human, he functions as a personified subjective factor: "Arnold Friend," she says, "is a fantastic figure: he is Death, he is the 'elf-knight' of the ballads, he is the Imagination, he is a Dream, he is a Lover, a Demon, *and all that.*"[5]

If '*Where Are You Going, Where Have You Been?*' is a "portrait of a psychopathic killer masquerading as a teenager,"[6] it is clear that this portrait is created in the mind of Connie, the teen-age protagonist of the story, and that it exists *there only.* It is thus Connie's inner world that determines how Arnold is, or has to be, at least in her eyes, for her personal problems are so compelling that they effectively rearrange and remodel the world of objective reality. Arnold Friend's own part in the creation of his image—whether he deliberately set about to become the "fantastic" figure he is, or seems to be, as his model, Smitty, did—Miss Oates ignores altogether. She is interested only in Connie, Arnold's young victim, and in how Connie's psychological state shapes her perceptions. We find—as we might expect with a writer who characterizes the mode in which she writes as "psychological realism"[7]—that the "fantastic" or mythological qualities of Arnold Friend (and of all those in the story) are presented as subjective rather than objective facts, aspects of the transpersonal psyche projected outward, products of the unconscious mental processes of a troubled adolescent girl.

Toward Arnold Friend, and what he represents, Connie is ambivalent: she is both fascinated and frightened. She is, after all, at that confusing age when a girl feels, thinks, and acts both like a child, put off by a possible lover, and like a woman, attracted to him. Uncertain how to bridge the chasm between "home" and "anywhere that was not home," she stands—or wavers—at the boundary between childhood and adulthood, hesitant and yet anxious to enter the new world of experience which is opening before her:

> Everything about her had two sides to it, one for home and one for anywhere that was not home: her walk, which could be childlike and bobbing, or languid enough to make anyone think she was hearing music in her head; her mouth, which was pale and smirking most of the time, but bright and pink on these evenings out; her laugh, which was cynical and drawling at home—"Ha, ha, very funny,"—but high-pitched and nervous anywhere else, like the jingling of the charms on her bracelet.[8]

That her laugh is "high-pitched and nervous" when she is "anywhere that was not home" betrays the fact that Connie, like all young people, needs help as she begins to move from the past to the future, as she begins the perilous inward journey towards maturity. This journey is an essential part of the adolescent's search for personal identity, and though it is a quest that he must undertake by himself, traditionally it has been the responsibility of culture to help by providing symbolic maps of the territory through which he will travel, territory that lies on the other side of consciousness.

Such models of behavior and maps of the unknown are generally provided by the products of fantasy—myth, legend, and folklore. Folk fairy tales have been especially useful in this way. In his book, *The Uses of Enchantment: The Meaning and Importance of Fairy Tales* (1976), Bruno Bettelheim argues that children's fairy tales offer "symbolic images" that suggest "happy solutions"[9] to the problems of adolescence. Indeed, Joyce Carol Oates herself has Hugh Petrie, the caricaturist in her novel *The Assassins* (1975) observe that "fairy tales are analogous to life as it is lived in the family."[10] In her fiction both short and long Miss Oates makes frequent use of fairy tale material. Again and again she presents characters and situations which parallel corresponding motifs from the world of folk fantasy. And never is this more true than in the present story—never in all the eight novels and eleven collections of short stories which she has written at last count. Woven into the complex texture of *Where Are You Going, Where Have You Been?* are motifs from such tales as *The Spirit in the Bottle, Snow White, Cinderella, Sleeping Beauty, Rapunzel, Little Red Riding Hood,* and *The Three Little Pigs.*[11] *The Pied Piper of Hamelin,* which ends tragically and so according to Bettelheim does not qualify as a proper fairy tale,[12] serves as the "frame device" that contains all the other tales.

There is a terrible irony here, for although the story is full of fairy tales, Connie, its protagonist, is not. Connie represents an entire generation of young people who have grown up—or tried to—without the help of those bedtime stories which not only entertain the child, but also enable him vicariously to experience and work through problems which he will encounter in adolescence. The only "stories" Connie knows are those of the sexually provocative but superficial lyrics of the popular songs she loves or of the equally insubstantial movies she attends. Such songs and movies provide either no models of behavior for her to imitate, or dangerously inappropriate ones. Connie has thus been led to believe that life and, in particular, love will be "sweet, gentle, the way it was in the movies and promised in songs." She has no idea that life actually can be just as grim as in folk fairy tales. The society that is depicted in *Where Are You Going, Where Have You Been?* has failed to make available to children like Connie maps of the unconscious such as fairy tales provide, because it has failed to recognize that in the unconscious past and future coalesce,[13] and that, psychologically, where the child is going is where he has already been. Since Connie has been left—in the words of yet another of the popular songs—to "wander through that wonderland alone"—it is small wonder, considering her lack of spiritual preparation, that Connie's journey there soon becomes a terrifying schizophrenic separation from reality, with prognosis for recovery extremely poor.

The fact that the Oates story, like the magazine article which inspired it, is framed around the motif of the Pied Piper is significant, for this device serves to fix blame for the catastrophe which the story describes. The motif suggests that the adults of Connie's world have made the same mistake as the Burghers[14] of Hamelin seven centuries before: having failed to live up to their moral obligations by refusing to "pay the piper," they themselves—albeit unknowingly—have unleashed the very force which will prove destructive to their children. What kind of force this is, and its particular implications for Connie, we can understand more clearly by interpreting the symbolism underlying the fate of the legendary children of Hamelin: led outside the comfortable sanity of their walled city, the children disappear into that emblem of the devouring unconscious, the Koppenberg ('head mountain'), victims, we would say, of an acute, collective psychosis. Assuming that the eternal patterns recur, each time as though for the first and last time, then this will be Connie's fate too, and her own psychosis will likewise have no remission. Certainly Arnold Friend is such that Connie cannot keep from following him, perhaps because in following him she is following the popular music she loves, music with which he is not only closely identified, but of which he is the personification. Thus, when Connie, "hearing music in her head," wanders into the bottle-shaped drive-in restaurant, charmed by "the music that made everything so good: the music . . . always in the background, like music at a church service," it is there that she first sees him. He later arrives at her house with a transistor radio which is playing "the same program that was playing inside the house," a program which leaves Connie feeling "bathed in a glow of slow-pulsed joy that seemed to rise mysteriously out of the music itself." Arnold even talks in a "simple lilting voice, exactly as if he were reciting the words to a song." There are many more passages of this kind, but let these suffice to show that Arnold is, indeed, depicted as a Pied Piper, incarnated by society's refusal to live up to its cultural obligation to provide what is needed to help the adolescent make it safely through to adulthood.

The help provided by fairy tales proper is such that a child can learn to compensate even when adult society makes errors of the gravest sort, capping with a happy ending a situation which might otherwise prove tragic for the child. Accordingly, the force which lures all save one of the unwitting children of Hamelin to their psychological death in the Koppenberg[15] is identical to that which the child is taught to tame in the fairy tale *Spirit in the Bottle.* For Connie, the "bottle" is the drive-in restaurant where the teen-agers hang out, a restaurant "shaped like a big bottle, though squatter than a real bottle . . . [and] on its cap a revolving figure of a grinning boy holding a hamburger aloft." The boy on the bottle-cap reminds us of "the boy named Eddie" inside the restaurant who, appropriately, sits *eddying* on his stool, "turning himself jerkily around in semicircles and then stopping and turning back again," motion which suggests that bottled up sexual pressures are building, ever more insistent in their demand for release. Eddie takes Connie off for some petting, some rubbing that arouses her sexuality, too, until in her mind his face dissolves "into a single face that was not even a face but an idea, a feeling, mixed up with the urgent insistent pounding of the music and the humid night air of July." On this same visit to the restaurant Connie arouses Arnold Friend, who wags his finger at her, laughs, and says, "'Gonna get you, baby'," and who at this moment reveals that he is not only the Pied Piper, but also that hostile spirit in the bottle which is described in the fairy tale.

When the woodcutter's son discovers *his* mysterious bottle and releases a spirit which likewise threatens to destroy *him,* he manages to entrap the spirit once again, agreeing to release it only when it agrees to share its special powers with him, powers which enable the boy to become the "greatest physician in the land." As in the fairy tale, Connie has uncorked the bottle, but because she is unacquainted with this part of the psyche, she is not equipped to recognize the grinning boy atop the bottle-cap or the laughing Arnold Friend as a potentially destructive force which must be controlled if it is to make a positive contribution to her personality. What complicates the attempt to control this force is that it disguises itself as mere sexuality, as is evident from the fairy tale in the fact that the bottle is clearly phallic and the boy's handling of it masturbatory: if we consider that what leads to the boy's taking flight and finding the bottle is his father's belittling him for incompetence at chopping wood, we can say that, psychologically, the boy is seeking compensation in an eroticised flood of negative content from the unconscious. Bettelheim points out that a fairy tale like *Spirit in the Bottle* deals with two problems that confront the child as he struggles to establish a sense of identity: parental belittlement, and integration of a divided personality.[16] In Connie's case, her mother's belittling remarks that "Connie couldn't do a thing, her mind was all filled with trashy daydreams," certainly have contributed to Connie's two-sidedness, with her one personality "for home" and another for "anywhere that was not home," a division also apparent in the relationship between Connie and the "girl friend" who accompanies her to the bottle-shaped restaurant—the two are so poorly differentiated as to suggest a mere *doubling* of Connie, rather than two separate individuals. While such personality division may at first glance seem pathological, it is not, according to Bettelheim, necessarily abnormal, since "the manner in which the child can bring some order into his world view is by dividing everything into opposites," and that "in the later oedipal[17] and post oedipal ages, this splitting extends to the child himself."[18] In *Spirit in the Bottle,* the degraded hero, reacting to the anguish of being regarded by his parent as stupid and incompetent, withdraws into himself, undergoes a split into positive and negative aspects, de-energizes the negative (as represented by the spirit that comes out of the bottle), and then successfully reintegrates his personality, achieving a durable and socially productive synthesis. Had Connie been familiar with this fairy tale, she would have known that however deplorable her situation might seem at a given moment, the means toward an eventual happy solution is in learning to interact with the unconscious in such a way as to emulate the woodcutter's son, who, *by asserting rational control over the terms of the spirit's release into consciousness,* is able to demonstrate to himself and the world that he is not only wiser and better than his parent, but positively the "greatest physician in the land."

Knowledge of this tale alone, however, would not suffice, for it is merely a beginning: to be assured of safe passage through what Bettelheim terms "that thorniest of thickets, the oedipal period,"[19] a child like Connie would need to have absorbed the wisdom of the other fairy tales to which Miss Oates alludes, tales such as *Snow White, Cinderella, Rapunzel,* and *Little Red Riding Hood.* By their applicability to Connie's situation, these tales reveal that at its deepest level Connie's most compelling psychological problem is *unresolved oedipal conflict, aggravated by sibling rivalry.*

Suggestive of *Snow White* is Connie's "habit of craning her neck to glance into mirrors, or checking other people's faces to make sure her own was all right" (as though other people's faces were mirrors, too); and we are told also that her mother, "who noticed everything and knew everything"—as though with the wicked queen's magic power—"hadn't much reason any longer to look at her own face," and so was jealous of her daughter's beauty and "always after Connie." Arnold Friend's sunglasses also mirror everything, which means that, in this instance, he personifies the Magic Mirror, and, of course, he finds Connie the fairest one of all. In his words, "Seen you that night and thought, that's the one, yes sir, I never needed to look anymore." Though he thus serves as Prince, there is a hint of the dwarf motif in Arnold's short stature and obvious phallicism; and most particularly is this true of his friend, Ellie Oscar, a case of arrested development, whose face is that of a "forty-year-old baby." Connie's "Someday My Prince Will Come" daydreams, plus the many references to how dazed and sleepy she always is, especially the day Arnold comes for her, when she "lay languidly about the airless little room" and "breathed in and breathed out with each gentle rise and fall of her chest"—these, too, suggest *Snow White* and, for that matter, *Sleeping Beauty,* whose heroine in the Brothers Grimm is, like Connie, fifteen.

The oedipal implications of *Snow White* are evident in the fact that, as Bettelheim points out, the queen's Magic Mirror speaks not with the mother's but the daughter's voice, revealing the jealous child's own sense of inferiority and frustration projected onto her mother. The father's romantic feelings for the daughter are never at issue in such a fairy tale, and he is generally depicted as weak, ineffectual, and oblivious to the struggle that ensues between mother and daughter[20]—exactly as in Miss Oates' story:

> Their father was away at work most of the time and when he came home he wanted supper and he read the newspaper at supper and after supper he went to bed. He didn't bother talking much to them, but around his bent head Connie's mother kept picking at her until Connie wished her mother was dead and she herself was dead and it was all over.

It would be difficult to find a more striking emblem of mother-daughter oedipal conflict than in this passage, where the second death wish serves as punishment for the first.

Bettelheim observes that whenever the child's feeling of "degradation" is the result of "oedipal entanglement of father and daughter," the "Cinderella" theme emerges.[21] Unlike *Snow White,* however, *Cinderella* centers on the "agonies and hopes which form the essential content of sibling rivalry . . . [since] 'having lived among the ashes' was a symbol of being debased in comparison to one's siblings."[22] In this case, the relationship between Connie and her sister June is a classical statement of the pattern:

> Her sister June was twenty-four and still lived at home. She was a secretary in the high school Connie attended, and if that wasn't bad enough—with her in the same building—she was so plain and chunky and steady that Connie had to hear her praised all the time by her mother and her mother's sisters. June did this, June did that. . . .

Although grown up, June has not only not left home, but, in a sense, she is still in high school: this suggests that June is an even greater victim of oedipal entanglement than Connie—or, to put it another way, that June is Connie projected nine years into the future. What we have is thus a feminine version of the tale *Two Brothers* in which the personality is split between "striving for independence and self-assertion" (Connie) and "the opposite tendency to remain safely home, tied to the parents" (June).[23] Implied also is the dichotomy underlying *Sinbad the Seaman and Sinbad the Porter,* in which the former character represents the "pleasure-oriented id" (Connie) and the latter the "reality-oriented ego" (June).[24] In this instance the ego is oriented toward the reality of permanent oedipal fixation, and therefore constitutes a negative personality, conforming to the Jungian concept of the *shadow*.[25] Perhaps the saddest commentary on the situation in Miss Oates' story is the fact that the personality receiving positive reinforcement is Connie's shadow: "If June's name was mentioned her mother's tone was approving, and if Connie's name was mentioned it was disapproving."

The theme of debasement with respect to one's siblings is, of course, not the only link between this story and *Cinderella*. Connie, with her other personality for "anywhere that was not home," suggests *Cinderella*, too, especially in the magical transformation from child to woman which she undergoes on her nights out. The description of the drive-in restaurant, with its music, and the boys with whom the girls pair up, and their feeling that the event is a wonderful experience which must end too soon—all of this brings to mind Cinderella's ball, particularly since it is here that Connie meets Arnold Friend, her "Prince Charming." And it is this meeting which sends him seeking her out and finding her, barefoot, in the kitchen. Certainly the "convertible jalopy painted gold" suggests *Cinderella*, though in the fairy tale it is Cinderella herself who has the "convertible" vehicle. This gold-painted car reminds us of a royal chariot, too, especially with the horn sounding as though to announce the arrival of royalty when the car comes up Connie's drive. Still more obvious in its reference to the fairy tale is the drawing on the car of "a round, grinning face that reminded Connie of a pumpkin, except it wore sunglasses" and was signed "ARNOLD FRIEND." It is also pertinent that Arnold proclaims that he has come to take her away, and that, as he talks, Connie notices "He had the voice of the man on the radio now," a man who has been mentioned several times, whose name suggests royalty epitomized, a man called "Bobby King."

If Connie is Cinderella, she is also, by virtue of her "long dark blond hair that drew anyone's eye to it," Rapunzel. On the day of Arnold's arrival, Connie "washed her hair so that it could dry all day long in the sun." At the first sound of the car, "her fingers snatched at her hair, checking it, and she whispered, 'Christ. Christ,' wondering how she looked." While she talks with Arnold, she makes the most of her hair: "Connie smirked and let her hair fall loose over one shoulder." Later, frightened by the desire she has aroused in him, she argues that her father is coming back to the house for her, that she has had to wash her hair in preparation for his return, but Arnold says, "No, your daddy is not coming and yes, you had to wash your hair and you washed it for me. It's nice and shining and all for me. I thank you sweetheart." Again, at the very end of the story, Connie watches "this body and this head of long hair moving out into the sunlight where Arnold Friend waited." It is obvious that Connie's *crowning glory* is, indeed, her hair, that she uses it to draw boys to her, among them Arnold Friend, and that Arnold, like the Prince in the fairy tale, takes her away from a place where she feels "locked inside." The fact that in the fairy tale the Prince is temporarily blinded by thorns when he falls from the tower where Rapunzel is locked is perhaps echoed in Arnold's peculiar eyes, "like holes . . . like chips of broken glass," which he covers with those dark glasses.

Why Arnold Friend is conjured up when it is, as she claims, her father that Connie is waiting for, becomes clear if we consider that Arnold, the Prince of *Snow White, Sleeping Beauty, Cinderella,* and *Rapunzel,* is also the Big Bad Wolf of *Little Red Riding Hood,* a tale which, according to Bettelheim, "deals with the daughter's unconscious wish to be seduced by her father (the wolf)."[26] If Arnold represents an erotic transformation of Connie's father, then this suggests that Connie's oedipal death-wish for her mother has undergone psychological realization. This in turn sheds light on that curious conversation between Arnold and Connie concerning "that old woman down the road" whom Connie insists is dead ("'She's dead—she's—she isn't here any more—'"), but about whom Arnold says "'But don't you like her, I mean, you got something against her? Some grudge or something?'" Connie's overreaction, so revealing in its guilt and terror, tells us that she has displaced onto the "old woman" the homicidal impulses unconsciously intended for her mother, an indiscretion for which she is already punishing herself through Arnold Friend. Bettelheim observes that when Little Red Riding Hood is swallowed up by the wolf, she is being "punished for arranging for the wolf to do away with a mother figure."[27]

Since one of Arnold's more lupine[28] characteristics is his *hairiness,* it is odd, though appropriate psychologically, considering that Arnold is experienced as a transformation of her "nice old bald-headed daddy," that Connie cannot keep from seeing "as a wig" Arnold's shaggy, shabby, black hair." But Arnold's hairiness is not the only sign that Connie's daddy-substitute is wolvish. He also has trouble standing and moving about, which suggests a four-footed animal masquerading as a man. When he first gets out of his car, he moves "carefully, planting his feet firmly on the ground." Later, he stands "in a strange way, leaning back against the car as if he were balancing himself." Later still, "He wobble[s] in his high boots and grab[s] hold of one of the porch posts." No wonder Connie has the uneasy feeling that "his feet do not go all the way down" into those boots as they should. Then, of course, there are Arnold's teeth, so "big and white," and his way of "sniffing" at Connie as though "she were a treat he was going to gobble up." What could be more reminiscent of the Wolf in *Little Red Riding Hood?* And we should add that Arnold's talk of tearing Connie's house down reminds us of the Wolf in *The Three Little Pigs,* also. When Connie tries to lock the screen, Arnold says:

> "But why lock it . . . It's just a screen door. It's just nothing . . . I mean, anybody can break through a screen door and glass and wood and iron or anything else if he needs to, anybody at all, and specially Arnold Friend. If the place got lit up with a fire, honey, you'd come runnin' out into my arms."

Later, in a statement that accurately epitomizes Connie's entire situation, he says: "'This place you are now—inside your daddy's house—is nothing but a cardboard box I can knock down any time. You know that and always did know it'."

If the structure of Connie's life—and of her psyche—were not, indeed, as flimsy as cardboard, she might be able to deal with Arnold Friend even as Beauty deals with the Beast who is *her* daddy-substitute; she might learn to love him for himself and so transform him into a Prince again. But Connie lacks the familial and psychic strength which allows Beauty and her love to mature.[29] She is still just as "little" as Little Red Riding Hood. And, as we shall see, her confrontation with "the Beast"—with the wolvish Arnold Friend—makes her more childlike, not less; she regresses to what Bettelheim describes as a "more primitive, earlier form of existence,"[30] as Red Riding Hood does under similar circumstances. Of course, "in typical fairy-story fashion" Red Riding Hood's regression is "impressively exaggerated." She goes all the way back to "the pre-birth existence in the womb" when she is swallowed by the Wolf (an act which has sexual significance, too). And she must then be cut from that "womb" by the Woodcutter, to emerge as a "born again" Red Riding Hood, a child who has learned that she is a child and still too young to deal with the Wolf.[31] Miss Oates is not free to exaggerate so fantastically, but she can and does suggest that Connie's psychological experience parallels Red Riding Hood's—in all respects save one. In Connie's case, Arnold Friend is the Woodcutter as well as the Wolf.

Connie begins to regress to a more childlike state as soon as she realizes that Arnold is more Wolf than Prince, more interested in animal sex than happy-ever-after romance. When he suddenly announces, "'I'm your lover. You don't know what that is yet but you will'," she is frightened, and when he proceeds to explain "what that is" in some detail, she is more frightened still. Her flirtatious words and gestures give way to the frantic words and gestures of a child—and a very young child at that: "'Shut up! You're crazy!' Connie said. . . . She put her hands up against her ears as if she'd heard something terrible, something not meant for her. 'People don't talk like that, you're crazy,' she muttered." Furthermore, while she is saying this, she "back[s] away from the door," and so backs away from that symbolic threshold between "home" and "not home," childhood and womanhood, where she has been hovering ever since Arnold arrived. She has not locked the door, though, and when she remembers that fact and tries to do so, with fingers clumsy as a child's, she fails. A "wave of dizziness and fear" has left her sweating, "panting," "shaking"—utterly unable to save herself from the Wolf. Of course, we must not forget that this Wolf actually embodies Connie's own sexual impulses, a fact which implies that her childlike inability to save herself from him is complicated by a womanly desire to give herself to him. And, indeed, the very portions of the text which suggest that Connie is feeling like a terrified child simultaneously suggest that she is feeling like a woman thoroughly aroused by Arnold Friend and the sex he offers. The "wave of dizziness," the sweating, "panting," and "shaking" all characterize a woman well on the way to orgasm.

Connie's progression towards orgasm and her regression towards the womb both reach their climax in that decidedly schizophrenic moment when she tries to call her mother on the telephone. Miss Oates describes it thus:

> . . . she ran into the back room and picked up the telephone. Something roared in her ear, a tiny roaring, and she was so sick with fear that she could do nothing but listen to it—the telephone was clammy and very heavy and her fingers groped down to the dial but were too weak to touch it. She began to scream into the phone, into the roaring. She cried out, she cried for her mother, she felt her breath start jerking back and forth in her lungs as if it were something Arnold Friend was stabbing her with again and again with no tenderness. A noisy sorrowful wailing rose all about her and she was locked inside it the way she was locked inside this house.
>
> After a while she could hear again. She was sitting on the floor with her wet back against the wall.

If the spasms which set Connie's "breath . . . jerking back and forth" as if Arnold were "stabbing her . . . again and again" suggest that she is experiencing something like the moment of climax in the sexual act, they also indicate that she is succumbing to sexual appetite exactly as Red Riding Hood does when she climbs into bed with the Wolf. Of course, Red Riding Hood is seeking the safety of a mother-figure's arms, the safety of a womb, not sex. This is true of Connie, too. The little girl in her is acting littler all the time, and now, more like a baby than a child, she is crying for her mother, trying to reach her mother through the umbilical-like cord on a phone she has forgotten how to use. She cannot reach her mother, but she does manage to reach the momentary safety of a womb of sorts. The lines which suggest that she is experiencing something like orgasm also suggest that she is experiencing something like birth—but in reverse. The description of the "breath . . . jerking back and forth in her lungs" in spasms that set her "wailing" reminds us of the moment of birth; and it is followed by a description that makes Connie sound like an unborn baby (rather than a newborn one), for she collapses into an unconscious and embryonic heap on the floor of the house where she feels "locked inside," even as a baby is "locked inside" a womb.

Connie does not stay in that "womb," however. The child in Connie may want to stay there, but the woman in Connie wants to be born. And the same spasms that suggest a birth-in-reverse suggest a birth-in-progress, too, a birth in which the two Connies who have thus far existed together in the one

Connie, with the woman "locked inside" the womb of the child, are finally torn apart. As the story moves towards its conclusion, we note that the child who has thus become mother of the woman feels "hollow." She feels as if her "heart" and "body" are not "really hers" any more. They belong to that womanly part of her which now seems to be someone else entirely—someone who pushes her way out of the womb-like house where she has spent her formative years even as she has pushed her way out of the womb of the child:

> She put out her hand against the screen. She watched herself push the door slowly open as if she were back safe somewhere inside the house . . . watching this body and this head of long hair moving out into the sunlight where Arnold Friend waited.

Arnold Friend has not had to pull Connie out of the womb with the physical force which the Woodcutter uses in the fairy tale. We should remember that he has threatened to use such physical force if necessary, but his psychological force (as an embodiment of Connie's own impulses) proves to be more than sufficient to ensure that the birth takes place, whether the embryonic woman is really ready to be born or not.

Of course she is not ready to be born—despite the fact that it is only as a newborn that brown-eyed Connie can be Arnold's "sweet little blue-eyed girl." Connie has not developed enough to survive in the world outside the womb—in the world outside the conscious personality—and it is not surprising that she gazes upon this world in utter bewilderment: "—so much land that Connie had never seen before and did not recognize except to know that she was going to it."[32] Had she been nurtured on fairy tales instead of popular songs and movies she would not feel at such a loss; she would have "been" to this world before, through the vicarious experience offered by fairy tales, and she would have some sense of how to survive there now. Connie lacks the benefit of such experience, however, and even Arnold Friend appears to realize how that lack has hampered her development. He certainly speaks to the supposed woman as though she were still a child: "'Now, turn this way. That's right. Come over here to me. . . . and let's see a smile, try it, you're a brave, sweet little girl'." How fatherly he sounds. And how like the Woodcutter. But we know that he is still the Wolf, and that he still intends to "gobble up" this "little girl" as soon as he gets the chance. Connie is not going to live happily ever after. Indeed, it would seem that she is not going to live at all. She simply does not know how. She is stranded in Fairyland, without a map.[33]

Notes

[1] "Interview with Joyce Carol Oates about *Where Are You Going, Where Have You Been?"* in *Mirrors: An Introduction to Literature,* ed. John R. Knott, Jr., and Christopher R. Keaske, 2nd ed. (San Francisco: Canfield Press, 1975), pp. 18–19.

[2] Don Moser, "The Pied Piper of Tucson," *Life,* 60, no. 9 (March 4, 1966), 18–19, 22–24, 80c–d.

[3] The raising of a human to divine status—Ed.

[4] Going beyond the individual or personal—Ed.

[5] Interview in *Mirrors,* p. 19. For a perceptive analysis of Arnold Friend as a demonic figure, a subject which will not be developed here, see Joyce M. Wegs, "Don't You Know Who I Am?" The Grotesque in Oates's 'Where Are You Going, Where Have You Been?'," *The Journal of Narrative Technique,* 5 (January 1975), 66–72.

[6] Wegs, p. 69.

[7] Joyce Carol Oates, "Preface," *Where Are You Going, Where Have You Been?: Stories of Young America* (Greenwich, CT: Fawcett Publications, 1974), p. 10.

[8] Joyce Carol Oates, "Where Are You Going, Where Have You Been?," *Where Are You Going, Where Have You Been?: Stories of Young America* (Greenwich, CT: Fawcett Publications, 1974), p. 13. All further references are to this edition of the story and will appear in the text of the essay. The story was originally published in *Epoch,* Fall 1966. It has since been included in *Prize Stories: The O. Henry Awards* 1968; in *The Best American Short Stories of 1967;* and in a collection of Oates' stories, *The Wheel of Love* (New York: Vanguard Press, 1970; Greenwich, CT: Fawcett Publications, 1972). The story is also being anthologized with increasing frequency in collections intended for use in the classroom, such as Donald McQuade and Robert Atwan, *Popular Writing in America: The Interaction of Style and Audience* (New York: Oxford University Press, 1974).

[9] Bruno Bettelheim, *The Uses of Enchantment: The Meaning and Importance of Fairy Tales* (New York: Alfred A. Knopf, 1976), p. 39.

[10] Joyce Carol Oates, *The Assassins* (New York: Vanguard Press, 1975), p. 378.

[11] At the MLA convention in New York, on December 26, 1976, I got a chance to ask Joyce Carol Oates if the many allusions to various fairy tales in *Where Are You Going, Where Have You Been?* were intentional. She replied that they were. (Gretchen Schulz)

[12] Bettelheim, n. 34, p. 316.

[13] Grow together; unite—Ed.

[14] Townspeople—Ed.

[15] According to the legend, one of the children of Hamelin does survive, though against his will. He is a *lame* boy who falls so far behind the other children that before he can reach the opening into the Koppenberg, it closes, swallowing all but himself. Psychologically, the boy's "lameness" can be interpreted as an unconscious protective mechanism which is capable of thwarting the boy's conscious will, thus saving him from destruction. This is protection exactly of the sort that properly internalized fairy tales provide,

and its chief advantage is that it is not subject to the ego's often erring judgment, since it operates beyond the effective jurisdiction of consciousness.

[16] Bettelheim, pp. 66 ff.; n. 6, pp. 311–312; and *passim.*

[17] Refers to ages from about 3 to 6 when a child often has sexual feelings toward the parent of the opposite sex, while fearing the parent of the same sex as a rival—Ed.

[18] Bettelheim, p. 74.

[19] Bettelheim, p. 73.

[20] Bettelheim, pp. 207, 114.

[21] Bettelheim, p. 245.

[22] Bettelheim, p. 236.

[23] Bettelheim, p. 91.

[24] Bettelheim, p. 85.

[25] C. G. Jung, *The Archetypes and the Collective Unconscious,* 2nd ed., and *Aion,* 2nd ed., Collected Works of C. G. Jung, Vol. IX, pts. I & II (Princeton, NJ: Princeton University Press, 1968), *passim.*

[26] Bettelheim, p. 175.

[27] Bettelheim, p. 172.

[28] Wolfish.

[29] Bettelheim, pp. 303–309, *passim.*

[30] Bettelheim, p. 180.

[31] Bettelheim, p. 180.

[32] There is a fascinating and, it seems, rather significant echo between this line and the passage in Hemingway's *The Snows of Kilimanjaro,* where at the moment of his death from gangrene, Harry imagines that the overdue plane that was to take him to the hospital in Arusha arrives, and shortly after taking off with Harry aboard, turns to the left (away from Arusha), and heads instead for the summit of Mt. Kilimanjaro: "Then they began to climb and they were going to the East it seemed, and then it darkened and they were in a storm, the rain so thick it seemed like flying through a waterfall, and then they were out and Compie (the pilot) turned his head and grinned and pointed and there, ahead, all he could see, as wide as all the world, great, high, and unbelievably white in the sun, was the square top of Kilimanjaro. *And then he knew that there was where he was going* [italics mine]." Ernest Hemingway, "The Snows of Kilimanjaro," *The Fifth Column and the First Forty-nine Stories* (New York: Charles Scribner's Sons, 1938), p. 174.

[33] Concerning the plight of the Connie's of the world, Bettelheim states thus: ". . . unfed by our common fantasy heritage, the folk fairy tale, the child cannot invent stories on his own which help him cope with life's problems. All the stories he can invent are just expressions of his own wishes and anxieties. Relying on his own resources, all the child can imagine are elaborations of where he presently is, since he cannot know where he needs to go, or how to go about getting there" (pp. 121–122).

Connie's Tambourine Man: A New Reading of Arnold Friend

Mike Tierce and John Michael Crafton

The critical reception of Joyce Carol Oates' "Where Are You Going, Where Have You Been?" reveals a consistent pattern for reducing the text to a manageable, univocal[1] reading. Generally, this pattern involves two assumptions: Arnold *must* symbolize Satan and Connie *must* be raped and murdered. No critic has yet questioned Joyce Wegs' assertion that "Arnold is clearly a symbolic Satan."[2] Marie Urbanski argues that Arnold's "feet resemble the devil's cloven hoofs," Joan Winslow calls the story "an encounter with the devil," Tom Quirk maintains the story describes a "demoniac character," and Christina Marsden Gillis refers to "the satanic visitor's incantation."[3] Wegs' assertion that Arnold is "a criminal with plans to rape and probably murder Connie"[4] is also accepted at face value. Gillis assumes that Arnold "leads his victim . . . to a quick and violent sexual assault,"[5] and Quirk refers to "the rape and subsequent murder of Connie."[6] Even though Gretchen Schulz and R. J. R. Rockwood correctly claim that the portrait of Arnold "is created in the mind of Connie . . . and that it exists *there only,*" they still persist in having Arnold as a demon and Connie as doomed: "But we know that he is still the Wolf, and that he still intends to 'gobble up' this 'little girl' as soon as he gets the chance. Connie is not going to live happily ever after. Indeed, it would seem that she is not going to live at all."[7]

While all of these critics insist on seeing satanic traces in Arnold, they refuse, on the other hand, to see that these traces are only part of a much more complex, more dynamic symbol. There are indeed diabolic shades to Arnold, but just as Blake and Shelley could see in Milton's Satan[8] a positive, attractive symbol of the poet, the rebellious embodiment of creative energy, so we should also be sensitive to Arnold's multifaceted and creative nature. Within the frame of the story, the fiction of Arnold burns in the day as the embodiment of poetic energy. The story is dedicated to Bob Dylan, the troubadour, the artist. Friend is the artist, the actor, the rhetorician, the teacher, all symbolized by Connie's overheated imagination. We should not assume that Arnold is completely evil because she is afraid of him. Her limited perceptions remind us of Blake's questioner in "The Tyger" who begins to perceive the frightening element of the experiential world but also is rather duped into his fear by his own limitations. Like the figure in Blake, Connie is the framer, the story creator—and the diabolic traces in her fiction frighten her not because they are the manifestations of an outside evil but because they are the symbolic extrapolations of her own psyche.

If the adamant insistence that Arnold Friend is Satan is rejected, then who is this intriguing mysterious visitor? In *Enter Mysterious Stranger: American Cloistral Fiction,* Roy Male asserts that many mysterious intruders throughout American literature "are almost always potential saviors, destroyers, or ambiguous combinations of both, and their initial entrance, however much it may be displaced toward realism, amounts to the entrance of God or the devil on a machine."[9] And if Arnold Friend is *not* satanic, then his arrival could be that of a savior. This possibility moreover is suggested by Connie's whispering "Christ. Christ"[10] when Arnold first arrives in his golden "machine." Not only is "33" part of Arnold's "secret code" of numbers, but his sign, an "X" that seems to hover in the air, is also one of the symbols for Christ. Because music is closely associated with religion—"the music was always in the background, like music at a church service"—it also adds a religious element to Arnold's arrival. The key question then is who is this musical messiah, and the key to the answer is the dedication "For Bob Dylan"—the element of the story so unsatisfactorily accounted for by our predecessors. Not only does the description of Arnold Friend also fit Bob Dylan—a type of rock-and-roll messiah—but three of Dylan's songs (popular when the story was written) are very similar to the story itself.

In the mid-sixties Bob Dylan's followers perceived him to be a messiah. According to his biographer, Dylan was "a rock-and-roll king."[11] It is no wonder then that Arnold speaks with "the voice of the man on the radio," the disc jockey whose name, Bobby King, is a reference to "Bobby" Dylan, the "king" of rock-and-roll. Dylan was more than just a "friend" to his listeners; he was "Christ revisited," "the prophet leading [his followers] into [a new] Consciousness."[12] In fact, "people were making him an idol; . . . thousands of men and women, young and old, felt their lives entwined with his because they saw him as a mystic, a messiah who would lead them to salvation."[13]

That Oates consciously associates Arnold Friend with Bob Dylan is clearly suggested by the similarities of their physical descriptions. Arnold's "shaggy, shabby black hair that looked crazy as a wig," his "long and hawklike nose," his unshavened face, his "big and white" teeth, his lashes, "thick and black as if painted with a black tarlike material" and his size ("only an inch or so taller than Connie") are all characteristic of Bob Dylan. Even Arnold's "fast, bright monotone voice" is suggestive of Dylan, especially since he speaks "in a simple lilting voice, exactly as if he were reciting the words to a song."

Dylan then provides a physical model for Arnold's appearance and a historical referent for Arnold's existence. Yet more profoundly, the myth of Dylan's being organized or somehow controlled by his music is reflected by Connie, Arnold, and Ellie being organized or perhaps even unified by the almost mystical music heard throughout the story. Connie, for example, notices the way Arnold "tapped one fist against another in homage to the perpetual music behind him." Since this "perpetual music" is the one thing that Connie can "depend upon," it even becomes her breath of life; she is "bathed in a glow of slow-pulsed joy that seemed to rise mysteriously out of the music itself, . . . breathed in and breathed out with each gentle rise of her chest." Paying "close attention" to the words and singing along with the songs played on the "*XYZ* Sunday Jamboree," Connie spends her Sunday afternoon worshiping "the music that made everything so good." And when her two visitors arrive, "the same program . . . playing inside the house" is also playing on Ellie Oscar's radio. In fact, "the music from [Connie's] radio and [Ellie's] blend together." Ellie is so closely associated with the radio that without it pressed up against his ear, he grimaces "as if . . . the air was too much for him." Both Ellie's and Arnold's existences seem to depend completely on the "perpetual music"; consequently, Oates appears to be suggesting that they are not literally present. They are instead part of Connie's musically induced fantasy—another of her so-called "trashy daydreams."

Oates points out that Connie spends her summer "thinking, dreaming of the boys she met." But because of Connie's gradually changing desires, "all the boys fell back and dissolved into a single face that was not even a face but an idea, a feeling, mixed up with the urgent insistent pounding of the music." This "urgent" feeling reflects Connie's desire for something more sexually stimulating than the kissing sessions she spends with "boys" like Eddie. As Freud points out, "the motive forces of phantasies are unsatisfied wishes, and every single phantasy is the fulfillment of a wish, a correlation of unsatisfying realty. . . . In young women the erotic wishes predominate almost exclusively."[14] Although we acknowledge the sexist nature of Freud's generalization, his point seems to apply to Connie. Furthermore, Roy Male suggests that even though "there is no logical reason for the entrance of a stranger, it is equally true that he comes as if in answer to some unuttered call." Arnold is described as "talking right through Connie's voice" because that is the only voice he has. His arrival is the answer to Connie's "unuttered" call and to her "erotic" desires. Arnold's "face" is therefore "familiar" because it is the "face" that replaces the "boys" in her fantasies. Not only is the emphasis placed on Arnold's face reinforced by "a drawing of a round grinning face" on his car, but when Connie first encounters Arnold at Napolean's drive-in restaurant, he is described as "a face just a few feet from hers"—perhaps her own distorted reflection in a car windshield.

Connie not only turns away from Arnold's face "without Eddie noticing anything," but many other elements in the story suggest that Arnold is just another "shadowy vision of [Connie] herself." For example,

Arnold is described as being "just a blur . . . that . . . had come from nowhere . . . and belonged nowhere and that everything about him . . . was only half real." His "fake" laughter suggests that his threatening presence is "all a joke." He opens the door to his car carefully because it might fall off, he cannot walk without stumbling, his feet seem not to be in his boots, and he wears a mask and make-up. He even touches his sunglasses "as if to make sure they were still there." He also magically knows Connie's name, her best friend's name, her other friends' names, and where her parents are and when they will return. Part of the action that takes place also suggests a dream-like experience. Arnold's asking Connie if she has something against a dead woman, Connie's inability to dial the telephone, and Arnold's promise not to come into the house are all tinged with a sense of unreality. Even the fact that the phrase "as if" is used over thirty times suggests that there is something dubious about Connie's experience.

In order to reinforce the idea that Arnold's visit is another fantasy, Oates parallels the actual description of one of Connie's other daydreams to the description of her finally joining Arnold Friend at the story's end:

> Connie sat with her eyes closed in the sun, dreaming and dazed with the warmth about her as if this were a kind of love, the caresses of love, and her mind slipped over onto thoughts of the boy she had been with the night before and how nice he had been, how sweet it always was, not the way someone like June would suppose but sweet, gentle, the way it was in movies and promised in songs; and when she opened her eyes she hardly knew where she was, the back yard ran off into weeds and a fence-like line of trees and behind it the sky was perfectly blue and still. The asbestos "ranch house" that was now three years old startled her—it looked small. She shook her head as if to get awake.
>
> "My sweet little blue-eyed girl," he said in a half-sung sigh that had nothing to do with her brown eyes but was taken up just the same by the vast sunlit reaches of the land behind him and on all sides of him—so much land that Connie had never seen before and did not recognize except to know that she was going to it.

The fence-like line of trees is replaced by "the vast sunlit reaches of the land" surrounding Arnold Friend. Through her encounter with this mysterious stranger, Connie frees herself from the sense of confinement she feels in her father's house. As Roy Male so aptly explains it, the "mysterious strangers who are potential saviors" force the "insider" to undergo a transformation, which "may involve the effort of the insider to break out of his fixed orientation."[15] The Dylanesque music initiates such a breakthrough for Connie. She no longer has to "dawdle in the doorway." As Dylan suggests in "Mister Tambourine Man," once she answers the call by forcing open the screen door, "there are no fences facin'" her any longer. She broadens her horizons to include the "vast sunlit reaches of the land" all around her.

The reference to "Mister Tambourine Man" implies another connection between the story and Dylan. A few of his song lyrics are very similar to the story itself. Oates herself suggests that part of the story's inspiration was "hearing for some weeks Dylan's song 'It's All Over Now, Baby Blue.'"[16] Such lines as "you must leave now," "something calls for you," "the vagabond who's rapping at your door," and "go start anew" are suggestive of the impending change awaiting Connie. Two other Dylan songs are equally as applicable though. The following lines from "Like a Rolling Stone"—the second most popular song of 1965 (the story was first published in 1966)—are also very similar to Connie's situation at the end of the story:

> You used to be so amused
> At Napoleon in rags and the
> language that he used
> Go to him now, he calls you, you
> can't refuse
> When you got nothing, you got
> nothing to lose
> You're invisible now, you got no
> secrets to conceal.

But Dylan's "Mr. Tambourine Man"—the number ten song in 1965—is even more similar. The following stanza establishes the notion of using music to rouse one's imagination into a blissful fantasy world:

> Take me on a trip upon your magic
> swirlin' ship,
> My senses have been stripped,
> My hands can't feel to grip,
> My toes too numb to step,
> Wait only for my boot heels to be
> wanderin'.
> I'm ready to go anywhere,
> I'm ready for to fade
> Into my own parade.
> Cast your dancin' spell my way,
> I promise to go under it.
> Hey, Mister Tambourine Man, play a
> song for me,
> I'm not sleepy and there ain't no
> place I'm going to.
> Hey, Mister Tambourine Man, play a
> song for me.
> In the jingle, jangle morning I'll
> come followin' you.

Arnold Friend's car—complete with the phrase "MAN THE FLYING SAUCERS"—is just such "a magic swirlin' ship." Arnold is the personification of popular music, particularly Bob Dylan's music; and as such, Connie's interaction with him is a musically induced fantasy, a kind of "magic carpet ride" in "a convertible jalopy painted gold." Rising out of Connie's radio, Arnold Friend/Bob Dylan is a magical, musical messiah; he persuades Connie to abandon her father's house. As a manifestation of her own desires, he frees her from the limitations of a fifteen-year-old girl, assisting her maturation by stripping her of her childlike vision.

Notes

[1] Having only one meaning.

[2] Joyce M. Wegs, "'Don't You Know Who I Am?' The Grotesque in Oates's 'Where Are You Going, Where Have You Been?'" in *Critical Essays on Joyce Carol Oates,* ed. Linda W. Wagner (Boston: G. K. Hall, 1979), p. 90. First printed in *Journal of Narrative Technique,* 5 (1975), 66–72.

[3] Marie Urbanski, "Existential Allegory: Joyce Carol Oates' 'Where Are You Going, Where Have You Been?'" *Studies in Short Fiction,* 15 (1978), p. 202; Joan Winslow, "The Stranger Within: Two Stories by Oates and Hawthorne," *Studies in Short Fiction,* 17 (1980), p. 264; Tom Quirk, "A Source for 'Where Are You Going, Where Have You Been?'" *Studies in Short Fiction,* 18 (1981), p. 416; Christina Marsden Gillis, "'Where Are You Going, Where Have You Been?': Seduction, Space, and a Fictional Mode," *Studies in Short Fiction,* 18 (1981), p. 70.

[4] Wegs, p. 89.

[5] Gillis, p. 65.

[6] Quirk, p. 416.

[7] Gretchen Schulz and R. J. R. Rockwood, "In Fairyland, without a Map: Connie's Exploration Inward in Joyce Carol Oates' 'Where Are You Going, Where Have You Been?'" *Literature and Psychology,* 30 (1980), pp. 156 & 165 & 166, respectively.

[8] In *Paradise Lost,* Milton clearly intends Satan to be a symbol of archetypal evil. Blake and Shelley, as true Romantics, saw in their predecessor's portrait of Lucifer a duality that embodied positive as well as negative traits.

[9] Roy Male, *Enter Mysterious Stranger: American Cloistral Fiction* (Norman: University of Oklahoma Press, 1979), p. 21.

[10] Joyce Carol Oates, "Where Are You Going, Where Have You Been?" in *The Wheel of Love* (New York: Vanguard Press, 1970), p. 40. Hereafter cited parenthetically within the text.

[11] Anthony Scaduto, *Bob Dylan* (New York: Grosset and Dunlop, 1971), p. 222.

[12] Scaduto, p. 274.

[13] Scaduto, p. 229.

[14] Sigmund Freud, "Creative Writers and Day-Dreamers," in *Criticism: The Major Statements,* ed. Charles Kaplan (New York: St. Martin's Press, 1975), p. 468.

[15] Male, p. 10.

[16] "Interview with Joyce Carol Oates about 'Where Are You Going, Where Have You Been?'" in *Mirrors: An Introduction to Literature,* eds. John R. Knott, Jr., and Christopher R. Keaske, 2d ed. (San Francisco: Canfield Press, 1975), pp. 18–19.

IT'S ALL OVER NOW, BABY BLUE

Bob Dylan

You must leave now, take what you need you think will last
But whatever you wish to keep, you better grab it fast
Yonder stands your orphan with his gun
Crying like a fire in the sun.
Look out, the saints are comin' through
And it's all over now, baby blue.

The highway is for gamblers, better use your sins
Take what you have gathered from coincidence
The empty-handed painter from your streets
Is drawing crazy patterns on your sheets
This sky too is folding under you
And it's all over now, baby blue.

All your seasick sailors they are rowing home
Your empty-handed army men are going home
The lover who has just walked out your door
Has taken all his blankets from the floor
The carpet too is moving under you
And it's all over now, baby blue.

Leave your stepping stones behind, something calls for you
Forget the dead you've left, they will not follow you
The vagabond who's rapping at your door
Is standing in the clothes that you once wore
Strike another match, go start anew
And it's all over now, baby blue.

"Don't You Know Who I Am?" The Grotesque in Oates's "Where Are You Going, Where Have You Been?"

Joyce M. Wegs

Joyce Carol Oates's ability to absorb and then to transmit in her fiction the terror which is often a part of living in America today has been frequently noted and admired. For instance, Walter Sullivan praises her skill by noting that "horror resides in the transformation of what we know best, the intimate and comfortable details of our lives made suddenly threatening."[1] Although he does not identify it as such, Sullivan's comment aptly describes a classic instance of a grotesque intrusion: a familiar world suddenly appears alien. Oates frequently evokes the grotesque in her fiction, drawing upon both its traditional or demonic and its contemporary or psychological manifestations.[2] In the prize-winning short story, "Where Are You Going, Where Have You Been?", Oates utilizes the grotesque in many of its forms to achieve a highly skillful integration of the multiple levels of the story and, in so doing, to suggest a transcendent reality which reaches beyond surface realism to evoke the simultaneous mystery and reality of the contradictions of the human heart. Full of puzzling and perverse longings, the heart persists in mixing lust and love, life and death, good and evil. Oates's teenage protagonist, Connie, discovers that her dream love-god also wears the face of lust, evil and death.

Centering the narrative on the world of popular teenage music and culture, Oates depicts the tawdry world of drive-in restaurants and shopping plazas blaring with music with a careful eye for authentic surface detail. However, her use of popular music as a thematic referent is typical also of her frequent illumination of the illusions and grotesquely false values which may arise from excessive devotion to such aspects of popular culture as rock music, movies, and romance magazines. In all of her fiction as in this story, she frequently employs a debased religious imagery to suggest the gods which modern society has substituted for conventional religion. Oates delineates the moral poverty of Connie, her fifteen-year-old protagonist, by imaging a typical evening Connie spends at a drive-in restaurant as a grotesquely parodied religious pilgrimage. Left by her friend's father to stroll at the shopping center or go to a movie, Connie and her girlfriend immediately cross the highway to the restaurant frequented by older teenagers. A grotesque parody of a church, the building is bottle-shaped and has a grinning boy holding a hamburger aloft on top of it. Unconscious of any ludicrousness, Connie and her friend enter it as if going into a "sacred building"[3] which will give them "what haven and blessing they yearned for." It is the music which is "always in the background, like music at a church service" that has invested this "bright-lit, fly-infested" place with such significance. Indeed, throughout the story the music is given an almost mystical character, for it evokes in Connie a mysterious pleasure, a "glow of slow-pulsed joy that seemed to rise mysteriously out of the music itself."

Although the story undoubtedly has a moral dimension,[4] Oates does not take a judgmental attitude toward Connie. In fact, much of the terror of the story comes from the recognition that there must be thousands of Connies. By carefully including telltale phrases, Oates demonstrates in an understated fashion why Connies exist. Connie's parents, who seem quite typical, have disqualified themselves as moral guides for her. At first reading, the reader may believe Connie's mother to be concerned about her daughter's habits, views, and friends; but basically their arguments are little more than a "pretense of exasperation, a sense that they . . . [are] tugging and struggling over something of little value to either of them." Connie herself is uncertain of her mother's motives for constantly picking at her; she alternates between a view that her mother's harping proceeds from jealousy of Connie's good looks now that her own have faded and a feeling that her mother really prefers her over her plain older sister June because she is prettier. In other words, to Connie and her mother, real value lies in beauty. Connie's father plays a small role in her life, but by paralleling repeated phrases, Oates suggests that this is precisely the problem. Because he does not "bother talking much" to his family, he can hardly ask the crucial parental questions, "Where are you going?" or "Where have you been?" The moral indifference of the entire adult society is underscored by Oates's parallel description of the father of Connie's friend, who also "never . . . [bothers] to ask" what they did when he picks up the pair at the end of one of their evenings out. Similarly, on Sunday morning, "none of them bothered with church," not even that supposed paragon, June.

Since her elders do not bother about her, Connie is left defenseless against the temptations represented by Arnold Friend. A repeated key phrase emphasizes her helplessness. As she walks through the parking lot of the restaurant with Eddie, she can not "help but" look about happily, full of joy in a life characterized by casual pickups and constant music. When she sees Arnold in a nearby car, she looks away, but her instinctive flirtatiousness triumphs and she can not "help but" look back. Later, like Lot's wife leaving Sodom and Gomorrah,[5] she cannot "help but look back" at the plaza and drive-in as her friend's father drives them home. In Connie's case, the consequences of the actions she can not seem to help are less biblically swift to occur and can not be simply labeled divine retribution.

Since music is Connie's religion, its values are hers also. Oates does not include the lyrics to any popular songs here, for any observer of contemporary America could surely discern the obvious link between Connie's high esteem for romantic love and youthful beauty and the lyrics of scores of hit tunes. The superficiality of Connie's values becomes terrifyingly apparent when Arnold Friend, the external embodiment of the teenage ideal celebrated in popular songs, appears at Connie's home in the country one Sunday afternoon when she is home alone, listening to music and drying her hair. It is no accident that Arnold's clothes, car, speech, and taste in music reflect current teenage chic almost exactly, for they constitute part of a careful disguise intended to reflect Arnold's self-image as an accomplished youthful lover.

Suspense mounts in the story as the reader realizes along with Connie that Arnold is not a teenager and is really thirty or more. Each part of his disguise is gradually revealed to be grotesquely distorted in some way. His shaggy black hair, "crazy as a wig," is evidently really a wig. The masklike appearance of his face has been created by applying a thick coat of makeup; however, he has carelessly omitted his throat. Even his eyelashes appear to be made-up, but with some tarlike material. In his clothing, his disguise appears more successful, for Connie approves of the way he dresses, as "all of them dressed," in tight jeans, boots, and pullover. When he walks, however, Connie realizes that the runty Arnold, conscious that the ideal teenage dream lover is tall, has stuffed his boots; the result is, however, that he can hardly walk and staggers ludicrously. Attempting to bow, he almost falls. Similarly, the gold jalopy covered with teenage slang phrases seems authentic until Connie notices that one of them is no longer in vogue. Even his speech is not his own, for it recalls lines borrowed from disc jockeys, teenage slang, and lines from popular songs. Arnold's strange companion, Ellie Oscar, is just as grotesque as Arnold. Almost totally absorbed in listening to music and interrupting this activity only to offer threatening assistance to Arnold, Ellie is no youth either; he has the "face of a forty-year-old baby." Although Arnold has worked out his disguise with great care, he soon loses all subtlety in letting Connie know of his evil intentions; he is not simply crazy but a criminal with plans to rape and probably to murder Connie.

However, Arnold is far more than a grotesque portrait of a psychopathic killer masquerading as a teenager; he also has all the traditional sinister traits of that arch-deceiver and source of grotesque terror, the devil. As is usual with Satan, he is in disguise; the distortions in his appearance and behavior suggest not only that his identity is faked but also hint at his real self. Equating Arnold and Satan is not simply a gratuitous connection designed to exploit traditional demonic terror, for the early pages of the story explicitly prepare for this linking by portraying popular music and its values as Connie's perverted version of religion. When Arnold comes up the drive, her first glance makes Connie believe that a teenage boy with his jalopy, the central figure of her religion, has arrived; therefore, she murmurs "Christ. Christ" as she wonders about how her newly-washed hair looks. When the car—a parodied golden chariot?—stops, a horn sounds "as if this were a signal Connie knew." On one level, the horn honks to announce the "second coming" of Arnold, a demonic Day of Judgment.[6] Although Connie never specifically recognizes Arnold as Satan, her first comment to him both hints at his infernal origins and faithfully reproduces teenage idiom: "Who the *hell* do you think you are?" (emphasis mine). When he introduces himself, his name too hints at his identity, for "friend" is uncomfortably close to "fiend"; his initials could well stand for Arch Fiend. The frightened Connie sees Arnold as "only half real": he "had driven up her driveway all right but had come from nowhere before that and belonged nowhere." Especially supernatural is his mysterious knowledge about her, her family, and her friends. At one point, he even seems to be able to see all the way to the barbecue which Connie's family is attending and to get a clear vision of what all the guests are doing. Typical of his ambiguous roles is his hint that he had something to do with the death of the old woman who lived down the road. It is never clear whether Arnold has killed her, has simply heard of her death, or knows about it in his devil role of having come to take her away to hell. Although Arnold has come to take Connie away, in his traditional role as evil spirit, he may not cross a threshold uninvited; he repeatedly mentions that he is not going to come in after Connie, and he never does. Instead, he lures Connie out to him. Part of his success may be attributed to his black magic in having put his sign on her—X for victim. Because the devil is not a mortal being, existing as he does in all ages, it is not surprising that he slips in remembering what slang terms are in vogue. Similarly, his foolish attempt at a bow may result from a mixup in temporal concepts of the ideal lover. In addition, his clumsy bow may be due to the fact that it must be difficult to manipulate boots if one has cloven feet!

Although Oates attempts to explain the existence of Connie, she makes no similar effort to explain the existence of Arnold, for that would constitute an answer to the timeless and insoluble problem of evil in the world. As this story shows, Oates would agree with Pope Paul VI's recent commentary on the "terrible reality" of evil in the world, but she would not, I feel sure, endorse his view of this evil as being literally embodied in a specific being. Pope Paul describes evil as "not merely a lack of something, but an effective agent, a living spiritual being, perverted and perverting. A terrible reality. Mysterious and frightening."[7] Oates's description of her own views on religion is in terms strikingly similar to the language used by Pope Paul. To her, religion is a "kind of psychological manifestation of deep powers, deep imaginative, mysterious powers, which are always with us, and what has in the past been called supernatural. I would prefer simply to call natural. However, though these things are natural, they are still inaccessible and cannot be understood, cannot be controlled."[8] Thus, although Arnold is clearly a symbolic Satan, he also functions on a psychological level.

On this level, Arnold Friend is the incarnation of Connie's unconscious erotic desires and dreams, but in uncontrollable nightmare form. When she first sees Arnold in the drive-in, she instinctively senses his sinister attraction, for she cannot "help glancing back" at him. Her "trashy daydreams" are largely filled with blurred recollections of the caresses of the many boys she has dated. That her dreams are a kind of generalized sexual desire—although Connie does not consciously identify them as such—is made evident by Oates's description of Connie's summer dreams: "But all the boys fell back and dissolved into a single face that was not even a face but an idea, a feeling, mixed up with the urgent insistent pounding of the music and the humid night air of July." What is frightening about Arnold is that he voices and makes explicit her own sexual desires; teenage boys more usually project their similar message with "that sleepy dreamy smile that all the boys used to get across ideas they didn't want to put into words." Connie's reaction to his bluntness is one of horror: "People don't talk like that, you're crazy."

Connie's fear drives her into a grotesque separation of mind from body in which her unconscious self takes over and betrays her. Terror-stricken, she cannot even make her weak fingers dial the police; she can only scream into the phone. In the same way that she is Arnold's prisoner, locked inside the house he alternately threatens to knock down or burn down, she is also a prisoner of her own body: "A noisy sorrowful wailing rose all about her and she was locked inside it the way she was locked inside this house." Finally, her conscious mind rejects any connection with her body and its impulses; her heart seems "nothing that was hers" "but just a pounding, living thing inside this body that wasn't really hers either." In a sense, her body with its puzzling desires "decides" to go with Arnold although her rational self is terrified of him: "She watched herself push the door slowly open as if she were back safe somewhere in the other doorway, watching this body and this head of long hair moving out into the sunlight where Arnold Friend waited."

Oates encourages the reader to look for multiple levels in this story and to consider Arnold and Connie at more than face value by her repeated emphasis on the question of identity. The opening of the story introduces the concept to which both Connie and her mother seem to subscribe—being pretty means being someone. In fact, her mother's acid questions as she sees Connie at her favorite activity of mirror-gazing—"Who are you? You think you're so pretty?"—also introduce the converse of this idea, namely, that those who lack physical beauty have no identity. As does almost everything in the story, everything about Connie has "two sides to it." However, Connie's nature, one for at home and one for "anywhere that was not home," is simple in comparison to that of Arnold. Connie's puzzled questions at first query what role Arnold thinks he is playing: "Who the hell do you think you are?" Then she realizes that he sees himself all too literally as the man of her dreams, and she becomes more concerned about knowing his real identity. By the time that Arnold asks, "Don't you know who I am?" Connie realizes that it is no longer a simple question of whether he is a "jerk" or someone worth her attention but of just how crazy he is. By the end she knows him to be a murderer, for she realizes that she will never see her family again. However, only the reader sees Arnold's Satan identity. Connie's gradual realization of Arnold's identity brings with it a recognition of the actual significance of physical beauty: Arnold is indeed someone to be concerned about, even if he is no handsome youth. At the conclusion Connie has lost all identity except that of victim, for Arnold's half-sung sigh about her blue eyes ignores the reality of her brown ones. In Arnold's view, Connie's personal identity is totally unimportant.

Dedicated to contemporary balladeer Bob Dylan, this story in a sense represents Oates's updated prose version of a ballad in which a demon lover carries away his helpless victim. By adding modern psychological insights, she succeeds in revealing the complex nature of the victim of a grotesque intrusion by an alien force; on one level, the victim actually welcomes and invites this demonic visitation. Like Bob Dylan, she grafts onto the ballad tradition a moral commentary which explores but does not solve the problems of the evils of our contemporary society; an analogous Dylan ballad is his "It's a Hard Rain's a Gonna' Fall." Even the title records not only the ritual parental questions but also suggests that there is a moral connection between the two questions: where Connie goes is related to where she has been. Oates does not judge Connie in making this link, however; Connie is clearly not in complete control over where she has been. The forces of her society, her family, and her self combine to make her fate inescapable.

Notes

[1] Walter Sullivan, "The Artificial Demon: Joyce Carol Oates and the Dimensions of the Real," *The Hollins Critic,* 9, No. 4 (Dec., 1972), p. 2.

[2] Joyce Markert Wegs, "The Grotesque in Some American Novels of the Nineteen-Sixties: Ken Kesey, Joyce Carol Oates, Sylvia Plath," Diss., University of Illinois, 1973.

[3] Joyce Carol Oates, "Where Are You Going, Where Have You Been?" *The Wheel of Love* (1970; rpt. Greenwich, CT: Fawcett, 1972), p. 31. All subsequent references to the story appear within parentheses in the text.

[4] See Walter Sullivan, "Where Have All the Flowers Gone?: The Short Story in Search of Itself," *Sewanee Review,* 78, No. 3 (Summer, 1970), p. 537.

[5] Lot and his family were spared when God destroyed the wicked cities of Sodom and Gomorrah, but Lot's wife was turned into a pillar of salt when she disobeyed God's injunction not to look back at the cities. See Genesis 19:24–26.

[6] The time of Christ's return; when all people on earth will be judged.

[7] Andrew M. Greeley, "The Devil, You Say," *The New York Times Magazine,* 4 Feb., 1973, p. 26, quotes an address by Pope Paul on 15 Nov., 1972, as reported in the Vatican newspaper.

[8] Linda Kuehl, "An Interview with Joyce Carol Oates," *Commonweal,* 91 (5 Dec., 1969), p. 308.

WRITING ASSIGNMENTS

1. How is "Where Are You Going, Where Have You Been?" similar to and different from Anne Tyler's "Teenage Wasteland"?
2. Is Arnold Friend meant to be the devil? Is he an antisocial hoodlum? Is he a rapist and murderer (see the March 4, 1966, *Life* Magazine article "The Pied Piper of Tucson" and "Killing for Kicks" in the March 14, 1966, issue of *Newsweek*)? Is he actually Bob Dylan (as Tierce and Crafton suggest in their article)? Or is he just a misunderstood social misfit who terrifies Connie more because of her innocence than because of his evil?
3. In a note accompanying the article she coauthored, Gretchen Schulz says that Oates told her the references to fairy tales in the story are intentional. Do you think Oates's comment is accurate? Does it matter whether or not the allusions are intentional?
4. Many critical articles see "Where Are You Going, Where Have You Been?" as heavily symbolic, even allegorical, with elements of myth, dream, and fairy tale woven throughout. Is this kind of analysis necessary, or could the story be seen in much simpler terms?
5. Who is the story's central character, Arnold Friend or Connie?
6. Dark undertones aside, in what sense is this simply an initiation story, the coming of age of a typical 1960s teenager?
7. What roles are played in the story by music, sex, the weather, contemporary slang, and physical appearance?
8. Why does Connie's family play such a minor role in the story? How would expanding their roles change the story?
9. What aspects of teenage culture have changed in the nearly thirty years since Oates wrote the story? Which have stayed the same? Given the scope of the changes, is the story dated?
10. Most critics see the end of the story as alarmingly negative, suggesting rape and even murder. Do you agree?
11. Feminist critics might see this story as a familiar tale of a young woman's seduction by a man who uses threats of physical violence to coerce her into giving in to his will. In what sense is this a story of male power and female powerlessness?

12. Do you agree with Oates that the dramatic differences in the endings of the film and the story are justified by the differences between the 1960s and the 1980s?

13. How is the so-called generation gap—the failure of one generation to understand another's culture, customs, and heroes—important to the story?

Michele Olivari
Professor Biemiller
English 102
8 March 1994

Mesmerizing Men and Vulnerable Teens: Power Relationships in "Where Are You Going, Where Have You Been?" and "Teenage Wasteland"

Both Joyce Carol Oates's "Where Are You Going, Where Have You Been?" (1966) and Anne Tyler's "Teenage Wasteland" (1984) feature adolescents engaged in constant conflict with their parents. Both stories are set in "teenage wastelands" in which the protagonists ignore limits established by authority figures and avoid making decisions or finding a direction for their lives. The most striking similarity between the two stories, however, is the presence of a hypnotic older man—one who exerts enormous influence over the teenagers, pushing them out of their passive states and causing them to take action. Ironically, the actions in both cases, although decisive, have terrifying consequences.

Arnold Friend, the mysterious loner who pursues Connie in "Where Are You Going, Where Have You Been" is characterized by Gretchen Schulz and R. J. R. Rockwood as the fairy tale wolf who "intends to 'gobble up' this 'little girl' as soon as he gets the chance" (547). Many other critics, as Mike Tierce and John Michael Crafton point out, see

Olivari 2

Arnold as the devil; Tierce and Crafton, however, prefer to see him as a Bob Dylan figure "—a type of rock and roll messiah—" (562). Oates herself, in stating that Arnold is based on a "charismatic mass murderer" (544), acknowledges both the threat he poses and his seductive powers. Regardless of whether Arnold is murderer, devil, wolf, or musical messiah, it is clear that he is a strong, controlling personality who has an unnaturally powerful hold over Connie. In a less dramatic way, Cal, the tutor in "Teenage Wasteland," has just such a hold over Donny. Both men, supported by background music, use their power to mesmerize young people, separating them from home and family and seducing them into following different—and dangerous—paths. In both stories, it is the adolescents' tendency to drift without an anchor that makes them vulnerable.

Both Connie and Donny are passive dreamers, stuck in numbing adolescence, waiting for something to happen. Meanwhile, both break the rules set by their parents. Connie is fifteen, and her mind is "all filled with trashy daydreams" (531). At night she sneaks out to forbidden hangouts, lying to her parents about where she is going. As she drifts through her unstructured summer days, she is "dazed with the warmth about her" (534) and caught up in the music she listens to and in her romantic fantasies. Donny is also stalled, caught in a cycle of failure and defeat, "noisy, lazy, and disruptive" (504) and unresponsive in school, cutting classes, smoking, and drinking beer.

Both Connie and Donny are emotionally separated from their parents. Connie's mother constantly nags her and compares her unfavorably to her sister June; her father does not even talk to them, choosing instead to read his newspaper and avoid conflict. In "Teenage Wasteland" Daisy's primary attitude toward her son Donny is disappointment. Ignoring his potential, she sees only "his pathetically poor posture, that slouch so forlorn that his shoulders [seem] about to meet his chin" (507). She feels sorry for him, but she is helpless to rescue him, let alone give him the emotional support he needs. Like Connie's mother, she clearly disapproves of her child's behavior. Despite her efforts to defend and encourage him, she is ashamed of his failures and upset at how they reflect upon her as a parent. Both Connie and Donny are drifting, unconnected to people or social institutions, and both are allowed to drift by weak, ineffective parents whom they neither respect nor admire. Both Connie and Donny, therefore, are vulnerable to the power of a hypnotic older man.

Arnold Friend, a strange-looking man who acts like a teenager, has great power over Connie. Initially, she is drawn to him by how he looks and dresses, and because of the music they share; later, his claims to know all about her, to know what she wants (which she herself does not know) draw her

Olivari 4

closer to him. Although she begins by flirting with him as she does with other boys, it does not take her long to realize he is different. At first "his face [is] a familiar face, somehow" (536), and "she recognize[s] most things about him" (537), but her confidence turns to fear when she realizes he is older than he appears (538) By now, though, she is under his spell. Little by little, things that have been comforting and familiar—the music, Arnold's clothing and mannerisms, even Connie's own kitchen—become "only half real" (539), as Arnold himself is. As Arnold becomes more and more threatening, Connie becomes more and more helpless; toward the end of the story, cut off from everything she has known, she is "hollow with what had been fear, but what [is] now an emptiness" (542). With Arnold's power the only thing she can recognize, she crosses the line into uncertainty—and, perhaps, death.

Cal Beadle, Donny's tutor, has none of the frightening mannerisms of Arnold Friend, and he has no sinister intentions. Nevertheless, he is also a controlling figure. Like Arnold, Cal is an older man who dresses and acts as adolescents do and listens to the music they like. He immediately sides with Donny, setting himself in opposition to authority figures and social institutions, such as school and the family. This attitude makes it possible—and even acceptable—for Donny to do the same thing. Never blaming, or even criticizing

Olivari 5

Donny, Cal suggests that Donny's parents are too controlling and advises they "give him more rope" (507). But many of Cal's "kids," like Donny, are allowed to continue their anti-social and self-destructive patterns of behavior, remaining under Cal's loose supervision for years. Cal does not help Donny to function in his world; he shelters him from it. Still, Donny sides with Cal, adopting his attitudes and expressions: it becomes "Cal this, Cal that, Cal says this, Cal and I did that" (508). Eventually, Cal becomes the role model Donny's own parents have failed to provide. Donny comes to depend on Cal, even going straight to Cal's house when he is expelled from school, and Cal comes to enjoy that dependence. But Cal does not necessarily have Donny's best interests at heart. Daisy, who despite her own failures with Donny seems to know him (and Cal) well, sees Cal as predatory and controlling, characterizing his smile as "feverish and avid—a smile of hunger" (511). Although Cal does not cause Donny to leave home, he makes it impossible for him to stay. Once he has convinced Donny that it is acceptable to reject the values established by his parents and teachers, Donny's departure becomes inevitable. Having removed all Donny's anchors, Cal then removes himself from Donny's life, deciding the teenager is "emotionally disturbed" (511) and thus absolving himself of blame. At this point, Donny, "exhausted and defeated" (511), has no real choice but to disappear.

Olivari 6

Both Arnold Friend and Cal Beadle—Arnold odd-looking and out of date, Cal estranged from his "controlling" wife and surrounded by teenagers—seem to exist outside the adult world and its rules and values. Perhaps as a result, each has a need for power, a desire to control. Each selects someone weaker, less confident, and more confused than himself, a teenager with strained family relationships and no focused goals. Clearly, critics' characterization of Arnold Friend, and the hypnotic power those characterizations suggest, apply not just to Arnold but also to Cal. Even though Cal is just a catalyst and means Donny no harm, his casual dismissal of him after he has separated the boy from all that is familiar to him pushes Donny from the known and safe to the unknown and dangerous. It is to this uncertain world that Connie too is driven: a place she "[does] not recognize except to know that she [is] going to it" (543).

Olivari 7

Works Cited

Kirszner, Laurie G. and Stephen R. Mandell, eds. Fiction: Reading, Reacting, Writing. 2nd. ed. Fort Worth: Harcourt, 1994.

Oates, Joyce Carol. "When Characters from the Page Are Made Flesh on the Screen." Kirszner and Mandell. 543–46.

---. "Where Are You Going, Where Have You Been?" Kirszner and Mandell. 531–43.

Schulz, Gretchen and R. J. R. Rockwood, "In Fairyland, without a Map: Connie's Exploration Inward in Joyce Carol Oates's 'Where Are You Going, Where Have You Been?'" Kirszner and Mandell. 547–60.

Tierce, Mike and John Michael Crafton. "Connie's Tambourine Man: A New Reading of Arnold Friend." Kirszner and Mandell. 561–66.

Tyler, Anne. "Teenage Wasteland." Kirszner and Mandell. 504–11.

APPENDIX A

DOCUMENTING SOURCES

Documentation is the acknowledgment that information you use to support ideas in a paper comes from an outside source. In general you should give credit to your sources whenever you quote, paraphrase, summarize, or in any other way incorporate the ideas of others into your work. Not to do so—on purpose or by accident—is to commit **plagiarism,** to appropriate the intellectual property of others. By following accepted standards of documentation, you not only help avoid plagiarism, but also show your readers that you write with care and precision. In addition, you enable them to distinguish your ideas from those of your sources and, if they wish, to consult the sources you cite.

Not all ideas from your sources need to be documented. You can assume that certain ideas—facts from encyclopedias, textbooks, newspapers, magazines, and dictionaries, or even from television and radio—are common knowledge. Even if the information is new to you, it need not be documented as long as it is generally available and you do not use the exact wording of your source. Information that is in dispute or that is the original contribution of a particular person, however, *must* be documented. You need not, for example, document the fact that Arthur Miller's *Death of a Salesman* was first performed in 1949 or that it won a Pulitzer Prize for drama. (You could find this information in any current encyclopedia.) You would, however, have to document a critic's interpretation of a performance or a scholar's analysis of an early draft of the play.

Students of literature use the documentation style recommended by the Modern Language Association of America (MLA), a professional organization of more than 25,000 teachers and students of English and other languages. This method of documentation, the one that you should use any time you write a literature paper, has three parts: *parenthetical references in the text, a list of works cited,* and *explanatory notes.*

PARENTHETICAL REFERENCES IN THE TEXT

MLA documentation uses references inserted in parentheses within the text that refer to a list of works cited at the end of the paper. A typical **parenthetical reference** consists of the author's last name and a page number.

> Gwendolyn Brooks uses the sonnet form to create poems that have a wide social and aesthetic range (Williams 972).

If you use more than one source by the same author, include a shortened title in the parenthetical reference. In the following entry, "Brooks's Way" is a shortened form of the complete title of the article "Gwendolyn Brooks's Way with the Sonnet."

> Brooks not only knows Shakespeare, Spenser, and Milton, she also knows the full range of African-American poetry (Williams, "Brooks's Way" 972).

If the author's name or the title of the work is included in the text, only a page reference is necessary.

> According to Gladys Margaret Williams in "Gwendolyn Brooks's Way with the Sonnet," Brooks combines a sensitivity to poetic forms with a depth of emotion appropriate for her subject matter (972–73).

Keep in mind that you punctuate parenthetical references differently with paraphrases and summaries, direct quotations run in with the text, and quotations of more than four lines.

With paraphrases and summaries

Place the parenthetical documentation one space after the last word of the sentence and before the final punctuation:

> In her works Brooks combines the pessimism of Modernist poetry with the optimism of the Harlem Renaissance (Smith 978).

With direct quotations run in with the text

Place the parenthetical documentation one space after the quotation marks and before the final punctuation:

> According to Gary Smith, Brooks's A Street in Bronzeville "conveys the primacy of suffering in the lives of poor Black women" (980).

According to Gary Smith, the poems in <u>A Street in Bronzeville,</u> "served notice that Brooks had learned her craft . . ." (978).

Along with Thompson we must ask, "Why did it take so long for critics to acknowledge that Gwendolyn Brooks is an important voice in twentieth-century American poetry" (123)?

With quotations set off from the text

Omit the quotation marks and place the parenthetical documentation two spaces after the final punctuation.

For Gary Smith, the identity of Brooks's African-American women is inextricably linked with their sense of race and poverty:

> For Brooks, unlike the Renaissance poets, the victimization of poor Black women becomes not simply a minor chord but a predominant theme of <u>A Street in Bronzeville</u>. Few, if any, of her female characters are able to free themselves from a web of poverty that threatens to strangle their lives. (980)

[Note that quotations of more than four lines are indented ten spaces from the margin and are not enclosed within quotation marks.]

SAMPLE REFERENCES

The following formats are used for the parenthetical references required in papers about literature.

An entire work

August Wilson's play <u>Fences</u> treats many themes frequently expressed in modern drama.

[When citing an entire work, include the name of the author in the text instead of in a parenthetical reference.]

A work by two or three authors

> Myths cut across boundaries and cultural spheres and reappear in strikingly similar forms from country to country (Feldman and Richardson 124).

> The effect of a work of literature depends on the audience's predispositions that derive from membership in various social groups (Hovland, Janis, and Kelley 87).

A work by more than three authors

> Hawthorne's short stories frequently use a combination of allegorical and symbolic methods (Guerin et al. 91).

[The abbreviation *et al.* is Latin for "and others."]

A work in an anthology

> In his essay "Flat and Round Characters" E. M. Forster distinguishes between one-dimensional characters and those that are well developed (Stevick 223–31).

[This note cites the anthology, edited by Stevick, in which Forster's essay appears.]

A work with volume and page numbers

> In 1961 one of Albee's plays, <u>The Zoo Story,</u> was finally performed in America (Eagleton 2:17).

An indirect source

> Wagner observed that myth and history stood before him "with opposing claims" (qtd. in Winkler 10).

[The abbreviation *qtd. in* (quoted in) indicates that the quoted material was not taken from the original source.]

A play or poem with numbered lines

> "Give thy thoughts no tongue," says Polonius, "Nor any unproportioned thought his act" (I.iii.59–60).

[The parentheses contain the act, scene, and line numbers, separated by periods.]

> "I muse my life-long hate, and without flinch / I bear it nobly as I live my part," says Claude McKay in his bitterly ironic poem "The White City" (3–4).

[Notice that a slash {/} is used to separate lines of poetry run in with the text. The parenthetical reference cites the lines quoted.]

THE LIST OF WORKS CITED

Parenthetical references refer to a **list of works cited** that includes all the sources used in your paper. (If your list includes all the works consulted, whether you cite them or not, use the title *Works Consulted.*) Begin the works cited list on a new page, continuing the page numbers of the paper. For example, if the text of the paper ends on page 6, the works cited section will begin on page 7.

Arrange entries alphabetically, according to the last name of each author (or the first word of the title if the author is unknown). Articles—*a, an,* and *the*—at the beginning of a title are not considered first words. Thus *A Handbook of Critical Approaches to Literature* would be alphabetized under *H.* In order to conserve space, publishers' names are abbreviated—for example, *Harcourt* for Harcourt Brace College Publishers. Double-space the entire works cited list between and within entries. Begin each entry at the left margin, and indent subsequent lines five spaces. The entry itself generally has three divisions—author, title, and publishing information—separated by a period and two spaces.

A book by a single author

> Kingston, Maxine Hong. The Woman Warrior: Memoirs of a Girlhood among Ghosts. New York: Knopf, 1976.

A book by two or three authors

> Feldman, Burton, and Robert D. Richardson. The Rise of Modern Mythology. Bloomington: Indiana UP, 1972.

[Notice that only the *first* author's name is in reverse order.]

A book by more than three authors

> Guerin, Wilfred, et al., eds. A Handbook of Critical Approaches to Literature. New York: Harper, 1979.

Two or more works by the same author

Novoa, Juan-Bruce. Chicano Authors: Inquiry by Interview. Austin, U of Texas P, 1980.

---. "Themes in Rudolfo Anaya's Work." Address given at New Mexico State University. Las Cruces, 11 Apr. 1987.

[List two or more works by the same author in alphabetical order by title. Use three hyphens followed by a period to take the place of the author's name in second and subsequent entries.]

An edited book

Oosthuizen, Ann, ed. Sometimes When it Rains: Writings by South African Women. New York: Pandora, 1987.

A book with a volume number

Eagleton, T. Allston. A History of the New York Stage. Vol. 2. Englewood Cliffs: Prentice, 1987. 3 vols.

[All three volumes have the same title.]

Durant, Will, and Ariel Durant. The Age of Napoleon: A History of European Civilization from 1789 to 1815. New York: Simon, 1975. Vol. 11 of The Story of Civilization. 11 vols.

[Each volume has a different title.]

A short story in an anthology

Salinas, Marta. "The Scholarship Jacket." Nosotros: Latina Literature Today. Ed. Maria del Carmen Boza, Beverly Silva, and Carmen Valle. Binghamton: Bilingual Press, 1986. 68–70.

[Place the inclusive page numbers two spaces after the year of publication.]

A poem in an anthology

Simmerman, Jim. "Child's Grave, Hale County, Alabama." The Pushcart Prize, X: Best of the Small

Presses. Ed. Bill Henderson. New York: Penguin, 1986. 198–99.

A play in an anthology

Hughes, Langston. Mother and Child. Black Drama Anthology. Ed. Woodie King and Ron Miller. New York: NAL, 1986. 399–406.

An article in an anthology

Forster, E. M. "Flat and Round Characters." The Theory of the Novel. Ed. Philip Stevick. New York: Free, 1980. 223–31.

More than one article from the same anthology

If you are using more than one selection from an anthology, cite the entire anthology. In addition, list the individual selections separately (in alphabetical order according to the author's last name) without including the anthology title or any publication information. Cite only the author, title, anthology editor's last name, and the inclusive page numbers on which the selection appears.

Kirszner, Laurie G., and Stephen R. Mandell, eds. Literature: Reading, Reacting, Writing. 2nd ed. Fort Worth: Harcourt, 1994.

Rich, Adrienne. "Diving into the Wreck." Kirszner and Mandell. 811–813.

A translation

Carpentier, Alejo. Reasons of State. Trans. Francis Partridge. New York: Norton, 1976.

An article in a journal

LeGuin, Ursula K. "American Science Fiction and the Other." Science Fiction Studies 2 (1975): 208–10.

An article in a magazine

Milosz, Czeslaw. "A Lecture." The New Yorker 22 June 1992: 32.

"Solzhenitsyn: An Artist Becomes an Exile." Time 25 Feb. 1974: 34+.

[34+ indicates that the article appears on pages that are not consecutive; in this case the article begins on page 34 and then continues on page 37. An unsigned article is entered by title on the works cited list.]

An article in a daily newspaper

Oates, Joyce Carol. "When Characters from the Page Are Made Flesh on the Screen." New York Times 23 March 1986, sec. 2:1+.

An encyclopedia article

"Dance Theatre of Harlem." Encyclopaedia Britannica: Micropaedia. 1985 ed.

[You do not need to include publication information for well-known reference books.]

Grimstead, David. "Fuller, Margaret Sarah." Encyclopedia of American Biography. Ed. John A. Garraty. New York: Harper, 1974.

[Include publication information when citing reference books that are not well known.]

An interview

Brooks, Gwendolyn. "Interview." Triquarterly 60 (1984): 74–92.

A lecture or address

Novoa, Juan-Bruce. "Themes in Rudolfo Anaya's Work." Address given at New Mexico State University. Las Cruces, 11 Apr. 1987.

EXPLANATORY NOTES

You can use explanatory notes, indicated by a superscript (a raised number) in the text, to cite several sources at once or to provide commentary or explanations that do not fit smoothly into your paper. The full text of these notes appears on the first numbered page following the last page of the paper. (If your paper has no explanatory notes, the works cited page follows the last page of the paper.) Like works cited entries, explanatory notes are double spaced within and between entries. However, the first line of each explanatory note is indented five spaces, with subsequent lines flush with the left-hand margin.

TO CITE SEVERAL SOURCES

In the paper

Surprising as it may seem, there have been many attempts to define literature.[1]

In the note

[1]Arnold 72; Eagleton 1–2; Howe 43–44; and Abrams 232–34.

FOR EXPLANATIONS

In the paper

In recent years gothic novels have achieved great popularity.[3]

In the note

[3]Gothic novels, works written in imitation of medieval romances, originally relied on supernatural occurrences. They flourished in the late eighteenth and early nineteenth centuries.

SAMPLE LITERATURE PAPER WITH MLA DOCUMENTATION

The following research paper, written for an introduction to literature course, follows MLA documentation format.

Flemming 1

Jennifer Flemming
Professor Jussawalla
English 3112
12 May 1993

Double space

Rudolfo Anaya's Bless Me, Ultima:
A Microcosmic Representation of Chicano Literature

Chicano authors have sometimes been called "noble savages," and they have been denied credit and recognition in the fields of literature and culture. Some scholars and teachers consider Chicano literature as "newly emerged" from recent political developments and therefore lacking in maturity and universal appeal, although others have traced its growth and development in the Southwest since the 16th century. The fact that most Chicano literature is based on social protest and is associated with political events also elicits less than positive responses from literary critics. The political nature of the literature causes it to be viewed as not quite legitimate. However, Chicano literature is neither "newly emerged" and thus lacking in maturity nor merely reflective of recent sociopolitical movements. On the contrary, Chicano literature not only records the Mexican-American experience in the American Southwest but also demonstrates the universality of that experience. Rudolfo Anaya's Bless Me, Ultima, which records the Mexican-American experience while describing the emotions universal to most ten-year-old boys, exemplifies the dual role of the best Chicano literature.

Flemming 2

Paredes and Paredes's definition of Chicano literature ties it to the Chicano's key role in the cultural development of the American Southwest:

> People like to record their experiences; Mexican-Americans have been no exception. They have had much to write about. Their lives have sometimes been stormy and often tragic, but always vital and intriguing. It is hardly surprising that Mexican-Americans have literary talents, for they are heirs to the European civilization of Spain and the Indian civilizations of Mexico, both of which produced great poets and storytellers. Furthermore, they have also been in contact with the history and literature of the United States. . . . (1)

Indent 10 spaces

Double space

This connection of the development of the literature with the locale is made by Luis Leal in his article "Mexican American Literature: A Historical Perspective" when he notes that Chicano literature had its origin when the Southwest was settled by the inhabitants of Mexico during colonial times (22). He emphasizes that the literature originated both from the contact of the colonial Mexicans with the Native Americans and from the contact with the Anglo culture that was moving westward. In fact, many of the themes of Chicano literature emphasize the coming in contact of two vastly different cultures. This is particularly true of Anaya's Bless Me, Ultima, which also reflects the universal emotions and feelings generated as a result of the clash of cultures.

Flemming 3

A recording of the experience of the Southwest is found in Anaya's Bless Me, Ultima, which ultimately develops universal themes of initiation and maturation (Novoa, "Themes"). In his novel about a young boy, Antonio, who moves from innocent adolescence to the ambiguous and morally corrupt adult world, the author expresses his culture's indigenous beliefs, myths, and legends.

Antonio's father tells him of the coming of the Spanish colonizers to the Valley, their contact with the American Indian culture which Ultima—an older grandmother figure—exemplifies, and the changes brought about in the village and the town by the coming of the Tejanos (Texans of Mexican descent). Yet the theme is universal, transcending the boundaries of his village. The events that result from the clash between the old and the new could take place anywhere in the world because they deal with religious hatred and with the conflicts between different ways of life.

The novel relates the story of a young boy and his friendship with a curandera (charlatan) named Ultima who comes to live with Antonio and his family. The arrival of Ultima has an enormous impact on him because he feels a kinship with her. For instance, through Ultima, Antonio—now nicknamed Tony—comes in contact with the local Indian religions. Ultima teaches him about herbs and shares with him her knowledge of their special magical properties. She also introduces Antonio to Narcisso, the Indian who teaches him the myth of the Golden

Flemming 4

Carp: "The people who killed the carp of the river . . . were punished by being turned into fish themselves. After that happened many years later, a new people came to live in this valley" (Anaya 110). This myth encapsulates the history of the Indian people, the Hispanic colonizers, and the Anglo settlers of New Mexico. Tony sees the reflection of the myth in his day-to-day life. The Indians and the Hispanics of the valley are gradually replaced by the "new people," the Anglos. This stirs in him deep love for his land, his people, and his lifestyle.

But at school he is teased for believing in these myths. His classmates, who have already laughed at his lunch of tortillas and his inability to speak English, taunt him about Ultima. Calling her a bruja (witch) they say, "Hey, Tony, can you make the ball disappear?" "Hey, Tony, do some magic" (Anaya 102). Tony suffers the angst of a ten-year-old taunted by these voices. He begins to suffer doubts about his identity and the rightness of his beliefs.

At the end of the book, when Ultima is killed by the townspeople for being a witch, Antonio falls to his knees to pray for her and in facing her death reaches his maturation. He knows what is right for him: "I praised the beauty of the Golden Carp" (Anaya 244).

Anaya has said, "When people ask me where my roots are, I look down at my feet. . . . They are here, in New Mexico, in the Southwest" (Novoa, Chicano Authors 185). The author's message is clear and undeniable: one must go back to one's roots, despite the conflicting pull of Americanization. It is this same message of faith and hope that Ultima, on her deathbed, gives to Antonio: Learn to accept life's experiences and feel the strength of who you are. In the character of Ultima, however, Anaya has created a symbol of beauty, harmony, understanding, and the power of goodness that transcends the limits of time and space and religious beliefs.

From the above examples it can be seen that Anaya is capable of producing Chicano literature that has universal appeal and themes. Anaya's novel records the Mexican-American experience of the Southwest while creating characters and portraying emotions of universal appeal. The social protest against Americanization is secondary to the treatment of myth and emotions.

Chicano literature cannot be considered just a by-product of the recent struggle for civil rights. This is not to minimize or deny the effects of the Chicano political movement and the new sense of awareness and direction that it has sparked (which includes the proliferation of Chicano literary texts). Although Chicano literature may appear to emphasize social protest and criticism of the dominant Anglo culture, or seem to be introspectively searching for self-definition, it will not be found lacking in universal appeal (Leal, Decade 42).

Flemming 6

Works Cited

Double space

Indent five spaces

Three hyphens indicaate author's name is exactly the same as previous entry

Anaya, Rudolfo. Bless Me, Ultima. Berkeley: Tonatiuh, 1972.

Leal, Luis, et al. A Decade of Chicano Literature. Santa Barbara: La Causa, 1982.

---. "Mexican American Literature: A Historical Perspective." Modern Chicano Writers. Ed. Joseph Sommers and Tomas Ybarra-Fausto. Englewood Cliffs: Prentice, 1979. 18-40.

Novoa, Juan-Bruce. Chicano Authors: Inquiry by Interview. Austin: U of Texas P, 1980.

---. "Themes in Rudolfo Anaya's Work." Address given at New Mexico State University. Las Cruces, 11 Apr. 1987.

Paredes, Americo and Raymond Paredes. Mexican-American Authors. Boston: Houghton, 1973.

APPENDIX B

LITERARY HISTORY: ARISTOTLE TO THE TWENTIETH CENTURY

The standard literary *canon* (the works of authors commonly read and taught) has been, until very recently, mainly male, white, upper class, and European—with some American influence. The canon readers have been exposed to determines their understanding of what constitutes good literature. Most readers are not aware that the fiction, drama, and poetry now designated as "classics" represent a series of choices about literary worth made over a long period of time. During the past twenty-five years or so, many challenges to the traditional canon have been made. To understand both the development of the traditional canon and the challenges to that canon, it is important to understand the history of Western literary criticism.

BEGINNINGS: THE GREEKS AND ROMANS (c. 450 B.C.–A.D. 400)

The Western tradition begins with the Greeks. In the *Republic* Plato (427–347 B.C.) described the ideal state as well as the role of philosophers and poets. His pupil, Aristotle (384–322 B.C.), was by far the most significant classical influence on Europeans of the Middle Ages and the Renaissance. Even today drama critics and students pay careful attention to the theories presented in Aristotle's *Poetics* about how literature imitates life, how an audience responds with pity and fear to a tragedy, and how a well-written play is constructed.

The Romans contributed works on what would now be called "loftiness of style" (*On the Sublime,* Longinus, first century A.D.) and a treatise on the art of poetry (*Ars Poetica,* Horace, 65–8 B.C.). These writers were typically more interested in the craft of poetry—in how one might construct a poem that would have a pleasing effect on a reader—than in the power of the poet. In contrast to the Greek philosophical approach, Roman literary criticism was more like a practical handbook.

THE MIDDLE AGES (c. A.D. 400–1500)

After the fall of the West Roman Empire in the fifth century A.D., Christianity became the unifying force of Western culture. The literature of the European Middle Ages was for the most part didactic and exemplary. It was intended to demonstrate moral virtue in the hopes that people would follow the behavior patterns it praised. Much literature of this period took the form of morality and mystery plays, both of which had religious themes. Worldly art was discouraged because the clergy who kept learning alive during these hard times felt that the role of literature was to instruct people in the way to lead a virtuous life. Significant departures from moralistic literature appeared in the French romances, which depicted adventures undertaken in the cause of love, and in Chaucer's *Canterbury Tales,* which drew on English, French, and Italian sources. These served as an antidote to the traditional cautionary plays and tales. It is not surprising, given the strong moral purpose of most literature of the Middle Ages, that literary criticism was not a priority of the intellectual life of the period.

THE RENAISSANCE (c. 1500–1660)

During the fourteenth and fifteenth centuries, Europe emerged from the church-centered Middle Ages with a rebirth (*renaissance* is French for "rebirth") of learning. Renewed access to Greek and Roman writers led Renaissance humanists to a broad interest in intellectual considerations. Sir Philip Sidney's (1554–1586) *The Defense of Poesy* (c. 1580) is usually considered the most important work of literary criticism from this period. In his *Defense* Sidney argues that poetry must serve not simply to give pleasure, but also to contribute positively to the life of society. Unlike the writers of medieval allegories, however, Sidney believed that literature could—and should—have a moral impact without being didactic or prescriptive. Despite Sidney's contributions, Aristotle continued to be the undisputed arbiter of critical questions, although his role was complicated by the emergence of William Shakespeare (1564–1616) as a dramatist of exceptional talent.

Shakespeare's work posed a problem because many critics realized that he was a fine playwright despite his frequent disregard for Aristotle's rules governing well-constructed plays. As a result, a concern of criticism up to the eighteenth century became the reconciling of Aristotle's standards with the challenges of contemporary playwriting.

THE ENLIGHTENMENT (1660–1798)

Samuel Johnson (1709–1784), who devoted much of the preface of his edition of Shakespeare's plays to the question of the bard's departures from Aristotle's rules, was a major critical figure of the Enlightenment, a period of neoclassicism characterized by a revitalized interest in the values and ideas of the classical world, particularly of the Romans. Along with Johnson, poets John Dryden (1631–1700) and Alexander Pope (1688–1744), as well as philosopher Edmund Burke (1729–1797), compared contemporary practice with the ideals of their Roman forebears.

Burke, for instance, took on the subject of Longinus's *On the Sublime* in his own treatise, *The Origin of Our Ideas of the Sublime and the Beautiful* (1757). Eighteenth-century critics stressed the value of reason and what they called "common sense." Their architectural style, familiar to us in buildings like the Capitol building in Washington, D.C., provides a visual example of what they sought in literature: clarity, symmetry, discipline. They demanded that a play or poem be tightly constructed and favored the heroic couplet (two lines of rhymed iambic pentameter) as the perfect building block with which to construct didactic poems such as Pope's famous *Essay on Criticism* (1711), a scathing statement of neoclassical literary principles.

Thomas Paine's *Common Sense: Addressed to the Inhabitants of America* (1776) inspired his fellow Americans to revolution, and his *Rights of Man* (1791, 1792) made a stirring case for freedom as the right of every individual. The literature of the American Revolutionary Age, when Paine, Thomas Jefferson, Alexander Hamilton, Philip Freneau, and Joel Barlow were writing, reflected the patriotic concerns of the infant democracy.

THE ROMANTIC PERIOD (1798–1837)

Perhaps as an inevitable counterreaction to the Enlightenment came the Romantics. They believed that poetry was *not* an objective construction like a building with a precise and unchanging meaning but, instead, a subjective creation whose meaning depends on the poet's emotional state and a reader's personal response. Romantic poet William Blake (1757–1827) illustrated the conflict between romanticism and neoclassicism through his ardent dislike of the criticism of Enlightenment artist Joshua Reynolds. In his notes on Reynolds's views, Blake observed that the emphasis on materialism and on physical evidence (empiricism) impoverishes art. Blake believed that the neoclassicists denied both imagination and subjective experience their preeminent role in the creative process. He felt that the artist must begin from the most concrete and minute sensory experience in order to reach the truth. Unlike most eighteenth-century writers, Blake and his fellow Romantics believed in the importance of the individual example rather than the general principle.

Like Blake, Samuel Taylor Coleridge (1772–1834) and William Wordsworth (1770–1850) placed value on the mysterious and on the significance of the common person's experience. Wordsworth in particular stressed the importance of concrete, simple language and offered, in his preface to the second edition of *Lyrical Ballads* (1800), a definition of poetry that has since become famous. A poem, Wordsworth says, should originate in "the spontaneous overflow of powerful feelings" whose energy comes from "emotion recollected in tranquility." George Gordon, Lord Byron (1788–1824), who himself lived a flamboyant life of publicly expressed powerful emotions, created in his poetry the melancholy

Romantic hero, defiant and haunted by secret guilt. Percy Bysshe Shelley (1792–1822) makes perhaps the greatest claims for the poet's power and obligation to society in "A Defense of Poetry" (1821), where he argues that the "great instrument of moral good is the imagination."

The difference in attitude between neoclassicists and Romantics can also be seen through a comparison of the Shakespearean criticism of Samuel Johnson and Samuel Taylor Coleridge. In his *Preface to Shakespeare* (1765) Johnson argues that Shakespeare's faults include being much more concerned with pleasing an audience than with teaching it morals; he observes that often virtue is not rewarded, nor wickedness suitably punished. Additionally, Johnson notes, Shakespeare's diction is too elevated, and he lets the characters in the tragedies talk too much without advancing the action.

Coleridge, on the other hand, sees in the tragic character of Hamlet the prototype of the Romantic hero and argues in his lecture "Shakespeare's Judgment Equal to his Genius" (1836) that Shakespeare knew exactly what he was doing in describing how people actually behave rather than how they ought to behave.

John Keats (1795–1821), another Romantic poet, continued Coleridge's defense of Shakespeare. Keats believed that Shakespeare's intensity, particularly evident in the tragedies, moved his work onto another level altogether, where such judgments become irrelevant and the work itself takes on life through its relationship with "beauty and truth" rather than with teaching proper patterns of behavior.

The Romantics in general, both in Britain and in the United States, made claims for the poet as particularly close to God and nature. The American philosopher Ralph Waldo Emerson (1803–1882) thought nature offered to the poet a mystical symbolism, while Henry David Thoreau (1817–1862) extolled the view that man should live close to nature and follow his personal conscience, rather than the dictates of society. Mary Shelley (1797–1851) and Edgar Allan Poe (1809–1849) were influential in another strand of romanticism: the macabre, melancholy, and mysterious.

THE VICTORIAN PERIOD (1837–1901)

The literary problem facing the post-Romantic generation of critics was the familiar one of dealing with a world where sublime isolation and communing with nature were less and less possible, even as ideals. During the Victorian era rapid industrialization, poverty, population growth, and mass transportation contributed to a general sense that the world was changing rapidly, and people had difficulty coping with these changes. In England critics like poet Matthew Arnold (1822–1888) argued that literature could help anchor people to their world and that literary criticism, as an occupation, should be a "disinterested endeavor" whose responsibility was to minister to a modern society that had lost its faith in other things, particularly religion. Although Arnold differed in many ways from the Romantics, he too believed in the ability of poetry to help us live productive, satisfying lives.

Just before the turn of the nineteenth century, the pendulum swung back from the Arnoldian view that poetry has moral utility—and that the best of it is serious and elevating—to the view that art should exist for its own sake. The dichotomy seen by the Romantics between intellect and feeling became in the 1890s the split between art and the domain of science. Oscar Wilde (1854–1900), Stéphane Mallarmé (1842–1898), and Charles Baudelaire (1821–1867) all dealt with this dichotomy by retreating altogether to the world of art and denying connection with anything else. These members of the symbolist movement valued suggestion, private symbols, and evocative references in their poetry. They attempted to connect their writing with a spiritual world they believed existed but knew was not accessible by the rational methods of science.

Charles Darwin (1809–1882) popularized a biological theory of natural selection in his landmark *Origin of Species* (1859), and his theories influenced novels and poetry of the latter part of the century. Those who believed natural selection contradicted the Bible were outraged, and others interpreted his theories as evidence of latent bestiality in humans. The certainty that mankind was the center of the universe was undermined, as was the conviction that the universe had been intelligently planned for a good purpose.

American writers of the late nineteenth century, including William Dean Howells and Henry James, were noted for realism; others, including naturalists Frank Norris and Theodore Dreiser, explored the idea of individuals being at the mercy of their instinctual drives and of external sociological forces.

THE MODERN PERIOD (1901–Present)

In the next major attempt to demonstrate some objective significance to poetry, T. S. Eliot (1888–1965) argued against the lingering Romantic idea that a poem is the original child of a poet's inspiration. Instead, he proposed in "Tradition and the Individual Talent" (1917) that the poem supersedes the poet, who is merely the agent of its creation. Eliot argues that Wordsworth is wrong to put the poet in the central role of life-experiencer and recreator. According to Eliot, the poem itself will join the tradition, and it will be up to the *critic* to make sense of that tradition. To continue with the example of Shakespeare, Eliot's analysis of *Hamlet* focuses neither on the character of Hamlet and his personal agony (as did the Romantics) nor on the moral tone of the play (as did the neoclassicists), but rather on the story of Hamlet as treated by dramatists before Shakespeare. Eliot concludes that the problems with Shakespeare's play come about because he cannot successfully incorporate the early source materials with his own desire to write a play about the effect of Gertrude's guilt on her son. Thus Eliot judges Shakespeare within a literary and historical tradition rather than within a moral or personal context.

The twentieth century has produced many important critics and theoreticians of literature who built upon the legacy of the past, though some only to the extent that they attempt to contradict earlier approaches. The dominant critical views, which are discussed more fully in Appendix C, can be divided into three groupings: formal, those concerned with the structure or form of texts (formalism, structuralism, deconstruction); social, those concerned with texts in relation to social contexts (new historicism, feminism, Marxism); and personal, those concerned with the interaction of the individual (author or reader) and texts (reader-response criticism, psychoanalytic criticism).

Each of these theoretical approaches can be traced to precursors in the writings of authors in the early part of the twentieth century or before. Mary Wollstonecraft's *A Vindication of the Rights of Women* (1792), for example, was an early forerunner of feminism. Virginia Woolf wrote a number of essays, including *A Room of One's Own* (1929), on the effects upon women of the patriarchal Western society. She pointed out deeply entrenched attitudes and beliefs of male-oriented society that hindered women in the pursuit of realizing their creative possibilities.

Formalism, which acquired prominence in English and American criticism in the middle part of the century, actually began in the early part of the century in Moscow and Petrograd, and was initially a term used in a negative fashion because the techniques focused on patterns and devices in a work of literature and ignored the subject matter. Soon, however, formalism's logical appeal took hold, and it was advocated by Victor Shklovsky, Boris Eichenbaum, and Roman Jakobson in the 1920s.

The roots of psychoanalytic criticism can be traced to the psychological criticism of the early nineteenth century. Thomas Carlyle suggested in 1827 that the best criticism of the day was psychological, deriving meaning from a poem by analyzing the mental state and personality structure of the author.

Marxist criticism is based on the writings of Karl Marx and Friedrich Engels; they borrowed their key term *ideology* from French philosophers of the late eighteenth century who used it to label the study of how sense perceptions develop into concepts. And the term Marxism itself was used in the same period to mean a rigidly held set of political ideas. Marx and Engels adapted and changed the terms, investing them with new meaning that built upon meanings already present in the culture.

Though many literary theorists since Aristotle have stressed the importance of structure, the roots of structuralist criticism can be traced more directly to Russian formalists and French anthropologist Claude Levi-Strauss (1908–   ), who posited that all cultural phenomena have an underlying structural system. Deconstruction both reacts against the tenets of structuralism and builds upon the theories of German philosophers Friedrich Nietzsche (1844–1900) and Martin Heidegger

(1889–1976), who questioned the validity and verifiability of "truth," "knowledge," and other basic philosophical concepts.

Reader-response criticism is a late-twentieth-century approach, beginning in the 1960s, which focuses on the reader and the reader's process and experience, rather than on the text or the text and its historical context. And new historicism is an even more recent mode of literary study, beginning in the 1980s, that reacts to formalism, structuralism, and deconstruction, arguing that the historical context is an integral part of a literary work and that the text cannot be considered in isolation.

The theoretical positions and techniques of each of these approaches to the study of literature are considered in some detail in Appendix C.

APPENDIX C

TWENTIETH-CENTURY LITERARY THEORIES

As you become aware of various schools of literary criticism and read essays applying their principles, you see new ways to think about fiction, poetry, and drama. Just as you value the opinions of your peers and your professors, you will also find that the ideas of literary critics can enrich your own reactions and evaluations of literature. Keep in mind that no single literary theory offers the "right" way of approaching what you read; no single critic provides the definitive analysis of any short story, poem, or play. As you become aware of the richly varied possibilities of twentieth-century criticism, you will begin to recognize new possibilities, ask new questions, and discover new complexities in the works you read.

FORMALISM

Formalism stresses the importance of literary form in determining the meaning of a work. Each piece of literature is considered by itself, in isolation. Formalist scholars consider biographical, historical, and social questions to be irrelevant to the real meaning of a play, short story, novel, or poem. For example, a formalist would see the relationship between Adam and Eve in *Paradise Lost* as entirely unrelated to Milton's own marital concerns, and theological themes in the same work would be viewed as entirely separate from Milton's deep involvement with the Puritan religious and political cause in seventeenth-century England. Milton's intentions and readers' responses to the famous epic poem would also be regarded by formalists as irrelevant. Instead, formalists ask an interpreter to read the text closely, paying attention to organization and structure, to verbal nuances (suggested by connotation and figurative language), and to multiple meanings (often created through the writer's use of paradox and irony). The formalist critic tries to reconcile the tensions and oppositions inherent in the text in order to develop a unified reading.

The formalist movement in English language criticism began in England with I. A. Richards's *Practical Criticism* (1929). To explain and introduce his theory, Richards asked students to interpret famous poems without telling them the poet's names. Of course this strategy encouraged close reading of the text rather than reliance on a poet's reputation, biographical data, or historical context. The American formalist movement, called *new criticism,* was made popular largely by college instructors who realized that formalist criticism provided a useful way for students to work along with an instructor in interpreting a literary work rather than passively listening to a lecture on biographical, literary, and historical influences. In fact, the new critical theorists Cleanth Brooks and Robert Penn Warren put together a series of textbooks (*Understanding Poetry, Understanding Fiction,* and *Understanding Drama,* first published in the late 1930s) used in colleges for years. After the 1950s, many new critics began to reevaluate their theories and to broaden their approaches. Although few scholars currently maintain a strictly formalist approach, nearly every critical movement of this century, including feminist, Marxist, psychoanalytic, structuralist, and deconstructionist criticism, owes a debt to the close reading techniques introduced by the formalists.

A FORMALIST READING: KATE CHOPIN'S "THE STORM" (p. 143)

A formalist critic reading Chopin's "The Storm," might well begin by noting the story's three distinctive sections. What relationship do the sections bear to one another? What do we learn from the word choice, the figures of speech, and the symbols in these sections? And, most important, how do these considerations lead readers to a unified view of the story?

In the first section of "The Storm," the reader meets Bobinôt and his son Bibi. The description of the approaching clouds as "sombre," "sinister," and "sullen" suggests an atmosphere of foreboding, yet the initial alliteration of these words also introduces a poetic tone. The conversation between father and son in the final part of this section contrasts, yet does not conflict, with the rather formal language of the introduction. Both Bobinôt and Bibi speak in Cajun dialect, suggesting their humble origins, yet their words have a rhythm that echoes the poetic notes struck in the description of the storm. As the section closes, Bobinôt, thinking of his wife, Calixta, at home, buys a can of the shrimp he knows she likes and holds the treasure "stolidly," ironically suggesting the protection he cannot offer his wife in his separation from her during the coming storm.

The long second section brings the reader to the story's central action. Calixta, as she watches the rain, sees her former lover, Alcée, riding up to seek shelter. Just as in the first section, the language of the narrator is somewhat formal and always poetic, filled with sensuous diction and images. For instance, we see Calixta "unfasten[ing] her white sacque at the throat" and, later, Alcée envisions her lips "as red and moist as pomegranate seed." Again, paralleling the first section, the conversation of the characters is carried on in dialect, suggesting their lack of sophistication and their connection to the powerful natural forces that surround them. The lovemaking that follows, then, seems both natural and poetic. There is nothing sordid about this interlude and, as the final sections of the story suggest through their rather ordinary, matter-of-fact language, nothing has been harmed by Calixta and Alcée's yielding to passion.

In Section 3, Bobinôt brings home the shrimp, symbol of his love for Calixta, and, although we recognize the tension between Bobinôt's shy, gentle approach and Alcée's passion, the reader can accept the final sentence as literal rather than ironic. The "storms" (both the rain and the storm of passion) have passed, and no one has been hurt. The threat suggested in the opening sentences has been diffused; both the power and the danger evoked by the poetic diction of the first two sections have disappeared, to be replaced entirely by the rhythms of daily life and speech.

For Further Reading: Formalism

Brooks, Cleanth. *The Well Wrought Urn.* 1947.
Empson, William. *Seven Types of Ambiguity.* 1930.
Stallman, Robert W. *Critiques and Essays in Criticism. 1920–1948.* 1949.
Wellek, René. *A History of Modern Criticism. Vol. 6.* 1986.
Wimsatt, W. K. *The Verbal Icon.* 1954.

READER-RESPONSE CRITICISM

Reader-response criticism suggests a critical view that opposes formalism, seeing the reader's interaction with the text as central to interpretation. Unlike formalists, reader-response critics do not believe that a work of literature exists as a separate, closed entity. Instead, they consider the reader's contribution to the text as essential. A poem, short story, novel, or play is not a solid fabric, but rather a series of threads separated by gaps that readers must fill in, drawing on their own experiences and knowledge.

As we read realistic fiction (where the world of the text closely resembles what we call reality), we may not notice that we are contributing our interpretation. As we read one sentence and then the next, we develop expectations; and, in realistic stories, these expectations are generally met. Nevertheless, nearly every reader supplies personal meanings and observations, making each reader's experience unique and distinctive from every other reader's experience with the same work. For example, imagine Shakespeare's *Romeo and Juliet* as it might be read by a fourteen-year-old high school student and by her father. The young woman, whose age is the same as Juliet's, is almost certain to identify closely with the female protagonist and to "read" Lord Capulet, Juliet's father, as overbearing and rigid. The young reader's father, however, may be drawn to the poignant passage where Capulet talks with a prospective suitor, urging that he wait while Juliet has time to enjoy her youth. Capulet describes the loss of his other children and calls Juliet "the hopeful lady of my earth." While the young woman reading this line may interpret it as yet another indication of Capulet's possessiveness, her father may see it as a sign of love and even generosity. The twentieth-century father may "read" Capulet as a man willing to risk offending a friend in order to keep his daughter safe from the rigors of early marriage (and early childbearing). Whose interpretation is correct? Reader-response theorists would say that both readings are entirely possible and, therefore, equally "right."

The differing interpretations produced by different readers can be seen as simply the effect of the different personalities (and personal histories) involved in constructing meaning from the same series of clues. Not only does the reader "create" the work of literature, in large part, but the literature itself may work on the reader as he or she reads, altering the reader's experience, and thus the reader's interpretation. For example, the father reading *Romeo and Juliet* may alter his sympathetic view of Capulet as he continues through the play and observes the old Lord's later, angry exchanges with Juliet.

Reader-response theorists believe in the importance of recursive reading—that is, reading and rereading with the idea that no interpretation is carved in stone. A second or third interaction with the text may well produce a new interpretation. This changing view is particularly likely when the rereading takes place significantly later than the initial reading. For example, if the young woman just described reread *Romeo and Juliet* when she was middle-aged and herself the mother of teenage children, her reaction to Capulet would quite likely be different from her reaction when she read the work at age fourteen.

In one particular application of reader-response theory, the idea of developing readings is applied to the general reading public rather than to individual readers. *Reception theory,* as proposed by Hans Robert Jauss ("Literary History as a Challenge to Literary Theory" in *New Literary History,*" Vol. 2. 1970–71), suggests that each new generation reads the same works of literature differently. Because each age of readers has experienced different historical events, read different books, and been aware of different critical theories, each generation will view the same works very differently from its predecessors. Certainly a quick look back at the summary of literary history in Appendix B will support the credibility of this idea. Consider, for example, the changing views toward Shakespeare from the seventeenth to the twentieth centuries.

Reader-response criticism has received serious attention since the 1960s, with Norman Holland's *The Dynamics of Literary Response* (1968) formulating the theory. The German critic Wolfgang Iser (*The Implied Reader,* 1974) argued that in order to be an effective reader, one must be familiar with the conventions and "codes" of writing. This, then, is one reason for studying literature in a classroom, not to produce only approved interpretations, but to develop strategies and information that will make sense of a text. Stanley Fish, an American critic, goes even further, arguing that there may not be any "objective" text at all (*Is There a Text in This Class?,* 1980). Fish says that no two readers read the same book, though readers can be trained to have relatively similar responses to a text if they have had relatively similar experiences. For instance, if readers have gone to college and taken an introduction to literature course, where they have learned to respond to the various elements of literature such as character, theme, irony, and figurative language, they are likely to have similar responses to a text.

READER-RESPONSE READINGS: KATE CHOPIN'S "THE STORM" (p. 143)

To demonstrate possible reader-response readings, we can look at the same story previously considered from a formalist perspective. (Of course, if several formalist critics read the story, they too would each write a somewhat different interpretation.)

Written by a 25-Year-Old Man; Has Studied American Literature: In Kate Chopin's "The Storm," attention must be paid to the two adult male characters, Bobinôt and Alcée. Usually in a love triangle situation one man is portrayed more sympathetically than the other. But Chopin provides us with a dilemma. Alcée is not merely the cavalier seducer; he genuinely cares for Calixta. Neither is he the brooding hero. There is nothing gruff or angry about Alcée, and he returns to his family home with no apparent harm done following the passionate interlude. On the other hand, Bobinôt is not a cruel or abusive husband. We can see no clear reason for Calixta's affair except for her desire to fulfill a sexual longing for Alcée.

Written by an 18-Year-Old Man; First-Year Literature Course: Bibi doesn't seem to be a very important character in the story, but we should pay attention to him as a reflection of his father. At the beginning of the story, Bibi worries about his mother and he expresses his concern to his father. Bobinôt tries to reassure his son, but he gets up and buys a treat for Calixta as much to comfort himself as to get something for her. Then Bibi sits with his father, and it seems as if he has transferred all his worries to Bobinôt. In the third section of the story, after Calixta and Alcée have had their love affair, Bibi and Bobinôt come home. They both seem like children, worried about how Calixta will react. She, of course, is nice to them because she feels so guilty. At the end of Section 3, both father and son are happy and enjoying themselves. You can't help but feel great sympathy for them both because they are so loving and simple and because they have been betrayed by Calixta, who has not behaved the way a loving mother and wife should.

Written by a 45-Year-Old Woman; Has Studied Kate Chopin's Life and Work: A decade after the controversial novel *The Awakening* was published in 1899, one critic protested, "To think of Kate Chopin, who once contented herself with mild yarns about genteel Creole life . . . blowing us a hot blast like that!" (qtd. in Gilbert and Gubar 981).

This literary observer was shocked, as one might expect from an early-twentieth-century reader, by Chopin's frank picture of sexual relations, and particularly of the sexual feelings of the novel's heroine. One cannot help but wonder, however, whether the scandalized reader was really widely acquainted with Chopin.

Certainly he could not have read "The Storm." This short story is surprising for many reasons, but primarily because it shows a woman who is neither evil nor doomed enjoying, even glorying in, her sexuality. Calixta is presented as a good wife and loving mother, concerned about her husband and son who are away from home during the storm. Yet her connection to Bobinôt and Bibi does not keep her from passionately enjoying her interlude with Alcée. She goes to his arms unhesitatingly, with no false modesty or guilt (feigned or real) to hold her back. Somehow, this scenario does not seem to fit the definition of "a mild yarn about genteel Creole life."

For Further Reading: Reader-Response Criticism

Bleich, David. *Subjective Criticism.* 1978.
Iser, Wolfgang. *The Act of Reading: A Theory of Aesthetic Response.* 1978.
Rosenblatt, Louise. *The Reader, the Text, the Poem.* 1978.
Sulleiman, Susan, and Inge Crosman, eds. *The Reader in the Text.* 1980.
Tomkins, Jane P., ed. *Reader-Response Criticism.* 1980.

SOCIOLOGICAL CRITICISM

Like reader-response criticism, **sociological criticism** takes issue with formalism. Sociological theorists maintain that the literary work cannot be separated from the social context in which it was created. Literature reflects society and derives its essential existence and significance from the social situations to which it responds. Sociological critics speculate about why a particular work might have been written and explore the ways in which it reacts to a specific situation.

For instance, a sociological literary scholar might note with interest that Shakespeare's history plays about Richard II, Henry IV, and Henry V deal with the consequences of uncertain royal succession and usurpation. These dramas were written during the final reigning years of Queen Elizabeth I, a monarch who had not produced an heir and refused to designate one. Although the plays cited were set considerably before Elizabeth's time, a sociological critic might conclude that they reflect the English concern about the threat of monarchic chaos should Elizabeth die with no clear line of succession.

In the twentieth century two strong arms of sociological criticism have emerged as dominant: feminist criticism and Marxist criticism. They are particularly forceful theories because most of their practitioners have a strong commitment to these ideologies, which they apply as they read literature. Feminism and Marxism share a concern with segments of society that have been underrepresented and often ignored. These views are, of course, supported by modern critical theories such as the reader-response idea of gaps in the text that must be filled in through the reader's own experience and knowledge. In addition, the techniques of New Criticism (in particular, close reading of the text), psychoanalysis, and structuralism have allowed sociological critics to focus on what had been overlooked or skewed in traditional readings and to analyze how the experience of marginal and minority groups has been represented in literature.

FEMINIST CRITICISM

Feminist criticism began as a defined approach to literature in the late 1960s, although throughout the nineteenth century, women such as the Brontë sisters, George Eliot (Mary Ann Evans), Elizabeth Barrett Browning, and Christina Rossetti struggled for the right to be taken as seriously as their male counterparts. In addition, in 1929 Virginia Woolf, an experimental novelist and literary critic, published *A Room of One's Own,* a collection of essays describing the difficulties that women writers faced and defining a tradition of literature written by women.

Modern feminist criticism began with works such as Mary Ellman's *Thinking About Women* (1968), which focuses on the negative female stereotypes in books authored by men and points out alternative feminine characteristics suggested by women authors. Another pioneering feminist work was Kate Millet's *Sexual Politics* (1969), which analyzes the societal mechanisms that perpetuate male domination of women. Since that time feminist writings, though not unified in one theory or methodology, have appeared in ever growing numbers. Some feminist critics have adapted psychoanalytic, Marxist, or other post-structuralist theories, and others have broken new ground. In general, feminist critics take the view that our culture—and by extension our literature—is primarily patriarchal (controlled by males).

What is at issue is not anatomical sex, but gender. As Simone de Beauvoir explained, a person is not born feminine, as our society defines it, but rather becomes so because of cultural conditioning. According to feminist critics, paternalist Western culture has defined the feminine as "other" to the male, as passive and emotional in opposition to the masculine as dominating and rational.

Feminist critics claim that paternalist cultural stereotypes pervade works of literature in the canon. Feminists point out that, until very recently, the *canon* (the accepted body of significant literary works) has consisted of works almost exclusively written by males and has focused on male experiences. Female characters, when they do appear, are often subordinate to male characters. A female reader of these works must either identify with the male protagonist or accept a marginalized role.

One response of feminist critics is to reread works in the traditional canon. As Judith Fetterley explains in *The Resisting Reader* (1978), the reader "revisions" the text, focusing on the covert sexual bias in a literary work. For example, a feminist scholar might study Shakespeare's *Macbeth,* looking closely at the role played by Lady Macbeth and arguing that she was not, in fact, simply a cold-hearted villain. Instead, a feminist might see her as a victim of the circumstances of her time: Women were not permitted to follow their own ambitions but were relegated to supporting roles, living their lives through achievements of their husbands and sons.

A second focus of feminist scholars has been the redefinition of the canon. By seeking out, analyzing, and evaluating little-known works by women, feminist scholars have rediscovered women writers who were ignored or shunned by the reading public and by critics of their own times. Thus writers such as Kate Chopin (whose short story "The Storm" has been discussed above) and Charlotte Perkins Gilman (see "The Yellow Wall-Paper," p. 159), who wrote during the late nineteenth and early twentieth centuries, are now recognized as worthy of study and consideration.

A FEMINIST READING: TILLIE OLSEN'S "I STAND HERE IRONING" (p. 150)

To approach Tillie Olsen's "I Stand Here Ironing," feminist scholars might focus on the episodes in the story where the narrator describes her relationships and encounters with men.

Some readings of Tillie Olsen's "I Stand Here Ironing" suggest that the narrator makes choices which doom her older daughter to a life of misunderstood confusion. If we look at the narrator's relationships with the men in her life, however, we can see that she herself is the story's main victim.

At nineteen she is a mother, abandoned by her husband who leaves her a note saying that he "could no longer endure sharing want" with his wife and infant daughter. This is the first desertion we hear about in the narrator's life, and although she agonizingly describes her painful decisions and the mistakes she makes with Emily, we cannot help but recognize that she is the one who stays and tries to make things right. Her actions contrast sharply with those of her husband, who runs away, implying that his wife and daughter are burdens too great for him to bear.

The second abandonment is more subtle than the first but no less devastating. After the narrator has remarried, she is once again left alone to cope with a growing family while Bill goes off to war. True, this desertion comes for a "noble" purpose and is probably not voluntary, but Emily's mother must, nevertheless, seek one of the low-paying jobs available to women to supplement her allotment checks. This time she is again forced to leave her children because her husband must serve the needs of the male-dominated military establishment.

The narrator is alone at crucial points in Emily's life and must turn away from her daughter simply in order to survive. Although she has been brought up in a world that teaches women to depend on men, she learns she is ultimately alone. Although the desertions she endures are not always intentional, she must bear the brunt of circumstances that are not her choice but are, rather, foisted on her by the patriarchal society in which she lives.

For Further Reading: Feminist Criticism

Benstock, Shari, ed. *Feminist Issues in Literary Scholarship.* 1987.
Eagleton, Mary, ed. *Feminist Issues in Literary Theory: A Reader.* 1986.
Gilbert, Sandra, and Susan Gubar. *The Madwoman in the Attic.* 1979.
———, eds. *The Norton Anthology of Literature by Women.* 1985.
Jacobus, Mary. *Reading Woman: Essays in Feminist Criticism.* 1986.
Miller, Nancy, K., ed. *The Poetics of Gender.* 1986.
Showalter, Elaine. *A Literature of Their Own.* 1977.
———. *Sisters Choice: Tradition and Change in American Women's Writing.* 1991.

MARXIST CRITICISM

Scholars influenced by Marxist criticism base their readings of literature on the social and economic theories of Karl Marx (*Das Kapital,* 1867–94) and his colleague and coauthor Friedrich Engels (*The Communist Manifesto,* 1884). Marx and Engels believed that the dominant capitalist middle class would eventually be challenged and overthrown by the working class. In the meantime, however, middle-class capitalists exploit the working class, who produce excess products and profits yet do not share in the benefits of their labor. Marx and Engels further regarded all parts of the society in which they lived—religious, legal, educational, governmental—as tainted by what they saw as the corrupt values of middle-class capitalists.

Marxist critics apply these views to their readings of poetry, fiction, and drama. They attempt to analyze the literary works of any historical era as products of the ideology, or network of concepts, that supports the interests of the cultural elite and suppresses those of the working class. Some Marxist critics see all Western literature as distorted by the privileged views of the elite class, but most believe that at least some creative writers reject the distorted views of their society and instead see clearly the wrongs to which working class people have been subjected. For example, George Lukacs, a Hungarian Marxist critic, proposed that great works of literature create their own worlds, which reflect life with clarity. These great works, though not written by Marxists, can be studied for their revealing examples of class conflict and other Marxist concerns. A Marxist critic would certainly look with favor on Charles Dickens, who in nearly every novel pointed out inequities in the political, legal, and educational establishments of his time. Those who remember Oliver Twist's pitiful plea for "more" workhouse porridge (refused by evil Mr. Bumble, who skims money from funds intended to feed the impoverished inmates) cannot help but see fertile ground for the Marxist critic, who would certainly applaud Dickens's scathing criticism of Victorian social and economic inequality.

Although Marxist criticism developed in the 1920s and 1930s in Germany and the Soviet Union, British and American Marxism has received greatest attention since 1960 with works such as Raymond Williams's *Culture and Society, 1780–1950* (1960) and Terry Eagleton's *Criticism and Ideology* (1976).

A MARXIST READING: TILLIE OLSEN'S "I STAND HERE IRONING" (p. 150)

The Marxist theorist reading Tillie Olsen's "I Stand Here Ironing" might concentrate on the episodes demonstrating how both the narrator's and Emily's fates have been directly affected by the capitalist society in which they lived.

Tillie Olsen's "I Stand Here Ironing" stands as a powerful indictment of the capitalist system. The narrator and her daughter Emily are repeatedly exploited and defeated by the pressures of the economic system in which they live.

The narrator's first child, Emily, is born into the world of the 1930s depression—an economic disaster brought on by the excesses and greed of Wall Street. When the young mother is deserted by her husband, there are no government programs in place to help her. She says it was the "pre-relief, pre-WPA world of the depression" that forced her away from her child and into "a job hashing at night." Although she is willing to work, she is paid so poorly that she must finally send Emily to live with her husband's family. Raising the money to bring Emily back takes a long time, and after this incident Emily's health, both physical and emotional, is precarious.

After Emily's episode with the measles, we get a hard look at what the few social programs that existed were like. The child is sent—at the urging of a government social worker—to a convalescent home. The narrator notes bitterly, "They still send children to that place. I see pictures on the society page of sleek young women planning affairs to raise money for it, or dancing at the affairs, or decorating Easter eggs or filling Christmas stockings for the children." The privileged class basks in the artificial glow of their charity work for the poor, yet the newspapers never show pictures of the hospitalized children who are kept isolated from anyone they loved and forced to eat "runny eggs . . . or mush with lumps." Here again the mother is separated from her daughter by a system that discriminates against the poor. Because the family cannot afford private treatment, Emily is forced to undergo treatment in a public institution that not only denies her any contact with her family, but also cruelly forbids her to save the letters she receives from home. Normal family relationships are severely disrupted by an uncaring economic structure that offers the poor only grudging and punitive aid.

It is clear that the division between mother and daughter is initiated and exacerbated by the social conditions in which they live. Because they are poor, they are separated at crucial times and, therefore, never get to know each other fully. Thus neither can truly understand the ordeals the other has been forced to endure.

For Further Reading: Marxist Criticism

Bullock, Chris, and David Peck, eds. *Guide to Marxist Literary Criticism.* 1980.
Eagleton, Terry. *Marxism and Literary Criticism.* 1976.
Jameson, Fredric. *Marxism and Form.* 1971.
Strelka, Joseph P., ed., *Literary Criticism and Sociology.* 1973.
Williams, Raymond. *Marxism and Literature.* 1977.

NEW HISTORICISM

New historicist critics focus on a text in relation to the historical and cultural contexts of the period in which it was created and periods in which it was critically evaluated. These contexts are not considered simply as "background" to a text but as integral parts of a text. History itself is not an entity composed of objective fact; rather, like literature, history is interpreted and reinterpreted depending on the power structure of a society.

Louis Althusser, for example, suggests that ideology intrudes in the discourse of an era, positioning readers in a way that "subjects" them to the interests of the ruling establishment. Michel Foucault reflects that the discourse of an era defines the nature of "truth" and what behaviors are acceptable, sane, or criminal. "Truth," for Foucault, is produced by interaction of power and the systems in which the power flows, and it changes as society changes. Mikhail Bakhtin suggests that all discourse is dialogic, meaning that any discourse contains within it many independent and sometimes conflicting voices.

Literature, in new historical criticism, is not "trans-historical"; that is, it does not exist outside time and place and cannot be interpreted without reference to the era in which it was written. Criticism likewise cannot be evaluated without reference to the time and place in which it was written. A fallacy of much criticism, according to new historicists, is to consider a literary text as an organic whole, ignoring the diversity of conflicting voices in a text or in the cultural context in which a text is embedded. Indeed, Stephen Greenblatt prefers the term "cultural poetics" to new historicism because it acknowledges the integral role literature and art play in the culture of any era of history. Works of art and literature, according to Greenblatt, actively foster subversive elements or voices but somehow "contain" those forces in ways that defuse challenges to existing culture.

New historicists also point out that readers, like texts, are influenced and shaped by the cultural context of their eras. A thoroughly objective "reading" of a text is, then, impossible. All readers to some degree "appropriate" a text. Acknowledging this problem, some new historicists present their criticism of texts as "negotiations" between past and present contexts. Thus criticism of a particular work of literature would involve both the cultural contexts of the era in which the text was written and the critic's present cultural context; and the critic would acknowledge how the latter context influences the interpretation of the former.

Beginning in the early 1970s, feminist critics adopted some new historicist positions, focusing on male-female power conflicts. And critics interested in multicultural texts stressed the role of the dominant white culture in suppressing or marginalizing the texts of non-whites. Marxist critics, including Raymond Williams, have adopted the term "cultural materialism" in discussing their mode of new historicism, which focuses on the political significance of a literary text.

A NEW HISTORICIST READING: "THE YELLOW WALL-PAPER" (p. 155)

A new historicist scholar might write an essay about "The Yellow Wall-Paper" as an illustration of the destructive effects of the patriarchical culture of the late nineteenth century upon women. This reading would be vastly different from that of most nineteenth-century critics who interpreted the story as a harrowing case study of female mental illness. Even earlier twentieth century readings have considered the narrator's mental illness caused by her individual psychological problems. New historicist critics might focus on the social conventions of the time, which produced conflicting discourses that drove the narrator to madness.

The female narrator of "The Yellow Wall-Paper," who is writing in her private journal (which is the text of the short story), explains that her husband, a physician, has diagnosed her as having a "temporary nervous depression—a slight hysterical tendency." She says she should believe such a "physician of high standing" and cooperate with his treatment, which is to confine her to a room in an isolated country estate and compel her to rest and have no visitors and not to write. The "cure" is intended to reduce her nervousness, she further explains. But as the story unfolds, the narrator relates that she suspects the treatment will not cure her because it leaves her alone with her thoughts without even her writing to occupy her mind. Her husband's "cure" forces her into a passive role and eliminates any possibility of asserting her own personality. However, she guiltily suggests that her own lack of confidence in her husband's diagnosis may be what is preventing her cure.

The text of "The Yellow Wall-Paper" can, then, be divided into at least two conflicting discourses: 1) the husband, who speaks with the authority of a highly respected physician and a husband, two positions reinforced by the patriarchical culture of the time; and 2) the narrator, whose own hesitant personal female voice contradicts the masculine voice or discourse but undermines itself because it keeps reminding her that women should obey their husbands and physicians.

A third discourse underlies the two dominant ones—that of the gothic horror tale, a popular genre of the late nineteenth century. The narrator in "The Yellow Wall-Paper" is isolated against her will in a room with barred windows in an almost deserted palatial country mansion she describes as "the most beautiful place"; she is at the mercy of her captor, in this case her husband; she is not sure whether she is hallucinating and thinks the mansion may be haunted; she does not know whom to trust, not being sure whether her husband really wants to "cure" her or to punish her for expressing her rebellion.

The narrator learns to hide her awareness of the conflicting discourses. She avoids mentioning her thoughts and fears about her illness or her fancies about the house being haunted, and she hides her writing. She speaks reasonably and in "a very quiet voice." But this inability to speak freely to anyone is a kind of torture, and alone in her room with the barred windows, she takes up discourse with the wallpaper. At first she describes it as "one of those sprawling flamboyant patterns committing every artistic sin." But she is fascinated by the pattern, which has been distorted by mildew and by portions that have been torn away. The narrator begins to strip off the wallpaper to free a woman she thinks is trapped inside; and, eventually, she visualizes herself as that woman, trapped, yet freed by the destruction of the wallpaper. The narrator retreats, or escapes into madness, driven there by the multiple discourses she cannot resolve.

For Further Reading: New Historicist Criticism

Geertz, Clifford. "Thick Description: Toward an Interpretive Theory of Culture," in *The Interpretation of Cultures*. 1973.

Greenblatt, Stephen, ed. *Representing the English Renaissance*. 1988.

Rabinov, Paul, ed. *The Foucault Reader*. 1986.

Veeser, H. Aram, ed. *The New Historicism*. 1989.

PSYCHOANALYTIC CRITICISM

Psychoanalytic criticism focuses on a work of literature as an expression in fictional form of the inner workings of the human mind. The premises and procedures used in psychoanalytic criticism were developed by Sigmund Freud (1846–1939), though some critics disagree strongly with his conclusions and their therapeutic and literary applications. Feminists, for example, take issue with Freud's notion that women are inherently masochistic. Some of the major points of Freud's theories depend on the idea that much of what is most significant to us does not take place in our conscious life. Freud believed that we have been forced (mostly by the rigors of having to live in harmony with other people) to repress much of our experience and many of our desires in order to coexist peacefully with others.

Some of this repressed experience Freud saw as available to us through dreams and other unconscious structures. He believed that literature could often be interpreted as the reflection of our unconscious life. Freud himself was among the first psychoanalytic critics, often using the techniques developed for interpreting dreams to interpret literature. Among other analyses, he wrote an insightful study of Dostoevsky's *The Brothers Karamazov* as well as brief commentaries on several of Shakespeare's plays, including *A Midsummer Night's Dream, Macbeth, King Lear,* and *Hamlet.* The latter study may have inspired a classic of psychoanalytic criticism: Ernest Jones's *Hamlet and Oedipus* (1949), in which Jones explains Hamlet's strange reluctance to act against his Uncle Claudius as resulting from Hamlet's unresolved longings for his mother and subsequent drive to eliminate his father. Since Hamlet's own father is dead, Jones argues that Claudius becomes, in the young man's subconscious mind, a father substitute. Hamlet, then, cannot make up his mind to kill his uncle because he does not see a simple case of revenge (for Claudius's murder of his father) but rather a complex web that includes incestuous desire for his own mother (now wed to Claudius). Jones continues his analysis to include the suggestion that Shakespeare himself experienced such a conflict and reflected his own Oedipal feelings in *Hamlet.*

A French psychoanalyst, Jacques Lacan (1901–1981), combined Freudian theories with structuralist literary theories to argue that the essential alienating experience of the human psyche is the acquisition of language. Lacan believes that once you can name yourself and distinguish yourself from others, you have entered the difficult social world that requires you to repress your instincts. Like Lacan, who modified and adapted psychoanalytic criticism to connect it to structuralism, many twentieth-century literary scholars, including Marxists and feminists, have found useful approaches in psychoanalytic literary theory (see, for example, Mary Jacobus's *Reading Woman: Essays in Feminist Criticism,* 1986).

PSYCHOANALYTIC TERMS

To fully appreciate psychoanalytic criticism, you should understand the following terms:

- *id*—The part of the mind that determines sexual drives and other unconscious compulsions that urge individuals to unthinking gratification.
- *ego*—Conscious mind that strives to deal with the demands of the id and to balance its needs with messages from the superego.
- *superego*—Part of the unconscious that seeks to repress the demands of the id and to prevent gratification of basic physical appetites. The superego, then, is a sort of censor that represents the prohibitions of society, religion, family beliefs, and so on.

- *condensation*—A process that takes place in dreams (and in literature) when several elements from the repressed unconscious are linked together to form a new, yet disguised, whole.
- *symbolism*—Use of representative objects to stand for forbidden (often sexual) objects. This process takes place in dreams and in literature. For instance, a pole, knife, or gun may stand for the penis.
- *displacement*—Substitution of a socially acceptable desire for a desire that is not acceptable. Again, this process may take place in dreams or in literature. For example, a woman who experiences sexual desires for her son may instead dream of caressing a neighbor who has the same first name as (or who looks like) her son.
- *Oedipus complex*—Repressed desire of a son to unite sexually with his mother and kill his father. According to Freud, all young boys go through this stage, but most resolve these conflicts before puberty.
- *projection*—Defense mechanism in which people mistakenly see in others antisocial impulses they fail to recognize in themselves.

A PSYCHOANALYTIC READING: EDGAR ALLAN POE'S "THE CASK OF AMONTILLADO" (p. 180)

Since Edgar Allan Poe died in 1849, six years before Freud was born, Poe could not possibly have known Freud's work. Nevertheless, psychoanalytic critics argue that the principles discovered by Freud and those who followed were always inherent in human nature. Therefore, it is perfectly plausible to use modern psychiatric terms when analyzing a work that was written before their invention.

Montresor, the protagonist of Poe's "The Cask of Amontillado," has long fascinated readers who have puzzled over his motives for the story's climactic action when he imprisons his rival, Fortunato, and leaves him to die. Montresor claims that Fortunato has insulted him and has dealt him a "thousand injuries." Yet when we meet Fortunato, although he appears something of a pompous fool, none of his actions—or even his comments—seems powerful enough to motivate Montresor's thirst for revenge.

If, however, we consider a defense mechanism, first named "projection" and described by Sigmund Freud, we gain a clearer picture of Montresor. Those who employ projection are often people who experience antisocial impulses yet are not conscious of these impulses. It seems highly likely that Fortunato has not persecuted Montresor; rather, Montresor himself has experienced the impulse to act in a hostile manner toward Fortunato. We know, for instance, that Fortunato belongs to the exclusive order of masons because he gives Montresor the secret masonic sign. Montresor's failure to recognize the sign shows that he is only a mason in the grimmest literal sense. Montresor clearly resents Fortunato's high standing and projects onto Fortunato all of his own hostility toward those who (he thinks) have more or know more than he does. Thus he imagines that Fortunato's main business in life is to persecute and insult him.

Montresor's obsessive behavior further indicates his pathology. He plans Fortunato's punishment with the cunning one might ordinarily reserve for a major battle, cleverly figuring out a way to keep his servants from the house and to lure the ironically named Fortunato to his death. Each step of the revenge is carefully plotted. This is no sudden crime of passion, but rather the diabolically anticipated act of a deeply disturbed mind.

If we understand Montresor's need to take all of the hatred and anger that is inside himself and to rid himself of those socially unacceptable emotions by projecting them on to someone else, then we can see how he rationalizes as deserved revenge a crime that seems otherwise nearly unmotivated. By killing Fortunato, Montresor symbolically kills the evil in himself. It is interesting to note that the final lines of the story support this reading. Montresor observes that "for half of a century no mortal has disturbed" the bones. In other words, these unacceptable emotions have not again been aroused. His last words, a Latin phrase from the mass for the dead meaning "rest in peace," suggest that only through his heinous crime has he found release from the torment of his own hatred.

For Further Reading: Psychoanalytic Criticism

Freud, Sigmund. *The Interpretation of Dreams.* 1900.

Gardner, Shirley N., ed. *The (M)other Tongue: Essays in Feminist Psychoanalytic Interpretation.* 1985.

Kris, Ernst. *Psychoanalytic Explorations in Art.* 1952.

Nelson, Benjamin, ed. *Sigmund Freud on Creativity and the Unconscious.* 1958.

Wright, Elizabeth. *Psychoanalytic Criticism: Theory in Practice.* 1984.

STRUCTURALISM

Structuralism is a literary movement with roots in linguistics and anthropology that concentrates on literature as a system of signs which have no inherent meaning except in their agreed-upon or conventional relation to one another. Structuralism is usually described by its proponents not as a new way to interpret literary works, but rather as a way to understand how works of literature come to have meaning for us. Because structuralism developed from linguistic theory, some structuralists use linguistic approaches to literature. That is, they talk about literary texts using terms employed by linguists (such as *morpheme* and *phoneme*) as they study the nature of language. Many structuralists, however, use the linguistic model as an analogy. To understand the analogy, then, you need to know a bit of linguistic theory.

The French linguist Ferdinand de Saussure (*Course in General Linguistics,* 1915) suggested that the relationship between an object and the name we use to designate it is purely arbitrary. What, for example, makes "C-A-T" signify a small, furry animal with pointed ears and whiskers? It is only our learned expectation that makes us associate "cat" with the family feline pet. Had we grown up in France, we would make the same association with *chat,* or in Mexico with *gato*. Therefore, the words we use to designate objects (linguists call these words *signs*) make sense only within the large context of our entire language system and would not be understood as meaningful by someone who did not know that language system. Further, Saussure pointed out, signs become truly useful only when we use them to designate difference. For instance, "cat" becomes useful when we want to differentiate a small furry animal that meows from a small furry animal that barks. Saussure was interested in how language, as a structure of conventions, worked. He asked intriguing questions about the underlying rules that allowed this made-up structure of signs to work, and his pioneering study caught the interest of scholars in many fields.

Many literary scholars saw linguistic structuralism as analogous to the study of literary works. Literary structuralism leads readers to think of poems, short stories, novels, and dramas not as self-contained and individual entities that have some kind of inherent meaning, but rather as part of a larger literary system. In order to fully appreciate and analyze the work, the reader must understand the system within which it operates. Like linguistic structuralism, literary structuralism focuses on the importance of difference. We must, for example, understand the difference between the structure of poetry and the structure of prose before we can make sense of a sentence like this:

> so much depends
> upon
> a red wheel
> barrow
>
> (from William Carlos Williams, "Red Wheelbarrow," p. 694)

Readers unacquainted with the conventions of poetry would find these lines meaningless and confusing, although if they knew the conventions of prose they would readily understand this sentence:

> So much depends upon a red wheelbarrow.

The way we interpret any group of "signs," then, depends on how they are structured and on the way we understand the system that governs their structure.

Structuralists believe that literature is basically artificial because although it uses the same "signs" as our everyday language, which has as its purpose giving information, the purpose of literature is *not* primarily to relay data. For example, a poem like Dylan Thomas's "Do Not Go Gentle into That Good Night" (p. 601) is written in the linguistic form of a series of commands, yet the poem goes much further than that. Its meaning is created not only by our understanding the lines as a series of commands, but also by our recognition of the poetic form, the rhyming conventions, and the figures of speech Thomas uses. We can only fully discuss the poem within the larger context of our literary knowledge.

A STRUCTURALIST READING: WILLIAM FAULKNER'S "BARN BURNING" (p. 187)

A structuralist reading tries to bring to light some of the assumptions about language and form that we are likely to take for granted. Looking at the opening paragraph of Faulkner's "Barn Burning," a structuralist critic might first look at an interpretation that reads the passage as a stream of Sarty's thoughts. The structuralist critic might then consider the assumptions a reader would have to make to see what Faulkner has written as the thoughts of an illiterate child. Next, the structuralist might look at evidence to suggest the language in this section operates outside the system of language that would be available to Sarty and that, therefore, "Barn Burning" opens not with a simple recounting of the main character's thoughts but rather with something far more complex.

The opening paragraph of William Faulkner's "Barn Burning" is often read as an excursion into the mind of Sarty, the story's young protagonist. When we read the passage closely, however, we note that a supposedly simple consciousness is represented in a highly complex way. For Sarty—uneducated and illiterate—the "scarlet devils" and "silver curve of fish" on the labels of food tins serve as direct signs appealing to his hunger. It is unlikely, however, that Sarty could consciously understand what he sees and express it as metaphor. We cannot, then, read this opening passage as a recounting of the thoughts that pass through Sarty's mind. Instead, these complex sentences and images offer possibilities that reach far outside the limits of Sarty's linguistic system.

Because our own knowledge is wider than Sarty's, the visual images the narrator describes take on meanings for us that are unavailable to the young boy. For example, like Sarty, we know that the "scarlet devils" stand for preserved ham. Yet the devils also carry another possible connotation. They may indicate evil and thus serve to emphasize the despair and grief Sarty feels are ever-present. So, then, we are given images that flash through the mind of an illiterate young boy, apparently intended to suggest his poverty and ignorance (he cannot read the words on the labels), yet we are led to see a highly complicated set of meanings. When we encounter later in the passage Sarty's articulated thought, "our enemy . . . ourn! mine and hisn both! . . . ," his down-to-earth dialect shows clearly the sharp distinction between the system of language the narrator uses to describe Sarty's view of the store shelves and the system of language Sarty uses to describe what he sees and feels.

For Further Reading: Structuralism

Barthes, Roland. *Critical Essays*. 1964.
Culler, Jonathan. *Structuralist Poetics*. 1975.
Hawkes, Terence. *Structuralism and Semiotics*. 1977.
Pettit, Philip. *The Concept of Structuralism: A Critical Analysis*. 1975.
Scholes, Robert. *Structuralism in Literature: An Introduction*. 1974.

DECONSTRUCTION

Deconstruction is a literary movement developed from structuralism. It argues that every text contains within it some ingredient undermining its purported system of meaning. In other words, the structure that seems to hold the text together is unstable because it depends on the conclusions of a particular ideology (for instance, the idea that women are inferior to men or that peasants are content with their lowly position in life), conclusions that are not really as natural or inevitable as the text may pretend. The practice of finding the point at which the text falls apart because of these internal inconsistencies is called deconstruction.

Deconstructive theorists share with formalists and structuralists a concern for the work itself rather than for biographical, historical, or ideological influences. Like formalists, deconstructionists focus on possibilities for multiple meanings within texts. However, while formalists seek to explain paradox by discovering tensions and ironies that can lead to a unified reading, deconstructionists insist on the primacy of multiple possibilities. Any given text is capable of yielding many divergent readings, all of which are equally valid and yet all of which may in some way undermine and oppose one another.

Like structuralists, deconstructionists see literary texts as part of larger systems of discourse. A key structuralist technique is identifying opposites in an attempt to show the structure of language used in a work. Having identified the opposites, the structuralist rests the case. Deconstructionists, however, go further. Jacques Derrida, a French philosopher, noticed that these oppositions do not simply reflect linguistic structures but are the linguistic response to the way people deal with their beliefs (their ideologies). For instance, if you believe strongly that democracy is the best possible form of government, you tend to lump other forms of government into the category of nondemocracies. If a government is nondemocratic, that—not its other distinguishing characteristics—would be significant to you. This typical ideological response operates in all kinds of areas of belief, even ones we are not aware of. Deconstructionists contend that texts tend to give away their ideological basis by means of this opposition.

Derrida called this distinction between "A" and "Not-A" (rather than "A" and "B") *différance,* a word he coined to suggest a concept represented by the French verb *différer,* which has two meanings: "to be different" and "to defer." (Note that in Derrida's new term an "a" is substituted for an "e"—a distinction that can be seen in writing, but not heard in speaking.) When a deconstructionist uncovers *différance* through careful examination of a text, he or she also finds an (often unwitting) ideological bias. Deconstructionists argue that the reader must transcend such ideological biases and must instead acknowledge contradictory possibilities as equally worthy of consideration. No one meaning can or should be designated as correct.

Deconstruction, then, is not really a system of criticism (and, in fact, deconstructionists resist being labeled as a school of criticism). Rather, deconstruction offers a way to take apart a literary text and thereby reveal its separate layers. Deconstructionists often focus on the metaphorical nature of language, claiming that all language is basically metaphoric because the sign we use to designate any given object or action stands apart from the object itself. In fact, deconstructionists believe that all writing is essentially literary and metaphorical because language, by its very nature, can only *stand for* what we call reality or truth; it cannot *be* reality or truth.

A major contribution of deconstructive critics lies in their playful approach to language and to literary criticism. They refuse to accept as absolute any one way of reading poetry, fiction, or drama, and they guard against what they see as the fixed conclusions and arbitrary operating assumptions of many schools of criticism.

A DECONSTRUCTIONIST READING: FLANNERY O'CONNOR'S "A GOOD MAN IS HARD TO FIND (p. 230)

A deconstructionist reading of Flannery O'Connor's "A Good Man is Hard to Find" might challenge the essentially religious interpretations the author offered of her own stories in essays and letters. A deconstructionist critic might argue that the author's reading of the story is no more valid than anyone else's, and that the story can just as legitimately be read as an investigation of the functions of irony in language.

Flannery O'Connor has explained that the grotesque and violent aspects of her stories are intended to shock the reader into recognizing the inhospitable nature of the world and thereby the universal human need for divine grace. The last sentence of "A Good Man is Hard to Find" is spoken by The Misfit, who has just murdered a family of travelers: "It's no real pleasure in life."

However, the language of O'Connor's stories is extremely ironic. That is, her narrators and characters often say one thing but mean another. So it is possible that their statements are not empirically true but are representations of a persona or elements of a story they have created using language.

The Grandmother, for example, lives almost entirely in fictions—newspaper clippings, stories for the grandchildren, her belief that The Misfit is a good man. On the other hand, The Misfit is more literal than the Grandmother in his perception of reality. He knows, for example, whether the car has turned over once or twice. But he too is posing, at first as the tough guy who rejects religious and societal norms by saying, "It's nothing for you to do but enjoy the few minutes you got left the best way you can—by killing somebody or burning down his house or doing some other meanness to him. No pleasure but meanness." Finally, he poses as the pessimist—or, according to O'Connor's reading, the Christian—who claims, "It's no real pleasure in life." The contradictions in The Misfit's language make it impossible to tell which of these façades is "real."

For Further Reading: Deconstruction

Abrams, M. H. "Rationality and the Imagination in Cultural History." *Critical Inquiry* 2 (1976): 447–64. (Abrams claims deconstructionists are parasites who depend on other critics to come up with interpretations that can be deconstructed.)

Arac, Jonathan, Wlad Godzich, and Wallace Martin, eds. *The Yale Critics: Deconstruction in America.* 1983.

Berman, Art. *From the New Criticism to Deconstruction.* 1988.

Culler, Jonathan. *On Deconstruction: Theory and Criticism After Structuralism.* 1982.

Jefferson, Ann. "Structuralism and Post-Structuralism." *Modern Literary Theory: A Comparative Introduction.* 1982.

Johnson, Barbara. *The Critical Difference: Essays in the Contemporary Rhetoric of Reading.* 1980.

Leitsch, Vincent B. *Deconstructive Theory and Practice.* 1982.

Miller, J. Hillis. "The Critic as Host." In *Deconstruction and Criticism.* Ed. Harold Bloom, et al. 1979. (response to Abrams article above)

Norris, Christopher. *Deconstruction: Theory and Practice.* 1982.

GLOSSARY OF LITERARY TERMS

Allegorical figure or framework See **Allegory**.

Allegory Narrative with two parallel and consistent levels of meaning, one literal and one figurative, in which the figurative level offers a moral or political lesson; Edmund Spenser's *The Faerie Queen* and Nathaniel Hawthorne's "Young Goodman Brown" are examples of allegory. An **allegorical figure** has only one meaning (for instance, it may represent good or evil), as opposed to a **symbol**, which may suggest a complex network of meanings. An **allegorical framework** is the system of ideas that conveys the allegory's message.

Alliteration Repetition of initial sounds in a series of words, as in Blake's "The Chimney Sweeper": "So your chimneys I sweep, and in soot I sleep." Alliteration may be reinforced by repeated sounds within and at the ends of words.

Allusion Reference, often to literature, history, mythology, or the Bible, that is unacknowledged in the text but that the author expects a reader to recognize. An example of allusion in a title is Charles Baxter's "Gryphon" (a mythical beast). Some modern writers, notably T.S. Eliot and James Joyce, use allusions drawn from their private reading, expecting few readers to understand them.

Ambiguity Intentional device in which authors evoke a number of possible meanings of a word or grammatical structure by leaving unclear which meaning they intend.

Antagonist Character who is in conflict with or opposition to the protagonist; the villain. Sometimes the antagonist may be a force or situation (war or poverty) rather than a person.

Antihero Modern character who possesses the opposite attributes of a hero. Rather than being dignified and powerful, the antihero tends to be passive and ineffectual. Gregor Samsa, the main character in "The Metamorphosis," is an antihero.

Archetype Image or symbol that is so common or significant to a culture that it seems to have a universal importance. The psychologist Carl Jung felt that because archetypes are an inherent part of psyches, we recognize them subconsciously when we encounter them and therefore give them a greater meaning than they would otherwise possess. Many archetypes appear in classical myths (for example, a journey to the underworld).

Assonance Repetition of vowel sounds in a series of words: "creep three feet."

Atmosphere Tone or mood of a literary work, often established by the setting and language. Atmosphere is the emotional aura that determines readers' expectations about a work—for example, the eerie atmosphere established in Poe's "The Cask of Amontillado."

Beast fable Short tale, usually including a moral, in which animals assume human characteristics—for example, "The Gentlemen of the Jungle" by Jomo Kenyatta.

Carpe diem Literally, "seize the day"; the philosophy that gave its name to a kind of seventeenth-century poetry arguing that one should enjoy life today before it passes one by, as seen in Herrick's "To the Virgins, to Make Much of Time." The term is also applied to fiction.

Character Fictional representation of a person, usually but not necessarily in a psychologically realistic way. E. M. Forster classified characters as **Round** (well developed, closely involved in the action and responsive to it) or **Flat** (static, stereotypical, or operating as **Foils** for the protagonist). Characters can also be classified as **Dynamic** (growing and changing in the course of the action) or **Static** (remaining unchanged). Also, a brief satirical sketch illustrating a type of personality, popular in eighteenth-century England.

Characterization Way in which writers develop their characters and reveal those characters' traits to readers.

Cliché Overused phrase or expression.

Climax Point of greatest tension or importance, where the decisive action of a play or story takes place.

Conflict Struggle between opposing forces (protagonist and antagonist) in a work of literature.

Connotation Meaning that a word suggests beyond its literal, explicit meaning, carrying emotional associations, judgments, or opinions. Connotations can be positive, neutral, or negative. For example, *family* has a positive connotation when it describes a group of loving relatives; a neutral connotation when it describes a biological category; and a negative connotation when it describes an organization of criminals.

Convention See **Literary convention**.

Conventional symbol See **Symbol**.

Crisis Peak or moment of tension in the action of a story; the point of greatest tension is the climax.

Deconstruction Type of theory and analysis according to which no work of literature can mean what it seems to say because of the ambiguous nature of language itself.

Denotation Dictionary meaning of a word; its explicit, literal meaning.

Denouement See **Resolution**.

Deus ex machina Literally, "the god out of the machine": any improbable resolution of plot involving the intervention of some force or agent hitherto extraneous to the story.

Dialect Particular regional variety of language, which may differ from the more widely used standard or written language in its pronunciation, grammar, or vocabulary. The characters in Flannery O'Connor's "A Good Man Is Hard to Find" speak in a regional dialect.

Diction Word choice of an author, which determines the level of language used in a piece of literature. **Formal diction** is lofty and elaborate (typical of Shakespearean nobility); **informal diction** is idiomatic and relaxed (like the dialogue in John Updike's "A&P"). **Jargon** is the specialized diction of a professional or occupational group (such as computer hackers). **Idioms** are the colloquial expressions, including slang, of a particular group or society.

Double entendre Phrase or word with a deliberate double meaning, one of which is usually sexual.

Dramatic irony See **Irony**.

Dynamic character See **Character**.

Epiphany Term created by James Joyce and now used generally to describe a sudden moment of revelation about the deep meaning inherent in common things, such as the boy's realization at the end of "Araby."

Euphemism Word consciously chosen for its pleasant **Connotations**; often used for subjects like sex and death whose frank discussion is somewhat taboo in our society. For example, a euphemism for "to die" is "to pass away" or "to go to one's reward."

Exposition First stage of a plot, where the author presents the information a reader or viewer will need to understand the characters and subsequent action.

Fable Short didactic story, often involving animals or supernatural beings and stressing plot above character development, whose object is to teach a pragmatic or moral lesson. Aesop's "The Tortoise and the Hare" is an example of a fable.

Fairy tale See **Folktale**.

Fantasy Nonrealistic piece of literature that depends on whimsical plot, supernatural or mythical characters, and implausible actions, usually with a happy ending.

Feminist criticism Theory and practice that seeks to do justice to female points of view, concerns, and values in literature by reorienting both women and men as readers, reconsidering the treatment of women as literary characters, re-evaluating women writers, revising the literary canon, and speculating about the relationships between gender and language.

Fiction Form of narrative that is primarily imaginative, though its form may resemble that of factual writing like history and biography.

Figures of speech Expressions that suggest more than their literal meanings. The primary figures of speech are **Hyperbole**, **Metaphor**, **Metonymy**, **Personification**, **Simile**, **Synechdoche**, and **Understatement**.

Flashback Variation on chronological order that presents an event or situation that occurred before the time in which the story's action takes place.

Flat character See **Character**.

Foil Minor character whose role is to highlight the main character by giving readers a chance to compare and contrast their qualities. In a modern comedic team, the "straight man" can be seen as a foil for the other member.

Folktale Contemporary version of an old, even ancient, oral tale that can be traced back centuries through many different cultures. Folktales include fairy tales, myths, and fables.

Foot See **Meter**.

Foreshadowing Presentation early in a story of situations, characters, or objects that seem to have no special importance but in fact are later revealed to have great significance. For example, a casual mention of a character's unusually accurate memory for faces may become significant only when his or her fate turns out to hinge on recognizing a person from the distant past.

Formal diction See **Diction**.

Formalism Type of theory and analysis that emphasizes the formal patterns and technical devices of literature rather than its subject matter and social values.

Genre Category of literature. Fiction, drama, and poetry are the three major genres; subgenres include the novel, the farce, and the lyric poem.

Hermeneutics Traditionally, the use of the Bible to interpret other historical or current events; in current critical theory, the principles and procedures followed to determine the meaning of a text.

Hyperbole Figurative language that depends on intentional overstatement; Mark Twain often used it to create humor; Jonathan Swift used it for **Satire**.

Imagery Words and phrases that describe the concrete experience of the five senses, most often sight. A **pattern of imagery** is a group of related images developed throughout a work.

In medias res Latin phrase describing works like Homer's *Iliad* that begin in the middle of the action in order to catch a reader's interest.

Informal diction See **Diction**.

Irony Literary device or situation that depends on the existence of at least two separate and contrasting levels of meaning or experience. **Dramatic** or **tragic irony**, depends on the audience's knowing something the protagonist has not yet realized (and thus experiencing simultaneously its own interpretation of the events and that of the protagonist). **Situational irony** exists when what happens is at odds with what the story's situation leads readers to expect will happen. **Verbal irony** occurs when what is said is in contrast with what is meant. It can be expressed as **understatement**, **hyperbole**, or **sarcasm**.

Jargon Specialized language associated with a particular trade or profession.

Literary canon Group of literary works generally acknowledged to be the best and most significant to have emerged from our history. The canon tends to be conservative (it is difficult to add to or remove works from it), and it reflects ideological positions that are not universally accepted.

Literary convention Something whose meaning is so widely understood within a society that authors can expect their audiences to accept and comprehend it unquestioningly—for example, the division of plays into acts with intermissions, or the fact that stepmothers in fairy tales are likely to be wicked.

Literary criticism Descriptions, analyses, interpretations, or evaluations of works of literature by experts in the field.

Literary symbol See **Symbol**.

Marxist criticism Readings of literature based on the social and economic theories of Karl Marx, who in conjunction with Frederick Engels predicted that the dominant capitalist middle class will eventually be challenged and overthrown by the working class, from whose labor the middle class profits unfairly.

Metaphor Concise form of comparison equating two things that may at first seem completely dissimilar, often an abstraction and a concrete image—for example, "My love's a fortress." Some people consider metaphor to be the essential element of poetry. An *extended metaphor* is a comparison used throughout a work; in Tillie Olsen's "I Stand Here Ironing," the mother compares her daughter to a dress waiting to be ironed, thus conveying her daughter's vulnerability. See **Simile**.

Metonymy Figure of speech in which the term for one thing can be applied to another with which it is closely associated—for example, using "defend the flag" to mean "defend the nation."

Mimesis Aristotle's term for the purpose of literature, which he felt was "imitation" of life; literature represents the essence of life and we are affected by it because we recognize (perhaps in another form) elements of our own experiences.

Mood Atmosphere created by the elements of a literary work (setting, characterization, imagery, tone, and so on).

Motivation Reasons behind a character's behavior that make us accept or believe that character.

Myth Anonymous story reflecting the religious and social values of a culture or explaining natural phenomena, often involving gods and heroes.

Narrative The "storytelling" of a piece of fiction; the forward-moving recounting of episode and description. When an event that occurred earlier is told during a later sequence of events, it is called a **Flashback**; suggesting earlier in a narration something that will occur later on is called **Foreshadowing**. The piece of fiction itself is a *narrative* and the storyteller is the **Narrator**.

Narrator Person who tells the story. See **Point of view**.

Naturalism Nineteenth-century movement whose followers believed that life should not be idealized when depicted in literature. Rather, literature should show that human experience is a continual (and for the most part losing) struggle against an implacable natural world. Émile Zola, Jack London, and Stephen Crane are important practitioners of naturalism.

New historicism Type of theory and analysis that concentrates on the historical and cultural context of literary works in terms of both production and, later, interpretation and evaluation.

Novel Fictional narrative, traditionally realistic, relating a series of events or following the history of a character or group of characters through a period of time.

Novella Extended short story, usually concentrated in episode and action (like a short story) but involving greater character development (like a novel); Franz Kafka's "The Metamorphosis" is a novella.

Oxymoron Phrase combining two seemingly incompatible elements: "crashing silence."

Parable Story that uses analogy to make a moral point, such as the parable of the prodigal son in the New Testament.

Paradox Seemingly contradictory situation.

Parody "Take-off" or exaggerated imitation of a serious piece of literature for humorous effect.

Pastoral romance Prose tale set in an idealized rural world; popular in Renaissance England.

Pattern of imagery See **Imagery**.

Persona Narrator or speaker of a poem or story; in Greek tragedy, the persona was a mask worn by an actor.

Personification Attributing of human qualities to things that are not human: "the river wept."

Picaresque Episodic, often satirical work about a rogue or rascal—for example, Cervante's *Don Quixote*. The form emerged in sixteenth-century Spain.

Plot Way in which the events of the story are arranged. When there are two stories of more or less equal importance, the work has a **Double plot**; when there is more than one story but one string of events is clearly the most significant, the other stories are called **Subplots**. Plot in fiction often follows the pattern of action in drama, rising to a **Climax** and then falling to a resolution.

Point of view Perspective from which a story is told. The storyteller may be a character in the story (*first-person narrator*) or someone who does not figure in the action (*third-person narrator*), in which case he or she may know the actions and internal doings of everyone in the story (*omniscient narrator*) or some part of these (*limited omniscient narrator*). Rarely, there may be a *second-person narrator* who uses "you" and the imperative mood throughout the story.

The narrator may be an *observer* or a *participant*. If he or she is untrustworthy (stupid or bad, for instance), one has an *unreliable narrator;* narrators who are unreliable because they do not understand what they are reporting (children, for instance) are called *naive narrators*. If the perspective on the story is the same as one would get by simply watching the action unfold on stage, the point of view is *dramatic* or *objective*.

Protagonist Principal character of a drama or fiction; the hero. The *tragic hero* is the noble protagonist in classical Greek drama who falls because of a tragic flaw.

Psychoanalytic criticism Readings of literature based on the theories and methods of Sigmund Freud, particularly those concerning family relationships and dream analysis.

Reader response criticism Type of theory and analysis according to which some or all of the meanings of a literary work are the creation of the reader, and hence no single "correct" reading of a text exists.

Realism Writing that stresses careful description of setting and the trappings of daily life, psychological probability, and the lives of ordinary people. Its practitioners believe they are presenting life "as it really is."

Resolution Also called the **Denouement**, this is the final stage in the plot of a drama or fiction. Here the action comes to an end and remaining loose ends are tied up.

Rhetoric Organization, strategy, and development of literary works, guided by an eye to how such elements will further the writer's intended effect on the reader.

Romance Type of narrative that deals with love and adventure in a nonrealistic way, most popular in the Middle Ages but sometimes used by more modern authors, such as Hawthorne, to separate themselves from the drabness of ordinary life.

Romanticism Eighteenth- and nineteenth-century literary movement that valued subjectivity, individuality, the imagination, nature, excess, the exotic, and the mysterious.

Round character See **Character**.

Sarcasm Form of irony in which apparent praise is used to convey strong, bitter criticism.

Satire Literary attack on folly or vanity by means of ridicule; usually intended to improve society.

Setting Background against which the action of a piece of literature takes place: the historical time, locale, season, time of day, interior decoration, and so on.

Short story Fictional narrative centered on one climatic event and usually developing only a single character in depth; its scope is narrower than that of the **novel**, and it often uses setting and characterization more directly to make its theme clear.

Simile Comparison of two seemingly unlike things using the words *like* or *as*: "My love is like an arrow through my heart." See **Metaphor**.

Situational irony See **Irony**.

Sociological criticism Type of theory and analysis according to which a literary work cannot be separated from the social context in which it was created.

Speaker See **Persona**.

Static character See **Character**.

Stock character Stereotypical character who behaves consistently and whom the audience of a drama can recognize and classify instantly: the town drunk, the nerd, and so on.

Stream of consciousness Form of narration controlled not by external events but by the thoughts and subjective impressions of the narrator, commonly found in modern literature, such as the work of Virginia Woolf and James Joyce.

Structuralism Type of theory and analysis that applies the concepts of linguistics to the interpretation of literature.

Structure Formal pattern or arrangement of elements to form a whole in a piece of literature.

Style Way an author selects and arranges words to express ideas and, ultimately, theme.

Surrealism Literary movement that allows unconventional use of syntax, chronology, juxtaposition, and bizarre, dreamlike images in prose and poetry.

Symbol Person, object, action, or idea whose meaning transcends its literal or denotative sense in a complex way. For instance, if someone wears a rose in a lapel to a dance, the rose may simply be a decoration, but it becomes a symbol when it takes on a range of paradoxical and complementary meanings. A symbol is invested with significance beyond what it could carry on its own: A swastika, for instance, is a powerful and frightening symbol as a result of Hitler's Nazism. **Universal symbols**, such as the grim reaper, may be called **Archetypes**; **Conventional symbols**, such as national flags, evoke a general and agreed-upon response from most people. In addition to having the same associations as conventional symbols, **literary symbols** may derive additional associations through their use in particular literary works.

Synechdoche Figure of speech in which a part of something is used to represent the whole—for example, "hired hand" represents a laborer.

Tale Short story often involving mysterious atmosphere and supernatural or inexplicable events, such as "The Tell-Tale Heart" by Edgar Allan Poe.

Theme Central or dominant idea of a piece of literature, made concrete by the details and emphasis in the work itself.

Tone Attitude of the speaker or author of a work toward the subject itself or the audience, as can be determined from the word choice and arrangement of the piece.

Tragedy Literary work, especially a play, that recounts the downfall of an individual. Greek tragedy demanded a noble protagonist whose fall could be traced to a tragic personal flaw. Shakespearean tragedy also treats noble figures, but the reasons for their tragedies may be less clear cut than in Greek drama. Domestic or modern tragedy tends to deal with the fates of ordinary people.

Understatement Intentional downplaying of a situation's significance, often for ironic or humorous effect, as in Mark Twain's famous comment on reading his own obituary, "The reports of my death are greatly exaggerated."

Universal symbol See **Symbol**.

Verbal irony See **Irony**.

ACKNOWLEDGMENTS

Chinua Achebe, "Vengeful Creditor" from *Girls at War and Other Stories* by Chinua Achebe. Copyright © 1972, 1973 by Chinua Achebe. Reprinted by permission of Doubleday, a division of Bantam, Doubleday, Dell Publishing Group, Inc.

Charles Baxter, "Gryphon" from *Through The Safety Nets* by Charles Baxter. Copyright © 1985 by Charles Baxter. All rights reserved. Reprinted by permission of Viking Penguin, a division of Penguin Books USA, Inc.

Tadeusz Borowski, "Silence" from *This Way for the Gas, Ladies and Gentlemen and Other Stories* by Tadeusz Borowski, selected and translated by Barbara Vedder. Copyright © 1959 by Maria Borowski. Translation Copyright © 1967 by Penguin Books, Ltd. Reprinted by permission of Viking Penguin, a division of Penguin Books USA, Inc.

T. Coraghessan Boyle, "Greasy Lake" from *Greasy Lake and Other Stories* by T. Coraghessan Boyle. Copyright © 1982 by T. Coraghessan Boyle. Reprinted by permission of Viking Penguin, a division of Penguin Books USA, Inc.

Ethan Canin, "The Carnival Dog, the Buyer of Diamonds" from *Emperor of the Air* by Ethan Canin. Copyright © 1988 by Ethan Canin. Reprinted by permission of Houghton Mifflin Company. All rights reserved.

Bob Dylan, "It's All Over Now, Baby Blue" by Bob Dylan. Copyright © 1964 by Bob Dylan. Reprinted by permission of Warner/Chapell Music, Inc.

Louise Erdrich, "Fleur" from *Tracks* by Louise Erdrich. Copyright © 1988 by Louise Erdrich. First published in *Esquire,* August 1986. Copyright © 1986 by Louise Erdrich. Reprinted by permission of the author.

William Faulkner, "Barn Burning" and "A Rose for Emily" from *Collected Stories of William Faulkner* by William Faulkner. Copyright © 1930 and renewed 1958 by William Faulkner. Reprinted by permission of Random House, Inc.

Nadine Gordimer, "Once Upon a Time" from JUMP by Nadine Gordimer. Copyright © 1991 Felix Licensing, B. V. Reprinted by permission of Farrar, Straus, & Giroux, Inc.

Ernest Hemingway, "A Clean, Well-Lighted Place." Reprinted with permission of Charles Scribner's Sons, an imprint of Macmillan Publishing Company, from WINNER TAKE NOTHING by Ernest Hemingway. Copyright © 1933 by Charles Scribner's Sons; renewal Copyright © 1961 by Mary Hemingway.

Isabel Huggan, "Celia Behind Me" from *The Elizabeth Stories* by Isabel Huggan. Copyright © 1984 by Isabel Huggan. Reprinted by permission of Viking Penguin, a division of Viking Books USA, Inc.

Shirley Jackson, "The Lottery" from *The Lottery* by Shirley Jackson. Copyright © 1949 by Shirley Jackson. Copyright renewed © 1976, 1977 by Lawrence Hyman, Mrs. Sarah, and Mrs. Joanne Schnauzer. Reprinted by permission of Stares, & Giro, Inc.

James Joyce, "Araby" from *Dubliners* by James Joyce. Copyright © 1916 by B. W. Huebsch, Inc. Definitive Text Copyright © 1967 by the Estate of James Joyce. Reprinted by permission of Viking Penguin, a division of Penguin Books USA, Inc.

Cynthia Kadohata, "Jack's Girl" by Cynthia Kadohata. Copyright © 1987 by Cynthia Kadohata. Reprinted with the permission of Wylie, Aitken, & Stone, Inc.

Franz Kafka, "The Metamorphosis" from *THE METAMORPHOSIS, THE PENAL COLONY, AND OTHER STORIES* by Franz Kafka, translated by Willa and Edwin Muir. Copyright © 1975 by Schoken Books, Inc. Reprinted by permission of Schoken Books, published by Pantheon Books, a division of Random House, Inc.

David Michael Kaplan, "Doe Season" from *Comfort* by David Michael Kaplan. Copyright © 1985 by David Michael Kaplan. Reprinted by permission of Viking Penguin, a division of Penguin Books USA, Inc.

Jamaica Kincaid, "Girl" from AT THE BOTTOM OF THE RIVER by Jamaica Kincaid. Copyright © 1978, 1983 by Jamaica Kincaid. Reprinted by permission of Farrar, Straus, & Giroux, Inc.

Salvatore La Puma, "Gravesend Bay" from *The Boys of the Bensonhurst* by Salvatore La Puma. Copyright © 1987 by and reprinted by permission of The University of Georgia Press.

D. H. Lawrence, "The Rocking Horse Winner" from *The Complete Short Stories of D. H. Lawrence* by D.H. Lawrence. Copyright © 1933 by the Estate of D. H. Lawrence, renewed © 1961 by Angelo Ravagli & C. Montague Weekley, Executors of the Estate of Frieda Lawrence Ravagli. Reprinted by permission of Viking Penguin, a division of Penguin USA, Inc.

Doris Lessing, "Woman on the Roof" from *STORIES* by Doris Lessing. Copyright © 1978 by Doris Lessing. Reprinted by permission of Alfred A. Knopf, Inc.

Gabriel García Márquez, "The Handsomest Drowned Man in the World" from *Leaf Storm and Other Stories* by Gabriel García Márquez. Copyright © 1972 by Gabriel García Márquez. Reprinted by permission of Harper and Row, Inc.

James Alan McPherson, "A Loaf of Bread" from ELBOW ROOM by James Alan McPherson. Copyright © 1977 by James Alan McPherson. By permission of Little, Brown and Company.

Lorrie Moore, "How to Talk to Your Mother (Notes)" from *Self-Help* by Lorrie Moore. Copyright © 1985 by M. L. Moore. Reprinted by permission of Alfred A. Knopf, Inc.

Alice Munro, "Boys and Girls" from *Dance of the Happy Shades* by Alice Munro. Copyright © 1986 by Alice Munro. Originally published in *The Montrealer.* Reprinted by arrangement with Virginia Barber Literary Agency, Inc. All rights reserved.

V. S. Naipaul, "B. Wordsworth," excerpt from "Miguel Street" from THREE NOVELS by V. S. Naipaul. Copyright © 1959 by V. S. Naipaul. Reprinted by permission of Alfred A. Knopf, Inc.

Joyce Carol Oates, "Where Are You Going, Where Have You Been?" from *The Wheel of Love and Other Stories* by Joyce Carol Oates. Copyright © 1970 by Joyce Carol Oates. Reprinted by permission of John Hawkins and Associates, Inc. "When Characters from the Page Are Made Flesh on the Screen" from *The New York Times,* March 23, 1986 by Joyce Carol Oates. Copyright © 1986 by The New York Times Company. Reprinted by permission.

Tim O'Brien, "The Things They Carried" from *Esquire Magazine* by Tim O'Brien. Reprinted by permission of International Creative Management, Inc. Copyright © 1986 by Tim O'Brien.

Flannery O'Connor, "A Good Man is Hard to Find" from *A GOOD MAN IS HARD TO FIND AND OTHER STORIES* by Flannery O'Connor, Copyright © 1953 by Flannery O'Connor and renewed 1981 by Mrs. Regina O'Connor, reprinted by permission of Harcourt Brace Jovanovich, Inc.

Tillie Olson, "I Stand Here Ironing" from *Tell Me A Riddle* by Tillie Olson. Copyright © 1957, 1960, 1961, 1965 by Tillie Olson. Used by permission of Delacorte Press/Seymour Lawrence, a division of Bantam, Doubleday, Dell Publishing Group, Inc.

Simon J. Ortiz, "Kaiser and The War" by Simon J. Ortiz. Copyright © by Simon J. Ortiz. Reprinted by permission of the author.

INDEX OF AUTHORS AND TITLES

KEY TERMS